Courts, Judges, and Politics

An Introduction to the Judicial Process

Courts, Judges, and Politics

An Introduction to the Judicial Process

Fourth Edition

Walter F. Murphy
Princeton University

C. Herman Pritchett
University of California, Santa Barbara

Random House　　　　　　New York

To Justice William Brennan, Jr.
Defender of the Constitutional Faith

Fourth Edition
9 8 7 6 5 4 3
Copyright © 1961, 1974, 1979, 1986 by Random House, Inc.

Library of Congress Cataloging-in-Publication Data

Murphy, Walter F., 1929–
  Courts, judges and politics.

  Bibliography: p.
  Includes index.
  1. Judicial process—United States. 2. Law and
politics. I. Pritchett, C. Herman (Charles Herman),
1907–   . II. Title.
KF8700.A7M8 1986   347.73'1   85-14404
ISBN 0-394-34740-4   347.3071

Manufactured in the United States of America

Preface

More than a quarter of a century ago, we developed this book out of a need for teaching materials on the judicial process. In 1961, Random House scattered the first edition to students and faculty. As in each of the intervening editions, we have responded to constant bombardments of judicial opinions and scholarly literature by making drastic changes in the specific cases and readings included here. We have, however, barely altered the basic framework of the book as we originally conceived it. The judiciary, as George Washington wrote to Chief Justice John Jay in 1789, is "the Key-stone of our political fabric," and the essence of its political functions remain pretty much constant, even as the forms of those functions change.

Indeed, the importance of courts and judges in the American political system has, if anything, increased over the decades. Most issues of domestic public policy, from affirmative action to abortion, to questions of the authority of the police and the rights of the criminally accused, to public endorsements of religious symbols, regularly—almost daily—come before the courts, as do broader problems of political structure such as federal regulation of campaign financing, federal control over state action, and congressional control over administrative discretion. Even the current Supreme Court, headed by a Chief Justice and largely staffed by associate justices who label themselves apostles of judicial self-restraint, finds itself deeply immersed in public policy. As we try to show, such immersion is not the result of judicial willfulness or misplaced ambition, but an inevitable part of the American political system.

We have chosen the materials in this book to illustrate the processes by which judges, especially, but by no means exclusively, those of the United States Supreme Court, play policy-making roles. Each chapter begins with an essay by the editors that endeavors to put the chapter's readings into an analytical focus. As far as possible, we have chosen selections that present alternative points of view—that, in effect, debate each other and perhaps the editors as well. Our reprinting a particular piece does not imply that we agree with it, only that we think it raises an important point that intelligent people must consider. Similarly, our placement of articles in debates is not meant to indicate what conclusions we believe students should draw. Our strategy has been to place first the selection that states a thesis, then to follow with a critique of that thesis.

As in previous editions, Part One offers an introduction to the judiciary's participation in the resolution of social conflict—an intrinsically political function. Part Two deals with the organization and staffing of courts, while Part Three examines judicial power—access to, instruments of, and limitations on that power. Part Four examines the distinctive methods that characterize judicial decision making, and Part Five concludes with analyses of the proper functions of judges in a constitutional democracy.

One note about style: In editing cases we have cut many references to cases and similar material and all citations to those sources. To save space and the burden of skipping over ellipses we have not marked such excisions. Our use of ellipses indicates that we have cut substantive matter rather than documentation.

As usual, our debts are as numerous as they are large. We are obliged to Rosemary A. Little of the Firestone Library and her assistants Melissa Hendrich and Lisa Parrish for speedy and efficient help in locating legal esoterica; to John E. Finn, Esq., now of the University of Michigan, for watching over the manuscript like a good shepherd; to Brenda Rodriguez and JoAnn Visnyiczke of Trenton, N. J., for preparing the text of the third edition to be translated into the fourth; to Stacie Scofield of Princeton University for cheerful patience in photocopying and rephotocopying materials; to Nancy Grandjean for help in preparing the table of cases; to Prof. Jennifer Nedelsky, formerly of Princeton University now of the Law School of the University of Toronto, for reading and commenting on part of the manuscript; to Susan Llewellyn for painstaking copyediting; to Robert B. Dishman (University of New Hampshire), George H. Gadbois, Jr. (University of Kentucky), Jill Norgren (John Jay College of Criminal Justice), and Harold J. Spaeth (Michigan State University) for trenchant critiques of the third edition and careful readings of the manuscript of the fourth. Our students were kind enough to register their views about what needed to be done. We have taken some, but not all, of their advice.

We also record our obligation to Bertrand W. Lummus and Lisa Moore of Random House for encouraging us to undertake this fourth edition.

We, of course, take full, if reluctant, responsibility for errors of commission and omission. For these and other failings that might go unnoticed except by our wives, we ask forgiveness and firmly resolve to do penance, sin no more, and mend, if not our lives, future editions.

Walter F. Murphy
PRINCETON, N.J.

C. Herman Pritchett
SANTA BARBARA, CAL.

July 4, 1985

Contents

PART ONE
Jurisprudence and Social Conflict

1
Political Jurisprudence

The title of this book may seem irreverent; surveys of public opinion indicate that Americans think a linkage between courts and politics is a bad thing. But we do not use the term "politics" in a pejorative sense to refer to jobbery or partisan manipulations. Quite the contrary. We use the word in much the same way Aristotle did, that is, as one of the most important and possibly noble of human undertakings: the processes concerned with the authoritative determination of a society's goals and ideals, mobilization of its resources to achieve those goals and ideals, and distribution of rights, duties, costs, benefits, rewards, and punishments among members of that society.

Obviously courts and judges are major participants in these processes. But much conventional wisdom has held that their role, though essential, is secondary and subsidiary to that of the real policy-forming instruments of government, the executive and the legislature. Judges, some writers have said, do not create or originate. They merely interpret and apply "the Law" as promulgated in constitutions, statutes, and previous decisions.

But interpretation and application of "the Law" are far from being automatic processes. "The Law," after all, is not "a brooding omnipresence in the sky," but something that other humans have found and made and probably not completely found or made. Thus judges have to make choices, often hard choices, in determining what the law is. Some constitutional clauses, like those of the Fifth and Fourteenth Amendments that forbid the federal and state governments to deprive a person of "life, liberty, or property, without due process of law," cry out for interpretation that goes far beyond parsing sentences or searching for largely lost legislative history to discover specific intentions of particular framers. Statutes are frequently no less general in their commands. The Sherman Antitrust Act, for example, forbids "every contract, combination in the form of trust or otherwise, or conspiracy

2

in restraint of trade." In fact, however, all contracts restrain trade to some extent, if only by limiting alternative agreements. Thus it should have come as no surprise that shortly after the Sherman Act became law, the Supreme Court ruled that, for the statute to be enforceable, judges had to read into it a "rule of reason." The Act could mean only that "unreasonable" restraints of trade were unlawful.

In the context of interpretation and discretion, some authors differentiate between broad or vague clauses, like those in the Fifth and Fourteenth Amendments, and more specific ones, such as the Third Amendment's prohibition against quartering troops in unwilling civilians' homes during peace. The first kind of clause obviously confers far greater discretion on judges than does the second. As Justice Felix Frankfurter explained the "two clause" theory in *United States v. Lovett* (1946), constitutional issues arising from broad standards of fairness written into the Constitution permit relatively wide play for individual legal judgments. But specific provisions adopted to prevent the recurrence of historic grievances were defined by history, and judges must respect those limits.

Along with discretion, judges also have power that fits nicely into Harold Lasswell's definition of politics as "who gets what, when, and how." Individual judicial decisions determine a great deal about who gets what from and pays what to the governmental system. Who owes taxes or military service, who is entitled to pensions, unemployment benefits, or welfare are matters that judges frequently decide, just as in civil (noncriminal) disputes between individuals, judges determine who owns a piece of property or what obligations a contract imposes, or how much Citizen A must pay Citizen B for damaging his car.

As later chapters show in some detail, the effects of judicial decisions that apparently concern only two private citizens or a single citizen and a governmental agency may ripple out to include large segments of the population, perhaps even the nation as a whole. Insofar as judicial decisions relate to the legitimate power of governmental officials vis-à-vis each other or private citizens, those rulings may preserve or alter existing structures of authority—the formal and informal means by which a polity is governed. Insofar as judges in justifying their decisions announce fundamental principles, they may affect a nation's ideals and ultimate goals.

SCHOOLS OF JURISPRUDENCE

On reflection, much of what we have just said may seem to consist of truisms. Who could deny such plain reality? The answer is that a venerable legal tradition denies that a judge should properly function as more than "the mouth of the law." Judicial decisions, so this tradition argues, affect public policy only if "the Law" so commands.

Mentioned in Class

Sir William Blackstone (1723–1780) was among the more eloquent writers who denied that wise and virtuous judges exercised real discretion. Blackstone's influence has been great in part because he was restating an already established and respected point of view. In part, that influence has also been due to his stating a comforting hope as an actual fact; that is, that the word "law" connotes something known, something sure, something solid on which people can lean in time of trouble. The true function of judges, he explained in his *Commentaries on the Laws of England,* was only to "declare" the law. Judges were "the depositories of the law; the living oracles who are bound by oath to decide according to the law of the land." Their task, Blackstone stressed, was not to decide cases according to their private ideas or values, nor were they "delegated to pronounce a new law, but to maintain and expound the old one." (Reading 1.1.)

SOCIOLOGICAL JURISPRUDENCE AND JUDICIAL REALISM

While some practicing politicians, judges, and scholars have accepted the declaratory theory of judging, others have angrily attacked it. In England, Jeremy Bentham (1748–1832) spent much of his time ridiculing Blackstone. In America, Thomas Jefferson bitterly attacked Chief Justice John Marshall's claims to be a Blackstonian judge, by merely applying objectively the Constitution and statutes of the United States. In Marshall's hands, Jefferson complained, the Constitution was "a thing of putty" and the law "nothing more than an ambiguous text, to be explained by his sophistry into any meaning which may subserve his personal malice." What Jefferson perceived was that the concepts embodied in the Constitution were broad and that Marshall was interpreting those concepts as would a stolid, conservative Federalist.

Several generations later, Oliver Wendell Holmes, Jr. (1841–1935), accepted judicial lawmaking as a fact of life, but he did so without Jefferson's partisan rancor. Indeed, Holmes contended that "the Law" had no existence apart from the decisions of courts. In a famous and influential sentence he wrote: "The prophecies of what the courts will do in fact, and nothing more pretentious, are what I mean by the law." (Reading 1.4.) Nor were judges moved merely by logic. As he explained:

> The life of the law has not been logic; it has been experience. The felt necessities of the time, the prevalent moral and political theories, intuitions of public policy, avowed or unconscious, even the prejudices which judges share with their fellow-men, have had a good deal more to do than the syllogism in determining the rules by which men should be governed.[1]

[1] *The Common Law* (Boston: Little, Brown, 1881), p. 1.

The appointment of Holmes to the Supreme Court in 1903 gave him the best pulpit in the land for announcing and amplifying his conception of the judicial function and for challenging the declaratory theory. He not only opposed many specific decisions of the Court but spoke out against his brethren's claims that they were not choosing among competing political values and public policies. When by a five-to-four vote the justices held unconstitutional a ten-hour statute for bakers in New York, Holmes charged that the decision was based not on law but upon an economic theory—moreover, "an economic theory which a large part of the country does not entertain." When the Court struck down a state tax in *Baldwin v. Missouri* (1930), Holmes in his last dissent denied that the Fourteenth Amendment "was intended to give us *carte blanche* to embody our economic or moral beliefs in its prohibitions."

Holmes thought that the future of the law belonged to "the man of statistics and the master of economics." Roscoe Pound (1870–1964), who was to become dean of the Harvard Law School, believed that it was sociology that would shape the development of the law, and he is regarded as the founder of sociological jurisprudence in the United States. His principal concern centered on the relationships between the legal system and the society of which it is a part. Pound saw legal development as the product of a series of adjustments made necessary by the function of law as a controlling and stabilizing force in a constantly changing society. Law, he argued, cannot control society if it does not satisfy fundamental social needs for both stability and change. Because understanding the precise nature of those needs depends heavily upon sociological knowledge and analysis, Pound concluded that lawyers and judges had to broaden their thinking to include comprehension of the actual effects of legal rules on society. Indeed, he came to see the study of law as one of the social sciences, living in union—or sin—with economics, history, sociology, and political science.

As did Holmes, Pound stressed the critical significance of the judge in providing the really creative element in law. He believed that, historically, legislation had failed to meet the requirements of social change; moreover, the complex conditions of modern life made legislators incapable of drafting statutes that could effectively encompass all eventualities. Judges, deciding on a case by case basis were in a better position than legislators to achieve the continual adjustment needed if a legal system was to harmonize rather than clash with its larger social system. But, Pound emphasized, to play that creative role judges had to abandon Blackstone's "slot machine theory" of judicial decision making and acquire the learning necessary to become informed "social engineers."

Justice Benjamin N. Cardozo (1870–1938) agreed with Pound about the nature of law and the creative tasks of judges. While he was still a judge on the New York Court of Appeals, Cardozo wrote a classic analysis of judicial decision making. (Reading 1.5.) Again it was Blackstone's concept of law as a fixed and immutable set of principles against which Cardozo contended. Some principles—in fact, a great many—he admitted, are well established, and these permit law to exercise a stabilizing influence on society. But often legal principles are not definite; then judges must create new rules or refashion old ones. It was in the exposition of how judges make these creative choices that Cardozo was so effective.

During the 1920s, dissidents, calling themselves "legal realists," broke from the sociological school and mounted a fresh assault on the still highly orthodox declaratory theory. Although realists formed a professionally and intellectually diverse group, which included political scientists, philosophers, economists, and psychologists, most of them were law professors. Taking their cue from Holmes's dictum that law consisted of "prophecies of what the courts will do in fact," they launched a vigorous effort to widen the vista of legal reasoning with the aid of the other social sciences, Freudian psychology, and philosophical pragmatism. Legal realism included several varieties of jurisprudence, and it has been described more as a cynical state of mind than a movement. In general, however, realists argued that judicial decisions and their actual effects on social behavior were the proper foci of legal study. They rejected emphasis on legal rules as traditionally conceived. Their science of law was to be based on observed facts. As Karl Llewellyn, one of the most influential of realists, put it:

> The main thing is what officials [i.e., judges] are going to do. . . . The main thing is seeing what officials do, do about disputes, or about anything else; and seeing that there is a certain regularity in their doing—a regularity which makes possible prediction of what they and other officials are about to do tomorrow.[2]

Finding out what judges do required improved methods of research and analysis, and the realists were responsible for substantial empirical and quantitative studies of the actual administration of justice. Some of them stressed the importance of trial courts, as opposed to appellate tribunals, which had been at the center of lawyers' interests for several generations. Others wrote about law from the outside, as would social psychologists or cultural anthropologists. In 1930 Jerome Frank (who later became a judge on the United States Court of Appeals for the Second Circuit) produced the clearest statement of a realist position in his seminal work *Law and the Modern Mind*. There he tried to further understanding of judges and their lawmaking by

[2] *The Bramble Bush* (New York: Oceana Publications, 1951), p. 13.

applying Freudian psychology and Jean Piaget's theories of child development to empirical data on judicial behavior.

Since the late 1960s a cluster of younger law school professors, calling themselves the Critical Legal Studies movement, has renewed and extended the realist critique.[3] Although, like the realists, members of Critical Legal Studies speak with diverse and frequently discordant voices, they tend to agree that legal concepts are inherently indeterminant and cannot logically govern decisions in individual cases. More specifically, most of the adherents of CLS are from the political left and initially many were neo-Marxists. Thus their early critiques tended to see law as protecting the interests of the dominant classes in society to the serious disadvantage of labor, ethnic minorities, women, and the poor. More recent CLS writings tend to stress the open-endedness of all legal systems and the consequent spuriousness of any claim to a system of "justice" based on neutral applications of coherent principles—the foundation of most conventional legal arguments. Like realism, Critical Legal Studies has focused more on attacking ("trashing" is the word many prefer) accepted notions than on constructing new theories.

POLITICAL JURISPRUDENCE

The searing, often scathing, attacks of realists and the CLS have at least cleared a great deal of rubble from the paths that lead toward understanding courts. Today, sociological jurisprudence's view of law as one form of social control has triumphed in American law schools and pretty much in American courts. Another major thread of sociological jurisprudence, the argument that a judge is inevitably a social engineer, is also dominant, though to a lesser extent, in American law schools. But even more than are commentators, judges are deeply troubled by the implications of their roles as social engineers. Some of their concern no doubt stems from the realists' success in demonstrating not only that judges have a wide range of discretion, but also that subconscious forces struggling within a judge's own psyche play a major part in shaping judicial decisions.

In this book we shall be concerned with courts for many of the same reasons as the realists, followers of sociological jurisprudence, and even the CLS. Because judges often affect public policy, they are important political actors; because they have discretion, who they are and how they are chosen make a difference to the kinds of public policy the country enjoys or from which it suffers. For the same reasons, we are also interested in how individuals, groups, and public officials

---

[3] See especially, Note, " 'Round and 'Round the Bramble Bush: From Legal Realism to Critical Legal Scholarship," 95 *Harvard Law Review* 1669 (1982); David Kairys, ed., *The Politics of Law* (New York: Pantheon Books, 1982); and Symposium, "Critical Legal Studies," 36 *Stanford Law Review* 1 (1984).

can energize and utilize judicial power as well as in the sorts of instruments that judges have at their disposal to shape specific policies and general values. In short, this book will examine the judicial process as one of the formal institutions that speed or retard societal change.

By so doing, we hope to encourage students to try to discover a political jurisprudence in judicial decisions and writings, that is, to look for a central set of politically relevant ideas and values that give order and coherence to the work of judges. Most basically, where the substance of judicial decisions is involved, those who want to understand how courts and judges participate in governing society should look for the principal values that decisions are advancing or restricting. For instance: Is the Supreme Court putting equality ahead of such competing values as individual liberty? Is the Court giving priority to the needs of people who want stability over the needs of those who want social change? Are the justices insisting that freedom of political communication takes precedence over all other values, even the right to privacy? Somewhat less basic are substantive questions about particular public policies and the power of specific governmental officials. To what extent and during what periods of time can a state regulate abortion? What positive action does a school board have to take to overcome racial imbalance in its classrooms? Does the treatment of prisoners constitute cruel and unusual punishment? Does prayer in the public schools amount to an establishment of religion?

By directing attention to these sorts of issues, we also hope to encourage students to ask normative questions: What theories and values *should* judges be advancing? What functions are proper to judges in a constitutional democracy and what functions are improper? By what standards does one draw clear distinctions between the proper and improper? How (and why) do particular lines of decision support or undermine values and policies central to a viable constitutional democracy?

THE COMMON LAW TRADITION

Most of the introductory essays and readings in the remainder of this book attempt to deal with—or at least indirectly raise—these sorts of questions. Before turning to them, it would be helpful to say a few words about the peculiarities of the American legal and governmental systems that enhance the political power that judges exercise.

First of all, the colonists brought with them from England the so-called common law, the British system (or lack of a system) of judge-made rules that had slowly developed over the centuries and still continues to develop. Soon after the Norman Conquest of England, royal officials, who only by rough analogy could be called judges in the modern sense, cooperated with the king to settle private disputes and sometimes to decide punishment for what we would call—although they did not—public offenses. These officials claimed to apply the common custom of the realm rather than the parochial traditions of a particular shire or village. Which custom was common and which was local depended in large part on the perceptions, experiences, values, and personal judgments of the officials, for neither sound data nor objective standards were available.

Because one set of judges decided the more important cases involving what we would call private litigation, their rulings eventually did become common law if not common custom. During the same period these judges began to follow a doctrine known as *stare decisis,* according to which they applied the rules announced in previous decisions to settle new cases. As we shall see in Chapter 10, deciding precisely what a previous case stands for and how its rule is to be applied to a new situation is hardly a simple matter. Furthermore, even a rigid doctrine of stare decisis allows a judge considerable discretion, but the use of precedents has given the common law a degree of continuity across both space and time.

Judicial discretion takes on added significance when one realizes exactly what is meant by the statement that the common law is largely judge-made. It was not until well into the nineteenth century that either the British Parliament or the American Congress began to pass many statutes dealing with the everyday affairs of private citizens. Centuries after it had become an important governmental institution, Parliament met principally to levy taxes, raise armies and navies, declare war, or conclude peace. Occasionally, it would pass a legal monument such as the Bill of Rights of 1689 or the Act of Settlement of 1701. Judges formulated most of the rules, not only in the field of private law, such as property, trespass, wills, contracts, employer-employee relations, but also on public law issues that in the United States would be regarded as constitutional in character. For example, the basic rights of persons accused of criminal offenses are stated in the so-called Judges' Rules, which originated in a letter written by the Lord Chief Justice in 1906 to the Chief Constable of Birmingham in response to a request for advice.

THE CIVIL LAW TRADITION[4]

The common law has taken root only in nations that were colonized or conquered by the British. The other and more widespread major legal system of the Western world is the civil law. The name "civil" came in the Middle Ages to distinguish this legal mode from canon (ec-

4 See especially, John Henry Merryman, *The Civil Law Tradition* (Stanford, California: Stanford University Press, 1969).

clesiastical) law, and its use has spread around the European continent, to Latin America, by French colonization to the Canadian province of Quebec, Louisiana in the United States, and parts of Africa, and by formal adoption, to other countries such as Japan and Turkey.

The roots of the civil law begin in Roman jurisprudence as rediscovered and reinterpreted by lawyer–scholars of the Middle Ages. The model of the civil law is a code—a lucid, detailed, and all-encompassing set of interlocking regulations that ideally lay down in general principle, if not in specific terms, the rules for settling all possible disputes among human beings. Its first incarnation was in the volumes promulgated by the Emperor Justinian in the sixth century; its modern reincarnations came first in the *Code Napoléon* in the early years of the nineteenth century and then in the German codes promulgated ninety years later. Napoleon wanted his Code to be so clear that the peasant in the field could understand it. Stendahl said that he read a page of the Code every day to improve his style. (Reading 1.6.)

The hero of the common law has been the judge and to a lesser extent his squire, the practicing attorney. But the hero of the civil law has been and remains the scholar, the writer who understands the basic philosophical principles that tie the whole system together into a coherent intellectual whole. His nominal superior but actual assistant is the legislator who adopts the scholar's analysis and gives it binding force within the community. Whereas the common law grew—and grew slowly—out of the muck and mire of courtroom battles over real disputes involving live human beings and their interests, the civil law was formulated in the antiseptic atmosphere of the university. Thus the civil law has been less dependent than the common law on practical efforts to settle immediate human conflict and more dependent on abstract intellectualizing and deep learning.

The judge, according to the official doctrine of the civil law, is little more than a skilled technician. Because the Code is supposedly clear, detailed, and complete, the judge's main function is to discover the appropriate provisions of the Code and apply them to the case at hand. Such a task requires a fine eye, but no creativity.

Several very different threads were woven into this normative pattern of a restricted judicial function. The absolutist notion of the law as the will of the sovereign came first. When the emperor—whether he was Roman, French, or German—had spoken, it was the task of all citizens, including magistrates, to obey, not to add to or subtract from his words as embodied in the law. Later, when democratic ideas were victorious, the same argument was made in relation to the will of the people as expressed through their elected legislators. Judges, as appointed officials, had no authority to amend the decisions of chosen representatives of the citizenry.

At the heart of the civil law system was a concept beyond both democratic and authoritarian ideologies: law was precisely what that term meant, a system, closed, self-contained, and self-sustained, a neatly ordered body of principles hierarchically arranged, with the less fundamental principles logically deduced from the more fundamental. Any judicial tampering with this system, even a charitable effort to ease the law's commands in a particular case, was bound to do more harm than good in the long run by destroying the intellectual integrity and conceptual purity of the entire corpus.

THE AMERICAN SYSTEM

Almost all scholars now agree that judges in civil law systems have always exercised considerable discretion. No code has been so complete, no scholar so prescient as to anticipate all disputes that have later arisen. Nevertheless, judicial freedom runs against the normative grain of the official doctrine of the civil law. On the other hand, the common law, despite Blackstone and his followers, has been much more hospitable to the notion of the judge as a social engineer. Such hospitality has attracted different sorts of men (and now women) to the bench in common law countries than in those that use the civil law. Common law judges tend to have been attorneys in active practice or lawyers who have gone into politics, people used to public battling over questions of policy. In the civil law countries, students decide to become judges at the end of their professional training, and, if their grades are high enough, immediately enter into a largely anonymous civil service in which promotion is dependent upon a mixture of seniority and professional skill in interpreting the relevant codes. Opinions of the court are unsigned and dissents almost unknown—indeed, in most civil law countries the bench and the various divisions of the practicing bar would view a dissenting opinion as either madness or heresy. For if the law is clear, judges cannot disagree (at least publicly) about its meaning.

American acceptance of the common law thus entailed a different, much more activist and prestigious model of the judge and so attracted people to the bench who, as a group, have been temperamentally different from their civil law colleagues. Moreover, the Constitution of 1787 established a new and hybrid form of government, one that combined popular participation (an element that grew into full-scale democracy, but only after many decades) and the notion of limited political power, whether that power was exercised by a few public officials acting on behalf of their own selfish interests or by all public officials acting on behalf of the wishes of the overwhelming majority of the people. The structure that emerged from the Convention at Philadelphia and has evolved since that time is obviously not one of pure democracy in which the people rule directly. Nor is it merely a system of representative democracy in which those elected by popular vote govern. Rather it is what the framers called "free government," and what most modern writers would label constitutional democracy.

In the name of the people, the Constitution grants, organizes, and allots political power. But the Constitution also limits legitimate political power. Division of the national government into three separate institutions sharing overlapping grants of power and prohibitions in the body of the Constitution as well as in the Bill of Rights and the post–Civil War amendments combine with federalism to restrict authority, even the authority of a massive majority of the people to obtain the public policies they ardently desire. A concerted, organized, and skillfully led majority could, of course, succeed in its goals, even if those goals contradicted explicit constitutional commands, but that sort of action, unless it first amended the Constitution, would be an exercise of brute force rather than of authority.

Judges, at least since 1803, when Chief Justice John Marshall wrote the opinion of the Court in *Marbury v. Madison* (Reading 1.3), have claimed that the Constitution authorizes courts to interpret the Constitution and thus to declare invalid acts of the legislature and executive. Whether the framers and ratifiers of the Constitution so intended can be endlessly debated. In No. 78 of *The Federalist* Alexander Hamilton provided the classic statement of the case for judicial review. (Reading 1.2.) We make only two points here. First, Marshall's claim has been successful. Judges have for generations routinely exercised the power of judicial review. Second, whatever the framers might have had specifically in mind, judicial review fits neatly into their general scheme of giving each branch of the national government a set of checks on the operations of the other two.

In sum, in the American system "the people shall govern," but only within the limits set by the Constitution. And judges, whatever was historically intended, can define the limits set by the Constitution. To be sure, this power is not unrestricted. Congress and the President and even the states have their own weapons, described and discussed in Chapter 7, that they can deploy against judges. But with that much said, judges have a duty, a constitutional duty, when a case is properly before them, to try to stop any governmental agency, no matter how representative of the popular will, from doing certain forbidden things or doing proper things in a forbidden fashion. Those kinds of decisions, especially when justified by opinions that become part of the national culture, can affect not only particular public policies and mark divisions of authority among governmental institutions; the decisions can also help to shape and define more general values such as equality, privacy, security, property, and liberty—the kinds of values that politics is ultimately all about.

SELECTED REFERENCES

Cardozo, Benjamin N. *The Nature of the Judicial Process.* New Haven, Connecticut: Yale University Press, 1921.

Dworkin, Ronald. *Taking Rights Seriously.* Cambridge, Mass.: Harvard University Press, 1977.

Frank, Jerome. *Law and the Modern Mind.* New York: Brentano's, 1930.

———. *Courts on Trial.* Princeton, New Jersey: Princeton University Press, 1949.

Friedman, Lawrence M. *History of American Law.* New York: Simon & Schuster, 1973.

Grossman, Joel B., and Joseph Tanenhaus (eds.). *Frontiers of Judicial Research.* New York: Wiley, 1969. Chs. 1, 2.

Hart, H. L. A. *The Concept of Law.* Oxford: Oxford University Press, 1961.

Llewellyn, Karl N. *The Bramble Bush.* New York: Oceana Publications, 1951.

———. *The Common Law Tradition: Deciding Appeals.* Boston: Little, Brown, 1960.

Merryman, John Henry. *The Civil Law Tradition.* Stanford, California: Stanford University Press, 1969.

Murphy, Walter F., and Joseph Tanenhaus. *The Study of Public Law.* New York: Random House, 1972. Ch. 1.

———. *Comparative Constitutional Law.* New York: St. Martin's Press, 1977. Chs. 1–6.

Neely, Richard. *How Courts Govern America.* New Haven: Yale University Press, 1981.

Pound, Roscoe. *An Introduction to the Philosophy of Law.* New Haven, Connecticut: Yale University Press, 1922.

———. "A Survey of Social Interests," 57 *Harvard Law Review* 1 (1943).

Pritchett, C. Herman. "Public Law and Judicial Behavior," 30 *Journal of Politics* 480 (1968).

Rawls, John. *A Theory of Justice.* Cambridge, Mass.: Harvard University Press, 1971.

Rembar, Charles. *The Law of the Land: The Evolution of Our Legal System.* New York: Simon & Schuster, 1980.

Rumble, Wilfred E., Jr. *American Legal Realism.* Ithaca, New York: Cornell University Press, 1968.

Shapiro, Martin. *Courts: A Comparative and Political Analysis.* Chicago: University of Chicago Press, 1981.

———. *Law and Politics in the Supreme Court.* New York: Free Press, 1964. Ch. 1.

Stone, Julius. *Social Dimensions of Law and Justice.* Stanford, California: Stanford University Press, 1966.

Symposium. "Critical Legal Studies," 36 *Stanford Law Review* 1 (1984).

Wasserstrom, Richard A. (ed.). *Morality and the Law.* Belmont, California: Wadsworth Publishing Co., 1971.

1.1   *"[Judges] are the depositaries of the laws; the living oracles . . ."*

COMMENTARIES ON THE LAWS OF ENGLAND

Sir William Blackstone

. . . But here a very natural, and very material, question arises: how are these customs and maxims to be known, and by whom is their validity to be determined? The answer is, by the judges in the several courts of justice. They are the depositaries of the laws; the living oracles, who must decide in all cases of doubt, and who are bound by an oath to decide according to the law of the land. Their knowledge of that law is derived from experience and study . . . and from being long personally accustomed to the judicial decisions of their predecessors. And indeed these judicial decisions are the principal and the most authoritative evidence, that can be given, of the existence of such a custom as shall form a part of the common law. The judgment itself, and all the proceedings previous thereto, are carefully registered and preserved, under the name of *records,* in public repositories set apart for that particular purpose; and to them frequent recourse is had, when any critical question arises, in the determination of which former precedents may give light or assistance. . . . For it is an established rule to abide by former precedents, where the same points come again in litigation: as well to keep the scale of justice even and steady, and not liable to waver with every new judge's opinion; as also because the law in that case being solemnly declared and determined, what before was uncertain, and perhaps indifferent, is now become a permanent rule which it is not in the breast of any subsequent judge to alter or vary from according to his private sentiments: he being sworn to determine, not according to his own private judgment, but according to the known laws and customs of the land; not delegated to pronounce a new law, but to maintain and expound the old one. Yet this rule admits of exception, where the former determination is most evidently contrary to reason; much more if it be clearly contrary to the divine law. But even in such cases the subsequent judges do not pretend to make a new law, but to vindicate the old one from misrepresentation. For if it be found that the former decision is manifestly absurd or unjust, it is declared, not that such a sentence was *bad law,* but that it was

American ed. (Chicago: Callaghan & Cockcroft, 1871), I, 69–70. Sir William Blackstone was an eighteenth-century English jurist whose *Commentaries* (1765–1768) became one of the most influential writings in Anglo-American legal theory.

not law; that is, that it is not the established custom of the realm, as has been erroneously determined. . . .

1.2   *"[Courts] may truly be said to have neither FORCE nor WILL, but merely judgment . . ."*

THE FEDERALIST, NO. 78

Alexander Hamilton

. . . Whoever attentively considers the different departments of power must perceive that, in a government in which they are separated from each other, the judiciary, from the nature of its functions, will always be the least dangerous to the political rights of the Constitution; because it will be least in capacity to annoy or injure them. The Executive not only dispenses honors, but holds the sword of the community. The legislature not only commands the purse, but prescribes the rules by which the duties and rights of every citizen are to be regulated. The judiciary, on the contrary, has no influence over either the sword or the purse; no direction either of the strength or of the wealth of the society; and can take no active resolution whatever. It may truly be said to have neither FORCE nor WILL, but merely judgment; and must ultimately depend upon the aid of the executive arm for the efficacy of its judgment. . . .

Some perplexity respecting the rights of the courts to pronounce legislative acts void, because contrary to the constitution, has arisen from an imagination that the doctrine would imply a superiority of the judiciary to the legislative power. It is urged that the authority which can declare the acts of another void, must necessarily be superior to the one whose acts may be declared void. As this doctrine is of great importance in all the American constitutions, a brief discussion of the ground on which it rests cannot be unacceptable.

There is no position which depends on clearer principles, than that every act of a delegated authority, contrary to the tenor of the commission under which it is exercised, is void. No legislative act, therefore, contrary to the Constitution, can be valid. To deny this, would be to affirm that the deputy is greater than his principal; that the servant is above his master; that the representatives of the people are superior to the people themselves; that men acting by virtue of powers may do not only what their powers do not authorize, but what they forbid.

If it be said that the legislative body are themselves the constitutional judges of their own powers, and that the construction put on them is conclusive upon the other departments, it may be answered, that this cannot be the natural presumption, where it is not to be collected from any particular provisions in the Constitution. It is not otherwise to be supposed, that the Constitution could intend to enable the representatives of the people to substitute their *will* to that of their constituents. It is far more rational to suppose, that the courts were designed to be an intermediate body between the people and the legislature, in order, among other things, to keep the latter within the limits assigned to their authority. The interpretation of the laws is the proper and peculiar province of the courts. A constitution is, in fact, and must be regarded by the judges, as a fundamental law. It therefore belongs to them to ascertain its meaning, as well as the meaning of any particular act proceeding from the legislative body. If there should happen to be an irreconcilable variance between the two, that which has the superior obligation and validity ought, of course, to be preferred; or, in other words, the Constitution ought to be preferred to the statute, the intention of the people to the intention of their agents.

Nor does this conclusion by any means suppose a superiority of the judicial to the legislative power. It only supposes that the power of the people is superior to both; and that where the will of the legislature, declared in its statutes, stands in opposition to that of the people, declared in the Constitution, the judges ought to be governed by the latter rather than the former. They ought to regulate their decisions by the fundamental laws, rather than by those which are not fundamental. . . .

1.3   *"It is, emphatically, the province and duty of the judicial department, to say what the law is."*

MARBURY V. MADISON

1 Cranch 137, 2 L. Ed. 60 (1803)

Before going out of office after their crushing defeat in 1800, the Federalists enacted the Judiciary Act of 1801. While this law made several needed reforms, its creation of many new judicial posts—to which Adams nominated and the lame-duck Senate confirmed deserving Federalists—made it vulnerable to a charge of court packing. In signing and delivering the commissions the night before Jefferson's inauguration, Adams's Secretary of State, John Marshall, neglected to deliver a number of appointments to justice-of-the-peace courts in the District of Columbia. The new Secretary of State, James Madison, refused to deliver some of these commissions. William Marbury, one of the disappointed appointees, brought suit in the Supreme Court under a provision of the Judiciary Act of 1789 that Marbury claimed gave the Court original jurisdiction in such cases.

It was expected that Marshall and the other Federalist justices would order the commission delivered and that Jefferson would defy the Court's authority. Marshall

opened his opinion with a 9,000-word indictment of Jefferson's ethics, asserting that
Marbury was entitled to his commission. Next the Chief Justice held that the laws of the
United States afforded Marbury a remedy. The third point was whether Marbury had
sought the proper remedy. Marshall stated that that portion of the Act of 1789 on which
Marbury relied enlarged the original jurisdiction of the Supreme Court as defined in
Article III of the Constitution. This apparent conflict raised the issue of whether the
justices should follow a statute when it ran counter to their interpretation of the Constitution.

MR. CHIEF JUSTICE MARSHALL delivered the opinion of the
Court. . . .

The question whether an act, repugnant to the constitution, can
become the law of the land, is a question deeply interesting to the
United States; but, happily, not of an intricacy proportioned to its
interest. It seems only necessary to recognize certain principles,
supposed to have been long and well established, to decide it. That
the people have an original right to establish for their future government, such principles as, in their opinion, shall most conduce to their
own happiness, is the basis on which the whole American fabric has
been erected. The exercise of this original right is a very great exertion; nor can it, nor ought it, to be frequently repeated. The principles, therefore, so established, are deemed fundamental: and as the
authority from which they proceed is supreme, and can seldom act,
they are designed to be permanent.

This original and supreme will organizes the government, and
assigns to different departments their respective powers. It may
either stop here, or establish certain limits not to be transcended by
those departments. The government of the United States is of the
latter description. The powers of the legislature are defined and
limited; and that those limits may not be mistaken, or forgotten, the
constitution is written. To what purpose are powers limited, and to
what purpose is that limitation committed to writing, if these limits
may, at any time, be passed by those intended to be restrained? The
distinction between a government with limited and unlimited powers is abolished, if those limits do not confine the persons on whom
they are imposed, and if acts prohibited and acts allowed, are of equal
obligation. It is a proposition too plain to be contested, that the
constitution controls any legislative act repugnant to it; or that the
legislature may alter the constitution by an ordinary act.

Between these alternatives, there is no middle ground. The constitution is either a superior paramount law, unchangeable by ordinary means, or it is on a level with ordinary legislative acts, and, like
other acts, is alterable when the legislature shall please to alter it. If
the former part of the alternative be true, then a legislative act,
contrary to the constitution, is not law; if the latter part be true, then

Constitution expresses the fundamental principles. All law should be based on it.

written constitutions are absurd attempts, on the part of the people, to limit a power, in its own nature, illimitable.

Certainly, all those who have framed written constitutions contemplate them as forming the fundamental and paramount law of the nation, and consequently, the theory of every such government must be, that an act of the legislature repugnant to the constitution is void. This theory is essentially attached to a written constitution, and is, consequently, to be considered, by this court, as one of the fundamental principles of our society. It is not, therefore, to be lost sight of, in the further consideration of this subject.

If an act of the legislature, repugnant to the constitution, is void, does it, notwithstanding its invalidity, bind the courts, and oblige them to give it effect? Or, in other words, though it not be law, does it constitute a rule as operative as if it was a law? This would be to overthrow, in fact, what was established in theory; and would seem, at first view, an absurdity too gross to be insisted on. It shall, however, receive a more attentive consideration.

It is, emphatically, the province and duty of the judicial department, to say what the law is. Those who apply the rule to particular cases, must of necessity expound and interpret that rule. If two laws conflict with each other, the courts must decide on the operation of each. So, if a law be in opposition to the constitution; if both the law and the constitution apply to a particular case, so that the court must either decide that case, conformably to the law, disregarding the constitution; or conformably to the constitution, disregarding the law; the court must determine which of these conflicting rules governs the case: this is of the very essence of judicial duty. If then, the courts are to regard the constitution, and the constitution is superior to any ordinary act of the legislature, the constitution, and not such ordinary act, must govern the case to which they both apply.

Those, then, who controvert the principle, that the constitution is to be considered, in court, as a paramount law, are reduced to the necessity of maintaining that courts must close their eyes on the constitution, and see only the law. This doctrine would subvert the very foundation of all written constitutions. . . . It would declare, that if the legislature shall do that which is expressly forbidden, such act, notwithstanding the express prohibition, is in reality effectual. It would be giving to the legislature a practical and real omnipotence, with the same breath which professes to restrict their powers within narrow limits. . . .

The judicial power of the United States is extended to all cases arising under the constitution. Could it be the intention of those who gave this power, to say, that in using it, the constitution should not be looked into? That a case arising under the constitution should be decided, without examining the instrument under which it arises?

This is too extravagant to be maintained. In some cases, then, the constitution must be looked into by the judges. And if they can open it at all, what part of it are they forbidden to read or to obey?

There are many other parts of the constitution which serve to illustrate this subject. It is declared that "no tax or duty shall be laid on articles exported from any state." Suppose, a duty on the export of cotton, of tobacco, or of flour; and a suit intended to recover it. Ought judgment to be rendered in such a case? ought the judges to close their eyes on the constitution, and only see the law?

The constitution declares "that no bill of attainder or *ex post facto* law shall be passed." If, however, such a bill should be passed, and a person should be prosecuted under it; must the court condemn to death those victims whom the constitution endeavors to preserve?

"No person," says the constitution, "shall be convicted of treason, unless on the testimony of two witnesses to the same overt act, or on confession in open court." Here, the language of the constitution is addressed especially to the courts. It prescribes, directly for them, a rule of evidence not to be departed from. If the legislature should change that rule, and declare one witness, or a confession out of court, sufficient for conviction, must the constitutional principle yield to the legislative act?

From these, and many other selections which might be made, it is apparent that the framers of the constitution contemplated that instrument as a rule for the government of courts, as well as of the legislature. Why otherwise does it direct the judges to take an oath to support it? This oath certainly applies, in an especial manner, to their conduct in their official character. How immoral to impose it on them, if they were to be used as the instruments, and the knowing instruments, for violating what they swear to support! . . . Why does a judge swear to discharge his duties agreeably to the constitution of the United States, if that constitution forms no rule for his government? if it is closed upon him, and cannot be inspected by him? If such be the real state of things, this is worse than solemn mockery. To prescribe, or to take the oath, becomes equally a crime.

It is also not entirely unworthy of observation, that in declaring what shall be the supreme law of the land, the constitution itself is first mentioned; and not the laws of the United States, generally, but those only which shall be made in pursuance of the constitution, have that rank.

Thus, the particular phraseology of the constitution of the United States confirms and strengthens the principle, supposed to be essential to all written constitutions, that a law repugnant to the constitution is void; and that courts, as well as other departments, are bound by that instrument.

The rule must be discharged.

1.4   *"The prophecies of what the courts will do in fact . . . are what I mean by the law."*

THE PATH OF THE LAW

The problem with law today is that there is no theory

Oliver Wendell Holmes, Jr.

When we study law we are not studying a mystery but a well known profession. We are studying what we shall want in order to appear before judges, or to advise people in such a way as to keep them out of court. The reason why it is a profession, why people will pay lawyers to argue for them or to advise them, is that in societies like ours the command of the public force is intrusted to the judges in certain cases, and the whole power of the state will be put forth, if necessary, to carry out their judgments and decrees. People want to know under what circumstances and how far they run the risk of coming against what is so much stronger than themselves, and hence it becomes a business to find out when this danger is to be feared. The object of our study, then, is prediction, the prediction of the incidence of the public force through the instrumentality of the courts.

The means of the study are a body of reports, of treatises, and of statutes, in this country and in England, extending back for six hundred years, and now increasing annually by hundreds. In these sibylline leaves are gathered the scattered prophecies of the past upon the cases in which the axe will fall. These are what properly have been called the oracles of the law. Far the most important and pretty nearly the whole meaning of every new effort of legal thought is to make these prophecies more precise, and to generalize them into a thoroughly connected system. . . . The primary rights and duties with which jurisprudence busies itself again are nothing but prophecies. One of the many evil effects of the confusion between legal and moral ideas, about which I shall have something to say in a moment, is that theory is apt to get the cart before the horse, and to consider the right or the duty as something existing apart from and independent of the consequences of its breach, to which certain sanctions are added afterward. But, as I shall try to show, a legal duty so called is nothing but a prediction that if a man does or omits certain things he will be made to suffer in this or that way by judgment of the court; —and so of a legal right. . . .

The first thing for a business-like understanding of the matter is to understand its limits, and therefore I think it desirable at once to

10 *Harvard Law Review* 39 (1897). Copyright 1897, Oliver Wendell Holmes, Jr. Holmes was Justice, Massachusetts Supreme Judicial Court, 1882–1899; Chief Justice, Massachusetts Supreme Judicial Court, 1899–1902; and Associate Justice, U.S. Supreme Court, 1902–1932.

point out and dispel a confusion between morality and law, which sometimes rises to the height of conscious theory, and more often and indeed constantly is making trouble in detail without reaching the point of consciousness. You can see very plainly that a bad man has as much reason as a good one for wishing to avoid an encounter with the public force, and therefore you can see the practical importance of the distinction between morality and law. A man who cares nothing for an ethical rule which is believed and practiced by his neighbors is likely nevertheless to care a good deal to avoid being made to pay money, and will want to keep out of jail if he can.

I take it for granted that no hearer of mine will misinterpret what I have to say as the language of cynicism. The law is the witness and external deposit of our moral life. Its history is the history of the moral development of the race. The practice of it, in spite of popular jests, tends to make good citizens and good men. When I emphasize the difference between law and morals I do so with reference to a single end, that of learning and understanding the law. For that purpose you must definitely master its specific marks, and it is for that that I ask you for the moment to imagine yourselves indifferent to other and greater things.

I do not say that there is not a wider point of view from which the distinction between law and morals becomes of secondary or no importance, as all mathematical distinctions vanish in presence of the infinite. But I do say that that distinction is of the first importance for the object which we are here to consider,—a right study and mastery of the law as a business with well understood limits, a body of dogma enclosed within definite lines. I have just shown the practical reason for saying so. If you want to know the law and nothing else, you must look at it as a bad man, who cares only for the material consequences which such knowledge enables him to predict, not as a good one, who finds his reasons for conduct, whether inside the law or outside of it, in the vaguer sanctions of conscience. . . . The prophecies of what the courts will do in fact, and nothing more pretentious, ~Law~ are what I mean by the law. . . .

. . . You may assume, with Hobbes and Bentham and Austin, that all law emanates from the sovereign, even when the first human beings to enunciate it are the judges, or you may think that law is the voice of the Zeitgeist, or what you like. It is all one to my present purpose. . . . In every system there are such explanations and principles to be found. It is with regard to them that a second fallacy comes in, which I think it important to expose.

The fallacy to which I refer is the notion that the only force at work in the development of the law is logic. In the broadest sense, indeed, that notion would be true. . . . The danger of which I speak is not the admission that the principles governing other phenomena also govern the law, but the notion that a given system, ours, for instance, can be worked out like mathematics from some general axioms of conduct. This is the natural error of the schools, but it is not confined to them. I once heard a very eminent judge say that he never let a decision go until he was absolutely sure that it was right. . . .

This mode of thinking is entirely natural. The training of lawyers is a training in logic. The processes of analogy, discrimination, and deduction are those in which they are most at home. The language of judicial decision is mainly the language of logic. And the logical method and form flatter that longing for certainty and for repose which is in every human mind. But certainty generally is illusion, and repose is not the destiny of man. Behind the logical form lies a judgment as to the relative worth and importance of competing legislative grounds, often an inarticulate and unconscious judgment, it is true, and yet the very root and nerve of the whole proceeding. You can give any conclusion a logical form. You always can imply a condition in a contract. But why do you imply it? It is because of some belief as to the practice of the community or of a class, or because of some opinion as to policy, or, in short, because of some attitude of yours upon a matter not capable of exact quantitative measurement, and therefore not capable of founding exact logical conclusions. Such matters really are battle grounds where the means do not exist for determinations that shall be good for all time, and where the decision can do no more than embody the preference of a given body in a given time and place. We do not realize how large a part of our law is open to reconsideration upon a slight change in the habit of the public mind. No concrete proposition is self-evident, no matter how ready we may be to accept it, not even Mr. Herbert Spencer's Everyman has a right to do what he wills, provided he interferes not with a like right on the part of his neighbors. . . .

I think that the judges themselves have failed adequately to recognize their duty of weighing considerations of social advantage. The duty is inevitable, and the result of the often proclaimed judicial aversion to deal with such considerations is simply to leave the very ground and foundation of judgments inarticulate, and often unconscious, as I have said. When socialism first began to be talked about, the comfortable classes of the community were a good deal frightened. I suspect that this fear has influenced judicial action both here and in England, yet it is certain that it is not a conscious factor in the decisions to which I refer. . . . I cannot but believe that if the training of lawyers led them habitually to consider more definitely and explicitly the social advantage on which the rule they lay down must be justified, they sometimes would hesitate where now they are confident, and see that really they were taking sides upon debatable and often burning questions.

So much for the fallacy of logical form. Now let us consider the present condition of the law as a subject for study, and the ideal toward which it tends. . . . The development of our law has gone on for nearly a thousand years, like the development of a plant, each generation taking the inevitable next step, mind, like matter, simply obeying a law of spontaneous growth. It is perfectly natural and right that it should have been so. Imitation is a necessity of human nature. . . . Most of the things we do, we do for no better reason than that our fathers have done them or that our neighbors do them, and the same is true of a larger part than we suspect of what we think. The reason is a good one, because our short life gives us no time for a better, but it is not the best. It does not follow, because we all are compelled to take on faith at second hand most of the rules on which we base our action and our thought, that each of us may not try to set some corner of his world in the order of reason, or that all of us collectively should not aspire to carry reason as far as it will go throughout the whole domain. In regard to the law, it is true, no doubt, that an evolutionist will hesitate to affirm universal validity for his social ideals, or for the principles which he thinks should be embodied in legislation. He is content if he can prove them best for here and now. He may be ready to admit that he knows nothing about an absolute best in the cosmos, and even that he knows next to nothing about a permanent best for men. Still it is true that a body of law is more rational and more civilized when every rule it contains is referred articulately and definitely to an end which it subserves, and when the grounds for desiring that end are stated or are ready to be stated in words.

At present, in very many cases, if we want to know why a rule of law has taken its particular shape, and more or less if we want to know why it exists at all, we go to tradition. We follow it into the Year Books, and perhaps beyond them to the customs of the Salian Franks, and somewhere in the past, in the German forests, in the needs of Norman kings, in the assumptions of a dominant class, in the absence of generalized ideas, we find out the practical motive for what now best is justified by the mere fact of its acceptance and that men are accustomed to it. The rational study of law is still to a large extent the study of history. . . . It is a part of the rational study, because it is the first step toward an enlightened scepticism, that is, toward a deliberate reconsideration of the worth of those rules. When you get the dragon out of his cave on to the plain and in the daylight, you can count his teeth and claws, and see just what is his strength. But to get him out is only the first step. The next is either to kill him, or to tame him and make him a useful animal. For the rational study of the law the black-letter man may be the man of the present, but the man of the future is the man of statistics and the master of economics. It is revolting to have no better reason for a rule of law than that so it was laid down in the time of Henry IV. It is still more revolting if the grounds upon which it was laid down have vanished long since, and the rule simply persists from blind imitation of the past. . . .

1.5   *"We cannot transcend the limitations of the ego . . ."*

THE NATURE OF THE JUDICIAL PROCESS

Benjamin N. Cardozo (N.Y. Court of Appeals)

The work of deciding cases goes on every day in hundreds of courts throughout the land. Any judge, one might suppose, would find it easy to describe the process which he had followed a thousand times and more. Nothing could be farther from the truth. Let some intelligent layman ask him to explain: he will not go very far before taking refuge in the excuse that the language of craftsmen is unintelligible to those untutored in the craft. Such an excuse may cover with a semblance of respectability an otherwise ignominious retreat. It will hardly serve to still the pricks of curiosity and conscience. In moments of introspection . . . the troublesome problem will recur, and press for a solution. What is it that I do when I decide a case? To what sources of information do I appeal for guidance? In what proportions do I permit them to contribute to the result? In what proportions ought they to contribute? If a precedent is applicable, when do I refuse to follow it? If no precedent is applicable, how do I reach the rule that will make a precedent for the future? . . . At what point shall the quest be halted by some discrepant custom, by some consideration of the social welfare, by my own or the common standards of justice and morals? Into that strange compound which is brewed daily in the cauldron of the courts, all these ingredients enter in varying proportions. I am not concerned to inquire whether judges ought to be allowed to brew such a compound at all. I take judge-made law as one of the existing realities of life. There before us is the brew. Not a judge on the bench but has had a hand in the making. The elements have not come together by chance. *Some* principle, however unavowed and inarticulate and subconscious, has regulated the infusion. It may not have been the same principle for all judges

New Haven, Connecticut: Yale University Press, 1921, pp. 9–13, 18–21, 43, 66–67, 105–106, 113–114, 141, 161–162. Copyright © 1921 by Yale University Press. Reprinted with permission. Benjamin N. Cardozo was Judge, New York Court of Appeals, 1913–1926; Chief Judge, New York Court of Appeals, 1926–1932; and Associate Justice, U.S. Supreme Court, 1932–1939.

at any time, nor the same principle for any judge at all times. But a choice there has been, not a submission to the decrees of Fate; and the considerations and motives determining the choice, even if often obscure, do not utterly resist analysis. . . . [T]here will be need to distinguish between the conscious and the subconscious. . . . More subtle are the forces so far beneath the surface that they cannot reasonably be classified as other than subconscious. It is often through these subconscious forces that judges are kept consistent with themselves, and inconsistent with one another. . . . There is in each of us a stream of tendency, whether you choose to call it philosophy or not, which gives coherence and direction to thought and action. Judges cannot escape that current any more than other mortals. All their lives, forces which they do not recognize and cannot name, have been tugging at them—inherited instincts, traditional beliefs, acquired convictions; and the resultant is an outlook on life, a conception of social needs, a sense in James's phrase of "the total push and pressure of the cosmos," which, when reasons are nicely balanced, must determine where choices shall fall. In this mental background every problem finds its setting. We may try to see things as objectively as we please. None the less, we can never see them with any eyes except our own. . . .

We reach the land of mystery when constitution and statute are silent, and the judge must look to the common law for the rule that fits the case. He is the "living oracle of the law" in Blackstone's vivid phrase. Looking at Sir Oracle in action, viewing his work in the dry light of realism, how does he set about his task?

The first thing he does is to compare the case before him with the precedents, whether stored in his mind or hidden in books. I do not mean that precedents are ultimate sources of the law, supplying the sole equipment that is needed for the legal armory, the sole tools . . . "in the legal smithy." Back of precedents are basic jural conceptions which are postulates of judicial reasoning, and farther back are the habits of life, the institutions of society, in which those conceptions have had their origin, and which, by a process of interaction, they have modified in turn. None the less, in a system so highly developed as our own, precedents have so covered the ground that they fix the point of departure from which the labor of the judge begins. Almost invariably, his first step is to examine and compare them. If they are plain and to the point, there may be need of nothing more. *Stare decisis* is at least the everyday working rule of our law. . . . It is a process of search, comparison, and little more. Some judges seldom get beyond that process in any case. Their notion of their duty is to match the colors of the case at hand against the colors of many sample cases spread out upon their desk. The sample nearest in shade supplies the applicable rule. But, of course, no system of living law can be evolved by such a process, and no judge of a high court worthy of his office views the function of his place so narrowly. If that were all there were to our calling, there would be little of intellectual interest about it. The man who had the best card index of the cases would also be the wisest judge. It is when the colors do not match, when the references of the index fail, when there is no decisive precedent, that the serious business of the judge begins. He must then fashion Law for the litigants before him. In fashioning it for them, he will be fashioning it for others. . . . Every judgment has a generative power. It begets its own image. . . .

. . . We go forward with our logic, with our analogies, with our philosophies, till we reach a certain point. At first, we have no trouble with the paths; they follow the same lines. Then they begin to diverge, and we must make a choice between them. History or custom or social utility or some compelling sentiment of justice or sometimes perhaps a semi-intuitive apprehension of the pervading spirit of our law must come to the rescue of the anxious judge, and tell him where to go. . . .

The final cause of law is the welfare of society. The rule that misses its aim cannot permanently justify its existence. "Ethical considerations can no more be excluded from the administration of justice . . . than one can exclude the vital air from his room and live." Logic and history and custom have their place. We will shape the law to conform to them when we may; but only within bounds. The end which the law serves will dominate them all. . . . I do not mean, of course, that judges are commissioned to set aside existing rules at pleasure in favor of any other set of rules which they may hold to be expedient or wise. I mean that when they are called upon to say how far existing rules are to be extended or restricted, they must let the welfare of society fix the path, its direction and distance. . . .

There has been much debate among foreign jurists whether the norms of right and useful conduct, the patterns of social welfare, are to be found by the judge in conformity with an objective or a subjective standard. . . . So far as the distinction has practical significance, the traditions of our jurisprudence commit us to the objective standard. I do not mean, of course, that this ideal of objective vision is ever perfectly attained. We cannot transcend the limitations of the *ego* and see anything as it really is. None the less, the ideal is one to be striven for within the limits of our capacity. This truth, when clearly perceived, tends to unify the judge's function. His duty to declare the law in accordance with reason and justice is seen to be a phase of his duty to declare it in accordance with custom. It is the customary morality of right-minded men and women which he is to enforce by his decree. . . .

My analysis of the judicial process comes then to this, and little more: logic, and history, and custom, and utility, and the accepted standards of right conduct, are the forces which singly or in combination shape the progress of the law. Which of these forces shall dominate in any case must depend largely upon the comparative importance or value of the social interests that will be thereby promoted or impaired. . . .

If you ask how [the judge] is to know when one interest outweighs another, I can only answer that he must get his knowledge just as the legislator gets it; from experience and study and reflection; in brief, from life itself. Here, indeed, is the point of contact between the legislator's work and his. The choice of methods, the appraisement of values, must in the end be guided by like considerations for the one as for the other. Each indeed is legislating within the limits of his competence. No doubt the limits for the judge are narrower. He legislates only between gaps. He fills the open spaces in the law. How far he may go without traveling beyond the walls of the interstices cannot be staked out for him upon a chart. He must learn it for himself as he gains the sense of fitness and proportion that comes with years of habitude in the practice of an art.

. . . [Yet] the judge, even when he is free, is still not wholly free. He is not to innovate at pleasure. He is not a knight-errant roaming at will in pursuit of his own ideal of beauty or of goodness. He is to draw his inspiration from consecrated principles. He is not to yield to spasmodic sentiment, to vague and unregulated benevolence. He is to exercise a discretion informed by tradition, methodized by analogy, disciplined by system, and subordinated to "the primordial necessity of order in the social life." Wide enough in all conscience is the field of discretion that remains. . . .

Our survey of judicial methods teaches us, I think, the lesson that the whole subject matter of jurisprudence is more plastic, more malleable, the moulds less definitively cast, the bound of right and wrong less preordained and constant, than most of us . . . have been accustomed to believe. . . . So also the duty of a judge becomes itself a question of degree, and he is a useful judge or a poor one as he estimates the measure accurately or loosely. He must balance all his ingredients, his philosophy, his logic, his analogies, his history, his customs, his sense of right, and all the rest, and adding a little here and taking out a little there, must determine, as wisely as he can, which weight shall tip the scales. . . .

1.6   *"The legitimacy of a child . . . may be disputed."*

THE NAPOLEONIC CODE: BOOK I

Title VII of the Napoleonic Code, decreed on March 23, 1803, deals with the law of "Paternity and Filiation." Chapter 1, entitled "Of Filiation of Children legitimate or born in Marriage," illustrates the style and logic of the Code.

312. A child conceived during marriage has the husband for its father.

Nevertheless he may disown the child, if he prove that, during the time which elapsed from the three hundredth to the one hundred and eightieth day before the birth of the child, he was, either by reason of distance, or in consequence of any accident, under the physical impossibility of cohabiting with his wife.

313. The husband cannot, by alledging his natural impotence, disown the child: he cannot disown it for cause of adultery, unless the birth has been concealed from him, in which case he shall be allowed to offer all the facts necessary to prove that he is not the father of it.

314. The child born before the one hundred and eightieth day of the marriage, can not be disowned by the husband in the following cases: 1. if he had knowledge of the pregnancy before the marriage; 2. if he has been privy to the act of birth, and if this act be signed by him, or contain his declaration that he knows not how to sign; 3. if the child be declared incapable of living.

315. The legitimacy of a child born three hundred days after the dissolution of marriage, may be disputed.

316. In the various cases wherein the husband is authorised to disclaim, he must do it, within the month, if he is upon the spot where the child is born; within two months after his return, if he was absent at the time; within two months after the discovery of the fraud, if the birth of the child was concealed from him.

317. If the husband be dead without having made his disclaimer, but being still within the time allowed for the purpose, the heirs shall have two months to contest the legitimacy of the child, reckoning from the time when such child shall have taken possession of the property of the husband, or from the period when the heirs were disturbed in such possession by the child.

2
Courts and Social Policy

The essential characteristics of institutions called courts, according to Martin Shapiro, are: (1) an independent judge applying (2) preexisting norms after (3) adversary proceedings in order to achieve (4) a dichotomous decision—one party right and one party wrong.[1] The almost universal existence of courts as thus described (or courtlike structures) suggests that they fulfill a basic need in social organization. It is tempting to go back to primitive societies for clues as to why courts develop and what their role is.

ORIGIN AND ROLE OF COURTS

William Seagle speculates that courts originate when society loses its foundation of kinship bonds, and relations become less personalized as the size and complexity of the social organization increases.[2] Glendon Schubert thinks that the need for courts is a direct function of the concentration of people and wealth. He regards it as significant that the Cheyenne Indians as a nomadic tribe had no need for courts, whereas the Barotse of Northern Rhodesia (now Zambia), as subsistence farmers, did.[3] "Once people stop wandering around the landscape," says Theodore L. Becker, "up go the courts."[4]

Cultural anthropologists have made intensive inquiries into judicial systems of primitive societies. Max Gluckman studied the judicial process among the Barotse and concluded that it corresponded with judi-

[1] *Courts: A Comparative and Political Analysis* (Chicago: University of Chicago Press, 1981), p. 1.
[2] *The Quest for Law* (New York: Knopf, 1941), p. 92.
[3] *Judicial Policy-Making* (Chicago: Scott, Foresman, 1965), p. 12.
[4] *Comparative Judicial Politics* (Chicago: Rand McNally, 1970), p. 103.

29

cial processes in Western society more than it differed from them.[5] Paul Bohannon examined justice and judgment among the Tiv in northern Nigeria and concluded that it would be "sociological over-simplification of the most blatant sort" to undertake to show similarities between Tiv law and Western law.[6] Victor Ayoub reviewed both studies and drew the conclusion that the main function of a court is to conciliate and to reintroduce harmony into the social relations of the contending parties, so that in effect the community will again function smoothly. But analogy between primitive and modern judicial systems, he thought, "seems neither to explain nor confirm. It serves only to suggest."[7]

Universal or not, it is clear that nearly all complex societies entrust agencies commonly called courts with a significant role in the resolution of conflicts. Their function is to decide disputes among individuals about personal or property rights as well as to assess blame and punishment upon transgressors against the community, in accordance with the laws, customs, traditions, taboos, or holy books of the society. Courts offer an alternative to force. The judicial process gains respect because it is a more predictable, fairer, and less disruptive means of settling disputes than combat. As George Christie says, "The primary social purpose of the judicial process is deciding disputes in a manner that will, upon reflection, permit the loser as well as the winner to feel that he has been fairly treated."[8]

Acceptance of judicial decisions as fair derives, first, from the status and prestige of the decision maker. In some societies the temporal chief may also act as judge, but it generally becomes necessary to treat the task of judging as a specialized role, allocated on the basis of seniority, reputation for learning or wisdom, confidence of the ruling powers, spiritual leadership, or consensus of the community. However selected, judges occupy a position of high status, often wear distinctive uniforms, are addressed deferentially, and can enforce respect for their office by punitive powers.

It is not, however, merely because judges are regarded as wise or trained in the law that the judicial process is thought to produce fair decisions. Judicial rulings are the end product of a distinctive process of varying degrees of complexity that determines facts and shapes issues for the ultimate decision maker. The proceeding before the judge is typically an adversary one, pitting two parties against each other, each intent upon establishing the rightness of its own contentions and the errors of its opponent's. In simpler societies—and occa-

5 "The Judicial Process Among the Barotse of Northern Nigeria," in Glendon A. Schubert, *Judicial Behavior: A Reader in Theory and Research* (Chicago: Rand McNally, 1964), p. 104.

6 "Justice and Judgment Among the Tiv," in Schubert, op. cit., p. 123.

7 "The Judicial Process in Two African Tribes," in Schubert, op. cit., p. 127.

8 "Objectivity in the Law," 78 *Yale Law Journal* 1311, 1329 (1969).

sionally even in the Western world—parties may themselves present their case, but generally they are represented by counsel skilled in the substantive rules and procedural technicalities of the law. Witnesses offer evidence as to the facts in dispute, and experts in the field of controversy provide technological information. Lay participants may perform a valued role, either as jurors who "find" the facts or as auxiliary judges. Only after these procedures, which are in part ritualistic as well as instrumental, and on the basis of the record that has been made, may a judge announce a decision and give reasons for it. Even then, the possibility exists of testing the fairness of the decision by appeal to a higher court.

case proceedings

The foregoing account of the judicial process is, of course, an idealized one. Judges may not be wise or learned. They may be irascible, prejudiced, and/or open to bribes. They are almost by definition representatives of the Establishment, likely to deal harshly with dissenters. Judicial proceedings have the reputation of being slow and expensive. Lawyers have perennially been targets of sarcasm and abuse because of a popular conception of their craft as devious, pettifogging, and manipulative. In Act 4 of Shakespeare's *King Henry the Sixth, Part II,* Dick the Butcher proposes to Jack Cade, "The first thing we do, let's kill all the lawyers." Moreover, legal rules themselves may not be fair or reasonable. Told in Dickens's *Oliver Twist* that the law assumed a man controlled the actions of his wife, Mr. Bumble made a classic response: "If the law says that, sir, then the law is a ass."

There is, then, a darker side to the judicial process, which the chapters that follow will try not to minimize. Critics have contended that in no other serious field of human endeavor where truth must be established or facts verified are the methods of the law courts used. These charges ignore the fact that the purpose of the judicial process is not solely to establish truth, but also to make societal exercise of compulsion acceptable. Because the scientific method in particular has been contrasted favorably with the ritualistic and argumentative procedures of the courts, there is no little irony in the proposal made in 1976 by a responsible group of physical scientists that courtlike adversary proceedings be set up as a method for resolving factual disputes about certain scientific issues so as to provide a sounder basis for public decisions.[9]

ALTERNATIVES TO LITIGATION

Most Americans probably regard courts and judges as the usual instruments for resolving social conflict, but a panoply of alternative modes is readily available. Direct negotiation, bargaining, mediation, and even violence still abound in almost every industrial nation. Police,

[9] 193 *Science* 653 (Aug. 20, 1976).

social workers, parole officers, and visiting nurses spend a large share of their time acting as informal mediators among neighbors and relatives, quieting disputes before they produce grist for judicial mills. Modern societies also use elections and referenda to help settle conflict, not only about who will govern but also about what public policies will prevail. Statutes may provide for compulsory arbitration in labor disputes or labor and management may include such provisions in their contracts.

It should be kept in mind that even the most formal processes have informal aspects. For instance, in civil suits, that is, legal actions in which one party (private citizen, group, corporation, or governmental agency) seeks compensation from another party, filing papers in court may be only one step toward an informal settlement, a bargaining ploy by one side.

Even criminal cases become matters of negotiation. The majority of convictions—and in some jurisdictions as many as nine out of ten— come from pleas of guilty that result from bargaining. The prosecutor reduces the charges against the defendant in return for a plea of guilty on the lesser charge. The defendant may rather accept a year in jail than risk five to ten years' imprisonment. Letting a criminal off with a light sentence may displease a prosecutor, but his office is likely to be understaffed and overworked. Moreover, he too faces a risk: a verdict of not guilty. The trial judge, whose swollen docket may have several hundred cases pending, is typically only too happy to see a bargain struck.

Alexis de Tocqueville gave a classic description of the American addiction to "lawing" in 1835. (Reading 2.1.) Today our degree of reliance on courts for dispute settlement can be better appreciated by comparison with certain other cultures. Japan, for example, is relatively suit-free, with a heritage of avoiding open confrontation. It is a nonadversarial, nonlitigious society, with only 10,000 lawyers in the entire country, compared with half a million in the United States. Private disputes are typically decided in out-of-court negotiation. (Reading 2.2.)

In American courts, by contrast, football fans upset over a call in a championship game sued the referee and the National Football League for "consumer fraud." A twenty-year-old man sued his parents for $350,000 because they had not brought him up properly. Parents of a child conceived a year after the mother had a sterilization operation sued the doctors for the expenses of rearing the child. The financial risk of malpractice suits has driven many physicians to abandon the practice of obstetrics. A comparatively small company raised the funds to sue a giant computer corporation by selling partnership shares in the lawsuit to some sixty investors. A clergyman who had counseled a young man was sued for malpractice by his parents after the youth committed suicide. (Reading 2.3.) In 1983 the Supreme Court, its patience exhausted, took the unusual action of fining a litigant $500 for filing frivolous lawsuits in the federal courts.[10]

The litigation explosion has encouraged organized efforts to promote alternative settlement processes or voluntary mechanisms for settling disputes. The movement, supported by Chief Justice Burger, has generated a new professional journal, *The Journal of Dispute Resolution,* and its own acronym—ADR (Alternative Dispute Resolution). Since the movement aims to reduce the amount of litigation, its principal emphasis is on negotiation and mediation prior to suit. But Professor Owen Fiss of the Yale Law School doubts that out-of-court settlement is always preferable to judgment by a court, and he does not think that settlement should be "institutionalized on a wholesale and indiscriminate basis."[11]

SEPARATION OF POWERS

In their formal as well as informal roles as resolvers of conflict, judges often affect public policy. Indeed, to settle a specific case they may deem it necessary to construct, interpret, and apply general rules—functions that violate notions of "separation of powers," which civics textbooks (and often judges themselves) praise. But "separation of powers" is a very fuzzy concept and a poor prescription for governing in the real world. Unlike Caesar's Gaul, governmental power cannot be neatly divided into three parts: legislative, executive, and judicial. It is impossible to draw a sharp line between legislating and adjudicating or between administering and either of the other two. (See the speech of Judge Frank Johnson, Reading 2.4.) How can an executive enforce a law without interpreting it? When a policeman decides not to ticket a driver who is exceeding the speed limit by only five miles an hour, is the officer legislating, administering, or adjudicating? How can judges help but make law when they decide what a vaguely worded statute means in a situation that its drafters never foresaw? As we shall see in Chapters 11 and 12, in a modern society interpretation of statutes, orders, or constitutional clauses is inherently a creative activity.

The features of conflict resolution peculiar to the judicial process can perhaps be better appreciated when compared to the legislative institutions that share these responsibilities. The conventional wisdom has it that legislatures make law while the courts enforce law. It is more accurate to suggest, as J. Woodford Howard, Jr., does, that the two processes are distinguished more by their procedures. While judicial

---

[10] *Tatum v. University of Nebraska* (1983). In both *Talamini v. Allstate Insurance Co.* (1985) and *Crumpacker v. Indiana* (1985), minority justices favored imposing fines for allegedly frivolous appeals, but the prevailing view stressed freedom of access to the courts as "a cherished value in our democratic society."

[11] "Against Settlement," 93 *Yale Law Journal* 1073 (1984).

procedures have historically been applied to a relatively narrow range of social conflicts, the two processes are complementary, and American courts have historically shared in the broader aspects of policy determination. (Reading 2.5.)

CHARACTERISTICS OF COURTS: LIMITS AND POSSIBILITIES FOR POLICY MAKING

The first and perhaps the most important characteristic of courts is that they cannot initiate action. Unlike legislators and administrators, judges may not—like legendary knights—ride off in search of someone in distress to rescue; they must wait for someone to appear in court and complain. Chapter 5 discusses in more detail limitations on how and when individuals may bring lawsuits; here we note only that one cannot energize judicial power merely by alleging some general wrong. A person in distress cannot obtain a judicial hearing merely by protesting, say, a lack of protection against menacing dragons.

To have a "case," someone must point to a specific and personal legal right that is being violated. For example, one might specify the dragon or dragons that are causing trouble and assert as a legally protected right something as concrete as the right to enjoy one's own property in peace. As a far less probable alternative, the aggrieved party might point to the existence of a statute that imposes a nondiscretionary duty on some official to exterminate dragons.

In addition, the person in distress must ask for a remedy—a cure or solution—that the court can grant. The judge cannot order Ye Blue Knight to go forth and slay—or even arrest—one Oliver Dragon, again except in the unlikely event that a statute clearly imposes a nondiscretionary duty on Blue Knight so to act. If there is a relevant statute but one that allows the officer of the law some discretion in carrying out the task of ridding the world of dragons, then the person with the complaint must go not to court but to law-enforcement officials and request action. If there is no statute at all, one must petition one's local legislator for action. Indeed, even if Blue Knight, acting as both police officer and prosecutor, brings Dragon into court, there is nothing the judge can do unless the knight can offer convincing evidence that Dragon has violated a criminal statute.

Normally, there are two remedies that, in our hypothetical situation, a plaintiff (one who initiates a civil action) can legitimately request from a judge. First, one can request that the court require payment of money by Dragon as compensation for injuries caused to the right to enjoy one's property. Second, and either alternatively or additionally, one can petition the court to issue an injunction ordering Dragon to cease and desist from trespassing and causing fright with his fiery snorts. (In such an instance, the "plaintiff" is called a petitioner.)

A third characteristic of the judicial process concerns the kind of evidence that a court will hear and the procedures by which it will receive and weigh evidence. In most trials in nations that follow the common law, much of the evidence is oral. Were the distressed person in our example to seek monetary damages against Dragon, the person would be required to testify, under oath, in response to questions from his or her attorney, to having witnessed Dragon, on a certain date at a particular time, in the act of trespassing. On that occasion, the testimony would continue, Dragon threatened bodily harm by hissing and snorting flame and smoke, thus depriving the plaintiff from that time forward of the peaceful enjoyment of the property.

At the conclusion of the replies to questions of the aggrieved person's own attorney, counsel for Dragon could conduct cross-examination. The purpose could be to expose a contradiction (Was the plaintiff not at fair on the alleged day?); to make the person concede the possibility of error in testimony (Was the dragon encountered really Oliver and not his cousin Henry—for after all, do not all dragons look alike?); or to impugn credibility (Was plaintiff really frightened? Had he or she not at fair last year bested all the other archers in a round robin?).

Furthermore, the other side must have the same full opportunity to present its evidence, subject, again, to cross-examination. Oliver Dragon might claim that for fifteen centuries he and his ancestors had used the stream by plaintiff's castle to cool their engines and that the smoke and fire that had been seen was only steam from his overheated radiator.

Of course, the dispute might necessarily involve some documentary evidence. Dragon might claim that the Romans had given his ancestors title to the stream and produce a grant dated 25 B.C. In rebuttal, plaintiff's attorney might introduce property-tax receipts for a period of three centuries. Whatever the specifics, the basic point is that all the evidence, oral or written, that the court may weigh in its decision is introduced in the presence of both sides, and each litigant has full opportunity to examine and rebut the evidence and arguments of the other. Although they may "notice" notorious circumstances like a war or a depression (see Chapter 9 for elaboration), judges, again unlike administrators or legislators, cannot legitimately consider information denied to one of the parties or base a decision on evidence not submitted in open court.

A fourth distinguishing mark of the judicial process is that the proceedings are adversary. In legal systems based on common law, attorneys for the two sides produce the evidence, define the issues, and formulate the arguments. They battle as equals, with the judge acting more as an umpire than as a participant. The adversary nature of proceeding is less sharp under civil (Roman) law, as practiced in Europe, Latin America, Quebec, parts of Africa, and to some extent Louisiana. In that legal system, the judge plays a far more active role

in civil suits, both in introducing evidence and in questioning witnesses. Civil law judges are also more active in criminal cases, but the
central actor in criminal trials is the procurator, whose tasks are much
broader than those of the American prosecutor and include introducing evidence and arguments for as well as against the defendant. To
say that the procurator controls the trial is an exaggeration, but under
civil law the defense attorney does not have an equal part in the
drama.

A fifth characteristic that sets the judicial process apart from legislative or administrative processes is that the parties—even governmental officials—may legitimately contact the judge or jury only under
tightly structured circumstances. Individuals, pressure groups, or public officials may file lawsuits, urge or help others to do so, or even ask
a judge to allow them to intervene in a case already in progress if the
ultimate decision in that litigation would directly affect their interests.
But lobbying in the sense typically used to describe informal presenta-
tions of views to legislators and administrators is taboo in the judicial
process. It is a serious crime for a litigant even to try to communicate
with the jury or any of its members except in open court under the
watchful eyes of the judge and opponent's counsel. A litigant or the
litigant's attorney may talk to the judge in the judge's chambers, but
normally only in the presence of the attorney for the other side.

A sixth set of distinguishing marks is more subtle and involves the
decision itself. When a legislature attacks the cause of social conflict,
it may issue a sweeping pronouncement in the form of a statute that
regulates the future conduct of all persons within its territory. An
administrative order, detailing more specific rules to carry out a legislative mandate, may be equally far reaching. In contrast, a judicial
decision typically relates to past conduct (Dragon should not have
trespassed on the estate), although it may also forbid future actions
similar to the one that triggered the lawsuit (Dragon is permanently
enjoined from trespassing on the estate).

Furthermore, a judicial decision, unlike a statute or administrative
order, does not bind everyone but only the parties to the case, their
employees, agents, successors in office, and those who cooperate with
any of these people. If it had been Oliver Dragon whom the court
forbade to trespass on the estate, Henry Dragon—as long as he is not
working with or for Oliver—may trespass without violating the judicial
order. The aggrieved property owner will have to go to court and
begin a new lawsuit to stop Henry from trespassing.

Here one encounters a seventh distinction that further differentiates
judicial from legislative ways of coping with conflict, although less so
than from administrative means. At the same time, this seventh distinction blurs the sixth. If a jury decides a dispute, it simply reports its
verdict and in civil suits its award, usually no more than a single
phrase—"Guilty as charged"—or statement—"We find for the plain-

tiff and award plaintiff $10,000 against Oliver Dragon." The jury gives no explanation of or justification for its collective decision.

On the other hand, when judges instruct juries on legal issues and even more so when judges decide cases without juries, they must provide reasons for their choices. Indeed, federal rules of procedure require federal judges to write out their findings of fact and their conclusions of law, and usually judges preface these with more detailed explanations of their reasoning, called an opinion. That opinion should be an intellectually coherent and convincing statement. It is not supposed to be a psychological explanation of why the judge decided one way or the other, but a justification for that decision, phrased in terms of legal principles. Legislators may produce similar statements, and some of the best of these far surpass most judicial opinions in intellectual quality. But whereas a judge, as a matter of course, is supposed to offer such a principled justification for every decision,[12] a legislator need not do so. Indeed, it is perfectly acceptable for a legislator, if later questioned about a vote, to say only, "It benefited *my* constituents." That the proposal injured 99 percent of other citizens is unfortunate—not illegal and possibly not unethical, merely unfortunate.

Publication of a judicial opinion blurs the sixth distinction because, in effect, such an opinion announces or clarifies general rules that the judge intends to apply to future cases. In doing so, especially if the tribunal is the highest court of a state or nation, the impact of an opinion may be similar to that of a statute in the sense of serving as a guide for future conduct of *all* persons within the court's jurisdiction. Thus we return to the problem—and the fact—of judicial lawmaking and judicial policy making.

LAW COURTS AND PUBLIC POLICY

For centuries, common law courts only decided cases between private citizens or criminal offenses that did not involve high matters of state like treason. The judicial procedures we know originally developed out of attempts to cope with social conflict revolving around a limited number of parties arguing about specific factual questions: Did Dragon hiss and spew smoke and fire at the plaintiff? Would such a hissing and spouting create mortal fear in the average, reasonable person? Did the Dragon family have a historic right, legitimated by long and unchallenged use (prescription), to the stream? Under all the circum-

---

[12] There are, of course, exceptions to the rule requiring judges to explain their decisions, the most obvious being the practice of the U.S. Supreme Court in refusing to hear certain cases. Because of the thousands of cases on their docket, the justices usually offer no explanation when they exercise their discretion not to hear a particular case.

stances of the case how much money would fairly compensate plaintiff for the loss of peaceful enjoyment of the property?

Of course—and here we again wander into the province of judicial policy making—larger issues lurk beneath such specific inquiries. What proof is sufficient to establish ownership of property? Does long and unchallenged usage of land or a stream confer legal title? If so, how long is long? Suppose the court found that the land belonged to the plaintiff but that Oliver Dragon had a prescriptive right to use the stream to replenish his cooling system. What then if the owner decided to build a mill on the property and dammed the stream so that the flow of water was changed? Could Dragon sue for damages to his radiator? What about the family who owned the next parcel of land downstream and used the water to fill the moat around its castle and to irrigate its crops? Could that family sue the person who built the dam?

It is evident that the narrow case of *Property Owner v. Dragon* could ignite a series of questions whose answers might affect all people who own property with a stream running through it, as well as affect technological development in an age whose primary sources of energy for manufacturing were muscle and water power. Deciding these issues, even between two private citizens, means preferring one sort of interest or right or value over another sort. Because legal rules are seldom, if ever, neutral in not preferring one interest, right, value, or group over another, conflict between two private citizens can rapidly escalate into conflicts between competing groups or even social and economic classes—upstreamers against downstreamers, mill owners against farmers, early mill owners against later mill owners. Thus, in the aggregate and over time, judicial decisions on such issues inevitably affect general public policy and economic development. (Reading 2.6.)

JUDICIAL SUPERVISION OF GOVERNMENTAL ACTION

But what happens when a private citizen goes into court and asks the judge to order the government to pay damages or to halt a particular policy? When, for instance, a group of poor people file a civil suit, alleging that a town has drafted its zoning ordinances so that they, and others who are economically underprivileged, cannot live in the town? Or suppose both litigants are governmental officials, as, for example, when a state officer asks a court to forbid the Attorney General of the United States to enforce a particular federal statute because, the state officer claims, that statute encroaches on authority reserved to the states. Obviously in these sorts of situations, the potential for judicial policy making is both far more direct and vastly greater than in the average suit between private citizens. Where only individuals are involved, it usually takes a line of decisions handed down over a period of some years to make a deep impact on public policy, but where judges forbid a public official to enforce a statute or order the government to act in a positive fashion, they are immediately and deeply involved in shaping public policy.

The British have never accepted judicial power in that naked a form. There Parliament is supreme; while judges can interpret acts of Parliament—Chapter 11 will show that is no small thing—British judges cannot invalidate a legislative act.[13] In the United States, of course, judges have such authority. The American concept of constitutionalism—a belief in the necessity of limitations on all government, even popular government—coupled with faith in the existence of certain natural, "unalienable rights" encouraged a search for some institution above the legislature and executive to keep both under control. Specific institutional arrangements such as federalism and divisions of authority among several branches of government also created a need for an umpire to draw jurisdictional lines. The existence of a written constitution that proclaimed itself "the supreme law of the land" persuaded judges to offer themselves humbly as chaste guardians of all that was holy and basic in the political system. "It is, emphatically, the province and duty of the judicial department," Chief Justice John Marshall modestly said as he asserted authority to declare unconstitutional acts of other branches of the government, "to say what the law is." (Reading 1.3.) And, of course, as Marshall immediately pointed out, the Constitution proclaims itself law, "The supreme law of the land."

Acceptance of Marshall's tenuous logic—the Constitution itself is silent on judicial review—resulted in a quantum leap in the power of American judges to resolve issues of social—and political—conflict. For the Constitution is not only "supreme law," embodying many of society's basic political values, it is also written in terse but very broad concepts that cry out for interpretation.

For a variety of reasons, judges, until the last few decades of the nineteenth century, seldom used this vast constitutional authority to invalidate federal statutes. But, when after the Civil War the industrial revolution created a mass of new problems with which legislators tried to cope by regulating business and labor, judges attacked with gusto. The dominant judicial belief held that social conflict between labor and management was inevitable, and best solved by bargaining on an individual level. A series of judicial decisions left government, state or federal, with only a small legitimate role in resolving such conflict.

---

[13] This situation may change. As a member of the European Economic Community, Britain, like the other signatories, agreed to a treaty that specifically claims to be superior to the domestic law of any member state. Thus, it is possible that a British court interpreting the treaty may find an act of Parliament inconsistent with that treaty and so invalid.

This aggressive judicial attitude quickly faded away after 1937, when the United States Supreme Court retreated in the face of President Franklin D. Roosevelt's effort to increase the number of justices from nine to fifteen.

Roosevelt did not succeed in his "Court-packing" plan, but he still achieved victory on the substantive issue of economic regulation. A majority of the "Old Court" and all of the younger justices who came to the bench in the years since 1937 left economic affairs to legislative regulation and turned their attention to other issues, in particular the Bill of Rights and the Fourteenth Amendment's guarantee—for decades a hollow guarantee—of equal protection of the laws. The great change in political attitudes toward governmental regulation of the economy that had provided the intellectual force behind the New Deal also came to the bench with some of these younger judges. They did not merely tolerate regulation, they endorsed the new philosophy of the welfare state that governmental intervention in economic and social affairs was not something to be dreaded but encouraged, perhaps demanded.

In a more extreme form, the new theory held that government, especially the federal government, had a positive obligation to regulate the economy as well as a duty to protect not only rights listed in the Constitution but also rights—such as those to a minimum income and a decent education—that make possible fruitful use of those rights mentioned in the Constitution. Moreover, government should protect its citizens not only against discrimination by its officials or those of subordinate agencies but also against other private citizens. Government also has the obligation, so many argue, to compensate for past discrimination.

This philosophy spread unevenly through layers of government and society, but, without a doubt, during the years of Earl Warren's chief justiceship (1953–1969), the Supreme Court encouraged judges to take a forceful role in effectuating much of this new public philosophy. Not all judges, of course, responded positively, and certainly the Supreme Court in more recent years has striven forcefully to dampen judicial enthusiasm for reform. But the activity begun by the Warren Court, in spite of greater restraint on the Burger Court, built up a momentum that has been difficult to stop.

Groups who lack the numbers, prestige, and money needed for clout in the legislative and administrative processes have been crowding the courtrooms, urging judges to protect "the living Constitution," to make it "relevant" to current problems, and to take over important governmental functions when elected officials fail in their duties. Racial minorities, prisoners, patients in mental hospitals, political dissidents, and conservationists have been among the most obvious, but by no means the only, members of the chorus cheering judges on.

JUDICIAL RESPONSES TO DEMANDS FOR SOCIAL REFORM

In response, judges have been using their power in ways their predecessors only a generation earlier would have considered revolutionary. The Supreme Court's decisions striking down racial segregation in public facilities, establishing the formula of "one person, one vote" for electoral districts, broadening traditional guarantees to those accused of crime, and expanding the concept of privacy to include a woman's right to dispose of her fetus have all made dramatic impacts on American society. Judges have also been active at state and local levels—for example, operating public schools, city jails, public housing, and state hospitals.[14]

In *Wyatt v. Stickney* (1971), a widely publicized instance of judicial involvement, federal district judge Frank M. Johnson issued a precedent-breaking order asserting the constitutional rights of patients committed to state hospitals "to receive such individual treatment as will give each of them a realistic opportunity to be cured or to improve his or her mental condition." His order detailed minimum constitutional standards for treatment and accommodations and required human rights committees to monitor their enforcement. (Reading 2.7.) The Supreme Court joined in concern over commitment practices when, in *O'Connor v. Donaldson* (1975), it held that patients who were not dangerous to others could not be confined in institutions against their will if they did not receive therapy.[15]

In the process judges have been transformed from umpires into managers of litigation, playing a critical role in shaping lawsuits and influencing results. (Readings 2.8, 2.9.) The nature of the remedies that judges offer has also changed significantly. First of all, the injunction —a judicial order to a named person commanding performance, or sometimes nonperformance, of specified actions—has historically been an "extraordinary writ," a directive issued only under truly unusual circumstances. Now, as Abram Chayes says, the "extraordinary" character of such writs "has faded."[16]

Perhaps more important, judges traditionally issued injunctions to

---

[14] One of the more spectacular situations occurred in Boston, where two judges named Garrity, Paul and W. Arthur, unrelated, one federal and one state, took over and for years made operating decisions concerning the jails, schools, public housing, and even the sewer system. As housing court judge Paul Garrity said, he took over public housing when he could no longer put up with "the turkeys who were running it—all either stonewalling or incompetent." (*New York Times,* October 2, 1984; November 30, 1984.)

[15] In *Pennhurst State School and Hospital v. Halderman* (1981), however, the Court narrowly interpreted a federal statutory "bill of rights" for the developmentally disabled so as not to create for the mentally retarded any substantive right to appropriate treatment in the least restrictive environment.

[16] "The Role of the Judge in Public Law Litigation," 89 *Harvard Law Review* 1281, 1292 (1976).

bar continuance of particular actions begun in the past or to prohibit acts about to be begun—forbidding, for instance, an official at the polls to refuse to give a ballot to a qualified black voter. As prohibitions, injunctions were typically *negative* orders. It is true, of course, that even in the past many injunctions have commanded positive action. Even more often, use of a double negative in the text of a writ has required positive action. To forbid an official to refuse to give a ballot to a black voter means the official must give that voter a ballot. Nevertheless, the usual purpose of an injunction has been to maintain the status quo or to return the parties in the suit to the relation that had existed before one of them had taken the injurious action. (See Chapter 6.)

In recent years, however, the sorts of decrees involved in operating schools, jails, and hospitals or in redistricting states have required positive action not merely in the sense of demanding that officials undo some particular past wrong. These writs have also ordered those officials to pursue into the indefinite future new and complicated public policies that judges think are necessary to achieve ends that the Constitution requires. Such commands relegate vast power to judges and turn high governmental officers into subordinates. The impact of such injunctions on people not directly involved in the litigation also increases markedly. The state legislature, for instance, may be forced to raise taxes to finance the execution of a court's orders or to find the money by reducing the budgets of other agencies or by curtailing certain public services.

One might cogently argue that in the cases that have spawned such sweeping decrees, judges have done no more than mandate policies that elected officials should have been—but were not—carrying out of their own free will. United States District Judge Frank M. Johnson made precisely that point in defending his orders regarding reform of "barbaric and shocking" conditions in Alabama's prisons and mental hospitals. (Reading 2.4.)

But many, including judges and serious scholars, have been troubled by the specter, perhaps the reality, of government by the judiciary. (Reading 2.10.) With the pressures of the Reagan administration for less active federal participation in social policies, and the increasing number of Reagan's nominees at all levels of federal courts, the direction, though not the fact, of judicial policy making has sharply changed. In an address delivered in 1984, Justice John Paul Stevens, often in the minority on the Burger Court, criticized his colleagues for their "far-reaching pronouncements" and their "enthusiastic attempts to codify the law instead of merely performing the judicial task of deciding the cases that come before them."

Government by judiciary, then, is practiced by both liberals and conservatives. The substantive issues concern choices among vital values: what portion of its citizens' incomes shall a state spend for public education, mental health, and care of prisoners? Where is the point beyond which it becomes dysfunctional to raise taxes? What forms of education are best for American society? Legislatures have usually had the final word here, but these sorts of inquiries also raise questions of equal protection of the laws, or at least equal benefit from the laws. And these latter are certainly issues that normally fall within the jurisdiction of courts.

Bluntly put, the people who settle the critical conflicts within a society are the people who in fact, if not in name, govern that society. This truism raises fundamental questions: When does an oath of fidelity to the Constitution allow or even compel judges to substitute their notions of the public good for those of legislators? To what extent should judges govern in a constitutional democracy? More practically, to what degree can judges in a constitutional democracy, operating within the limitations of the judicial process, carry out effective government?

SELECTED REFERENCES

Ackerman, Bruce A. *Social Justice in the Liberal State.* New Haven: Yale University Press, 1981.

Auerbach, Jerold S. *Justice Without Law.* New York: Oxford University Press, 1983.

Bentley, Arthur F. *The Process of Government.* Chicago: University of Chicago Press, 1908.

Black, Donald. *The Behavior of Law.* New York: The Academic Press, 1976.

Canon, Bradley C. "Defining the Dimensions of Judicial Activism," 66 *Judicature* 237 (1983).

Cover, Robert M. "The Origins of Judicial Activism in the Protection of Minorities," 91 *Yale Law Journal* 1287 (1982).

Fletcher, William A. "The Discretionary Constitution: Institutional Remedies and Judicial Legitimacy," 91 *Yale Law Journal* 635 (1982).

Halpern, Stephen C., and Charles M. Lamb (eds.). *Supreme Court Activism and Restraint.* Lexington, Mass.: D. C. Heath & Co., 1982.

Horowitz, Donald L. *The Courts and Social Policy.* Washington, D.C.: The Brookings Institution, 1977.

———."Decreeing Institutional Change: Judicial Supervision of Public Institutions," 1983 *Duke Law Journal* 1265.

Horwitz, Morton J. *The Transformation of American Law.* Cambridge, Massachusetts: Harvard University Press, 1977.

Howard, J. Woodford, Jr. "Adjudication Considered as a Process of Conflict Resolution," 18 *Journal of Public Law* 339 (1969).

Lieberman, Jethro K. *The Litigious Society.* New York: Basic Books, 1981.

Mason, Alpheus T. *Harlan Fiske Stone: Pillar of the Law.* New York: Viking, 1956.

Miller, Arthur S. *Toward Increased Judicial Activism: The Political Role of the Supreme Court.* Westport, Conn.: Greenwood Press, 1982.

Murphy, Walter F., and Joseph Tanenhaus. *The Study of Public Law.* New York: Random House, 1972. Chs. 1, 2, 8.

Pritchett, C. Herman. "Public Law and Judicial Behavior," 30 *Journal of Politics* 480 (1968).

Sarat, Austin, and Joel B. Grossman. "Courts and Conflict Resolution: Problems in the Mobilization of Adjudication," 69 *American Political Science Review* 1200 (1975).

Shapiro, Martin. *Courts: A Comparative and Political Analysis.* Chicago: University of Chicago Press, 1981.

White, G. Edward. *The American Judicial Tradition: Profiles of Leading American Judges.* New York: Oxford University Press, 1976.

Yarbrough, Tinsley E. *Judge Frank Johnson and Human Rights in Alabama.* University: University of Alabama Press, 1981.

2.1

"He only judges the law because he is obliged to judge a case."

JUDICIAL POWER IN THE UNITED STATES

Alexis de Tocqueville

... I am not aware that any nation of the globe has hitherto organized a judicial power on the principle adopted by the Americans. The judicial organization of the United States is the institution which the stranger has the greatest difficulty in understanding. He hears the authority of the judge invoked in the political occurrences of every day, and he naturally concludes that in the United States judges are important political functionaries; nevertheless, when he examines the nature of the tribunals, they offer nothing which is contrary to the usual habits and privileges of those bodies; and the magistrates seem to him to interfere in public affairs by chance, but by a chance which recurs every day. . . .

The first characteristic of judicial power in all nations is the duty of arbitration. But rights must be contested in order to warrant the interference of a tribunal; and an action must be brought to obtain the decision of a judge. As long, therefore, as a law is uncontested, the judicial authority is not called upon to discuss it. . . . When a judge in a given case attacks a law relating to that case, he extends the circle of his customary duties, without however stepping beyond it; since he is in some measure obliged to decide upon the law, in order

Democracy in America (1835), Ch. 6. Alexis de Tocqueville was a French political analyst whose observations of nineteenth-century American society have become classic.

to decide the case. But if he pronounces upon a law without resting upon a case, he clearly steps beyond his sphere, and invades that of the legislative authority.

The second characteristic of the judicial power is that it pronounces on special cases. . . .

The third characteristic of the judicial power is its inability to act unless it is appealed to. . . . This characteristic is less general than the other two; but notwithstanding the exceptions, I think it may be regarded as essential. The judicial power is by its nature devoid of action; it must be put in motion in order to produce a result. When it is called upon to repress a crime, it punishes the criminal; when a wrong is to be redressed, it is ready to redress it; when an act requires interpretation, it is prepared to interpret it; but it does not pursue criminals, hunt out wrongs, or examine into evidence of its own accord. . . .

The Americans have retained these three distinguishing characteristics of the judicial power. . . . [A judge's] position is therefore perfectly similar to that of the magistrate of other nations; and he is nevertheless invested with immense political power. . . . The cause of this difference lies in the simple fact that the Americans have acknowledged the right of the judges to found their decisions on the Constitution, rather than on the laws. In other words, they have left judges at liberty not to apply such laws as may appear to them to be unconstitutional.

I am aware that a similar right has been claimed—but claimed in vain—by courts of justice in other countries; but in America it is recognized by all the authorities; and not a party, nor so much as an individual, is found to contest it. This fact can only be explained by the principles of the American constitutions. . . . In the United States, the Constitution governs the legislator as much as the private citizen: as it is the first of laws, it cannot be modified by a law; and it is therefore just that the tribunals should obey the Constitution in preference to any law. . . .

Whenever a law which the judge holds to be unconstitutional is argued in a tribunal of the United States, he may refuse to admit it as a rule; this power is the only one which is peculiar to the American magistrate, but it gives him immense political influence. Few laws can escape his searching analysis; for there are few which are not prejudicial to some private interest or other, and none which may not be brought before a court of justice by the choice of the parties, or by the necessity of the case. But from that time a judge has refused to apply any given law in a case, that law loses a portion of its moral sanction. The persons to whose interests it is prejudicial learn that means exist of evading its authority; and similar suits are multiplied, until it becomes powerless. One of two alternatives must then be resorted to: the people must alter the Constitution, or the legislature must repeal the law.

The political power which the Americans have entrusted to their courts of justice is therefore immense; but the evils of this power are considerably diminished by the obligation which has been imposed of attacking the laws through the courts of justice alone. If the judge had been empowered to contest the laws on the ground of theoretical generalities, if he had been enabled to open an attack or to pass a censure on the legislator, he would have played a prominent part in the political sphere; and as the champion or the antagonist of a party, he would have arrayed the hostile passions of the nation in the conflict. But when a judge contests a law, applied to some particular case in an obscure proceeding, the importance of his attack is concealed from the public gaze; his decision bears upon the interest of an individual, and if the law is slighted it is only collaterally. Moreover, although it be censured, it is not abolished; its moral force may be diminished, but its cogency is by no means suspended; and its final destruction can only be accomplished by the reiterated attacks of judicial functionaries. It will readily be understood that by connecting the censureship of the laws with the private interests of members of the community, and by intimately uniting the prosecution of the law with the prosecution of an individual, the legislation is protected from wanton assailants and from the daily aggressions of party-spirit. The errors of the legislator are exposed whenever their evil consequences are most felt; and it is always a positive and appreciable fact which serves as the basis of a prosecution.

I am inclined to believe this practice of the American courts to be at once the most favorable to liberty as well as to public order. If the judge could only attack the legislator openly and directly, he would sometimes be afraid to oppose any resistance to his will; and at other moments party-spirit might encourage him to brave it every day. The laws would consequently be attacked when the power from which they emanate is weak, and obeyed when it is strong. That is to say, when it would be useful to respect them, they would be contested; and when it would be easy to convert them into an instrument of oppression, they would be respected. But the American judge is brought into the political arena independently of his own will. He only judges the law because he is obliged to judge a case. The political question which he is called upon to resolve is connected with the interest of the parties, and he cannot refuse to decide it without abdicating the duties of his post. He performs his functions as a citizen by fulfilling the strict duties which belong to his profession as a magistrate. It is true that upon this system the judicial censureship which is exercised by the courts of justice over legislation cannot extend equally to all laws, in as much as some of them can never give rise to that precise species of contestation which is termed a lawsuit; and even when such a contestation is possible, it may happen that no one cares to bring it before a court of justice. The Americans have often felt this disadvantage, but they have left the remedy incomplete, lest they should give it efficacy which might in some cases prove dangerous. Within these limits, the power vested in the American courts of justice of pronouncing a statute to be unconstitutional forms one of the most powerful barriers which has ever been devised against the tyranny of political assemblies.

2.2 *". . . lawyers are avoided as symbols of discord."*

USING A LAWYER IN JAPAN IS EMBARRASSING

Sam Jameson and David Holley

TOKYO—In the United States, a wronged citizen wants his day in court, and when he goes he usually takes a lawyer with him. But in Japan, trials are considered *dakatsu*, which means "abominable, detestable," and lawyers are avoided as symbols of discord.

"This is a homogenous society," James S. Adachi, an American who has practiced law in Japan for 32 years, said in an interview. "People feel they are all part of one family. If there are problems, they will be settled within the family. The Japanese feel that an outsider, like a lawyer, is not required."

These attitudes are borne out by statistics. Although California has one lawyer for every 333 citizens, the proportion in Japan is one to 10,170.

"I have begun to wonder if there is really a need for us," lawyer Minoru Koyama said.

Koyama was educated under American-inspired concepts of a government of laws, not of men. He said he had been taught to believe that the traditional Japanese values of personal obligation and human pity were weak pillars on which to build a social order dedicated to justice for all.

Now he is not so sure. Japanese society, after all, is functioning very well, he said. And with very few lawyers.

Japan has 11,314 lawyers, compared with 450,000 in the United States and 66,000 in California.

Some lawyers see all this as a crisis, Koyama said, adding:

"I myself feel there is a danger that Japanese lawyers will become unable to make a living."

Demand for lawyers is so limited that specialization, which is common in the United States, is an impossibility in Japan.

"A Japanese lawyer could not make a living by specializing," Koyama said. "He handles everything from criminal cases to patents."

The limited number of lawyers in Japan is a phenomenon almost without parallel in other countries. It is due in part to the fact that Japan allows its citizens to take a variety of legal actions without using a lawyer.

A couple can get a divorce without using a lawyer and without going to court. Japanese do not need a lawyer to draw up a will, nor do they need court sanction to dispose of the assets in a will. Lawyers play no role in land sales in Japan. Japanese companies, in their dealings with one another, make virtually no use of lawyers. Lawyers need not be involved in setting up a company.

According to Motoharu Furukawa, a prosecutor in the Justice Ministry, the law specifies just one instance in which a lawyer must be used—in the defense of accused criminals.

Adachi, the American lawyer, said that in the United States, "lawyers and government, including the Congress, have created situations in which lawyers are necessary. Lawyers in the United States have made themselves necessary."

Japan operates as if it intended to make sure that lawyers never become necessary.

The Japanese equivalent of the American bar examination sets what can only be described as "genius" standards for passing.

In 1977, 51% of those who took the California bar exam passed. A mere 1.6% passed the equivalent test in Japan—the entrance exam to the Legal Training & Research Institute. . . .

Japanese universities' faculties of law resemble American undergraduate political science departments and most of their graduates seek jobs in government or business.

Still, every year a staggering number of applicants take the test to enter the government's Legal Training & Research Institute. This year, 29,390 took the test. All but about 10% were eliminated by a first-stage multiple-choice test of 90 questions. Only 485 survived the second stage, 11 days of essay and oral testing—and not all the survivors will become lawyers. . . .

"There is consciousness that those who pass should attain a certain standard," Matsuda said. "Those who cannot achieve that level must be rejected."

Students admitted to the institute spend two years in courses similar to those offered at law schools in the United States. The Japanese, however, put more emphasis on trial procedures.

Admission to the institute is virtually a "free pass" into the profession—as a judge, a prosecutor or a lawyer. Students are paid $9,650 by the state while studying and the institute's final examination is a formality. With few exceptions, only graduates of the institute can become lawyers.

Social values that are unique to Japan play a major role in retaining the high standards for lawyers.

"The system has continued as it exists now for many years," Matsuda said, "but no shortage has developed in the number of judges, prosecutors or lawyers."

Since feudal times, he went on, people have considered trials to be dakatsu. Even today, Matsuda said, to use the word that means "a court affair" is to arouse "an emotional feeling of revulsion."

Koyama said that the airing of personal problems in front of third persons is embarrassing to Japanese.

Even with urbanization, Matsuda said, ties with neighbors and with relatives remain strong.

"Crimes between people with close relationships seldom occur in Japan," he said.

It is precisely that kind of relationship, however, which lawyers like Koyama see as impeding justice in terms of individual rights.

Too often, Koyama said, individuals stop short of insisting on their rights in order to preserve the appearance of harmony in personal relationships.

In rural divorce proceedings, Koyama said, if couples cannot agree on the terms of the divorce or on the divorce itself, "locally influential" persons often act as mediators.

"These," he said, "are actually local bosses who frequently tell one party or the other, 'You do this,' or 'You do that.' This may be an aspect of Japanese culture, but we evaluate it very negatively.

"Local bosses frequently give advice that couples should quit arguing and make up. It would be fine if the people involved actually did make up, but what often happens is that they just act as if they have made up, because they have been told to by that kind of person.

"This is medieval, sentimental. It's in areas like this where the difference between consciousness of one's rights in the United States and Japan comes into play."

In the city, too, justice often assumes the form of harmony rather than a clear-cut ruling of right or wrong.

Police will usually encourage the parties involved in a traffic accident to work out a settlement while the policeman is writing up his report, Adachi said.

The most dramatic difference between Japan and the United States—in the way they use lawyers and in their attitudes toward lawyers—is found in corporate law, the field where most American lawyers find work.

Adachi said that in the United States lawyers are used as "preventive medicine," but in Japan they are used as doctors operating on seriously ill patients.

The concept of using lawyers to avoid disputes is alien to Japanese, even to lawyers. Asked how Japanese companies use lawyers, Koyama replied, "I don't understand what you mean."

Adachi said, "When negotiating a contract, the Japanese don't think they are negotiating as adversaries. They could take offense if a lawyer were brought in."

Lavish incomes are rare, but lawyers in their mid-30s earn on the average about $20,000 a year—well above the average income of $13,700 for salaried employees. The lawyer in his mid-40s averages about $40,000 a year, Koyama estimated.

Lawyers also stand out in one other aspect. The individuality that lawyers such as Koyama hope to see develop in society as a whole appears to be a hallmark of the legal profession.

"As a lawyer, one's time is one's own," Koyama said. "You can help people. You get a sense of justice. And you have the pride of knowing that you're not being used by anyone.

"As an individual, you can even take on the nation itself."

2.3   *"Why are so many people involved in legal disputes?"*

DIVERSE AMERICAN SOCIETY MAY ASK TOO MUCH OF LEGAL SYSTEM

Charles H. Whitebread and John Heilman

California Chief Justice Rose Elizabeth Bird recently proposed that sufficient tax revenues be generated to pay the full cost of trial courts. Her idea was designed to eliminate filing and user fees and to ensure equal access to civil courts for all Californians, especially the middle class. It drew strong criticism from some lawyers and laymen who felt that litigants, not taxpayers, should bear the costs of civil courts.

Regardless of the merits of the proposal, the debate may serve only to cloud the real issue: Why are so many people involved in legal disputes? Until that question is answered, the issue of who should pay for our dispute-resolution system is premature. Indeed, before any

Los Angeles Times, December 21, 1983. Copyright, 1983, Los Angeles Times. Reprinted by permission. Charles H. Whitebread is the George T. Pfleger Professor of Law at USC and John Heilman is a practicing attorney in Beverly Hills and Mayor Pro Tempore of the City of West Hollywood.

meaningful reform of our civil courts, we must address the issue of why our society is so litigious.

The fact that Americans are extremely litigious cannot be disputed. In the last 10 years we have heard constant complaints about crowded court calendars and burgeoning dockets. On the federal level there have even been proposals to create an intermediate appellate court between the Court of Appeals and the Supreme Court.

In state and local systems numerous proposals have been made and enacted to relieve congestion in the courts. Among these have been mandatory arbitration and the use of neighborhood dispute-resolution centers. But while some of these programs are quite successful, they have not had much effect on our litigiousness. The system is still overcrowded—and, as Bird has pointed out, there are people who want to use the courts but are deterred by high filing and user fees.

Why are Americans so litigious? One obvious explanation is that the structure and nature of our society are different. We are truly a melting pot of economic classes, and the juxtaposition of different cultures and values can often result in conflict. In addition, our traditions of independence and rugged individualism often mean that Americans are more likely to challenge the social order to correct a perceived wrong. When this is combined with our supposed materialism, a great deal of litigation may ensue.

Another potential explanation lies in the breakdown of other, less formal, methods of resolving disputes. In many societies strong extended families probably resolve many disputes and prevent others from occurring. But in the United States, with a high divorce rate and few extended families, the institution of the family rarely serves to resolve or avoid disputes, and in many cases may actually cause or exacerbate the sort of conflict that leads to litigation.

Neighborhood pressure often resolves disputes, but in the United States our neighborhoods (such as they are) may actually increase litigiousness by bringing together people who have little in common. The transient nature of our society aggravates the problem because people feel less compunction about resorting to the legal system; after all, one or all of the disputants may leave the community. Obviously, people who have lived and worked in the same neighborhood for many years have a greater incentive to keep the peace by resolving their disputes outside the courts.

In our legal system lawyers are permitted to take cases on a contingent-fee basis. (Cases may be filed in which attorneys' fees are paid out of any potential recovery.) Generally this means that an attorney will take a case with an agreement to accept one-third of any recovery as a legal fee. Obviously the contingent fee lets some people pursue litigation that they otherwise could not afford.

At the same time, our strong commitment to equality generates pressure on the legal system to guarantee equality of access to our courts. Everyone must have his day in court. Certainly our notion of equality, foreign to so many societies, contributes to the high volume of lawsuits in our courts. And we don't assess costs against the losing parties. Elsewhere, notably in England, losing parties must pay the cost of litigation. This discourages some people from bringing frivolous lawsuits, and encourages others to settle quarrels without resort to the legal system. (By contrast, we sometimes award attorneys' fees to victorious litigants. Fees are even awarded at times to encourage certain types of litigation that are deemed socially advantageous.)

So what are we trying to accomplish with our legal system? Like no other society, we have attempted to use it to right all the wrongs and to remedy all the injustices of our society. And we use it not only more frequently but also for a greater variety of issues. We use law to eradicate inequality, and we use law to regulate a host of social, economic and even medical problems that are customarily resolved in non-legal ways in other countries.

Perhaps this litigiousness signifies the disintegration of our social fabric into competing materialistic factions. Or perhaps it is a sign of strength. Maybe the frequent resort to the legal system is the only way in which our diverse social factions can coexist in a peaceful and civilized manner.

Maybe—but maybe our legal system is overburdened because we ask it to do too much. Now may be the time to question whether the law can ever do all that we want it to do.

2.4   ". . . the federal judiciary has responded cautiously but unwaveringly. . . ."

THE ROLE OF THE JUDICIARY WITH RESPECT TO THE OTHER BRANCHES OF GOVERNMENT

Frank M. Johnson, Jr.

It is impossible to draw a sharp line between legislating, adjudicating and administering.

During the past two decades federal judges have again come under attack by politicians and various special interest groups. Members of Congress have attempted to limit federal court jurisdiction in the civil and human rights areas. State legislatures have called for a

The John A. Sibley Lecture in Law, University of Georgia, 1977. Frank M. Johnson, Jr., has been U.S. District Judge for the Middle District of Alabama since 1955. Reprinted with permission.

constitutional convention to nullify the results reached in *Baker v. Carr*. [Reading 5.11.]

I submit to you that the attacks now being made are not based upon any new concepts or theories, but are in substance the same as those that have been made since the adoption of the Constitution. Furthermore, I would suggest that in many instances the individuals and groups making the most vocal attacks against the courts are those who have forced the courts to take positive action in the first place.

The renewal of the criticism is prompted by the fact that the past several decades have been extremely active and dynamic ones for the federal judiciary in the area of constitutional law. The general citizenry, demonstrating a new awareness of rights or increasingly affected by government controls and dependent upon government programs and services, has looked more and more to the federal courts for the guarantee of rights or for protection against unconstitutional conduct on the part of the states' and federal executive and legislative branches. The organized Bar has, in the finest tradition of the legal profession, repeatedly called upon the federal courts to extend and to expand to all groups and persons in our society the freedoms and protections afforded by the Constitution. True to its constitutional imperative, the federal judiciary has responded cautiously but unwaveringly, adjudicating and upholding the rights of, among many others, black persons and women to equal educational and employment opportunities; the involuntarily committed mentally ill to minimum care and treatment; and incarcerated offenders to a safe and decent environment.

Involving, as they do, judicial review of legislative and executive action and resolution of oft-times complex and controversial issues, it is not surprising that these constitutional adjudications have generated much discussion and debate. . . . This debate, both sides of which have merit, centers on the proper role and function of the federal judiciary with respect to the other branches of government.

The power of the federal judiciary to review and to decide matters involving the legislative and executive branches of government is circumscribed by two basic constitutional doctrines. The first, the doctrine of separation of powers, reflects the deeply held belief of our founding fathers that the powers of government should be separate and distinct, with the executive, the legislative, and the judicial departments being independent and coordinate branches of government. It is this doctrine which is responsible, in great part, for the creation and maintenance of the federal courts as courts of only limited jurisdiction.

The second doctrine, which also reflects the founding fathers' distrust of centralized government, is commonly referred to as "Our Federalism." This doctrine, incorporated in the Tenth Amendment to the Constitution, restricts the power of the federal courts to intervene in the functions and affairs of the states and their political subdivisions.

In deference to these constitutional doctrines, the federal courts have traditionally been reluctant to intervene in the affairs and activities of the other branches of government. . . .

Yet, these doctrines serve only to restrain, not to interdict, the exercise of judicial power. The authors of the Constitution never intended for these or any other doctrines to render impotent the power of the federal judiciary to restrain unconstitutional action on the part of governmental institutions. Had they, in fact, desired to insulate governmental conduct from judiciary scrutiny, the founding fathers would have adopted a constitution modeled after the Articles of Confederation, which document vested all judicial authority in the legislative branch of government.

Instead, the founding fathers prudently and discerningly perceived that the survival of our republican form of government depended on the supremacy of the Constitution and that maintaining the supremacy of the Constitution depended, in turn, on a strong and independent judiciary, possessing the power and the authority to resolve disputes of a constitutional nature between the states, between the states and the national government, and, most importantly, between individuals and governmental institutions. These crucial features of our form of government are embraced in Article VI, Section 2, of the Constitution, which establishes the Constitution as the supreme law of the land; and in Article III, Section 2, of the Constitution, which extends to the federal courts jurisdiction over all cases arising under our Constitution and laws.

In granting to the federal judiciary the power to decide cases arising under our Constitution and laws, the framers of the Constitution fully recognized that the exercise of such power would inevitably thrust the courts into the political arena. In fact . . . this grant of power was, in effect, a mandate to the federal courts to check and to restrain any infringement by the legislative and executive branches on the supremacy of the Constitution. James Madison, in cautioning his colleagues that the protections afforded by the Bill of Rights would be hollow without a judiciary to uphold them, referred to the federal judiciary as "an impenetrable bulwark against every assumption of power in the legislative or executive; [the courts] will be naturally led to resist every encroachment upon [the Bill of] rights."

Thus, the judiciary's role as defender of the Bill of Rights and its occasional intrusion in the affairs of the legislative and executive branches of government result not from an arrogation of power but from compliance with a constitutional mandate. . . .

Nor did the founding fathers fail to recognize that the exercise of this power by the judiciary would, at times, create strains and ten-

sions between the federal courts and the executive and legislative
branches at the national level and between these courts and the
various governmental institutions at the state and local levels. It was
their sound and reasoned judgment, however, that the need to maintain the supremacy and integrity of the Constitution far outweighed
any disadvantages resulting from this grant of power. The wisdom
and correctness of this decision, attested to by the ability of our
nation to survive each constitutional crisis which has arisen and by
the strength and stability of our form of government over the past
200 years, is reflected in this observation by de Tocqueville:

> The peace, the prosperity and the very existence of the Union, are in-
> vested in the hands of the . . . judges. Without their active co-operation
> the constitution would be a dead letter: the executive appeals to them for
> assistance against the encroachments of the legislative powers; the legisla-
> ture demands their protection from the designs of the executive; they
> defend the Union from the disobedience of the states, the states from the
> exaggerated claims of the Union, the public interest against the interests
> of private citizens. . . .

And, it should be added, the interests of private citizens against
governments. . . .

The role of the federal courts in deciding constitutional questions
is and always has been an activist one. It is not a role which has been
usurped by the judiciary, . . . but is one which is inextricably intertwined with its duty to interpret the Constitution. The federal courts
have never acted directly on the states or assumed jurisdiction of
mere political issues, but in cases involving individual rights and
liberties, these courts are compelled to construe the law in order to
determine such rights and [liberties]. As Chief Justice Marshall so
eloquently expressed it . . . :

> As this Court has never grasped at ungranted jurisdiction, so will it never,
> we trust, shrink from the exercise of that which is conferred upon it.

In describing the role of the federal judiciary in deciding constitutional issues, I ascribe no particular political or social philosophy to
the word "activist." . . . The "activism" I refer to is measured not by
the end result but by how and under what circumstances [the] result
is achieved.

Once having decided the issues, the court must then concern
itself with the second and final phase of the adjudicatory process—
the formulation and entry of an appropriate decree. If the evidence
fails to disclose a constitutional violation, or if the evidence discloses
a constitutional violation which can effectively be remedied by an
award of damages or the issuance of a prohibitory injunction, the
court's role is a limited one terminating upon entry of the decree. If
the constitutional or statutory violation is one, however, which can

be adequately remedied only by the issuance of a decree providing for affirmative, ongoing relief, the court's involvement is necessarily enlarged and prolonged.

The federal judiciary finds itself today being increasingly called upon to fashion and to render this latter type of decree, that is, one of an ongoing, remedial relief. This trend, I assure you, results not from the judiciary's masochistic yearning for hard work, but from several relatively recent developments in the law.

The most significant procedural change has been the adoption and promulgation by Congress and the courts of liberalized standing and joinder requirements. Under [traditional] code pleading, for example, litigation involved but two individuals or at least two competing interests, diametrically opposed, with the winner taking all. Today, however, there are often competing, if not conflicting, interests among members of the same class, among different classes, and among parties and intervenors. This has made the task of formulating appropriate relief an increasingly complex and difficult one.

A significant development in the substantive area has been the shift in subject matter from business and economic issues to social issues. During the latter part of the Nineteenth Century and the first half of this century, the major focus . . . of constitutional law was on the power of Congress and the states to enact statutes regulating and restricting private businesses and property. . . . Since only property rights were at stake, an award of damages to compensate the litigant for any economic loss and the issuance of a prohibitory injunction to restrain the operation of the statute provided the litigant with all the relief to which he was entitled.

During the past several decades, however, there have been in our society a growing awareness of and concern for the rights and freedoms of the individual. This awareness and this concern are reflected in the steady shift in emphasis in constitutional litigation from property rights to individual rights. Congress has enacted social welfare statutes in such areas as education, voting, consumer protection, and environmental protection. Speaking through these enactments, Congress has made clear its desire that freedom, justice, and equality become a reality to and for all Americans. In many instances the responsibility for seeing that this salutary goal is accomplished lies with the federal judiciary.

The traditional forms of relief—an award of damages and the issuance of a prohibitory injunction—while adequate to remedy most constitutional violations of a business or economic nature, are but ingredients in remedying constitutional and statutory violations of a personal and social nature. The prisoner, who lives in constant fear for his life and safety because of inadequate staffing and overcrowded conditions, will not have his rights protected merely by an award of damages for the past injury sustained by him. If we, as judges, have learned anything from *Brown v. Board of Education* and its progeny, it is that prohibitory relief alone affords but a hollow protection to the basic and fundamental rights of citizens to equal protection of the law.

Once a constitutional deprivation has been shown, it becomes the duty of the court to render a decree which will as far as possible eliminate the effects of the past deprivations as well as bar like deprivations in the future. Because of the complexity and nature of the constitutional rights and issues involved, the traditional forms of relief have proven totally inadequate. The courts have been left with two alternatives. They could throw up their hands in frustration and claim that, although the litigants have established a violation of constitutional or statutory rights, the courts have no satisfactory relief to grant them. This would, in addition to constituting judicial abdication, make a mockery of the Bill of Rights. Utilizing their equitable powers, the federal courts have pursued the only reasonable and constitutionally acceptable alternative—fashioning relief to fit the necessities of the particular case.

With the acknowledgment that they are professionally trained in the law, not in penology, medicine, or education, the federal courts have approached these areas cautiously and hesitatingly. Further recognizing that many of the issues they are being asked to decide call for sensitive social and political policy judgments, the courts have shown great deference to those charged with making these judgments and have intervened only when a constitutional or statutory violation has clearly and convincingly been established.

Nor have the courts attempted to enter these often murky and uncharted waters without navigational aids. In addition to evidence from experts, the parties, intervenors, and *amici* are invited to submit their recommendations and suggestions, usually in the form of proposed plans. This process, in addition to minimizing the need for judicial resolution of many of the remedial issues, increases the likelihood of voluntary compliance by the parties with the decree eventually adopted and entered by the court. The courts have also turned to outside sources for advice and assistance. Biracial committees are, for example, now routinely provided for in school desegregation decisions in the Fifth Circuit. In addition to putting forward their own remedial suggestions, these outside groups can and do play an invaluable role in implementing and, if necessary, monitoring the decree. . . .

2.5   *"Adjudication . . . serves less to avoid conflict than to channel and resolve disputes already begun."*

ADJUDICATION CONSIDERED AS A PROCESS OF CONFLICT RESOLUTION

J. Woodford Howard, Jr.   American courts share in the broader aspects of policy determination

Adjudication is a method of peaceful conflict resolution in which parties present arguments and evidence to a neutral third party for a decision in their favor according to established procedures and rules of law.

Because it exists to settle disputes, adjudication by definition is the child of conflict. Because Anglo-American practice anchors it in the adversary system, even its internal mechanisms are stylized forms of combat. But it should be emphasized that adjudication is only one among many methods of conflict resolution in free societies. For varying purposes we resort to voting, bargaining, mediation, lotteries, and even restricted private warfare. These processes, however different in character, are often related in practice. Each may be applied before major public controversies are settled (if ever). While the typical adjudication involves application of a general rule to a particular case, it is seldom invoked until prior methods have failed and it may well be followed by the loser's resort to another method or forum. Adjudication usually comes somewhere in the middle of conflict resolution sequences. Thus it serves less to avoid conflict than to channel and resolve disputes already begun.

Any avoidance functions of adjudication lie largely in preventing conflict enlargement or using it in conjunction with other methods of settlement. Litigation may deflect controversies away from the political arena or confirm results there reached. Thus it may coopt legitimate dissent. Threats of litigation, in turn, may be a powerful stimulus to settlement by negotiation. Indeed, pretrial settlement of the vast majority of civil and criminal cases is an administrative prerequisite for keeping the courts of this country open. On the other hand, the choice of adjudication may inject new elements of conflict—institutional conflict—into a public dispute. And no one should assume either that a law suit will end any quarrel or, in the words of Brooks Adams, that "the universe will obey the judicial decree." Adjudication, in short, should be conceived as merely a specialized form of third-party decision-making, one method in a stream of public and private alternatives, the successful use of which depends on a complex calculus.

18 *Journal of Public Law* 339 (1969). J. Woodford Howard, Jr., is Thomas P. Stran Professor of Political Science, Johns Hopkins University.

In summary, the argument is that adjudication and legislation differ as methods of conflict resolution. The differences lie less in substantive policy outcomes than in procedures of decision-making which, ex hypothesis, affect those outcomes. Specifically, such institutionally-defined procedures at every stage of the decisional process as representation, problem identification, fact-finding, conversion, and fashioning remedies, serve to regulate the thought processes and control the discretion of adjudicators in order to maximize the opportunity for impartial and informed decision according to the evidence presented by the parties and rules of law. It follows that judges are highly dependent on other actors within the legal system who condition and implement judicial choices. It also follows that adjudication is a highly specialized type of third-party decision-making which may be applied successfully to a relatively narrow range of social conflicts. It does not follow, however, that any particular outcome can be guaranteed by either adjudication or legislation. Neither is one process necessarily more restrained than the other. Rather they operate under different sets of constraints. Nor can we say that organizational arrangements are more or less important than attitudinal or ideological variables in causal explanation of decisions reached. Rather, organizational variables interact with personal ones and condition the way they operate. If anything meaningful remains in the venerable separation of powers theory it is that the richest ore may be found in procedures than in formal powers.

2.6   *". . . each decision is just a nudge to the legal culture."*

DISPUTES AND RULES

Frank H. Easterbrook

judicial decisions on certain issues inevitably affect general public policy and economic development.

Judges both resolve disputes and create rules. For a long time courts portrayed rule creation as a by-product of dispute resolution. The court had to decide the case, and in order to show that its decision was not capricious it often had to announce a rule to govern future cases. The need to decide impelled the creation of a rule. This is appropriate for a court with mandatory jurisdiction. But the Supreme Court possesses discretionary jurisdiction, designed so that

Excerpted from "Foreword: The Court and the Economic System," 98 *Harvard Law Review* 4 (1984). Copyright © 1984 by the Harvard Law Review Association. Frank H. Easterbrook is Lee and Brena Freeman Professor of Law, University of Chicago.

the Justices may concentrate on creating rules for the guidance of others. Today cases often are just excuses for the creation or alteration of rules. Good or bad, this is the consequence of certiorari jurisdiction.

The dispute-resolution and rule-creation functions of the Court tug the Justices in different directions. Dispute resolution is backward looking, an exercise in apportioning gains and losses given the occurrence of some known injury or conflict. The "equities" of the dispute—the good faith of the parties, their knowledge of the rules, and so on—will seem important to a fair disposition. Rule creation is forward looking, and a rule knows not its subjects. The rule seeks to induce people to become informed or change their positions. A judge often is torn between doing justice in the case—that is, adjusting the apportionment of benefits and detriments among people who, by the time of litigation, are trapped in positions no longer within their control—and applying a rule that creates additional benefits for people who can alter their behavior in the future.

Lower courts may adhere to the traditional model of dispute resolution with the assurance that their opinions are not a large source of rules. The Supreme Court has no such comfort. The pressure to use cases as occasions for the creation of rules grows continuously. The dockets of the lower courts expand as legal rules govern more and more conflicts. The Supreme Court cannot hear more cases, though, and it copes by deciding more things in each case. As it announces more rules and tries to explicate its reasons more fully —the better to govern future disputes—it puts greater strains both on its ability to resolve disputes and on internal harmony. The more the Court tries to say, the more grounds for disagreement. Justices may complain that the Court's reasons are broader than necessary to resolve the dispute at hand (which often is true but beside the point) or even that the opinions contain hints of things to come.

Many have written about the growth of the rule-creation function and about how constitutional decisions influence the structure and conduct of government. Yet constitutional rules are unusual, because their addressees are the lower courts. The Supreme Court tells lower courts which statutes to invalidate, what injunctions to issue, what evidence to exclude. The constitutional rules do not directly influence the conduct of those outside the judicial system. Legislatures go on passing laws, fobbing off constitutional questions on the courts. Constitutional rules directed to the police or to the administrators of schools do not affect the nominal addressees of those rules. The exclusion of evidence does not harm the officer on the beat or the injunction the superintendent of schools; their salaries are secure, and a complex of immunities protects their wealth. The Court's constitutional decisions affect conduct (beyond that of the parties to the case) only through a series of intermediaries—those who promulgate administrative rules, those who train and supervise administrators, those who enforce the law, those who practice it, and other process providers. Incremental changes, not strong private incentives, transmit the effects of the Court's decisions. If the Court's decisions are unclear or its signals mixed, that is regrettable but remediable; each decision is just a nudge to the legal culture.

2.7

"There can be no legal (or moral) justification for the State of Alabama's failing to afford treatment . . . to the several thousand patients . . ."

constitutional standards for treatment and accomodations of patients and for a human rights committee to enforce standards

WYATT V. STICKNEY

325 F. Supp. 781 (Middle District, Alabama, 1971)

This case began as a labor dispute in 1970 when reductions in revenue from Alabama's tax on cigarettes precipitated a cut in the state's budget for mental health. Plans to cope with the problem included dismissal of ninety-nine employees from Bryce Hospital. These employees and a group of patients then filed a class action in a United States District Court against the governor, the Mental Health Board, and several other state officials. In passing, plaintiffs alleged that reducing the staff would leave patients without adequate care.

At a pretrial conference in his chambers, the presiding judge, Frank M. Johnson, Jr. (see Reading 2.4), indicated that he thought that state courts could adequately protect any rights of employees possibly injured by the dismissals; but he also expressed concern about the general level of care at Bryce. Largely in response to these remarks, plaintiffs amended their suit to focus on the claim that patients had a constitutional right to adequate treatment, a right that Alabama was denying them. They asked the court to enjoin the state from sending any more patients to Bryce and to appoint a special master to determine the adequacy of current treatment at the mental hospital and the means the state should use to raise those practices to meet minimal medical and constitutional standards.

JOHNSON, CHIEF JUDGE

Bryce Hospital is located in Tuscaloosa, Alabama, and is a part of the mental health service delivery system for the State. . . . Bryce Hospital has approximately 5,000 patients, the majority of whom are involuntarily committed through civil proceedings by the various probate judges in Alabama. Approximately 1,600 employees were assigned to various duties at the Bryce Hospital facility when this case was heard. . . .

During October 1970, the Alabama Mental Health Board and the administration of the Department of Mental Health terminated 99 of these employees. These terminations were made due to budgetary considerations. . . . The employees who were terminated included 41 persons who were assigned to duties . . . not involving direct patient care. . . . Twenty-six persons were discharged who were involved in patient activity and recreational programs. . . . The remaining 32 employees who were discharged included 9 in the department of psychology, 11 in the social service department . . . three registered nurses, two physicians, one dentist and six dental aides. After the termination of these employees, there remained at Bryce Hospital 17 physicians, approximately 850 psychiatric aides, 21 registered nurses, 12 patient activity workers, and 12 psychologists . . . together with 13 social service workers. Of the employees remaining whose duties involved direct patient care in the hospital therapeutic programs, there are only one Ph.D. clinical psychologist, three medical doctors with some psychiatric training (including one board eligible but no board-certified psychiatrist) and two M.S.W. social workers. . . .

Included in the Bryce Hospital patient population are between 1,500 and 1,600 geriatric patients who are provided custodial care but no treatment. The evidence is without dispute that these patients are not properly confined at Bryce Hospital since these geriatric patients cannot benefit from any psychiatric treatment or are not mentally ill. Also included in the Bryce patient population are approximately 1,000 mental retardates, most of whom receive only custodial care without any psychiatric treatment. . . .

The evidence further reflects that Alabama ranks fiftieth among all the states in the Union in per-patient expenditures per day. This Court must, and does, find from the evidence that the programs of treatment in use at Bryce Hospital . . . were scientifically and medically inadequate. These programs of treatment failed to conform to any known minimums established for providing treatment for the mentally ill.

The patients at Bryce Hospital, for the most part, were involuntarily committed through noncriminal procedures and without the constitutional protections that are afforded defendants in criminal proceedings. When patients are so committed for treatment purposes they unquestionably have a constitutional right to receive such individual treatment as will give each of them a realistic opportunity to be cured or to improve his or her mental condition. Rouse v. Cameron . . . Covington v. Harris. . . . Adequate and effective treatment is constitutionally required because, absent treatment, the hospital is transformed "into a penitentiary where one could be held indefinitely for no convicted offense." Ragsdale v. Overholser. . . . The purpose of involuntary hospitalization for treatment purposes is *treatment* and not mere custodial care or punishment. This is the only justification, from a constitutional standpoint, that allows civil commitments to mental institutions. . . . [T]he failure of Bryce Hospital to supply adequate treatment is due to a lack of operating funds. The failure to provide suitable and adequate treatment to the mentally ill cannot be justified by lack of staff or facilities. . . . In *Rouse* the Court [of Appeals for the District of Columbia Circuit] stated:

> We are aware that shortage of psychiatric personnel is a most serious problem today in the care of the mentally ill. In the opinion of the American Psychiatric Association no tax-supported hospital in the United States can be considered adequately staffed. We also recognize that shortage cannot be remedied immediately. But indefinite delay cannot be approved. "The rights here asserted are . . . *present* rights . . . and, unless there is an overwhelming compelling reason, they are to be promptly fulfilled." Watson v. City of Memphis . . . (1963). (Emphasis in original.)

There can be no legal (or moral) justification for the State of Alabama's failing to afford treatment—and adequate treatment from a medical standpoint—to the several thousand patients who have been civilly committed to Bryce's for treatment purposes. To deprive any citizen of his or her liberty upon the altruistic theory that the confinement is for humane therapeutic reasons and then fail to provide adequate treatment violates the very fundamentals of due process. . . .

Judge Johnson deferred a decision on plaintiffs' request for a special master. Instead he ordered the defendants within six months to implement fully their own plan to bring the level of care up to minimal standards. The judge also invited the United States, through the Department of Justice and the Department of Health, Education, and Welfare, to assist the court in evaluating defendants' plans and to aid the hospital in qualifying for federal financial aid.

In September 1971 the defendants submitted their final report. Judge Johnson found that they had "failed to promulgate and implement a treatment program satisfying minimum medical and constitutional requisites." 334 F. Supp. 1341 (1971). The court ordered new hearings in which both sides and amici curiae, who now included the National Mental Health Law Project and the American Civil Liberties Union as well as federal officials, presented evidence. When the proceedings were finished, Johnson said that he believed he had heard testimony from "the foremost authorities on mental health in the United States." (In the meantime, plaintiffs had amended their complaint to include within their "class" patients at Searcy Hospital, another state institution.)

"Not only are the lives of the patients currently confined . . . at stake, but also at issue are the well-being and security of every citizen of Alabama."

WYATT V. STICKNEY

344 F. Supp. 373 (1972)

JOHNSON, CHIEF JUDGE. . . .

In addition to asking that their proposed standards be effectuated, plaintiffs and amici have requested other relief designed to guarantee the provision of constitutional and humane treatment. Pursuant to one such request for relief, this Court has determined that it is appropriate to order the initiation of human rights committees to function as standing committees of the Bryce and Searcy facilities. The Court will appoint the members of these committees who shall have review of all research proposals and all rehabilitation programs, to ensure that the dignity and the human rights of patients are preserved. The committees also shall advise and assist patients who allege that their legal rights have been infringed or that the Mental Health Board has failed to comply with judicially ordered guidelines. At their discretion, the committees may consult appropriate, independent specialists who shall be compensated by the defendant Board. Seven members shall comprise the human rights committee for each institution, the names and addresses of whom are set forth in Appendix B to this decree. Those who serve on the committees shall be paid on a per diem basis and be reimbursed for travel expenses. . . .

This Court will reserve ruling upon other forms of relief advocated by plaintiffs and amici, including their prayer for the appointment of a master and a professional advisory committee to oversee the implementation of the court-ordered minimum constitutional standards. Federal courts are reluctant to assume control of any organization, but especially one operated by a state. This reluctance, combined with defendants' expressed intent that this order will be implemented forthwith and in good faith, causes the Court to withhold its decision on these appointments. Nevertheless, defendants, as well as the other parties and amici in this case, are placed on notice that unless defendants do comply satisfactorily with this order, the Court will be obligated to appoint a master.

Because the availability of financing may bear upon the implementation of this order, the Court is constrained to emphasize at this juncture that a failure by defendants to comply with this decree cannot be justified by a lack of operating funds. . . .

Despite the possibility that defendants will encounter financial difficulties in the implementation of this order, this Court has decided to reserve ruling also upon plaintiffs' motion that defendant Mental Health Board be directed to sell or encumber portions of its land holdings in order to raise funds. Similarly, this Court will reserve ruling on plaintiffs' motion seeking an injunction against the treasurer and the comptroller of the State. . . . The Court stresses, however, the extreme importance and the grave immediacy of the need for proper funding of the State's public mental health facilities. The responsibility for appropriate funding ultimately must fall, of course, upon the State Legislature and, to a lesser degree, upon the defendant Mental Health Board of Alabama. For the present time, the Court will defer to those bodies in hopes that they will proceed with the realization and understanding that what is involved in this case is not representative of ordinary governmental functions such as paving roads and maintaining buildings. Rather, what is so inextricably intertwined with how the Legislature and Mental Health Board respond to the revelations of this litigation is the very preservation of human life and dignity. Not only are the lives of the patients currently confined at Bryce and Searcy at stake, but also at issue are the well-being and security of every citizen of Alabama. As is true in the case of any disease, no one is immune from the peril of mental illness. The problem, therefore, cannot be overemphasized and a prompt response from the Legislature, the Mental Health Board and other responsible State officials, is imperative.

In the event, though, that the Legislature fails to satisfy its well-defined constitutional obligation, and the Mental Health Board . . . fails to implement fully the standards herein ordered, it will be necessary for the Court to take affirmative steps, including appointing a master, to ensure that proper funding is realized. . . .[1]

This Court now must consider that aspect of plaintiffs' motion . . . seeking an injunction against further commitments to Bryce and Searcy until such time as adequate treatment is supplied in those hospitals. Indisputably, the evidence in this case reflects that no treatment program at the Bryce-Searcy facilities approaches constitutional standards. Nevertheless, because of the alternatives to commitment . . . the Court is fearful that granting plaintiffs' request at the present time would serve only to punish and further deprive Alabama's mentally ill. . . .

To assist the Court in its determination of how to proceed henceforth, defendants will be directed to prepare and file a report within six months from the date of this decree detailing the implementation of each standard herein ordered. This report shall be comprehensive and shall include a statement of the progress made on each standard not yet completely implemented, specifying the reasons for incomplete performance. The report shall include also a statement of the financing secured since the issuance of this decree and of defendants' plans for procuring whatever additional financing might be required. Upon the basis of this report and other available information, the Court will evaluate defendants' work and, in due course, determine the appropriateness of appointing a master and of granting other requested relief.

[1]The Court understands and appreciates that the Legislature is not due back in regular session until May, 1973. Nevertheless, special sessions of the Legislature are frequent occurrences in Alabama, and there has never been a time when such a session was more urgently required. If the Legislature does not act promptly to appropriate the necessary funding for mental health, the Court will be compelled to grant plaintiffs' motion to add various State officials and agencies as additional parties to this litigation, and to utilize other avenues of fund raising.

Accordingly, it is the order, judgment and decree of this Court:

1. That defendants be and they are hereby enjoined from failing to implement fully and with dispatch each of the standards set forth in Appendix A attached hereto and incorporated as a part of this decree;

2. That human rights committees be and are designated and appointed. . . . These committees shall have the purposes, functions, and spheres of operation previously set forth in this order. . . .

3. That the court costs incurred in this proceeding, including a reasonable attorneys' fee for plaintiffs' lawyers, be and they are hereby taxed against the defendants;

4. That jurisdiction of this cause be and the same is hereby specifically retained. . . .

APPENDIX A

Minimum Constitutional Standards for Adequate Treatment of the Mentally Ill . . .

II. *Humane Psychological and Physical Environment*
1. Patients have a right to privacy and dignity.
2. Patients have a right to the least restrictive conditions necessary to achieve the purposes of commitment.
3. No person shall be deemed incompetent to manage his affairs, to contract, to hold professional or occupational or vehicle operator's licenses, to marry and obtain a divorce, to register and vote, or to make a will *solely* by reason of his admission or commitment to the hospital.
4. Patients shall have the same rights to visitation and telephone communications as patients at other public hospitals, except to the extent that the Qualified Mental Health Professional responsible for formulation of a particular patient's treatment plan writes an order imposing special restrictions. The written order must be renewed after each periodic review of the treatment plan if any restrictions are to be continued. Patients shall have an unrestricted right to visitation with attorneys and with private physicians and other health professionals.
5. Patients shall have an unrestricted right to send sealed mail. Patients shall have an unrestricted right to receive sealed mail from their attorneys, private physicians, and other mental health professionals, from courts, and government officials. Patients shall have a right to receive sealed mail from others, except to the extent that the Qualified Mental Health Professional responsible for formulation of a particular patient's treatment plan writes an order imposing special restrictions on receipt of sealed mail. The written order must be renewed after each periodic

review of the treatment plan if any restrictions are to be continued.

6. Patients have a right to be free from unnecessary or excessive medication. No medication shall be administered unless at the written order of a physician. . . .

7. Patients have a right to be free from physical restraint and isolation. Except for emergency situations, in which it is likely that patients could harm themselves or others and in which less restrictive means of restraint are not feasible, patients may be physically restrained or placed in isolation only on a Qualified Mental Health Professional's written order which explains the rationale for such action. . . .

19. *Physical Facilities*

A patient has a right to a humane psychological and physical environment within the hospital facilities. These facilities shall be designed to afford patients with comfort and safety, promote dignity, and ensure privacy. The facilities shall be designed to make a positive contribution to the efficiency attainment of the treatment goals of the hospital.

A. *Resident Unit*

The number of patients in a multi-patient room shall not exceed six persons. There shall be allocated a minimum of 80 square feet of floor space per patient in a multi-patient room. Screens or curtains shall be provided to ensure privacy within the resident unit. Single rooms shall have a minimum of 100 square feet of floor space. Each patient will be furnished with a comfortable bed with adequate changes of linen, a closet or locker for his personal belongings, a chair, and a bedside table.

B. *Toilets and Lavatories*

There will be one toilet provided for each eight patients and one lavatory for each six patients. A lavatory will be provided with each toilet facility. The toilets will be installed in separate stalls to ensure privacy, will be clean and free of odor, and will be equipped with appropriate safety devices for the physically handicapped.

C. *Showers*

There will be one tub or shower for each 15 patients. If a central bathing area is provided, each shower area will be divided by curtains to ensure privacy. Showers and tubs will be equipped with adequate safety accessories.

D. *Day Room*

The minimum day room area shall be 40 square feet per patient. Day rooms will be attractive and adequately furnished with reading lamps, tables, chairs, television and other recreational facilities. They will be conveniently located to patients' bedrooms and shall have outside windows. There shall be at least one day room area on each bedroom floor in a multi-story hospital. Areas used for corridor traffic cannot be counted as day room space; nor can a chapel with fixed pews be counted as a day room area.

E. *Dining Facilities*

The minimum dining room area shall be ten square feet per patient. The dining room shall be separate from the kitchen and will be furnished with comfortable chairs and tables with hard, washable surfaces. . . .

The order went on to list in detail standards for record keeping, linen service, housekeeping, heating, air conditioning, hot water, fire and safety regulations, nutrition, and number and qualifications of staff; it also required that a comprehensive, frequently reviewed plan of treatment be developed for each patient.

Alabama then appealed to the United States Court of Appeals for the Fifth Circuit. That court, *Wyatt v. Aderholt,* 503 F. 2d 1305 (1974), unanimously affirmed that "civilly committed mental patients have a constitutional right to such individual treatment as will help each of them to be cured or to improve his or her mental condition." Furthermore, speaking through Judge Minor Wisdom, the court held: "That being the case, the state may not fail to provide treatment for budgetary reasons alone."

The Court of Appeals found that the matter of a proper remedy raised "profound questions" about the role of the federal judiciary in managing state institutions. But because the state had conceded that its treatment fell below minimal constitutional requirements, the circuit judges said: "We need not and do not reach a decision as to whether the standards prescribed by the district court are constitutionally minimum requirements or whether it is within the province of a federal district court . . . to prescribe standards as distinguished from enjoining the operations of such institutions while constitutional rights are being violated."

According to a close analysis of the first two years of implementation of *Wyatt,* Judge Johnson's decree effected "substantial improvements" in conditions in the mental hospital, making it "safer, more sanitary, and generally more habitable for the residents. But a large disparity still exists between the existing institution and the standards contained in the decree. . . ." Note, "The Wyatt Case: Implementation of a Judicial Decree Ordering Institutional Change," 84 *Yale L. J.* 1338 (1975). (The authors of this piece, written anonymously, as is the custom with student-authored articles in law reviews, were Diane S. Kaplan and Richard S. Zuckerman.)

2.8   *"Management is a new form of 'judicial activism'. . . ."*

MANAGERIAL JUDGES

Judith Resnik

Until recently, the American legal establishment embraced a classical view of the judicial role. Under this view, judges are not supposed

96 *Harvard Law Review* 374 (1982). Copyright © 1982 by the Harvard Law Review Association. Judith Resnik is Associate Professor of Law, University of Southern California.

to have an involvement or interest in the controversies they adjudicate. Disengagement and dispassion supposedly enable judges to decide cases fairly and impartially. The mythic emblems surrounding the goddess Justice illustrate this vision of the proper judicial attitude: Justice carries scales, reflecting the obligation to balance claims fairly; she possesses a sword, giving her great power to enforce decisions; and she wears a blindfold, protecting her from distractions.

Many federal judges have departed from their earlier attitudes; they have dropped the relatively disinterested pose to adopt a more active, "managerial" stance. In growing numbers, judges are not only adjudicating the merits of issues presented to them by litigants, but also are meeting with parties in chambers to encourage settlement of disputes and to supervise case preparation. Both before and after the trial, judges are playing a critical role in shaping litigation and influencing results.

Several commentators have identified one kind of lawsuit—the "public law litigation" or "structural reform" case—in which federal judges have assumed a new role. In these cases, judges actively supervise the implementation of a wide range of remedies designed to desegregate schools and to reform prisons and other institutions. Some commentators have questioned the legitimacy of judges' dominance in what is now generally acknowledged to be a "new model of civil litigation." Few, however, have scrutinized the managerial aspects of such postdecision judicial work. Even less attention has been paid to the role judges now play in the pretrial phases of both complex and routine cases.

I believe that the role of judges before adjudication is undergoing a change as substantial as has been recognized in the posttrial phase of public law cases. Today, federal district judges are assigned a case at the time of its filing and assume responsibility for shepherding the case to completion. Judges have described their new tasks as "case management"—hence my term "managerial judges." As managers, judges learn more about cases much earlier than they did in the past. They negotiate with parties about the course, timing, and scope of both pretrial and posttrial litigation. These managerial responsibilities give judges greater power. Yet the restraints that formerly circumscribed judicial authority are conspicuously absent. Managerial judges frequently work beyond the public view, off the record, with no obligation to provide written, reasoned opinions, and out of reach of appellate review.

This new managerial role has emerged for several reasons. One is the creation of pretrial discovery rights. The 1938 Federal Rules of Civil Procedure embodied contradictory mandates: a discovery system ("give your opponent all information relevant to the litigation") was grafted onto American adversarial norms ("protect your client zealously" and therefore "withhold what you can"). In some cases, parties argued about their obligations under the discovery rules; such disputes generated a need for someone to decide pretrial conflicts. Trial judges accepted the assignment and have become mediators, negotiators, and planners—as well as adjudicators. Moreover, once involved in pretrial discovery, many judges became convinced that their presence at other points in a lawsuit's development would be beneficial; supervision of discovery became a conduit for judicial control over all phases of litigation and thus infused lawsuits with the continual presence of the judge-overseer.

Partly because of their new oversight role and partly because of increasing case loads, many judges have become concerned with the volume of their work. To reduce the pressure, judges have turned to efficiency experts who promise "calendar control." Under the experts' guidance, judges have begun to experiment with schemes for speeding the resolution of cases and for persuading litigants to settle rather than try cases whenever possible. During the past decade, enthusiasm for the "managerial movement" has become widespread; what began as an experiment is likely soon to become obligatory. Unless the Supreme Court and Congress reject proposed amendments to the Federal Rules, pretrial judicial management will be required in virtually all cases.

In the rush to conquer the mountain of work, no one—neither judges, court administrators, nor legal commentators—has assessed whether relying on trial judges for informal dispute resolution and for case management, either before or after trial, is good, bad, or neutral. Little empirical evidence supports the claim that judicial management "works" either to settle cases or to provide cheaper, quicker, or fairer dispositions. Proponents of judicial management have also failed to consider the systemic effects of the shift in judicial role. Management is a new form of "judicial activism," a behavior that usually attracts substantial criticism. Moreover, judicial management may be teaching judges to value their statistics, such as the number of case dispositions, more than they value the quality of their dispositions. Finally, because managerial judging is less visible and usually unreviewable, it gives trial courts more authority and at the same time provides litigants with fewer procedural safeguards to protect them from abuse of that authority. In short, managerial judging may be redefining *sub silentio* our standards of what constitutes rational, fair, and impartial adjudication.

2.9   *". . . judicial action only achieves . . . legitimacy by responding to, indeed by stirring the deep and durable demand for justice in our society."*

THE ROLE OF THE JUDGE IN PUBLIC LAW LITIGATION

Abram Chayes

[handwritten: judges are managers of litigation, playing a critical role in shaping lawsuits and influencing results]

. . . I would . . . argue that just as the traditional concept [of the judicial function] reflected and related to a system in which social and economic arrangements were remitted to autonomous private action, so the new model reflects and relates to a regulatory system where such arrangements are the product of positive [governmental] enactment. In such a system, enforcement and application of law is necessarily implementation of regulatory policy. Litigation inevitably becomes an explicitly political forum and the court a visible arm of the political process.

A FIRST APPRAISAL

A. Trial Balance

One response to the [new] positive law model of litigation would be to condemn it as an intolerable hodge-podge of legislative, administrative, executive, and judicial functions addressed to problems that are by their nature inappropriate for judicial resolution. Professor Lon Fuller has argued that when such functions are given to the judiciary they are parasitic, in the sense that they can be effectively carried out only by drawing on the legitimacy and moral force that courts have developed through the performance of their inherent function, adjudication according to the traditional conception. A certain limited amount of such parasitism can be accommodated, but too much undermines the very legitimacy on which it depends, because the nontraditional activities of the judiciary are at odds with the conditions that ensure the moral force of its decisions.

From one perspective, the Burger Court may be seen to be embarked on some such program for the restoration of the traditional forms of adjudication. . . .

In any event, I think, we have invested excessive time and energy in the effort to define—on the basis of the inherent nature of adjudication, the implications of a constitutional text, or the functional characteristics of courts—what the precise scope of judicial activity

89 *Harvard Law Review* 1281 (1976). Reprinted with permission of the author. Abram Chayes is Professor of Law at Harvard University.

ought to be. Separation of powers comes in for a good deal of veneration in our political and judicial rhetoric, but it has always been hard
to classify all government activity into three, and only three, neat
and mutually exclusive categories. In practice, all governmental officials, including judges, have exercised a large and messy admixture
of powers, and that is as it must be. That is not to say that institutional
characteristics are irrelevant in assigning governmental tasks or that
judges should unreservedly be thrust directly into political battles.
But such considerations should be taken as cautionary, not decisive;
for despite its well rehearsed inadequacies, the judiciary may have
some important institutional advantages for the tasks it is assuming:

First, and perhaps most important, is that the process is presided
over by a judge. His professional tradition insulates him from narrow
political pressures, but, given the operation of the federal appointive
power and the demands of contemporary law practice, he is likely
to have some experience of the political process and acquaintance
with a fairly broad range of public policy problems. Moreover, he is
governed by a professional ideal of reflective and dispassionate analysis of the problem before him and is likely to have had some experience in putting this ideal into practice.

Second, the public law model permits ad hoc applications of
broad national policy in situations of limited scope. The solutions can
be tailored to the needs of the particular situation and flexibly administered or modified as experience develops. . . .

Third, the procedure permits a relatively high degree of participation by representatives of those who will be directly affected by
the decision, without establishing a *liberum veto.*

Fourth, the court, although traditionally thought less competent
than legislatures or administrative agencies in gathering and assessing information, may have unsuspected advantages in this regard.
Even the diffused adversarial structure of public law litigation furnishes strong incentives for the parties to produce information. If the
party structure is sufficiently representative of the interests at stake,
a considerable range of relevant information will be forthcoming.
And, because of the limited scope of the proceeding, the information
required can be effectively focused and specified. Information produced will not only be subject to adversary review, but . . . the judge
can engage his own experts to assist in evaluating the evidence.
Moreover, the information that is produced will not be filtered
through the rigid structures and preconceptions of bureaucracies.

Fifth, the judicial process is an effective mechanism for register-
ing and responding to grievances generated by the operation of
public programs in a regulatory state. Unlike an administrative bureaucracy or a legislature, the judiciary *must* respond to the complaints of the aggrieved. It is also rather well situated to perform the
task of balancing the importance of competing policy interests in a

specific situation. The legislature, perhaps, could balance, but it cannot address specific situations. The bureaucracy deals with specific situations, but only from a position of commitment to particular policy interests.

Sixth, the judiciary has the advantage of being non-bureaucratic. It is effective in tapping energies and resources outside itself and outside the government in the exploration of the situation and the assessment of remedies. It does not work through a rigid, multilayered hierarchy of numerous officials, but through a smallish, representative force, assembled ad hoc, and easily dismantled when the problem is finally resolved.

The foregoing enumeration is admittedly one-sided. It surely does not warrant unqualified endorsement of the public law litigation model in its present form. For one thing, the returns are not all in, and those we have show varying degrees of success. . . .

There are also counter-instances and counter-arguments for each of the advantages of the public law model suggested above. Can the disinterestedness of the judge be sustained, for example, when he is more visibly a part of the political process? Will the consciously negotiated character of the relief ultimately erode the sense that what is being applied is law? Can the relatively unspecialized trial judge, even with the aid of the new authority and techniques being developed in public law litigation, respond adequately to the demands for legislative and predictive fact-finding in the new model? Against the asserted "responsiveness" of the courts, it may be argued that the insensitivity of other agencies represents a political judgment that should be left undisturbed. And although the courts may be well situated to balance competing policy interests in the particular case, if as is often true the decree calls for a substantive commitment of resources, the court has little basis for evaluating competing claims on the public purse. . . .

One issue, because it is the center of much current theoretical discussion, deserves somewhat fuller treatment, even in this preliminary effort. Public law litigation, because of its widespread impact, seems to call for adequate representation in the proceedings of the range of interests that will be affected by them. At the stage of relief in particular, if the decree is to be quasi-negotiated and party participation is to be relied upon to ensure its viability, representation at the bargaining table assumes very great importance, not only from the point of view of the affected interests but from that of the system itself. . . . [T]he tendency, supported by both the language and the rationale of the Federal Rules of Civil Procedure, is to regard anyone whose interests may be significantly affected by the litigation to be presumptively entitled to participate in the suit on demand. In a public law system, persons are usually "affected" by litigation in terms of an "interest" that they share with many others similarly situated, whether organized or unorganized. . . . Participation of those affected by the decision has a reassuringly democratic ring, but when participation is mediated by group representatives, often self-appointed, it gives a certain pause. . . .

The real problem . . . is the inevitable incompleteness of the interest representation. What about those who do not volunteer—most often the weak, the poor, the unorganized? A first response is that these groups are unlikely to be better off in any other process to which the policy issue might be remitted for decision. On this score, neither the judiciary nor the administrative agencies . . . need entertain feelings of inferiority to the typical bureaucratic decision or local governing board action, or even to the operation of "de-regulated" private activity. And to retreat to the notion that the legislature itself—Congress!—is in some mystical way adequately representative of all the interests at stake, particularly on issues of policy implementation and application, is to impose democratic theory by brute force on observed institutional behavior.

Moreover, a number of techniques are available to the judge to increase the breadth of interests represented in a suit, if that seems desirable. He can, for example, refuse to proceed until new parties are brought in. . . . In class actions, the judge may order such "notice as may be required for the protection of members of the class or otherwise for the fair conduct of the action," including "sampling notice" designed to apprise the judge of significant divisions of interest among the putative class, not brought to light by its representatives. And that notice is supposed to be reasonably calculated to inform absentees of their potential interest in the litigation, which is more than can be said of notification of administrative proceedings in the Federal Register. The judge can also appoint guardians *ad litem* for unrepresented interests. And as we have seen, he can and does employ experts and amici to inform himself on aspects of the case not adequately developed by the parties. Finally, the judge can elicit the views of public officials at all levels.

There is also a basis for thinking that the judge may have some success in identifying unrepresented interests that ought to be involved. The diversity of his work load may induce a certain breadth of perspective, in contrast to the specialized administrator. Courts have been somewhat more successful than some agencies in deriving policy guidance from opaque statutory provisions, a guidance that may help inform the choice of interests to be represented. The relatively defined focus even of public law litigation and its often local setting may help in identifying and defining affected interests.

The foregoing is at best a fragmentary and impressionistic response. . . . Moreover, most of it relates to the *potential* of the judicial system. A critical question for research is whether this potential is or can be exploited to produce a party structure that is adequately representative in light of the consequences of public law litigation without introducing so much complexity that the procedure falls of its own weight.

Even if one could be reasonably confident of the capacity of the court to construct ad hoc a kind of mini-legislature for the situation in litigation, I take it an even more fundamental query remains. In reaching a decision, what weight is to be assigned to the interests represented? A part of the answer may be found in the suggestion that the decision, or at least the remedy, involves a species of negotiation among the parties. But on this issue, the argument is familiar and powerful that Congress, whatever its makeup, is the institution authoritatively empowered in our system to balance incommensurable political values and interests. Here we confront, finally, the question of the legitimacy of judicial action in public law litigation.

* * * * *

Despite the foregoing reservations, I am inclined . . . to urge a hospitable reception for the developments I have described and a willingness to accept a good deal of disorderly, pragmatic institutional overlap. After all, the growth of judicial power has been, in large part, a function of the failure of other agencies to respond to groups that have been able to mobilize considerable political resources and energy. And, despite its new role, the judiciary is unlikely to displace its institutional rivals for governing power or even to achieve a dominant share of the market. In the circumstances, I would concentrate not on turning the clock back (or off), but on improving the performance of public law litigation, both by practical attention to the difficulties noted in this Article and by a more systematic professional understanding of what is being done. . . .

In my view, judicial action only achieves . . . legitimacy by responding to, indeed by stirring, the deep and durable demand for justice in our society. I confess some difficulty in seeing how this is to be accomplished by erecting the barriers of the traditional conception to turn aside, for example, attacks on exclusionary zoning and police violence, two of the ugliest remaining manifestations of official racism in American life. In practice, if not in words, the American legal tradition has always acknowledged the importance of substantive results for the legitimacy and accountability of judicial action. Otherwise it could not praise *Marbury v. Madison* as creative judicial statesmanship while condemning *Lochner v. New York** as abuse of power. Perhaps the most important consequence of the inevitably exposed position of the judiciary in our contemporary regulatory state is that it will force us to confront more explicitly the qualities

---

*Lochner v. New York (1905) was among the most famous of the Supreme Court's decisions that, near the turn of the century, tried to write laissez-faire economics into American constitutional law.—Eds.

of wisdom, viability, responsiveness to human needs—the justice—
of judicial decisions. . . .

2.10   *"Courts see the tips of icebergs and the bottoms of barrels."*

THE HAZARDS OF JUDICIAL
GUARDIANSHIP   *The problems of potential government
by the judiciary*

Donald L. Horowitz

Judges may be performing new roles . . . but they continue to act very
much within the framework of an old process, a process that evolved,
not to devise new programs or to oversee administration, but to
decide controversies. The constraints of that process operate to limit
the range of what can reasonably be expected from courts. The
principal limitations derive from the way in which cases get to court,
the way in which issues are framed and reasons adduced, and the
provisions for effectuating court decisions.

COURTS AND PRIVATE INITIATIVE

Courts are public decision makers, yet they are wholly dependent on
private initiative to invoke their powers: they do not self-start. Parties affected by administrative action choose to seek or not to seek
judicial redress on the basis of considerations that may bear no relation to the public importance of the issues at stake, to the recurring
character of the administrative action in question, or to the competence of courts to judge the action or to change it. This basic feature
of judicial review has a number of important consequences.

First of all, the fact that judges do not choose their own menu
makes it difficult for them to concentrate in a sustained way on any
policy area. Judicial action tends to be spotty and uneven; some
agencies may be subject to frequent correction in the courts, others
to virtually none at all. The decisions that emerge are ad hoc; they
are rarely informed by a comprehensive view of the agency's work,
and they cannot aspire to anything approaching the status of a coher-

Reprinted from 37 *Public Administration Review* 148 © (1977) by The American
Society for Public Administration, 1225 Connecticut Avenue, N.W., Washington, D.C.
All rights reserved.

Donald L. Horowitz is Professor of Law, Duke University Law School. His book,
The Courts and Social Policy (Washington, D.C.: The Brookings Institution, 1977), was
awarded the Louis Brownlow Prize of the National Academy of Public Administration
as that year's best book in the field.

ent policy. One of the catchwords of the administrative state—and now perhaps one of its biggest disappointments—was "planning." Few agencies do the kind of program planning that was once expected of them. But if this is a deficiency of the administrative process in need of rectification, the courts, whose own process is fundamentally passive and piecemeal, are not the place to seek it.

The fact that courts do not deal with anything resembling a random sample of the work of administrative agencies affects their perspective in another way. They are put in the position of having to prescribe on the basis of very special, indeed often highly atypical, cases—cases that come to decision one at a time. . . . [T]hey base their inferences on a skewed sample. Courts see the tips of icebergs and the bottoms of barrels. If their perspective is detached, it is not necessarily well informed.

PROBLEMS OF JUDICIAL PROCEDURE

As courts decide only special cases, so do they decide them in a special way. The framing of issues is geared to the litigant and his complaint. The mission of the courts is to set wrongs right. This means that the facts of the single case are highlighted, the facts of all cases slighted. The judicial process has a bias toward the particular and against the recurrent. Judicial standards of relevance are strict. In consequence, everything that can be labeled context or background is relegated to a distant second place in litigation. Elaborate provision is made for proving and weighing the events that give rise to the litigation. Virtually no provision is made for proving anything more general about administrative behavior. Courts are, for example, often ignorant of the scope and nuances of the programs they find themselves judging, and nothing in the rituals of litigation alerts them to this omission. On the contrary, everything pushes them toward a narrow focus on the case before them. It is this feature of adjudication that so often gives outsiders the impression that courts are fascinated by questions that are at best tangential to policy.

The sources of judicial reasoning do, of course, reside in general principles. But those principles are to be found in yet more particular cases—often cases far afield from the administrative action being challenged. The principles tend to cut across the functional divisions along which agencies are organized and policies are formulated. For purposes of decision, reality is organized in terms of categories that seem to make no sense except in court. Thus, perhaps the only thing that social security recipients, produce handlers, and environmentalists have in common is that all must be accorded hearings by the administrators whose actions affect their interests—though the "actions," the "effects," and the "interests" may be completely different in kind. No doubt the propensity of courts to seek their analogies in far-flung places contributes to the development of an integrated jurisprudence, and there is much to be said for it in these terms. But this propensity again detracts from judicial attention to the program being reviewed. It also diminishes the value of the judicial decision as guidance to the administrator as he manages his program.

Judicial decisions thus embrace a limited species of reasoning. Equally important, they are *all reasoning*. The judicial process is tied to reason as the mode of decision and can scarcely be described apart from its resort to reason. Yet there are some questions that lend themselves to other modes of decision—particularly to negotiation and compromise. Sometimes that is the only way to satisfy conflicting interests and keep them from turning against the political system. Sometimes reason provides no clues to an appropriate answer. There may be a shortage of knowledge sufficient to provide answers or a shortage of resources to find the answers at the time that they are needed, at a cost that makes sense. The administrative process has at least its fair share of such problems. Courts are not the place to look for their solution.

Perhaps the ultimate hazard of relying on courts to guard the public interest is that their decisions stand a good chance of being ineffective or effective in ways not intended. Some administrators have been known to act on the view that courts decide only individual cases. A succession of cases repudiating the lawfulness of agency policy brings a series of concessions to individual litigants but no change in policy. Those with the resources, initiative, and foresight to bring suit may force a "policy change" applicable only to their cases.

Even more generous views of the authority of courts to lay down policy can raise problems of uniformity. Decisions of the federal courts, short of the Supreme Court, are binding only in the circuit or district in which the court sits. Although this principle is a useful safeguard against settling difficult policy questions prematurely, it also permits recalcitrant bureaucrats to wait until at least several courts have spoken before bringing general policies into line with court decisions. Typically, this time is measured in years, and there are some agencies that do not feel obliged to alter their course until the Supreme Court itself has spoken. Given the multitude of issues competing for Supreme Court consideration, this may be never. The fact that courts decide one case at a time, against agencies with varying degrees of responsiveness to judicial decisions, makes it hard for courts to force policy changes all by themselves.

There is, however, a problem of impact beyond this. It lies in the propensity of all policies to have unanticipated consequences. In this respect, policies enunciated by courts are no different from the policies that emanate from other decision makers. But the courts are

usually short of machinery to detect and correct unintended consequences after they have occurred. They have no monitoring mechanisms, no inspectors, no grapevines. Quite the opposite: judicial
proprieties foster isolation of the decision maker from the environment in which his/her decisions must operate. Unless a litigant provides the courts with feedback about the consequences of their
decisions, there is every likelihood that they will pass unnoticed—
and unaltered. Here, again, private initiative seems inadequate to
protect public interests.

CONCLUSION

Different institutions tend to perform well at different kinds of tasks.
Each has its own characteristic modes of operating, and these leave
an indelible stamp on the matters they touch. In the case of the
courts, I have argued, their procedures remain attuned to the disposition of individual controversies. This means that they function on
a basis that is too intermittent, too spotty, too partial, too ill-informed
for them to have a major constructive impact on administrative performance. They can stop action in progress, they can slow it down,
and they can make it public (their exposing function has been too
little noted). Perhaps most important, they can bring moral judgment to bear, for moral evaluation is a traditional judicial strength.
But courts cannot build alternate structures, for the customary
modes of judicial reasoning are not adequate for this. When it comes
to framing and modifying programs, administrators are far better
situated to see things whole, to obtain, process, and interpret complex or specialized data, to secure expert advice, to sense the need
to change course, and to monitor performance after decision. Courts
can limit the discretion of others, but they find it harder to exercise
their own discretion where that involves choosing among multiple,
competing alternatives.

Although the tendency to resort to the courts for the vindication
of broad public interests continues unabated, the impact of judicial
intervention on administrative behavior remains uncertain. There
has surely been no rush in the federal agencies to embrace judicially
enunciated standards of performance beyond what is minimally required by individual decrees. Even then, many government lawyers
and program managers have been inclined to read judicial opinions
as narrowly as the words would warrant, secure in the knowledge
that many things escape the attention of the courts, that judicial
correction comes, not every budget session, but every-so-often and,
at that, frequently in a different court and usually in a fresh factual
setting.

But it is wrong to reckon the benefits and costs only by the effects
of judicial action inside the departments and agencies. The growing

judicial role has implications for the courts, too. They have so far been remarkably slow to enhance their ability to meet the new burdens they face. It is, as I have suggested, the fact that they continue to face new challenges with the old machinery very much intact that limits their ability to handle complex data, to monitor the consequences of their decrees, or to do the other things that might make them more effective partners in the process of defining the public interest.

Yet even in this failing there is something to be celebrated. The outstanding characteristic of the judicial process remains the way in which it generalizes from the particular instance. So committed are the courts to the individual case that all their machinery is tuned to resolving it. From the standpoint of policy making, this is a weakness. Retooling the judicial process means essentially giving it the capacity to function more systematically in terms of general categories, to draw probabilistic inferences, to forecast effects. Should retooling proceed beyond marginal improvements, it seems highly likely that it will occur at the expense of the commendable attention currently given to the individual case and that courts, in trying to improve other institutions, will become much more like them. The distinctiveness of the judicial process—that which unfits it for much of the important work of government—lies in its willingness to expend social resources on individual complaints one at a time. That distinctiveness is worth preserving.

PART TWO
The Federal Courts

3
Judicial Organization

The task of judging in the United States is performed under organizational arrangements more complex and confusing than those encountered in almost any other country. There are, first of all, two complete systems of courts—federal and state—with all the attendant problems of defining their respective jurisdictions. Then there are fifty separate state systems, which with few exceptions are based upon models and assumptions dating from the eighteenth century, if not earlier. Each of these systems is composed of various levels of courts arrayed in a hierarchical structure that provides channels of communication among courts and ensures a measure, but only a measure, of control by higher courts over lower ones.

LAW AND EQUITY

A preliminary word should be said concerning an English heritage that had a substantial effect on judicial organization and jurisdiction. Historic English practice created a dichotomy between cases in law and cases in equity. In its early development the common law had gone through periods of extreme rigidity during which courts simply turned would-be litigants away if their suits could not be settled by issuance of certain specific technical writs or orders. These litigants began appealing to the king for his personal justice. By the fourteenth century such petitions for grace were being referred to the king's chancellor for settlement. Out of this practice, courts of chancery, or equity, grew up alongside the courts of law.

The purpose of equity, then as now, is to provide a more flexible set of remedies than the common law (or perhaps statutory law) offers. The common law's typical prescription for an injury to a legally protected right is to order the offender to pay a sum of money to the injured person. But some injuries cannot be made whole by money.

82

Patients confined to a mental hospital where treatment is poor need the help of trained medical personnel, not money. Blacks who are prevented from voting need to have their political rights restored, not monetary compensation for their loss of political influence.

For persons suffering injuries that cannot be calculated in dollars and cents, equity offers the remedy of an injunction, a judicial order commanding named persons to perform or not to perform certain specific actions. Chapter 6 says more about this kind of order; for present purposes the most important point is that the judge can tailor an injunction's exact terms to fit individual cases.

While in England courts of law and courts of equity were separate systems staffed by different judges, the first United States Congress enacted a major reform in judicial administration by providing that federal courts would have jurisdiction both in law and equity, a practice now followed in almost all American states and even in England. The proceedings and, more significantly, the remedies in law and equity remain very different, but the legislation eliminated a whole set of courts at each level, a considerable saving of public funds. This merging of functions means that in a complex case the litigant can file a single complaint asking for both legal and equitable remedies rather than plodding through the delay and confusion of two separate trials, perhaps followed by separate appeals to different courts, processes that might result in contradictory decisions.

To avoid unnecessary friction with courts of common law, English judges of the old chancery (equity) courts would refuse to hear a case unless the litigant could show that the injury being suffered or immediately threatened was irreparable (that is, an injury for which money would not adequately compensate) and that the common law offered no other remedy that was suitable. Despite the merger of the two kinds of courts, American judges still treat orders in equity as "extraordinary writs" and in form, though not always in substance, require the traditional showings before hearing a case in equity.

THE JUDICIAL SYSTEM IN THE STATES

The American approach to judicial organization has been strongly localistic. The pattern was established when the country was sparsely settled and methods of communication and transportation were primitive. Courts needed to be close to be convenient, and the result was widespread adoption of the justice-of-the-peace system to provide courts on a neighborhood basis. At the next higher level courts tended to be established with relation to the distance a man could travel in a day on horseback. These local courts and judicial districts have proved very difficult to modify, because judges, clerks, and staff members, as well as practicing attorneys, have a vested interest in continuing the system.

Another dominant characteristic of state judicial systems has been layers of courts, often with overlapping jurisdiction. Justices of the peace or other part-time magistrates, where they still exist, constitute the lowest level of trial courts. They typically are authorized to grant money judgments up to a certain amount (often about $300), and as criminal courts they can try only minor offenses. They are not courts of record, and if one of their decisions is appealed, an entirely new trial must be held in the next highest court. Municipal or county courts are the courts of first instance for most civil, criminal, and probate proceedings. Circuit or district courts are also trial courts, usually covering several counties and handling the more important civil and criminal business.

At the appellate level states typically provide a set of intermediate appellate courts in addition to a supreme court. The easy availability of appellate review and the tremendous volume of appeals carried to higher courts are characteristics in which the American legal system differs markedly from English and Continental systems of justice. This practice grew first of all from the widespread assumption that litigants were entitled to carry disputes through all levels of courts. Perhaps more important, however, was the view that the appellate judges had of their own function. Their job was primarily, as Willard Hurst says, "to declare the law, rather than merely to decide the case." So appellate judges did not see cases as a whole. They saw rather a succession of legal issues that it was their job to settle. If appellate judges found a legal error in the trial, they would return the case to the trial court for further proceedings, and the later decision might in turn be appealed on other legal issues.

American appellate procedure was further complicated by choice of the writ of error as the main instrument for securing review. This writ was one of the most technical in English law, and it limited the reviewing court to a consideration of the formal record of the case. An appeal thus takes on the status almost of a new and more expensive lawsuit as assignments of error are prepared, records printed, and evidence transcribed. Because of the convoluted technicalities required to invoke appellate jurisdiction properly, courts still decide many appeals simply on the basis of error in procedure without even discussing the substantive problems over which the litigants are wrangling.

THE FEDERAL COURT SYSTEM

Federalism does not require that each of the two levels of government have a complete judicial system. In fact, most federations have a complete set of state or provincial courts, topped by a single federal supreme court, sometimes with the addition of one or more specialized federal tribunals.

The American Constitution made possible a similar arrangement, because it established only one national court, the Supreme Court, and left it up to Congress to decide whether to create any federal courts inferior to the Supreme Court. Few actions of the First Congress were more portentous for the development of American federalism than its decision in the Judiciary Act of 1789 to set up a complete system of lower federal courts that would interpret and apply some aspects of federal law.

From this beginning the federal court system has developed into a three-tiered structure with many features typical of bureaucratic organizations. (Reading 3.1.) The district courts, one or more of which is located in every state, are the trial courts of the federal system. (Readings 3.2 and 3.3.) Initially, there were also federal circuit courts that were trial courts for some classes of cases, but they were finally abolished by statute in 1911. Appeals from the decisions of the district courts go to the courts of appeals, created by Congress in 1891, and known until 1948 as circuit courts of appeals. For judicial purposes the country is divided into eleven numbered circuits; a twelfth court of appeals sits in the District of Columbia. There are from three to twenty-three judges for each circuit. Usually the judges sit in panels of three to hear cases, though for exceptionally important matters they may sit *en banc*, that is, all together.

The character of the appeals courts' business varies from circuit to circuit. The Second Circuit, sitting in New York, is known as the nation's "commercial court," because so much corporate litigation comes to that court for review. For obvious reasons litigation involving the federal government is heavily concentrated in the court of appeals for the District of Columbia. Up to 1981 the court of appeals for the Fifth Circuit, based in New Orleans, covered the six states of the Old South and had the most judges and the heaviest case load of all the circuits.[1] This was the court that had the primary responsibility of supervising the Southern district judges who were carrying out the Supreme Court's rulings against racial segregation.[2] In 1978 new judicial authorizations brought the Fifth Circuit up to an unwieldy twenty-six judges. There had long been pressure, primarily from conservative quarters, to split the Fifth, and it finally succeeded. The states of Texas, Louisiana, and Mississippi remained in the Fifth Circuit, while Georgia, Florida, and Alabama became a new Eleventh Circuit, headquartered in Atlanta.[3]

---

[1] J. Woodford Howard, Jr., has made an intensive study of the work of these three courts; *Courts of Appeals in the Federal Judicial System* (Princeton: Princeton University Press, 1981). See also Lawrence Baum, Sheldon Goldman, and Austin Sarat, "The Evolution of Litigation in the Federal Courts of Appeals, 1895–1975," 16 *Law and Society Review* 291 (1981–82).

[2] See Jack W. Peltason, *Fifty-Eight Lonely Men: Southern Federal Judges and School Desegregation* (New York: Harcourt, Brace & World, 1961).

[3] The Ninth Circuit, on the West Coast, has twenty-three judges. In 1978 Congress authorized courts with more than fifteen judges to constitute "administrative units"

As J. Woodford Howard, Jr., points out (Reading 3.4), decisions of the courts of appeals make national law in the great majority of cases, because less than 1 percent of their decisions are successfully appealed. The Supreme Court tends to grant review on issues where two or more courts of appeals have arrived at conflicting interpretations of law and also when it is in disagreement with the result reached below. Consequently it is not surprising that the Supreme Court reverses the courts of appeals in the majority of the cases it accepts.

Under supervision of the district courts and appointed by district judges is a corps of some 500 United States magistrates (most of them serving part-time), who relieve district judges of certain routine duties. They try minor offenses, conduct pretrial conferences, handle immigration matters, and screen petitions for habeas corpus. The Federal Magistrates Act of 1976 authorized district judges to delegate to magistrates many additional duties, such as general supervision of the criminal calendar (the list or docket of lawsuits scheduled for trial) and motions to expedite or postpone the trial of cases.

In 1979 Congress further expanded the authority of magistrates, allowing them to preside at jury and nonjury trials with the consent of both parties, at misdemeanor trials if the defendant consents, and at petty-offense juvenile trials if the juvenile consents. Direct appeals go from magistrates to a federal court of appeals. District judges continue to appoint magistrates, but candidates must be screened by merit selection panels.[4]

In certain situations federal statutes have provided for three-judge district courts, typically composed of two circuit judges and one district judge. First authorized in 1903 to try cases arising under the Sherman Antitrust Act, they were subsequently required for other types of proceedings—such as challenges to the constitutionality of state and federal statutes—where Congress was reluctant to have deci-

---

within the court and to perform *en banc* functions by less than the total number of members.

There are also a number of specialized courts in the federal system, including the Customs Court, the U.S. Claims Court, and the U.S. Court of Appeals for the Federal Circuit, which hears customs and patent appeals and cases from the appellate division of the Claims Court. The Tax Court is actually not in the judicial branch; it is rather an executive agency that hears protests against decisions of the Internal Revenue Service.

[4] See "Note: Federal Magistrates and the Principles of Article III," 97 *Harvard Law Review* 1947 (1984). The position of federal referee in bankruptcy should also be noted. Referees were given the status of "adjuncts" to federal district judges by the Bankruptcy Act of 1978, but the Supreme Court ruled this status unconstitutional in *Northern Pipeline Construction Co. v. Marathon Pipe Line Co.* (1982), because the bankruptcy judges did not enjoy tenure for "good behavior" or protection from reduction in salary as required for all judges by Article III. The Court postponed the effect of its decision several times to allow Congress to pass remedial legislation, but the final deadline passed before Congress acted in 1984, which meant that the act had to restore the bankruptcy judges to their positions retroactively and perhaps unconstitutionally.

sions made by a single district judge. There was a right of appeal from a three-judge court directly to the Supreme Court.

Staffing three-judge courts drained judicial resources, and the right of direct appeal burdened the Supreme Court. As civil rights litigation increased, so did the number of three-judge courts, reaching a peak of 321 in 1973. A long effort to reduce the three-judge-court requirement succeeded in 1976, when Congress eliminated the obligation to set up such courts whenever an injunction suit challenged the constitutionality of state or federal legislation. The act did not affect the necessity of convening a three-judge court to hear challenges to congressional or state legislative apportionment, or cases specifically mandated by Congress, as in the Civil Rights Act of 1964 or the Voting Rights Act of 1965.[5]

THE SUPREME COURT

At the apex of the federal hierarchy is the Supreme Court, headed by the Chief Justice of the United States. The Court was created directly by Article III of the Constitution, but the number of its members is determined by congressional statute. The office of chief justice, strangely enough, is not mentioned in Article III, but is assumed to exist by Article I, Section 3, which provides that the chief justice shall preside over impeachment proceedings in the Senate if the President is on trial.

For a half century the office was designated only as Chief Justice of the Supreme Court, but in the Civil War period Salmon P. Chase successfully claimed the more grandiloquent title of Chief Justice of the United States. The responsibilities of the office are in fact much wider than simply being presiding officer and manager of Court affairs. The chief is a ceremonial figure and third-ranking government official after the President and Vice President. As we shall see, he is concerned with the organization and operation of the entire judicial establishment, which he undertakes to represent before Congress, the bar, and the public generally.[6]

The Supreme Court is primarily an appellate court, but the Constitution does define two categories of cases that can be heard in the Court's original jurisdiction, that is, without prior consideration by any other tribunal. These are cases in which a state is a party and those affecting ambassadors, public ministers, and consuls. Generally, however, the Court does not have to accept a suit invoking its original jurisdiction unless it feels there is a compelling reason of public policy.

[5] In 1982 there were sixty-two three-judge courts, forty-two of which dealt with reapportionment issues resulting from the 1980 census. The number dropped to twenty-seven in 1983, primarily because there were only nine reapportionment cases. Voting rights were at issue in fourteen.

[6] See the excellent discussion by Peter G. Fish, *The Office of Chief Justice of the United States* (Charlottesville, Va.: The Miller Center, University of Virginia, 1984).

All the remaining business of the Supreme Court comes to it in its appellate jurisdiction, which it exercises, as the Constitution says, "with such Exceptions, and under such Regulations as the Congress shall make." In the post–Civil War period Congress used this authority over the Court's appellate jurisdiction to withdraw from judicial consideration a politically embarrassing case in which the Court had already heard argument. The Supreme Court in *Ex parte McCardle* (1869) agreed that such action was within congressional power, though the circumstances were so exceptional as to make it hazardous to generalize from this single ruling.

Cases reach the Supreme Court in two ways—by "appeal" and through grant of the writ of certiorari.[7] Federal statutes appear to give litigants a right to have their cases reviewed by the Supreme Court on "appeal" when (1) a lower federal court declares unconstitutional a state or federal statute; (2) a state's highest court invalidates a federal statute, treaty, or executive order; or (3) a state's highest court sustains the constitutionality of a state statute. There is more appearance of a right here than reality, however. Pleading overwork and a snowstorm of frivolous appeals, for several decades the justices have been treating appeals as within the discretion of the Court to grant or deny. Indeed, the justices dismiss most of them, particularly those from state courts sustaining the constitutionality of state statutes, offering only the cryptic explanation: "Want of a substantial federal question."

Most cases come to the Court by way of a petition for certiorari (from the Latin, "to be made more certain"). The losing litigant in a United States court of appeals, one of the special federal courts, or the highest court of a state (if a question of federal treaty, statutory, or constitutional law is involved) may request the Supreme Court to take the case. If four justices, one less than a majority, vote affirmatively, the Court accepts the case, and it is placed on the calendar for argument.

The Court receives from four to five thousand cases each year and denies or dismisses well over 95 percent of them. Denial of certiorari does not necessarily mean that the Court agrees with the decision below; it simply means that, for whatever reasons, four justices did not find that the case merited the Court's scarcest resource, time. In general the Court accepts only cases that present substantial issues of law or policy. (Reading 3.5.) On some occasions, however, the Court has refused to review decisions raising issues of major importance, usually because the justices felt it would be imprudent for them to become involved at that particular juncture.[8]

---

[7] A third avenue, now rarely used, is "certification," which occurs when a United States court of appeals certifies to the Supreme Court a question of law that the lower-court judges regard as too important or difficult for them to decide.

[8] The Court's decision-making procedures, and particularly the handling of certiorari petitions, are discussed in more detail in Chapter 13.

To a certain extent the statistics on the Court's burgeoning caseload are misleading, since by far the largest increase is in *in forma pauperis* petitions—those filed without payment of the customary fees. These petitions are typically written by prison inmates seeking review of their convictions. The Court reviews these requests in the same way as paid petitions. Sometimes they provide the occasion for dramatic decisions. *Gideon v. Wainwright* (1963)—the case that held that all persons accused of felonies have a right to be represented by counsel and that a state must provide free counsel if the defendant cannot hire his own attorney—reached the Supreme Court in the form of a petition hand-printed in pencil by Clarence Gideon while in the Florida penitentiary. But, the petitions *in forma pauperis* seldom present valid claims.

ORGANIZATIONAL PROBLEMS

The Supreme Court's heavy caseload was the subject of a 1972 report by a prestigious committee headed by Paul A. Freund of the Harvard Law School. The Freund committee concluded that the Court was seriously overburdened, and proposed to relieve the situation by creation of a new National Court of Appeals immediately below the Supreme Court. Staffed by seven senior circuit judges on a rotating basis, the court would resolve conflicting rulings among the circuits and screen appeals, passing perhaps four hundred of the most important cases on to the Supreme Court.[9] The proposal was not favorably received. Critics, including former Chief Justice Earl Warren, argued that deciding which cases to decide was an essential function of the Supreme Court and that cutting off access to the Court and denying the justices control over their docket would seriously damage the power and prestige of the high court. (Reading 3.6.)

In 1975 a federal commission headed by Senator Roman L. Hruska proposed an alternative plan which also called for creation of a new court. Subordinate to the Supreme Court and composed of seven full-time judges, it would decide significant cases assigned to it by the Supreme Court or the various courts of appeals.[10] This suggestion also received little support, although Chief Justice Burger, who made improvement of federal judicial administration a major concern, favored it.

In 1983 Burger updated these proposals with a revised plan for an "inter-circuit tribunal" to resolve differences among the federal courts of appeals. This new court was to be staffed from the corps of sitting

[9] Federal Judicial Center, *Report of the Study Group on the Caseload of the Supreme Court* (Washington, D.C.: Administrative Office of U.S. Courts, 1972).

[10] Commission on Revision of the Federal Court Appellate System, *Structure and Internal Procedures: Recommendations for Change* (Washington, D.C., 1975).

judges on a rotating basis.[11] Another suggestion came from Justice Stevens, who proposed creation of a new court having the sole task of screening certiorari petitions and selecting those to be decided by the Court. None of these proposals, however, attracted substantial support; and a recent decline in the number of cases filed with the Court and in its backlog makes reorganization even less likely.

Almost a half century before Burger, Chief Justice Taft had also sought, with some success, to improve the administration of the federal courts. In 1922 he secured congressional approval for creation of the Conference of Senior Circuit Justices, which was to meet annually in Washington under the chairmanship of the chief justice to oversee the functioning of the federal courts. Congress authorized the Administrative Office of the United States Courts in 1939. The same statute provided for a judicial council in each circuit, with general supervisory responsibilities for the district courts within that circuit, and an annual conference in each circuit, attended by all the circuit and district judges along with representatives of the bar.

The name of the Conference of Senior Circuit Judges was subsequently changed to the Judicial Conference of the United States, and its membership was increased by adding an elected district judge from each circuit. The Conference meets twice a year and, under the leadership of the chief justice, performs important oversight and planning functions for the court system. The Federal Judicial Center was established in 1967; among its functions is conducting seminars for newly appointed federal district judges. Congress has created the position of court executive in each circuit, and state-federal judicial councils provide liaison between federal and state judges in nearly all of the states. Finally, a National Center for State Courts was created in 1971, at Burger's suggestion, by state judges and judicial administrators to provide research and training services for the state courts, as the Federal Judicial Center does for the federal system.

FEDERAL JURISDICTION

The jurisdiction of federal courts is defined by Article III of the Constitution on two different bases: subject matter and nature of the parties involved. The classifications by subject matter are (1) all cases in law and equity arising under the Constitution; (2) all cases in law and equity arising under the laws of the United States; (3) all cases in law and equity arising under treaties made under the authority of the United States; and (4) all cases of admiralty and maritime jurisdiction.

[11] See Symposium on Intercircuit Tribunal Proposal, 11 *Hastings Constitutional Law Quarterly* 359–509 (1984).

Any case falling in these four fields can be brought into the federal courts, regardless of who the parties to the controversy may be.

Issues arising under the first three of these headings—Constitution, laws, and treaties—are referred to generally as "federal questions." A plaintiff seeking to bring a case into the federal courts on one of these grounds must set forth on the face of his complaint a substantial claim as to the federal question involved—a claim whose solidity, as just noted, the Supreme Court often denies.

Second, Article III establishes federal jurisdiction on the basis of the nature of the parties involved in a dispute and authorizes federal courts to hear controversies (1) to which the United States is a party; (2) between two or more states; (3) between a state and citizens of another state; (4) between citizens of different states; (5) between a state, or the citizens thereof, and foreign states, citizens, or subjects; and (6) affecting ambassadors, other public ministers, and consuls. Disputes involving these classes of parties can be brought into federal courts, regardless of the subject matter of the case.

Of these classes, the first and the fourth generate by far the most litigation. The United States enters federal courts as a party plaintiff in a great number of civil and criminal suits every year, and it can also be haled into court as a defendant in situations where it has waived its sovereign immunity and given its consent to be sued. Even where Congress has not consented to the government's being sued, it may still be possible to sue individual officials acting for the government, particularly if they are alleged to be acting beyond their statutory authority or under an unconstitutional statute.

Suits between citizens of different states are commonly referred to as arising under the "diversity of citizenship" jurisdiction of the federal courts. The original purpose of opening federal courts to such parties was to provide a neutral forum, since state courts might be biased in favor of their own citizens and against "strangers" from other states. Today there is less likelihood of such bias, and there is considerable opposition to diversity jurisdiction on the ground that it congests the federal courts with a tremendous number of cases growing out of essentially local issues that federal judges must determine according to state law.

There is strong pressure from judges to limit or abolish diversity jurisdiction. The American Law Institute has proposed that a plaintiff be denied the right to file a diversity action in the federal court of his or her own state, and Congress has given serious consideration to restricting or eliminating diversity jurisdiction. But practicing lawyers generally oppose any limitation, contending that some local prejudice still persists and that federal judges are likely to be superior to state judges. Of the 261,485 private civil cases filed in the federal district courts in 1984, 56,856 were diversity cases.

THE EXTENSION OF FEDERAL JURISDICTION

Congress initially relied on state courts to vindicate many essential rights arising under the Constitution and federal laws. In the aftermath of the Civil War, however, congressional trust in the willingness of state judges to protect federal rights receded. Five civil rights acts passed between 1866 and 1875 greatly enlarged the jurisdiction of federal courts. But much of the legislative product of Radical Reconstruction was declared unconstitutional by a hostile Supreme Court, or repealed by later Congresses operating in the context of Northern white apathy and Southern white opposition.

Some of the provisions of the civil rights acts did survive, however. Section 1 of the Act of 1866 guarantees all citizens the same rights as white citizens to make and enforce contracts and to inherit, purchase, lease, or sell real and personal property. The provisions as to contracts were subsequently reenacted as Section 16 of the Voting Rights Act of 1870 and codified as section 1981 of Title 42 of the United States Code (42 U.S.C. § 1981). They were notably enforced in *Runyon v. McCrary* (1976) to forbid racially discriminatory admissions practices in private schools. The language on property rights was also codified (42 U.S.C. § 1982) and served as the basis for the decision in *Jones v. Alfred H. Mayer Co.* (1968) forbidding racial discrimination in private housing.

Also surviving is section 1 of the Civil Rights Act of 1871, which authorizes anyone deprived of constitutional rights by a person acting "under color of any statute, ordinance, regulation, custom, or usage, of any state," to bring suit for damages, suit in equity, or other proper proceeding for redress (42 U.S.C. § 1983). The same section gives federal district courts original jurisdiction over such actions (28 U.S.C. § 1343(a)). In the leading case of *Monroe v. Pape* (1961) the Supreme Court held that police brutality constituted action "under color of" law within the meaning of section 1983. This ruling unleashed a flood of litigation in federal courts by private citizens claiming denial of their civil rights, an increase from 270 in 1961 to 9,938 in 1983. The Burger Court regarded these civil rights cases as a burden on the federal judiciary and by decisions such as *Paul v. Davis* (1976) and *Rizzo v. Goode* (1976) sought to reduce their number. (Reading 3.7.)

The Enforcement Act of 1870 and the Civil Rights Act of 1866, now codified as 18 U.S.C. §§ 241 and 242, authorize federal criminal prosecutions for violation of civil rights. Section 241 provides a fine of up to $5,000 and imprisonment for up to ten years for a conspiracy by two or more persons to "injure, oppress, threaten, or intimidate any citizen" from exercising, or because of exercising, any right or privilege secured by the Constitution or laws of the United States. Section 242 provides a fine of $1,000 or one year in prison, or both, for any person who, acting "under color of any law, statute, ordinance, regulation, or custom," willfully deprives any inhabitant of the United States of any of the rights, privileges, or immunities secured or protected by the Constitution or laws of the United States.

In *United States v. Classic* (1941), the Supreme Court sustained combined use of sections 241 and 242 to prosecute state officials for fraud in an election. *Screws v. United States* (1945) upheld use of section 242 against a local sheriff for beating a prisoner to death, although the Court reversed the conviction because the trial judge had not instructed the jury that they had to find that the sheriff had "willfully" deprived the prisoner of his rights. *United States v. Price* (1966) affirmed convictions under both sections for the murder of civil rights workers in Mississippi.

The final congressional effort in the post–Civil War period was the Civil Rights Act of 1875, which bestowed on federal courts the broad jurisdiction that had lain dormant in the Constitution since 1789. Under this act any suit asserting a right under the Constitution, laws, or treaties of the United States can begin in federal courts, and any such action started in state courts can be removed by the defendant to the federal courts for disposition.

SUPREME COURT REVIEW OF STATE COURTS

Although the Judiciary Act of 1789 set up a complete system of federal courts, it did not grant to the federal system all the jurisdiction to which federal courts were entitled by the Constitution. As just noted, jurisdiction over practically all the important "federal questions" (that is, questions in law and equity arising under the Constitution, laws, and treaties of the United States) was left in the first instance to state courts. In this situation it was essential that the Supreme Court be able to enforce the national supremacy clause of the Constitution (Article VI) by having power to review state court decisions, and § 25 of the Judiciary Act specifically provided for such review. (Reading 3.8.)

In spite of § 25 and the supremacy clause, Supreme Court review of state court decisions met strong opposition. Between 1789 and 1860 the courts of seven states denied the authority of the Supreme Court to decide cases on writs of error to state courts, and the legislatures of eight states adopted resolutions or statutes against this power. Between 1821 and 1882 bills were introduced in ten sessions of Congress to deprive the Court of this jurisdiction. The broadest basis for these attacks was the constitutional theory of the Kentucky and Virginia Resolutions of 1798 that each state had a right, equal to that of the federal government, to abide by its own interpretation of the Constitution. The Supreme Court, however, in two classic cases coming from the highest court of Virginia—*Martin v. Hunter's Lessee* (1816) and *Cohens v. Virginia* (1821)—decisively rejected these contentions.

The Kentucky and Virginia Resolutions also claimed for each state the right to nullify any federal act that it believed had encroached on its own authority. Such a claim was implicit in much of the opposition to the Court's reviewing state decisions and in some conflicts was quite explicit. Understandably, the Supreme Court has always given very short constitutional shrift to such arguments. Even Roger Brooke Taney, probably the most ardent states' righter among chief justices, denounced efforts by state judges in Wisconsin to nullify the Fugitive Slave Act and defy the Supreme Court. For a unanimous Court in *Ableman v. Booth* (1859) Taney wrote: "The sphere of action appropriate to the United States is as far beyond the reach of the judicial process issued by a State judge or a State court, as if the line of division was traced by landmarks and monuments visible to the eye."

A century later, Arkansas tried to nullify the Court's rulings in the School Segregation cases. In *Cooper v. Aaron* (1958) the justices responded by publishing an opinion signed by each member of the Court (usually one justice speaks for the Court or for the majority of the justices if they are not unanimous) saying that "the federal judiciary is supreme in the exposition of the law of the Constitution" and that no state official can disobey a federal constitutional ruling "without violating his undertaking to support" that Constitution.

RELATION OF FEDERAL AND STATE COURTS

In 1793 the Supreme Court accepted original jurisdiction of a suit, *Chisholm v. Georgia,* against the state of Georgia brought by two citizens of South Carolina trying to collect a debt. This action was based on Article III's authorization for federal courts to adjudicate controversies "between a State and citizens of another State." Congress reacted quickly by adopting the Eleventh Amendment guaranteeing state immunity to suit. Suits brought by other states or the United States are not prohibited, however, and states can consent to be sued. Moreover, the Supreme Court can review state court judgments in suits to which a state is a party, since supremacy of federal law requires review of federal questions presented by such judgments. Also, federal legislation can create rights enforceable against states or state officials in spite of the Eleventh Amendment.

The principles of federalism, says Laurence H. Tribe, require that federal courts further "the twin policies of preserving the integrity of state law and respecting the institutional autonomy of state judicial systems." Potential conflicts between federal and state courts are limited by the principle of comity, "the fundamental premise of judicial federalism which holds that, since both federal and state courts have a duty to enforce the Constitution, there is no constitutional basis, in the absence of some infirmity in the state judicial process itself, for preferring federal courts to state courts as adjudicators of federal constitutional claims."[12] Consequently, state courts are entitled to interpret their own statutes and constitutional provisions, and if their reasoning rests on "independent and adequate" state grounds, state court decisions are not subject to federal court review.[13]

One of the most significant manifestations of comity is the judge-made rule of abstention. In *Railroad Commission v. Pullman Co.* (1941) the Court, speaking through Justice Felix Frankfurter, held that when the constitutionality of a state law was challenged, a federal court might suspend action to allow state courts an opportunity to adopt a construction of the challenged law that would avoid or modify the constitutional problem. Abstention is not a consistent practice; it is an instrument of judicial diplomacy. The Warren Court was less likely to defer to state courts than the Burger Court.

INJUNCTIONS AGAINST STATE COURTS

A statute of 1793 (28 U.S.C. § 2283) forbade federal courts to grant injunctions staying proceedings in a state court "except as expressly authorized by Act of Congress, or where necessary in aid of its jurisdiction, or to protect or effectuate its judgments." The Supreme Court in *Osborn v. Bank of the United States* (1824) asserted power to restrain state officials from bringing criminal or civil proceedings in state courts to enforce an invalid state statute, but under that decision an injunction could issue only *after* a federal court had found the state statute unconstitutional. In 1908 *Ex parte Young* abandoned this requirement. There the Court held that a federal court could enjoin the attorney general of a state from enforcing a state statute in state courts *pending* a determination of its constitutionality.[14]

Because of exceptions in the anti-injunction act of 1793, federal courts have had considerable leeway in issuing injunctions against state courts, but in pursuance of the principle of comity have largely restrained exercise of their authority by the policy of "equitable ab-

[*Principle of Comity?*]

[12] *American Constitutional Law* (Mineola, N. Y.: Foundation Press, 1978), pp. 147–148.
[13] Nevertheless, the Burger Court in several rulings challenged state courts that had reversed criminal convictions on state grounds. Thus in *Michigan v. Long* (1983) the Court ruled that in a state court judgment where nonfederal grounds are interwoven with federal grounds, the Supreme Court would take jurisdiction.
[14] The principle of *Ex parte Young* has been applied in many subsequent cases, but it was substantially limited in *Pennhurst State School & Hospital v. Halderman* (1984), a class action brought by mentally retarded Pennsylvania citizens challenging the conditions of their confinement in a state institution. Although lower courts allowed claims for damages and injunctive relief, the Supreme Court reversed, holding that the violations complained of were of state law, not the federal Constitution, and consequently that the suit was against the state and barred by the Eleventh Amendment. The rhetoric of this five-to-four decision was unusually bitter, Justice Stevens for the minority charging that there was "absolutely no authority" for the Court's "voyage into the sea of undisciplined lawmaking." See David L. Shapiro, "Wrong Turns: The Eleventh Amendment and the *Pennhurst* Case," 98 *Harvard Law Review* 61 (1984).

stention." This practice is based on the contention that what Justice Hugo L. Black called "Our Federalism" forbids federal courts to interfere with a state's good-faith administration of its criminal laws. Issuance of an injunction by a federal court cuts short the normal adjudication of issues and constitutional defenses in state courts and under traditional equity rules can be justified only if the defendants are threatened with irreparable injury should the state prosecution be allowed to proceed. Consequently, a federal judge will seldom enjoin a state criminal prosecution.[15]

FEDERAL HABEAS CORPUS REVIEW OF STATE CRIMINAL CONVICTIONS

Although the existence of independent and adequate state grounds bars direct appellate Supreme Court review of federal questions otherwise presented in a state decision, it does not necessarily limit the collateral availability of federal writs of habeas corpus.

The historic purpose of habeas corpus was to challenge detention by executive authorities of a person imprisoned, and until 1867 the writ was not available against any sentence imposed by a court of competent jurisdiction. But in that year Congress, anticipating Southern resistance to new civil rights legislation and constitutional guaranties, conferred on federal courts broad authority to issue writs of habeas corpus for prisoners in custody "in violation of the Constitution or of any treaty or law of the United States." As Justice Brennan commented in *Fay v. Noia* (1963): "A remedy almost in the nature of removal from the state to the federal courts of state prisoners' constitutional contentions seems to have been envisaged."

The result was that defendants convicted in state criminal proceedings had two separate channels for seeking federal judicial redress. First, they could petition for direct review by the United States Supreme Court of an adverse decision by the highest state court. If this route failed, prisoners could attack their convictions collaterally by seeking habeas corpus from the federal court for the district in which they were held, with appeal to the court of appeals and finally to the Supreme Court once again. The major accommodation between the two systems required by the Supreme Court, as stated in *Fay v. Noia*, was that the defendants exhaust their state remedies before seeking habeas corpus in federal court.

Applications from convicted state prisoners for habeas corpus from federal courts increased rapidly as the Supreme Court became more sensitive to the rights of accused persons. In 1941 federal judges

---

[15] One of the exceptional cases was *Dombrowski v. Pfister* (1965), a ruling by the Warren Court that opened the way for greater federal protection of civil rights by allowing increased federal judicial intervention in state proceedings. But a few years later, in *Younger v. Harris* (1971) and in other cases decided the same day, the Court severely limited *Dombrowski* and adopted a stricter view of its comity obligations.

received 127 such petitions; in 1984 the number was 8,349, and the most common allegation was that evidence used to convict had been secured by unreasonable searches in violation of the Fourth and Fourteenth Amendments.

Justice Robert H. Jackson complained in *Brown v. Allen* (1953) about the multiplicity of petitions, "so frivolous, so meaningless, and often so unintelligible that this worthlessness of the class discredits each individual application." In *Schneckloth v. Bustamonte* (1973) Justice Lewis Powell, with the support of the other three justices chosen by Richard Nixon, attacked "the escalating use, over the past two decades, of federal habeas corpus to reopen and readjudicate state criminal judgment." He contended that the Court had extended habeas corpus "far beyond its historic bounds and in disregard of the writ's central purpose," resulting in unwise use of limited judicial resources, repetitive criminal litigation, and friction between federal and state systems of justice.

Powell was victorious in 1976. In *Stone v. Powell* the Court held by a vote of six to three that if a defendant had been given a "full and fair" opportunity to argue the constitutional issue in state court, collateral attacks on a state conviction through federal habeas corpus would no longer be permitted where the only challenge to the conviction was the contention that evidence had been secured in violation of the Fourth Amendment.[16] (Reading 3.9.)

In *Stone* Justice Powell reasoned that state judges could be relied on to protect constitutional rights as effectively as federal judges, but sponsors of civil liberties litigation generally preferred to bring their suits in federal courts. (Reading 3.10.) But experience with the Burger Court and lower federal judges chosen by Ronald Reagan has led many civil rights lawyers to avoid taking cases to federal courts, for fear that favorable rulings of the Warren Court would be reversed; and there has been new interest in and exploitation of civil rights protections available in state constitutions. (Reading 3.11.)

SELECTED REFERENCES

Ball, Howard. *Courts and Politics: The Federal Judicial System.* Englewood Cliffs, N.J.: Prentice-Hall, 1980.

Bator, Paul M., Paul J. Mishkin, David L. Shapiro, and Herbert Wechsler. *Hart and Wechsler's The Federal Courts and the Federal System.* Mineola, New York: Foundation Press, 1973.

Baum, Lawrence, Sheldon Goldman, and Austin Sarat. "Research Note: The Evolution of Litigation in Federal Courts of Appeals, 1895–1975," 16 *Law and Society Review* 291 (1981–1982).

[16] Availability of federal habeas corpus relief for state prisoners was further limited by 1982 rulings of the Supreme Court in *Engle v. Isaac* and *United States v. Frady,* which held that a state judge's instructions to a jury could not be attacked by habeas corpus if the defendant's lawyers had failed to object to the instructions at the trial.

Black, Charles L., Jr. "The National Court of Appeals: An Unwise Proposal," 83 *Yale Law Journal* 883 (1974).

Carp, Robert A., and C. K. Rowland. *Policymaking and Politics in the Federal District Courts.* Knoxville, Tenn.: University of Tennessee Press, 1983.

Casper, Gerhard, and Richard A. Posner. *The Workload of the Supreme Court.* Chicago: American Bar Foundation, 1976.

Clark, David S. "Adjudication to Administration: A Statistical Analysis of Federal District Courts in the Twentieth Century," 55 *Southern California Law Review* 65 (1981).

"Developments in the Law—Section 1983 and Federalism," 90 *Harvard Law Review* 1133 (1977).

Douglas, William O. "The Supreme Court and Its Caseload," 45 *Cornell Law Quarterly* 401 (1960).

———. *We the Judges.* New York: Doubleday, 1956. Ch. 3.

Dubois, Philip L. (ed.). *The Politics of Judicial Reform.* Lexington, Mass.: Lexington Books, 1982.

Fish, Peter G. *The Office of Chief Justice of the United States.* Charlottesville, Va.: Miller Center, University of Virginia, 1984.

———. *The Politics of Federal Judicial Administration.* Princeton, N.J.: Princeton University Press, 1973.

Frankfurter, Felix, and James M. Landis. *The Business of the Supreme Court.* New York: Macmillan, 1928.

Friendly, Henry J. *Federal Jurisdiction: A General View.* New York: Columbia University Press, 1973.

Goldberg, Arthur J. "Measuring the Supreme Court's Workload," 11 *Hastings Constitutional Law Quarterly* 353 (1984).

Griswold, Erwin N. "Helping the Supreme Court by Reducing the Flow of Cases Into the Courts of Appeals," 67 *Judicature* 58 (1983).

Hart, Henry M., Jr. "The Time Chart of the Justices," 73 *Harvard Law Review* 84 (1959).

Hellman, Arthur D. "Caseload, Conflicts, and Decisional Capacity," 67 *Judicature* 28 (1983).

Howard, J. Woodford, Jr. "Query: Are Heavy Caseloads Changing the Nature of Appellate Justice?" 66 *Judicature* 57 (1982).

Landever, Arthur R. "Chief Justice Burger and Extra-Case Activism," 20 *Journal of Public Law* 523 (1971).

"Masters and Magistrates in the Federal Courts," 88 *Harvard Law Review* 779 (1975).

Mayers, Lewis. *The American Legal System.* New York: Harper, 1956.

McGowan, Carl. *The Organization of Judicial Power in the United States.* Evanston, Illinois: Northwestern University Press, 1967.

Note. "Federal Question Abstention: Justice Frankfurter's Doctrine in an Activist Era," 80 *Harvard Law Review* 604 (1967).

Note. "Of High Designs: A Compendium of Proposals to Reduce the Workload of the Supreme Court," 97 *Harvard Law Review* 307 (1983).

Porter, Mary Cornelia, and G. Alan Tarr (eds.). *State Supreme Courts: State Supreme Courts and the Federal System.* Westport, Conn.: Greenwood Press, 1982.

Posner, Richard A. *The Federal Courts.* Cambridge, Mass.: Harvard University Press, 1985.

Rebell, Michael A., and Arthur R. Block. *Educational Policy-Making and the Courts.* Chicago: University of Chicago Press, 1982.

Report of the Study Group on the Caseload of the Supreme Court.
Washington, D.C.: Federal Judicial Center, 1972.
Rosenbloom, David H. *Public Administration and the Law: Bench v.
Bureau in the United States.* New York: Marcel Dekker, 1983.
Swindler, William F. "The Chief Justice and Law Reform, 1921–
1971," in Philip B. Kurland (ed.), *The Supreme Court Review,
1971.* Chicago: University of Chicago Press, 1971. Pp. 241–264.
Wheeler, Russell R., and Howard R. Whitcomb (eds.). *Judicial Ad-
ministration.* Englewood Cliffs, N.J.: Prentice-Hall, 1977.

3.1   *"The judiciary should be seen as a coordinate source of
government power . . . subject to the same forces that
have shaped the executive and legislative branches."*

THE BUREAUCRATIZATION OF THE JUDICIARY

Owen M. Fiss

The history of the twentieth century is largely the history of increasing bureaucratization. Almost every phase of American life has come
to be dominated by large-scale, complex organizations—the corporation, the labor union, the university, the public hospital, and even our
national political agencies. The national executive does not simply
consist of the President and a small group of trusted advisers, but is
instead composed of a vast, sprawling conglomerate of administrative agencies, which are staffed by more than three million (civilian)
employees. We have come to accept this and often refer to the
executive branch as "The Bureaucracy," but a similar development
has occurred within the legislature. In addition to some 500 senators
and representatives, Congress now consists of about 40,000 employees, more than 300 committees and subcommittees, and 8 internal agencies (like the General Accounting Office and the
Congressional Budget Office). Against this background, an account of
the judiciary, such as Cardozo's, that focuses exclusively on the agony
of a lonely, isolated judge seems somewhat dated. Today the judiciary must be seen as a large-scale, complex organization.

My claim is not that the bureaucratic character of the modern
judiciary is a legacy of the New Deal. . . . The interaction between
the judiciary and the distinctive forms of government power legitimated by the New Deal may have contributed to and indeed exacer-
bated the bureaucratization of the judiciary; but I do not believe that

92 *Yale Law Journal* 1442 (1983). Reprinted by permission of The Yale Law
Journal Company and Fred B. Rothman & Company from *The Yale Law Journal,* Vol.
92, p. 1442. Owen M. Fiss is Alexander M. Bickel Professor of Public Law, Yale Law
School.

this particular interaction is the basic cause of the phenomenon. I attribute it instead to the growing size and complexity of American society. The judiciary should be seen as a coordinate source of government power—an integral part of the state—subject to the same forces that have shaped the executive and legislative branches. The bureaucratization of the judiciary does not stem from the bureaucratization of the political agencies of the state, or from the interaction of the judiciary with them; it is instead a parallel development caused by the same forces—not the New Deal, not the advent of the administrative or activist state, but the very character of modern life itself.

From this perspective, this essay can be seen as a case study of the bureaucratization of governmental power. . . . It is, however, a case study with a special twist because in the context of the judiciary, bureaucratization poses a unique challenge to the legitimacy of governmental power. The legislative and executive branches derive their legitimacy from their responsiveness to popular will, and bureaucratization acts as a screen that impairs the responsiveness of officials within these branches. With the judiciary, however, the impact of bureaucratization is felt in another domain altogether: Bureaucratization tends to corrode the individualistic processes that are the source of judicial legitimacy.

The foundation of judicial power is process. Judges are entrusted with power because of their special competence to interpret public values embodied in authoritative texts, and this competence is derived from the process that has long characterized the judiciary and that limits the exercise of its power. One aspect of that process is independence. Judicial independence is not threatened by bureaucratization, and, indeed, today the independence of the judiciary from the political branches might depend on its capacity to develop the organizational resources usually associated with a bureaucracy. But a second aspect of the legitimating process of the judiciary is threatened. I am referring to the obligation of a judge to engage in a special dialogue—to listen to all grievances, hear from all the interests affected, and give reasons for his decisions. By signing his name to a judgment or opinion, the judge assures the parties that he has thoroughly participated in that process and assumes individual responsibility for the decision. We accept the judicial power on these terms, and yet bureaucratization raises the spectre that the judge's signature is but a sham and that the judge is exercising power without genuinely engaging in the dialogue from which his authority flows.

Not all organizational relationships are bureaucratic. The allocation of power to both state and federal courts creates a complex set of organizational relationships among the judges of the two political systems, but I regard these relationships more as coordinate than bureaucratic. Similarly, I do not regard as bureaucratic the organizational relationships that arise from the fact that appellate courts today generally act through groups of judges. Interactions among the members of each group may create relationships that threaten the integrity of the judicial process, when, for example, compromises must be made to secure a majority, but I regard these relationships as more collegial or committee-like than bureaucratic. For me, the feature that distinguishes bureaucracy from these other organizational relationships is hierarchy: The bureaucratic relationship is vertical rather than horizontal.

"Bureaucracy" is a term often used with pejorative connotations, because of the pathologies or dysfunctions connected with complex organizations, but I intend it more descriptively. I will use the term "bureaucracy" to refer to a complex organization with three features: (1) a multitude of actors; (2) a division of functions or responsibilities among them; and (3) a reliance upon a hierarchy as the central device to coordinate their activities. In stressing the hierarchical element, I do not mean to claim that hierarchy is the only coordinating device, for in bureaucracies of professionals, like the judiciary, hierarchy is often supplemented by a common culture— a set of shared norms and ideals. But this qualification does not destroy the central importance of hierarchy to the organization and the usefulness of the concept in analyzing a series of organizational relationships that characterize the modern judiciary.

I focus on the federal judiciary because it is often thought to be the fullest embodiment of the judicial ideal and also because it is considered the least bureaucratic of all our judicial systems. In this system, three hierarchical relationships can be identified: judge-judge, judge-staff, and what I shall call "judge-subjudge." Of all the hierarchical relationships, the first—the relationship between judges on different levels of the judicial system—is the weakest and, as is often true in bureaucratic organizations, those at the bottom of the hierarchy have considerably more power than the organizational chart indicates. There is a gap between formal power and real power. This gap stems in part from the fact that the Supreme Court lacks the time, resources, and information needed to supervise the lower courts effectively. The Supreme Court fully considers around 150 cases a year while the federal courts of appeals alone produce 10,000 judgments a year. Nor can the courts of appeals fill the supervisory void left by the Supreme Court. They are not organized to exercise managerial duties. Each court of appeals consists of a multitude of judges, who do not speak with one voice, and the control of each court is confined to a geographical region of the country and does not extend as broadly as federal law must—to the entire nation.

The hierarchy among judges is further weakened by the absence of any sanctioning system. Contrary to the practice in most bureaucracies, those higher up in the judicial hierarchy have no authority over the appointment, removal, promotion, or pay of those below. Sometimes the especially obedient are rewarded by compliments in appellate opinions; sometimes the especially recalcitrant are publicly reprimanded; and sometimes judges high in the hierarchy will be consulted when a judge below seeks to move up. For the most part, however, the hierarchical control over judges is exercised through review of the work product of those below. And although the conscientious do not take such review lightly, it must be seen as a rather weak and indirect instrument of control. In 1980, Congress gave the judicial councils of the circuits power to investigate complaints against lower judges, but the sanctions stop short of removal. The statute surrounds the judge accused of misbehavior with elaborate procedural protections, nearly equivalent to those available in a criminal prosecution, and specifically provides that a complaint may be dismissed if it relates to the merits of a decision. In many respects, the new legislation stands as a symbol of the weakness of the controls of one judge over another.

The second hierarchical relationship is that between a judge and his staff. Some of that staff—for example, the clerk of the court, the bailiff, and the judge's secretary—generally do not participate in the decisional process, and for the purposes of examining how bureaucratization affects the integrity of that process, they can be safely ignored. Law clerks, however, cannot be ignored. One must begin an analysis of their role by making a distinction between two types of law clerks: "elbow clerks," who are chosen by and work under the direct supervision of a particular judge, and "staff attorneys," who are not assigned to any particular judge but belong to what has become known as the "central legal staff." The staff attorneys seem to be confined to the courts of appeals.

The role of staff in the decisional process is not publicly or formally defined, and in any event, varies from judge to judge and from court to court. Elbow clerks may write memoranda recommending how cases should be decided (referred to as "bench memoranda"), discuss cases with the judge, research issues that are not fully briefed, and draft opinions. Staff attorneys might do the same, but their primary function is to screen cases for appellate courts. A staff attorney usually prepares a memorandum for a panel of judges recommending whether a case should be disposed of summarily through issuance of a judgment order, rather than being fully argued and decided with a full opinion.

The third hierarchical relationship in the federal system is that between judges and certain auxiliary personnel such as magistrates, bankruptcy judges, and special masters, all of whom I call . . . "subjudges." Subjudges participate in the decisional process, but fall somewhere between law clerks and judges in terms of their power. In contrast to law clerks, subjudges are formally and publicly entrusted with some measure of decisional power, and yet are distinguished from judges because of special restrictions on their power. The scope of their jurisdiction is especially limited (e.g., bankruptcy, pretrial discovery, habeas corpus petitions, or the trial of petty crimes). Their decisions are subject to review by a judge under more stringent standards than when one judge is reviewing the work of another judge. Subjudges serve for limited terms and are subject to the hierarchical controls—appointment and dismissal—that are not exercised by one judge over another. As a consequence, the hierarchy between judges and subjudges, like that between judge and staff, is stronger than the hierarchy among judges.

Putting together these three hierarchical relationships—judge-judge, judge-staff, and judge-subjudge—one can discern the familiar bureaucratic structure: a pyramid. The federal judicial system consists of three tiers of courts—the Supreme Court, the courts of appeals, and the district courts. Within each of these tiers is a shadow consisting of the law clerks or staff. The bottom tier has a second shadow, consisting of the subjudges, who are primarily used and supervised by the district judges. As a purely formal matter, this bureaucratic structure is not new. Almost every element of it can be traced back to the turn of the century, when Congress created the circuit courts of appeals and transformed the federal judicial system from a two-tiered to a three-tiered system. What is new, and what has provoked the bureaucratization debate of recent years, is not the formal structure itself, but rather its internal density—the proliferation of participants within the structure.

In 1900, there were just over 100 federal judges—9 at the Supreme Court, 24 circuit judges, and 77 district judges. Today there are more than 850. In 1900, there were only 9 "stenographic clerks" —one for each justice. The modern law clerk can be seen to have evolved from that position, but today the role of the clerk has become more important in the decisional process and the number of law clerks has greatly increased. There are approximately 1,600 elbow clerks; some judges have two, others three, and some four. The Chief Justice has five. The staff attorney is also new. Today there are 112 such clerks, and it seems likely that their number will grow now that the position has been institutionalized and the need for screening cases has become more important.

Within recent years, a great deal of attention has focused on special masters. This is probably due to the hotly contested and protracted nature of the cases in which they are involved (e.g., school desegregation) rather than their number; in fact, their closest historical counterparts—the receivers of the railroad reorganizations at the turn of the century—were fairly numerous. Attention has also focused on the subjudges used in the bankruptcy system, who for most of the twentieth century have been known as referees but are today called judges, even though they do not enjoy the full protection of Article III. In 1982, the Supreme Court declared unconstitutional the 1978 statute that effectuated this change of title and that also entrusted these officials with what the Court considered Article III duties. Congress now has the choice, over which it has been especially divided, of elevating the bankruptcy judges to full judicial status, with life tenure and protection against pay reduction, or limiting their powers and duties.

It seems to me, however, that the most significant federal subjudges are neither the special masters nor the bankruptcy judges, but the magistrates. They are not specialists but, in background and work, generalists much like the federal district judges. Magistrates handle matters as varied as habeas petitions and social security claims; they manage pretrial discovery, adjudicate petty crimes and, with the consent of the parties, can try all matter of civil cases. The present scheme contemplates close to 500 magistrates, which makes them almost as numerous as district judges (though almost half now serve on a part-time basis). The commissioners, whom the magistrates succeeded, were also quite numerous (in 1900 they numbered over 1,100), but this statistic obscures important distinctions. The contemporary magistrate is a lawyer and charged with more significant decisional responsibility than were the commissioners; and the magistrates' role will probably increase as Congress entrusts them with more responsibility and as the Supreme Court continues to remove the constitutional objections to this legislative program. It is likely that, in time, the elaboration of the magistrate system will create a permanent corps of subjudges and that the second shadow on the bottom level of the pyramid will become a fourth, but somewhat irregular, tier of the federal system.

3.2   "Federal judges are both masters . . . and servants. . . ."

FEDERAL DISTRICT COURTS IN THE TWENTIETH CENTURY

David S. Clark

In 1900, 102 federal trial judges terminated 29,094 civil and criminal cases. Most judges presided over their own district courts like lords over their fiefs. The criminal docket was substantially more impor-

"Adjudication to Administration: A Statistical Analysis of Federal District Courts in the Twentieth Century," 55 *Southern California Law Review* 65 (1981). Reprinted with the permission of the *Southern California Law Review*. David S. Clark is Professor of Law, The University of Tulsa College of Law.

tant than the civil, which suffered from notorious delay. The United States Government, as chief litigant, concerned itself largely with internal revenue, post office, and customs matters. Many of these were probably routine, and the average annual workload of 285 cases per judge provided sufficient time for more difficult litigation. Private civil suits constituted about one-third of the caseload, and 54% of these cases were either dismissed or discontinued. By comparison, 31% of the government civil cases and 28% of the criminal suits were dismissed. The federal judiciary at the turn of the century was a specialized court system primarily servicing the United States Government in areas of traditional federal concern.

During the twentieth century, three forces transformed federal judges from adjudicators to administrators. The first factor contributing to bureaucratization of the federal judiciary was the political movement for judicial reform and its emphasis on efficient caseload management. This trend was apparent from the beginning of the twentieth century. Roscoe Pound's speech in 1906 on popular dissatisfaction with the administration of justice set the tone for the Progressive Era's structural and administrative reform of the federal courts. William Taft continued the reformist pressure for centralized control, which by 1922 resulted in an annual conference of senior circuit judges under the direction of the Chief Justice. This evolved in the late 1930's into the Judicial Conference of the United States and the Administrative Office of the United States Courts. Along with the Federal Judicial Center, added in 1967, these organizations have developed policies that have gradually been implemented by standardized rules limiting the autonomy of each judge. Bureaucratic coordination has occurred as advisory committees have made procedural rules and managerial guidelines to control judicial behavior. Moreover, the role of the chief judge in each district has become more administrative as the number of trial judges in each district has increased.

In addition to this centralized guidance, federal courts in the 1970's have obtained the staffing necessary for bureaucratic institutions. From 1970 to 1980, personnel in the federal judiciary increased by 111%, from 6,887 to 14,451. Federal judges are both masters of and servants to this growing number of employees.

Second, the federal judiciary has become more bureaucratic by increasing the use of routinized administrative techniques in dealing with its caseload. Certain types of cases that lend themselves to routine treatment have been given a high priority by Congress, the Supreme Court, or the Department of Justice: liquor prohibition cases during the 1920's are the classic example. Thus, federal court workloads grew 279% from 1917 to 1932, reaching a total of 152,585 cases, or 948 per judge. Prisoner petitions in the 1960's are another illustration: 93% of these cases were terminated before trial in 1967.

By the late 1970's, moreover, most prisoner matters were handled by the federal magistrate corps, a system of full-time judicial officers. Today the United States Government is using the federal courts to collect defaulted student loans and overpaid veteran benefits, with approximately 20,000 of these cases in 1980. These student and veteran contract suits were settled without court action in 79% of the cases.

Finally, the rise of public law litigation in the 1960's has moved the trial judge into an active posture in managing class action or other complex lawsuits involving group interests. In 1980, for example, 1,568 class action suits were filed in federal courts and 2,480 were terminated. Although each judge terminated only about five of these cases on the average, the cases may be extremely time consuming and disproportionately important in their impact on the community. More than any other type of case, class action suits have shaped the current image of the federal judge as an administrator who may run a prison or manage a school desegregation plan.

Bureaucratization presents a special issue for federal courts, since their proper functioning within our constitutional allocation of powers depends to some degree on their independence and prestige, which in turn depend on the citizenry's faith that federal judges are making judicial and not political decisions. To the extent that the trend toward administration alters the traditional mode of adjudication, it may threaten the effectiveness of the courts.

Henry Jacoby has written:

> The concept of bureaucracy and all that it entails has emerged as a central social issue in the mid-twentieth century. Complaint about its growing influence in the world arises from man's feeling that he no longer controls his own destiny. Each member of contemporary society is part of a large conglomerate whose self-expression and sense of existence depends on the operation of complicated governmental machinery.

Federal trial courts have become part of this complicated government machinery. At the same time, federal judges provide vital protection for the individual and for disadvantaged groups in society. They are, therefore, part of the problem of general bureaucratization as well as part of the solution against powerlessness. Abram Chayes has stated that "judicial action only achieves . . . legitimacy by responding to, indeed by stirring, the deep and durable demand for justice in our society." This is the meaning behind the principle in Magna Carta that "to none will we deny, or delay, right or justice." Nevertheless, federal judges are still fallible human beings. Skepticism is appropriate, but realism demands that we consider the alternatives. Owen Fiss persuasively argues:

The legislative and executive branches of government, as well as private institutions, have a voice; so should the courts. Judges have no monopoly on the task of giving meaning to the public values of the Constitution, but neither is there reason for them to be silent. They too can make a contribution to the public debate and inquiry.

Of the three major forces altering the federal judiciary in the twentieth century, the judicial efficiency movement, particularly its call for more judges and staff, may be the most threatening to the prestige and legitimacy of the judiciary. The federal trial judiciary has traditionally been a small group of elite jurists with sufficient independence for principled decisionmaking. The ability of federal judges to communicate adequately with their colleagues lessens as the number of judges grows. Large staffs further increase the distance between a judge and his caseload. Parajudges and law clerks are assigned judicial tasks, and the judge himself may become the courthouse satrap.

If the size of the federal judiciary should be small to counteract the organizational dynamics of larger institutions and to guarantee what remains of its adjudicatory function, then a solution must be found for the problem of growing caseloads. Strong arguments can be made that federal courts should retain their purview over public law disputes. The victims of majoritarian decisions—e.g., ethnic minorities, prisoners, and the infirm or retarded inmates of institutions—have nowhere else to turn for redress of their constitutional rights. Society today is dominated by large scale organizations; federal courts provide the countervailing power. Public law suits, however, are fairly small in number. The remaining district court docket is subject to unpredictable fluctuations that depend largely upon decisions made by Congress, the Justice Department, and the Supreme Court. For example, the question of whether the 20,000 student and veteran contract collection suits brought by the United States Government, the 17,000 state prisoner petitions, or the 17,000 diversity jurisdiction contract cases terminated in 1980 are suitable for federal court resolution involves a complicated dialogue among the three branches of government. Many of the cases terminated in 1980 could easily have been diverted to state courts or local decision-making institutions without sacrificing federalism or other constitutional principles.

The federal district courts in the twentieth century have exhibited tremendous resilience in coping with widely varying workloads. Success in this endeavor, especially in reducing delay in processing cases after the mid-1920's, has been achieved partly by the courts' bureaucratization. Bureaucracy, however, brings its own dangers: Max Weber's image of mankind imprisoning itself in an iron cage of its own making illustrates this danger. In the future, the federal judiciary must face the delicate task of retaining the benefits of administrative efficiency without becoming itself another insensitive bureau.

3.3 *"The District Court gives more scope to a judge's initiative and discretion."*

THE IMPORTANCE OF THE TRIAL JUDGE

Charles E. Wyzanski, Jr.   *The district courts are the trial courts of the federal system*   January 12, 1959

Dear Lev:

I am deeply appreciative of your suggestion that my name be presented to the President and the Attorney General for their consideration whether to nominate me as a judge of the United States Court of Appeals for the First Circuit. . . . That you regard me as worthy of that high office is a great compliment. And were I to be appointed to a judgeship in that Court, I should regard it as both an honor and an opportunity for public service.

Yet I am persuaded that it is in both the public interest and my interest for me to decline to allow my name to be considered for the United States Court of Appeals. . . .

The District Court for the District of Massachusetts seems to me to offer at least as wide a field for judicial service as the Court of Appeals for the First Circuit. The District Court gives more scope to a judge's initiative and discretion. His width of choice in sentencing defendants is the classic example. But there are many other instances. In civil litigation a District Judge has a chance to help the lawyers frame the issues and develop the facts so that there may be a meaningful and complete record. He may innovate procedures promoting fairness, simplification, economy, and expedition. By instructions to juries and, in appropriate cases, by comments on the evidence he may help the jurors better to understand their high civic function. He is a teacher of parties, witnesses, petitioners for naturalization, and even casual visitors to his court. His conduct of a trial may fashion and sustain the moral principles of the community. More even than the rules of constitutional, statutory, and common law he applies, his character and personal distinction, open to daily inspection in his courtroom, constitute the guarantees of due process.

Letter to Senator Leverett Saltonstall, January 12, 1959. Charles E. Wyzanski, Jr., is United States District Judge (senior status) for the District of Massachusetts.

Admittedly, the Court of Appeals stands higher than the District Courts in the judicial hierarchy, and Congress by attaching a larger compensation to the office of Circuit Judge has expressed its view of the relative importance of the two courts. Yet not all informed persons would concur in that evaluation. My revered former chief, Judge Augustus N. Hand, always spoke of his service in the District Court as being more interesting as well as more revealing of his qualities, and more enjoyable, than his service in the Court of Appeals. . . .

Although less spectacular litigation may ordinarily be carried from the District Court to the Court of Appeals, statistics will show how small a percentage of a reasonably good trial judge's decrees are in fact appealed. The District Judge so often has the last word. Even where he does not, heed is given to his estimates of credibility, his determination of the facts, his discretion in framing or denying relief upon the facts he found. . . .

The District Judge is in more direct relation than is the judge of the Court of Appeals to the bar and its problems. It is within the proper function of a District Court not merely by rules and decisions, but by an informed, intelligent, and energetic handling of his calendar to effectuate prompt as well as unbiased justice. It is the vigor of the District Court more than the action of the Court of Appeals which governs the number of cases which are ripe for appeal, and the time between the beginning of an action and a final judgment in an appellate court. And, paradoxically, it is not infrequently the alertness of the District Judge and his willingness to help counsel develop uncertain points of law (even though the development of such points inevitably increases the risks of error by the trial judge and of reversal by the appellate court) which makes a case significant in the progress of the law when it reaches a court of last resort.

While it may well be true that the highest *office* for a judge is to sit in judgment on other judges' errors, it is perhaps a more challenging *task* to seek, from minute to minute, to avoid one's own errors. And the zest of that task is enhanced by the necessity of reacting orally, instead of after the reflection permitted under the appellate judge's uninterrupted schedule of reading and writing.

I realize that the trial judge lacks the opportunity to benefit from the collegiate discussion open to an appellate judge. His ties with his brethren are less intimate. Consequently, he runs the perils of excessive individualism. Few there are who can gently chide him on his foibles, remind him of the grace of manners, or warn against the nigh universal sin of pride.

Yet perhaps the trial judge's relative loneliness brings him closer to the tragic plight of man. Was not Wallace Stevens speaking for the trial judge when he wrote

"Life consists
Of propositions about life. The human
Reverie is a solitude in which
We compose these propositions, torn by dreams"? . . .
                              Sincerely,
                              Charles E. Wyzanski, Jr.

3.4   *"[The] federal judicial system . . . is more heterogeneous than hierarchical in practice. . . ."*

LITIGATION FLOW IN THREE UNITED STATES COURTS OF APPEALS

J. Woodford Howard, Jr.

[handwritten: Decisions of the court of appeals make national law in the great majority of cases]

This article reports some findings from an intensive quantitative study of the flow of litigation from federal district courts to three federal courts of appeals (District of Columbia, Second, and Fifth Circuits), and from the three appeals courts to the Supreme Court. The study covered all reported cases decided by the three appeals courts during fiscal years 1965, 1966, and 1967—a total of 4,945. The excerpt reprinted here deals only with the relation of the courts of appeals to the Supreme Court.

The most striking pattern is how little direct supervision the [Supreme Court] Justices exercised over the three courts of appeals. Litigants appealed 1,004 or 1-in-5 of these circuit decisions [4,945] to the Supreme Court, which granted certiorari in 9.2% of those appealed. Discounting 11 dismissals, the Court intervened in 92 cases or 1.9% of the entire sample* . . . affirming 0.5% and disturbing 1.4%. In effect, the three tribunals became courts of last resort in 98.1% of the cases and made decisions that formally prevailed in 98.6%. . . .

The upshot is uneven supervision of circuit courts by the Justices. . . . For three years, these courts of appeals were left to their own devices in broad ranges of litigation. The Justices exercised no review at all over their treatment of insurance and marine contracts, workmen's compensation, fair labor standards, parole, social security, suffrage, and school desegregation. . . . Notwithstanding the high court's propensity to reverse [circuit court decisions], the Justices intervened so rarely and selectively in these federal appeals that controls on the discretion of circuit judges would appear to depend less on fear of formal reversal than on the informal constraints em-

8 *Law and Society Review* 33 (1973). Reprinted with permission. J. Woodford Howard, Jr., is Thomas P. Stran Professor of Political Science, Johns Hopkins University.

*In 1984 the figure was less than 1 percent.—Eds.

bodied in the notion of "judicial role." . . . Supreme Court review looms as too irregular for rotating circuit judges to worry greatly about reversal or second-guessing Justices. . . .

These frequencies, of course, do not mean that circuit judges were 49 times more influential over federal appeals than the Supreme Court. Just as intermediate appellate courts are highly dependent on litigants and tribunals below, so are they theoretically bound by other Supreme Court decisions in like circumstances and influenced by the decisions of other circuits, too. One Supreme Court decision may control dozens of similar circuit cases, and in a case-law system we cannot assume that a lower court must be reversed in order to follow a higher one. Nor is each appeal in the circuit component of equal significance. . . . Yet these frequencies do help to establish the opportunities of circuit courts to affect national law and further understanding of their appellate roles. . . . The Justices exert direct control over so little federal litigation that those concerned with the distribution of individual justice or the administration of national policy through law should look not only up but down and around. . . .

Circuit judges filter issues on their way to the Supreme Court; they have substantial opportunity to create and to resist judicial policy when the Justices cannot or will not intervene, which is nearly all the time. . . . As courts of last resort in the overwhelming majority of cases, they *make* national law residually and regionally. Whether courts of appeals are conceived of as political actors with distinct constituencies or as functionaries in a legal bureaucracy, the magnitude of their finality in contexts of regional recruitment and organization produces a federal judicial system that is more heterogeneous than hierarchical in practice. . . .

3.5   *"A review on writ of certiorari is not a matter of right. . . ."*

U.S. SUPREME COURT RULE 17: CONSIDERATIONS GOVERNING REVIEW ON CERTIORARI

Supreme court accepts only cases that present substantial issues of law or policy

RULE 17. CONSIDERATIONS GOVERNING REVIEW ON CERTIORARI

.1. A review on writ of certiorari is not a matter of right, but of judicial discretion, and will be granted only when there are special and important reasons therefor. The following, while neither controlling nor fully measuring the Court's discretion, indicate the character of reasons that will be considered.

(a) When a federal court of appeals has rendered a decision in conflict with the decision of another federal court of appeals on the same matter; or has decided a federal question in a way in conflict with a state court of last resort; or has so far departed from the accepted and usual course of judicial proceedings, or so far sanctioned such a departure by a lower court, as to call for an exercise of this Court's power of supervision.

(b) When a state court of last resort has decided a federal question in a way in conflict with the decision of another state court of last resort or of a federal court of appeals.

(c) When a state court or a federal court of appeals has decided an important question of federal law which has not been, but should be, settled by this Court, or has decided a federal question in a way in conflict with applicable decisions of this Court.

.2. The same general considerations outlined above will control in respect of petitions for writs of certiorari to review judgments of the United States Court of Appeals for the Federal Circuit, the United States Court of Military Appeals, and of any other court whose judgments are reviewable by law on writ of certiorari. (Amended August 1, 1984.)

3.6   *"The Court's calendar mirrors the ever-changing concerns of this society. . . ."*

SOME THOUGHTS ON THE SUPREME COURT'S WORKLOAD

William J. Brennan, Jr.

In 1972 the Freund Committee (see p. 89) proposed to relieve the Supreme Court of its burden of reviewing over 4,000 petitions annually by creating a new National Court of Appeals which would select perhaps 400 of the most important cases to pass on to the Supreme Court for decision. There was little support for this proposal, but in 1982 Justice John Paul Stevens revived the idea, saying:[1]

> I favor the creation of a new court to which the Supreme Court would surrender . . . the power to decide what cases the Supreme Court should decide on the merits. . . . I believe an independent tribunal that did not have responsi-

66 *Judicature* 230 (1983). Reprinted from *Judicature*, the journal of the American Judicature Society. William J. Brennan, Jr., is an Associate Justice of the Supreme Court of the United States.
[1]"Some Thoughts on Judicial Restraint," 66 *Judicature* 177 (1982).

bility for deciding the merits of any case would do a far better job of selecting those relatively few cases that should be decided by the Supreme Court of the United States. . . .

Justice Brennan responded in an address before the Third Circuit Judicial Conference on September 9, 1982:

I completely disagree with my respected and distinguished colleague. I dissented from the form in which the Freund Committee made the proposal and feel even more strongly that adoption of Justice Stevens' proposal would destroy the role of the Supreme Court as the framers envisaged it.

Justice Stevens believes that the screening function "is less important work than studying and actually deciding the merits of cases that have already been accepted for review and writing opinions explaining those decisions." Apart from the fact that the plan would clearly violate the constitutional provision establishing "one Supreme Court," and therefore require a constitutional amendment, I reject Justice Stevens' fundamental premise that consideration given to the cases actually decided on the merits is compromised by the pressures of processing the inflated docket of petitions and appeals. . . .

If the screening function were to be farmed out to another court, some enormous values of the Supreme Court decisional process would be lost. Under the present system, a single justice may set a case for discussion at conference, and, in many instances that justice succeeds in persuading three or more of his colleagues that the case is worthy of plenary review. Thus the existing procedure provides a forum in which the particular interests or sensitivities of individual justices may be expressed, and therefore has a flexibility that is essential to the effective functioning not only of the screening process but also of the decisional process which is an inseparable part.

Similarly, the artificial construction of the Supreme Court's docket by others than the members of the Court would seriously undermine the important impact dissents from denials of review frequently have had upon the development of the law. Such dissents often herald the appearance on the horizon of possible re-examination of what may seem to the judges of another court doing the screening work to be an established and unimpeachable principle. Indeed, a series of dissents from denials of review played a crucial role in the Court's reevaluation of the reapportionment question, and the question of the applicability of the Fourth Amendment to electronic searches. The history of the role of such dissents on the right to counsel in criminal cases and the application of the Bill of Rights to the states surely is too fresh in mind to ignore.

Moreover, the assumption that the judges of a national court of appeals could accurately select the "most review-worthy" cases wholly ignores the inherently subjective nature of the screening process. The thousands upon thousands of cases docketed each term simply cannot be placed in a computer that will instantaneously identify those that I or any one of my colleagues would agree are "most review-worthy." A question that is "substantial" for me may be wholly insubstantial to some, perhaps all, of my colleagues. As Chief Justice Warren said:

> The delegation of the screening process to the National Court of Appeals would mean that the certiorari "feel" of the rotating panels of that Court would begin to play a vital role in the ordering of our legal priorities and control of the Supreme Court docket. More than that, this lower court "feel" would be divorced from any intimate understanding of the concerns and interests and philosophies of the Supreme Court Justices; and that "feel" could reflect none of the other intangible factors and trends within the Supreme Court that often play a role in the certiorari process.

I repeat that a fundamental premise of Justice Stevens' proposal is that the screening function plays only a minor and separable part in the exercise of the Court's fundamental responsibilities. I think that premise is clearly, indeed dangerously, wrong. In my experience over more than a quarter century, the screening process has been, and is today, inextricably linked to the fulfillment of the Court's essential duties and is vital to the effective performance of the Court's unique mission "to define the rights guaranteed by the Constitution, to assure the uniformity of federal law, and to maintain the constitutional distribution of powers in our federal union."

The choice of issues for decision largely determines the image that the American people have of their Supreme Court. The Court's calendar mirrors the ever-changing concerns of this society with ever more powerful and smothering government. The calendar is therefore the indispensable source for keeping the Court abreast of these concerns. Our Constitution is a living document and the Court often becomes aware of the necessity for reconsideration of its interpretation only because filed cases reveal the need for new and previously unanticipated applications of constitutional principles. To adopt Justice Stevens' proposal to limit the Court's consideration to a mere handful of the cases selected by others would obviously result in isolating the Court from many nuances and trends of legal change throughout the land.

The point is that the evolution of constitutional doctrine is not merely a matter of hearing arguments and writing opinions in cases granted review. The screening function is an inseparable part of the whole responsibility; to turn over that task to a national court of appeals is to rend a seamless web. And how traumatic and difficult must be the screening task of the judges of a court of appeals required to do major Supreme Court work without being afforded even the slightest glimpse of the whole picture of a justice's function.

It is not only that constitutional principles evolve over long periods and that one must know the history of each before he feels competent to grapple with their application in new contexts never envisioned by the framers. It is also that he must acquire an understanding of the extraordinarily complex factors that enter into the distribution of judicial power between state and federal courts and other problems of "Our Federalism." The screening function is an indispensable and inseparable part of the entire process and it cannot be withdrawn from the Court without grave risk of impairing the very core of the Court's unique and extraordinary functions.

3.7

". . . federal courts must be constantly mindful of the special delicacy of the adjustment to be preserved between federal equitable power and State administration of its own law.'"

RIZZO V. GOODE

423 U.S. 362, 96 S. Ct. 598, 46 L. Ed. 2d 561 (1976)

Plaintiffs representing residents of Philadelphia brought two class action suits under 42 U.S.C. § 1983 against the mayor and police of the city alleging that the defendants had approved or condoned systematic violation of the constitutional rights of minorities and the poor by the police. The district court made extensive findings of fact relating to some forty incidents of police misconduct over a one-year period. The court found a "pattern of frequent police violations" of constitutional rights, particularly against poor blacks and persons protesting police actions. Holding existing grievance and discipline procedures inadequate, the court ordered defendants to draw up a detailed plan to improve them. The Court of Appeals for the Third Circuit affirmed.

MR. JUSTICE REHNQUIST delivered the opinion of the Court. . . .

The central thrust of respondents' efforts in the two trials was to lay a foundation for equitable intervention, in one degree or another, because of an assertedly pervasive pattern of illegal and unconstitutional mistreatment by police officers. This mistreatment was said to have been directed against minority citizens in particular and against all Philadelphia residents in general. The named individual and group respondents (hereafter individual respondents) were certified to represent these two classes. The principal petitioners here—the Mayor, the City Managing Director, and the Police Commissioner—were charged with conduct ranging from express authorization or encouragement of this mistreatment to failure to act in a manner so as to assure that it would not recur in the future. . . .

These actions were brought, and the affirmative equitable relief fashioned, under the Civil Rights Act of 1871, 42 U.S.C. § 1983. It provides that "[e]very person who, under color of [law] subjects, or causes to be subjected, any . . . person [within the jurisdiction of the United States] to the deprivation of any rights . . . secured by the Constitution and laws, shall be liable to the party injured in an action at law [or] suit in equity. . . ." The plain words of the statute impose liability—whether in the form of payment of redressive damages or being placed under an injunction—only for conduct which "subjects or causes to be subjected" the complainant to a deprivation of a right secured by the Constitution.

The findings of fact made by the District Court at the conclusion of these two parallel trials—in sharp contrast to that which respondents sought to prove with respect to petitioners—disclose a central paradox which permeates that Court's legal conclusions. Individual police officers *not named as parties* to the action were found to have violated the constitutional rights of particular individuals, only a few of whom were parties plaintiff. As the facts developed, there was no affirmative link between the occurrence of the various incidents of police misconduct and the adoption of any plan or policy by petitioners—express or otherwise—showing their authorization or approval of such misconduct. Instead, the *sole* causal connection found by the District Court between petitioners and the individual respondents was that in the absence of a change in police disciplinary procedures, the incidents were likely to continue to occur, *not* with respect to them but as to the members of the classes they represented. In sum, the genesis of this lawsuit—a heated dispute between individual citizens and certain policemen—has evolved into an attempt by the federal judiciary to resolve a "controversy" between the entire citizenry of Philadelphia and the petitioning elected and appointed officials over what steps might, in the Court of Appeals' words, "appeared to have the potential for prevention of future police misconduct." . . . The lower courts have, we think, overlooked several significant decisions of this Court in validating this type of litigation and the relief ultimately granted.

We first of all entertain serious doubts whether on the facts as found there was made out the requisite Art. III case or controversy between the individually named respondents and petitioners. . . . [F]or the individual respondents' claim to "real and immediate" injury rests not upon what the named petitioners might do to them in the future—such as set a bond on the basis of race—but upon what one of a small, unnamed minority of policemen might do to them in the future because of that unknown policeman's perception of departmental disciplinary procedures. . . .

Going beyond considerations concerning the existence of a live controversy and threshold statutory liability, we must address an additional and novel claim advanced by respondent classes. They

assert that given the citizenry's "right" to be protected from unconstitutional exercises of police power, and the "need for protection
from such abuses," respondents have a right to mandatory equitable
relief in some form when those in supervisory positions do not institute steps to reduce the incidence of unconstitutional police misconduct. The scope of federal equity power, it is proposed, should be
extended to the fashioning of prophylactic procedures for a state
agency designed to minimize this kind of misconduct on the part of
a handful of its employees. But on the facts of this case, not only is
this novel claim quite at odds with the settled rule that in federal
equity cases "the nature of the violation determines the scope of the
remedy," . . . important considerations of federalism are additional
factors weighing against it. Where, as here, the exercise of authority
by state officials is attacked, federal courts must be constantly mindful of the "special delicacy of the adjustment to be preserved between federal equitable power and State administration of its own
law." . . . When a plaintiff seeks to enjoin the activity of a government
agency, even within a unitary court system, his case must contend
with "the well-established rule that the Government has traditionally been granted the widest latitude in the 'dispatch of its own
internal affairs,' *Cafeteria and Restaurant Workers Union Local 473
A.F.L.–C.I.O. v. McElroy.* . . . The District Court's injunctive order
here, significantly revising the internal procedures of the Philadelphia police department, was indisputably a sharp limitation on the
department's "latitude in the 'dispatch of its own internal affairs.' "
    When the frame of reference moves from a unitary court system,
governed by the principles just stated, to a system of federal courts
representing the Nation, subsisting side by side with 50 state judicial,
legislative, and executive branches, appropriate consideration must
be given to principles of federalism in determining the availability
and scope of equitable relief. . . .
    Thus the principles of federalism which play such an important
part in governing the relationship between federal courts and state
governments, though initially expounded and perhaps entitled to
their greatest weight in cases where it was sought to enjoin a criminal
prosecution in progress, have not been limited either to that situation
or indeed to a criminal proceeding itself. We think these principles
likewise have applicability where injunctive relief is sought not
against the judicial branch of the state government, but against those
in charge of an executive branch of an agency of state or local governments such as respondents here. . . .
    Contrary to the District Court's flat pronouncement that a federal
court's legal power to "supervise the functioning of the police department . . . is firmly established," it is the foregoing cases and
principles that must govern consideration of the type of injunctive
relief granted here. When it injected itself by injunctive decree into

the internal disciplinary affairs of this state agency, the District Court departed from these precepts.

For the foregoing reasons the judgment of the Court of Appeals which affirmed the decree of the District Court is

Reversed.

MR. JUSTICE STEVENS took no part in the consideration or decision of this case.

MR. JUSTICE BLACKMUN, with whom MR. JUSTICE BRENNAN and MR. JUSTICE MARSHALL join, dissenting.

To be sure, federal court intervention in the daily operation of a large city's police department, as the Court intimates, is undesirable and to be avoided if at all possible. The Court appropriately observes, however . . . that what the Federal District Court did here was to engage in a careful and conscientious resolution of often sharply conflicting testimony and to make detailed findings of fact, now accepted by both sides, that attack the problem that is the subject of the respondents' complaint. The remedy was one evolved with the defendant officials' assent, reluctant though that assent may have been, and it was one that the Police Department concededly could live with. Indeed, the District Court, in its memorandum of October 5, 1973, stated that "the resolution of all the disputed items was more nearly in accord with the defendants' position than with the plaintiffs' position," and that the relief contemplated by the earlier order of March 14, 1973, see 357 F.Supp. 1289 (E.D. Pa.), "did not go beyond what the defendants had always been willing to accept." App. 190a. No one, not even this Court's majority, disputes the apparent efficacy of the relief or the fact that it effectuated a betterment in the system and should serve to lessen the number of instances of deprival of constitutional rights of members of the respondent classes. What is worrisome to the Court is abstract principle, and, of course, the Court has a right to be concerned with abstract principle that, when extended to the limits of logic, may produce untoward results in other circumstances on a future day. . . .

But the District Court here, with detailed, careful and sympathetic findings, ascertained the existence of violations of citizens' *constitutional* rights, of a *pattern* of that type of activity, of its likely continuance and recurrence, and of an official indifference as to doing anything about it. . . .

I would regard what was accomplished in this case as one of those rightly rare but nevertheless justified instances . . . of federal court "intervention" in a state or municipal executive area. The facts, the deprival of constitutional rights, and the pattern are all proved in sufficient degree. And the remedy is carefully delineated, worked out within the administrative structure rather than superimposed by edict upon it, and essentially, and concededly, "livable." In the City of Brotherly Love—or in any other American city—no less should be expected. It is a matter of regret that the Court sees fit to nullify what so meticulously and thoughtfully has been evolved to satisfy an existing need relating to constitutional rights that we cherish and hold dear.

3.8   *"[A state decision] may be re-examined and reversed or affirmed in the Supreme Court of the United States."*

JUDICIARY ACT OF 1789, SECTION 25

1 U.S. Statutes at Large 85–86   *[handwritten: Supreme Court has the power to review state court decisions]*

That a final judgment or decree in any suit, in the highest court of law or equity of a State in which a decision in the suit could be had, where is drawn in question the validity of a treaty or statute of or an authority exercised under the United States, and the decision is against their validity; or where is drawn in question the validity of a statute of, or an authority exercised under any State, on the ground of their being repugnant to the constitution, treaties or laws of the United States, and the decision is in favor of their validity, or where is drawn in question the construction of any clause of the constitution, or of a treaty, or statute of, or commission held under the United States, and the decision is against the title, right, privilege or exemption specifically set up or claimed by either party, under such clause of the said constitution, treaty, statute or commission, may be re-examined and reversed or affirmed in the Supreme Court of the United States. . . .* *[handwritten: If a court has the right to review it, then doesn't a citizen have the right to appeal it]*

[handwritten margin note: 3 categories of decisions of which a court may review]

[handwritten margin note: gets dismissed]

3.9   *"In sum, there is 'no intrinsic reason why the fact that a man is a federal judge should make him more competent, or conscientious, or learned . . . than his neighbor in the state courthouse.'"*

STONE V. POWELL

[handwritten: habeas corpus would no longer be permitted on the contention that the evidence was secured illegally (4th Amendment)]

428 U.S. 465, 96 S. Ct. 3037, 49 L. Ed. 2d 1067 (1976)

Powell was convicted of second degree murder, and the California supreme court denied review. Instead of petitioning the Supreme Court for a writ of certiorari, Powell asked a federal district court to issue a writ of habeas corpus. He contended that

*Under § 25, denial of a federal right by the highest court of a state in the three categories specified was reviewable in the Supreme Court as of right (on writ of error). A 1914 act permitted review by certiorari and also where the state court had *upheld* the federal right. But an act of 1916 withdrew appeal as of right in cases of the third category, leaving certiorari as the only avenue of review. See Felix Frankfurter and James M. Landis, *The Business of the Supreme Court* (New York: Macmillan), pp. 211–213.

[handwritten margin note: – Basement of East Campus Library. Public Document Room – Law Review in the law magazine]

How did the case get from the Court of Appeals to the S.C.

Cardozo

evidence used to convict him had been secured by a search in connection with an illegal arrest and should have been excluded at the trial under the rule announced in *Mapp v. Ohio* (1961). The district judge denied this claim but was reversed by the Court of Appeals for the Ninth Circuit. Members of the Supreme Court, particularly Chief Justice Burger and Justice Powell, had been increasingly critical of the exclusionary rule, which Justice Cardozo had once criticized as requiring courts to let the criminal go free because the constable had blundered. The Court majority took this opportunity to restrict the application of the exclusionary rule when state convictions were subjected to Fourth Amendment challenges on federal habeas corpus. The decision featured a bitter attack on the ruling by Brennan and a rebuttal by Powell, principally in footnotes to his opinion for the Court.

MR. JUSTICE POWELL delivered the opinion of the Court. . . .

Footnote 37. The dissent characterizes the Court's opinion as laying the groundwork for a "drastic withdrawal of federal habeas jurisdiction, if not for all grounds . . . then at least [for many]. . . ." It refers variously to our opinion as a "novel reinterpretation of the habeas statutes," . . . as a "harbinger of future eviscerations of the habeas statutes," . . . as "rewriting Congress' jurisdictional statutes . . . and [barring] access to federal courts by state prisoners with constitutional claims distasteful to a majority" of the Court . . . and as a "denigration of constitutional guarantees [that] must appall citizens taught to expect judicial respect" of constitutional rights. . . .

what about law created by Congress on p. 96

With all respect, the hyperbole of the dissenting opinion is misdirected. Our decision today is *not* concerned with the scope of the habeas corpus statute as authority for litigating constitutional claims generally. We do reaffirm that the exclusionary rule is a judicially created remedy rather than a personal constitutional right, . . . and we emphasize the minimal utility of the rule when sought to be applied to Fourth Amendment claims in a habeas corpus proceeding. . . . In sum, we hold only that a federal court need not apply the exclusionary rule on habeas review of a Fourth Amendment claim absent a showing that the state prisoner was denied an opportunity for a full and fair litigation of that claim at trial and on direct review. Our decision does not mean that the federal court lacks jurisdiction over such a claim, but only that the application of the rule is limited to cases in which there has been both such a showing and a Fourth Amendment violation.

14th Amendment

unfair or incomplete trial litigation

Footnote 35. The policy arguments . . . in support of the view that federal habeas corpus review is necessary to effectuate the Fourth Amendment stem from a basic mistrust of the state courts as fair and competent forums for the adjudication of federal constitutional rights. The argument is that state courts cannot be trusted to effectuate Fourth Amendment values through fair application of the rule, and the oversight jurisdiction of this Court on certiorari is an inadequate safeguard. The principal rationale for this view emphasizes the broad differences in the respective institutional settings within which federal judges and state judges operate. Despite differences in institutional environment and the unsympathetic attitude to federal constitutional claims of some state judges in years past, we are unwilling to assume that there now exists a general lack of appropriate sensitivity to constitutional rights in the trial and appellate courts of the several States. State courts, like federal courts, have a constitutional obligation to safeguard personal liberties and to uphold federal law. *Martin v. Hunter's Lessee* [1816]. . . . Moreover, the argument that federal judges are more expert in applying federal constitutional law is especially unpersuasive in the context of search-and-seizure claims, since they are dealt with on a daily basis by trial level judges in both systems. In sum, there is "no intrinsic reason why the fact that a man is a federal judge should make him more competent, or conscientious, or learned with respect to the [consideration of Fourth Amendment claims] than his neighbor in the state courthouse."

MR. JUSTICE BRENNAN, with whom MR. JUSTICE MARSHALL concurs, dissenting. . . .

The Court . . . argues that habeas relief for non-"guilt-related" constitutional claims is not mandated because such claims do not affect the "basic justice" of a defendant's detention . . . ; this is presumably because the "ultimate goal" of the criminal justice system is "truth and justice." . . . This denigration of constitutional guarantees and *constitutionally mandated procedures,* relegated by the Court to the status of mere utilitarian tools, must appall citizens taught to expect judicial respect and support for their constitutional rights. Even if punishment of the "guilty" were society's highest value—and procedural safeguards denigrated to this end—in a constitution that a majority of the members of this Court would prefer, that is not the ordering of priorities under the Constitution forged by the Framers, and this Court's sworn duty is to uphold that Constitution and not to frame its own. The procedural safeguards mandated in the Framers' Constitution are not admonitions to be tolerated only to the extent they serve functional purposes that ensure that the "guilty" are punished and the "innocent" freed; rather, every guarantee enshrined in the Constitution . . . is by it endowed with an independent vitality and value, and this Court is not free to curtail those constitutional guarantees even to punish the most obviously guilty. Particular constitutional rights that do not affect the fairness of fact-finding procedures cannot for that reason be denied at the trial itself. What possible justification then can there be for denying vindication of such rights on federal habeas when state courts do deny those rights at trial? To sanction disrespect and disregard for

the Constitution in the name of protecting society from law-breakers
is to make the government itself lawless. . . .

Enforcement of *federal* constitutional rights that redress constitutional violations directed against the "guilty" is a particular function of federal habeas review, lest judges trying the "morally
unworthy" be tempted not to execute the supreme law of the land.
State judges popularly elected may have difficulty resisting popular
pressures not experienced by federal judges given lifetime tenure
designed to immunize them from such influences, and the federal
habeas statutes reflect the Congressional judgment that such detached federal review is a salutary safeguard against *any* detention
of an individual "in violation of the Constitution or laws of the United
States."

Federal courts have the duty to carry out the congressionally
assigned responsibility to shoulder the ultimate burden of adjudging
whether detentions violate federal law, and today's decision substantially abnegates that duty. The Court does not, because it cannot,
dispute that institutional constraints totally preclude any possibility
that this Court can adequately oversee whether state courts have
properly applied federal law, and does not controvert the fact that
federal habeas jurisdiction is partially designed to ameliorate that
inadequacy. Thus, though I fully agree that state courts "have a
constitutional obligation to safeguard personal liberties and to uphold federal law," and that there is no "general lack of appropriate
sensitivity to constitutional rights in the trial and appellate courts of
the several States," . . . I cannot agree that it follows that, as the Court
holds today, federal court determinations of almost all Fourth
Amendment claims of state prisoners should be barred and that state
court resolution of those issues should be insulated from the federal
review Congress intended. . . .

Limiting [handwritten margin note]

3.10

"*. . . an elite tradition animates the federal judiciary,
instilling elan and a sense of mission in federal
judges. . . .*"

THE MYTH OF PARITY

state judges could be relied
on to protect constitutional
rights as effectively as
federal judges [handwritten margin note]

Burt Neuborne

In *Stone v. Powell,* Justice Powell . . . appeared to assume that state
and federal courts are functionally interchangeable forums likely to
provide equivalent protection for federal constitutional rights. If it

90 *Harvard Law Review* 1105 (1977). Reprinted by permission. Burt Neuborne
is Professor of Law, New York University.

existed, this assumed parity between state and federal courts . . . would render the process of allocating judicial business between state and federal forums an outcome-neutral exercise unrelated to the merits.

Unfortunately . . . the parity which Justice Powell celebrated in *Stone* exists only in his understandable wish that it were so. I suggest that the assumption of parity is . . . a dangerous myth, fostering forum allocation decisions which channel constitutional adjudication under the illusion that state courts will vindicate federally secured constitutional rights as forcefully as would the lower federal courts. . . . I hope to challenge the Court's present assumptions . . . by focusing on institutional characteristics relevant to assessing the relative competence of state and federal courts as constitutional enforcement mechanisms. . . .

The first step in assessing the relative institutional capacity of state and federal courts to enforce constitutional doctrine requires agreement on which state forum should be compared with the federal district courts to determine whether a comparative advantage exists. Generally, when the parity issue is discussed, it is in the context of a comparison that tends to measure the federal district courts against state appellate courts. While such a comparison makes sense in the context of habeas corpus, where the petitioner first will have pursued his federal claims unsuccessfully through the state court system, it is inappropriate in most constitutional cases. Even if one concedes parity between state appellate and federal district courts, corrective state appellate work does not adequately substitute for vigorous constitutional protection at the trial level. The expense, delay, and uncertainty which inhere in any appellate process render ultimate success after appeal far less valuable than speedy, accurate resolution below. Especially in the context of first amendment rights, by their nature fragile, the possibility of a lengthy, problematic appeal in order to reverse an adverse criminal or civil judgment may deter many individuals from effectively exercising their rights. Moreover, in many constitutional cases, the factfinding process plays a critical role in resolution of the controversy. These two factors combine to render the trial forum often the most critical stage, and thus the appropriate institutional comparison should be between federal district courts and their state trial counterparts.

A second preparatory step is to dispel the notion that acknowledging a comparative advantage to federal courts need imply that state trial judges violate their oaths by consciously refusing to enforce federal rights. We are not faced today with widespread state judicial refusal to enforce clear federal rights. When the mandates of the Federal Constitution are clear, most state judges respect the supremacy clause and enforce them. Constitutional litigation is, however, rarely about clear law. The disputes which propel parties raising constitutional questions into court frequently pit strong legal and moral claims against each other and resolution of those competing "legitimate" claims is the real stuff of constitutional litigation. Thus, one need not intimate that state trial judges act in bad faith. Our comparison need only suggest that given the institutional differences between the two benches, state trial judges are less likely to resolve arguable issues in favor of protecting federal constitutional rights than are their federal brethren.

As a final preparatory step, another notion—that federal district judges, when called upon to enforce the fourteenth amendment against local officials, resemble an alien, occupying army dispatched from Washington to rule over a conquered province—must be dispelled. Federal judges are chosen from the geographical area they serve. Generally, they are appointed with the consent and often at the behest of a senator representing the state in which they will sit, frequently after local officials and citizen groups have had the opportunity to make their views on the nominee known. To characterize federal judges as carpetbaggers, unaware of, and insensitive to, local concerns is thus inaccurate and serves to deflect attention from the relative efficacy of state and federal forums in enforcing constitutional norms.

Concentrating, therefore, on an institutional comparison at the trial level, disclaiming any intent to cast aspersions on the good faith of state judges, and recognizing that both state and federal trial judges have roots in the communities they serve, three sets of reasons support a preference for a federal trial forum. First, the level of technical competence which the federal district court is likely to bring to the legal issues involved generally will be superior to that of a given state trial forum. Stated bluntly, in my experience, federal trial courts tend to be better equipped to analyze complex, often conflicting lines of authority and more likely to produce competently written, persuasive opinions than are state trial courts. . . .

Because it is relatively small, the federal trial bench maintains a level of competence in its pool of potential appointees which dwarfs the competence of the vastly larger pool from which state trial judges are selected. There are about twice as many trial judges in California as in the entire federal system. As in any bureaucracy, it is far easier to maintain a high level of quality when appointing a relatively small number of officials than when staffing a huge department. Additionally, there is a substantial disparity between state and federal judicial compensation which allows the federal bench to attract a higher level of legal talent than state trial courts can hope to obtain.

The selection processes utilized to staff the respective judicial posts also incline toward a federal bench of higher professional distinction. While the federal selection process is not without flaws, it does focus substantially on the professional competence of the nominee. The selection processes for state trial courts are generally less concerned with gradations of professional competence once a minimum level has been attained. Neither elections nor an appointment process based largely on political patronage is calculated to make refined judgments on technical competence.

The competence gap does not stem solely from the differences in the native ability of the judges. While it is often overlooked, the caliber of judicial clerks exerts a substantial impact on the quality of judicial output. Federal clerks at both the trial and appellate levels are chosen from among the most promising recent law school graduates for one- to two-year terms. State trial clerks, on the other hand, when available at all, tend to be either career bureaucrats or patronage employees and may lack both the ability and dedication of their federal counterparts. Moreover, while the caseload burden of the federal courts is substantial, it pales when compared to the caseload of most state trial courts of general jurisdiction.

Even if state and federal forums were of equal technical competence, a series of psychological and attitudinal characteristics renders federal district judges more likely to enforce constitutional rights vigorously. First, although intangible, an elite tradition animates the federal judiciary, instilling elan and a sense of mission in federal judges and exerting . . . a palpable influence on the quality of the judicial product. As heirs of a tradition of constitutional enforcement, federal judges feel subtle, yet nonetheless real pressures to uphold that tradition. State trial judges, on the other hand, generally seem to lack a comparable sense of tradition or institutional mission.

Second, federal judges often display an enhanced sense of bureaucratic receptivity to the pronouncements of the Supreme Court. State judges, of course, almost always recognize that they too are bound not to disregard the Supreme Court's interpretation of the Federal Constitution. Their bureaucratic relationship with the Supreme Court is, however, more attenuated than that of a district court judge. Although the effects of this difference are difficult to isolate with certainty, in my experience federal judges appear to recognize an affirmative obligation to carry out and even anticipate the direction of the Supreme Court. Many state judges, on the other hand, appear to acknowledge only an obligation not to disobey clearly established law. While this distinction is subtle, in the doubtful case it can exert a discernible impact on the trial level outcome. Since civil liberties lawyers frequently are engaged in urging judges to recognize Supreme Court precedent, which, while not clearly dispositive, implies judgment for the constitutional plaintiff, the forum's recognition of an institutional duty to anticipate the as yet unexpressed views of the Supreme Court is critical.

Third, in seeking a federal forum, civil liberties lawyers hope to benefit from what can be described as an "ivory tower syndrome."

The scope of federal jurisdiction, even taking account of that over federal crimes and habeas corpus, is such that federal judges are insulated from the more cynicism-breeding dimensions of constitutional law. State trial judges, conversely, especially at the criminal, family, and lower civil court levels, are steadily confronted by distasteful and troubling fact patterns which can sorely test abstract constitutional doctrine and foster a jaded attitude toward constitutional rights. The fourth amendment's exclusionary rule, for example, will command greater allegiance from a judge who has not been repeatedly exposed to the reality of the social harms inflicted by some felons whom the rule requires to be freed. Similarly, the right to hold a political demonstration or a union organizing rally will seem more obvious to a judge who need not face the disorderly conduct arrests which may arise from them. Distance from the pressures and emotions generated by the application of constitutional doctrine is conducive to a generous reading and vigorous enforcement of constitutional rights. For state trial courts, which ordinarily must be responsible both for law enforcement and the day to day implementation of constitutional rights, no such distance is possible. Federal trial judges, on the other hand, because of the limited nature of their jurisdiction, enjoy a degree of distance enhancing the likelihood that they will liberally and assiduously perform their function of enunciating constitutional norms.

Finally, the differences in the backgrounds of the state and federal trial judges make it more likely that a federal judge will possess certain class-based predilections favorable to constitutional enforcement than will his state court counterpart. The federal bench is an elite, prestigious body, drawn primarily from a successful, homogeneous socioeducational class—a class strongly imbued with the philosophical values of Locke and Mill (which the Bill of Rights in large measure tracks). As such, when a plaintiff asserts a constitutional claim against a state official whose socioeducational background does not include obeisance to that libertarian tradition, a federal judge generally will protect the threatened constitutional value.

This is not to say that judges consciously shape rulings in constitutional cases according to the defendant's social class. Rather, I suggest only that if the defendant and the judge are of the same socioeducational class, a judge will tend to trust that the defendant shares his values and thus will not feel compelled to enforce them vigorously. If the defendant deviates from the judge's class, however, no assumption of shared values will exist—and indeed a suspicion of contrary values may exist—leading to stronger enforcement of the judge's values in the guise of constitutional adjudication.

Most of the constitutional rights which civil liberties lawyers seek to protect fit snugly within nineteenth-century liberal thought. And since a class disparity between federal trial judges and the individual targets of constitutional enforcement is more likely than one between state trial judges and constitutional defendants, this class phenomenon will assist the constitutional plaintiff more often in the federal courts.

Constitutional adjudication inherently involves persuading a judicial forum to counter the will of the majority as expressed through its representatives. To the extent that the forum is itself subject to the political pressures which shaped the judgment it is asked to review, its capacity to provide sustained enforcement of countermajoritarian constitutional norms will be diminished. When one compares the institutional structure of the federal trial bench with state court structures, the functional superiority of federal courts as checks on majoritarian excess is pronounced.

Federal district judges, appointed for life and removable only by impeachment, are as insulated from majoritarian pressures as is functionally possible, precisely to insure their ability to enforce the Constitution without fear of reprisal. State trial judges, on the other hand, generally are elected for a fixed term, rendering them vulnerable to majoritarian pressure when deciding constitutional cases. Thus, when arguable grounds supporting the majoritarian position exist, state trial judges are far more likely to embrace them than are federal judges. This insulation factor, I suggest, explains the historical preference for federal enforcement of controversial constitutional norms. While the level of hostility towards any given constitutional decision varies from locality to locality, from issue to issue, and over time, constitutional adjudication still frequently involves issues which raise strong political passions. Insulation from political pressures may not be necessary in all constitutional cases; yet, where such pressures are strong, insulated judicial forums are necessary if constitutional rights are to remain viable. . . .

3.11   *". . . the Supreme Court's answer is not presumptively the right answer. . . ."*

E PLURIBUS—CONSTITUTIONAL THEORY
AND STATE COURTS

Hans A. Linde

there has been new interest in and exploitation of civil rights protections available in state constitutions.

State courts function in a more complex legal world than the Supreme Court of the United States. The Supreme Court's agenda consists only of questions arising under the Constitution and the laws and treaties of the United States. The Court interprets the laws of

18 *Georgia Law Review* 165 (1984). Reprinted by permission. Hans A. Linde is Judge, Supreme Court of Oregon.

only one legislative body, the Congress, from which virtually all other government action must derive its authority, and the Court needs to attend to only one court's precedents and doctrines, its own. When state laws are the object of Supreme Court attention, their substance is not the Court's responsibility. This makes briefing a federal case, if not easy, at least relatively straightforward.

State courts, by contrast, face the legislative output not only of the state legislature but of many other elected bodies. Some of the acts of these bodies must be based on the statutes and some not. State courts also are responsible for the state's common law. As one common law court among equals, a state supreme court is accustomed to being offered precedent from other states, too often without regard to differences in the other state's written laws. Beyond this, every state court also is bound to apply federal law, not only the United States Constitution, acts of Congress, and treaties, but also federal regulations, executive actions, and caselaw based on nothing more than federal jurisdiction.

These complexities have changed the familiar work of common law courts and counsel, who habitually rely on case citations and quotations from prior opinions to solve all problems. The states themselves have increasingly complex laws and regulations. Add the fact that today's lawyers learned about public law first and perhaps only in a first-year course in constitutional law and sincerely believe that stating the desired outcome as a constitutional claim obviates any need to untangle lesser issues. It is not surprising, then, to find cases argued and decided on grounds drawn directly from Supreme Court opinions with neither counsel nor court stopping to examine the state's law. Nor is it surprising that state courts hesitate to add to the complexity by recognizing the separate level of the state's constitution ahead of the federal constitutional claim.

Yet in many states this reluctance is yielding to the original logic of the federal system. It once again is becoming familiar learning that the federal Bill of Rights was drawn from the earlier state declarations of rights adopted at the time of independence, that most protection of people's rights against their own states entered the federal Constitution only in the Reconstruction amendments of the 1860's, and that it took another hundred years and much disputed reasoning to equate most of the first eight amendments with due process under the fourteenth. Of course this did not repeal the guarantees found in the states' own constitutions. But, in fact, most state courts had a poor record of taking seriously the individual rights and fair procedures promised in their states' bills of rights. Those guarantees rarely seemed to demand anything other than the familiar and accepted practices in the local communities and courthouses. State courts issued and still issue gag orders against the press without much concern whether their constitutions guarantee freedom to speak, write, or publish on any subject whatever. State courts did not probe very deeply into what a state's promise of equal privileges and immunities might mean for blacks or for women. Issues such as prayer in the public schools or trials without counsel and the use of illegally seized evidence did not rank high among the state courts' priorities.

As a result, most of the individual rights and fair procedures that have occupied the Supreme Court's agenda for the past thirty years became associated entirely with federal law, even when they also were guaranteed in the state constitutions. Both academic commentary and lawyers' jargon reinforced the effect. People do not claim rights against self-incrimination; they "take the fifth" and expect "*Miranda* warnings." Unlawful searches are equated with fourth amendment violations. Journalists do not invoke freedom of the press; they demand their first amendment rights. All claims of unequal treatment are phrased as denials of equal protection of the laws.

This in turn creates a quandary for state courts, for lawyers, and, I might add, for law schools and students. The rediscovery of state constitutional law is still very new. Contemporary discussion in the law reviews began only in 1969. The latest bibliographies now list more than 60 items without claiming to be exhaustive. For state courts the problems are both practical and theoretical. Let me mention first the practical problems that a court must resolve before there can be any coherent view of the state's constitutional law.

Ordinarily an appeal is limited to issues properly raised first in the trial court and then on appeal. What should a state court do when faced with a constitutional claim that is phrased in federal terminology and cites only federal cases, though there could be an equivalent claim under the state constitution? Should the court translate such a claim into its state analogue, or should it proceed with the federal claim only? Must constitutional claims be identified by brand, or is there such a thing as generic constitutional law?

Obviously it is easier to ignore potential issues of state law when counsel cite only the familiar federal cases and formulas. But this course is less logical, because it places a state court in the position of holding that the state falls short of a national standard which the state law, if properly invoked, in fact would meet or exceed. When the state issue is omitted, an appellate opinion must take care to explain that it sets no precedent for the state's law. Moreover, in criminal cases, the bulk of all constitutional litigation, a failure to raise the possible state issue leaves open a later claim of inadequate assistance of counsel. If a court will decide only issues that the parties have argued, it needs a way to make parties argue the state law before the federal issue.

The practical problems intersect with the theoretical. In recent years some advocates and courts began to couple their customary briefing of a federal constitutional claim with a citation to the parallel clause of the state constitution and to conclude that the challenged action violated, for instance, both the fourth amendment and the state's guarantee against unreasonable searches or seizures. That proved to be bad practice because it is bad theory. The Supreme Court promptly disregarded such tacked-on state citations and at the end of the 1982 Term told state courts to speak "clearly and expressly" if their decisions are based on "bona fide separate, adequate, and independent grounds." This may lead a conscientious trial or intermediate court to divide every typical constitutional claim into its familiar federal component and a state parallel component and to decide both whenever the court has little precedent under state law. In the state's highest court, of course, a successful state claim makes the federal issue irrelevant.

Why do not state courts always apply state law before reaching a federal question? In fact they routinely do so with state statutes or constitutional provisions that have no federal parallel. But when the Supreme Court has decided a point, many state courts take the decision as a kind of benchmark, presumptively correct also for state law. When they depart from federal decisions, state courts often begin by explaining that the Supreme Court permits them to interpret their state's law in their own way—a sign of how far we have lost sight of basic federalism.

If state courts either follow the Supreme Court's lead or feel obliged to explain why not, the reason is not only that counsel fail to brief state law. In the past thirty years, there have been far more Supreme Court decisions on freedom of expression, on equal protection, and on criminal procedure than in any state court. As I have said, counsel or courts looking for scholarly help on these issues find only commentary on Supreme Court cases and doctrines. Our law clerks come prepared for nothing else. As Justice Charles G. Douglas of New Hampshire has deplored, "[t]he federalization of all our rights has led to a rapid withering of the development of state decisions based upon state constitutional provisions." Wisconsin's Justice Shirley Abrahamson also notes "an understandable human tendency on the part of state judges to view a Supreme Court decision on a particular topic as the absolute, final truth." And she adds: "It is easier for state judges and for lawyers to go along with the United States Supreme Court than to strike out on their own to analyze the state constitution."

Because the state is bound to comply with federal standards in any case, divergence from Supreme Court doctrines is criticized for making daily life in the trial courts more uncertain and difficult. Justice Stanley Mosk of the California Supreme Court, which has a distinguished but intermittent record of independent constitutional holdings, counters that such independent holdings can bring stability to the state's law in the face of frequent inconsistencies and changes in Supreme Court doctrines. It is an illusion to seek stability by following the Supreme Court in deciding a state claim; for once it has been decided, does the decision not continue to bind the state's courts even when Supreme Court doctrine changes? Still, most courts that take an independent course tend to look first to those doctrines and then discuss whether or why the state should, as it is put, "go further" than the Supreme Court. The effect is to make independent state grounds appear not as original state law, but as a kind of supplemental rights that require an explanation.

Justice Steward Pollock of the New Jersey Supreme Court recently discussed three different ways in which state courts deal with overlapping state and federal claims. The Vermont court, for example, has chosen to decide the state and federal claims in separate parts of one opinion. This, however, makes the discussion of the federal claim pure dicta when the state claim succeeds. A similar practice in California was criticized because it implies that the result could not be changed by amending the state constitution. The New Jersey court itself follows the supplemental approach I have mentioned, reaching a state claim only when federal doctrine fails to provide protection. Justice Pollock observes that state courts should not look to their own constitutions only when they wish to reach a result different from the United States Supreme Court. That practice runs the risk of criticism as being more pragmatic than principled. He believes that a court can develop criteria to decide when to diverge from federal law. But in my view, to ask when to diverge from federal doctrines is quite a different question from taking a principled view of the state's constitution; in fact, this supplemental or interstitial approach prevents a coherent development of the state's law.

My own view has long been that a state court always is responsible for the law of its state before deciding whether the state falls short of a national standard, so that no federal issue is properly reached when the state's law protects the claimed right. That approach has recently been followed by the Oregon Supreme Court. I think most courts would take that approach for granted when a state statute rather than a state constitution is involved. Of course we pay attention and respect to Supreme Court opinions on issues common to the two constitutions, and it is to be expected that on many such issues courts will reach common answers. The crucial step for counsel and for state courts, however, is to recognize that the Supreme Court's answer is not presumptively the right answer, to be followed unless the state court explains why not.

The right question is not whether a state's guarantee is the same as or broader than its federal counterpart as interpreted by the Supreme Court. The right question is what the state's guarantee means and how it applies to the case at hand. The answer may turn out the same as it would under federal law. The state's law may prove to be more protective than federal law. The state law also may be less protective. In that case the court must go on to decide the claim under federal law, assuming it has been raised.

This, in summary, is the complex world of the state court in our federal system, a system that leaves the individual states responsible both for most civil and criminal laws and also for their own constitutions, subject to several layers of federal law. You will appreciate the temptation to reduce the complexity by leaving at least one layer, constitutional law, to the specialists in Washington, D.C. Nevertheless, courts are resuming their responsibility for the constitutional law of their states.

4
Judicial Recruitment and Selection

In every Western nation judges form an elite group. They are usually distinguished from the rest of society by a unique uniform and by a specialized form of education, as well as by the degree of power that they exercise over the lives of their fellow citizens. Three means—or some combination of these—are generally used today to select judicial personnel: (1) establishing the judiciary as a separate profession, entrance to which is regulated much the same as in medicine or law; (2) allowing political officials to make appointments to the bench; or (3) permitting the people as a whole to elect their judges.

Nations using the civil law system set the judiciary apart as a distinct profession, one separate even from the practice of law. In West Germany, for example, to become a judge a young man or woman must be a university graduate with the equivalent of an undergraduate major in law, pass with exceptionally high marks a set of professional examinations, undergo several years of training that combine further study with apprenticeship, and finally sustain another set of rigorous examinations administered by the government. Once in the judicial profession, judges follow careers much like civil servants, moving slowly up the hierarchy from less important to more important courts as long as they receive good fitness reports from senior jurists in the system.

In Britain, on the other hand, judges from the time of the Norman Conquest have been appointed by the king. Indeed, through much of the Middle Ages judges were regarded merely as assistants to the sovereign in his personal administration of justice. Early English judges were often clergymen attending the royal household. But by the beginning of the fourteenth century kings were also staffing their courts from among the sergeants of the law who were trained in the Inns of the Court, a practice that slowly grew until judicial office became a virtual monopoly of the legal profession.

British judges held their positions only at the pleasure of the king, and their terms of office expired on the death of the sovereign who had appointed them. This dependence on royal favor frequently made for judicial subservience. Their long struggle for free government convinced the English that an independent judiciary was vital to the type of constitutional rule they desired; but not until 1701 did the Act of Settlement provide that judges should serve during good behavior, with removal contingent upon parliamentary approval. And it was not until 1760 that a judge's commission did not expire on the death of the king who had appointed him.

The British belief in the value of an independent judiciary was transplanted to America, and royal abuse of this principle was one of the grievances that gave a moral tinge to the Revolutionary cause. The Declaration of Independence accused George III of having "made Judges dependent on his Will alone, for the Tenure of their Offices, and the Amount and Payment of their Salaries."

After the Revolution American states generally provided that judges should be elected by one or both houses of the legislature or appointed by the governor with the consent of either a special legislative council or the legislature itself. Only one state allowed the governor full appointing power. At the Constitutional Convention in 1787 the Framers were presented with several plans for choosing federal judges. Those delegates, such as Franklin, Mason, Gerry, and Ellsworth, who opposed a strong executive, wanted to adhere to the dominant state practice and vest the appointing authority in Congress. Others, like Hamilton, Madison, and Morris, wanted the executive to appoint judges. It was Hamilton who first suggested that the President nominate and the Senate confirm, but this obvious compromise was twice rejected by the Convention before it was finally approved. Following British practice, the new Constitution provided that federal judges should serve during good behavior.

THE FEDERAL SYSTEM IN OPERATION

Because the Reagan administration substantially modified past practices in judicial selection, the traditional or pre-Reagan practices will be described first. The President's actual power to nominate federal judges, as compared with his legal power, varies with the court involved. The President has widest discretion in filling a vacancy on the Supreme Court. The Attorney General and his staff have generally acted for the President in originating or screening suggestions for nominees to the Court. In some instances politically influential friends of candidates waged intensive campaigns to gain the President's approval. Many considerations have shaped presidential choices, such as geographic or ethnic representation, anticipated reactions of the bar and the public, and the climate of opinion in the Senate. But by and large, the President's principal concern has tended to be the general ideology of the nominee and the way the nominee can be expected to vote on the Court. (Reading 4.1.)

President Nixon was very frank and explicit in declaring what qualifications he would look for in his nominees. During the 1968 campaign he attacked the record of the Warren Court, particularly its decisions on the rights of defendants in criminal cases, which he deplored as having weakened the "peace forces" in society. He promised that if elected he would appoint to the Court "strict constructionists who saw their duty as interpreting law and not making law." His first nominee, Warren E. Burger, fitted within the confines of this unrealistic description of judicial policy making, for as a judge on the Court of Appeals for the District of Columbia he had publicly attacked the Warren Court's decisions regarding criminal procedure. Nixon then announced that his next nominee would come from the South, and he made two unsuccessful efforts to appoint Southerners. Only after the Senate refused to confirm Clement F. Haynsworth, Jr., of South Carolina and G. Harrold Carswell of Florida did he turn to a non-Southerner, Harry A. Blackmun of Minnesota.

During Gerald Ford's two years as President, he had the opportunity to make one appointment, which went to John Paul Stevens, a moderate Republican who was sitting on the U.S. Court of Appeals for the Seventh Circuit. His selection was confirmed by the Senate 98 to 0. President Carter had no vacancies to fill on the Court. Through July, 1985, Ronald Reagan had only one nomination to make. He chose Sandra Day O'Connor, a state judge from Arizona, who was a conservative Republican and had been a classmate of Justice William H. Rehnquist at the Stanford Law School.

In the nomination of judges for lower federal courts, senators of the President's party play an important role, although not always a dominant one. After an exhaustive study of judicial appointments in the Eisenhower, Kennedy, and Johnson administrations, Harold W. Chase concluded: "[T]he time has come to set aside the simplistic explanation that senators alone determine the appointments to the federal bench. For better or worse, the process is much more complicated...."[1] Judge Joseph Samuel Perry provides an unusually frank account of his campaign for a federal judgeship. (Reading 4.2.)

When a vacancy occurs on a district court, a senator from the President's party from that state will normally submit one or more names of candidates to the Attorney General for consideration. But the Department of Justice, acting through the Deputy Attorney General,

---

[1] *Federal Judges* (Minneapolis: University of Minnesota Press, 1972), p. 47.

also conducts an active search for promising talent. If there is a conflict of views between the senator and the administration, the senator can threaten to block a nomination at the confirmation stage; and so a compromise is usually arranged.

If there are two senators from the President's party in a state, nominees must be satisfactory to both—though perhaps not the first choice of either—or be allotted alternately between the two. Even when both senators are from the opposition party, the President may have to come to terms with them. For example, both Presidents Nixon and Ford had an agreement with the two Democratic senators from California to permit the senators to nominate one Democrat for every two Republicans selected by the President.

Nominations for the courts of appeals differ in that each circuit covers more than one state, which means that senators from several states have potential interest in the appointments. It is generally true, however, that the judgeships in each circuit have been allocated by custom among the component states. Consequently, when a vacancy occurs, it is often claimed that the successor should be from the same state as the former incumbent, thus giving the administration senator from that state a prior claim to the position.

As a presidential candidate Jimmy Carter promised to remove federal judges from the political patronage system. After his election he set up by executive order the U.S. Circuit Nominating Commission, composed of panels in each circuit, appointed by the President and equally divided between lawyers and nonlawyers. These panels were free to search for candidates and to accept applications, not merely to screen persons suggested by senators or the administration. Carter, however, generally found that he had to defer to senatorial prerogative as far as district judges were concerned, though he did suggest to senators that they establish their own merit selection commissions for appointments in their states. Senators in at least eighteen states complied.

In 1978 Congress took long-delayed action to increase the number of federal judges, adding 117 district judges and 39 court of appeals judgeships. The Omnibus Judgeship Act required the President to establish standards for selection of judges on the basis of merit, and to give "due consideration to qualified individuals regardless of race, color, sex, religion, or national origin." Together with the usual number of vacancies, Carter was given an unprecedented opportunity to shape the federal judiciary, with special emphasis on the selection of women and minorities.[2]

---

[2] Sheldon Goldman, "Carter's Judicial Appointments: A Lasting Legacy," 64 *Judicature* 344 (1981). Carter's 262 nominees to district courts included 40 women, 38 blacks, and 16 Hispanics.

THE PRESIDENT AND THE SENATE

The Senate can impose effective restraints on executive discretion, even if it does not control the selection of judges. Washington saw one of his Supreme Court nominees rejected by the Senate, and in the nineteenth century over 25 percent of nominations to the Court failed to negotiate the senatorial maze—eight were rejected, five withdrawn because of opposition, and ten postponed or not acted upon. In contrast, during the first two-thirds of the twentieth century, the Senate rejected only one nominee to the Supreme Court. Judge John J. Parker was defeated in 1930, partly because of the opposition of labor and black organizations. There had also been strong opposition to Louis D. Brandeis in 1916 and to Charles Evans Hughes in 1931, but both were confirmed by substantial margins. It was, therefore, a stunning reversal of practice when within the space of two years, between 1968 and 1970, President Johnson and President Nixon each saw two of his nominees fail to win senatorial confirmation.

Johnson's trouble arose out of his effort to elevate his long-time friend and legal adviser Associate Justice Abe Fortas to the chief justiceship. In June 1968 Chief Justice Warren notified Johnson of his desire to retire, effective upon confirmation of his successor. Johnson transmitted Fortas's name to the Senate, at the same time nominating another old friend, Homer Thornberry of Texas (a judge of the Court of Appeals for the Fifth Circuit), to the post to be vacated by Fortas. Opposition to Fortas quickly developed, for a variety of reasons: partisan politics, objections to the liberal decisions in which Fortas had participated, revelation of Fortas's continuation as presidential adviser while on the bench (especially his support of Johnson's Vietnam policy), and argument that there was no vacancy since Warren had not actually retired. When a filibuster prevented the Senate from voting on the nomination, Fortas asked the President to withdraw his name. He remained on the Court as associate justice until his resignation eight months later (thus the vacancy for which Thornberry had been nominated was rendered nonexistent), and Warren continued as chief justice for one more term.

Nixon then filled the chief justice's post by nominating Warren Burger, who was confirmed almost without opposition. But the next vacancy was a different matter. In 1969 *Life* magazine revealed that Justice Fortas had agreed to accept an annual fee for advisory services to a private foundation funded by a man who was under federal investigation at the time and who was subsequently convicted for violations of the Securities and Exchange Act. This association was generally regarded as a clear breach of judicial propriety, even though Fortas had not participated in any cases involving the financier and had eventually returned the retainer as a result of public criticism. Fortas resigned, the first justice in Supreme Court history to leave under such circumstances.[3]

Nixon nominated Clement Haynsworth for Fortas's vacancy. But the Senate had been so alerted to the issues of judicial ethics by the Fortas affair, and the Democrats in the Senate so embarrassed by it, that Haynsworth's judicial record was subjected to intense scrutiny. Changes of ethical insensitivity, related to his stock holdings in companies involved in cases in which he had participated, as well as opposition to his conservative political views, led to his rejection by the Senate by the vote of fifty-five to forty-five.

Nixon's second "strict constructionist," G. Harrold Carswell, was also rejected by the Senate because of his lack of intellectual qualifications and past opposition to civil rights. Not since 1894 had two successive Supreme Court nominees been defeated in the Senate.

THE MECHANICS OF THE APPOINTING PROCESS

Prior to the Reagan administration, the President depended heavily on the Attorney General and his staff to screen candidates and maintain liaison with Congress and interested pressure groups. Under Reagan a joint White House–Justice Department committee took over this responsibility. In other respects the procedures remain largely unchanged. When the list of candidates has been narrowed, the FBI runs a full loyalty-security check, and the Department of Justice seeks the approval of the American Bar Association's Committee on Federal Judiciary. This committee then conducts its own inquiry, seeking the views of the legal profession.

When the nomination is sent to the Senate, the matter is referred to the Committee on the Judiciary. The committee chairman is allowed to read the FBI report, but other senators are not. At the same time, the committee clerk sends out a "blue slip" to the Senators from the nominee's state, asking their views. If there is objection, and the President nevertheless proceeds with the nomination, "senatorial courtesy" will normally be invoked to defeat confirmation of the appointment.

Next, the committee chairman appoints a subcommittee, which sets a date for hearings. In the case of lower-court judges these hearings are usually perfunctory if the Department of Justice has maintained proper liaison with senators. The senators from the nominee's state and a few other character witnesses testify in glowing terms. Only occasionally is there more than token opposition from senators, though not infrequently a few cranks ask to be heard. It sometimes happens, however, that senators use these hearings to exert legislative pressure on either the executive or the judiciary.

---

[3] Fortas's conduct might easily have stood the test of nineteenth-century judicial ethics, which, for example, allowed Justice Story to serve as director of a bank (and receive, as a gift, a clock that now adorns the justices' dining room).

In contrast to the usual bland character of hearings on lower-court nominees, proceedings on an appointment to the Supreme Court are often elaborate and explosive. Interest groups can use these hearings as a forum to voice their views on the course of constitutional law, and senators can utilize the publicity of the occasion to express opposition to the candidate, the President, or the Court. Thus in 1958 Southern senators tried to turn the hearings on Justice Potter Stewart into a debate on the merits of school desegregation. The hearings on the Fortas-Thornberry nominations ran for nine days and with supporting documents filled a volume of 1,284 pages. The hearings on Haynsworth, Carswell, and William Rehnquist, Nixon's fourth appointee, were also lengthy as well as heated.

Before the second administration of Franklin D. Roosevelt a Supreme Court nominee usually did not attend the hearings. Beginning with the nomination of Felix Frankfurter, however, it has become normal practice for the nominee to appear as a witness and be subjected to committee interrogation. Sandra Day O'Connor, the first woman nominee, extended the practice by making a series of visits to influential senators before her hearings. As a member of the Arizona legislature she had voted on an issue related to abortion, and anti-abortionists in the Senate hearings made persistent but unsuccessful efforts to get her to commit herself on this and other issues. (Reading 4.3.)

After the hearings the subcommittee reports to the full Committee on the Judiciary, and the question of confirmation is discussed and voted upon. Prior to 1929 the Senate held secret sessions on confirmation. Now, of course, the debate is open and may be highly dramatic. The debate on Carswell's nomination continued for almost four weeks and turned what had been expected to be a favorable vote into a rejection.[4]

JUDICIAL QUALIFICATIONS

The selection of federal judges is thus frankly a partisan process. In the twelve administrations from Harding to Reagan the percentage of judges appointed from the President's own party ranged from 87.2 (Hoover) to 97 (Reagan).

Generally, appointments go to persons of competence and integrity, but not necessarily to the most able members of the bar. Nominees to the lower federal courts have usually been judges, prosecuting attorneys, legislators, administrators, or lawyers in private practice who have been politically active.

Opinions differ about the value of prior judicial experience, and throughout its history only about half the members of the Supreme Court had previously been judges. (Reading 4.4.) President Eisen-

[4] The story is well told in Richard Harris, *Decision* (New York: E. P. Dutton, 1971).

hower, after appointing as Chief Justice Earl Warren, who had been California's attorney general and governor but not a judge, made judicial experience a prerequisite for his remaining four nominees. In fact, the policy of Republican presidents has generally been to nominate persons with prior judicial experience, whereas Democratic presidents have preferred nominees with broad political or administrative backgrounds.

Since 1946 the American Bar Association has had a Committee on Federal Judiciary, which has sought with varying degrees of success to influence the appointing process by expressing views on the qualifications of nominees. The committee at first hoped to be permitted to suggest candidates for vacancies, but neither Democratic nor Republican regimes would agree. The Truman administration, however, did consult with the ABA's committee, and under Eisenhower the committee came to have almost a veto power over nominations. The next three administrations displayed less deference. Eight of Kennedy's nominations were made despite committee ratings of the nominees as unqualified, and Johnson established a similar record.

The experience of the ABA committee with Nixon's recommendations for the Supreme Court was particularly difficult. In nominating Haynsworth and Carswell, the administration followed the established practice of giving the ABA committee no advance information about the individuals who were under consideration. Thus the committee could only conduct hurried consultations after the names of the nominees had been sent to the Senate, and it rated both nominees as qualified. After the Senate rejected them, Attorney General John N. Mitchell agreed to change the procedure and to consult with the committee while the list of possible nominees was being made up. When Justices Black and Harlan retired in 1971, Mitchell submitted to the ABA committee the names of six possible nominees, all of whom were either unknown nationally or obviously lacking in qualifications for the high court. The committee's response was to rate as unqualified the two candidates listed as preferred, ratings which were immediately leaked to the press. Nixon then dropped these candidates and, without notifying the committee, named two much abler conservatives, Lewis F. Powell, Jr., and William H. Rehnquist.

With Carter's nominating commissions and their concern for widening the opportunities for judicial selection, the ABA committee lost the monopoly it had enjoyed on the advisory function. Three nominees rated by the ABA as "unqualified" were confirmed by the Senate (in one case the ground for the rating was age, a standard subsequently abandoned by the committee).

A number of critics have questioned the propriety of giving the ABA a prominent part in recruiting judges. The organization includes in its membership fewer than half of the nation's practicing attorneys, and it espouses not merely professional "improvements" designed to benefit certain interests within the legal profession, but also controversial, and typically conservative, political goals.[5]

REAGAN'S RECORD

A major concern of the Reagan administration was to balance the "activist" Carter-appointed judges by conservatives who would practice judicial restraint and support Reagan's position on social and political issues. The 1980 Republican platform promised selection of judges "who respect traditional family values and the sanctity of innocent human life." During the campaign Reagan said that he would not adopt a single-issue litmus test for judges, but would look for nominees whose views were "broadly similar" to his own.

To ensure that nominees would meet this ideological test, the White House staff took a much more active role in the search for or approval of candidates than had been customary in the past. Creation of a nine-person joint White House–Department of Justice committee, called the President's Committee on Federal Judicial Selection, institutionalized and formalized an active White House role in judicial selection. "Legislative, patronage, political, and policy considerations are considered to an extent never before so systematically taken into account."[6] (Reading 4.5.)

Under Reagan's procedures, candidates supported by Republican senators or governors were rejected if they failed the ideological tests. Carter's emphasis on selection of women and minorities, while not abandoned, became a distinctly minor objective. As a Justice Department official said, "We're not going to sacrifice those things we feel most important simply to adjust the numbers." The record for Reagan's first term, during which he made 161 nominations, was 2 blacks, 8 Hispanics, and 17 women.[7] In general, Reagan's selections were white, male, rich, and almost 100 percent Republican. In a widely noted law school address, Justice Rehnquist defended the right of the President to try to "pack" the Supreme Court with justices who agree with him, though he questioned how successful such efforts would be. (Reading 4.6.)

Because of Reagan's emphasis on ideology, right-wing political and religious groups outside the usual channels of influence have sought, with considerable success, to break into the appointing proc-

---

[5] For an excellent analysis of the work of the ABA Committee, see Elliot E. Slotnick, "The American Bar Association Standing Committee on Federal Judiciary," 66 *Judicature* 349 (1983).

[6] Sheldon Goldman, "Reaganizing the Judiciary: The First Term Appointments," 68 *Judicature* 313 (1985).

[7] On the failure to appoint blacks, the Justice Department's special counsel for judicial selection explained that there are "just not that many" black Republicans who are "excited about the President's emphasis on judicial restraint." *Congressional Quarterly Weekly Report,* December 5, 1984, p. 3076.

ess. For example, three conservative Republican senators sent an eight-page questionnaire to an Hispanic New Jersey state official, who had been nominated by the President on the recommendation of the state's Republican governor. The questionnaire asked for such information as his views on abortion and a list of his political contributions for the past ten years. Senator J. Strom Thurmond, Republican chairman of the Judiciary Committee, protested that such inquiries should be confined to committee hearings.

Again, a New York official of the Legal Aid Society, proposed jointly by the New York senators, one Republican and one Democrat, was denied nomination on the ground that he was "not consistent with what the [White House] committee was looking for." The nomination of a Deputy Solicitor General who appeared "soft" on abortion and gun control was withdrawn by the White House after thirteen Republican senators wrote the President saying they would oppose his confirmation.

Another tactic of the Reagan administration was to choose as judges comparatively young persons who could anticipate a long-term incumbency. One study reported that 11.4 percent of Reagan's first-term nominees were under the age of 40, which could extend Reagan's influence over eight succeeding presidential terms. Also, as Goldman's study shows, by selecting persons with prior judicial experience or conservative law school professors with established reputations, the Reagan administration has minimized the possibility of "mistakes" concerning nominees' views.

While judicial selections in the past have usually been made on grounds of politics and policy, the procedures tended to be loose, and the pressures and recommendations to the President came from so many different sources—members of Congress, governors, active party officials, members of the bar—that the result was a valuable diversity on the federal bench. Reagan's policies and procedures guaranteed an ideological polarization, which, given the probability that he will have appointed more than half the entire federal bench by the end of his second term, promised to characterize the federal judiciary for several decades to come.

JUDICIAL SELECTION IN THE STATES

In the states judges are selected by election, by appointment, or by a combination of both methods. The practice of electing judges was one of the bequests of Jacksonian democracy. Prior to 1832 only one state chose all its judges by popular election, but every state admitted to the Union since 1846 has provided for the election of all or most of its judges. In 1977 election was the principal method of judicial selection in twenty-five states (on partisan ballot in thirteen states and nonpartisan in twelve); the legislatures elected the judges in four states; there was executive appointment in eight states; and a so-called merit plan existed in thirteen states.

The merit plan, also known as the Missouri plan, is a compromise between appointing and electing judges. Under this arrangement several commissions nominate judges at different court levels. The appellate commission consists of seven members: the chief justice of the state, three lawyers elected by the state bar association, and three persons appointed by the governor, none of whom can be a public officeholder or an official of a political party. With the exception of the chief justice, these members serve for six years, with their terms staggered so that two retire every other year. The commission nominates three persons for each judicial vacancy. The governor must appoint one of the three. At the first election after twelve months of service, the name of the new judge is put on the ballot with the question whether he or she should be retained in office. If elected, the judge then serves a definite term—twelve years for an appellate judge, six years for a trial judge. At the end of this term the incumbent is eligible for reelection. Whether the Missouri plan really recruits judges on the basis of merit is open to question. What is clear is that selection is no less political, although the political arena tends to be that of bar associations, rather than a public forum in which citizens have a check if not a voice.[8] (Reading 4.7.)

California has something like the Missouri plan in reverse. The governor has complete discretion in making appointments to the state's appellate courts, but once named, nominees are subjected to review by a three-person committee, composed of the attorney general, the chief justice (or senior supreme court justice if the chief justiceship is being filled), and the presiding justice of the appellate court affected by the nomination (or senior presiding judge where a supreme court nomination is at stake). Only once in California history has the committee rejected the governor's choice. Once confirmed, appellate court judges must face the voters for retention unopposed at the next general election. In 1982 a strong effort to defeat three of Governor Brown's liberal appointees narrowly failed.[9]

In some thirty-six states citizens without training in the law are empowered to sit as justices of the peace, magistrates, and police judges. A 1972 study of California's lay judges showed that 37 percent had no education beyond high school while 13 percent had even less. The Mississippi Judicial Commission was told in 1969 that "33 percent of the justices of the peace are limited in educational background to the extent that they are not capable of learning the necessary ele-

---

[8] See especially Richard A. Watson and Rondal G. Downing, *The Politics of the Bench and the Bar: Judicial Selection Under the Missouri Nonpartisan Court Plan* (New York: Wiley, 1969).

[9] See John H. Culver, "Politics and the California Plan for Choosing Appellate Judges," 66 *Judicature* 151 (1982).

Table 1   Appellate Court Selection Plans

ELECTED	MISSOURI PLAN	EXEC. APPOINTMENT WITH CONFIRMATION	LEGISLATURE SELECTS	CALIF. PLAN
Partisan	Alaska	Delaware (Sen)[4]	Connecticut (GA)	California
Alabama	Arizona	Maine (Sen)	Rhode Island	
Arkansas	Colorado	New Jersey (Sen)	South Carolina	
Georgia[1]	Florida	New Hampshire (Council)[5]	Virginia	
Illinois	Hawaii			
Mississippi[1]	Indiana			
New Mexico	Iowa			
North Carolina	Kansas			
Pennsylvania	Maryland[2]			
Texas	Massachusetts			
West Virginia[1]	Missouri			
Nonpartisan	Nebraska			
Idaho	New York			
Kentucky	Oklahoma[3]			
Louisiana	South Dakota			
Michigan	Tennessee			
Minnesota[1]	Vermont[2]			
Montana	Wyoming			
Nevada				
North Dakota				
Ohio				
Oregon				
Utah				
Washington				
Wisconsin				

[1]Interim vacancies are filled by the governor with the assistance of a nominating commission.

[2]Plus Senate confirmation.

[3]Intermediate appellate court judges are selected by nonpartisan elections.

[4]By executive order, appointments are made on a nonpartisan basis from nominees whose names are submitted by a judicial nominating commission.

[5]Gubernatorial nominees are approved by a five-member council elected by the people of the state.

SOURCE: John H. Culver, "Politics and the California Plan for Choosing Appellate Judges," 66 *Judicature* 157 (1982). Reprinted from *Judicature*, the journal of the American Judicature Society.

ments of law." While reports of national commissions have been unanimous in calling for elimination of nonlawyer judges, the Supreme Court held in *North v. Russell* (1976) that trial before a lay judicial officer did not violate due process provided there was a right of appeal to and a trial de novo before a lawyer-trained judge.

JUDICIAL SOCIALIZATION

Learning how to act like a judge in the United States is a matter of on-the-job training. As we have noted, in countries influenced by the civil law tradition, judging is a definite career which young men and women enter through a program of education and examination. England is like the United States in that judges are selected from the practicing bar, but there the selection is made from a very limited number (approximately 2,600 for the entire country) of barristers who have specialized in courtroom appearances and advocacy. In the United States lawyers who ascend the bench by election or appointment vary widely in legal training, experience, and ability.

How do American judges adjust to their new role? What do they need to learn if they are to cope with the demands of their new position? Carp and Wheeler suggest that new judges experience three general kinds of problems.[10] The first are of a legal nature, such as learning new areas of substantive law and procedures; for example, many lawyers have steered clear of criminal law practice, but as judges face a welter of such cases. The second are administrative in nature—supervision of court staff, efficient use of personnel and organization and planning of the court docket. The third type of problem is essentially psychological—maintaining a judicial bearing on and off the bench, learning to abandon the former role of partisan advocate for that of impartial umpire, and dealing with local pressures in controversial matters such as school integration.

For the federal bench there are some systematic efforts to ease the socialization process for new judges. The Federal Judicial Center in Washington presents annually a seminar for newly appointed district judges, where the topics range from judicial ethics to the use of jurors in multijudge courts. A Bench Book for United States District Judges was introduced by the Federal Judicial Center in 1969. Judges learn from each other and from their experienced staff members. In multijudge cities it is customary for the judges to meet on a regular basis to discuss common problems. Circuit judicial conferences are held at least once a year, attended by all the district and appellate judges in the circuit, along with the Supreme Court justice assigned to that circuit and special guests.

[10] Robert Carp and Russell Wheeler, "Sink or Swim: The Socialization of a Federal District Judge," 21 *Journal of Public Law* 359 (1972).

THE JUDICIAL ELITE: A COLLECTIVE PORTRAIT

John Schmidhauser has sketched a collective portrait of the ninety-one men who sat on the Supreme Court from 1789 to 1957.[11] He found that

> throughout the entire history of the Supreme Court, only a handful of its members were of essentially humble origin. Nine individuals selected in widely scattered historical periods comprise the total. The remaining eighty-two (90%) were not only from families in comfortable economic circumstances, but were chosen overwhelmingly from the socially-prestigeful and politically-influential gentry class in the late eighteenth and nineteenth century or the professionalized upper middle-class thereafter.

Equally meaningful for social origin was the fact that nearly two-thirds of the justices "were drawn from politically active families, and of perhaps greater significance, a third of this group were chosen from a relatively narrow circle of families—families which have been distinctive in their possession of traditions of judicial service."

The justices themselves have generally been politically active people. In fact, George Shiras was the only justice out of the ninety-one who had not participated in practical politics before going to the Court. Twenty-six out of the thirty-four pre–Civil War appointees had been primarily politicians, and the overall percentage for the 168 years covered by Schmidhauser's study was 53.9. This figure would be considerably larger if some or all of the twenty-four men who had pursued lower-court judicial careers were included in the "politician" category. Only four Supreme Court justices have been primarily law-school professors, and all were appointed by Franklin Roosevelt. Of the fourteen justices who were neither "politicians," lower-court judges, nor professors, eleven were chiefly corporation lawyers, and three were noncorporation lawyers.

As for religious persuasion, most Supreme Court justices have been members of high-status Protestant sects (Episcopalian, Presbyterian, French Calvinist, Congregationalist, or Unitarian), though in the twentieth century there has been a marked tendency for each President to keep a Catholic on the Court and since 1916 a Jew. President Nixon, however, broke this tradition and criticized the idea that there should be a Jewish or Catholic seat on the Court.

Ethnically, Schmidhauser found that only five justices were not natural-born American citizens, and three of these five were appointed by George Washington. Most of the justices—94.6 percent—came from predominantly western European stock—English, Welsh, Scotch-Irish, Irish, French, Dutch, or Scandinavian—and some 57.2 percent

---

[11] "The Justices of the Supreme Court: A Collective Portrait," 3 *Midwest Journal of Political Science* 1 (1959).

from British or Welsh backgrounds. Of the justices born in the United States, the majority have come from small towns or urban areas, with the percentage of rural-born justices steadily declining.

Noting the high educational level of Supreme Court appointees, Schmidhauser concluded that "the recruitment process has generally rewarded those whose educational backgrounds, both legal and non-legal, have comprised the rare combination of intellectual, social and political opportunities which have generally been available only to the economically comfortable and socially prominent segment of the American population."

Although Schmidhauser's study was published in 1959, there is little reason to think that subsequent appointments to the Supreme Court would affect his generalizations. Thurgood Marshall, nominated by Johnson in 1967, is the first and only black, Sandra O'Connor the first and only woman. Except for Arthur Goldberg and Abe Fortas, the other ten nominees since 1959 have been Protestants with names identified with Northern European origins. As of July 1985 no one of Italian or Slavic background had been nominated. The only person with an Hispanic name was Benjamin N. Cardozo (1932–1938), and he was a Sephardic Jew.

Looking at the entire history of the Court, one must conclude that the ability of its members has been reasonably high. Sixty-five law school deans and professors of law, history, and political science who were asked to evaluate the ninety-six justices on the Court from 1789 to 1969 ranked twelve as "great" and fifteen as "near great"—well over one-fourth of the group.[12] Only six were rated below average and eight as failures.

SELECTED REFERENCES

Abraham, Henry J. " 'A Bench Happily Filled': Some Historical Reflections on the Supreme Court Appointment Process," 66 *Judicature* 282 (1983).

————. *Justices and Presidents: A Political History of Appointments to the Supreme Court.* New York: Oxford University Press, 1974.

Abraham, Henry J., and Bruce A. Murphy. "The Influence of Sitting and Retired Justices on Presidential Supreme Court Nominations," 3 *Hastings Constitutional Law Quarterly* 37 (1976).

Adamany, David, and Philip DuBois. "Electing State Judges," 1976 *Wisconsin Law Review* 731.

Atkins, Burton, and Marc G. Gertz. "The Local Politics of Judicial Selection," 66 *Judicature* 39 (1982).

Berger, Raoul. *Impeachment: The Constitutional Problems.* Cambridge, Massachusetts: Harvard University Press, 1973.

---

[12] Albert P. Blaustein and Roy M. Mersky, "Rating Supreme Court Justices," 58 *American Bar Association Journal* 1183 (1972). In chronological order, the "great" justices were John Marshall, Joseph Story, Roger B. Taney, John M. Harlan I, Oliver W. Holmes, Jr., Charles E. Hughes, Louis D. Brandeis, Harlan F. Stone, Benjamin N. Cardozo, Hugo L. Black, Felix Frankfurter, and Earl Warren.

Bickel, Alexander M. "Mr. Taft Rehabilitates the Court," 79 *Yale Law Journal* 1 (1969).

Canon, Bradley C. "The Impact of Formal Selection Processes on the Characteristics of Judges," 6 *Law and Society Review* 579 (1972).

Carbon, Susan (ed.). "Women in the Judiciary," 65 *Judicature* 285 (1982).

Carmen, Ira H. "The President, Politics and the Power of Appointment: Hoover's Nomination of Mr. Justice Cardozo," 55 *Virginia Law Reveiw* 616 (1969).

Carp, Robert, and Russell Wheeler. "Sink or Swim: The Socialization of a Federal District Judge," 21 *Journal of Public Law* 359 (1972).

Chase, Harold W. *Federal Judges: The Appointing Process.* Minneapolis: University of Minnesota Press, 1972.

Cook, Beverly Blair. "The Socialization of New Federal Judges: Impact on District Court Business," 1971 *Washington University Law Quarterly* 253.

Danelski, David J. *A Supreme Court Justice Is Appointed.* New York: Random House, 1964.

Daniels, William J. "The Geographic Factor in Appointments to the United States Supreme Court: 1789–1976," 31 *Western Political Quarterly* 226 (1978).

DuBois, Philip L. *From Ballot to Bench.* Austin: University of Texas Press, 1980.

Ewing, Cortez A. M. *The Judges of the Supreme Court, 1789–1937.* Minneapolis: University of Minnesota Press, 1938.

Fowler, W. Gary. "Judicial Selection under Reagan and Carter: A Comparison of Their Initial Recommendation Procedures," 67 *Judicature* 265 (1984).

Goldman, Sheldon. "American Judges: Their Selection, Tenure, Variety and Quality," 61 *Current History* 1 (1971).

———. "Carter's Judicial Appointments: A Lasting Legacy," 64 *Judicature* 344 (1981).

———. "Reagan's Judicial Appointments at Mid-Term: Shaping the Bench in His Own Image," 66 *Judicature* 335 (1983).

Goulden, Joseph C. *The Benchwarmers: The Private World of the Powerful Judges.* New York: Weybright and Talley, 1974.

Grossman, Joel B. *Lawyers and Judges: The ABA and the Politics of Judicial Selection.* New York: Wiley, 1965.

Murphy, Walter F. "In His Own Image: Mr. Chief Justice Taft and Supreme Court Appointments," in Philip B. Kurland (ed.), *The Supreme Court Review, 1961.* Chicago: University of Chicago Press, 1961. Pp. 159–193.

Provine, Doris Marie. "Persistent Anomaly: The Lay Judge in the American Legal System." Denver, Colo.: Graphic Impressions.

Schmidhauser, John R. *The Supreme Court: Its Politics, Personalities, and Procedures.* New York: Holt, Rinehart and Winston, 1960.

Shogan, Robert. *A Question of Judgment: The Fortas Case and the Struggle for the Supreme Court.* Indianapolis: Bobbs-Merrill, 1972.

Slotnick, Elliot E. "The ABA Standing Committee on Federal Judiciary: A Contemporary Assessment," 66 *Judicature* 349 (1983).

———. "The Changing Role of the Senate Judiciary Committee in Judicial Selection," 62 *Judicature* 502 (1979).

———. "The Paths to the Federal Bench: Gender, Race, and Judicial Recruitment Variation," 67 *Judicature* 371 (1984).

Songer, Donald R. "The Policy Consequences of Senate Involvement in the Selection of Judges in the U. S. Courts of Appeals," 35 *Western Political Quarterly* 107 (1982).

Tribe, Laurence H. *God Save This Honorable Court: How the Choice of Justices Shapes Our History.* New York: Random House, 1985.

Vandenberg, Donna. "Voluntary Merit Selection," 66 *Judicature* 265 (1983).

Volcansek, Mary L. "An Exploration of the Judicial Election Process," 34 *Western Political Quarterly* 572 (1981).

Watson, Richard A., and Rondal G. Downing. *The Politics of the Bench and the Bar: Judicial Selection Under the Missouri Nonpartisan Plan.* New York: Wiley, 1969.

4.1   *"[A judge] is not . . . fitted for the position unless he is a party man, a constructive statesman . . ."*

THEODORE ROOSEVELT TO HENRY CABOT LODGE

July 10, 1902

PERSONAL

Dear Cabot:

. . . . Now as to Holmes . . . First of all, I wish to go over the reasons why I am in his favor. He possesses the high character and the high reputation both of which should if possible attach to any man who is to go upon the highest court of the entire civilized world. His father's name entitles the son to honor; and if the father had been an utterly unknown man the son would nevertheless now have won the highest honor. The position of Chief Justice of Massachusetts is in itself a guarantee of the highest professional standing. Moreover, Judge Holmes has behind him the kind of career and possesses the kind of personality which make a good American proud of him as a representative of our country. He has been a most gallant soldier, a most able and upright public servant, and in public and private life alike a citizen whom we like to think of as typical of the American character at its best. The labor decisions which have been criticized by some of the big railroad men and other members of large corporations constitute to my mind a strong point in Judge Holmes' favor. The ablest lawyers and greatest judges are men whose past has natu-

Henry Cabot Lodge, *Selections from the Correspondence of Theodore Roosevelt and Henry Cabot Lodge, 1894–1918* (New York: Charles Scribner's Sons, 1925), I, 517–519. Reprinted with permission. Henry Cabot Lodge (1850–1924) was a leading Republican and United States senator from Massachusetts.

rally brought them into close relationship with the wealthiest and most powerful clients, and I am glad when I can find a judge who has been able to preserve his aloofness of mind so as to keep his broad humanity of feeling and his sympathy for the class from which he has not drawn his clients. I think it eminently desirable that our Supreme Court should show in unmistakable fashion their entire sympathy with all proper effort to secure the most favorable possible consideration for the men who most need that consideration.

Finally, Judge Holmes' whole mental attitude, as shown for instance by his great Phi Beta Kappa speech at Harvard, is such that I should naturally expect him to be in favor of those principles in which I so earnestly believe.

. . . In the ordinary and low sense which we attach to the words "partisan" and "politician," a judge of the Supreme Court should be neither. But in the higher sense, in the proper sense, he is not in my judgment fitted for the position unless he is a party man, a constructive statesman, constantly keeping in mind his adherence to the principles and policies under which this nation has been built up and in accordance with which it must go on; and keeping in mind also his relations with his fellow statesmen who in other branches of the government are striving in cooperation with him to advance the ends of government. Marshall rendered such invaluable service because he was a statesman of the national type, like Adams who appointed him, like Washington whose mantle fell upon him. Taney was a curse to our national life because he belonged to the wrong party and faithfully carried out the criminal and foolish views of the party which stood for such a construction of the Constitution as would have rendered it impossible to preserve the national life. The Supreme Court of the sixties was good exactly in so far as its members represented the spirit of Lincoln.

This is true at the present day. The majority of the present Court who have, although without satisfactory unanimity, upheld the policies of President McKinley and the Republican party in Congress, have rendered a great service to mankind and to this nation. The minority—a minority so large as to lack but one vote of being a majority—have stood for such reactionary folly as would have hampered well-nigh helplessly this people in doing efficient and honorable work for the national welfare, and for the welfare of the islands themselves, in Porto Rico and the Philippines. No doubt they have possessed excellent motives and without a doubt they are men of excellent personal character; but this no more excuses them than the same conditions excused the various upright and honest men who took part in the wicked folly of secession in 1860 and 1861.

Now I should like to know that Judge Holmes was in entire sympathy with our views, that is with your views and mine and Judge Gray's, for instance, just as we know that ex-Attorney General

Knowlton is, before I would feel justified in appointing him. Judge Gray has been one of the most valuable members of the Court. I should hold myself as guilty of an irreparable wrong to the nation if I should put in his place any man who was not absolutely sane and sound on the great national policies for which we stand in public life.

Faithfully yours,
Theodore Roosevelt

4.2 *"As it turned out that proved to be pretty good strategy . . ."*

HOW I GOT TO BE A FEDERAL JUDGE

Joseph Samuel Perry

I thought that instead of giving a lecture on some philosophical question I would relate how I became a federal judge. Some of the younger lawyers might be interested in hearing about the avenue I travelled to that appointment. There are, of course, many avenues . . . but I will tell you how I got there.

To begin with, if you want to be appointed to that office in Illinois, you almost have to be a Democrat. There are some States where one could be a Republican, but not in Illinois. In Minnesota, for example, you could be appointed if you were a Republican—that is, if you were a dangerous Republican who might defeat some Democrat who wanted to be elected to a particular office.

I started out by being born a Republican. Now I know that doesn't sound very good for a fellow who was born in Alabama, but there is one county down there—Winston County—which was known as the Free State of Winston during the Civil War. They had no slaves and so they did not fight on the Confederate side in the Civil War. They either hid out in the bluffs or they ran across the border at night and fought in the Union Army. They still vote Republican and they have never elected a Democrat in the history of the county. Not even Roosevelt carried Winston County.

I was born right near the edge of that county and my grandfather, John Brown—no relation to the famous John Brown—was an old Republican, and my mother was a Republican, and so, as I say, I was born a Republican.

After my mother's death, which occurred when I was four, my

Speech before the Chicago Bar Association, November 20, 1951 (*The Chicago Daily News,* November 30, 1951). Joseph Samuel Perry was U.S. District Court Judge, Northern District of Illinois.

father moved down into a Democratic county where I "got educated." Of course, I became a Democrat. It was not until I was about
17 years old and went back to the vicinity of Winston County to teach
school that I learned that my mother's people had been Republicans
and that I had been born of a Republican mother.

After I enlisted in World War I and had served overseas, I returned and went to work in the coal mines. By that time, of course,
the unions had gotten there and I joined the union, as my friend here
said, and I was getting along fine. Then John Lewis came down and
called a strike in the summertime when we had very little work
anyway and when it couldn't hurt the coal company. That made me
mad. I got so mad that I quit coal mining and went to college and
got an education.

So that was another step forward. I came up here, went to the
University of Chicago and got a master's degree. Then I got a doctor's
degree and felt highly educated.

Then I moved out to DuPage County and, because of the college
education I had acquired, I almost became a Republican. However,
before I could completely backslide, my friend Elmer Schaefer, over
here—Walter Schaefer's brother—who had gone to law school with
me, began to work on me. He saw I was getting a little weak and he
induced me to rejoin and affiliate myself with the Democratic party.
And so, because I had a good evangelist working on me, I stuck with
the Democratic party.

Of course, I became active in DuPage County. I will be frank
about it. At first I talked around amongst the Republicans about
doing some work—there was no Democratic party out there—but
the Republicans didn't need me. Well, after I became converted to
the Democratic party again, or was saved again, so to speak, I proceeded to organize the Democratic party out there and to make it
tough for the Republicans. The result was that we finally had the
framework of a party. Later, with the aid of the late Governor Henry
Horner and a few other good Democrats, I landed in the legislature
and kept working along and served my term there. Then I got out
of politics and came back and practiced law.

And then I gambled. I saw a man—Paul Douglas—who looked as
though he might be elected to the United States Senate. I backed him
and as a result I had his support. My political friendship with my good
friend Scott Lucas, in the meantime, had grown bit by bit and Scott
was not mad at me.

Since we are talking confidentially I will be perfectly frank with
you folks in admitting that I tried to obtain this appointment seven
years ago and learned then that it requires not one but two senators.
At that time I was out of politics and they did not need me. Therefore, I decided that this time if I wanted that appointment I had
better get back into politics—which I did. When I learned, as I soon

did, that everyone shoots at the top man—that he is everyone's target —I went to each of the senators and said "Listen here, if you are going to back me, for heaven's sake don't make me number one. Be sure to back me and get me on the list but don't make me number one."

As it turned out that proved to be pretty good strategy because everybody else was shot off and, no use lying about it, I helped to shoot them off. The result of it was I landed on top. [Laughter.] I have the job now and I am going to stick.

4.3   *"... my own view in the area of abortion is that I am opposed to it. ..."*

HEARINGS BEFORE THE SENATE JUDICIARY COMMITTEE ON THE NOMINATION OF SANDRA DAY O'CONNOR

Sandra Day O'Connor, an Arizona state judge and former majority leader of the state senate, was nominated by President Reagan on July 7, 1981, to fill the post of Associate Justice vacated by the retirement of Potter Stewart. The Senate Judiciary Committee held hearings on September 9, 10, and 11, 1981, and the nomination was approved by the committee on September 15 by a vote of seventeen to zero, Senator Denton abstaining. The Senate confirmed Justice O'Connor by a vote of ninety-nine to zero on September 21. The chairman of the committee was J. Strom Thurmond of South Carolina.

Members of the committee asked Judge O'Connor for her views on such diverse subjects as judicial activism, the exclusionary rule, separation of powers, constitutional amendment by conventions, tuition tax vouchers, and fees for attorneys in civil rights cases; but controversy was almost wholly confined to the nominee's views on abortion and related votes she had cast as an Arizona legislator.

Testimony of Hon. Sandra Day O'Connor, Nominated to Be Associate Justice of the U.S. Supreme Court

Mr. Chairman and members of the Senate Judiciary Committee, I would like to begin my brief opening remarks by expressing my gratitude to the President for nominating me to be an Associate Justice of the U.S. Supreme Court, and my appreciation and thanks to you and to all the members of this committee for your courtesy and for the privilege of meeting with you.

As the first woman to be nominated as a Supreme Court Justice, I am particularly honored, and I happily share the honor with millions of American women of yesterday and of today whose abilities and whose conduct have given me this opportunity for service. As a citizen and as a lawyer and as a judge, I have from afar always regarded the Court with the reverence and with the respect to which it is so clearly entitled because of the function it serves. It is the institution which is charged with the final responsibility of insuring that basic constitutional doctrines will always be honored and enforced. It is the body to which all Americans look for the ultimate protection of their rights. It is to the U.S. Supreme Court that we all turn when we seek that which we want most from our Government: equal justice under the law.

If confirmed by the Senate, I will apply all my abilities to insure that our Government is preserved; that justice under our Constitution and the laws of this land will always be the foundation of that Government.

I want to make only one substantive statement to you at this time. My experience as a State court judge and as a State legislator has given me a greater appreciation of the important role the States play in our federal system, and also a greater appreciation of the separate and distinct roles of the three branches of government at both the State and the Federal levels. Those experiences have strengthened my view that the proper role of the judiciary is one of interpreting and applying the law, not making it.

If confirmed, I face an awesome responsibility ahead. So, too, does this committee face a heavy responsibility with respect to my nomination. I hope to be as helpful to you as possible in responding to your questions on my background and my beliefs and my views. There is, however, a limitation on my responses which I am compelled to recognize. I do not believe that as a nominee I can tell you how I might vote on a particular issue which may come before the Court, or endorse or criticize specific Supreme Court decisions presenting issues which may well come before the Court again. To do so would mean that I have prejudged the matter or have morally committed myself to a certain position. Such a statement by me as to how I might resolve a particular issue or what I might do in a future Court action might make it necessary for me to disqualify myself on the matter. This would result in my inability to do my sworn duty; namely, to decide cases that come before the Court. Finally, neither you nor I know today the precise way in which any issue will present itself in the future, or what the facts or arguments may be at that time, or how the statute being interpreted may read. Until those crucial factors become known, I suggest that none of us really know how we would resolve any particular issue. At the very least, we would reserve judgment at that time. . . .

The CHAIRMAN [Senator J. Strom Thurmond]. Judge O'Connor, there has been much discussion regarding your views on the subject of abortion. Would you discuss your philosophy on abortion, both personal and judicial, and explain your actions as a State senator in

Arizona on certain specific matters: First, your 1970 committee vote in favor of House bill No. 20, which would have repealed Arizona's felony statutes on abortion. Then I have three other instances I will inquire about.

Judge O'CONNOR. Very well. May I preface my response by saying that the personal views and philosophies, in my view, of a Supreme Court Justice and indeed any judge should be set aside insofar as it is possible to do that in resolving matters that come before the Court.

Issues that come before the Court should be resolved based on the facts of that particular case or matter and on the law applicable to those facts, and any constitutional principles applicable to those facts. They should not be based on the personal views and ideology of the judge with regard to that particular matter or issue.

Now, having explained that, I would like to say that my own view in the area of abortion is that I am opposed to it as a matter of birth control or otherwise. The subject of abortion is a valid one, in my view, for legislative action subject to any constitutional restraints or limitations.

I think a great deal has been written about my vote in a Senate Judiciary Committee in 1970 on a bill called House bill No. 20, which would have repealed Arizona's abortion statutes. Now in reviewing that, I would like to state first of all that that vote occurred some 11 years ago, to be exact, and was one which was not easily recalled by me, Mr. Chairman. In fact, the committee records when I looked them up did not reflect my vote nor that of other members, with one exception.

It was necessary for me, then, to eventually take time to look at news media accounts and determine from a contemporary article a reflection of the vote on that particular occasion. The bill did not go to the floor of the Senate for a vote; it was held in the Senate Caucus and the committee vote was a vote which would have taken it out of that committee with a recommendation to the full Senate.

The bill is one which concerned a repeal of Arizona's then statutes which made it a felony, punishable by from 2 to 5 years in prison, for anyone providing any substance or means to procure a miscarriage unless it was necessary to save the life of the mother. It would have, for example, subjected anyone who assisted a young woman who, for instance, was a rape victim in securing a D. & C. procedure within hours or even days of that rape.

At that time I believed that some change in Arizona statutes was appropriate, and had a bill been presented to me that was less sweeping than House bill No. 20, I would have supported that. It was not, and the news accounts reflect that I supported the committee action in putting the bill out of committee, where it then died in the caucus.

I would say that my own knowledge and awareness of the issues and concerns that many people have about the question of abortion has increased since those days. It was not the subject of a great deal of public attention or concern at the time it came before the committee in 1970. I would not have voted, I think, Mr. Chairman, for a simple repealer thereafter. . . .

Testimony of Dr. Carolyn F. Gerster, Vice President in Charge of International Affairs, National Right to Life Committee, Inc.

Dr. GERSTER. I would like to thank Senator Strom Thurmond and the members of the Senate Judiciary Committee for this opportunity to testify at the confirmation hearing.

I am an Arizona physician, cofounder, and first president of the Arizona Right to Life. I have served as director from Arizona to the national board since its formation in 1973. I was immediate past president and am currently vice president in charge of international affairs.

I would like to preface my written remarks by saying that, as a woman in a profession that is still dominated by men, I believe that the nomination of a woman Justice to the U.S. Supreme Court is about 200 years overdue, and I wish with all my heart that I could support the nomination of this fellow Arizonan.

I would like to comment on the Justice Department memorandum that has been mentioned by Senator Denton, a memorandum from Kenneth W. Starr dated July 7, 1981, summarizing his July 6 telephone investigation of Judge Sandra O'Connor's voting record in family-related issues during the period that she served in the Arizona State Senate. The memo reads in part:

> Judge O'Connor indicated, in response to my questions, that she had never been a leader or outspoken advocate on behalf of either pro-life or abortion rights organizations. She knows well the Arizona leader of the right-to-life movement, a prominent female physician in Phoenix, and has never had any disputes or controversies with her.

I was not contacted by the Justice Department for a verification. This statement has been understandably misunderstood by members of the legislature and the media to imply that Judge O'Connor and I share similar beliefs on the abortion issue.

I have known Sandra Day O'Connor since 1972. Our children were members of the same Indian Guide group. We attend the same church; we have the same friends. She is a very gracious and a very gifted lady.

Quite apart from our social contact, however, we were in an absolute adversary position during 1973 and 1974 due to Senator O'Connor's position on abortion-related legislation when she served as senate majority leader. The Justice Department memorandum is misleading and incomplete regarding Senator O'Connor's voting record from 1970 through 1974.

All of the votes cast on abortion-related bills during this period have been consistently supportive of legalized abortion, with the possible exception of senate bill 1333, which actually is interpreted as a conscience clause allowing physicians and hospital personnel the right to object on moral or religious grounds. What the Starr memorandum fails to mention is that this passed 30 to 0, supported by those on both sides of the abortion question.

In 1970, house bill 20 proposed to remove all restrictions from abortions done by a licensed physician, without regard to indication or duration of pregnancy. This bill, which predated the infamous 1973 U.S. Supreme Court decision by 3 years, if passed would have allowed abortion on demand to term. This was a radical concept when compared to existing State laws at that time.

The Justice Department memorandum states that "There is no record of how Senator O'Connor voted, and she indicated that she has no recollection of how she voted." Judge O'Connor has so stated in her testimony. As a reason she gives "the literally thousands of bills" that were presented during her 4 years.

This bill was controversial. It was news in Arizona. It was opposed by the Catholic bishop. It was the subject of editorials. She voted for it twice, in judiciary and again in the majority caucus. . . .

Rather than go on with my testimony which details the errors and omissions page by page of the Starr memorandum, paragraph by paragraph, as my time is growing short I will submit the manuscript. I can say that I came here prepared to tear up my testimony and to enthusiastically support Judge O'Connor's nomination. I believed that, as she had promised, that she would speak on substantive issues, primarily abortion, before this committee. We have not had that assurance.

I am aware that despite the commitment given by the present administration and reiterated in the Republican Party platform that "We will work for the appointment of judges at all levels of the judiciary who respect traditional family values and the sanctity of innocent human life," that there are members sitting here that do not agree with that. However, I think that all members of this committee agree that misrepresentation, evasion, and distortion of fact have no place in selection of a Justice to the U.S. Supreme Court. . . .

Testimony of Dr. John C. Willke, President, National Right to Life Committee, Inc.

Dr. WILLKE. Thank you, Mr. Chairman.

I am John Willke, physician and current president of the National

Right to Life Committee. I speak here for that committee, which is composed of the 50 State right-to-life organizations which contain almost 2,000 active chapters and an estimated millions of membership.

We are concerned. We exist as a movement because of the 1973 *Roe v. Wade* decision of the U.S. Supreme Court. Just as the *Dred Scott* decision of 1857 was a civil rights outrage in that century, so we see *Roe v. Wade* as a similar blot upon our Nation in this century. In *Dred Scott* the Supreme Court ruled that an entire class of living humans were chattel. This decision denied black Americans civil rights and equal protection by law.

Accordingly, let us flash back in time, if you please, to the post-Civil War era, and ask a question. Suppose a nominee to the U.S. Supreme Court at that time was being questioned and his qualifications examined. Suppose that that person as a legislator had previously voted for the continuation of slavery, not once but twice. Suppose also that he had voted on a memorial resolution asking the Congress to pass a constitutional amendment to abolish slavery, and that that nominee had voted against that resolution and for discrimination, not once but twice.

Would not then it be a proper question to that nominee to inquire whether that nominee still held those proslavery convictions? We believe so. We also believe that if such earlier actions were not totally repudiated by that nominee, that such person would be disqualified from sitting on the U.S. Supreme Court.

A century has passed. Another Supreme Court by a similar 7-to-2 decision—*Roe v. Wade*—has ruled that another entire class of living humans were to be reduced to the status of property of the owner —the mother; further, that the mother was given the newly created right to privacy, a right that allowed her to have her property—her unborn child—destroyed if she wished. Because of this ruling and because of the Court's interpretation of the word "health," we have a body count today of 1.5 million a year.

There are indeed some single issues which are so fundamental that they ought to be weighed very heavily in considering any lifetime appointment to the Federal bench, among these, racial justice. In 1948, G. Harold Carswell gave a speech in which he said, "I believe that segregation of the races is the proper and only practical and correct way of life in our States." During Senate consideration of his nomination 22 years later, he completely repudiated that position, and yet the matter weighed heavily upon the minds of many Senators, and quite properly so. Concern over that earlier commitment to racial injustice perhaps played an important role in the rejection of his nomination. . . .

We believe that recognition of the right to life of the unborn child is also just such a fundamental issue. Those who do not recognize this right, we suggest, should be disqualified from sitting on the Federal court.

A nominee now sits before this distinguished body. You must decide whether she is qualified to sit on the Court, and there are serious questions. Her record as a State legislator is very disturbing.

In 1970, as a State Senator, at that time only one-third of the States had legalized abortion and most laws were highly restrictive. New York, in that same year, had passed abortion on demand until 24 weeks and was to be the second last State that legalized abortion through statute. Thirty-three States subsequently voted on the issue and voted down proposed abortion laws. The nation had been shocked by this.

In this climate, Senator O'Connor voted for a bill that would have legalized abortion on demand in the entire 9 monnths of pregnancy. No statute remotely as radical had been considered elsewhere. This was not a casual vote on the floor; this was a vote on a committee, after having studied it.

Again, a year after the Supreme Court decision which did legalize abortion in the entire 9 months of pregnancy, she had an opportunity to vote against that sweeping decision. Again, on two occasions she voted to maintain what has been abortion permissive through the 9 months of pregnancy.

She had recently stated that she is personally opposed to abortion. In no way referring to the nominee, let me merely state that I have never met an abortion chamber operator or an abortionist who was not personally opposed to abortion. The simple fact is that such a personal statement does not in any way relate nor is an indicator of how such a person may view abortion for others, or in the case of a public servant, how they will vote or how they will rule.

Finally, the last point is that many legal scholars are quite convinced that the decision of the Supreme Court in *Roe v. Wade* was in fact raw judicial power and activism. The nominee here has been held up as a constructionist. It would seem to us that in fact, if she does not repudiate *Roe v. Wade,* that that fact alone denies that title and should deny her the nomination. . . .

Senator METZENBAUM. Dr. Gerster, it is nice to have you before us.

I have concerns, whether it has to do with right to life or any other single issue, as to what happens to the fabric of our democracy if we are to elect or defeat people, or nominees to the Supreme Court, based upon any one single issue. When Judge Mikva was before this committee the issue was gun control. Now Judge O'Connor is before this committee; the issue is right-to-life.

Both of you are very intelligent people. Both of you, I am sure, are good Americans, but I truly question whether you or anyone else should judge any particular individual for elective office or appointive office based upon one issue. The woman who is up for appointment does not meet my criteria as to what I think a Supreme Court Justice should be. I would not necessarily have appointed her, but that, in my opinion, is not the issue.

She has indicated by her comments that she and I differ strongly on the scope of the first amendment, which I hold very high. Should I, on that basis, vote against her? She has indicated her views with respect to capital punishment, busing, a number of other issues. She was not asked about gun control but, regardless of what the particular issue is, should any member of this committee vote for or against this woman and her confirmation based upon one single issue?

I asked her in the last couple of days about the question of access to the courts, I am concerned about whether or not the poor can get into the courtroom, whether or not they should be denied the right to be in the courtroom because a case is below $10,000 in value. She and I are diametrically opposed on that issue. She wrote an article in which she made that very clear. Should that be a basis for me to vote against her confirmation?

She belongs to some clubs that, in my opinion, are discriminatory. Should that be the basis on which I vote against her confirmation? She has different views than I do as to the role of the Government as it pertains to proper Government surveillance. Should that be the basis on which I vote against her confirmation?

More broadly, the polls indicate that there are a substantial block of Americans—I do not know whether it is a majority, I am told that it is a majority—who approve of abortion under certain circumstances. Should all of those people be denied appointment to the Supreme Court of the United States, or be denied the opportunity to be elected, because of the position that your organization has taken?

Frankly, it disturbs me, not because I do not respect full well your right to take any position that you want—to me, that is fundamental in this country—but what concerns me is that any group holds itself out and says that on the basis of this issue, this is more important than any other issue. That, I believe, is enough to disturb all of us because I think it strikes at the very heart of the system of government under which we live.

Since I do respect both of you as good Americans, I find something un-American about any particular candidate or any particular appointee being judged on the basis of one issue and one issue alone.

Dr. WILLKE. Senator—

Dr. GERSTER. I would like to address myself to that also.

Dr. WILLKE [continuing]. I think we have to make a distinction between single issue and disqualifying issue. It is our opinion that only once or twice in a century does an issue raise itself in our society that is of such overweening and overwhelming importance, that strikes so clearly to the very heart of the basis of our society and the basis of the freedoms that this Nation has been built upon, the most basic right of all, that unalienable one, to live.

In the last century I mentioned one that arose, and I am sure we have no disagreement here. For someone to have been proslavery after the Civil War was certainly a single issue but I do believe it would have been a disqualifying issue. . . .

I would suggest that the killing of 1.5 million innocent unborn babies a year is such an intolerable evil that it is that once-in-a-century issue. You must respect—and you have said you do and we appreciate the respect—that vast numbers of people in this Nation view that as such an abominable evil, so utterly intolerable, that in fact while being a single issue it is that once-in-a-century issue. It does in our minds disqualify a person from holding public office.

Senator METZENBAUM. It does not bother you that the gun control people think that is the most important issue? It does not bother you that the single issue prayer-in-the-school people think that is the most important issue? It does not bother you that there are so many groups who think that their issue is the only issue? Now you say that this has become the overriding, the paramount issue, but the fact is that a majority of people in this country have not indicated in the polls they agree with you, and seven Supreme Court Justices have not indicated that they agree with you. Yet you feel that by reason of your position that that is the paramount issue, and that should disqualify this woman from being confirmed to the Supreme Court.

4.4   *"Greatness in the law is not a standardized quality. . . ."*

THE SUPREME COURT IN THE MIRROR OF JUSTICES

Felix Frankfurter

. . . During the one hundred and sixty-seven years since the day appointed for its first session, ninety Justices have sat on the Supreme

105 *University of Pennsylvania Law Review* 781 (1957). Copyright 1957 University of Pennsylvania. Reprinted with permission. Felix Frankfurter was Associate Justice, Supreme Court of the United States, from 1939 until 1962.

Court. The number of men over so long a period would seem to be sufficient to afford some light on the kind of experience or qualifications that may be deemed appropriate for service on the Court. Indeed, the actualities about the men who were appointed to the Court may well be wiser guides than abstract notions about the kind of men who should be named. Of the ninety Justices I shall consider seventy-five, omitting contemporary and relatively recent occupants of the Court. . . . I refer to the suggestion, indeed the assumption that, since the Supreme Court is the highest judicial tribunal, prior "judicial service" is not only a desirable, but an indispensable, qualification.

What is the teaching of history on this? Of the seventy-five Justices, twenty-eight had not a day's prior judicial service. Seven more had sat on some bench from a few months to not more than two years. Nine sat six years or less. Measures have been proposed that would require "judicial service" of not less than five years in a lower federal court or as a member of the highest court of a State; some bills demand ten years of such service. A five-year requirement would have ruled out at least thirty-five of the seventy-five judges (in fact more, because several of the Justices who had had the judicial experience did not sit on a federal bench or on the highest court of a State), and the ten-year requirement would have barred certainly forty-five of our seventy-five Justices.

Who were these Justices who came on the Supreme Court without any "judicial service," without even the judicial experience of an Iredell, who at the age of twenty-six sat on the Superior Court of his State, North Carolina, only long enough—six months—to resign. They begin with . . . James Wilson and include Bushrod Washington, Marshall, Story, Taney, Curtis, Campbell, Miller, Chase, Bradley, Waite, Fuller, Moody, Hughes, Brandeis, Stone and Roberts. Of the twelve Chief Justices within our period five had not had any judicial experience at the time of their appointment as Chief Justice and two more had had none when they first came on the Court.

Apart from the significance of a Chief Justice as the administrative head of the Court, what of the quality of judicial service of the men who came on the Court totally devoid of judicial experience? Assessment of distinction in the realm of the mind and spirit cannot exclude subjective factors. Yet it is as true of judges as of poets or philosophers that whatever may be the fluctuations in what is called the verdict of history, varying and conflicting views finally come to rest and there arises a consensus of informed judgment. It would indeed be a surprising judgment that would exclude Marshall, William Johnson, Story, Taney, Miller, Field, Bradley, White (despite his question-begging verbosities), Holmes, Hughes, Brandeis and Cardozo in the roster of distinction among our seventy-five. I myself would add Curtis, Campbell, Matthews and Moody. (Some might prefer the first Harlan or Brewer or Brown.) Of the first twelve, five had had judicial experience and seven none before coming on the Court; of the other only Matthews can be counted a judge, for a brief period, before he came to Washington. Of the sixteen Justices whom I deem pre-eminent, only six came to the Court with previous judicial experience, however limited. It would require discernment more than daring, it would demand complete indifference to the elusive and intractable factors in tracking down causes, in short, it would be capricious, to attribute acknowledged greatness in the Court's history either to the fact that a Justice had had judicial experience or that he had been without it.

Greatness in the law is not a standardized quality, nor are the elements that combine to attain it. To speak only of Justices near enough to one's own time, greatness may manifest itself through the power of penetrating analysis exerted by a trenchant mind, as in the case of Bradley; it may be due to persistence in a point of view forcefully expressed over a long judicial stretch, as shown by Field; it may derive from a coherent judicial philosophy, expressed with pungency and brilliance, reinforced by the *Zeitgeist,* which in good part was itself a reflection of that philosophy, as was true of Holmes; it may be achieved by the resourceful deployment of vast experience and an originating mind, as illustrated by Brandeis; it may result from the influence of a singularly endearing personality in the service of sweet reason, as Cardozo proves; it may come through the kind of vigor that exerts moral authority over others, as embodied in Hughes.

The roll-call of pre-eminent members of the Supreme Court who had had no judicial experience in itself establishes, one would suppose, that judicial experience is not a prerequisite for that Court. It would be hard to gainsay that this galaxy outshines even the distinguished group that came to the Court with prior experience on state courts, though these judges included the great names of Holmes and Cardozo. It has been suggested that the appearance on the Court of Marshall, Story, Taney, Curtis, Campbell, Miller, Bradley, Hughes and Brandeis, all without prior judicial experience, is "a curious accident." But this accident has been thrown up by history over a period of one hundred and fifty years. . . .

. . . Apart from meaning that a man had sat on some court for some time "judicial service" tells nothing that is relevant about the qualifications for the functions exercised by the Supreme Court. While it seems to carry meaning, it misleads. . . . The Supreme Court is a very special kind of court. "Judicial service" as such has no significant relation to the kinds of litigation that come before the Supreme Court, to the types of issues they raise, to qualities that these actualities require for wise decision.

4.5

"Reagan will accomplish what only Roosevelt and Eisenhower accomplished during the last half century—naming a majority of the lower federal judiciary in active service."

REAGANIZING THE JUDICIARY: THE FIRST TERM APPOINTMENTS

Sheldon Goldman

Ronald Reagan's reelection by a landslide victory in 1984 was hailed by some observers as a significant political event comparable to Franklin Roosevelt's reelection in 1936. Both presidents received overwhelming electoral approval, which was widely interpreted as a mandate to continue along the course set in the first term. Both were enormously popular with the large majority of the populace, although both stimulated considerable antipathy and even denigration from a vocal minority opposed to Administration philosophy and policy. Both elections could be seen as confirming a new electoral era in national politics and new voting patterns among young voters and other population groups.

In addition, both presidents had spent their first terms dealing with economic crises and both used Keynesian economics (without credit to Keynes in the latter instance) to nurse the economy back to health. Both presidents had a view of the role of government, including the courts, that was radically different from their immediate predecessors in office. Indeed, both sought to change the direction of government, saw the courts as frustrating their policy agendas, and self-consciously attempted to use the power of judicial appointment to place on the bench judges sharing their general philosophy. And with both, their presidential campaigns saw the courts and judicial appointments emerge as issues.

Franklin Roosevelt left a major legacy with his court appointments that fundamentally reshaped constitutional law and whose judges numerically dominated the lower federal courts for close to a decade after his presidency. Ronald Reagan has already begun the groundwork for his judicial legacy. With just two terms in office as compared to Roosevelt's three plus, Reagan will accomplish what only Roosevelt and Eisenhower accomplished during the last half century—naming a majority of the lower federal judiciary in active service. This makes it all the more significant to inquire what has been the Reagan first term record in the realm of judicial selection.

Judicature, vol. 68 (April–May 1985), p. 313. Reprinted from *Judicature*, the journal of the American Judicature Society. Sheldon Goldman is professor of political science at the University of Massachusetts-Amherst.

What changes have occurred in the selection process? What is the professional, demographic, and attribute profile of the Reagan appointees and how do they compare with appointees of previous administrations? Has the Administration been successful in placing on the bench those in harmony with Administration philosophy? What can we expect in the second term? These are the questions that this article confronts. . . .*

SELECTION UNDER REAGAN

A striking characteristic of the judicial selection process in the Reagan Administration has been the formalization of the process by institutionalizing interaction patterns and job tasks that in previous administrations were more informal and fluid. There have also been changes of more substantive import.

The center of judicial selection activity in previous administrations was the Deputy Attorney General's Office, with an assistant to the deputy responsible for the details, and at times negotiations, associated with the selection process. During the Reagan Administration these responsibilities have shifted to the Office of Legal Policy. The Assistant Attorney General heading that office reports to the Deputy Attorney General but also has an independent role as a member of the President's Federal Judicial Selection Committee. Assisting the head of the Legal Policy division in matters concerning judicial selection is the Special Counsel for Judicial Selection, a post formally established in September of 1984. The Attorney General, Deputy Attorney General, the Assistant Attorney General for Legal Policy, the Special Counsel for Judicial Selection, and some of their assistants meet to make specific recommendations for judgeships to the President's Committee on Federal Judicial Selection.

The major substantive innovation in the selection process made by the Reagan Administration is the creation of the President's Committee on Federal Judicial Selection. This nine-member committee institutionalizes and formalizes an active White House role in judicial selection. . . . From the Justice Department are the Attorney General, Deputy Attorney General, Associate Attorney General, and the Assistant Attorney General for Legal Policy.

*The findings and analyses presented here concern all lifetime federal district and courts of appeals judges confirmed by the U.S. Senate of the 97th and 98th Congresses. The courts of appeals judges analyzed were only those appointed to the 11 numbered circuits and the Court of Appeals for the District of Columbia. Appointments to the Court of Appeals for the Federal Circuit, a court of specialized as opposed to general jurisdiction, were not included. The findings for the Reagan first term appointments are compared to those for the Johnson, Nixon, Ford, and Carter lifetime appointments to courts of general jurisdiction. During his first term Reagan named 129 to the district courts and 31 to the appeals courts.

The highest levels of the White House staff have played a continuing active role in the selection of judges. Legislative, patronage, political, and policy considerations are considered to an extent never before so systematically taken into account. This has assured policy coordination between the White House and the Justice Department, as well as White House staff supervision of judicial appointments.

The Committee does not merely react to the Justice Department's recommendations; it is also a source of names of potential candidacies and a vehicle for the exchange of important and relevant information. Furthermore, the president's personnel office conducts an investigation of prospective nominees *independent* of the Justice Department's investigation. It is perhaps not an overstatement to observe that the formal mechanism of the Committee has resulted in the most consistent ideological or policy-orientation screening of judicial candidates since the first term of Franklin Roosevelt.

It is also relevant to observe that this selection process innovation potentially contains an inherent source of tension as the perspective from the Justice Department can be quite different from that of the White House. . . .

Although the consequences of this shift is immediately apparent in terms of the screening of candidates, in the hands of a less ideologically oriented administration partisan patronage considerations could conceivably become the principal selection criterion. . . .

Another change in the process worthy of note is that the Reagan Administration is the first Republican Administration in 30 years in which the American Bar Association Standing Committee on Federal Judiciary was not actively utilized and consulted in the prenomination stage. From the Eisenhower Administration through the Ford Administration, Justice Department officials sounded out the ABA Standing Committee for tentative preliminary ratings of the leading candidates for a specific judgeship. These informal reports could be used by Justice officials in negotiations with senators and other officials of the president's party. At times they influenced the Justice officials' final selection. During the Carter Administration, however, this close working relationship ended as the Administration established its own judicial selection commission for appeals court appointments and most Democratic senators established analogous commissions for district court positions.

The Reagan Administration abolished the selection commission but has, with few exceptions, maintained a more formal relationship with the ABA Standing Committee and has not sought preliminary ratings on anyone but the individual the Administration has already settled on to nominate. This has also meant that unlike previous Republican Administrations which pledged not to nominate any person rated "Not Qualified" by the ABA Standing Committee, this administration has made no such pledge and is willing, if not persuaded by the Committee, to nominate the person of its choice even were the nominee rated "Not Qualified."

This is not to suggest that relations were cool with the ABA Committee. . . . Of course, the Administration has been concerned that its nominees receive high ABA ratings, but evidently it has not been willing to give the ABA Standing Committee an opportunity to influence the selection during the more fluid pre-nomination stage.

One further observation about the selection process is in order. The Reagan Administration repudiated the selection commission concept and in so doing abandoned the most potentially effective mechanism for expanding the net of possible judicial candidates to include women and racial minorities, groupings historically excluded from the judiciary. The Carter Administration's record in this regard was unprecedented, with Carter naming to the courts of appeals 11 women, nine black Americans (including one black woman), two Hispanics, and the first person of Asian ancestry (out of a total of 56 appointments). The Reagan record with regard to the appeals courts . . . falls markedly short of that.

DISTRICT COURT APPOINTMENTS

Occupation: If we look at the occupation at time of appointment we find that about 40 percent were members of the judiciary on the state bench or, in several instances, U.S. magistrates or bankruptcy judges. Only the Carter Administration of the past five administrations had a higher proportion of those who were serving as judges at the time they were chosen for the federal district bench. About eight per cent of the Reagan district court appointees were in politics or governmental positions but few of these were U.S. Attorneys; this also had been true for the Carter appointees but not for the appointees of previous administrations. It would appear, for whatever the reason, that the U.S. Attorney position is not the direct stepping-stone to a federal judgeship it once was, although both federal and state prosecutorial experience was prominent in the backgrounds of the judges. Also of note is that few law school professors were appointed, in contrast to the Reagan record for the courts of appeals. The Carter, Nixon, and Johnson Administrations appointed proportionately more law school professors than did Reagan in his first term.

Private law practice was the occupation at time of appointment for close to half the Reagan appointees. The range of the size of firm varied considerably, with close to 12 per cent affiliated with large firms (with 25 or more partners and/or associates) and a slightly lower proportion at the other end of the spectrum practicing in firms with four or fewer members or associates. This is roughly comparable to the distribution of the Carter appointees. . . .

Experience: Over 70 per cent of the first term Reagan district court appointments had either judicial or prosecutorial experience, a proportion comparable to the appointees of the Carter Administration, and the second highest of all five administrations' appointees. Of special interest and importance is that the proportion of those with judicial experience exceeded the proportion of those with prosecutorial experience—a trend begun only in the Carter Administration. Before Carter, prosecutorial experience was more frequent. . . . The result of this recent emphasis on judicial experience may be the growing professionalization of the American judiciary.

Education: The educational background of a majority of Reagan appointments to the district courts . . .was private school including the highly prestigious Ivy League schools. Only about one-third of Reagan appointees attended a public university for undergraduate work, whereas over 57 per cent of the Carter appointees attended public colleges—perhaps a reflection of poorer socioeconomic roots of a substantial segment of the Carter judges. Again, with law school education, the majority of the Reagan appointees attended private law schools while a bare majority of the Carter appointees attended public-supported law schools.

Although there are some problems with equating being able to attend a private undergraduate college with socioeconomic status, the argument can be made that it is a rough indicator. The findings for the Reagan appointees are consistent with earlier findings and compatible with findings from other studies suggesting that the socio-economic differences between the Republican and Democratic electorates are mirrored to some degree in the appointments of Republican and Democratic Administrations. . . . In sum, we can observe that with relatively few exceptions, there is a tendency for the typical Republican appointee to be of a higher socioeconomic status than the typical Democratic appointee. . . .

Affirmative action: The record of the Reagan first term district court appointments is a mixed one with regard to gender and race/ ethnicity. The Reagan Administration was, of course, responsible for the historic appointment of the first woman to the Supreme Court. At the district court level, the record . . . shows that the Reagan Administration's appointment of women was second only to the Carter Administration. Over nine per cent of the appointments went to women, and this suggests that the Administration, as well as some Republican senators, made an effort to recruit well qualified women. . . . It is also significant to note that by the end of the first term two women held important Justice Department positions that are concerned with judicial selection. . . .

The record as to black appointments, however, is markedly different. The Reagan first term record is not only the worst of all five administrations, . . . it is the worst since the Eisenhower Administration in which no blacks were appointed to life-time district court positions. Justice Department officials are aware of this poor record and have said they would like it to improve, but feel that it is extraordinarily difficult to find well qualified blacks who share the President's philosophy and are also willing to serve. Critics respond that the Administration has not made the recruitment of blacks a high priority in part because the black electorate votes overwhelmingly Democratic, and there is little political payoff in the appointment of blacks. In contrast, the proportion of Hispanics was second only to that of the Carter Administration. Some observers link that fact to the Republican Party effort to woo Hispanic voters in the 1984 election.

ABA ratings and other factors: When we examine the ratings of the ABA Standing Committee on Federal Judiciary we find that about seven per cent of the Reagan first term appointees to the district courts received the highest rating, that of Exceptionally Well Qualified. This is the best record since the Johnson Administration. The next highest rating, that of Well Qualified, was received by about 43 per cent, which means that half the Reagan appointees were in the top two categories. The Carter appointees received proportionately more Well Qualified ratings than did the Reagan appointees but fewer Exceptionally Well Qualified ratings. However, when the top two ratings are combined, 51 per cent of the Carter appointees fell into those categories—about the same as the Reagan appointees. . . .

In terms of party affiliation of district court appointees, approximately 97 per cent of the Reagan appointees were Republican, the highest partisanship level of all five administrations and the highest proportion of a president choosing members of his own party since Woodrow Wilson. The figures for previous prominent party activism suggest that the Reagan appointees had the highest proportion of all five administrations. However, there is no suggestion that the Reagan appointees with a record of party activism received their appointments solely because of their political activities. Instead, it must be recognized that a history of party activity is helpful to a judicial candidacy only when other factors are present such as distinguished legal credentials, and, particularly as far as the Reagan Administration is concerned, a judicial philosophy in harmony with that of the Administration. Suffice it to note that many of the Reagan appointees to both the district and appeals courts had impressive legal credentials as well as a background of partisan activism. . . . Also observe that about four out of ten Reagan appointees did *not* have a record of prominent partisan activism, although they of course had to receive sufficient political backing or clearance in order to have been nominated.

The religious origins or religious affiliation of the Reagan first term district court appointees differed markedly from the appointees of previous Republican administrations; Reagan appointed more Catholics and fewer Protestants—proportions similar to those of Democratic administrations. In fact, . . . the Republican Reagan Administration appointed proportionately more Catholics than did the Democratic Carter and Johnson Administrations. In the past, Republican administrations appointed more Protestants and fewer Catholics and Jews than did Democratic administrations; this could be attributed to the fact that the religious composition or mix of the parties was different and thus, to a large extent, so was the pool of potential judicial candidates from both parties. The finding for the Reagan appointees does not mean that the Administration gave greater preference to Catholics because of their religion than did previous Republican administrations, but rather that more Catholics have entered the potential pool from which Republican judicial nominees emerge thus increasing their proportion of appointees. This is consistent with the relatively heavy Catholic vote for Reagan in 1980 and especially 1984.

The average age of the Reagan appointees was about that of the Carter appointees and similar to that of the appointees of the previous three presidents.

. . . There were proportionately more millionaires among the Reagan district court appointees, over five times as many as the Carter appointees, and proportionately fewer Reagan appointees at the lower end of the economic spectrum. This suggests . . . that there is somewhat of a class difference between the Republican and Democratic appointees on the whole that is analogous to the socioeconomic differences among the electorates of the two parties. However, the findings also suggest that the Reagan and Carter appointees were for the most part drawn from the middle to upper classes.

APPEALS COURT APPOINTMENTS

Traditionally, senators of the president's party have had considerably less influence in the selection of appeals court as distinct from district court judges. This has meant that administrations have had more of an opportunity to pursue their policy agendas . . . by way of recruiting appeals judges who are thought to be philosophically sympathetic with such agendas. . . .

Occupation and experience: A striking finding . . . is that three out of five Reagan appeals court appointees and over half the Ford, Nixon, and Johnson appointees were already serving in the judiciary at the time of their appointment to the courts of appeals. Of the 19

Reagan appointees who were judges at the time of appointment, 16 were serving as federal district judges. . . . Just as with the selection of federal district judges, Justice Department officials felt more secure evaluating the candidacies of those with judicial track records. The Reagan Administration was particularly concerned not only with the professional quality of prospective nominees, but also with their judicial philosophy. As presidential counsel Fred F. Fielding noted, "We have an opportunity to restore a philosophical balance that you don't have across the board right now."

The promotion of a lower court judge to a higher court can also be seen as furthering the concept of a professional judiciary, although it does not appear that pure merit was the governing factor with the Reagan first term elevations. The same undoubtedly holds true for the appointments of other administrations. Politically, the elevation of a federal district judge enables an administration to make two appointments: the elevation that fills the appeals court position; and the appointment to fill the vacancy thus created on the federal district bench.

Another striking finding is the proportion of Reagan appeals court appointees who were law school professors at the time of appointment. Because Robert Bork had left his professorship at Yale Law School some six months before and at the time of selection was a senior partner in the Washington, D.C. firm of Kirkland & Ellis, he was not counted in the professor of law category. [See Reading 14.5.] Were he counted, the proportion of professors of law would be about one out of five Reagan appeals court appointees, a modern record.

Bork, as well as the five other law professors, were all known as conservative thinkers and advocates of judicial restraint with a tendency toward deference to government in matters of alleged civil liberties or civil rights violations. These appointees also had a track record of published works so that their candidacies could be evaluated as to their compatibility with the Administration's vision of the role of the courts. Further, the appointment of academics was expected to provide intellectual leadership on the circuits and a potential pool of candidates for vacancies that might occur on the Supreme Court. . . .

In terms of experience, about three out of four Reagan appointees had judicial or prosecutorial experience in their backgrounds, with judicial experience being the most prominent. . . . This also supports the suggestion that Justice officials were more concerned with judicial track records in evaluating ideological compatibility than with prosecutorial track records.

Education and affirmative action: The majority of the Reagan appointees as well as the Carter, Nixon, and Johnson appointees attended private schools for both their undergraduate and law school training. . . . However, the proportion of Reagan appointees with an

Ivy League law school education was the *lowest* of all five administrations. Although some of the appointees attended prestigious non-Ivy League law schools both public and private, it may be that the quality of legal education of the Reagan appeals court appointees, like that of the district court appointees, was on the whole somewhat lower than the Carter appointees. . . .

In terms of appointments of women and minorities, the first term Reagan record for the appeals courts can be seen as a dramatic retreat from the Carter record. Of 31 appeals court appointees only one was a woman, only one was black, and only one was Hispanic. . . .

ABA ratings and other factors: The proportion of Reagan appointees with the highest ABA rating, that of Exceptionally Well Qualified, was the highest since the Johnson Administration. However, the Reagan appointees also had the highest proportion of all five administrations of those with the lowest Qualified rating. Interestingly, all five who were professors of law at the time of their nominations were only rated Qualified despite their distinguished legal scholarly achievements. This suggests that the ABA ratings are biased against legal academics who are not active practitioners. . . .

None of the Reagan first term appointees to the appeals courts were Democrats. . . .

As for religious origin or affiliation, the Reagan appeals court appointments were somewhat similar to his district court appointments with the proportion of Catholics akin to that of the previous Democratic Administrations of Carter and Johnson.

Given the importance of the appeals courts and the desire of the Reagan Administration to place on the bench those with a judicial philosophy compatible with that of the Administration, one might expect that there would be an active effort to recruit younger people who could be expected to remain on the bench longer. There is a hint that this may have occurred. The average age of the Reagan appointees was 51.5, the lowest for all five administrations. . . .

The net worth of the Reagan appointees compared to the Carter appointees . . . and the differences between both groups of appointees are similar to those for the district court appointees. Over one in five Reagan appointees were millionaires as compared to one in ten Carter appointees. Two-thirds had a net worth between $200,-000 and under $1 million, compared to 56 per cent of the Carter appointees. At the lowest end of the net worth continuum, one in ten Reagan appointees had a net worth of under $200,000, compared to one in three of the Carter appointees.

The net worth findings for the appeals courts, as well as the district courts, underscore the importance of Chief Justice Warren Burger's urgent request that Congress dramatically increase the pay of the federal judiciary. . . . [T]here is a very real danger that the federal courts will soon become the preserve of the wealthy for only they will be able to afford the assumption of judicial office. If it is considered desirable that monetary considerations not affect judicial recruitment, then judicial salaries will have to be increased significantly.

IDEOLOGICAL SUCCESS?

We have thus far seen how the Reagan Administration has to some extent reshaped the judicial selection process, and we have examined the demographic and attribute profiles of the Reagan district and appeals court appointees as compared to those of four previous presidents. The questions remain, have the Reagan appointees met the expectations of the Administration? Have the Reagan appointees begun to shift the ideological balance on the lower courts?

The answers to these questions must await systematic empirical analysis; there is fragmentary evidence that has begun to emerge, however, that suggests that the Reagan Administration on the whole is satisfied. . . .

Ours is a historic political era that in the pendulum of American politics has come every 30 to 40 years. . . . Barring economic or military catastrophies, the cycle of conservative Republican domination may well last until the turn of the century. The Reagan Administration correctly sees the courts as having the power to further or hinder Administration goals; thus judicial appointments are of major importance for this Administration in its attempt to reshape public policy.*

4.6   *". . . a President who sets out to 'pack' the Court seeks to appoint people to the Court who are sympathetic to his political or philosophical principles. There is no reason in the world why a President should not do this."*

PRESIDENTIAL APPOINTMENTS TO THE SUPREME COURT

William H. Rehnquist

One of the proud and just boasts of the constitutional system of government which we have in the United States is that even the

*Statistical tables comparing the Reagan, Carter, Ford, Nixon, and Johnson appointees to the district courts and courts of appeals, and net worth of Reagan and Carter judicial appointees, are omitted. See 68 *Judicature* 313 (1985).

Speech at the College of Law, University of Minnesota, October 19, 1984. Reprinted by permisssion. William H. Rehnquist is Associate Justice, Supreme Court of the United States.

President is not above the law. The justness of the boast is rooted in decisions such as the Steel Seizure Case, in which the Court rebuffed the claims of President Truman, and in the Nixon Tapes Case, in which the Court rebuffed the claims of President Nixon. But though the President, the head of the Executive Branch, may be subject under our system to checks and balances administered by the Judicial Branch of government, the courts themselves are subject to a different form of check and balance administered by the President. Vacancies in the federal judiciary are filled by the President with the advice and consent of the United States Senate. Just as the courts may have their innings with the President, the President comes to have his innings with the courts. It seems fitting, particularly in the year of a presidential election, to inquire what history shows as to the propensity of presidents to "pack" the Court, and the extent to which they have succeeded in any such effort.

I use the word "pack" as the best verb available, realizing full well that it has a highly pejorative connotation. But it ought not to have such a connotation when used in this context; the second edition of Webster's unabridged dictionary, which happens to be the one I have in my study, defines the verb "pack" as "to choose or arrange (a jury, committee, etc.) in such a way as to secure some advantage, or to favor some particular side or interest." Thus a President who sets out to "pack" the Court seeks to appoint people to the Court who are sympathetic to his political or philosophical principles.

There is no reason in the world why a President should not do this. One of the many marks of genius which our Constitution bears is the fine balance struck in the establishment of the Judicial Branch, avoiding both subservience to the supposedly more vigorous Legislative and Executive Branches, on the one hand, and to total institutional isolation from public opinion, on the other. The performance of the Judicial Branch of the United States government for a period of nearly two hundred years has shown it to be remarkably independent of the other coordinate branches of that government. Yet the institution has been constructed in such a way that the public will, in the person of the President of the United States—the one official who is elected by the entire nation—have something to say about the membership of the Court, and thereby indirectly about its decisions.

Surely we would not want it any other way. We want our federal courts, and particularly the Supreme Court of the United States, to be independent of popular opinion when deciding the particular cases or controversies which come before them. The provision for tenure during good behavior and the prohibition against diminution of compensation have proved more than adequate to secure that sort of independence. The result is that judges are responsible to no electorate or constituency. But the manifold provisions of the Constitution with which judges must deal are by no means crystal clear in their import, and reasonable minds may differ as to which interpretation is proper. When a vacancy occurs on the Court, it is entirely appropriate that that vacancy be filled by the President, responsible to a national constituency, as advised by the Senate, whose members are responsible to regional constituencies. Thus, public opinion has some say in who shall become judges of the Supreme Court.

The answer to the first question I posed—have Presidents in the past attempted to "pack" the Court—is easy; the Presidents who have been sensible of the broad powers which they have possessed, and been willing to exercise those powers, have all but invariably tried to have some influence on the philosophy of the Court as a result of their appointments to that body. This should come as a surprise to no one.

The answer to the second question which I posed—how successful have Presidents been in their efforts to pack the Court—is more problematical. . . .

[H]istory teaches us, I think, that even a "strong" President determined to leave his mark on the Court—a President such as Lincoln or Franklin Roosevelt—is apt to be only partially successful. Neither the President nor his appointees can foresee what issues will come before the Court during the tenure of the appointees, and it may be that none had thought very much about these issues. Even though they agree as to the proper resolution of current cases, they may well disagree as to future cases involving other questions when, as judges, they study briefs and hear arguments. Longevity of the appointees, or untimely deaths such as those of Justice Murphy and Justice Rutledge, may also frustrate a President's expectations; so also may the personal antagonisms developed between strong-willed appointees of the same President.

All of these factors are subsumed to a greater or lesser extent by observing that the Supreme Court is an institution far more dominated by centrifugal forces, pushing towards individuality and independence, than it is by centripetal forces pulling for hierarchial ordering and institutional unity. The well-known checks and balances provided by the Framers of the Constitution have supplied the necessary centrifugal force to make the Supreme Court independent of Congress and the President. The degree to which a new Justice should change his way of looking at things when he "puts on the robe" is emphasized by the fact that Supreme Court appointments almost invariably come "one at a time," and each new appointee goes alone to take his place with eight colleagues who are already there. Unlike his freshman counterpart in the House of Representatives, where if there has been a strong political tide running at the time of a particular election there may be as many as forty or fifty or eighty new members who form a bloc and cooperate with one another, the new judicial appointee brings no cohorts with him.

A second series of centrifugal forces is at work within the Court itself, pushing each Member of the Court to be thoroughly independent of his colleagues. The Chief Justice has some authority that the Associate Justices do not have, but this is relatively insignificant compared to the extraordinary independence that each Justice has from every other Justice. Tenure is assured no matter how one votes in any given case; one is independent not only of public opinion, of the President, and of Congress, but of one's eight colleagues as well. When one puts on the robe, one enters a world of public scrutiny and professional criticism which sets great store by individual performance, and much less store upon the virtue of being a "team player."

The Supreme Court is to be independent of the legislative and executive branches of the government; yet by reason of vacancies occurring on that Court, it is to be subjected to indirect infusions of the popular will in terms of the President's use of his appointment power. But the institution is so structured that a brand-new presidential appointee, perhaps feeling himself strongly loyal to the President who appointed him, and looking for colleagues of a similar mind on the Court, is immediately beset with the institutional pressures which I have described. He identifies more and more strongly with the new institution of which he has become a member, and he learns how much store is set by his behaving independently of his colleagues. I think it is these institutional effects, as much as anything, which have prevented even strong Presidents from being any more than partially successful when they sought to "pack" the Supreme Court.

4.7   *"This is not to say that the merit plan is wholly meritless or evil."*

MR. JUSTICE MARSHALL COMMENTS ON THE MISSOURI PLAN

As you may know, exactly one month ago President Carter issued an executive order creating a new mechanism for selecting federal appellate judges. Under this order, each time a vacancy on a court of appeals occurs, a panel will be activated to report to the President the names of the five persons considered "best qualified" to fill the vacancy. These panels will consist of approximately equal numbers

Remarks by Mr. Justice Thurgood Marshall at the spring meeting of the American College of Trial Lawyers in Coronado, California, March 14, 1977. Reprinted with permission. Marshall was appointed to the Supreme Court in 1967 by President Johnson.

of lawyers and nonlawyers and will be drawn, in part, from the circuit in which the vacancy occurs. Presumably, the President will make every effort to select his nominees from these lists, as he did while Governor of Georgia.

The President's plan, you will note, to a large degree follows the so-called "merit plan" or "Missouri Plan" for selecting judges. This plan, first proposed by Dean Kales of Northwestern Law School in 1914, has spread rapidly in recent years; since 1970 the number of States using it has more than doubled, and almost half the States presently select some or all of their judges under the merit system. My aim, today, is to raise some questions—and express some reservations—about this system.

Of course, no one opposes selecting judges on merit; the alternative, after all, is a meritless selection system, hardly an appealing prospect. Nor can one quarrel with the goal, perhaps first voiced in this country by George Washington, of choosing "the fittest characters to expound the laws and dispense justice": again one need only consider the alternative. The crucial questions are what types of persons make "the fittest" judges, and by what process are they best elevated to the bench.

In theory, at least, the Missouri Plan speaks only to the second question—the question of process. Its answer is that "the fittest"—however defined—are best selected by creating a commission of lawyers and laymen to submit a small list of names to the executive from which he must choose judges. My concern, as I shall explain, is that this process will subtly influence the definition of "fitness," by giving preeminent weight to technical or professional selection criteria.

Insofar as the merit plan is designed simply to put an end to cronyism and patronage in judicial appointments, no one can quarrel with it. I can think of no task that judges are properly called upon to perform that requires prior experience as a friend or backer of the appointing official (or his party). I might add, however, that the one major study that has been done of the first 20 years of the merit plan in Missouri gives substantial reason to question whether the plan can remove friendship with the executive as a criterion for judicial selection.

But questions of effectiveness aside, creating an elaborate set of commissions with broad powers seems unnecessary simply to eliminate cronyism; I cannot help believing that there is an easier way. Perhaps for this reason, proponents of the merit plan never rest their defense on this limited, essentially negative ground. Rather, they contend that it is affirmatively desirable to have a group of lawyers and laypersons assigned the tasks of ferreting out candidates for judgeships, developing information about the candidates, and determining who is best qualified.

I see no basis for objecting to commissions which perform the first two tasks. But I know of no one who suggests that the commissions should simply gather names and information for use by the executive. The crux of the merit system, in the eyes of its advocates, is the selection function of the commissions.

It is this crux that I find troubling. That is not just because I come from Washington, where skepticism about committees is almost as prevalent as committees; indeed in Washington it is said that "nothing is impossible—until you assign it to a committee." I am troubled by judicial selection by committee because it seems to me that two biases, or risks of biases, inhere in the process: (1) objective criteria will be given undue weight; and (2) to the extent subjective factors are considered, they will be value-free or technical ones.

The temptation for committees to rely on objective criteria is obvious. Such criteria simplify the task of paring down long lists of names to manageable numbers. Moreover, they can avoid endless debates as to which candidates have demonstrated the best knowledge of the law, for example, by providing seemingly clear measurements.

Perhaps the clearest example of the over-emphasis on objective factors is the weight nominating committees have assigned to prior judicial experience. A national study of members of such commissions found that after mental and physical health, this was the background factor the commissioners considered most important. Similarly, the twenty-year study in Missouri found that 57% of the intermediate court judges and 70% of the Supreme Court judges appointed under the merit plan had prior judicial experience. Yet I know of no evidence indicating that appellate judges with prior experience make better judges than those lacking such experience; to the contrary, evaluations of Supreme Court Justices demonstrate, as Felix Frankfurter put it, that at least with respect to my court, "the correlation between prior judicial experience and fitness . . . is zero."

Much the same may be true of two other objective criteria on which many place great weight: the requirement that nominees have (1) "at least fifteen years significant legal experience," and, (2) for trial judges, that the nominees have had "substantial experience in the adversary system." The first of these requirements effectively excludes all lawyers under the age of 40 and many lawyer-politicians; the second excludes from the trial bench the overwhelming majority of lawyers. It is clear to me, however, that at the very least some of those disqualified for lack of experience—Learned Hand, for one— should not be excluded from consideration. Persons like Judge Hand either already have acquired or could readily acquire the knowledge that experience is thought to guarantee. On the other hand, some who are included by virtue of their experience actually should be disqualified on this basis. These persons have spent too many years learning undesirable practices or approaches. In fact, I know of no empirical evidence to justify either experience requirement. The study of Supreme Court Justices to which I earlier referred found that more of those appointed at a younger age (in this context, under 53) went on to greatness—including Justice Joseph Story, appointed at age 32.

But what troubles me most about the merit system is *not* that it precludes the appointment of some well-qualified persons who don't meet more-or-less arbitrary standards. I am more concerned that the merit plan may compel or induce the appointment of judges simply because they are technically well-qualified, without regard to their basic values, philosophy, or life experience.

It is to be expected that nominating commissions will tend to ignore value-related considerations. We live in an age in which values are viewed as subjective. Unless a nominating committee happens to be homogenous, therefore, it is unlikely to agree on the values that judges should hold. Moreover, even if the committee could agree, it would be improper for it to impose its values on the selection process. These committees typically are neither representative nor accountable bodies. The national study of state nominating committees found, for example, that 98% of the committee members are white, 90% are male, and that the lay members are largely businessmen and bankers.

Rather than looking to the values of would-be nominees, then, nominating committees may be expected to look exclusively to the nominees' professional abilities: their knowledge of the law, proficiency at writing, and ability to "think like a lawyer." As my late friend and colleague Judge Charles Clark put it with characteristic grace, such committees look "to the head exclusively and not to the heart." But as Charlie Clark also insisted, judging is more than just an exercise in technique or craft; it calls for value judgments. This is true of the trial judge required to decide, for example, whether the risk of prejudice outweighs the probative value of a piece of evidence, or whether the risk that an offender will commit more crimes outweighs the offender's interest in retaining his liberty before trial or pending appeal. It is equally true of the appellate judge, required to resolve conflicting claims between liberty and order, equality and efficiency, states' rights and federal power. Indeed studies of judicial behavior have uniformly found clear voting patterns traceable to the attitudes or values of the judges. Thus, as Judge Clark concluded, "it is of truly vital importance that the inner convictions or bias of candidates for judicial appointment be appraised."

Of course, nothing in the merit system necessarily disables the appointing official—who *is* popularly elected—from considering "inner convictions or bias" in making his selections. But it is at least possible that, by excluding values from their inquiry, nominating committees inadvertently will develop lists of ideologically similar persons. It is also possible that the members of a nominating committee will all agree as to the values that judges should hold, and will make their selections accordingly. In either event, the executive could be precluded from appointing judges who share his—and presumably his constituency's—basic philosophical orientation. And even when nominating committees produce ideologically diverse lists, the thrust of merit selection may persuade some appointing officials that it is somehow illegitimate for them to consider the attitudes or experiences of potential nominees. This, I submit, would be tragic. . . .

This is not to say that the merit plan is wholly meritless or evil. As I said at the outset, I intend only to raise questions and concerns —not to pass definitive judgments. And since I earlier referred to President Carter's executive order, I should note that it may avoid many of the problems I have noted, since it first guarantees women and minority groups representation on the nominating panels; second, requires the panels to recommend only those who have demonstrated "commitment to equal justice under laws"; and third, does not oblige the President to accept every panel's choices. Nevertheless, I am *not* persuaded that it is either necessary or desirable to give any nominating panel the power to choose the three or five most qualified persons; it seems to me sufficient to allow the panels to search for candidates, generate information, and perhaps make evaluations. But whatever one's ultimate views on the merit system I think it essential that the biases and risks inherent in the process be carefully exposed so that those involved in making selections can be attentive to them. . . .

PART THREE
Judicial Power

5
Access to
Judicial Power

As inheritors of the common law tradition, federal judges cannot apply their power until someone brings a case before them. Courts, as Justice Robert H. Jackson once said, lack a self-starter. Judges who act within the legal framework can only decide issues when they come to court in accordance with the jurisdictional rules that Congress has laid down. But even then the judicial process does not automatically go into operation. Judges, especially Supreme Court justices, have long felt that overuse can cheapen the value of their decisions, and they refuse to decide a dispute simply because someone has money enough to hire a lawyer. The limitations imposed on access to the courts are often stated in such technical language as "standing to sue," but fundamentally what is involved is a concern among judges to avoid involvement in controversies that, for whatever reason, they feel it imprudent to handle.

Most of the restrictions and standing requirements governing access to the courts date from the time when the typical litigants were those who went to court to promote or protect their own personal or proprietary interests. But lawsuits have increasingly been brought by individuals or groups who sue in a representative capacity to further broad social, economic, or ideological goals, requiring courts to make some accommodations in the traditional rules of access for these non-traditional plaintiffs.

JURISDICTION: CASES AND CONTROVERSIES

"Jurisdiction" refers to the persons about whom and the matters about which a court has authority to make decisions. Jurisdiction is defined by the Constitution, by statute, and by the common law, and judges acting within their jurisdiction are immune from legal responsibility for any consequences of their decisions. Upholding judicial immunity in

182

Bradley v. Fisher (1871), the Supreme Court said that the rule was not "for the protection of a malicious or corrupt judge, but for the benefit of the public, whose interest it is that the judges should be at liberty to exercise their functions with independence, and without fear of consequences." (Reading 5.1.)

So far as federal courts are concerned, jurisdiction is limited to "cases" and "controversies." These are technical terms that refer to real disputes in which the interests of two or more persons are in collision. Federal judges say they will not exert their power—and risk their prestige—to answer hypothetical, academic, or abstract questions or to hand down a decision where a judgment can have no practical effect.

Muskrat v. United States (1911) is one of the leading cases on the necessity of adverse interests. Congress had passed a statute authorizing Cherokee Indians to contest the validity of earlier legislation that had restricted their land rights. The Supreme Court, however, ruled that no actual controversy existed; for although both parties had real interests, there was no live disagreement between them, only an effort by both parties to obtain a ruling on the constitutionality of Indian regulations.[1]

The requirement of a case or controversy is also one of the reasons federal judges give for refusing advisory opinions. It is the practice in a few states—and in many foreign countries—for judges of the highest court to advise the executive or legislature, when so requested, as to their views on the constitutionality of proposed policy. Since the time of Chief Justice John Jay, however, federal judges have claimed that the absence of a case or controversy prevents them from performing a similar function. Nevertheless, on occasion judges have broken their own rule of judicial noninterference and have offered advice. Also, judges have occasionally conferred in private with political leaders and given informal rather than formal opinions.

Supreme Court justices have sometimes given advice in an institutional but indirect manner. The Judiciary Act of 1925 granting the Court wide discretion in controlling its docket was largely drafted by the justices on the Taft Court, and Taft and his associates openly lobbied for its passage. In 1937 when the Senate was considering Roosevelt's Court packing plan, Chief Justice Hughes sent an open letter to Senator Burton K. Wheeler advising that an increase in the

---

[1] In *Immigration and Naturalization Service v. Chadha* (1983) the House of Representatives had used the so-called "legislative veto" to force the INS to deport an alien whose deportation had been suspended by the Attorney General. Both the INS and Chadha agreed that the one-house veto was unconstitutional, and consequently counsel for the House contended that this was "a friendly, non-adversary proceeding." But the Court held that a live controversy—whether Chadha was to be deported—was presented and said: "It would be a curious result if, in the administration of justice, a person would be denied access to the courts because the Attorney General . . . agreed with the legal arguments asserted by the individual."

number of justices would not allow the allegedly overworked Court to sit in separate panels to hear cases, because the Constitution commands that there be "one Supreme Court." Chief Justice Burger has regarded it as part of his job to let Congress know what kind of legislation he thought would be good for the courts and what the impact of proposed legislation would be on the judicial establishment.

Judges have occasionally given advice to Congress in their opinions to guide future legislation. In 1922, for example, Chief Justice Taft, speaking for the Court in *Hill v. Wallace,* held that a federal statute regulating transactions in grain futures was unconstitutional. Such matters, Taft said, "cannot come within the regulatory power of Congress as such, unless they are regarded by Congress, from the evidence before it, as directly interfering with interstate commerce so as to be an obstruction or a burden thereon." Congress took the hint and a few months later passed the Grain Futures Act, declaring that grain-market manipulations were obstructing interstate commerce. In *Board of Trade v. Olsen* (1923), the Court promptly upheld the new statute.

In *Regents of the University of California v. Bakke* (1978) the Court held that a white applicant for admission to medical school had been unconstitutionally rejected because of preference given to minority applicants. But Justice Powell in his opinion volunteered the advice that the kind of affirmative action program operated by Harvard University would be constitutionally acceptable.

TEST CASES

Test cases deliberately contrived to secure a judicial ruling on a constitutional issue are perfectly proper and effective, provided that the constitutional "case or controversy" requirements are met. Such organizations as the American Civil Liberties Union or the National Association for the Advancement of Colored People are much concerned with finding good test cases involving constitutional issues on which they hope to draw a favorable ruling from the Supreme Court.[2]

---

[2] The planning that may go into setting up a test case is illustrated by the litigation aimed at establishing that James Joyce's novel *Ulysses,* which had been published in Paris in the 1920s, could be published in the United States without violating the obscenity laws. Random House bought the American rights from the Paris publisher and arranged to have one copy openly carried into the United States through Customs, where Random House expected it to be seized as an obscene book. The plan almost failed when a bored Customs official said: "Oh, for God's sake, everybody brings that in. We don't pay any attention to it." But the book's owner insisted, the book was seized, and the landmark ruling by Judge John M. Woolsey in *United States v. One Book Entitled "Ulysses"* (1934) was the result. (David Margolick, *New York Times,* December 6, 1983.)

INTEREST AND STANDING

In addition to demonstrating a clash of interests, a plaintiff must show that the interest asserted is a legally protected one. Traditionally, to acquire the status of a legal right, a claim had to be grounded in a specific statutory or constitutional provision or, more generally, to involve one of those property or pocketbook interests the common law recognized as deserving judicial protection.

But more than a legally protected right must be at stake. To gain standing to sue, a plaintiff must establish that the right or claim asserted is a personal one, not that of other parties or the public at large. A long-established exception to this requirement is the taxpayer's suit, a favorite method for initiating litigation in state courts to test state or local expenditures, bond issues, or special assessments. As the title implies, the only requirement is that of being a taxpayer in the jurisdiction involved.

Frothingham v. Mellon (1923) prohibited federal courts from entertaining taxpayers' suits as a method of testing congressional expenditures. This bar was maintained until 1968 when *Flast v. Cohen* relaxed the rule, at least to the extent of permitting suits to test whether congressional grants benefiting parochial schools amounted to an establishment of religion in violation of the First Amendment.

Flast symbolized what was at that time a general trend toward easing the requirements for judicial review. Congress, concerned about arbitrary and unreviewable actions of federal administrative agencies, had provided in the Administrative Procedure Act of 1946 that any person "suffering legal wrong because of agency action, or adversely affected or aggrieved within the meaning of a relevant statute, is entitled to judicial review thereof." The Supreme Court gave this provision a broad interpretation in *Association of Data Processing Service Organizations v. Camp* (1970), specifically rejecting the old standing test of a "recognized legal interest"; as Kenneth C. Davis said, "A huge portion of the former foundation of the law of standing was thus knocked out."[3] Supported by *Flast,* Raoul Berger asserted in 1969 that "the notion that the Constitution demands injury to a personal interest as a prerequisite to attacks on allegedly unconstitutional action is historically unfounded."[4]

There have been other occasional challenges to the direct injury–personal interest test for standing. For example, a denial of one party's constitutional rights, which might have repercussions adversely affecting the rights of a second party, might be sufficient to give the second party standing. Thus the Supreme Court allowed a private religious school in *Pierce v. Society of Sisters* (1925) to sue to enjoin enforce-

---

[3] "The Liberalized Law of Standing," 37 *University of Chicago Law Review* 450, 453 (1970).
[4] "Standing to Sue in Public Actions," 78 *Yale Law Journal* 816, 840 (1969).

ment of a state statute that infringed on parents' rights to send their children to schools of their own choice. Similarly, in *Peters v. Kiff* (1972) the Court recognized the standing of a white man to challenge the exclusion of blacks from the grand jury that indicted him and the trial jury that convicted him.[5]

Prisoners of course have access to courts to test the legality of their detention by habeas corpus or other postconviction remedies provided by law, but it is only recently that they have had standing to complain about the conditions of their incarceration. A number of such suits have been successful in state and lower federal courts, and a few have risen to the Supreme Court level. For example, in *Estelle v. Gamble* (1976) the Court ruled that deliberate indifference of prison officials to a prisoner's serious illness or injury would constitute cruel and unusual punishment in violation of the Eighth Amendment. *O'Connor v. Donaldson* (1975) was significant as the first recognition by the Supreme Court of the rights to treatment of persons committed to mental institutions.

More recently, however, the policy of the Burger Court has moved toward restoring strict standing requirements and limiting access to federal courts. In 1984, *Hudson v. Palmer* held that prison inmates had no reasonable expectation of privacy entitling them to protection of the Fourth Amendment against unreasonable searches of their cells and seizure of noncontraband private possessions. (Reading 14.4.)

ACCESS FOR INTEREST GROUPS

The problem of standing is likely to present special problems for interest groups or organizations which go to court to achieve public policies rather than merely to vindicate personal rights. Lawsuits are especially attractive instruments for groups whose small size, lack of prestige, and limited cash limit their influence in other political forums. While their supply of the usual political weapons may be short, these groups sometimes have moral, statutory, or constitutional claims that may be persuasive to judges. It is hardly necessary to mention the areas where resort to the judiciary achieved politically significant results that at the time could not have been wrung from legislative or executive officials—racial desegregation, legislative reapportionment, limitations on capital punishment, prison reform, and protection of illegitimate children against legal discrimination stand out among dozens of examples.

Nearly three-quarters of a century ago, Arthur F. Bentley provided the theoretical foundation for the representation of group interests

---

[5] *Singleton v. Wulff* (1976) recognized the right of physicians to challenge a state law excluding Medicaid payment for abortions that were not "medically indicated," on the ground that the physicians would suffer "concrete injury" from the operation of the statute.

through judicial action. He included courts in his general thesis concerning social pressures. Interest groups exert pressure to get the support of the law, and courts respond to these pressures:

> so far from being a sort of legal machine, [courts] are a functioning part of this government, responsive to the group pressures within it, representatives of all sort of pressures, and using their representative judgment to bring these pressures to balance, not indeed in just the same way, but on just the same basis that any other agency does.[6]

Subsequently David B. Truman, Jack W. Peltason, and Clement E. Vose refined and applied Bentley's insights to current techniques of group representation before courts.[7] (Reading 5.2.)

Some interest groups have litigation as one of their principal reasons for existence. These groups include the American Civil Liberties Union, the NAACP's Legal Defense and Education Fund, the Sierra Club, and a growing number of public-interest law firms or centers with both liberal and conservative orientations.[8]

Two general strategies are available to these groups. First, they may wait for cases to arise within their field of concern and then assume all or part of the task of representing a litigant in court. The ACLU typically relies on this tactic. Parties who believe that their constitutional rights are being violated by prosecution or other governmental coercive action come to the ACLU and request that it represent them in court action. The organization, having limited resources, generally agrees to handle only those cases in which it conceives that an important constitutional principle is at stake or may be established.

The alternative strategy is to go out looking for abuses that can be attacked by filing test cases. This tactic has been standard with the NAACP, particularly in the years immediately before and after the *Brown* decision, when it was necessary for NAACP attorneys to travel around the country looking for favorable situations in which to bring desegregation suits and for plaintiffs in whose names such suits could be filed. Authorities in several Southern states countered the NAACP's efforts by charging that its attorneys were engaged in fomenting litigation, an unethical and illegal practice under state laws. In *National Association for the Advancement of Colored People v. Button* (1963),

---

[6] *The Process of Government* (Chicago: University of Chicago Press, 1908), p. 393.

[7] David B. Truman, *The Governmental Process* (New York: Knopf, 1951), Ch. 15; Jack W. Peltason, *Federal Courts in the Political Process* (New York: Random House, 1955); Clement E. Vose, *Caucasians Only: The Supreme Court, the NAACP, and the Restrictive Covenant Cases* (Berkeley: University of California Press, 1959).

[8] Karen O'Connor and Lee Epstein, "The Rise of Conservative Interest Group Litigation," 45 *Journal of Politics* 479 (1983). Oliver A. Houck, "With Charity For All: Public Interest Law Firms," 93 *Yale Law Journal* 1415 (1984), questions whether "business" public-interest law firms should be entitled to tax exemption as public charities.

the Supreme Court held that these laws forbade only stirring up litigation for private gain; applying them to lawsuits brought to vindicate
associational rights would violate the First Amendment. As the Court
said, "for such a group [as the NAACP], association for litigation may
be the most effective form of political association."9 (Reading 5.3.)

Groups seeking to litigate public issues must demonstrate a legally
protected interest or right not shared with the public generally. This
problem has been particularly difficult for the conservationists and
ecologists who have been fighting environmental damage over wide
areas affecting great numbers of people. Judges have often accorded
standing to organizations such as the Sierra Club; but in one important
case, *Sierra Club v. Morton* (1972), the Supreme Court ruled that the
Club had failed to allege that its members would be affected by a
proposed ski resort in a national forest and consequently that the Club
lacked standing to protest the development under the Administrative
Procedure Act. Justice Douglas, dissenting, proposed that a river
should be given standing as a plaintiff to speak for "the ecological unit
of life that is part of it."10

In contrast to the *Sierra Club* ruling, *United States v. SCRAP*
(1973) granted standing to a volunteer group challenging the Interstate Commerce Commission's policy on railroad rates that made recy-
cling operations more expensive. Standing, the Court said, "is not
confined to those who show economic harm," adding, "aesthetic and
environmental well-being, like economic well-being, are important
ingredients of the quality of life in our society, and the fact that particular environmental interests are shared by the many rather than the few
does not make them less deserving of legal protection through the
judicial process."

Although environmentalists, buttressed by strong federal legislation, have been fairly successful in gaining access to the courts, many
interest groups have been unable to meet the standing requirements
as tightened by the Burger Court. Ad hoc citizens' organizations protesting against alleged governmental abuses or illegal actions have
often failed to achieve standing because they could not show they
suffered more harm or had a greater interest than the general public.
Thus in *Laird v. Tatum* (1972) the Court refused to hear a complaint
against Army surveillance of private citizens who were opposed to the
war in Vietnam; *United States v. Richardson* (1974) denied standing

9 In *In re Primus* (1978) an ACLU lawyer who had offered free legal assistance to a
South Carolina woman who had been sterilized as a condition of receiving public
medical assistance, had been publicly reprimanded by the state supreme court for
soliciting a client. The Supreme Court reversed, holding that solicitation of prospective litigants by nonprofit organizations that engage in litigation as a form of political
expression constitutes associational conduct entitled to First Amendment protection.
Compare *Ohralik v. Ohio State Bar Association* (1978).

10 By reason of the Endangered Species Act, this proposal has become a reality; see
Cabinet Mountains Wilderness/Scotchman's Peak Grizzly Bears v. Peterson (1982).

to a group seeking to compel publication of the CIA budget; and *Schlesinger v. Reservists Committee to Stop the War* (1974) rejected a suit asking the courts to declare it unconstitutional for members of Congress to hold commissions in the armed forces reserves.

Warth v. Seldin, decided by the Burger Court in 1975, further narrowed access to federal courts by holding that blacks, Puerto Ricans, and poor people, who were not residents of the town in which they worked, lacked standing to challenge that town's zoning laws. Plaintiffs had argued that the zoning regulations effectively excluded them from living in the town because the regulations banned low-cost housing. By a five-to-four vote the Supreme Court denied standing on the ground that they had not suffered "injury in fact" because they could not point to any particular low-cost housing project that would actually have been built but for the town's ordinances. (Reading 5.4.)

Continuing this strict attitude toward access, the Burger Court denied standing in two suits challenging Internal Revenue Service tax exemption practices. In *Simon v. Eastern Kentucky Welfare Rights Organization* (1975) an organization of low-income individuals, too poor to afford hospital services, had challenged tax exemptions granted to certain private hospitals. In *Allen v. Wright* (1984) parents of black children attending public schools in seven states brought a class-action suit asking for more rigorous enforcement of federal rules denying tax exemption to racially discriminatory private schools. The injury alleged was that black children were unable to attend fully desegregated public schools because large numbers of white children went to private schools that did not admit minority children. In a five-to-three ruling, Justice O'Connor held this injury only to be "abstract" though "stigmatic"; recognition of standing in such circumstances, she said, would transform the courts into "no more than a vehicle for the vindication of the value interests of concerned bystanders." (Reading 5.5.)

An attack on the Hyde Amendment, which forbade the use of federal funds to reimburse the costs of abortions under state Medicaid programs, partially failed for lack of standing in *Harris v. McRae* (1980). The case was brought by Medicaid recipients and church members who alleged, among other things, that the Hyde Amendment violated their free exercise of religious rights by incorporating into law the doctrines of the Roman Catholic Church. (Reading 5.6.) On the other hand, litigants bringing gender-discrimination suits have generally had no standing problems.

Valley Forge Christian College v. Americans United (1982) denied standing to a nonprofit organization, dedicated to the maintenance of the separation between church and state, to attack the transfer of an outmoded Armed Forces hospital to a religious educational institution. Justice Rehnquist rehearsed at length all the virtues of strict adherence to case or controversy limitations and to showing of an "actual injury" redressable by the courts. Justice Brennan, dissenting, protested the Court's failure to honor *Flast* and sharply criticized use of "standing to slam the courthouse door against plaintiffs who are entitled to full consideration of their claims on the merits."[11]

RIPENESS AND MOOTNESS

If governmental action is challenged in a lawsuit, the action must be sufficiently final to be "ripe" for review by federal courts. This rule forms the basis for the doctrine of exhaustion of administrative remedies, which requires that persons aggrieved by administrative decisions must have used all the procedures available for correcting the action administratively before they have standing to be heard in court.

The ripeness doctrine also bars access to court until the threat of adverse governmental action is immediate, as the experience of birth-control advocates in *Poe v. Ullman* (1961) demonstrates. (Reading 5.7.) Again, in *Communist Party v. Subversive Activities Control Board* (1961), the Supreme Court refused to consider the constitutionality of sanctions ordered by the Internal Security Act of 1952 against communist-action organizations, because the government's proceedings against the Communist party had not yet reached the sanctioning stage.

Conversely, events may have proceeded since the filing of the suit to a point where judicial action is no longer needed or cannot provide the relief requested. In these situations the case may be dismissed as moot. Judges occasionally resort to such holdings to avoid difficult decisions. Thus in *DeFunis v. Odegaard* (1974) a white applicant to a state law school who had been rejected for admission, contended that less qualified minority applicants had been accepted under an affirmative action program, and the trial judge ordered his admission. The university appealed, but by the time the case reached the Supreme Court DeFunis was in his third year of law school, and his graduation was guaranteed. By a five-to-four vote the Court, while recognizing that the same issue would be raised in subsequent suits, held this proceeding moot.

Kremens v. Bartley (1977) was a case where, as in *DeFunis,* the Court avoided a decision on the ground of mootness, leading Justice Brennan to protest that "the recent Art. III jurisdiction of this Court in

---

[11] But in two five-to-four rulings the Court rejected Rehnquist's position on standing. *Larson v. Valente* (1982) granted standing to Rev. Moon's Unification Church in a successful challenge to a Minnesota law imposing certain registration and reporting requirements on religious organizations that solicit more than 50 percent of their funds from nonmembers. And *Maryland v. Munson* (1984) struck down a state statute prohibiting charities from spending more than 25 percent of their gross income on fund raising. Rehnquist protested that the plaintiff had no standing—as a commercial fund-raising organization—to litigate the First Amendment issue.

such areas as mootness and standing is creating an obstacle course of confusing standardless rule to be fathomed by courts and litigants . . . without functionally aiding in the clear, adverse presentation of the constitutional questions presented."

Of course a strict application of the mootness doctrine would prevent many cases from ever being decided by the Supreme Court. In *Dunn v. Blumstein* (1972) a new resident of Tennessee challenged the law requiring one year's residence in the state as a qualification for voting. By the time the case got to the Supreme Court he had lived in the state for two years, but the Court did not regard the case as moot for that reason.[12] In *Roe v. Wade* (1973), one of the original decisions invalidating state laws regulating abortion, it was pregnancy that had given the plaintiff standing in 1970 when she filed the suit. The Supreme Court, deciding the case thirty-two months later, held that "pregnancy provides a classic justification for a conclusion of non-mootness." (Reading 5.8.)

In *Firefighters Local Union v. Stotts* (1984) the Court also rejected a claim of mootness. Under court order, the city of Memphis had employed some black firefighters to achieve a measure of racial balance. When a fiscal crisis required reduction in force, the federal district court sought to protect the positions of the newly hired blacks by ordering white firefighters to be laid off even though they had more seniority. In fact, under public pressure the white firefighters were promptly rehired, but the lawsuit they had begun and lost in the lower courts was nevertheless accepted by the Supreme Court and decided in their favor. While the immediate controversy was moot, the Court majority apparently saw this case as an important challenge to the principle of affirmative action.

CLASS ACTIONS

A critical resource for group litigants is the *class action,* a suit that one or several persons bring in their own behalf and in behalf "of all others similarly situated." The Federal Rules of Civil Procedure authorize class actions where a number of persons have a common legal right and the group is "so numerous as to make it impractical to bring them all before the court." Before allowing a class action to proceed, the judge must determine that such a class exists and that the plaintiffs are members of that class.

A class action permits the judge to make only one decision to settle

---

12 Donald Horowitz concludes that "the old prohibition on the decision of moot cases is now so riddled with exceptions that it is almost a matter of discretion whether to hear a moot case." *The Courts and Social Policy* (Washington, D.C.: The Brookings Institution, 1977), p. 8.

the rights of perhaps thousands of persons. From the interest group's viewpoint it also saves time and money. If, for instance, one black voter were to institute a class action against state officials and could prove that they were refusing to allow qualified blacks to vote, the injunction would require the officials to cease discrimination not only against the plaintiff but against *all* black voters. Other advantages include lessening the chance that a plaintiff will settle a case by compromise; usually the plaintiff cannot do so in a class action without the permission of the court. The class action also diminishes the possibility that a case will be dismissed as moot because the original plaintiff has died, moved away, or otherwise lost standing. To continue the suit under such circumstances, counsel need only substitute as plaintiff another member of the class.

In line with its efforts to reduce the work of federal judges, the Burger Court has limited class suits in federal courts. *Zahn v. International Paper Co.* (1973) was a diversity of citizenship suit, and in such suits the amount in controversy must be at least $10,000. But in *Zahn* the Court ruled that *every* member of the class action must have sustained $10,000 in damages, thereby precluding aggregation of a number of smaller claims in order to reach the $10,000 figure. In another class action, *Eisen v. Carlisle & Jacquelin* (1974), brought on behalf of all odd-lot purchasers of stock on the New York Stock Exchange over a four-year period, the Court held that the parties initiating a federal class action must notify, at their own expense, all other persons in the class—in this instance two and one-quarter million people.

Partly as a result of these decisions, recourse to class suits in the federal courts has subsided, decreasing from a high of 3,584 in 1976 to 988 in 1984. But the class suit remains an important instrument of redress. In 1976 a federal judge in the District of Columbia certified as a nationwide class action a suit on behalf of 750,000 low-income tenants against the Department of Housing and Urban Development, which ultimately settled in 1979 for $60 million. In 1980 a federal judge accepted 7,000 Vietnam veterans as a class in a suit against five companies that manufactured the allegedly carcinogenic defoliant Agent Orange used in Vietnam. In 1984 a federal judge in Philadelphia approved a suit against fifty-five asbestos manufacturers on behalf of the nation's primary and secondary schools—the first nationwide class action for property damage arising out of a product-liability question.[13]

The *Zahn* rule, moreover, does not apply to state courts, many of which operate under state laws facilitating the joining of consumers or others of like interest in class actions. Public prosecutors may also file suits on behalf of a class.

[13] *New York Times,* October 2, 1984.

AMICUS CURIAE BRIEFS

Persons or organizations not parties to a lawsuit may nonetheless gain the right to participate by securing status as amici curiae (friends of the court; singular, amicus curiae). As such they may submit briefs and perhaps even join in oral argument. The Supreme Court's rules provide that an amicus brief may be filed with the consent of the parties or, if either party refuses, by consent of the Court. The rules allow the Solicitor General to submit an amicus brief whenever he wishes. Indeed, the justices often invite him to do so because he can take a broader view of the controversy than the actual parties, and the expertise of his staff can repair deficiencies in litigants' arguments.[14] In the Reagan administration, the position of the Solicitor General was particularly important because of conservative pressures to file amicus briefs in cases raising controversial social issues. (Reading 5.9.)

When the Supreme Court reviews the constitutionality of an important policy operative in several states, it is customary for the attorney general of the state involved to ask his counterparts in other states to support his position by amicus briefs. Thus, when the New York public school prayer case came up in *Engel v. Vitale* (1962), twenty-two states submitted a brief asking that New York be permitted to continue the ceremony. In *Brewer v. Williams* (1977), where an admitted murderer's conviction was threatened on the ground of denial of counsel, attorneys general from twenty-one states plus the National District Attorneys Association and a citizens' group called Americans for Effective Law Enforcement filed amicus briefs. But in the landmark right to counsel case, *Gideon v. Wainwright* (1963), the effort of Florida's attorney general to secure support from other states backfired. Only two states responded favorably while, largely through the initiative of Walter F. Mondale, then attorney general of Minnesota, twenty-three states filed a brief supporting Gideon's constitutional right to counsel.

Among private organizations, the American Civil Liberties Union and its affiliates make probably the most frequent appearances as amici in Supreme Court litigation. In the seminal case of *Mapp v. Ohio* (1961), where the Court held that illegally seized evidence could not be used in state criminal trials, counsel for Mapp had not even raised the constitutional issue; it was a lawyer for the Ohio Civil Liberties Union, appearing as amicus, who had made this argument. In *DeFunis v. Odegaard* (1974) twenty-six briefs were filed in support of or in opposition to the University of Washington Law School's plan for preferential admission of minority students. But this record was far eclipsed in *Regents of the University of California v. Bakke,* involving the admission of minority students to medical school. In this case 58 amicus briefs were filed by more than 100 organizations, 42 of the

[14] Karen O'Connor, "The Amicus Curiae Role of the U. S. Solicitor General in Supreme Court Litigation," 66 *Judicature* 256 (1983).

briefs backing the university admissions policy and 16 supporting Bakke.

SOVEREIGN IMMUNITY

The doctrine of sovereign immunity imposes yet another possible limitation on judicial access. The Eleventh Amendment protects the states from suit in federal courts without their consent, and the courts have tacitly assumed that a similar immunity extends to the federal government. In 1855 Congress consented to suits against the government in the Court of Claims in actions arising out of governmental contracts, and the Federal Tort Claims Act of 1946 made the federal government subject to suit for torts (that is, wrongful acts) of its officials.

In addition to litigation permitted under these statutes, injured persons can sue governmental officers as individuals; and the officers can be held personally and financially liable for their actions if the harm done to the plaintiff was not officially authorized. Making such distinctions has involved courts in the difficult task of weighing the public interest in avoiding undue judicial interference with ongoing governmental programs against the desirability of providing judicial access to persons claiming that governmental action has harmed them.

Ex parte Young (1908), as noted in Chapter 3, held that a suit against the attorney general of a state to enjoin enforcement of an allegedly unconstitutional state statute did not conflict with the Eleventh Amendment. As Justice Douglas once commented on this ruling:

> Logic cannot justify the rule of *Ex parte Young.* I have never thought it was in full harmony with the Eleventh Amendment. *Ex parte Young* and its offspring do, however, reflect perhaps an even higher policy: the belief that courts must be allowed in the interest of justice to police unruly, lawless government officials who seek to impose oppressive laws on the citizen.[15]

Monroe v. Pape (1961) opened up the possibility of bringing suits for the violation of federally secured civil rights against individual defendants in spite of the fact that they held public office; in this instance defendants were Chicago police.[16] A state governor was similarly denied immunity in *Scheuer v. Rhodes* (1974), a suit brought against the governor and officers of the Ohio National Guard by the father of one of the Kent State students killed by National Guardsmen in 1970. The lower federal courts rejected the suit on the ground that it was in substance an action against the state, but the Supreme Court

---

[15] *We the Judges* (New York: Doubleday, 1956), p. 75.

[16] *Monroe v. Pape* held that municipal corporations are not liable for civil rights violations by their officials and employees, but the Court reversed this rule in *Monell v. Department of Social Services* (1978), making cities liable for civil rights violations by employees if carrying out official policy.

ruled that "a governor or other high executive officer" has no absolute immunity to suit for damages. Federal officials got the same treatment in *Butz v. Economou* (1978), which ruled that even cabinet officers may be subjected to civil suits if they deliberately violate an individual's constitutional rights.

POLITICAL QUESTIONS

In a different category from all of the traditional rules of access is a restriction based purely on policy judgments as to the proper role of the courts vis-à-vis the "political" branches of the government. This self-imposed limitation is known as the doctrine of "political questions."

When the Supreme Court has justified judicial restraint and noninvolvement on grounds that a case presents a political question, the Court's explanation has typically been that the issue was one whose settlement has been entrusted by the Constitution to another branch of the government, or that the problem is in a field where judges have no special competence, or that as a practical matter the issue is one with which the judicial process cannot cope.

The first explicit application of the political question doctrine was made by the Supreme Court in *Luther v. Borden* (1849). The case arose out of efforts in 1841 to reform the government of Rhode Island, which was still operating largely under a charter granted by the king in 1663. Liberal elements in the state joined in a rebellion led by Thomas Dorr, and for a time two rival governments coexisted, although not too peacefully.[17] *Luther v. Borden* originated as a suit by a private citizen against an official of the charter government for trespassing on his property. In his defense the official claimed that he was executing a command of the lawful state government.

A decision would have hinged on the question of which government was legitimate; but the Supreme Court refused to stir up the embers of this controversy, which as a practical matter had long been settled by the time the case reached Washington. Congress had already seated representatives elected under authority of the charter government, and the President had likewise recognized it as the legal government. These decisions by the political branches of the federal government, Chief Justice Taney held, were within their constitutional power to make and beyond the competence of courts to review.

For similar reasons the Court has held that the President and Congress have exclusive authority to decide whether a constitutional amendment has been properly ratified or whether the use of the referendum and recall destroyed the republican status of a state govern-

---

[17] For details see Marvin E. Gettleman, *The Dorr Rebellion* (New York: Random House, 1973), and John S. Schuckman, "The Political Background of the Political Question Doctrine: The Judges and the Dorr War," 16 *American Journal of Legal History* 111 (1972).

ment. In *Colegrove v. Green* (1946), a plurality of the Court used the doctrine of political questions to justify a refusal to consider whether gross disparities in population among congressional districts in Illinois violated the Constitution. (Reading 5.10.) In *Baker v. Carr* (1962), however, the Court reconsidered *Colegrove,* and in the process Justice Brennan developed a more restricted definition of political questions. He held for the majority that the doctrine amounted to nothing more than a general self-imposed obligation on the Court to show appropriate deference to the President and Congress. (Reading 5.11.)

Judicial deference has tended to be the rule particularly in the field of foreign affairs, where judges have generally disclaimed any competence and emphasized that the other branches of government have plenary authority. The Supreme Court has refused as political rather than justiciable issues decisions on questions involving the recognition of foreign governments, the authority of foreign diplomats, the validity of treaties, and the beginning and ending of wars.

Persistent efforts to get the Supreme Court to rule on the constitutionality of American military operations in Vietnam were uniformly unsuccessful. In *Katz v. Tyler* (1967) a draft objector claimed that the military action was a war of aggression outlawed by the 1945 Treaty of London (which makes soldiers in an aggressive war individually responsible as war criminals, even if they acted under orders). *Mora v. McNamara* (1967) was an action brought by three soldiers who refused to go to Vietnam on the ground that the war was unconstitutional because it had not been declared by Congress. *Massachusetts v. Laird* (1970) was an effort authorized by the legislature of Massachusetts to raise the same issue. *Sarnoff v. Schultz* (1972) sought to cut off funds for the military operations. *Holtzman v. Schlesinger* (1973) requested an injunction against the bombing of Cambodia. The Supreme Court denied certiorari in these and other similar cases, though Justice Douglas, supported on occasion by Justices Marshall, Brennan, Stewart, or Harlan—but never by all in the same case—thought the challenges should be heard.

COURT COSTS AND PUBLIC-INTEREST LAW ORGANIZATIONS

While not a legal principle, one of the most important barriers to judicial access has been the cost of lawsuits, a factor that has tended to exclude all except the reasonably well-to-do from initiating legal actions. This situation has been remedied to a limited extent by the growth of poverty law centers and public-interest law firms. Lawyers in these organizations contend that in bringing civil rights cases and public interest litigation generally, they are acting as "private attorneys general" to enforce public laws and their costs should be paid by the losing parties. This has not been the rule in American courts, and in *Alyeska Pipeline Service Co. v. Wilderness Society* (1975), a suit challenging the building of the Alaskan pipeline, the Supreme Court declared that "it would be inappropriate for the judiciary, without legislative guidance, to reallocate the burdens of litigation in [this] manner. . . ." Such "legislative guidance" was soon forthcoming. In 1976 Congress enacted a law permitting federal courts, at their discretion, to award attorneys' fees to a prevailing party who brought suit to enforce almost one hundred designated civil rights statutes.[18]

In 1964 the Office of Economic Opportunity began a government-financed legal services program. In 1975 this program was taken over by the Legal Services Corporation, created by Congress and headed by an eleven-member board of presidential appointees. Its activities, though supported by the organized bar, drew conservative opposition, and President Reagan, having failed to abolish the corporation, sought to limit its activities by appointing board members opposed to its program.[19]

SELECTED REFERENCES

Barker, Lucius J. "Third Parties in Litigation: A Systemic View of the Judicial Function," 29 *Journal of Politics* 41 (1967).

Berger, Raoul. "Standing to Sue in Public Actions," 78 *Yale Law Journal* 816 (1969).

Birkby, Robert H., and Walter F. Murphy. "Interest Group Conflict in the Judicial Arena: The First Amendment and Group Access to the Courts," 42 *Texas Law Review* 1018 (1964).

Consumer Class Actions. Washington, D.C.: American Enterprise Institute, 1977.

"Developments in the Law—Class Actions," 89 *Harvard Law Review* 1319–1644 (1976).

Henkin, Louis. "Is There a 'Political Question' Doctrine?" 85 *Yale Law Journal* 597 (1976).

Horn, Robert A. *Groups and the Constitution.* Stanford, Calif.: Stanford University Press, 1956.

Hutchinson, Diane Wood. "Class Actions: Joinder or Representational Device?" in Philip B. Kurland et al. (eds.), *1983 Supreme Court Review* 459. Chicago: University of Chicago Press, 1984.

Jaffe, Louis L. "Standing to Secure Judicial Review: Public Actions," 74 *Harvard Law Review* 1265 (1961).

[18] In *Blum v. Stenson* (1984) the Court held that the statute's authorization of "reasonable fees" to attorneys bringing federal civil rights suits required fees to be calculated according to market rates in the community. The prospect of winning awards motivates public-interest law firms to bring civil rights cases, but the awards (sometimes in excess of $1 million) may be a heavy burden on state and local governments. A claim of over $300,000 by Harvard professor Laurence Tribe for services in the case of *Larkin v. Grendel's Den* (1982) was resisted by Massachusetts and was eventually set by the court of appeals at $82,000. *New York Times,* December 11, 1984. See also *Webb v. Dyer County* (1985).

[19] Members of Congress charged that the corporation's funds, intended to support legal services for poor people, were granted by the board to groups more interested in promoting Reagan's policies. *New York Times,* October 22, 1984.

————. "The Citizen as Litigant in Public Actions," 116 *University of Pennsylvania Law Review* 1033 (1968).

Krislov, Samuel. "The Amicus Curiae Brief: From Friendship to Advocacy," 72 *Yale Law Journal* 694 (1963).

Monaghan, Henry P. "Constitutional Adjudication: The Who and When," 82 *Yale Law Journal* 1363 (1973).

Note. "Class Standing and the Class Representative," 94 *Harvard Law Review* 1637 (1981).

Note. "Conflicts in Class Actions and Protection of Absent Class Members," 91 *Yale Law Journal* 590 (1982).

Note. "Government Litigation in the Supreme Court: The Roles of the Solicitor General," 78 *Yale Law Journal* 1442 (1969).

Note. "In Defense of an Embattled Mode of Advocacy: An Analysis and Justification of Public Interest Practice," 90 *Yale Law Journal* 1436 (1981).

O'Connor, Karen. "The Amicus Curiae Role of the U. S. Solicitor General in Supreme Court Litigation," 66 *Judicature* 256 (1983).

O'Connor, Karen, and Lee Epstein. "Amicus Curiae Participation in U.S. Supreme Court Litigation," 16 *Law and Society Review* 311 (1981–1982).

Orren, Karen. "Standing to Sue: Interest Group Conflict in the Federal Courts," 70 *American Political Science Review* 723 (1976).

Peltason, Jack W. *Federal Courts in the Political Process.* New York: Random House, 1955.

Rosenberg, Mark L. "Class Actions for Consumer Protection," 7 *Harvard Civil Rights-Civil Liberties Law Review* 601 (1972).

Sorauf, Frank J. *The Wall of Separation: The Constitutional Politics of Church and State.* Princeton, N.J.: Princeton University Press, 1976.

————. "Winning in the Courts: Interest Groups and Constitutional Change," *This Constitution* (Fall 1984), p. 4.

Strum, Philippa. *The Supreme Court and "Political Questions."* University: University of Alabama Press, 1974.

Truman, David B. *The Governmental Process,* 2nd ed. New York: Knopf, 1971. Ch. 15.

Vose, Clement E. *Caucasians Only: The Supreme Court, the NAACP, and the Restrictive Covenant Cases.* Berkeley: University of California Press, 1959.

Wasby, Stephen L. "Civil Rights Litigation by Organizations," 68 *Judicature* 337 (1985).

5.1

"A judge is not free, like a loose cannon, to inflict indiscriminate damage whenever he announces that he is acting in his judicial capacity."

STUMP V. SPARKMAN

U.S. 98 S. Ct. 1099, 55 L. Ed. 2d 331 (1978)

In 1971 the mother of a fifteen-year-old girl presented to an Indiana circuit judge a petition to have a tubal ligation (sterilization) performed on her daughter, alleging that the girl was "somewhat retarded," had been associating with young men, and had stayed out overnight on several occasions. The operation, according to the petition, would be in the daughter's best interest "to prevent unfortunate circumstances." The petition was approved by the judge the same day it was presented and the operation was performed, the daughter having been informed that her appendix was being removed. Two years later she married, and her inability to become pregnant led to discovery that she had been sterilized by the 1971 operation. She and her husband filed suit in federal court against her mother, the judge, the doctors, and the hospital, charging violation of her civil rights. The district court held that no federal action would lie against any of the defendants because the circuit judge, the only state agent, was absolutely immune from suit. The Court of Appeals for the Seventh Circuit reversed, and the Supreme Court granted certiorari.

MR. JUSTICE WHITE delivered the opinion of the Court. . . .

The governing principle of law is well established and is not questioned by the parties. As early as 1872, the Court recognized that it was "a general principle of the highest importance to the proper administration of justice that a judicial officer, in exercising the authority vested in him, [should] be free to act upon his own convictions, without apprehension of personal consequences to himself." *Bradley v. Fisher.* For that reason the Court held that "judges of courts of superior or general jurisdiction are not liable to civil actions for their judicial acts, even when such acts are in excess of their jurisdiction, and are alleged to have been done maliciously or corruptly." Later we held that this doctrine of judicial immunity was applicable in suits under § 1 of the Civil Rights Act of 1871, 42 U.S.C. § 1983, for the legislative record gave no indication that Congress intended to abolish this long-established principle. *Pierson v. Ray* (1967).

The Court of Appeals correctly recognized that the necessary inquiry in determining whether a defendant judge is immune from suit is whether at the time he took the challenged action he had jurisdiction over the subject matter before him. . . . The scope of the judge's jurisdiction must be construed broadly where the issue is the immunity of the judge. A judge will not be deprived of immunity because the action he took was in error, was done maliciously, or was in excess of his authority; rather, he will be subject to liability only when he has acted in the "clear absence of all jurisdiction."...

We cannot agree that there was a "clear absence of all jurisdiction" in the DeKalb County Circuit Court to consider the petition presented by Mrs. McFarlin. As an Indiana circuit court judge, Judge Stump had "original exclusive jurisdiction in all cases at law and in equity whatsoever . . . ," jurisdiction over the settlement of estates and over guardianships, appellate jurisdiction as conferred by law, and jurisdiction over "all other causes, matters and proceedings where exclusive jurisdiction thereof is not conferred by law upon some other court, board or officer." This is indeed a broad jurisdictional grant; yet the Court of Appeals concluded that Judge Stump did not have jurisdiction over the petition authorizing Linda Sparkman's sterilization.

In so doing, the Court of Appeals noted that the Indiana statutes provided for the sterilization of institutionalized persons under certain circumstances . . . but otherwise contained no express authority for judicial approval of tubal ligations. It is true that the statutory grant of general jurisdiction to the Indiana circuit courts does not itemize types of cases those courts may hear and hence does not expressly mention sterilization petitions presented by the parents of a minor. But in our view, it is more significant that there was no Indiana statute and no case law in 1971 prohibiting a circuit court, a court of general jurisdiction, from considering a petition of the type presented to Judge Stump. The statutory authority for the sterilization of institutionalized persons in the custody of the State does not warrant the inference that a court of general jurisdiction has no power to act on a petition for sterilization of a minor in the custody of her parents, particularly where the parents have authority under the Indiana statutes to "consent to and contract for medical or hospital care or treatment of [the minor] including surgery." The District Court concluded that Judge Stump had jurisdiction to entertain and act upon Mrs. McFarlin's petition. We agree with the District Court, it appearing that neither by statute or case law has the broad jurisdiction granted to the circuit courts of Indiana been circumscribed to foreclose consideration of a petition for authorization of a minor's sterilization. . . .

Perhaps realizing the broad scope of Judge Stump's jurisdiction, the Court of Appeals stated that, even if the action taken by him was not foreclosed under the Indiana statutory scheme, it would still be "an illegitimate exercise of his common law power because of his failure to comply with elementary principles of procedural due process." This misconceives the doctrine of judicial immunity. A judge is absolutely immune from liability for his judicial acts even if his exercise of authority is flawed by the commission of grave procedural errors. The Court made this point clear in *Bradley*, where it stated that "this erroneous manner in which [the court's] jurisdiction was exercised, however it may have affected the validity of the act, did not make the act any less a judicial act; nor did it render the defendant liable to answer in damages for it at the suit of the plaintiff, as though the court had proceeded without having any jurisdiction whatever. . . ."

We conclude that the Court of Appeals, employing an unduly

restrictive view of the scope of Judge Stump's jurisdiction, erred in holding that he was not entitled to judicial immunity. Because the court over which Judge Stump presides is one of general jurisdiction, neither the procedural errors he may have committed nor the lack of a specific statute authorizing his approval of the petition in question rendered him liable in damages for the consequences of his actions.

The respondents argue that even if Judge Stump had jurisdiction to consider the petition presented to him by Mrs. McFarlin, he is still not entitled to judicial immunity because his approval of the petition did not constitute a "judicial" act. It is only for acts performed in his "judicial" capacity that a judge is absolutely immune, they say. We do not disagree with this statement of the law, but we cannot characterize the approval of the petition as a nonjudicial act.

Respondents themselves stated in their pleadings before the District Court that Judge Stump was "clothed with the authority of the state" at the time that he approved the petition and that "he was acting as a county circuit court judge." They nevertheless now argue that Judge Stump's approval of the petition was not a judicial act because the petition was not given a docket number, was not placed on file with the clerk's office, and was approved in an *ex parte* proceeding without notice to the minor, without a hearing, and without the appointment of a *guardian ad litem.*

This Court has not had occasion to consider, for purposes of the judicial immunity doctrine, the necessary attributes of a judicial act; but it has previously rejected the argument, somewhat similar to the one raised here, that the lack of formality involved in the Illinois Supreme Court's consideration of a petitioner's application for admission to the state bar prevented it from being a "judicial proceeding" and from presenting a case or controversy that could be reviewed by this Court. *In re Summers* (1945).

The relevant cases demonstrate that the factors determining whether an act by a judge is a "judicial" one relate to the nature of the act itself, *i.e.,* whether it is a function normally performed by a judge, and to the expectations of the parties, *i.e.,* whether they dealt with the judge in his judicial capacity. Here, both factors indicate that Judge Stump's approval of the sterilization petition was a judicial act. State judges with general jurisdiction not infrequently are called upon in their official capacity to approve petitions relating to the affairs of minors, as for example, a petition to settle a minor's claim. Furthermore, as even respondents have admitted, at the time he approved the petition presented to him by Mrs. McFarlin, Judge Stump was "acting as a county circuit court judge." ... Because Judge Stump performed the type of act normally performed only by judges and because he did so in his capacity as a circuit court judge, we find no merit to respondents' argument that the informality with which he proceeded rendered his action nonjudicial and deprived him of his absolute immunity.

Both the Court of Appeals and the respondents seem to suggest that, because of the tragic consequences of Judge Stump's actions, he should not be immune. For example, the Court of Appeals noted that "[t]here are actions of purported judicial character that a judge, even when exercising general jurisdiction, is not empowered to take" . . . and respondents argue that Judge Stump's action was "so unfair" and "so totally devoid of judicial concern for the interests and well-being of the young girl involved" as to disqualify it as a judicial act. . . . Disagreement with the action taken by the judge, however, does not justify depriving that judge of his immunity. Despite the unfairness to litigants that sometimes results, the doctrine of judicial immunity is thought to be in the best interests of "the proper administration of justice . . . [for it allows] a judicial officer, in exercising the authority vested in him [to] be free to act upon his own convictions, without apprehension of personal consequences to himself." *Bradley v. Fisher.* . . . The fact that the issue before the judge is a controversial one is all the more reason that he should be able to act without fear of suit.

The Indiana law vested in Judge Stump the power to entertain and act upon the petition for sterilization. He is, therefore, under the controlling cases, immune from damages liability even if his approval of the petition was in error. Accordingly, the judgment of the Court of Appeals is reversed and the case is remanded for further proceedings consistent with this opinion.

It is so ordered.

MR. JUSTICE BRENNAN took no part in the consideration or decision of this case.

MR. JUSTICE STEWART, with whom MR. JUSTICE MARSHALL and MR. JUSTICE POWELL join, dissenting.

It is established federal law that judges of general jurisdiction are absolutely immune from monetary liability "for judicial acts, even when such acts are in excess of their jurisdiction, and are alleged to have been done maliciously or corruptly." *Bradley v. Fisher.* But the scope of judicial immunity is limited to liability for "judicial acts," and I think that what Judge Stump did on July 9, 1971, was beyond the pale of anything that could sensibly be called a judicial act. . . .

The Court finds two reasons for holding that Judge Stump's approval of the sterilization petition was a judicial act. First, the Court says, it was "a function normally performed by a judge." Second, the Court says, the act was performed in Judge Stump's "judicial capacity." With all respect, I think that the first of these grounds is factually untrue and that the second is legally unsound.

When the Court says that what Judge Stump did was an act "normally performed by a judge," it is not clear to me whether the Court means that a judge "normally" is asked to approve a mother's decision to have her child given surgical treatment generally, or that a judge "normally" is asked to approve a mother's wish to have her daughter sterilized. But whichever way the Court's statement is to be taken, it is factually inaccurate. In Indiana, as elsewhere in our country, a parent is authorized to arrange for and consent to medical and surgical treatment of his minor child. And when a parent decides to call a physician to care for his sick child or arranges to have a surgeon remove his child's tonsils, he does not, "normally" or otherwise, need to seek the approval of a judge. On the other hand, Indiana did in 1971 have statutory procedures for the sterilization of certain people who were *institutionalized.* But these statutes provided for *administrative proceedings* before a board established by the superintendent of each public hospital. Only if after notice and an evidentiary hearing, an order of sterilization was entered in these proceedings could there be review in a circuit court.

In sum, what Judge Stump did on July 9, 1971, was in no way an act "normally performed by a judge." Indeed, there is no reason to believe that such an act has ever been performed by *any* other Indiana judge, either before or since.

When the Court says that Judge Stump was acting in "his judicial capacity" in approving Mrs. McFarlin's petition, it is not clear to me whether the Court means that Mrs. McFarlin submitted the petition to him only because he was a judge, or that, in approving it, he *said* that he was acting as a judge. But however the Court's test is to be understood, it is, I think, demonstrably unsound.

It can safely be assumed that the Court is correct in concluding that Mrs. McFarlin came to Judge Stump with her petition because he was a county circuit court judge. But false illusions as to a judge's power can hardly convert a judge's response to those illusions into a judicial act. In short, a judge's approval of a mother's petition to lock her daughter in the attic would hardly be a judicial act simply because the mother had submitted her petition to the judge in his official capacity.

If, on the other hand, the Court's test depends upon the fact that Judge Stump *said* he was acting in his judicial capacity, it is equally invalid. It is true that Judge Stump affixed his signature to the approval of the petition as "Judge, DeKalb Circuit Court." But the conduct of a judge surely does not become a judicial act merely on his own say-so. A judge is not free, like a loose cannon, to inflict indiscriminate damage whenever he announces that he is acting in his judicial capacity.

If the standard adopted by the Court is invalid, then what is the proper measure of a judicial act? Contrary to implications in the Court's opinion, my conclusion that what Judge Stump did was not a judicial act is not based upon the fact that he acted with informality, or that he may not have been "in his judge's robes," or "in the courtroom itself." . . . And I do not reach this conclusion simply "because the petition was not given a docket number, was not placed on file with the clerk's office, and was approved in an *ex parte* proceeding without notice to the minor, without a hearing, and without the appointment of a *guardian ad litem.*" It seems to me, rather that the concept of what is a judicial act must take its content from a consideration of the factors that support immunity from liability for the performance of such an act. Those factors were accurately summarized by the Court in *Pierson v. Ray* [1967]:

> [I]t 'is . . . for the benefit of the public, whose interest it is that the judges should be at liberty to exercise their functions with independence and without fear of consequences.' . . . It is a judge's duty to decide all cases within his jurisdiction that are brought before him, including controversial cases that arouse the most intense feelings in the litigants. His errors may be corrected on appeal, but he should not have to fear that unsatisfied litigants may hound him with litigation charging malice or corruption. Imposing such a burden on judges would contribute not to principled and fearless decision-making but to intimidation.

Not one of the considerations thus summarized in the *Pierson* opinion was present here. There was no "case," controversial or otherwise. There were no litigants. There was and could be no appeal. And there was not even the pretext of principled decision-making. The total absence of *any* of these normal attributes of a judicial proceeding convinces me that the conduct complained of in this case was not a judicial act.

The petitioners' brief speaks of an "aura of deism which surrounds the bench . . . essential to the maintenance of respect for the judicial institution." Though the rhetoric may be overblown, I do not quarrel with it. But if aura there be, it is hardly protected by exonerating from liability such lawless conduct as took place here. And if intimidation would serve to deter its recurrence, that would surely be in the public interest.

MR. JUSTICE POWELL, dissenting. . . .

5.2

". . . there is no incompatibility between the activity of organizations in litigation and the integrity or independence of the judiciary."

LITIGATION AS A FORM OF PRESSURE GROUP ACTIVITY

Clement E. Vose

Organizations support legal action because individuals lack the necessary time, money, and skill. . . . The form of group participation in court cases is set by such factors as the type of proceeding, standing of the parties, legal or constitutional issues in dispute, the characteristics of the organization, and its interest in the outcome. Perhaps the most direct and open participation has been by organizations which have been obliged to protect their own rights and privileges. . . . The cases have sometimes placed organizations as parties, but more often the organization supports a member or an officer in litigation. One example must suffice.

The constitutional concept of religious freedom has been broadened in recent years by the Supreme Court decisions in cases involving members of the sect known as Jehovah's Witnesses. Most of the cases began when a Jehovah's Witness violated a local ordinance or state statute. Since 1938, the Witnesses, incorporated as the Watch Tower Bible and Tract Society and represented by its counsel, Hayden Cooper Covington, have won forty-four of fifty-five cases in the United States Supreme Court. . . .

THE NAACP

Since 1909 the National Association for the Advancement of Colored People has improved the legal status of Negroes immeasurably by the victories it has won in more than fifty Supreme Court cases. During its early years, the NAACP relied upon prominent volunteer lawyers . . . to represent Negroes in the courts. Limited success coupled with its failure to win gains from Congress led the NAACP in the 1930's to make court litigation fundamental to its program. A separate organization, the NAACP Legal Defense and Educational Fund, was incorporated for this purpose. The goal of the NAACP was to make Negroes "an integral part of the nation, with the same rights and guarantees that are accorded to other citizens, and on the same

319 *The Annals of the American Academy of Political and Social Science* 20 (1958). Copyright 1958 the American Academy of Political and Social Science. Reprinted with permission. Clement E. Vose was John E. Andrus Professor of Government, Wesleyan University.

terms." This ambition meant that beginning in 1938 Thurgood Marshall as special counsel for the NAACP Legal Defense and Educational Fund held what was "probably the most demanding legal post in the country."

In aiming to establish racial equality before the law on a broad basis, the Legal Defense Fund has not functioned as a legal aid society. Limited resources have prevented the Fund from participating in all cases involving the rights of Negroes. As early as 1935 Charles Houston, an imaginative Negro lawyer who preceded Marshall as special counsel, set the tone of NAACP efforts when he declared that the legal campaign against inequality should be carefully planned "to secure decisions, rulings and public opinion on the broad principle instead of being devoted to merely miscellaneous cases."

By presenting test cases to the Supreme Court, the NAACP has won successive gains protecting the right of Negroes in voting, housing, transportation, education, and service on juries. Each effort has followed the development of new theories of legal interpretation and required the preparation of specific actions in the courts to challenge existing precedent. The NAACP Legal Defense Fund has accomplished these two tasks through the co-operation of associated and allied groups. First, as many as fifty Negro lawyers practicing in all parts of the country have been counsel in significant civil rights cases in the lower courts. Many of these men received their legal education at the Howard University Law School in Washington, D.C., and have shared membership in the National Bar Association since its founding in 1925. . . . Second, the NAACP has long benefited from its official advisory group, the National Legal Committee composed of leading Negro and white lawyers. . . . Third, other organizations with no direct connection with the Legal Defense Fund have sponsored a few cases. State and local chapters of the NAACP have often aided Negroes who were parties in cases, especially in the lower courts. The St. Louis Association of Real Estate Brokers was the chief sponsor of the important restrictive covenant case of *Shelley v. Kraemer.* A Negro national college fraternity, Alpha Phi Alpha, sponsored quite completely the successful attack on discrimination in interstate railway dining cars. . . .

THE AMERICAN LIBERTY LEAGUE

The experience of the American Liberty League, organized in 1934 by conservative businessmen to oppose the New Deal, provides another variation on the theme of organizations in litigation. When the League proved unable to prevent enactment of economic regulation by Congress, a National Lawyers' Committee was formed to question the constitutionality of the legislation. In August 1935, the National

Lawyers' Committee of fifty-eight members announced plans to prepare a series of reports to the public on whether particular federal laws were "consonant with the American constitutional system and American traditions." These reports "would be of a strictly professional nature and would in no case go into the question of social and economic advisability or the need for constitutional change to meet new conditions." This intention led the Committee during the next two years to conclude that a dozen New Deal statutes were unconstitutional.

The most celebrated Liberty League "brief" prepared by the National Lawyers' Committee questioned the constitutionality of the National Labor Relations Act. That analysis was prepared by a subcommittee of eight attorneys under the chairmanship of Earl F. Reed. It was then submitted to the other members and made public by Raoul E. Desverine, Chairman of the entire group, on Constitution Day, 1935. The reports of the Committee were given wide publicity through press releases, the distribution of pamphlets, and radio talks by leading conservative lawyers like James M. Beck. . . .

Members of the National Lawyers' Committee of the American Liberty League, but not the organization itself, participated in litigation. . . . Although the intention was to offer free legal services to citizens without funds to defend their constitutional rights, members of the National Lawyers' Committee actually represented major corporations which challenged the constitutionality of New Deal legislation in the Supreme Court. Earl F. Reed simply adapted the Liberty League report to apply to the specific facts of the case when he represented the Jones and Laughlin Steel Corporation against the National Labor Relations Board. Another member of the National Lawyers' Committee, John W. Davis, represented the Associated Press in a companion case.

ORGANIZATIONS AS "FRIENDS OF THE COURT"

The appearance of organizations as *amici curiae* has been the most noticed form of group representation in Supreme Court cases. . . . During the last decade *amici curiae* have submitted an average of sixty-six briefs and seven oral arguments in an average total of forty cases a term.

The frequent entrance of organizations into Supreme Court cases by means of the *amicus curiae* device has often given litigation the distinct flavor of group combat. This may be illustrated by the group representation in quite different cases. In 1943, when a member of the Jehovah's Witnesses challenged the constitutionality of a compulsory flag salute in the schools, his defense by counsel for the Watchtower Bible and Tract Society was supported by separate *amici*

curiae, the American Civil Liberties Union and the Committee on
the Bill of Rights of the American Bar Association. The appellant
state board of education was supported by an *amicus curiae* brief
filed by the American Legion. In 1951, in a case testing state resale
price maintenance, the United States was an *amicus* against a Louisiana statute while the Commonwealth of Pennsylvania, the Louisiana
State Pharmaceutical Association, American Booksellers, Inc., and
the National Association of Retail Druggists entered *amici curiae*
briefs in support of the statute. . . .

REGULATION OF ORGANIZATIONS IN THE COURTS

Judges, lawyers, legislators, and citizens have reacted to appearances
that organizational activity in court cases touches the integrity of the
judicial process. A number of limitations have resulted. But in protecting the legal system against these dangers, regulations may be
too harsh on organizations and interfere unduly with the freedom of
association their functioning represents. Especially is this true when
the barriers against group participation in litigation are erected by
legislative bodies, but it is not entirely absent when the rules are
established by bar associations or by courts themselves. Some practices by organizations require control, but most of the practices of
organizations in conducting litigation are perfectly compatible with
an independent judiciary. . . .

During the trial of the leaders of the Communist party under the
Smith Act in the Federal District Court for the Eastern District of
New York located at Foley Square in New York City, picketing and
parading outside the court was a daily occurrence. When the Senate
Judiciary Committee was considering bills to limit this practice, it
received many statements like the following: "Assuming under our
form of representative government pressure groups must be tolerated in our legislative and executive branches, I feel there is no good
reason why our courts should be subjected to such pressures." In
accord with this view, Congress, in 1950, enacted legislation prohibiting any person from parading, picketing, or demonstrating in or
near a federal courthouse with the intent of "interfering with, obstructing, or impeding" the administration of justice or of "influencing any judge, juror, witness, or court officer" in the discharge of his
duty.

In 1953, the National Committee to Secure Justice in the Rosenberg Case addressed a petition claimed to have the support of 50,000
persons to the Supreme Court. . . . No rule prevents groups from such
indecorous action but Justice Hugo Black has expressed the intense
disapproval of the Supreme Court. In 1951, when granting a stay of
execution to Willie McGhee, a Negro under the death penalty in
Mississippi, Justice Black lamented the "growing practice of sending
telegrams to judges in order to have cases decided by pressure."

Declaring that he would not read them, he said that "the courts of the United States are not the kind of instruments of justice that can be influenced by such pressures." Justice Black gave an implied warning to the bar by noting that "counsel in this case have assured me they were not responsible for these telegrams."

The offer of the National Lawyers' Committee of the American Liberty League to donate its services in test cases led a critic to make a formal complaint to the American Bar Association. The League was charged with unethical conduct for having "organized a vast free lawyers service for firms and individuals 'bucking' New Deal laws on constitutional grounds." The ABA Committee on Professional Ethics and Grievances ruled, in a formal opinion, that the activities of the Liberty League were perfectly proper, even laudable. The Committee found that neither the substance of the offer, to provide legal defense for "indigent citizens without compensation," nor the "proffer of service," even when broadcast over the radio, was offensive to the ethical code of the American bar. . . .

CONCLUSION

. . . Considering the importance of the issues resolved by American courts, the entrance of organizations into cases in these ways seems in order. Indeed the essential right of organizations to pursue litigation would appear to follow from the generous attitude of American society toward the freedom of individuals to form associations for the purpose of achieving common goals. Of course, traditional judicial procedures should be followed and the attorneys for organizations, as well as for individuals, must address their arguments to reason. If these standards of conduct are followed there is no incompatibility between the activity of organizations in litigation and the integrity or independence of the judiciary.

5.3   *". . . association for litigation may be the most effective form of political association."*

NATIONAL ASSOCIATION FOR THE ADVANCEMENT OF COLORED PEOPLE V. BUTTON

371 U.S. 415, 83 S. Ct. 328, 9 L. Ed. 2d 405 (1963)

Following the successful outcome of its suit in *Brown v. Board of Education* (1954, 1955), the NAACP began an active program to force desegregation of Southern schools by court action. Southern state officials retaliated by charging that NAACP lawyers were violating state laws forbidding the fomenting of litigation. The NAACP brought this suit against the attorney general of Virginia, seeking a declaratory judgment that the Virginia statute against the improper solicitation of legal business was unconstitutional.

MR. JUSTICE BRENNAN delivered the opinion of the Court. . . .

Typically, a local NAACP branch will invite a member of the legal staff to explain to a meeting of parents and children the legal steps necessary to achieve desegregation. The staff member will bring printed forms to the meeting authorizing him, and other NAACP or Defense Fund attorneys of his designation, to represent the signers in legal proceedings to achieve desegregation. On occasion, blank forms have been signed by litigants, upon the understanding that a member or members of the legal staff, with or without assistance from other NAACP lawyers, or from the Defense Fund, would handle the case. It is usual, after obtaining authorizations, for the staff lawyer to bring into the case the other staff members in the area where suit is to be brought, and sometimes to bring in lawyers from the national organization or the Defense Fund. In effect, then, the prospective litigant retains not so much a particular attorney as the "firm" of NAACP and Defense Fund lawyers, which has a corporate reputation for expertness in presenting and arguing the difficult questions of law that frequently arise in civil rights litigation.

These meetings are sometimes prompted by letters and bulletins from the Conference urging active steps to fight segregation. The Conference has on occasion distributed to the local branches petitions for desegregation to be signed by parents and filed with local school boards, and advised branch officials to obtain, as petitioners, persons willing to "go all the way" in any possible litigation that may ensue. While the Conference in these ways encourages the bringing of lawsuits, the plaintiffs in particular actions, as far as appears, make their own decisions to become such.

Statutory regulation of unethical and nonprofessional conduct by attorneys has been in force in Virginia since 1849. These provisions outlaw, *inter alia*, solicitation of legal business in the form of "running" or "capping." Prior to 1956, however, no attempt was made to proscribe under such regulations the activities of the NAACP, which had been carried on openly for many years in substantially the manner described. In 1956, however, the legislature amended, by the addition of Chapter 33, the provisions of the Virginia Code forbidding solicitation of legal business by a "runner" or "capper" to include, in the definition of "runner" or "capper," an agent for an individual organization which retains a lawyer in connection with an action to which it is not a party and in which it has no pecuniary right or liability. The Virginia Supreme Court of Appeals held that . . . the activities of NAACP, the Virginia Conference, the Defense Fund, and the lawyers furnished by them, fell within, and could constitutionally be proscribed by, the chapter's expanded definition of improper solicitation of legal business, and also violated Canons 35 and 47 of the American Bar Association's Canons of Professional Ethics, which the court had adopted in 1938. Specifically the court held that, under the expanded definition, such activities on the part of NAACP, the Virginia Conference, and the Defense Fund constituted "fomenting and soliciting legal business in which they are not parties and have no pecuniary right or liability, and which they channel to the enrichment of certain lawyers employed by them, at no cost to the litigants and over which the litigants have no control." . . .

We reverse the judgment of the Virginia Supreme Court of Appeals: We hold that the activities of the NAACP, its affiliates and legal staff shown on this record are modes of expression and association protected by the First and Fourteenth Amendments which Virginia may not prohibit, under its power to regulate the legal profession, as improper solicitation of legal business violative of Chapter 33 and the Canons of Professional Ethics.

We meet at the outset the contention that "solicitation" is wholly outside the area of freedoms protected by the First Amendment. To this contention there are two answers. The first is that a State cannot foreclose the exercise of constitutional rights by mere labels. The second is that abstract discussion is not the only species of communication which the Constitution protects; the First Amendment also protects vigorous advocacy, certainly of lawful ends, against governmental intrusion. . . . In the context of NAACP objectives, litigation is not a technique of resolving private differences; it is a means for achieving the lawful objectives of equality of treatment by all government, federal, state and local, for the members of the Negro community in this country. It is thus a form of political expression. Groups which find themselves unable to achieve their objectives through the ballot frequently turn to the courts. . . . under the conditions of modern government, litigation may well be the sole practicable avenue open to a minority to petition for redress of grievances.

We need not, in order to find constitutional protection for the kind of cooperative, organizational activity disclosed by this record, whereby Negroes seek through lawful means to achieve legitimate political ends, subsume such activity under a narrow, literal conception of freedom of speech, petition or assembly. For there is no longer any doubt that the First and Fourteenth Amendments protect certain forms of orderly group activity. . . .

The NAACP is not a conventional political party; but the litigation it assists, while serving to vindicate the legal rights of members of the American Negro community, at the same time and perhaps more importantly, makes possible the distinctive contribution of a minority group to the ideas and beliefs of our society. For such a group, association for litigation may be the most effective form of political association. . . .

The second contention is that Virginia has a subordinating interest in the regulation of the legal profession, embodied in Chapter 33, which justifies limiting petitioner's First Amendment rights. Specifically, Virginia contends that the NAACP's activities in furtherance of litigation, being "improper solicitation" under the state statute, fall within the traditional purview of state regulation of professional conduct. However, the State's attempt to equate the activities of the NAACP and its lawyers with common-law barratry, maintenance and champerty, and to outlaw them accordingly, cannot obscure the serious encroachment worked by Chapter 33 upon protected freedoms of expression. . . .

However valid may be Virginia's interest in regulating the traditionally illegal practices of barratry, maintenance and champerty, that interest does not justify the prohibition of the NAACP activities disclosed by this record. Malicious intent was of the essence of the common-law offenses of fomenting or stirring up litigation. And whatever may be or may have been true of suits against government in other countries, the exercise in our own, as in this case, of First Amendment rights to enforce constitutional rights through litigation, as a matter of law, cannot be deemed malicious. Even more modern, subtler regulations of unprofessional conduct or interference with professional relations, not involving malice, would not touch the activities at bar; regulations which reflect hostility to stirring up litigation have been aimed chiefly at those who urge recourse to the courts for private gain, serving no public interest. . . .

Resort to the courts to seek vindication of constitutional rights is a different matter from the oppressive, malicious, or avaricious use of the legal process for purely private gain. . . .

Reversed.

MR. JUSTICE DOUGLAS, concurring. . . .

MR. JUSTICE WHITE, concurring in part and dissenting in part. . . .

MR. JUSTICE HARLAN, whom MR. JUSTICE CLARK and MR. JUSTICE STEWART join, dissenting. . . .

"Without such limitations . . . courts would be called upon to decide abstract questions of wide public significance even though other governmental institutions may be more competent to address the questions . . ."

5.4

WARTH V. SELDIN

422 U.S. 490, 95 S. Ct. 2197, 45 L. Ed. 2d 343 (1975)

Various organizations and individuals resident in the metropolitan area of Rochester, New York, brought suit in a federal district court against Penfield, a town adjacent to

Rochester. Plaintiffs sought a declaratory judgment, an injunction, and monetary damages, alleging that the town's zoning ordinances effectively excluded persons of low and moderate income from living in the town and so violated their rights protected by both the Fourteenth Amendment and federal civil rights statutes. The district court dismissed the complaint for lack of standing, and the court of appeals affirmed. The United States Supreme Court granted plaintiffs' petition for certiorari.

MR. JUSTICE POWELL delivered the opinion of the Court. . . .

We address first the principles of standing relevant to the claims asserted by the several categories of petitioners in this case. In essence the question of standing is whether the litigant is entitled to have the court decide the merits of the dispute or of particular issues. This inquiry involves both constitutional limitations on federal court jurisdiction and prudential limitations on its exercise. In both dimensions it is founded in concern about the proper—and properly limited—role of the courts in a democratic society. See *Schlesinger v. Reservists Comm. to Stop the War* (1974); *United States v. Richardson* (1974).

In its constitutional dimension, standing imports justiciability: whether the plaintiff has made out a "case or controversy" between himself and the defendant within the meaning of Art. III. This is the threshold question in every federal case, determining the power of the court to entertain the suit. As an aspect of justiciability, the standing question is whether the plaintiff has "alleged such a personal stake in the outcome of the controversy" to warrant *his* invocation of federal court jurisdiction and to justify exercise of the court's remedial powers on his behalf. *Baker v. Carr* (1962). The Art. III judicial power exists only to redress or otherwise to protect against injury to the complaining party, even though the court's judgment may benefit others collaterally. A federal court's jurisdiction therefore can be invoked only when the plaintiff himself has suffered "some threatened or actual injury resulting from the putatively illegal action. . . ." *Linda R. S. v. Richard D.* (1973).

Apart from this minimum constitutional mandate, this Court has recognized other limits on the class of persons who may invoke the courts' decisional and remedial powers. First, the Court has held that when the asserted harm is a "generalized grievance" shared in substantially equal measure by all or a large class of citizens, that harm alone normally does not warrant exercise of jurisdiction. Second, even when the plaintiff has alleged injury sufficient to meet the "case or controversy" requirement, this Court has held that the plaintiff generally must assert his own legal rights and interests, and cannot rest his claim to relief on the legal rights or interests of third parties. Without such limitations—closely related to Art. III concerns but essentially matters of judicial self-governance—the courts would be called upon to decide abstract questions of wide public significance even though other governmental institutions may be more competent to address the questions and even though judicial intervention may be unnecessary to protect individual rights.

Although standing in no way depends on the merits of the plaintiff's contention that particular conduct is illegal, e.g., *Flast v. Cohen* (1968), it often turns on the nature and source of the claim asserted. The actual or threatened injury required by Art. III may exist solely by virtue of "statutes creating legal rights, the invasion of which creates standing. . . ." See *Linda R. S. v. Richard D.; Sierra Club v. Morton* (1972). Moreover, the source of the plaintiff's claim to relief assumes critical importance with respect to the prudential rules of standing that, apart from Art. III's minimum requirements, serve to limit the role of the courts in resolving public disputes. Essentially, the standing question in such cases is whether the constitutional or statutory provision on which the claim rests properly can be understood as granting persons in the plaintiff's position a right to judicial relief. In some circumstances, countervailing considerations may outweigh the concerns underlying the usual reluctance to exert judicial power when the plaintiff's claim to relief rests on the legal rights of third parties. In such instances, the Court has found, in effect, that the constitutional or statutory provision in question implies a right of action in the plaintiff. See *Pierce v. Society of Sisters* (1925); *Sullivan v. Little Hunting Park, Inc.* (1969). Moreover, Congress may grant an express right of action to persons who otherwise would be barred by prudential standing rules. Of course, Art. III's requirement remains: the plaintiff still must allege a distinct and palpable injury to himself, even if it is an injury shared by a large class of other possible litigants. E.g., *United States v. SCRAP* (1973). But so long as this requirement is satisfied, persons to whom Congress has granted a right of action, either expressly or by clear implication, may have standing to seek relief on the basis of the legal rights and interests of others, and, indeed, may invoke the general public interest in support of their claim. E.g., Sierra Club v. Morton. . . .

With these general considerations in mind, we turn first to the claims of Petitioners Ortiz, Reyes, Sinkler, and Broadnax, each of whom asserts standing as a person of low or moderate income and, coincidentally, as a member of a minority racial or ethnic group. We must assume, taking the allegations of the complaint as true, that Penfield's zoning ordinance and the pattern of enforcement by respondent officials have had the purpose and effect of excluding persons of low and moderate income, many of whom are members of racial or ethnic minority groups. We also assume, for purposes here, that such intentional exclusionary practices, if proved in a proper case, would be adjudged violative of the constitutional and statutory rights of the persons excluded.

But the fact that these petitioners share attributes common to persons who may have been excluded from residence in the town is an insufficient predicate for the conclusion that petitioners themselves have been excluded, or that the respondents' assertedly illegal actions have violated their rights. Petitioners must allege and show that they personally have been injured, not that injury has been suffered by other, unidentified members of the class to which they belong and which they purport to represent. . . .

We find the record devoid of the necessary allegations. As the Court of Appeals noted, none of these petitioners has a present interest in any Penfield property; none is himself subject to the ordinance's strictures; and none has ever been denied a variance or permit by respondent officials. Instead, they rely on little more than the remote possibility, unsubstantiated by allegations of fact, that their situation might have been better had respondents acted otherwise, and might improve were the court to afford relief. . . .

We hold only that a plaintiff who seeks to challenge exclusionary zoning practices must allege specific, concrete facts demonstrating that the challenged practices harm *him,* and that he personally would benefit in a tangible way from the courts' intervention. Absent the necessary allegations of demonstrable, particularized injury, there can be no confidence of "a real need to exercise the power of judicial review" or that relief can be framed "no broader than required by the precise facts to which the court's ruling would be applied."

The petitioners who assert standing on the basis of their status as taxpayers of the city of Rochester present a different set of problems. These "taxpayer-petitioners" claim that they are suffering economic injury consequent to Penfield's allegedly discriminatory and exclusionary zoning practices. Their argument, in brief, is that Penfield's persistent refusal to allow or to facilitate construction of low- and moderate-cost housing forces the city of Rochester to provide such housing in greater numbers than it otherwise would do; that to provide such housing, Rochester must allow certain tax abatements; and that as the amount of tax-abated property increases, Rochester taxpayers are forced to assume an increased tax burden in order to finance essential public services. . . .

But even if we assume that the taxpayer-petitioners could establish that Penfield's zoning practices harm them, their complaint nonetheless was properly dismissed. Petitioners do not, even if they could, assert any personal right under the Constitution or any statute to be free of action by a neighboring municipality that may have some incidental adverse effect on Rochester. On the contrary, the only basis of the taxpayer-petitioners' claim is that Penfield's zoning ordinance and practices violate the constitutional and statutory rights of third parties, namely, persons of low and moderate income who are said to be excluded from Penfield. In short the claim of these petitioners falls squarely within the prudential standing rule that normally bars litigants from asserting the rights or legal interests of others in order to obtain relief from injury to themselves. . . .

We turn next to the standing problems presented by the petitioner associations—Metro-Act of Rochester, Inc., one of the original plaintiffs; Housing Council in the Monroe County Area, Inc., which the original plaintiffs sought to join as a party-plaintiff; and Rochester Home Builders Association, Inc., which moved in the District Court for leave to intervene as plaintiff. . . . [All the associations were denied standing to seek relief from injuries to themselves or their members.]

The rules of standing, whether as aspects of the Art. III case or controversy requirement or as reflections of prudential considerations defining and limiting the role of the courts, are threshold determinants of the propriety of judicial intervention. It is the responsibility of the complainant clearly to allege facts demonstrating that he is a proper party to invoke judicial resolution of the dispute and the exercise of the court's remedial powers. We agree with the District Court and the Court of Appeals that none of the petitioners here has met this threshold requirement. Accordingly, the judgment of the Court of Appeals is

Affirmed.

MR. JUSTICE DOUGLAS, dissenting.

With all respect, I think that the Court reads the complaint and the record with antagonistic eyes. There are in the background of this case continuing strong tides of opinion touching on very sensitive matters, some of which involve race, some class distinctions based on wealth.

A clean, safe, and well-heated home is not enough for some people. Some want to live where the neighbors are congenial and have social and political outlooks similar to their own. This problem of sharing areas of the community is akin to that when one wants to control the kind of person who shares his own abode. Metro-Act of Rochester, Inc. and the Housing Council in the Monroe County Area, Inc.—two of the associations which bring this suit—do in my opinion represent the communal feeling of the actual residents and have standing. . . .

Standing has become a barrier to access to the federal courts, just as "the political question" was in earlier decades. The mounting caseload of federal courts is well known. But cases such as this one reflect festering sores in our society; and the American dream teaches that if one reaches high enough and persists there is a forum where justice is dispensed. I would lower the technical barriers and let the courts serve that ancient need. They can in time be curbed by legislative or constitutional restraints if an emergency arises.

We are today far from facing an emergency. For in all frankness, no Justice of this Court need work more than four days a week to carry his burden. I have found it a comfortable burden carried even in my months of hospitalization. . . .

I would reverse. . . .

MR. JUSTICE BRENNAN, with whom MR. JUSTICE WHITE and MR. JUSTICE MARSHALL join, dissenting.

In this case, a wide range of plaintiffs, alleging various kinds of injuries, claimed to have been affected by the Penfield zoning ordinance, on its face and as applied, and by other practices of the defendant officials of Penfield. Alleging that as a result of these laws and practices low- and moderate-income and minority people have been excluded from Penfield, and that this exclusion is unconstitutional, plaintiffs sought injunctive, declaratory, and monetary relief. The Court today, in an opinion that purports to be a "standing" opinion but that actually, I believe, has overtones of outmoded notions of pleading and of justiciability, refuses to find that any of the variously situated plaintiffs can clear numerous hurdles, some constructed here for the first time, necessary to establish "standing." While the Court gives lip-service to the principle, oft-repeated in recent years, that "standing in no way depends on the plaintiff's contention that particular conduct is illegal," in fact the opinion, which tosses out of court almost every conceivable kind of plaintiff who could be injured by the activity claimed to be unconstitutional, can be explained only by an indefensible hostility to the claim on the merits. I can appreciate the Court's reluctance to adjudicate the complex and difficult legal questions involved in determining the constitutionality of practices which assertedly limit residence in a particular municipality to those who are white and relatively well-off, and I also understand that the merits of this case could involve grave sociological and political ramifications. But courts cannot refuse to hear a case on the merits merely because they would prefer not to, and it is quite clear, when the record is viewed with dispassion, that at least three of the groups of plaintiffs have made allegations, and supported them with affidavits and documentary evidence, sufficient to survive a motion to dismiss for lack of standing. . . .

5.5   *"The issue before us is whether plaintiffs have standing to bring this suit."*

ALLEN V. WRIGHT

468 U.S. 737, 104 S. Ct. 3315, 82 L. Ed. 2d 556 (1984)

Parents of black children attending public schools brought a nationwide class action against the Internal Revenue Service in the Federal District Court for the District of

Columbia, alleging that it had not adopted the standards and procedures proper to meet its obligation to deny tax-exempt status to racially discriminatory private schools. The parents asserted that the IRS's failure harmed them directly and interfered with the ability of their children to be educated in desegregated public schools. The district judge dismissed the suit, holding that plaintiffs lacked standing to sue; but the Court of Appeals for the District of Columbia reversed. The Supreme Court granted certiorari.

JUSTICE O'CONNOR delivered the opinion of the Court. . . .

. . . The issue before us is whether plaintiffs have standing to bring this suit. We hold that they do not. . . .

Article III of the Constitution confines the federal courts to adjudicating actual "cases" and "controversies." As the Court explained in *Valley Forge Christian College v. Americans United for Separation of Church and State* (1982), the "case or controversy" requirement defines with respect to the Judicial Branch the idea of separation of powers on which the Federal Government is founded. The several doctrines that have grown up to elaborate that requirement are "founded in concern about the proper—and properly limited—role of the courts in a democratic society." *Warth v. Seldin* (1975).

> "All of the doctrines that cluster about Article III—not only standing but mootness, ripeness, political question, and the like—relate in part, and in different though overlapping ways, to an idea, which is more than an intuition but less than a rigorous and explicit theory, about the constitutional and prudential limits to the powers of an unelected, unrepresentative judiciary in our kind of government." *Vander Jagt v. O'Neil* (1983) (Bork, circuit judge, concurring.)

The case-or-controversy doctrines state fundamental limits on federal judicial power in our system of government.

The Art. III doctrine that requires a litigant to have "standing" to invoke the power of a federal court is perhaps the most important of these doctrines. "In essence the question of standing is whether the litigant is entitled to have the court decide the merits of the dispute or of particular issues." *Warth v. Seldin.* Standing doctrine embraces several judicially self-imposed limits on the exercise of federal jurisdiction, such as the general prohibition on a litigant's raising another person's legal rights, the rule barring adjudication of generalized grievances more appropriately addressed in the representative branches, and the requirement that a plaintiff's complaint fall within the zone of interests protected by the law invoked. . . . The requirement of standing, however, has a core component derived directly from the Constitution. A plaintiff must allege personal injury fairly traceable to the defendant's allegedly unlawful conduct and likely to be redressed by the requested relief.

Like the prudential component, the constitutional component of standing doctrine incorporates concepts concededly not susceptible of precise definition. The injury alleged must be, for example, " 'distinct and palpable,' " and not "abstract" or "conjectural" or "hypothetical." The injury must be "fairly" traceable to the challenged action, and relief from the injury must be "likely" to follow from a favorable decision. These terms cannot be defined so as to make application of the constitutional standing requirement a mechanical exercise.

The absence of precise definitions, however, as this Court's extensive body of case law on standing illustrates, hardly leaves courts at sea in applying the law of standing. Like most legal notions, the standing concepts have gained considerable definition from developing case law. In many cases the standing question can be answered chiefly by comparing the allegations of the particular complaint to those made in prior standing cases. More important, the law of Art. III standing is built on a single basic idea—the idea of separation of powers. It is this fact which makes possible the gradual clarification of the law through judicial application. Of course, both federal and state courts have long experience in applying and elaborating in numerous contexts the pervasive and fundamental notion of separation of powers.

Determining standing in a particular case may be facilitated by clarifying principles or even clear rules developed in prior cases. Typically, however, the standing inquiry requires careful judicial examination of a complainant's allegations to ascertain whether the particular plaintiff is entitled to an adjudication of the particular claims asserted. Is the injury too abstract, or otherwise not appropriate, to be considered judicially cognizable? Is the line of causation between the illegal conduct and injury too attenuated? Is the prospect of obtaining relief from the injury as a result of a favorable ruling too speculative? These questions and any others relevant to the standing inquiry must be answered by reference to the Art. III notion that federal courts may exercise power only "in the last resort, and as a necessity," and only when adjudication is "consistent with a system of separated powers and [the dispute is one] traditionally thought to be capable of resolution through the judicial process."

Respondents allege two injuries in their complaint to support their standing to bring this lawsuit. First, they say that they are harmed directly by the mere fact of Government financial aid to discriminatory private schools. Second, they say that the federal tax exemptions to racially discriminatory private schools in their communities impair their ability to have their public schools desegregated.

Because respondents have not clearly disclaimed reliance on either of the injuries described in their complaint, we address both allegations of injury. We conclude that neither suffices to support respondents' standing. The first fails under clear precedents of this Court because it does not constitute judicially cognizable injury. The second fails because the alleged injury is not fairly traceable to the assertedly unlawful conduct of the IRS.

Respondents' first claim of injury can be interpreted in two ways. It might be a claim simply to have the Government avoid the violation of law alleged in respondents' complaint. Alternatively, it might be a claim of stigmatic injury, or denigration, suffered by all members of a racial group when the Government discriminates on the basis of race. Under neither interpretation is this claim of injury judicially cognizable.

This Court has repeatedly held that an asserted right to have the Government act in accordance with law is not sufficient, standing alone, to confer jurisdiction on a federal court. In *Schlesinger v. Reservists Committee to Stop the War* (1974), for example, the Court rejected a claim of citizen standing to challenge Armed Forces Reserve commissions held by Members of Congress as violating the Incompatibility Clause of Art. I, § 6, cl. 2, of the Constitution. As citizens, the Court held, plaintiffs alleged nothing but "the abstract injury in nonobservance of the Constitution. . . ." More recently, in *Valley Forge,* we rejected a claim of standing to challenge a Government conveyance of property to a religious institution. Insofar as the plaintiffs relied simply on " 'their shared individuated right' " to a Government that made no law respecting an establishment of religion, we held that plaintiffs had not alleged a judicially cognizable injury. "[A]ssertion of a right to a particular kind of Government conduct, which the Government has violated by acting differently, cannot alone satisfy the requirements of Art. III without draining those requirements of meaning." Respondents here have no standing to complain simply that their Government is violating the law.

Neither do they have standing to litigate their claims based on the stigmatizing injury often caused by racial discrimination. There can be no doubt that this sort of noneconomic injury is one of the most serious consequences of discriminatory government action and is sufficient in some circumstances to support standing. . . . Our cases make clear, however, that such injury accords a basis for standing only to "those persons who are personally denied equal treatment" by the challenged discriminatory conduct.

In *Moose Lodge No. 107 v. Irvis* (1972), the Court held that the plaintiff had no standing to challenge a club's racially discriminatory membership policies because he had never applied for membership. In *O'Shea v. Littleton* (1974), the Court held that the plaintiffs had no standing to challenge racial discrimination in the administration of their city's criminal justice system because they had not alleged that they had been or would likely be subject to the challenged practices. The Court denied standing on similar facts in *Rizzo v.*

Goode (1976). In each of those cases, the plaintiffs alleged official racial discrimination comparable to that alleged by respondents here. Yet standing was denied in each case because the plaintiffs were not personally subject to the challenged discrimination. Insofar as their first claim of injury is concerned, respondents are in exactly the same position . . . they do not allege a stigmatic injury suffered as a direct result of having personally been denied equal treatment.

The consequences of recognizing respondents' standing on the basis of their first claim of injury illustrate why our cases plainly hold that such injury is not judicially cognizable. If the abstract stigmatic injury were cognizable, standing would extend nationwide to all members of the particular racial groups against which the Government was alleged to be discriminating by its grant of a tax exemption to a racially discriminatory school, regardless of the location of that school. All such persons could claim the same sort of abstract stigmatic injury respondents assert in their first claim of injury. A black person in Hawaii could challenge the grant of a tax exemption to a racially discriminatory school in Maine. Recognition of standing in such circumstances would transform the federal courts into "no more than a vehicle for the vindication of the value interests of concerned bystanders." *United States v. SCRAP* (1973). Constitutional limits on the role of the federal courts preclude such a transformation.

It is in their complaint's second claim of injury that respondents allege harm to a concrete, personal interest that can support standing in some circumstances. The injury they identify—their children's diminished ability to receive an education in a racially integrated school—is, beyond any doubt, not only judicially cognizable but, as shown by cases from *Brown v. Board of Education* (1954), to *Bob Jones University v. United States* (1983), one of the most serious injuries recognized in our legal system. Despite the constitutional importance of curing the injury alleged by respondents, however, the federal judiciary may not redress it unless standing requirements are met. In this case, respondents' second claim of injury cannot support standing because the injury alleged is not fairly traceable to the Government conduct respondents challenge as unlawful.

The illegal conduct challenged by respondents is the IRS's grant of tax exemptions to some racially discriminatory schools. The line of causation between that conduct and desegregation of respondents' schools is attenuated at best. From the perspective of the IRS, the injury to respondents is highly indirect and "results from the independent action of some third party not before the court," *Simon v. Eastern Kentucky Welfare Rights Org.* (1976).

The diminished ability of respondents' children to receive a desegregated education would be fairly traceable to unlawful IRS grants of tax exemptions only if there were enough racially discriminatory private schools receiving tax exemptions in respondents' communities for withdrawal of those exemptions to make an appreciable difference in public-school integration. Respondents have made no such allegation. It is, first, uncertain how many racially discriminatory private schools are in fact receiving tax exemptions. Moreover, it is entirely speculative, as respondents themselves conceded in the Court of Appeals, see n. 17, *supra,* whether withdrawal of a tax exemption from any particular school would lead the school to change its policies. It is just as speculative whether any given parent of a child attending such a private school would decide to transfer the child to public school as a result of any changes in educational or financial policy made by the private school once it was threatened with loss of tax-exempt status. It is also pure speculation whether, in a particular community, a large enough number of the numerous relevant school officials and parents would reach decisions that collectively would have a significant impact on the racial composition of the public schools.

The links in the chain of causation between the challenged Government conduct and the asserted injury are far too weak for the chain as a whole to sustain respondents' standing. . . . It involves numerous third parties (officials of racially discriminatory schools receiving tax exemptions and the parents of children attending such schools) who may not even exist in respondents' communities and whose independent decisions may not collectively have a significant effect on the ability of public-school students to receive a desegregated education.

The idea of separation of powers that underlies standing doctrine explains why our cases preclude the conclusion that respondents' alleged injury "fairly can be traced to the challenged action" of the IRS. *Simon v. Eastern Kentucky Welfare Rights Org.* That conclusion would pave the way generally for suits challenging, not specifically identifiable Government violations of law, but the particular programs agencies establish to carry out their legal obligations. Such suits, even when premised on allegations of several instances of violations of law, are rarely if ever appropriate for federal-court adjudication.

"Carried to its logical end, [respondents'] approach would have the federal courts as virtually continuing monitors of the wisdom and soundness of Executive action; such a role is appropriate for the Congress acting through its committees and the 'power of the purse'; it is not the role of the judiciary, absent actual present or immediately threatened injury resulting from unlawful governmental action." *Laird v. Tatum.*

The same concern for the proper role of the federal courts is reflected in cases like *O'Shea v. Littleton* (1974), *Rizzo v. Goode* (1976), and *City of Los Angeles v. Lyons* (1983). In all three cases plaintiffs sought injunctive relief directed at certain systemwide law enforcement practices. The Court held in each case that, absent an allegation of a specific threat of being subject to the challenged practices, plaintiffs had no standing to ask for an injunction. Animating this Court's holdings was the principle that "[a] federal court . . . is not the proper forum to press" general complaints about the way in which government goes about its business.

Case-or-controversy considerations, the Court observed in *O'Shea v. Littleton*, "obviously shade into those determining whether the complaint states a sound basis for equitable relief." The latter set of considerations should therefore inform our judgment about whether respondents have standing. Most relevant to this case is the principle articulated in *Rizzo v. Goode*:

> "When a plaintiff seeks to enjoin the activity of a government agency, even within a unitary court system, his case must contend with 'the well-established rule that the Government has traditionally been granted the widest latitude in the dispatch of its own internal affairs.' "

When transported into the Art. III context, that principle, grounded as it is in the idea of separation of powers, counsels against recognizing standing in a case brought, not to enforce specific legal obligations whose violation works a direct harm, but to seek a restructuring of the apparatus established by the Executive Branch to fulfill its legal duties. The Constitution, after all, assigns to the Executive Branch, and not to the Judicial Branch, the duty to "take Care that the Laws be faithfully executed." U.S. Const., Art. II, § 3. We could not recognize respondents' standing in this case without running afoul of that structural principle.

"The necessity that the plaintiff who seeks to invoke judicial power stand to profit in some personal interest remains an Art. III requirement." *Simon v. Eastern Kentucky Welfare Rights Org.* Respondents have not met this fundamental requirement. The judgment of the Court of Appeals is accordingly reversed, and the injunction issued by that court is vacated.

It is so ordered.

JUSTICE MARSHALL took no part in the decision of the case.
JUSTICE BRENNAN, dissenting.

Once again, the Court "uses 'standing to slam the courthouse door against plaintiffs who are entitled to full consideration of their claims on the merits.' " *Valley Forge Christian College v. Americans United for Separation of Church and State, Inc.* (1982) (BRENNAN, J., dissenting). And once again, the Court does so by "wax[ing] eloquent" on considerations that provide little justification for the decision at hand. This time, however, the Court focuses on "the idea of separation of powers," as if the mere incantation of that phrase provides an obvious solution to the difficult questions presented by these cases.

One could hardly dispute the proposition that Article III of the Constitution, by limiting the judicial power to "cases" or "controversies," embodies the notion that each branch of our National Government must confine its actions to those that are consistent with our scheme of separated powers. But simply stating that unremarkable truism provides little, if any, illumination of the standing inquiry that must be undertaken by a federal court faced with a particular action filed by particular plaintiffs. "The question whether a particular person is a proper party to maintain the action does not, by its own force, raise separation of powers problems related to improper judicial interference in areas committed to other branches of the Federal Government." *Flast v. Cohen* (1968).

The Court's attempt to obscure the standing question must be seen, therefore, as no more than a cover for its failure to recognize the nature of the specific claims raised by the respondents in these cases. By relying on generalities concerning our tripartite system of government, the Court is able to conclude that the respondents lack standing to maintain this action without acknowledging the precise nature of the injuries they have alleged. In so doing, the Court displays a startling insensitivity to the historical role played by the federal courts in eradicating race discrimination from our nation's schools—a role that has played a prominent part in this Court's decisions from *Brown v. Board of Education* through *Bob Jones University v. United States* (1983). Because I cannot join in such misguided decisionmaking, I dissent. . . .

5.6   *"[A]ppellees . . . failed to allege either that they are or expect to be pregnant. . . ."*

HARRIS V. MCRAE

448 U.S. 297, 100 S. Ct. 2671, 65 L. Ed. 2d 784 (1980)

The so-called Hyde Amendment, adopted by Congress in 1976 and reenacted in slightly different forms in succeeding years, forbade payment of federal funds to reimburse states under the Medicaid program for abortions, unless they had been necessary to save the life of the mother or the pregnancy had resulted from rape or incest. Numerous petitioners brought suit in a federal district court against the Secretary of Health, Education, and Welfare, challenging the constitutionality of the cutoff as violating the liberty protected by the due process clause of the Fifth Amendment and the equal protection of the laws that same clause guaranteed. In addition, they asserted that because the Hyde Amendment incorporated the Catholic Church's teachings on abortion, it established a religion, contrary to the First Amendment, and also interfered with their First Amendment right freely to exercise their religion.

The litigants included four women on Medicaid who wished to have abortions that did not fall within the Hyde Amendment's exceptions, two officers of the Women's

Division of the Board of Global Ministries of the United Methodist Church, and the Women's Division itself.

The district judge held the act was invalid and the court of appeals affirmed. The secretary of HEW appealed to the Supreme Court; and, by a five-to-four vote, the justices reversed on the first three points. They also considered the claim that the Hyde Amendment interfered with the free exercise of religion.

MR. JUSTICE STEWART delivered the opinion of the Court. . . .

We need not address the merits of the appellees' arguments concerning the Free Exercise Clause, because the appellees lack standing to raise a free exercise challenge to the Hyde Amendment. The named appellees fall into three categories: (1) the indigent pregnant women who sued on behalf of other women similarly situated, (2) the two officers of the Women's Division, and (3) the Women's Division itself. The named appellees in the first category lack standing to challenge the Hyde Amendment on free exercise grounds because none alleged, much less proved, that she sought an abortion under compulsion of religious belief. See *McGowan v. Maryland* [1961]. Although the named appellees in the second category did provide a detailed description of their religious beliefs, they failed to allege either that they are or expect to be pregnant or that they are eligible to receive Medicaid. These named appellees, therefore, lack the personal stake in the controversy needed to confer standing to raise such a challenge to the Hyde Amendment. See *Warth v. Seldin* [1975].

Finally, although the Women's Division alleged that its membership includes "pregnant Medicaid eligible women who, as a matter of religious practice and in accordance with their conscientious beliefs, would choose but are precluded or discouraged from obtaining abortions reimbursed by Medicaid because of the Hyde Amendment," the Women's Division does not satisfy the standing requirements for an organization to assert the rights of its membership. One of those requirements is that "neither the claim asserted nor the relief requested requires the participation of individual members in the lawsuit." *Hunt v. Washington Apple Advertising Comm'n.* [1972]. Since "it is necessary in a free exercise case for one to show the coercive effect of the enactment as it operates against him in the practice of his religion," *Abington School Dist. v. Schempp* [1963], the claim asserted here is one that ordinarily requires individual participation. In the present case, the Women's Division concedes that "the permissibility, advisability and/or necessity of abortion according to circumstance is a matter about which there is diversity of view within . . . our membership, and is a determination which must be ultimately and absolutely entrusted to the conscience of the individual before God." It is thus clear that the participation of individual members of the Women's Division is essential to a proper understanding and resolution of their free exercise claims. Accordingly, we conclude that the Women's Division, along with the other named appellees, lack standing to challenge the Hyde Amendment under the Free Exercise Clause.

5.7   *"What are these people—doctor and patients—to do?"*

THE CONNECTICUT BIRTH CONTROL CASES

A Connecticut statute, passed in 1879, prohibited the use of drugs or instruments to prevent conception or the giving of assistance or counsel in their use. Periodic efforts to repeal the statute having failed, the Connecticut Planned Parenthood League resorted to the courts. The first two suits sought declaratory judgment that the statute was unconstitutional. A declaratory judgment action must meet all the requirements of a case or controversy, but it asks the court to declare the rights of parties in controversy without requiring them to put themselves in jeopardy by taking action based on their legal contentions. The third suit was a criminal action for violation of the statute.

". . . the proceedings . . . present no constitutional question which appellant has standing to assert."

Tileston v. Ullman

318 U.S. 44, 63 S. Ct. 493, 87 L. Ed. 603 (1943)

PER CURIAM.*
This case comes here on appeal to review a declaratory judgment of the Supreme Court of Errors of Connecticut that §§ 6246 and 6562 of the General Statutes of Connecticut of 1930—prohibiting the use of drugs or instruments to prevent conception, and the giving of assistance or counsel in their use—are applicable to appellant, a registered physician, and as applied to him are constitutional.

The suit was tried and judgment rendered on the allegations of

---

*"Per curiam" means "by the Court." It designates an unsigned opinion, usually employed in less important or controversial cases, but sometimes used to record a limited consensus when the justices are badly divided. See, for example, the per curiam opinion in *New York Times Company v. United States* (1971).—Eds.

the complaint which are stipulated to be true. Appellant alleged that the statute, if applicable to him, would prevent his giving professional advice concerning the use of contraceptives to three patients whose condition of health was such that their lives would be endangered by child-bearing, and that appellees, law enforcement officers of the state, intend to prosecute any offense against the statute and "claim or make claim" that the proposed professional advice would constitute such offense. The complaint set out in detail the danger to the lives of appellant's patients in the event that they should bear children, but contained no allegations asserting any claim under the Fourteenth Amendment of infringement of appellant's liberty or his property rights. The relief prayed was a declaratory judgment as to whether the statutes are applicable to appellant and if so whether they constitute a valid exercise of constitutional power "within the meaning and intent of Amendment XIV of the Constitution of the United States prohibiting a state from depriving any person of life without due process of law." On stipulation of the parties the state superior court ordered these questions of law reserved for the consideration and advice of the Supreme Court of Errors. That court, which assumed without deciding that the case was an appropriate one for a declaratory judgment, ruled that the statutes "prohibit the action proposed to be done" by appellant and "are constitutional."

We are of the opinion that the proceedings in the state courts present no constitutional question which appellant has standing to assert. The sole constitutional attack upon the statutes under the Fourteenth Amendment is confined to their deprivation of life—obviously not appellant's but his patients. There is no allegation or proof that appellant's life is in danger. His patients are not parties to this proceeding and there is no basis on which we can say that he has standing to secure an adjudication of his patients' constitutional right to life, which they do not assert in their own behalf. No question is raised in the record with respect to the deprivation of appellant's liberty or property in contravention of the Fourteenth Amendment, nor is there anything in the opinion or judgment of the Supreme Court of Errors which indicates or would support a decision of any question other than those raised in the superior court and reserved by it for decision of the Supreme Court of Errors. That court's practice is to decline to answer questions not reserved.

Since the appeal must be dismissed on the ground that appellant has no standing to litigate the constitutional question which the record presents, it is unnecessary to consider whether the record shows the existence of a genuine case or controversy essential to the exercise of the jurisdiction of this Court.

Dismissed.

> *"Justiciability is . . . not a legal concept with a fixed content. . . ."*

Poe v. Ullman

367 U.S. 497, 81 S. Ct. 1752, 6 L. Ed. 2d 989 (1961)

The *Tileston* case failed because it had been brought by a doctor, who was held to have no standing to challenge the anticontraceptive law. The next test case was brought against Connecticut State's Attorney Abraham Ullman by Dr. C. Lee Buxton and two of his female patients, both of whom had experienced difficult and dangerous pregnancies. The women alleged that the state law threatened their health or lives by preventing the doctor from giving them birth-control advice and treatment. They asked for a declaratory judgment holding the statute to be unconstitutional.

MR. JUSTICE FRANKFURTER announced the judgment of the Court in an opinion which the CHIEF JUSTICE [WARREN], MR. JUSTICE CLARK, and MR. JUSTICE WHITTAKER join. . . .

Appellants' complaints in these declaratory judgment proceedings do not clearly, and certainly do not in terms, allege that appellee Ullman threatens to prosecute them for use of, or for giving advice concerning, contraceptive devices. The allegations are merely that, in the course of his public duty, he intends to prosecute any offenses against Connecticut law, and that he claims that use of and advice concerning contraceptives would constitute offenses. . . .

The Connecticut law prohibiting the use of contraceptives has been on the State's books since 1879. During the more than three-quarters of a century since its enactment, a prosecution for its violation seems never to have been initiated, save in *State v. Nelson*. The circumstances of that case, decided in 1940, only prove the abstract character of what is before us. There, a test case was brought to determine the constitutionality of the Act as applied against two doctors and a nurse who had allegedly disseminated contraceptive information. After the Supreme Court of Errors sustained the legislation on appeal from a demurrer to the information, the State moved to dismiss the information. Neither counsel nor our own researches have discovered any other attempt to enforce the prohibition of distribution or use of contraceptive devices by criminal process. The unreality of these law suits is illumined by another circumstance. We were advised by counsel for appellants that contraceptives are commonly and notoriously sold in Connecticut drug stores. Yet no prosecutions are recorded; and certainly such ubiquitous, open, public sales would more quickly invite the attention of enforcement officials than the conduct in which the present appellants wish to engage— the giving of private medical advice by a doctor to his individual patients, and their private use of the devices prescribed. The undeviating policy of nullification by Connecticut of its anti-contraceptive laws throughout all the long years that they have been on the statute books bespeaks more than prosecutorial paralysis. . . .

The restriction of our jurisdiction to cases and controversies within the meaning of Article III of the Constitution, see *Muskrat v. United States* [1911], is not the sole limitation on the exercise of our appellate powers, especially in cases raising constitutional questions. The policy reflected in numerous cases and over a long period was thus summarized in the oft-quoted statement of Mr. Justice Brandeis: "The Court [has] developed, for its own governance in the cases confessedly within its jurisdiction, a series of rules under which it has avoided passing upon a large part of all the constitutional questions pressed upon it for decision." *Ashwander v. Tennessee Valley Authority* [1936] (concurring opinion). In part the rules summarized in the Ashwander opinion have derived from the historically defined, limited nature and function of courts and from the recognition that, within the framework of our adversary system, the adjudicatory process is most securely founded when it is exercised under the impact of a lively conflict between antagonistic demands, actively pressed, which make resolution of the controverted issue a practical necessity. In part they derive from the fundamental federal and tripartite character of our National Government and from the role—restricted by its very responsibility—of the federal courts, and particularly this Court, within that structure.

These considerations press with special urgency in cases challenging legislative action or state judicial action as repugnant to the Constitution. "The best teaching of this Court's experience admonishes us not to entertain constitutional questions in advance of the strictest necessity." *Parker v. County of Los Angeles* [1949]. The various doctrines of "standing," "ripeness," and "mootness," which this Court has evolved with particular, though not exclusive, reference to such cases are but several manifestations—each having its own "varied application"—of the primary conception that federal judicial power is to be exercised to strike down legislation, whether state or federal, only at the instance of one who is himself immediately harmed, or immediately threatened with harm by the challenged action. . . .

. . . And with due regard to Dr. Buxton's standing as a physician and to his personal sensitiveness, we cannot accept, as the basis of constitutional adjudication, other than as chimerical the fear of enforcement of provisions that have during so many years gone uniformly and without exception unenforced.

Justiciability is of course not a legal concept with a fixed content or susceptible of scientific verification. Its utilization is the resultant of many subtle pressures, including the appropriateness of the issues for decision by the Court and the actual hardship to the litigants of denying them the relief sought. Both these factors justify withholding adjudication of the constitutional issues raised under the circumstances and in the manner in which they are now before the Court.

Dismissed.

MR. JUSTICE BLACK dissents because he believes that the constitutional questions should be reached and decided.

MR. JUSTICE BRENNAN, concurring in the judgment. . . .

MR. JUSTICE DOUGLAS, dissenting.

These cases are dismissed because a majority of the members of this Court conclude, for varying reasons, that this controversy does not present a justiciable question. That conclusion is too transparent to require an extended reply. . . .

. . . Plaintiffs in No. 60 are two sets of husband and wife. One wife is pathetically ill, having delivered a stillborn fetus. If she becomes pregnant again, her life will be gravely jeopardized. This couple has been unable to get medical advice concerning the "best and safest" means to avoid pregnancy from their physician, plaintiff in No. 61, because if he gave it he would commit a crime. The use of contraceptive devices would also constitute a crime. And it is alleged—and admitted by the State—that the State's Attorney intends to enforce the law by prosecuting offenses under the laws.

A public clinic dispensing birth-control information has indeed been closed by the State. Doctors and a nurse working in that clinic were arrested by the police and charged with advising married women on the use of contraceptives. That litigation produced *State v. Nelson* which upheld these statutes. . . .

The Court refers to the *Nelson* prosecution as a "test case" and implies that it had little impact. Yet its impact was described differently by a contemporary observer who concluded his comment with this sentence: "This serious setback to the birth control movement [the Nelson case] led to the closing of all the clinics in the state, just as they had been previously closed in the state of Massachusetts." At oral argument, counsel for appellants confirmed that the clinics are still closed. In response to a question from the bench, he affirmed that "no public or private clinic" has dared give birth-control advice since the decision in the *Nelson* case.

These, then, are the circumstances in which the Court feels that it can, contrary to every principle of American or English common law, go outside the record to conclude that there exists a "tacit agreement" that these statutes will not be enforced. No lawyer, I think, would advise his clients to rely on that "tacit agreement." No police official, I think, would feel himself bound by that "tacit agreement." . . .

When the Court goes outside the record to determine that Connecticut has adopted "The undeviating policy of nullification . . . of its anti-contraceptive laws," it selects a particularly poor case in which to exercise such a novel power. This is not a law which is a dead letter. Twice since 1940, Connecticut has reenacted these laws as part of general statutory revisions. Consistently, bills to remove the statutes from the books have been rejected by the legislature. In short, the statutes—far from being the accidental left-overs of another era—are the center of a continuing controversy in the State.

Again, the Court relies on the inability of counsel to show any attempts, other than the *Nelson* case, "to enforce the prohibition of distribution or use of contraceptive devices by criminal process." Yet, on oral argument, counsel for the appellee stated on his own knowledge that several proprietors had been prosecuted in the "minor police courts of Connecticut" after they had been "picked up" for selling contraceptives. The enforcement of criminal laws in minor courts has just as much impact as in those cases where appellate courts are resorted to. . . .

What are these people—doctor and patients—to do? Flout the law and go to prison? Violate the law surreptitiously and hope they will not get caught? By today's decision we leave them no other alternatives. It is not the choice they need have under the regime of the declaratory judgment and our constitutional system. It is not the choice worthy of a civilized society. A sick wife, a concerned husband, a conscientious doctor seek a dignified, discrete, orderly answer to the critical problem confronting them. We should not turn them away and make them flout the law and get arrested to have their constitutional rights determined. . . .

MR. JUSTICE HARLAN, dissenting. . . .
MR. JUSTICE STEWART, dissenting. . . .

"Here those doubts are removed. . . ."

Griswold v. Connecticut

381 U.S. 479, 85 S. Ct. 1678, 14 L. Ed. 2d 510 (1965)

Following the Supreme Court's ruling in *Poe v. Ullman* that the case was not justiciable, officials of the Planned Parenthood League of Connecticut decided that they would have to get arrested to refute Justice Frankfurter's theory that the Connecticut law was a dead letter. They opened a birth-control clinic with Dr. Buxton, one of the plaintiffs in *Poe,* as medical director. After the center had been open for ten days, Dr. Buxton and Ms. Griswold, executive director of the League, were arrested and convicted in state courts. On appeal to the Supreme Court the only standing problem was whether they could defend themselves by invoking the constitutional rights of the people whom the clinic served. This was a minor issue, however, compared with the Supreme Court's major holding that the Connecticut state statute was an unconstitutional invasion of privacy. (For the decision on the major issue, see Reading 14.3.)

MR. JUSTICE DOUGLAS delivered the opinion of the Court. . . .

We think that appellants have standing to raise the constitutional rights of the married people with whom they had a professional relationship. *Tileston v. Ullman* [1943] is different, for here the plaintiff seeking to represent others asked for a declaratory judgment. In that situation we thought that the requirements of standing should be strict, lest the standards of "case or controversy" in Article III of the Constitution become blurred. Here those doubts are removed by reason of a criminal conviction for serving married couples in violation of an aiding-and-abetting statute. Certainly the accessory should have standing to assert that the offense which he is charged with assisting is not, or cannot constitutionally be, a crime.

This case is more akin to *Truax v. Raich* [1915] where an employee was permitted to assert the rights of his employer; to *Pierce v. Society of Sisters* [1925] where the owners of private schools were entitled to assert the rights of potential pupils and their parents; and to *Barrows v. Jackson* [1952] where a white defendant, party to a racially restrictive covenant, who was being sued for damages by the covenantors because she had conveyed her property to Negroes was allowed to raise the issue that enforcement of the covenant violated the rights of prospective Negro purchasers to equal protection although no Negro was a party to the suit. The rights of husband and wife, pressed here, are likely to be diluted or adversely affected unless those rights are considered in a suit involving those who have this kind of confidential relation to them. . . .

5.8   *"Pregnancy provides a classic justification for a conclusion of nonmootness."*

ROE V. WADE

410 U.S. 113, 93 S. Ct. 705, 35 L. Ed. 2d 147 (1973)

A pregnant single woman challenged the constitutionality of Texas's criminal abortion laws, which proscribed procuring or attempting an abortion except on medical advice for the purpose of saving the mother's life.

MR. JUSTICE BLACKMUN delivered the opinion of the Court. . . .

Jane Roe, a single woman who was residing in Dallas County, Texas, instituted this federal action in March 1970 against the District Attorney of the county. She sought a declaratory judgment that the Texas criminal abortion statutes were unconstitutional on their face, and an injunction restraining the defendant from enforcing the statutes.

Roe alleged that she was unmarried and pregnant; that she wished to terminate her pregnancy by an abortion "performed by a competent, licensed physician, under safe, clinical conditions"; that she was unable to get a "legal" abortion in Texas because her life did not appear to be threatened by the continuation of her pregnancy; and that she could not afford to travel to another jurisdiction in order to secure a legal abortion under safe conditions. She claimed that the Texas statutes were unconstitutionally vague and that they abridged her right of personal privacy, protected by the First, Fourth, Fifth, Ninth, and Fourteenth Amendments. By an amendment to her complaint Roe purported to sue "on behalf of herself and all other women" similarly situated.

We are . . . confronted with issues of justiciability, standing, and abstention. [Has Roe] established that "personal stake in the outcome of the controversy," Baker v. Carr (1962), that insures that "the dispute sought to be adjudicated will be presented in an adversary context and in a form historically viewed as capable of judicial resolution," Flast v. Cohen (1968) and Sierra Club v. Morton (1972)? . . . A. Jane Roe. Despite the use of the pseudonym, no suggestion is made that Roe is a fictitious person. For purposes of her case, we accept as true, and as established, her existence; her pregnant state, as of the inception of her suit in March 1970 and as late as May 21 of that year when she filed an alias affidavit with the District Court; and her inability to obtain a legal abortion in Texas.

Viewing Roe's case as of the time of its filing and thereafter until as late as May, there can be little dispute that it then presented a case or controversy and that, wholly apart from the class aspects, she, as a pregnant single woman thwarted by the Texas criminal abortion laws, had standing to challenge those statutes. Indeed, we do not read the appellee's brief as really asserting anything to the contrary. The "logical nexus between the status asserted and claim sought to be adjudicated," Flast v. Cohen, and the necessary degree of contentiousness, Golden v. Zwickler (1969), are both present.

The appellee notes, however, that the record does not disclose that Roe was pregnant at the time of the District Court hearing on May 22, 1970, or on the following June 17 when the court's opinion and judgment were filed. And he suggests that Roe's case must now be moot because she and all other members of her class are no longer subject to any 1970 pregnancy.

The usual rule in federal cases is that an actual controversy must exist at stages of appellate or certiorari review, and not simply at the date the action is initiated.

But when, as here, pregnancy is a significant fact in the litigation, the normal 266-day human gestation period is so short that the pregnancy will come to term before the usual appellate process is complete. If that termination makes a case moot, pregnancy litigation seldom will survive much beyond the trial stage, and appellate review will be effectively denied. Our law should not be that rigid. Pregnancy often comes more than once to the same woman, and in the general population, if man is to survive, it will always be with us. Pregnancy provides a classic justification for a conclusion of nonmootness. It truly could be "capable of repetition, yet evading review."

We therefore agree with the District Court that Jane Roe had standing to undertake this litigation, that she presented a justiciable controversy, and that the termination of her 1970 pregnancy has not rendered her case moot. . . .

5.9

"It's a question of . . . how far you can push the Supreme Court. . . ."

NOT RIGHT ENOUGH?

Al Kamen

Solicitor General Rex E. Lee, who led the Reagan administration's often successful drive to push the Supreme Court in a conservative direction, has announced his resignation after four years as the government's leading litigator.

Lee began his tenure under fire from liberals and women's groups who accused him of being too conservative and of politicizing the relatively autonomous office.

But he leaves office under increasingly bitter attack from conservative hard-liners who demanded his ouster. They insist that, despite his successes, he has either ignored or not pushed enough for the administration's views on abortion, school prayer, busing, criminal law and civil rights.

His opponents within the administration often included Assistant Attorney General William Bradford Reynolds, frequently mentioned as a possible successor.

Lee says his long-expected departure is not related to administration infighting. "I can tell you categorically no one asked me to leave and I was not leaving under any kind of pressure," Lee states. "Four

Washington Post National Weekly Edition, May 13, 1985. Reprinted by permission. Al Kamen is a staff writer for the *Washington Post.*

years just seems like a good time to leave, and I literally cannot afford to stay any longer because of my family."

Lee has seven children, aged 6 to 22, three of whom will be in college this fall. Lee will leave in June to become a partner in the Washington office of a Chicago law firm.

Lee shares the administration's views against abortion, busing, racial quotas and judicial activism. He also favors loosening judicially imposed restraints on police and an increasing role for religion in public life, including prayer in the schools.

But the low-key Lee—a former law clerk to Supreme Court Justice Byron R. White, former head of the Justice Department's civil division and former dean of Brigham Young University Law School —also insisted on maintaining what he calls the solicitor general's traditional "unique relationship" of trust and confidence with the Supreme Court.

That did not set well with those who wanted stronger advocacy on behalf of an administration that, more than any since the New Deal, has brought its political and social agenda to the court.

Lee "misunderstands both his own role and that of the [Supreme] Court," James McClellan, head of the conservative Center for Judicial Studies, wrote last fall in an article calling for Lee's ouster.

Lee calls the disagreement largely tactical. "It's a question of what you can get away with, how far can you push the Supreme Court or move the Supreme Court in the direction you want to go."

Pushing too hard could lead to a fatal loss of credibility before the court, Lee says.

Lee's statistical record of success equals or exceeds that of any recent predecessor, according to longtime court-watchers. In the last Supreme Court term, the justices agreed to hear about 80 percent of the petitions for review filed by Lee's office. In contrast, they agreed to review about 3 percent of all the 3,878 other petitions filed.

Lee's office won 83 percent of the cases it filed or participated in.

Detractors say that record only shows he has been asking the Court merely for what it would easily give. Others explain his success rate by noting that his tenure coincided with a period when the Court itself was moving rightward, especially with the replacement of moderate conservative Justice Potter Stewart with the more conservative Sandra Day O'Connor.

But those who often oppose Lee before the court acknowledge his effectiveness.

"Although many conservatives will disagree, I think he has done the conservative cause far more good with his moderate approach," says Alan Morrison, director of the Public Citizen Litigation Group. "He and I continue to disagree on many issues, but he has been quite successful, winning a lot of 5-to-4 [Supreme Court] decisions that were not easy cases to win. The office has done well by its client [the administration]. Whether they have done well by the United States is another matter."

Paul D. Kamenar, legal director of the conservative Washington Legal Foundation, says Lee generally deserves "good marks" but agrees with other conservatives that Lee was "timid" in pushing administration goals.

Lee says his approach resulted in important victories in the last four years that enhanced the power of the executive over Congress and the discretion of executive branch agencies over the judiciary.

Other victories allowed for greater use in trials of illegally seized evidence, for parents to claim state tax deductions for parochial school expenses and for limits on affirmative action plans.

Lee says he felt that when he pushed too hard for limits on the constitutional right to abortion, the strategy backfired, leading to a ringing reaffirmation by the Court of the original 1973 decision. Lee cites that as the biggest loss in his four years.

Similarly, when the administration prevailed over the solicitor's office and pushed for tax exemptions for schools that discriminate, it lost overwhelmingly.

Lee says that if his client wanted everything but he as a lawyer knew that only something less was possible, it would make no sense to go for everything and lose.*

5.10   "Courts ought not to enter this political thicket."

COLEGROVE V. GREEN
328 U.S. 549, 66 S. Ct. 1198, 90 L. Ed. 1432 (1946)

At the time of this case, Congress had set the size of the House of Representatives at 435, with each state's share to be automatically reapportioned after every census. Although Congress had required that representatives be elected from single-member districts, it had not, since 1929, regulated the relative size of districts within individual states. The rurally dominated legislature of Illinois had refused to redistrict the state and thereby increase the political power of the Chicago area. As a result, in the mid-1940s the population of metropolitan districts ran as high as nine times that of rural, downstate districts. Protesting against this gerrymandering-by-default, three college professors from the Chicago area brought suit in 1946 in a federal district court to enjoin state officials from holding an election under the existing system. The special three-judge district court dismissed the suit, and the professors appealed to the Supreme Court.

*Mr. Lee resigned as Solicitor General in June 1985—Eds.

MR. JUSTICE FRANKFURTER announced the judgment of the Court and an opinion in which MR. JUSTICE REED and MR. JUSTICE BURTON concur. . . .

We are of opinion that the petitioners ask of this Court what is beyond its competence to grant. This is one of those demands on judicial power which cannot be met by verbal fencing about "jurisdiction." It must be resolved by considerations on the basis of which this Court, from time to time, has refused to intervene in controversies. It has refused to do so because due regard for the effective working of our Government revealed this issue to be of a peculiarly political nature and therefore not meet for judicial determination.

This is not an action to recover for damage because of the discriminatory exclusion of a plaintiff from rights enjoyed by other citizens. The basis for the suit is not a private wrong, but a wrong suffered by Illinois as a polity. In effect this is an appeal to the federal courts to reconstruct the electoral process of Illinois in order that it may be adequately represented in the councils of the Nation. Because the Illinois legislature has failed to revise its Congressional Representative districts in order to reflect great changes, during more than a generation, in the distribution of its population, we are asked to do this, as it were, for Illinois.

Of course no court can affirmatively remap the Illinois districts so as to bring them more in conformity with the standards of fairness for a representative system. At best we could only declare the existing electoral system invalid. The result would be to leave Illinois undistricted and to bring into operation, if the Illinois legislature chose not to act, the choice of members for the House of Representatives on a statewide ticket. The last stage may be worse than the first. The upshot of judicial action may defeat the vital political principle which led Congress, more than a hundred years ago, to require districting. . . . Assuming acquiescence on the part of the authorities of Illinois in the selection of its Representatives by a mode that defies the direction of Congress for selection by districts, the House of Representatives may not acquiesce. In the exercise of its power to judge the qualifications of its own members, the House may reject a delegation of Representatives-at-large. . . . Nothing is clearer than that this controversy concerns matters that bring courts into immediate and active relations with party contests. From the determination of such issues this Court has traditionally held aloof. It is hostile to a democratic system to involve the judiciary in the politics of the people. And it is not less pernicious if such judicial intervention in an essentially political contest be dressed up in the abstract phrases of the law.

The appellants urge with great zeal that the conditions of which they complain are grave evils and offend public morality. The Constitution of the United States gives ample power to provide against these evils. But due regard for the Constitution as a viable system precludes judicial correction. Authority for dealing with such problems resides elsewhere. Article I, section 4 of the Constitution provides that "The Times, Places and Manner of holding Elections for . . . Representatives, shall be prescribed in each State by the Legislature thereof; but the Congress may at any time by Law make or alter such Regulations . . ." The short of it is that the Constitution has conferred upon Congress exclusive authority to secure fair representation by the States in the popular House and left to that House determination whether States have fulfilled their responsibility. If Congress failed in exercising its powers, whereby standards of fairness are offended, the remedy ultimately lies with the people. Whether Congress faithfully discharges its duty or not, the subject has been committed to the exclusive control of Congress. An aspect of government from which the judiciary, in view of what is involved, has been excluded by the clear intention of the Constitution cannot be entered by the federal courts because Congress may have been in default in exacting from States obedience to its mandate. . . .

To sustain this action would cut very deep into the very being of Congress. Courts ought not to enter this political thicket. The remedy for unfairness in districting is to secure State legislatures that will apportion properly, or to invoke the ample powers of Congress. The Constitution has many commands that are not enforceable by courts because they clearly fall outside the conditions and purposes that circumscribe judicial action. Thus, "on Demand of the executive Authority," Art. IV, § 2, of a State it is the duty of a sister State to deliver up a fugitive from justice. But the fulfillment of this duty cannot be judicially enforced. *Commonwealth of Kentucky v. Dennison* [1861]. The duty to see to it that the laws are faithfully executed cannot be brought under legal compulsion. *State of Mississippi v. Johnson* [1867]. Violation of the great guaranty of a republican form of government in States cannot be challenged in the courts. *Pacific States Telephone & Telegraph Co. v. Oregon* [1912]. The Constitution has left the performance of many duties in our governmental scheme to depend on the fidelity of the executive and legislative action and, ultimately, on the vigilance of the people in exercising their political rights. Dismissal of the complaint is

Affirmed.

[JUSTICE RUTLEDGE concurred in the result. JUSTICES BLACK, DOUGLAS, and MURPHY dissented.]

5.11

"The nonjusticiability of a political question is primarily a function of the separation of powers."

BAKER V. CARR

369 U.S. 186, 82 S. Ct. 691, 7 L. Ed. 2d 663 (1962)

For sixteen years after *Colegrove* the Supreme Court did not disturb the opinion of the plurality that legislative reapportionment was a political question. However, the logic of this position was somewhat shaken in 1960 by *Gomillion v. Lightfoot,* in which the Court struck down an Alabama statute redrawing the boundaries of the city of Tuskegee so as to exclude almost all black residents, thereby preventing them from voting in city elections. Justice Frankfurter, writing for the Court, held that this was racial discrimination in violation of the Fifteenth Amendment and denied that judicial invalidation of the statute conflicted with *Colegrove.*

Baker v. Carr was an action brought by certain Tennessee voters challenging the failure of the state legislature to reapportion its membership since 1901, in spite of shifts and enlargements in the voting population since that time. The Tennesseans' suit was dismissed by a three-judge federal district court that relied on *Colegrove.* The voters then appealed to the Supreme Court.

MR. JUSTICE BRENNAN delivered the opinion of the Court. . . .

In holding that the subject matter of this suit was not justiciable, the District Court relied on *Colegrove v. Green* [1946], and subsequent *per curiam* cases. . . . We understand the District Court to have read the cited cases as compelling the conclusion that since the appellants sought to have a legislative apportionment held unconstitutional, their suit presented a "political question" and was therefore nonjusticiable. We hold that this challenge to an apportionment presents no nonjusticiable "political question. . . ."

Of course the mere fact that the suit seeks protection of a political right does not mean it presents a political question. Such an objection "is little more than a play upon words." *Nixon v. Herndon.* . . . Rather, it is argued that apportionment cases, whatever the actual wording of the complaint, can involve no federal constitutional right except one resting on the guaranty of a republican form of government, and that complaints based on that clause have been held to present political questions which are nonjusticiable.

We hold that the claim pleaded here neither rests upon nor implicates the Guaranty Clause and that its justiciability is therefore not foreclosed by our decisions of cases involving that clause. . . .

Our discussion . . . requires review of a number of political question cases, in order to expose the attributes of the doctrine—attributes which, in various settings, diverge, combine, appear, and disappear in seeming disorderliness. . . . That review reveals that in the Guaranty Clause cases and in the other "political question" cases, it

is the relationship between the judiciary and the coordinate
branches of the Federal Government, and not the federal judiciary's
relationship to the States, which gives rise to the "political question."

We have said that "in determining whether a question falls within
[the political question] category, appropriateness under our system
of government of attributing finality to the action of the political
departments and also the lack of satisfactory criteria for a judicial
determination are dominant considerations." *Coleman v. Miller*
[1939]. The nonjusticiability of a political question is primarily a
function of the separation of powers. Much confusion results from
the capacity of the "political question" label to obscure the need for
case-by-case inquiry. Deciding whether a matter has in any measure
been committed by the Constitution to another branch of government, or whether the action of that branch exceeds whatever authority has been committed, is itself a delicate exercise in constitutional
interpretation, and is a responsibility of this Court as ultimate interpreter of the Constitution. To demonstrate this requires no less than
to analyze representative cases and to infer from them the analytical
threads that make up the political question doctrine. We shall then
show that none of those threads catches this case.

Foreign relations. There are sweeping statements to the effect that
all questions touching foreign relations are political questions. Not
only does resolution of such issues frequently turn on standards that
defy judicial application, or involve the exercise of a discretion demonstrably committed to the executive or legislature; but many such
questions uniquely demand single-voiced statement of the Government's views. Yet it is error to suppose that every case or controversy
which touches foreign relations lies beyond judicial cognizance. Our
cases in this field seem invariably to show a discriminating analysis
of the particular question posed, in terms of the history of its management by the political branches, of its susceptibility to judicial handling in the light of its nature and posture in the specific case, and
of the possible consequences of judicial action. . . .

Dates of duration of hostilities. Though it has been stated broadly
that "the power which declared the necessity is the power to declare
its cessation, and what the cessation requires," here too analysis reveals isolable reasons for the presence of political questions, underlying this Court's refusal to review the political departments'
determination of when or whether a war has ended. Dominant is the
need for finality in the political determination. . . .

Validity of enactments. In *Coleman v. Miller,* this Court held that
the questions of how long a proposed amendment to the Federal
Constitution remained open to ratification, and what effect a prior

rejection had on a subsequent ratification, were committed to con-gressional resolution and involved criteria of decision that necessarily escaped the judicial grasp. . . .

The status of Indian tribes. This Court's deference to the political departments in determining whether Indians are recognized as a tribe, while it reflects familiar attributes of political questions . . . also has a unique element in that "the relation of the Indians to the United States is marked by peculiar and cardinal distinctions which exist nowhere else. . . ."

It is apparent that several formulations which vary slightly according to the settings in which the questions arise may describe a political question, although each has one or more elements which identifies it as essentially a function of the separation of powers. Prominent on the surface of any case held to involve a political question is found a textually demonstrable constitutional commitment of the issue to a coordinate political department; or a lack of judicially discoverable and manageable standards for resolving it; or the impossibility of deciding without an initial policy determination of a kind clearly for nonjudicial discretion; or the impossibility of a court's undertaking independent resolution without expressing lack of the respect due coordinate branches of government; or an unusual need for unquestioning adherence to a political decision already made; or the potentiality of embarrassment from multifarious pronouncements by various departments on one question.

Unless one of these formulations is inextricable from the case at bar, there should be no dismissal for nonjusticiability on the ground of a political question's presence. The doctrine of which we treat is one of "political questions," not one of "political cases." The courts cannot reject as "no law suit" a bona fide controversy as to whether some action denominated "political" exceeds constitutional authority. . . .

But it is argued that this case shares the characteristics of decisions that constitute a category not yet considered, cases concerning the Constitution's guaranty, in Art. IV, § 4, of a republican form of government. A conclusion as to whether the case at bar does present a political question cannot be confidently reached until we have considered those cases with special care. We shall discover that Guaranty Clause claims involve those elements which define a "political question," and for that reason and no other, they are nonjusticiable. In particular, we shall discover that the nonjusticiability of such claims has nothing to do with their touching upon matters of state governmental organization. . . .

[The opinion then reviewed at length *Luther v. Borden* (1849) and other cases involving the "republican form of government" issue.]

We come, finally, to the ultimate inquiry whether our precedents as to what constitutes a nonjusticiable "political question" bring the case before us under the umbrella of that doctrine. A natural beginning is to note whether any of the common characteristics which we have been able to identify and label descriptively are present. We find none: The question here is the consistency of state action with the Federal Constitution. We have no question decided, or to be decided, by a political branch of government coequal with this Court. Nor do we risk embarrassment of our government abroad, or grave disturbance at home if we take issue with Tennessee as to the constitutionality of her action here challenged. Nor need the appellants, in order to succeed in this action, ask the Court to enter upon policy determinations for which judicially manageable standards are lacking. Judicial standards under the Equal Protection Clause are well developed and familiar, and it has been open to courts since the enactment of the Fourteenth Amendment to determine, if on the particular facts they must, that a discrimination reflects *no* policy, but simply arbitrary and capricious action. . . .

Reversed and remanded.

MR. JUSTICE FRANKFURTER, whom MR. JUSTICE HARLAN joins, dissenting. . . . [This dissent is reprinted as Reading 8.2.]

6
Instruments of Judicial Power

The judge's chair is a seat of power. Not only do judges have power to make binding decisions; their decisions may also legitimate the use of power by other officials. Judges are the custodians of authority because their putative expertness in the law, their presumed independence from political control, and their ritualized fact-finding procedures supposedly make their judgments more objective than those of other officials.

The power that judges have, of course, is not physical power. They have a few officers of the court at their disposal, enough to keep order in the courtroom and to move prisoners safely in and out of the court. But generally judicial orders are obeyed without compulsion, because even the losers either believe in the fairness of the adjudicative process or recognize that nonacquiescence would be futile since the ample power of the executive branch usually stands ready to enforce a judicial decision.[1] The Constitution commands that the President "shall take care that the laws be faithfully executed," and specific congressional statutes direct executive assistance in carrying out judicial decisions. Without orders to the contrary, a marshal will enforce a court's decrees, and the Department of Justice will cooperate in protecting the integrity of the judicial process. Occasionally, as in 1809, when the governor of Pennsylvania used militia to defy the Supreme Court's judgment in *United States v. Peters,* or when mob violence prevented school desegregation in Little Rock in 1957 and at the University of Mississippi in 1962, additional force may be necessary to secure obedience to a court order. The marshal may summon a posse, as was done in the *Peters* case, or the President may send in

[1] Judges, of course, have power to command only the parties in the proceeding before them. Whether their decision in a particular case will become effective as a legal standard controlling conduct or be accepted as a precedent in subsequent litigation is another question, which will be examined in Chapter 8, "The Impact of Judicial Decisions," and Chapter 10, "Precedents and Legal Reasoning."

243

federal troops as he did in the Little Rock and Mississippi cases. But the fact that force must be used indicates that judicial authority is approaching its outer limits.

DECISIONS, OPINIONS, AND ORDERS

The judge's most visible function is to decide controversies brought before the court. A judge's authority varies, depending on the particular level of the court and on whether the case is heard with or without a jury. But even when the final decision is left to a jury, the judge's instructions to the jurors and rulings on what evidence they may or may not consider typically have great influence in determining the outcome of litigation.

The judge's capacity to command is made palatable by the general assumption that judicial decisions are based on reason and knowledge of the law. Federal rules of procedure require judges of district courts to file findings of fact and conclusions of law to explain their decisions, and judges of appellate courts typically support their rulings with lengthy essays—opinions—detailing their reasoning. Jurists have long recognized that carefully drafted explanations of their interpretations and applications of the law not only help demonstrate the correctness of particular decisions but can also increase their impact on public policy. John Marshall fully realized the potential of judicial opinions as instruments to achieve fundamental political goals. His opinions in *McCulloch v. Maryland* (1819) and *Gibbons v. Ogden* (1824)—marking the constitutional expanse of federal power—and *Marbury v. Madison* (1803)—first fully asserting judicial review—stand among the most significant of American political writings.

The compulsive element in every judicial decision is the order, which terminates the proceeding and appears at the conclusion of the written opinion. The order in most litigation is simple; it directs payment of a fine or a sum of money in settlement of a claim, prescribes imprisonment for a period, terminates a marriage, or settles a dispute about property. But on occasion an order can be quite complicated and lengthy—for example, a detailed set of instructions as to what specific steps must be taken to end racial segregation in a school system or to provide proper care and medical treatment for inmates of state mental institutions. At the Supreme Court level the order typically issued either affirms or reverses a contested decision of a lower court and remands the case to the lower court for further proceedings in conformity with the Supreme Court's holding.

THE INJUNCTION

Judges in the English common law invented a number of specialized orders, or writs, that were available to suitors for achieving particular purposes. In general, however, these writs were adapted only to the settlement of disputes over money or property or office. In many situations a case concerned not a past wrong that could be compensated for by money damages, but a continuing or potential source of injury that a complainant wanted to have stopped or prevented. Because writs at common law looked backward rather than forward, judicial intervention to control future action was not possible.

As explained in Chapter 3, this gap was filled by courts of equity, which developed the writ of injunction. An injunction is a command from a court directed to named defendants *forbidding* them to perform certain specified acts. It may also take the form of a mandatory injunction *commanding* performance of specific acts. Under traditional rules of equity, to obtain an injunction a litigant must show that he or she has a real right at stake, is suffering or is about to suffer "irreparable injury," there is no action at law that offers an adequate remedy (that is, the injury is of a type that cannot be compensated for by an award of money), and when "the equities are balanced," righting this wrong will outweigh any inconvenience or damage suffered by the defendant or by the public at large. (Reading 6.1.)

The injunction fulfills a very important function for public policy, since it is the principal instrument available to private parties for testing the legality of official action or restraining other private parties from committing allegedly illegal acts. The injunction is also widely used by public officials to compel compliance with the law. There are three types of injunctions:

1. *Ex parte restraining orders,* issued at the request of a complainant, without hearing the opposing party; these simply maintain the status quo until the court can hold a full hearing.
2. *Temporary injunctions,* issued after both parties have been heard, but controlling action only for a specified time, after which the situation will presumably have stabilized or no longer exist.
3. *Permanent injunctions,* controlling acts into the indefinite future.

While an injunction addresses named defendants, it binds not only the defendants but also their servants, agents, attorneys, and employees, as well as all other persons who, knowing the injunction is in effect, conspire with the defendants to violate it. If the defendant is a public official, the injunction will run against the office rather than the incumbent, thus binding successors in office. But the writ differs from a statute in that it does not bind all persons within a particular jurisdiction.

An important feature of an injunction is that the judge can draft a decree with specific provisions aimed to secure the goal that he or she believes equity requires. For example, in 1972 a federal judge in Mississippi issued an injunction aimed at ending discrimination against blacks in the hiring policies of the state highway patrol. The writ ordered the state to stop refusing to give employment applications to blacks, to withdraw a recruiting motion picture portraying an all-white patrol, to advertise vacancies thirty days in advance, and to make recruiting visits to black colleges. In 1974, three years after a similar order had been issued by Judge Frank Johnson in Alabama, that state had a larger percentage of blacks in its state police force than any other state in the nation.

Martin Luther King's famous Selma march in 1965 took place under the protection of a federal injunction forbidding Governor George Wallace to interfere. In *Allee v. Medrano* (1974) a federal district court enjoined the Texas Rangers from harassing a farmworkers' union. (Reading 6.2.) Prisoners have also been recently seeking injunctions to overcome what they—and federal judges—have found to be conditions so inhumane as to constitute "cruel and unusual punishment." Federal courts in Alabama, Arkansas, and Virginia, for instance, have not only barred such practices as the regular use of solitary confinement, bread and water, and enforced nudity and the crowding of prisoners in tiny cells, but have required state officials to provide more guards and better food, medical care, and recreational facilities, and to clean the prisons of their filth, rats, and roaches. (Reading 6.3.)

Although judges still call injunctions "extraordinary" writs, courts now issue them almost routinely. While traditional limitations on suits for injunctions have by no means disappeared, judges often relax them. For example, many judges treat the necessity of a showing of irreparable injury as a mere formality. In the mid-1930s, for instance, during the battle between the New Deal and the Supreme Court, district judges issued some 1,600 injunctions against enforcement of federal statutes. This tidal wave of restraining orders led Congress to enact a statute in 1937 requiring that a judge to whom such a request was made notify the Attorney General so that the United States could intervene and present argument. Congress also provided that only a special three-judge district court could issue such an injunction; but, as already noted, Congress repealed this latter provision in 1976.

Earlier, overuse of injunctions against labor unions to break strikes and hamper efforts to organize moved Congress to adopt the Norris-LaGuardia Act in 1932, which largely withdrew jurisdiction from federal courts to issue injunctions in labor disputes. There was some initial question whether this statute imposed an unconstitutional limit on judicial discretion and perhaps also on the rights of businessmen. *Truax v. Corrigan* (1921) had seemed to say that employers had a constitutionally protected right to seek an injunction in a dispute with their workers, for in that case the Supreme Court invalidated a state statute prohibiting state courts from enjoining certain kinds of actions in labor disputes. But in *Lauf v. E. G. Shinner & Co.* (1938) the Supreme Court sustained the Norris-LaGuardia Act as an exercise of congressional authority "to define and limit the jurisdiction of the inferior courts of the United States." Nevertheless, the Court has subsequently recaptured for federal judges a substantial measure of power to issue injunctions in labor disputes by narrowly interpreting the prohibitions of the Norris-LaGuardia Act or finding them in conflict with more recent congressional legislation.

In contrast to the Norris-LaGuardia Act's limitation on authority to issue injunctions, Congress in the Taft-Hartley Act of 1947 conferred on federal courts the authority to issue injunctions against strikes imperiling the national health or safety. Such injunctions, however, cannot be sought by private parties. Only the Attorney General of the United States can ask for the writ, and the order is limited to barring strikes during an eighty-day "cooling-off" period, so that negotiations to end the dispute can proceed. (Reading 6.4.)

Because the First Amendment protects the press against "prior restraint," *Near v. Minnesota* (1931) declared unconstitutional the use of injunctions against publications; and there have been few efforts to use this sanction against the news media. When the government sought an injunction in 1971 against publication of the so-called Pentagon Papers on the ground that their dissemination would irreparably damage the national interest, the Supreme Court majority rebuffed the government in *New York Times v. United States* (1971), holding that "any system of prior restraint of expression comes to this Court bearing a heavy presumption against its constitutional validity." Again in 1979 the government made an abortive attempt to ban publication of an article that purported to explain how to make an atomic bomb. (Reading 6.5.)

The government, however, did succeed in enjoining alleged breaches of contract by Frank W. Snepp, a former CIA employee who had, after leaving the agency—and in spite of his contractual obligation to submit any writings to the CIA for prepublication review— published a book about the disorderly American withdrawal from Vietnam in 1975. Justice Stevens, dissenting in *Snepp v. United States* (1980), charged that the government, without any showing that there was no adequate remedy at law, had "jumped to the conclusion that equitable relief is necessary."[2]

The effectiveness of injunctions is largely due to the fact that violations of their terms are punishable as contempt of court. A person can violate an unconstitutional statute with impunity, provided its invalidity is established when a prosecution is brought. But, as *Walker v. City of Birmingham* (1967) demonstrates, an injunction, even though it palpa-

---

[2] In the *Snepp* case, the Court ruled that the author must surrender all present and future profits from his book to the government; and anything that he might write in the future on any subject had to be submitted to the CIA for clearance.

bly infringes on constitutional rights, must be obeyed until its invalidity is established on appeal to a higher court. (Reading 6.6.) It was this procedure of appeal rather than violation of an order of doubtful validity that the *New York Times* successfully followed in 1971 after the Nixon administration had obtained an injunction against further publication of *The Pentagon Papers*.

Litigants may join a request for declaratory judgment to a petition for an injunction. As its title implies, a declaratory judgment is in effect a statement by a court that "declares" the rights of parties to a dispute. A declaratory judgment is not an advisory opinion. A real controversy between opposing parties asserting a legally protected right must exist. The assumption behind this kind of ruling is that once the persons involved know precisely what their rights are, they will obey the law, and so no coercive order will be needed. Somewhat illogically, however, a person requesting a declaratory judgment may also seek an injunction to require the opposing party to carry out the terms of the declaration. In *Samuels v. Mackell* (1971), for example, several persons who had been indicted in a New York court on charges of criminal anarchy filed suit in a federal district court seeking both a declaratory judgment that the New York criminal anarchy act was unconstitutional and an injunction forbidding the prosecutor from continuing to enforce the statute.

THE CONTEMPT POWER

The contempt power is one of the oldest of judicial weapons. Its purpose is to provide judges with the means to protect the dignity of the court and to punish disobedience of their orders. There is a distinction between criminal and civil contempt, a distinction which, though often difficult to discern, is nonetheless important. The major difference is one of purpose. The aim of a criminal contempt charge is to vindicate the dignity of the court, while a civil contempt action is intended to protect the rights of one of the litigants. The two types of action also differ as to procedure. In criminal cases the judge or some other governmental official generally initiates prosecution; the usual presumption of innocence present in a criminal trial applies and, to convict, the court must find the defendant guilty beyond a reasonable doubt. Civil contempt proceedings are commonly initiated by one of the parties to a suit, and the court can make a judgment on the preponderance of the evidence. Although the President may pardon a person found guilty of criminal contempt of a federal court, it is doubtful that he can pardon in civil contempt cases, at least where the offended party is a private citizen.

Perhaps the most important difference between the two types of contempt action lies in the punishment meted out. Within limits set by Congress, federal judges may impose fines or prison sentences for criminal contempt as in other criminal cases. Judges have the same option in civil cases, again within limits set by Congress; but here their power is far more extensive. Because the object of a civil contempt action is to secure the rights of one of the parties, the sentence is normally conditional. The judge may, for example, sentence recalcitrants to be imprisoned until they agree to comply with the court's orders. These orders, of course, could mean life imprisonment, a possibility that judges have recognized. The usual judicial explanation is that such prisoners carry the keys to their cells in their own pockets. They will be released as soon as they consent to obey the judge. Such an indeterminate sentence is obviously a more powerful sanction than a specific fine or jail term.

The simplest kind of contempt issue is presented when an individual is disrespectful or disorderly in the courtroom. (Readings 6.7 and 6.8.) In this situation the judge has traditionally had the power immediately and summarily, without notice, hearing, or representation by counsel, to charge, try, convict, and sentence the contemnor to jail for a specified term. If it is the defendant who is in contempt, his removal to jail would normally bring the trial to a halt. To prevent aborting the proceedings, judges have in some cases dealt with obstreperous defendants by chaining or gagging them in court and continuing the trial. In *Illinois v. Allen* (1970) the Supreme Court reluctantly approved of such a practice. The Court expressed preference for the contempt remedy and held that under extreme provocation the trial could continue in the absence of the defendant without violation of his constitutional rights.

To avoid problems that arise if defendants or counsel are held in contempt during a trial, some judges have delayed contempt citations until the end of a trial. The question raised by such action is whether, since the trial is over and there is no longer any need for quick action, the individual charged with contempt should not have the usual procedural rights of the criminally accused as well as the benefit of having the case heard by a different judge who could take a more objective view of the controversy. While the Supreme Court, in *Sacher v. United States* (1952), initially upheld summary conviction at the close of a trial, more recently, in *Mayberry v. Pennsylvania* (1971), it ruled that when the contempt charge is postponed until the end of the trial, the fact of contempt should be tried by a different judge. (Reading 6.8.)

Disturbances within the courtroom are usually called "direct" contempts. Disobedience of a judicial order occurring outside the courtroom is an "indirect" contempt; under the federal rules of criminal procedure, the latter can be prosecuted only after notice, with representation by counsel, and with trial by a different judge if the alleged contempt involved disrespect to or criticism of a judge. Formerly, a common use of the power to punish indirect contempts was against newspapers that published criticisms of judges or judicial actions, but *Bridges v. California* (1941) held that the right to criticize judicial proceedings was protected by the First and Fourteenth Amendments and that only a "clear and present danger" to the orderly administration of justice could justify convictions in such instances.

Historically, there has been no right to a jury trial in contempt cases. The explanation has been that judicial authority would be seriously impaired if a judge had to depend upon a jury's verdict for defense of the court's dignity and authority. In certain statutes, however, Congress has required a jury trial in contempt proceedings arising out of disobedience to federal court orders if the conduct complained of also constitutes a criminal offense under federal or state laws. Under the Civil Rights Act of 1957, for instance, no sentence for criminal contempt exceeding a $300 fine or forty-five days of imprisonment can be imposed without a jury trial.

The Supreme Court has also been concerned about the absence of procedural due process in punishment of criminal contempt. In *Green v. United States* (1958), where individuals who had disobeyed a court order were sentenced to three years for contempt, Justice Black charged that a system that permitted a judge to prosecute for contempt, sit in judgment on the charges, and punish as the court saw fit amounted to "autocratic omnipotence." This was a minority view at the time, but eight years later, in *Cheff v. Schnackenberg* (1966), the Court ruled that sentences of over six months for contempt could not be imposed without a jury trial. In the aftermath of the Chicago Seven trial of 1969 Judge Julius Hoffman sought to avoid the six-month limit by assessing contempt sentences, each of six months or less, for a number of individual acts by defendants and their counsel and cumulating them for total sentences of up to forty-eight months. The Court of Appeals, however, reversed.

The Supreme Court promptly extended these limitations on the punishment of criminal contempts to state courts. *Bloom v. Illinois* (1968) enforced the six-month rule, and *Codispoti v. Pennsylvania* (1974) required a jury trial if the sentences imposed aggregated more than six months, even though no sentence for more than six months was imposed for any one act of contempt. In *Taylor v. Hayes* (1974) sentences on an attorney initially totaling four and one-half years were subsequently reduced by the judge to six months; but, because of his personal embroilment with the attorney, the Supreme Court held that a different judge should try the contempt.

Refusal to testify before a grand jury may be punished as civil contempt after the prosecutor has obtained a judicial order requiring the testimony. Imprisonment is limited to the term of the grand jury, but a determined prosecutor can repeat the process before the next grand jury and so continue the imprisonment. The New Jersey Crime Commission kept a taciturn Mafia godfather, affectionately known as

"Princeton Sam," in jail for five years by this method, until the state supreme court ruled in 1975 that the confinement had lost its "coercive power."

In *Branzburg v. Hayes* (1972) newspaper reporters had been subpoenaed by grand juries and asked to give information concerning stories they had written. The reporters refused on the ground that the First Amendment gives newspeople immunity from being forced to reveal their sources. By a five-to-four vote the Supreme Court upheld the convictions. The majority saw no First Amendment problem and declined "to grant newsmen a testimonial privilege that other citizens do not enjoy."

This ruling unleashed a flood of subpoenas against journalists and encouraged judges to issue "gag orders" forbidding publication of information about pending criminal trials. In a noteworthy incident a Los Angeles journalist, William Farr, was jailed for civil contempt for refusing to reveal the sources of a news story about the celebrated Manson trial that he had published in defiance of the trial judge's order. With neither judge nor newsman willing to yield, the possibility that Farr might spend the rest of his life in jail led Justice William O. Douglas to grant his release after forty-eight days of confinement, pending outcome of his appeal. Eventually a different state judge ruled that further imprisonment would serve no purpose.

The Supreme Court's decision in *Nebraska Press Association v. Stuart* (1976) may have substantially ended the use of gag orders. The opinion of the Chief Justice held only that the strong presumption against prior restraints had not been overcome in that case, but four, and possibly five, justices went even further and indicated that they could never accept gag orders as constitutional. Still, the way was left open for judges to issue orders restraining the press's sources—police, attorneys, and witnesses—orders that can be enforced by contempt citations without direct coercion of the news media.[3]

THE WRIT OF HABEAS CORPUS

Another major instrument of judicial power to affect public affairs is the writ of habeas corpus. Called by Blackstone "the great writ of liberty," habeas corpus is an order from a judge directing a jailer or other official who has custody of a prisoner to bring that prisoner to court so that the judge may determine the legality of his detention. Originally the purpose of habeas corpus was to protect the jurisdiction of the English common law courts against encroachments by courts of

---

[3] In 1978 a reporter for the *New York Times,* Myron Farber, was jailed for civil contempt by a New Jersey judge for refusing to turn over his notes, which the defense claimed were relevant in a first-degree murder trial. See *New York Times v. New Jersey* (1978).

chancery or by the Crown. Gradually, however, the purpose of the writ shifted to become the classic means of protecting individuals against unlawful imprisonment. The Habeas Corpus Act of 1679 established the writ as one of the fundamental rights of English government, and American colonial practice generally accorded the writ the same high standing. Article I of the Constitution provides that the privilege of the writ of habeas corpus may not be suspended "unless when in cases of rebellion or invasion the public safety may require it."

As we saw in Chapter 3, modern American practice, while retaining the writ as protection against executive authority, has also made habeas corpus a means of tighter federal judicial control over state court proceedings, although the Supreme Court's decision in *Stone v. Powell* (1976) and subsequent cases makes the writ less available for this purpose.

As a potential judicial weapon against executive power, habeas corpus poses a threat of intragovernmental conflict, and on occasion the conflict has become a reality. In 1861, for instance, Chief Justice Taney ruled in *Ex parte Merryman* that only Congress, and not the President, could suspend the writ. Lincoln met this challenge to his war power by ignoring the Chief Justice's order. Shortly thereafter the President averted another judicial rebuke by putting a District of Columbia judge under virtual house arrest to prevent him from hearing a habeas corpus petition. After the war the full Supreme Court sustained Taney's doctrine in *Ex parte Milligan* (1866), but this decision could undo little of the military rule that Lincoln had imposed on the border states. This experience was repeated almost exactly in World War II, when executive suspension of habeas corpus in Hawaii was invalidated only after the war was over. It would thus appear, as Clinton Rossiter has said, that the fate of habeas corpus in times of emergency depends on what executives do and not on what judges say.[4]

SELECTED REFERENCES

Cover, Robert, and T. Alexander Aleinikoff, "Dialectical Federalism: Habeas Corpus and the Court," 86 *Yale Law Journal* 1035 (1977).

Duker, William F. *A Constitutional History of Habeas Corpus.* Westport, Conn.: Greenwood Press, 1980.

Fiss, Owen M. *The Civil Rights Injunction.* Bloomington: Indiana University Press, 1978.

————. *Injunctions.* Mineola, N.Y.: Foundation Press, 1972.

Frankfurter, Felix, and Nathan Greene. *The Labor Injunction.* New York: Macmillan, 1930.

Freund, Paul A. "The Year of the Steel Case," 66 *Harvard Law Review* 89 (1952).

---

[4] *The Supreme Court and the Commander in Chief,* expanded ed. (Ithaca, N.Y.: Cornell University Press, 1976), p. 39.

Gewirtz, Paul. "Remedies and Resistance," 92 *Yale Law Journal* 585 (1983).

Goldfarb, Ronald L. *The Contempt Power.* New York: Columbia University Press, 1963.

Kuhns, Richard B. "The Summary Contempt Power," 88 *Yale Law Journal* 39 (1978).

Leubsdorf, John. "The Standard for Preliminary Injunctions," 91 *Harvard Law Review* 525 (1978).

McDowell, Gary. *Equity and the Constitution: The Supreme Court, Equitable Relief, and Public Policy.* Chicago: University of Chicago Press, 1982.

McFeeley, Neil D. "A Change of Direction: Habeas Corpus from Warren to Burger," *Western Political Quarterly* 174 (1979).

Note. "Developments in the Law: Federal Habeas Corpus," 83 *Harvard Law Review* 1038 (1970).

Note. "Developments in the Law: Injunctions," 78 *Harvard Law Review* 99 (1965).

Note. "The Federal Anti-Injunction Statute and Declaratory Judgments in Constitutional Litigation," 83 *Harvard Law Review* 1870 (1970).

Schuck, Peter. *Suing Government: Citizen Remedies for Official Wrongs.* New Haven: Yale University Press, 1983.

Turner, James. "Habeas Corpus After *Stone v. Powell,*" 13 *Harvard Civil Rights-Civil Liberties Law Review* 521 (1978).

6.1   *"The structure of an institutional suit tends to be sprawling. . . ."*

THE DISCRETIONARY CONSTITUTION

William A. Fletcher

Federal courts have been asked with increasing frequency in recent years to grant injunctive decrees that would restructure public institutions in accordance with what are asserted to be the commands of the federal Constitution. This type of litigation has become such a familiar part of the legal landscape that it has acquired a distinct vocabulary: the lawsuit is called an "institutional suit," and a resulting remedial injunction an "institutional decree." The variety and importance of the institutions involved, the range of issues that courts must address, and most important, the broad discretionary powers trial courts must exercise in framing remedial decrees set modern institutional suits substantially apart from other forms of litigation. These suits pose a number of difficult problems concerning the appropriate role of federal judicial power in our society.

Reprinted by permission of the Yale Law Journal Company and Fred B. Rothman & Company from *The Yale Law Journal*, vol. 91, pp. 635ff. William A. Fletcher is Professor of Law, Boalt Hall, University of California, Berkeley.

Institutional suits . . . are typically brought against state officials to enforce asserted constitutional norms. Frequently, such suits are filed only after the plaintiffs have unsuccessfully exerted pressure on the political branches of the state government to correct the problems of which they complain. Sometimes, as part of a general attack, such suits are filed concurrently with the exertion of pressure on the political branches. The subject matter of these suits and the litigants' desire to influence political as well as judicial action frequently result in extensive news coverage of the problems giving rise to the litigation, and, though sometimes to a lesser degree, of the litigation itself.

The structure of an institutional suit tends to be sprawling, with a large number of parties, intervenors, and amici. The actual trial, during which plaintiffs seek to establish the existence of a constitutional violation, often involves many witnesses and extensive testimony. The judge, both before and during trial, frequently encourages the participants to work out a settlement. He or she may also be reluctant to set an early trial date or to expedite the trial itself if it appears that the state, through either its political branches or its judiciary, is likely to arrive at an acceptable solution on its own.

If the court does find a constitutional violation, that finding is typically only a prelude to a drawn-out and complex process of devising a decree directing the defendants to reform their institution and practices. The remedial decree, rather than the finding of a constitutional violation, is commonly perceived as the key to the success or failure of the litigation. At this stage of the suit additional parties are frequently permitted to intervene, making the already unwieldy structure of the litigation even more cumbersome. In formulating the decree, the judge usually asks the parties to agree on a "plan." If the parties do agree, the judge issues an injunction that incorporates their agreement. When soliciting plans from the parties or formulating the decree itself, the court frequently hears additional evidence and expert testimony concerning the possible effects of contemplated decrees; sometimes the court appoints its own experts, special masters or committees; and sometimes it threatens to impose draconian decrees that not even the plaintiffs want.

What the remedial decree may seek to accomplish, and the means chosen, vary. A decree may be extremely detailed. In a prison or mental hospital case, for instance, it may specify precise staffing ratios, the temperatures in rooms or cells, the types and quantities of food to be served, the manner of determining types of and times for isolation or solitary confinement, and a variety of other things. Once the decree is issued, the judge sometimes appoints a special master to supervise its implementation, or in certain cases, a "receiver" to take over and run the state institution for a time. Ordinarily, the decree stays in effect for a number of years, and the parties are required periodically to submit to the court reports or other evidence of their compliance. Sometimes the decree is amended as conditions change, or as it becomes apparent that the original decree is inadequate to accomplish its purpose.

An institutional suit is much more than a conventional courtroom dispute in which one party asserts that another has broken a legal rule and in which the court can provide a determinate and easily administered remedy. It has been argued that little of importance differentiates modern institutional decrees from many well-established judicial practices that intrude deeply into the affairs of public and private entities. But the fundamental difficulty with constitutional institutional decrees lies not in the depth of their intrusion into the political affairs of the states, but rather in the *manner* of their intrusion. In reorganizing and redirecting the governmental functions of a political branch of a state, a federal court must rely largely on its own ingenuity in discovering the likely consequences of its remedial decree, and on its own intuitions in evaluating the desirability of those consequences. Owen Fiss describes an institutional suit and decree as "the initiation of a relationship between the judge and an institution—a declaration that the judge will henceforth manage the reconstruction of an ongoing social institution." In such a role, a judge moves far beyond the normal competence and authority of a judicial officer, into an arena where legal aspirations, bureaucratic possibilities, and political constraints converge, and where ordinary legal rules frequently are inapplicable.

6.2   *"Where, as here, there is a persistent pattern of police misconduct, injunctive relief is appropriate."*

ALLEE V. MEDRANO

416 U.S. 802, 94 S. Ct. 2191, 40 L. Ed. 2d 566 (1974)

In 1966 and 1967 members of the United Farm Workers Organizing Committee, AFL-CIO, were engaged in an effort to organize into the union the predominantly Mexican-American farmworkers of the lower Rio Grande Valley. This effort led to considerable controversy and conflict with state and local authorities. The union organizers brought a civil rights action in federal court attacking the constitutionality of certain Texas statutes and alleging that members of the Texas Rangers and Starr County law officers had "conspired to deprive [the organizers] of their rights under the First and Fourteenth Amendments, by unlawfully arresting, detaining and confining them without due process and without legal justification, and by unlawfully threatening, harassing, coercing, and physically assaulting them to prevent their exercise of the rights of free speech and assembly."

A three-judge court convened and found that the law enforcement officials had taken sides "in what was essentially a labor-management controversy" and that these were not a series of isolated incidents but a prevailing pattern throughout the controversy. The court declared five Texas statutes unconstitutional and in addition permanently enjoined the defendants from a variety of unlawful practices that formed the core of the alleged conspiracy. The terms of what Chief Justice Burger called "this remarkable injunction" were as follows:

> It is further ordered, adjudged and decreed by the Court that Defendants, their successors, agents and employees, and persons acting in concert with them, are permanently enjoined and restrained from any of the following acts or conduct directed toward or applied to Plaintiffs and the persons they represent, to wit:
>
> A. Using in any manner Defendants' authority as peace officers for the purpose of preventing or discouraging peaceful organizational activities without adequate cause.
> B. Interfering by stopping, dispersing, arresting, or imprisoning any person, or by any other means, with picketing, assembling, solicitation, or organizational effort without adequate cause.
> C. Arresting any person without warrant or without probable cause which probable cause is accompanied by intention to present appropriate written complaint to a court of competent jurisdiction.
> D. Stopping, dispersing, arresting or imprisoning any person without adequate cause because of the arrest of some other person.
> E. As used in this Paragraph 16, Subparagraphs A, B and D above, the term "adequate cause" shall mean (1) actual obstruction of a public or private passway, road, street, or entrance which actually causes unreasonable interference with ingress, egress, or flow of traffic; or (2) force or violence, or the threat of force or violence, actually committed by any person by his own conduct or by actually aiding, abetting, or participating in such conduct by another person; or (3) probable cause which may cause a Defendant to believe in good faith that one or more particular persons did violate a criminal law of the State of Texas other than those specific laws herein declared unconstitutional, or a municipal ordinance.

MR. JUSTICE DOUGLAS delivered the opinion of the Court. . . .

We first consider the provisions of the federal court decree enjoining police intimidation of the appellees. . . . The complaint charged that the enjoined conduct was but one part of a single plan by the defendants, and the District Court found a pervasive pattern of intimidation in which the law enforcement authorities sought to suppress appellees' constitutional rights. In this blunderbuss effort the police not only relied on statutes the District Court found constitutionally deficient, but concurrently exercised their authority under valid laws in an unconstitutional manner. . . . That part of the decree in question here prohibits appellants from using their authority as peace officers to arrest, stop, disperse, or imprison appellees, or otherwise interfere with their organizational efforts, without "adequate cause." "Adequate cause" is defined as (1) actual obstruction of public or private passways causing unreasonable interference, (2) force or violence, or threat thereof, actually committed by any person, or the aiding and abetting of such conduct, or, (3) probable cause to believe in good faith that a criminal law of the State of Texas has been violated, other than the ones struck down in the remainder of the decree. On its face the injunction does no more than require the police to abide by constitutional requirements; and there is no contention that this decree would interfere with law enforcement by restraining the police from engaging in conduct that would be otherwise lawful.

Thus the only question before us is whether this was an appropriate exercise of the federal court's equitable powers. We first note that this portion of the decree creates no interference with prosecutions pending in the state courts, so that the special considerations relevant to cases like *Younger v. Harris* [1971] do not apply here. Nor was there any requirement that appellees first exhaust state remedies before bringing their federal claims under the Civil Rights Act of 1871 to federal court. *McNeese v. Board of Education* [1963]; *Monroe v. Pape* [1961]. Nonetheless there remains the necessity of showing irreparable injury, "the traditional prerequisite to obtaining an injunction" in any case.

Such a showing was clearly made here as the unchallenged findings of the District Court show. The appellees sought to do no more than organize a lawful union to better the situation of one of the most economically oppressed classes of workers in the country. Because of the intimidation by state authorities, their lawful effort was crushed. The workers, and their leaders and organizers were placed in fear of exercising their constitutionally protected rights of free expression, assembly, and association. Potential supporters of their cause were placed in fear of lending their support. If they were to be able to regain those rights and continue furthering their cause by constitutional means, they required protection from appellants' concerted conduct. No remedy at law would be adequate to provide such protection. *Dombrowski v. Pfister* [1965].

Isolated incidents of police misconduct under valid statutes would not, of course, be cause for the exercise of a federal court's equitable powers. But "[w]e have not hesitated on direct review to strike down applications of constitutional statutes which we have found to be unconstitutionally applied." *Cameron v. Johnson* [1968]. Where, as here, there is a persistent pattern of police misconduct, injunctive relief is appropriate. In *Hague v. Committee for Industrial Organization* [1939], we affirmed the granting of such relief under strikingly similar facts. There also law enforcement officials set out to crush a nascent labor union. The police interfered with the lawful distribution of pamphlets, prevented the holding of public meetings, and ran some labor organizers out of town. The District Court declared some of the municipal ordinances unconstitutional. In addition, it enjoined the police from "exercising personal restraint over [the plaintiffs] without warrant or confining them without lawful arrest and production of them for prompt judicial hearing . . . or interfering with their free access to the streets, parks, or public places of the city," or from "interfering with the right of the [plaintiffs], their agents and those acting with them, to communicate their views as individuals to others on the streets in an orderly and peaceable manner." The lower federal courts have also granted such relief in similar cases. . . .

In summary, we affirm the decree granting injunctive relief against police misconduct. . . .

It is so ordered.

MR. JUSTICE POWELL took no part in the consideration or decision of this case.

MR. CHIEF JUSTICE BURGER, with whom MR. JUSTICE WHITE and MR. JUSTICE REHNQUIST join, concurring in the result in part and dissenting in part. . . .

6.3

"Each unit used to house prisoners in segregation shall be maintained reasonably free of rodents, birds, insects and other vermin."

TOUSSAINT V. MC CARTHY

U.S. District Court for the Northern District of California, October 18, 1984

Practices in California's San Quentin and Folsom prisons with respect to "segregation" of inmates (solitary confinement), reviewed and limited by a federal district court in *Wright v. Enomoto*, 462 F. Supp. 397 (1976), were again at issue in this class-action suit filed by prisoners. In deciding the case Judge Stanley A. Weigel made a personal inspection of prison conditions.

JUDGMENT OF PERMANENT INJUNCTION

Based upon the Findings of Fact and Conclusions of Law this day filed:

IT IS HEREBY ORDERED, ADJUDGED, and DECREED as follows:

Defendants, the Director of the California Department of Corrections, the Wardens of the California State Prison at San Quentin and the California State Prison at Folsom, their agents, servants, employees, successors in office and all persons acting in their aid or in participation with them, are advised, enjoined and ordered as follows:

II

Defendants, by immediate and continuous efforts, shall provide as follows with respect to all present and future members of the plaintiff class:

1. Each prisoner, upon initial assignment to segregation and upon each cell transfer while remaining in segregation, shall be provided with a clean cell, furnished with at least a bed, cot or bunk and a clean, untorn mattress, a clean, untorn blanket, a clean, untorn pillow, a properly functioning toilet and a properly functioning sink.

2. No prisoner assigned to segregation shall be involuntarily double-celled with another prisoner in any cell smaller than seventy (70) square feet.

3. All cells in which prisoners assigned to segregation are housed shall be provided with adequate heat and adequate ventilation. Defective or clearly inadequate heating and ventilating equipment and broken windows shall be repaired or replaced promptly.

4. Each facility used to house prisoners assigned to segregation shall be equipped with adequate plumbing and sewage disposal systems. Leaking pipes and fixtures, clogged or defective drains and clogged or defective sewer lines shall be repaired or replaced promptly.

5. Any prisoner assigned to a cell in which there is no significant source of natural light, or from which all significant natural light can be excluded without the control of the prisoner, shall have under his control at all times a source of artificial light adequate to illuminate the cell. All cells used to house prisoners assigned to segregation shall be equipped with a source of artificial illumination sufficient to permit the occupant to read comfortably while seated or lying on his bunk or bed. All electric lights inside cells shall be connected to a functioning on-off switch that is under the control of the occupant during hours when the use of such lights is permitted.

6. Defendants shall undertake immediate steps to abate the levels of noise prevailing in five-tier cell blocks used to house segregated inmates. The following specific measures shall be undertaken unless and until defendants reduce the noise to acceptable levels by alternate means: (1) Inmates shall not be permitted to employ any loud-speaking device, including, for example, those devices included in televisions, radios, and stereophonic equipment, unless the device is incapable of producing sound noticeably audible to any person outside the cell of the inmate using the device. (2) Defendants shall install sound-absorbing wall coverings in all five-tier units. (3) Defendants shall provide each inmate assigned to segregation and housed in a five-tier cell block with a set of medically approved sound exclusion devices such as, for example, earplugs. If earplugs are used, they shall be issued monthly.

7. Each facility used to house prisoners in segregation shall be equipped with electrical wiring reasonably safe from danger of fire or electrocution.

8. Each facility used to house prisoners in segregation shall be reasonably safe from danger of death or serious injury caused by fire. Defendants shall develop and rehearse plans for the speedy egress of all segregated inmates in the event of serious fire.

9. Each prisoner assigned to segregation shall be provided with clean, untorn clothing reasonably appropriate in size. Such clothing shall be laundered on a regular, not less than bi-weekly, basis. Blankets shall be laundered not less than once every six months. Towels and sheets shall be laundered not less than once every two weeks. This provision does not require defendants to relieve any prisoner of the consequences to that prisoner of damage done deliberately by the prisoner to clothes, blankets, towels or sheets.

10. Each prisoner assigned to segregation and housed in a cell without hot running water shall be permitted no less than three (3) showers each week. All shower facilities used by prisoners assigned to segregation shall be maintained in reasonably sanitary condition with adjustable hot and cold running water. Defendants shall ensure that each prisoner assigned to segregation is supplied with adequate quantities of materials necessary to sound personal hygiene.

11. Each facility used to house segregated inmates shall be maintained in sanitary condition. Defendants shall undertake the following specific measures to ensure adequate sanitation: (1) Each prisoner shall be required to maintain his cell in reasonably sanitary condition. (2) Each prisoner shall be provided with a container in which to store garbage. Garbage shall be collected from each cell on a regular basis not less than once every day. (3) Tiers and floors shall be maintained in a reasonably clean and sanitary condition. (4) "Pipe chases" or service areas shall be maintained in reasonably clean and sanitary condition, free of sewage, refuse, standing or leaking water, or any other noxious substance (including gases). (5) Standing water shall be promptly removed from any portion of any unit in which it may accumulate. If necessary, drains shall be installed to carry out this provision.

This provision does not require defendants to relieve any prisoner of the consequences to that prisoner of any damage, misbehavior, or failure to perform required cleaning tasks done or omitted deliberately by that prisoner.

12. Each unit used to house prisoners in segregation shall be maintained reasonably free of rodents, birds, insects and other vermin. Unless and until the intendment of this provision is accomplished by alternate means, defendants shall employ on a full-time basis at each prison at least one person whose exclusive duty is to manage the task of eradicating vermin.

13. All food shall be stored, prepared and served under healthful, sanitary conditions, free of spoilage or vermin infestation.

14. Each prisoner assigned to segregation shall be provided with an opportunity for outdoor exercise at least:

(a) one (1) hour every day, for a minimum total of eight (8) hours per week; or

(b) two (2) hours every other day, for a minimum total of eight (8) hours per week; or

(c) three times per week, for a minimum of one (1) hour each time, for a minimum total of ten (10) hours per week.

The provision of exercise may be suspended for a period not to exceed ten days as to any prisoner if the suspension is based upon genuine reasons of discipline, inmate safety or prison security. When weather is inclement during a period of outdoor exercise, exercising inmates shall be issued suitable rain gear.

15. In the absence of specific and compelling security reasons, documented in writing, all prisoners assigned to segregation shall be permitted to visit and use an adequate prison law library as reasonably necessary. Any prisoner denied direct access to the law library for documented reasons of security shall be permitted to order at least five books per week from that library. Books so ordered shall be delivered promptly and without fail. Each prisoner assigned to segregation shall be provided upon request with a complete listing of all books available in the prison law library and all books, if any, available to prisoners from other sources.

IV

A. Pursuant to Fed. R. Civ. P. 53, the Court will appoint a Special Master (referred to herein as "Monitor") to monitor the progress of defendants in carrying out the provisions of this Permanent Injunction. Among the duties of the Monitor shall be to inspect each facility affected by this Injunction, to report to the Court from time to time concerning the state of compliance with this Permanent Injunction and the state of conditions of confinement in segregation at San Quentin and Folsom, and to advise the Court concerning any modifications to this Permanent Injunction that may appear necessary or that may be requested by a party. Defendants shall honor all requests by the Monitor for admission into any part of any facility affected by this Permanent Injunction. Defendants shall likewise honor all requests by the Monitor for the production of documents relevant to the state of compliance with this Injunction or the state of conditions of confinement in segregation. The duties of the Monitor shall continue until such time as he may be relieved by the Court or until the

Court may adopt the Monitor's written report that defendants are in full compliance with the Permanent Injunction and that conditions of confinement in segregation units at San Quentin and Folsom do not violate the Constitution. . . .

V

Defendants shall provide a copy of this Permanent Injunction to each member of the plaintiff class at San Quentin and Folsom within ten days of the date of this Injunction, and shall post a copy in each segregation unit where it may readily be seen by class members. Defendants shall also provide a copy of this Permanent Injunction to every employee of the California Department of Corrections at San Quentin and/or Folsom.

No person who has notice of this Permanent Injunction shall fail to comply with the letter and spirit hereof nor shall any person subvert the letter or spirit hereof by any sham, indirection or other artifice.

VII

The Court retains jurisdiction to modify this Injunction at any time and from time to time on its own motion or upon the motion of any party in the interest of effectuating its intendments or in the interest of furthering the ends of justice under all applicable law.

Dated: October 18, 1984.

STANLEY A. WEIGEL, Senior Judge

6.4   *"If the federal court is to be merely an automaton stamping the papers an Attorney General presents, the judicial function rises to no higher level than an IBM machine."*

UNITED STEELWORKERS V. UNITED STATES
361 U.S. 39, 80 S. Ct. 1, 4 L. Ed. 2d 12 (1959)

In 1959, after a long series of wage negotiations, the United Steelworkers called a strike. The Attorney General filed suit in the United States District Court for the Western District of Pennsylvania, asking for an eighty-day injunction under Section 208 of the Taft-Hartley Act. In support of his petition the Attorney General produced affidavits from the Secretary of Defense and other high governmental officials stating that a steel strike would not only disrupt the national economy but would also imperil national defense, particularly NATO commitments and various missile and atomic-energy programs. The district judge granted the injunction, and the Court of Appeals affirmed. The steelworkers petitioned the Supreme Court for certiorari, asserting, among other points,

that the conditions the Taft-Hartley law had laid down for the issuance of an injunction
had not been met; and that even if such conditions had been met, the injunction provisions of the statute were unconstitutional because they imposed duties on federal courts
that were essentially legislative or executive in nature.

upholds injunction

PER CURIAM. . . . . . . In pertinent part § 208 provides that if the
District Court "finds that . . . [a] threatened or actual strike or lock-
out—

i. affects an entire industry or a substantial part thereof engaged in
    trade, commerce, transportation, transmission, or communication
    among the several States or with foreign nations, or engaged in
    the production of goods for commerce; and
ii. if permitted to occur or to continue, will imperil the national
    health or safety, it shall have jurisdiction to enjoin any such strike
    or lock-out, or the continuing thereof, and to make such other
    orders as may be appropriate. . . ."

The arguments of the parties here and in the lower courts have
addressed themselves in considerable part to the propriety of the
District Court's exercising its equitable jurisdiction to enjoin the
strike in question once the findings set forth above had been made.
These arguments have ranged widely into broad issues of national
labor policy, the availability of other remedies to the executive, the
effect of a labor injunction on the collective bargaining process, consideration of the conduct of the parties to the labor dispute in their
negotiations, and conjecture as to the course of those negotiations in
the future. We do not believe that Congress in passing the statute
intended that the issuance of injunctions should depend upon judicial inquiries of this nature. . . .

The statute imposes upon the courts the duty of finding, upon the
evidence adduced, whether a strike or lock-out meets the statutory
conditions of breadth of involvement and peril to the national health
or safety. We have accordingly reviewed the concurrent findings of
the two lower courts. Petitioner here contests the findings that the
continuation of the strike would imperil the national health and
safety. The parties dispute the meaning of the statutory term "national health"; the Government insists that the term comprehends
the country's general well-being, its economic health; petitioner
urges that simply the physical health of the citizenry is meant. We
need not resolve this question, for we think the judgment below is
amply supported on the ground that the strike imperils the national
safety. Here we rely upon the evidence of the strike's effect on
specific defense projects; we need not pass on the Government's
contention that "national safety" in this context should be given a
broader construction and application.

The petitioner suggests that a selective reopening of some of the steel mills would suffice to fulfill specific defense needs. The statute was designed to provide a public remedy in times of emergency; we cannot construe it to require that the United States either formulate a reorganization of the affected industry to satisfy its defense needs without the complete reopening of closed facilities, or demonstrate in court the unfeasibility of such a reorganization. There is no room in the statute for this requirement which the petitioner seeks to impose on the Government.

We are of opinion that the provision in question as applied here is not violative of the constitutional limitation prohibiting courts from exercising powers of a legislative or executive nature, powers not capable of being conferred upon a court exercising solely "the judicial power of the United States." Petitioner contends that the statute is constitutionally invalid because it does not set up any standard of lawful or unlawful conduct on the part of labor or management. But the statute does recognize certain rights in the public to have unimpeded for a time production in industries vital to the national health or safety. It makes the United States the guardian of these rights in litigation. The availability of relief, in the common judicial form of an injunction, depends on findings of fact, to be judicially made. Of the matters decided judicially, there is no review by other agencies of the Government. We conclude that the statute entrusts the courts only with the determination of a "case or controversy," on which the judicial power can operate, not containing any element capable of only legislative or executive determination. We do not find that the termination of the injunction after a specified time, or the machinery established in an attempt to obtain a peaceful settlement of the underlying dispute during the injunction's pendency, detracts from this conclusion. . . .

Affirmed.

Concurring opinion of MR. JUSTICE FRANKFURTER and MR. JUSTICE HARLAN. . . .

MR. JUSTICE DOUGLAS, dissenting.

Great cases, like this one, are so charged with importance and feeling that, as Mr. Justice Holmes once remarked, they are apt to generate bad law. We need, therefore, to stick closely to the letter of the law we enforce to keep this controversy from being shaped by the intense interest which the public rightfully has in it. . . .

It is plain that the President construed the word "health" to include the material well-being or public welfare of the nation. When the Attorney General moved under § 208 for an injunction in the District Court based on the opinion of the President and the conclusions of the board of inquiry, the union challenged the conclusion that "the national health or safety" was imperiled, as those words are used in the Act. The District Court found otherwise, stating five ways in which a continuance of the strike would, if permitted to continue, imperil "the national health and safety." . . .

. . . It is obvious that "national health" was construed to include the economic well-being or general welfare of the country. . . .

To read "welfare" into "health" gives that word such a vast reach that we should do it only under the most compelling necessity. We must be mindful of the history behind this legislation. Re Debs . . . stands as ominous precedent for the easy use of the injunction in labor disputes. Free-wheeling Attorneys General used compelling public demands to obtain the help of courts in stilling the protests of labor. The revulsion against that practice was deep; and it led ultimately to the enactment of the Norris-LaGuardia Act. We deal of course with a later Congress and an Act that sets aside by § 208(b) pro tanto the earlier Act. What Congress has created Congress can refashion. But we should hesitate to conclude that Congress meant to restore the use of the injunction in labor disputes whenever that broad and all-inclusive concept of the public welfare is impaired. The words used—"national health or safety"—are much narrower. . . .

Nor can this broad injunction be sustained when it is rested solely on "national safety." The heart of the District Court's finding on this phase of the case is in its statement, "Certain items of steel required in top priority military missile programs are not made by any mill now operating, nor available from any inventory or from imports." Its other findings, already quoted, are also generalized. One cannot find in the record the type or quantity of the steel needed for defense, the name of the plants at which those products are produced, or the number or the names of the plants that will have to be reopened to fill the military need. We do know that for one and a half years ending in mid-1959 the shipments of steel for defense purposes accounted for less than 1% of all the shipments from all the steel mills. If 1,000 men, or 5,000 men, or 10,000 men can produce the critical amount the defense departments need, what authority is there to send 500,000 men back to work?

. . . Will a selective reopening of a few mills be adequate to meet defense needs? Which mills are these? Would it be practical to reopen them solely for defense purposes or would they have to be reopened for all civilian purposes as well? This seems to me to be the type of inquiry that is necessary before a decree can be entered that will safeguard the rights of all the parties. Section 208(a) gives the District Court "jurisdiction to enjoin" the strike. There is no command that it *shall* enjoin 100% of the strikers when only 1% or 5% or 10% of them are engaged in acts that imperil the national "safety." We are dealing here with equity practice which has several hundred years of history behind it. We cannot lightly assume that Congress intended to make the federal judiciary a rubber stamp for the President. His findings are entitled to great weight; and I along with my Brethren accept them insofar as national "safety" is concerned. But it is the Court, not the President, that is entrusted by Article III of the Constitution to shape and fashion the decree. . . . If the federal court is to be merely an automaton stamping the papers an Attorney General presents, the judicial function rises to no higher level than an IBM machine. . . .

An appeal to the equity jurisdiction of the Federal District Court is an appeal to its sound discretion. One historic feature of equity is the molding of decrees to fit the requirements of particular cases. Equity decrees are not like the packaged goods this machine age produces. They are uniform only in that they seek to do equity in a given case. We should hesitate long before we conclude that Congress intended an injunction to issue against 500,000 workers when the inactivity of only 5,000 or 10,000 of the total imperils the national "safety." That would be too sharp a break with traditional equity practice for us to accept, unless the statutory mandate were clear and unambiguous. . . .

6.5   *"A mistake in ruling against The Progressive will seriously infringe cherished First Amendment rights."*

UNITED STATES V. PROGRESSIVE, INC.

467 F. Supp. 990 (1979)

In 1979 *Progressive* magazine proposed to publish an article entitled "The H-Bomb Secret." The article, which was popularly thought to explain how to make the bomb, was written by a man with no special training or access to secret data, but the government contended that the publication would do immediate and irreparable harm, and applied to a federal district court in Wisconsin for an injunction against publication.

MEMORANDUM AND ORDER

WARREN, District Judge.

On March 9, 1979, this Court, at the request of the government, but after hearing from both parties, issued a temporary restraining order enjoining defendants, their employees, and agents from publishing or otherwise communicating or disclosing in any manner any restricted data contained in the article: "The H-Bomb Secret: How We Got It, Why We're Telling It."

In keeping with the Court's order that the temporary restraining order should be in effect for the shortest time possible, a preliminary injunction hearing was scheduled for one week later, on March 16, 1979.

In order to grant a preliminary injunction, the Court must find that plaintiff has a reasonable likelihood of success on the merits, and that the plaintiff will suffer irreparable harm if the injunction does not issue. In addition, the Court must consider the interest of the public and the balance of the potential harm to plaintiff and defendants. . . .

Under the facts here alleged, the question before this Court involves a clash between allegedly vital security interests of the United States and the competing constitutional doctrine against prior restraint in publication.

In its argument and briefs, plaintiff relies on national security, as enunciated by Congress in The Atomic Energy Act of 1954, as the basis for classification of certain documents. Plaintiff contends that, in certain areas, national preservation and self-interest permit the retention and classification of government secrets. The government argues that its national security interest also permits it to impress classification and censorship upon information originating in the public domain, if when drawn together, synthesized and collated, such information acquires the character of presenting immediate, direct and irreparable harm to the interests of the United States.

Defendants argue that freedom of expression as embodied in the First Amendment is so central to the heart of liberty that prior restraint in any form becomes anathema. They contend that this is particularly true when a nation is not at war and where the prior restraint is based on surmise or conjecture. While acknowledging that freedom of the press is not absolute, they maintain that the publication of the projected article does not rise to the level of immediate, direct and irreparable harm which could justify incursion into First Amendment freedoms.

Hence, although embodying deep and fundamental principles of democratic philosophy, the issue also requires a factual determination by a federal court sitting in equity. At the level of a temporary restraining order, or a preliminary injunction, such matters are customarily dealt with through affidavits.

Thus far the affidavits filed are numerous and complex. They come from individuals of learning and renown. They deal with how the information at issue was assembled, what it means, and how injurious the affiant believes it to be. . . .

From the founding days of this nation, the rights to freedom of speech and of the press have held an honored place in our constitutional scheme. The establishment and nurturing of these rights is one of the true achievements of our form of government.

Because of the importance of these rights, any prior restraint on publication comes into court under a heavy presumption against its constitutional validity. *New York Times v. United States* (1971).

However, First Amendment rights are not absolute. They are not boundless.

In *Near v. Minnesota* (1931), the Supreme Court specifically recognized an extremely narrow area, involving national security, in which interference with First Amendment rights might be tolerated and a prior restraint on publication might be appropriate. The Court stated:

> "When a nation is at war many things that might be said in time of peace are such a hindrance to its effort that their utterance will not be endured so long as men fight and that no Court could regard them as protected by any constitutional right. No one would question but that a government might prevent actual obstruction to its recruiting service or the publication of the sailing dates of transports or the number and location of troops."

Thus, it is clear that few things, save grave national security concerns, are sufficient to override First Amendment interests. A court is well admonished to approach any requested prior restraint with a great deal of skepticism.

Juxtaposed against the right to freedom of expression is the government's contention that the national security of this country could be jeopardized by publication of the article.

The Court has grappled with this difficult problem and has read and studied the affidavits and other documents on file. After all this, the Court finds concepts within the article that it does not find in the public realm—concepts that are vital to the operation of the hydrogen bomb.

Does the article provide a "do-it yourself" guide for the hydrogen bomb? Probably not. A number of affidavits make quite clear that a *sine qua non* to thermonuclear capability is a large, sophisticated industrial capability coupled with a coterie of imaginative, resourceful scientists and technicians. One does not build a hydrogen bomb in the basement. However, the article could possibly provide sufficient information to allow a medium size nation to move faster in developing a hydrogen weapon. It could provide a ticket to by-pass blind alleys.

The defendants have also relied on the decision in the *New York Times* case. In that case, the Supreme Court refused to enjoin the *New York Times* and the *Washington Post* from publishing the contents of a classified historical study of United States decision-making in Viet Nam, the so-called "Pentagon Papers."

This case is different in several important respects. In the first place, the study involved in the *New York Times* case contained historical data relating to events that occurred some three to twenty years previously. Secondly, the Supreme Court agreed with the lower court that no cogent reasons were advanced by the government as to why the article affected national security except that publication might cause some embarrassment to the United States.

A final and most vital difference between these two cases is the fact that a specific statute is involved here. Section 2274 of The Atomic Energy Act prohibits anyone from communicating, transmitting or disclosing any restricted data to any person "with reason to believe such data will be utilized to injure the United States or to secure an advantage to any foreign nation."

The case at bar is so difficult precisely because the consequences of error involve human life itself and on such an awesome scale.

A mistake in ruling against *The Progressive* will seriously infringe cherished First Amendment rights. If a preliminary injunction is issued, it will constitute the first instance of prior restraint against a publication in this fashion in the history of this country, to this Court's knowledge. Such notoriety is not to be sought. It will curtail defendants' First Amendment rights in a drastic and substantial fashion. It will infringe upon our right to know and to be informed as well.

A mistake in ruling against the United States could pave the way for thermonuclear annihilation for us all. In that event, our right to life is extinguished and the right to publish becomes moot.

In the *Near* case, the Supreme Court recognized that publication of troop movements in time of war would threaten national security and could therefore be restrained. Times have changed significantly since 1931 when *Near* was decided. Now war by foot soldiers has been replaced in large part by war by machines and bombs. No longer need there be any advance warning or any preparation time before a nuclear war could be commenced.

In light of these factors, this Court concludes that publication of the technical information on the hydrogen bomb contained in the article is analogous to publication of troop movements or locations in time of war and falls within the extremely narrow exception to the rule against prior restraint.

Because of this "disparity of risk," because the government has met its heavy burden of showing justification for the imposition of a prior restraint on publication of the objected-to technical portions of the Morland article, and because the Court is unconvinced that suppression of the objected-to technical portions of the Morland article would in any plausible fashion impede the defendants in their laudable crusade to stimulate public knowledge of nuclear armament and bring about enlightened debate on national policy questions, the Court finds that the objected-to portions of the article fall within the narrow area recognized by the Court in *Near v. Minnesota* in which a prior restraint on publication is appropriate.

The government has met its burden under section 2274 of The Atomic Energy Act. In the Court's opinion, it has also met the test enunciated by two Justices in the *New York Times* case, namely grave, direct, immediate and irreparable harm to the United States.

The Court has just determined that if necessary it will at this time assume the awesome responsibility of issuing a preliminary injunction against *The Progressive*'s use of the Morland article in its current form.

FINDINGS OF FACT

5. In view of the showing of . . . harm made by the United States, a preliminary injunction would be warranted even in the absence of statutory authorization because of the existence of the likelihood of direct, immediate and irreparable injury to our nation and its people.

6. The facts and circumstances as presented here fall within the extremely narrow recognized area, involving national security, in which a prior restraint on publication is appropriate. Issuance of a preliminary injunction does not, under the circumstances presented to the Court, violate defendants' First Amendment rights.*

6.6

"*. . . respect for judicial process is a small price to pay for the civilizing hand of law. . . .*"

WALKER V. CITY OF BIRMINGHAM
388 U.S. 307, 87 S. Ct. 1824, 18 L. Ed. 2d 1210 (1967)

Martin Luther King, Jr., and other black ministers planned to protest racial discrimination in Birmingham, Alabama, by holding peaceful demonstrations on Good Friday and Easter Sunday, 1963. Requests for a parade permit were twice denied. The Birmingham ordinance authorized refusal of permits when required by considerations of "public welfare, peace, safety, health, decency, good order, morals or convenience. . . ." Convinced that no permit could be secured, the ministers proceeded with their plans. On Wednesday before Good Friday, city officials secured an ex parte injunction from the state circuit court forbidding all persons having notice of the order from holding demonstrations without a permit, and copies of the injunction were served on the ministers. Nevertheless, the planned demonstrations for the Easter weekend were carried out, and some minor violence resulted. On Monday the court found the ministers in contempt for violation of the injunction.

*Before a full hearing regarding the issuance of a permanent injunction was held, the government abandoned these proceedings, apparently because similar information regarding nuclear weapons was being published in other sources.—Eds.

Mr. Justice Stewart delivered the opinion of the court. . . .

In the present case . . . we are . . . asked to say that the Constitution compelled Alabama to allow the petitioners to violate this injunction, to organize and engage in these mass street parades and demonstrations, without any previous effort on their part to have the injunction dissolved or modified, or any attempt to secure a parade permit in accordance with its terms . . . we cannot accept the petitioners' contentions in the circumstances of this case.

Without question the state court that issued the injunction had, as a court of equity, jurisdiction over the petitioners and over the subject matter of the controversy. And this is not a case where the injunction was transparently invalid or had only a frivolous pretense to validity. We have consistently recognized the strong interest of state and local governments in regulating the use of their streets and other public places. When protest takes the form of mass demonstrations, parades, or picketing on public streets and sidewalks, the free passage of traffic and the prevention of public disorder and violence become important objects of legitimate state concern. . . .

The generality of the language contained in the Birmingham parade ordinance upon which the injunction was based would unquestionably raise substantial constitutional issues concerning some of its provisions. The petitioners, however, did not even attempt to apply to the Alabama courts for an authoritative construction of the ordinance. Had they done so, those courts might have given the licensing authority granted in the ordinance a narrow and precise scope . . . it could not be assumed that this ordinance was void on its face.

The breadth and vagueness of the injunction itself would also unquestionably be subject to substantial constitutional question. But the way to raise that question was to apply to the Alabama courts to have the injunction modified or dissolved. The injunction in all events clearly prohibited mass parading without a permit, and the evidence shows that the petitioners fully understood that prohibition when they violated it.

The petitioners also claim that they were free to disobey the injunction because the parade ordinance on which it was based had been administered in the past in an arbitrary and discriminatory fashion. In support of this claim they sought to introduce evidence that, a few days before the injunction issued, requests for permits to picket had been made to a member of the city commission. One request had been rudely rebuffed, and this same official had later made clear that he was without power to grant the permit alone, since the issuance of such permits was the responsibility of the entire city commission. Assuming the truth of this proffered evidence, it does not follow that the parade ordinance was void on its face. The petitioners, moreover, did not apply for a permit either to the commission itself or to any commissioner after the injunction issued. Had they done so, and had the permit been refused, it is clear that their claim of arbitrary or discriminatory administration of the ordinance would have been considered by the state circuit court upon a motion to dissolve the injunction.

This case would arise in quite a different constitutional posture if the petitioners, before disobeying the injunction, had challenged it in the Alabama courts, and had been met with delay or frustration of their constitutional claims. But there is no showing that such would have been the fate of a timely motion to modify or dissolve the injunction. . . .

The rule of law that Alabama followed in this case reflects a belief that in the fair administration of justice no man can be judge in his own case, however exalted his station, however righteous his motives, and irrespective of his race, color, politics, or religion. This Court cannot hold that the petitioners were constitutionally free to ignore all the procedures of the law and carry their battle to the streets. One may sympathize with the petitioners' impatient commitment to their cause. But respect for judicial process is a small price to pay for the civilizing hand of law, which alone can give abiding meaning to constitutional freedom.

Affirmed.

MR. CHIEF JUSTICE WARREN, whom MR. JUSTICE BRENNAN and MR. JUSTICE FORTAS join, dissenting. . . .
MR. JUSTICE DOUGLAS, with whom the CHIEF JUSTICE, MR. JUSTICE BRENNAN, and MR. JUSTICE FORTAS concur, dissenting. . . .

The record shows that petitioners did not deliberately attempt to circumvent the permit requirement. Rather they diligently attempted to obtain a permit and were rudely rebuffed and then reasonably concluded that any further attempts would be fruitless.

The right to defy an unconstitutional statute is basic in our scheme. Even when an ordinance requires a permit to make a speech, to deliver a sermon, to picket, to parade, or to assemble, it need not be honored when it is invalid on its face.

By like reason, where a permit has been arbitrarily denied one need not pursue the long and expensive route to this Court to obtain a remedy. The reason is the same in both cases. For if a person must pursue his judicial remedy before he may speak, parade, or assemble, the occasion when protest is desired or needed will have become history and any later speech, parade, or assembly will be futile or pointless.* . . .

*When later reviewing a conviction, growing out of the same incident, for violating the ordinance itself, the Court unanimously held that ordinance unconstitutional. *Shuttlesworth v. Birmingham* (1969).—Eds.

MR. JUSTICE BRENNAN, with whom the CHIEF JUSTICE, MR. JUS-
TICE DOUGLAS, and MR. JUSTICE FORTAS join, dissenting. . . .

6.7   *"Language likely to offend the sensibilities of some listeners is now fairly commonplace. . . ."*

EATON V. CITY OF TULSA

415 U.S. 697, 94 S. Ct. 1228, 39 L. Ed. 2d 693 (1974)

Eaton was charged with violation of a municipal ordinance. While he was on the witness
stand for cross-examination by the prosecutor, the following exchange occurred:

Q: What did you do?

A: I sensed something behind me and turned maybe enough to look
over my shoulder. At the time I turned and looked over my
shoulder I could see this guy's face and shoulders coming at me;
almost simultaneously he hit me and he knocked me over on my
back a bench down. Luckily, somebody grabbed him and pulled
him back, and I got up off my back after being knocked down
on my back, wrenched my elbow, got up to a vertical posture
where I would have some kind of defensibility and moved up to
where I had some square footing.

Q: What's defensibility?

A: I think that would be a place where you were able to get your
feet to stand square so you would be half ready for some chicken
shit that had jumped you from behind.

The Court: Mr. Eaton, you will have until tomorrow morning to show me why
you should not be held in direct contempt of this Court. I'm not
going to put up with that kind of language in this Court.

The witness: That's fine. I don't feel as though I need to put up with why I
received this.

The Court: Mr. Eaton, did you hear what I just said?

The witness: Yes, sir.

The Court: That kind of language you used in this Court, I will not put up
with any more of that talk in this courtroom. That was not responsive to any type of question whatsoever and I'm not going to
have profanity in this courtroom and you're going to be held in
direct contempt of this Court unless you can show me by tomorrow morning, cause why you should not be.

The witness: Fine. I'm not going to show you anything in the morning any
more than I can show you now, but I think me being asked to
speculate as to why someone would jump on me from behind is
not within any kind of realm of prosecution—

The Court: The Court will be in recess.

Eaton was prosecuted and convicted for direct contempt "by his insolent behavior during open court and in the presence of the judge, to wit, by using the language 'chicken-shit'. . . ."

PER CURIAM. . . .

This single isolated usage of street vernacular, not directed at the judge or any officer of the court, cannot constitutionally support the conviction of criminal contempt. "The vehemence of the language used is not alone the measure of the power to punish for contempt. The fires which it kindles must constitute an imminent, not merely a likely, threat to the administration of justice." *Craig v. Harney* (1947). In using the expletive in answering the question on cross-examination "[i]t is not charged that [petitioner] here disobeyed any valid court order, talked loudly, acted boisterously, or attempted to prevent the judge or any other officer of the court from carrying on his court duties." *Holt v. Virginia* (1965). In the circumstances, the use of the expletive thus cannot be held to "constitute an imminent . . . threat to the administration of justice." . . .

The motion to proceed *in forma pauperis* and the petition for certiorari are granted, the judgment is reversed, and the case is remanded for further proceeding not inconsistent with this opinion.

MR. JUSTICE POWELL, concurring.

I concur in the Court's *per curiam* opinion. I write briefly only to make clear my understanding of the limited scope of its holding. Whether the language used by petitioner in a courtroom during trial justified exercise of the contempt power depended upon the facts. Under the circumstances here, the imposition of a contempt sanction against petitioner denied him due process of law.

The phrase "chicken shit" was used by petitioner as a characterization of the person whom petitioner believed assaulted him. As noted in the Court's opinion, it was not directed at the trial judge or anyone officially connected with the trial court. But the controlling fact, in my view, and one that should be emphasized, is that petitioner received no prior warning or caution from the trial judge with respect to court etiquette. It may well be, in view of contemporary standards as to the use of vulgar and even profane language, that this particular petitioner had no reason to believe that this expletive would be offensive or in any way disruptive of proper courtroom decorum. Language likely to offend the sensibility of some listeners is now fairly commonplace in many social gatherings as well as in public performances.

I place a high premium on the importance of maintaining civility and good order in the courtroom. But before there is resort to the summary remedy of criminal contempt, the court at least owes the party concerned some sort of notice or warning. No doubt there are circumstances in which a courtroom outburst is so egregious as to justify a summary response by the judge without specific warning, but this is surely not such a case.

MR. JUSTICE REHNQUIST, with whom the CHIEF JUSTICE [BURGER] and MR. JUSTICE BLACKMAN join, dissenting. . . .

Even the Court appears to shy away from a flat rule, analogous to the hoary doctrine of the law of torts that every dog is entitled to one bite, to the effect that every witness is entitled to one free contumacious or other impermissible remark. . . .

6.8   *"Don't argue with me."*

FISHER V. PACE, SHERIFF OF JASPER COUNTY, TEXAS

336 U.S. 155, 69 S. Ct. 425, 93 L. Ed. 569 (1949)

warning was given

MR. JUSTICE REED delivered the opinion of the Court.

While participating as counsel in the trial of a cause the petitioner, Joe J. Fisher, was adjudged guilty of contempt committed in the presence of the court by the District Court of Jasper County, Texas. The petitioner's client was the plaintiff in an action under the state workmen's compensation law. The case was being tried before a jury and the parties had stipulated as to the average weekly wage of the claimant and the rate of compensation per week. The only remaining questions to be determined were as to the extent and duration of the incapacity resulting from an injury to the claimant's foot. . . .

Thereafter petitioner began his opening argument to the jury during which the following occurrence took place, as shown by the trial court's order of contempt and commitment:

[By MR. FISHER:] "Now bear in mind, gentlemen, that this is what we call a specific injury . . . and the law states the amount of maximum compensation which a person can receive for such an injury, that is, one hundred and twenty-five weeks. . . . That is all we are asking. Now that means one hundred and twenty-five weeks times the average weekly compensation rate.

By MR. COX: Your Honor please—

By THE COURT: Wait a minute.

By MR. COX: The jury is not concerned with the computation; it has only one series of issues. That is not before the jury.

By THE COURT: That has all been agreed upon.

By MR. FISHER: I think it is material, Your Honor, to tell the jury what the average weekly compensation is of this claimant so they can tell where he is.

By THE COURT: They are not interested in dollars and cents.

By MR. FISHER: They are interested to this extent—

By THE COURT: Don't argue with me. Go ahead. I will give you your exception to it.

By MR. FISHER: Note our exception.

By THE COURT: All right.

[By MR. FISHER:] This negro, as I stated, can only recover one hundred and twenty-five weeks compensation, at whatever compensation the rate will figure under the law.

By MR. COX: I am objecting to that discussion, Your Honor, as to what the plaintiff can recover.

By THE COURT: Gentlemen! Mr. Fisher, you know the rule, and I have sustained his objection.

By MR. FISHER: I am asking—

By THE COURT: Don't argue with me. Gentlemen, don't give any consideration to the statement of Mr. Fisher.

By MR. FISHER: Note our exception. I think I have a right to explain whether it is a specific injury or general injury.

By THE COURT: I will declare a mistrial if you mess with me two minutes and a half, and fine you besides.

By MR. FISHER: That is all right. We take exception to the conduct of the Court.

By THE COURT: That is all right; I will fine you $25.00.

By MR. FISHER: If that will give you any satisfaction.

By THE COURT: That is $50.00; that is $25.00 more. Mr. Sheriff come get it. Pay the clerk $50.00.

By MR. FISHER: You mean for trying to represent my client?

By THE COURT: No sir; for contempt of Court. Don't argue with me.

By MR. FISHER: I am making no effort to commit contempt, but merely trying to represent the plaintiff and stating in the argument—

By THE COURT: Don't tell me. Mr. Sheriff, take him out of the courtroom. Go on out of the courtroom. I fine you three days in jail.

By MR. FISHER: If that will give you any satisfaction; you know you have all the advantage by you being on the bench.

By THE COURT: That will be a hundred dollar fine and three days in jail. Take him out.

By MR. FISHER: I demand a right to state my position before the audience.

By THE COURT: Don't let him stand there. Take him out. . . .

Historically and rationally the inherent power of courts to punish contempts in the face of the court without further proof of facts and without aid of jury is not open to question. This attribute of courts is essential to preserve their authority and to prevent the administration of justice from falling into disrepute. Such summary conviction and punishment accords due process of law.

There must be adequate facts to support an order for contempt in the face of the court. Contrary to the contention of the petitioner the state Supreme Court evaluated the facts to decide whether there was sufficient evidence to support the judgment of the trial court and held that there was. . . . After a careful analysis of the facts as disclosed by the judgment of the trial court, the conclusion was reached that the conduct of the petitioner was clearly sufficient to support the power of the court to punish summarily the contempt committed in its presence.

The judgment of the Supreme Court of Texas must be affirmed. In a case of this type the transcript of the record cannot convey to us the complete picture of the courtroom scene. It does not depict such elements of misbehavior as expression, manner of speaking, bearing, and attitude of the petitioner. Reliance must be placed upon the fairness and objectivity of the presiding judge. The occurrence must be viewed as a unit in order to appraise properly the misconduct, and the relationship of the petitioner as an officer of the court must not be lost sight of. . . .

. . . On objection of the opposing counsel petitioner was stopped by the trial judge, but in the face of the court's decision he persisted in trying to tell the jury the effect of their answers. . . . In addition to this stubborn effort to bring excluded matter to the knowledge of the jury, the petitioner twice refused to heed the court's admonition not to argue the point. . . .

. . . We see nothing in [the Supreme Court of Texas'] opinion or conclusion that indicates any disregard of petitioner's rights. The conduct of a judge should be such as to command respect for himself as well as for his office. We cannot say, however, that mildly provocative language from the bench puts a constitutional protection around an attorney so as to allow him to show the contempt for judge and court manifested by this record, particularly the last few sentences of the altercation.

The judgment of the Supreme Court of Texas accordingly is

Affirmed.

MR. JUSTICE DOUGLAS, with whom **MR. JUSTICE BLACK** concurs, dissenting.

The power to punish for contempt committed in open court was recognized long ago as a means of vindicating the dignity and authority of the court. But its exercise must be narrowly confined lest it become an instrument of tyranny. Chief Justice Taft in *Cooke v. United States* [1925] warned that its exercise by a federal court is "a delicate one and care is needed to avoid arbitrary or oppressive conclusions." The same restraint is necessary under our constitutional scheme when state courts are claiming the right to take a person by the heels and fine or imprison him for contempt without a trial or an opportunity to defend. . . .

It is said that the statement was improper under Texas practice. But it took a ruling of the Texas Supreme Court to make it so, and even then Justice Sharp dissented. If Texas law on the point is so uncertain that the highest judges of the State disagree as to what is the permissible practice, is a lawyer to be laid by the heels for pressing the point? Yet it was for pressing the point of law on which the Supreme Court of Texas divided that Fisher was held in contempt. . . .

This lawyer was the victim of the pique and hotheadedness of a judicial officer who is supposed to have a serenity that keeps him above the battle and the crowd. This is as much a perversion of the judicial function as if the judge who sat had a pecuniary interest in the outcome of the litigation. . . .

MR. JUSTICE MURPHY, dissenting. . . .

A trial judge must be given wide latitude in punishing interference with the orderly administration of justice. But the summary nature of contempt proceedings, the risk of imprisonment without jury, trial, or full hearing, make this the most drastic weapon entrusted to the trial judge. To sanction the procedure when it is patent that there has been no substantial interference with the trial, when a judge has used his position and power to successively increase the penalty for simple objections, is, I believe, a denial of the due process of law. . . .

MR. JUSTICE RUTLEDGE, dissenting. . . .

Lawyers owe a large, but not an obsequious, duty of respect to the court in its presence. But their breach of this obligation in no case justifies correction by an act or acts from the bench intemperate in character, overriding judgment. Since the case comes here upon the sequence of events taken as an entirety, I do not undertake to separate one portion of the judgment from another. Accordingly, as the case stands here, I must take the entire sentence as infected with the fault I have noted. It follows, in my view, that the judgment should be reversed. Whatever the provocation, there can be no due process in trial in the absence of calm judgment and action, untinged with anger, from the bench.

6.9   *"Many of the words leveled at the judge . . . were highly personal aspersions, even 'fighting words' . . ."*

MAYBERRY V. PENNSYLVANIA

400 U.S. 455, 91 S. Ct. 499, 27 L. Ed. 2d 532 (1971)

MR. JUSTICE DOUGLAS delivered the opinion of the Court.

Petitioner and two codefendants were tried in a state court for prison breach and holding hostages in a penal institution. While they had appointed counsel as advisers, they represented themselves. The trial ended with a jury verdict of guilty of both charges on the 21st day, which was a Friday. The defendants were brought in for sentencing on the following Monday. Before imposing sentence on the verdicts the judge pronounced them guilty of criminal contempt. He found that petitioner had committed one or more contempts on 11 of the 21 days of trial and sentenced him to not less than one nor more than two years for each of the 11 contempts or a total of 11 to 22 years. . . .

Petitioner's conduct at the trial comes as a shock to those raised in the Western tradition that considers a courtroom a hallowed place of quiet dignity as far removed as possible from the emotions of the street.

On the first day of the trial petitioner came to the side bar to make suggestions and obtain rulings on trial procedures. Petitioner said: "It seems like the court has the intentions of railroading us" and moved to disqualify the judge. The motion was denied. Petitioner's other motions, including his request that the deputy sheriffs in the courtroom be dressed as civilians, were also denied. Then came the following colloquy:

MR. MAYBERRY: I would like to have a fair trial of this case and like to be granted a fair trial under the Sixth Amendment.

THE COURT: You will get a fair trial.

MR. MAYBERRY: It doesn't appear that I am going to get one the way you are overruling all our motions and that, and being like a hatchet man for the State.

THE COURT: The side bar is over.

MR. MAYBERRY: Wait a minute, Your Honor.

THE COURT: It is over.

MR. MAYBERRY: You dirty sonofabitch. . . .

The fifth charge relates to a protest which the defendants made that at the end of each trial day they were denied access to their legal documents—a condition which the trial judge shortly remedied. The following ensued:

MR. MAYBERRY: You're a judge first. What are you working for? The prison authorities, you bum?

MR. LIVINGSTON: I have a motion pending before Your Honor.

THE COURT: I would suggest—

MR. MAYBERRY: Go to hell. I don't give a good God damn what you suggest, you stumbling dog.

Meanwhile one defendant told the judge if he did not get access to his papers at night he'd "blow your head off." Another defendant said he would not sit still and be "kowtowed and be railroaded into a life imprisonment." Then the following transpired:

MR. MAYBERRY: You started all this bullshit in the beginning.

THE COURT: You keep quiet.

MR. MAYBERRY: Wait a minute.

THE COURT: You keep quiet.

MR. MAYBERRY: I am my own counsel.

THE COURT: You keep quiet.

MR. MAYBERRY: Are you going to gag me?

THE COURT: Take these prisoners out of here. We will take a ten minute recess, members of the jury. . . .

As the court prepared to charge the jury, petitioner said:

Before Your Honor begins the charge to the jury defendant Mayberry wishes to place his objection on the record to the charge and to the whole proceedings from now on, and he wishes to make it known to the Court now that he has no intention of remaining silent while the Court charges the jury, and that he is going to continually object to the charge of the Court to the jury throughout the entire charge, and he is not going to remain silent. He is going to disrupt the proceedings verbally throughout the entire charge of the Court, and also he is going to be objecting to being forced to terminate his defense before he was finished.

The court thereupon had petitioner removed from the courtroom and later returned gagged. But petitioner caused such a commotion under gag that the court had him removed to an adjacent room where a loudspeaker system made the courtroom proceedings audible. The court phrased this contempt charge as follows:

On December 9, 1966, you have constantly, boisterously, and insolently interrupted the Court during its attempts to charge the jury, thereby creating an atmosphere of utter confusion and chaos.

These brazen efforts to denounce, insult, and slander the court and to paralyze the trial are at war with the concept of justice under law. Laymen, foolishly trying to defend themselves, may understandably create awkward and embarrassing scenes. Yet this is not the character of the record revealed here. We have here downright insults of a trial judge, and tactics taken from street brawls and transported to the courtroom. This is conduct not "befitting an American courtroom," as we said in *Illinois v. Allen* [1970], and criminal contempt is one appropriate remedy.

As these separate acts or outbursts took place, the arsenal of authority described in *Allen* was available to the trial judge to keep order in the courtroom. He could, with propriety, have instantly acted, holding petitioner in contempt, or excluding him from the courtroom, or otherwise insulating his vulgarity from the courtroom. . . .

. . . Where, however, he does not act the instant the contempt is committed, but waits until the end of the trial, on balance, it is generally wise where the marks of the unseemly conduct have left personal stings to ask a fellow judge to take his place. . . .

. . . [A] judge, vilified as was this Pennsylvania judge, necessarily becomes embroiled in a running, bitter controversy. No one so cruelly slandered is likely to maintain that calm detachment necessary for fair adjudication. . . .

. . . Many of the words leveled at the judge in the instant case were highly personal aspersions, even "fighting words"—"dirty sonofabitch," "dirty tyrannical old dog," "stumbling dog," and "fool." He was charged with running a Spanish Inquisition and told to "Go to hell" and "Keep your mouth shut." Insults of that kind are apt to strike "at the most vulnerable and human qualities of a judge's temperament." *Bloom v. Illinois* [1968].

Our conclusion is that by reason of the Due Process Clause of the Fourteenth Amendment a defendant in criminal contempt proceedings should be given a public trial before a judge other than the one reviled by the contemnor. In the present case that requirement can be satisfied only if the judgment of contempt is vacated so that on remand another judge, not bearing the sting of these slanderous remarks and having the impersonal authority of the law, sits in judgment on the conduct of petitioner as shown by the record.

Vacated and remanded.

7
Limitations on Judicial Power

In his dissent to *United States v. Butler* (1936), one of the Supreme Court's anti–New Deal decisions, Justice Harlan F. Stone warned his colleagues: "The only check upon our own exercise of power is our own sense of self-restraint." But within months the Court had surrendered to the New Deal in the famous "switch in time that saved nine." In earlier chapters we have noted some of the political limitations on judicial power, such as those inherent in the appointing process. This chapter will seek to recognize more explicitly the limitations imposed on the courts by the American political and institutional setting.

INTERNAL CHECKS

We should begin by recognizing the relevance of what Stone called "self-restraint" as an operative force in judicial decision making. Internal restraints revolve around that set of standards judges think should govern their conduct on and off the bench. Robert A. Dahl has stressed the importance in preserving political stability in America of democratic beliefs among political elites. These political professionals, Dahl says, accept certain rules of the game—that restrict their own power —respecting the results of an election or allowing the opposition to speak, for example.[1] Judges, too, typically internalize certain limitations as befitting appointive officials in a representative constitutional democracy.

We know that Stone himself found much of the New Deal politically distasteful; yet, because he could not find any constitutional prohibitions against these policies, he voted to sustain them. In much the same fashion Oliver Wendell Holmes dissented against rulings reading

[1] *Who Governs* (New Haven: Yale University Press, 1961), espec. chaps. 27–28.

laissez faire into the Constitution. He, in fact, distrusted governmental intervention in economic processes (the Sherman Act he characterized as "humbug"); but as he noted in one of his most biting dissents: "The Fourteenth Amendment does not enact Mr. Herbert Spencer's Social Statics." During his service on the Court (1939–1962), Felix Frankfurter made a fetish of proclaiming his self-control in matters constitutional. His opinion in *Haley v. Ohio* (1948) presents one such effort at do-it-yourself psychoanalysis, as does Justice Harry Blackmun's opinion in the capital punishment controversy. (Reading 7.1.) Other chapters reprint much material that is relevant to such a discussion; here we want only to underline the importance of such self-limiting concepts.

INSTITUTIONAL CHECKS

The judicial system itself imposes certain institutional as well as moral restrictions on a judge. The limitations on trial judges are most evident. In all important criminal cases as well as in many civil suits, litigants have a right to trial by jury. While a judge may shield the jurors from some untrustworthy evidence and give them detailed explanations of "the law," the final decision is theirs. Moreover, under existing legal rules, a judge is not supposed to overturn a jury's verdict if it appears that reasonable people could reasonably have arrived at such a conclusion.

The right of a losing litigant (except, of course, the prosecution in a criminal case) to appeal a decision puts another limitation on a trial judge. While appellate judges must give certain presumptions to the judgment of a colleague who presided over the actual combat, reversals of lower-court rulings are quite common.

Appellate judges also operate within a network of restrictions. Probably the most effective limitation is the staffing of all appellate courts by more than one judge. Justices of the Supreme Court who wish to have their jurisprudence translated into public law must muster at least four colleagues behind their reasoning.

Judges at all levels have felt free to criticize the work of other courts, though it was somewhat unusual when an Alabama federal district judge in 1983 told the Supreme Court that its rulings on prayer in the public schools were wrong and based on a mistaken reading of history. (Reading 7.2.) In 1984 Justice Rehnquist explained why the Supreme Court had reversed twenty-seven of twenty-eight rulings by the Court of Appeals for the Ninth Circuit when reviewed by the Supreme Court in the preceding term: "When all is said and done, some panels of the Ninth Circuit have a hard time saying no to any litigant with a hard luck story."[2]

---

[2] *Los Angeles Times*, August 16, 1984. Was Appeals Court Judge Antonin Scalia artfully challenging the Supreme Court's view on libel when he wrote that *New York*

Court of Appeals Judge Robert Bork's decision in *Dronenburg v. Zech* (1984) was an implied criticism of the Supreme Court's failure to provide a clear ruling on the constitutional status of homosexuality. While the Supreme Court in *Doe v. Commonwealth's Attorney for Richmond* (1976) had summarily affirmed a district court judgment upholding a Virginia statute making private consensual homosexual conduct a criminal offense, the Court had provided no reconciliation of this position with its discovery—or recognition—of the constitutional right to privacy in *Griswold v. Connecticut* (1965). In *Dronenburg,* Judge Bork, noted scholar, former Solicitor General, and probable Supreme Court appointee, filled this gap in constitutional theory, concluding "that we can find no constitutional right to engage in homosexual conduct and that, as judges, we have no right to create one."[3]

Lower-court judges can hamper and even frustrate the commands of higher courts. This potential should not be surprising, since bureaucratic resistance in administrative hierarchies is a well-documented fact of life. Moreover, the Supreme Court usually does not issue a final order when it decides a case but only remands it to a lower court for "proceedings consistent with this opinion." Not infrequently, a party who wins on appeal to the Supreme Court still winds up the loser on return to the lower court. Ernesto Miranda—the defendant whose name has since 1966 been attached to the famous warning about rights to silence and to free counsel the Court has required police to give people whom they arrest—was convicted again when he was retried.

Lower courts can also drag their heels. For six years, Alabama judges resisted the Supreme Court's rulings protecting the right of the NAACP to operate within the state. (Reading 7.3.) In 1955, Georgia's supreme court authorized an execution that the United States Supreme Court had explicitly warned was unconstitutional. (Reading 7.4.)

Apart from evasion or even attacks on a higher court, there is ample room for conflict when a trial judge senses a shift in the Supreme Court's policy. "It is a little difficult," Charles Curtis once observed, "for the lower court to have to follow the Supreme Court of the next succeeding year." Two schools of thought tell lower courts how to handle such problems. One, represented by Jerome Frank, feels that "when a lower court perceives a pronounced new doctrinal trend in Supreme Court decisions, it is its duty, cautiously to be sure, to follow

---

Times v. Sullivan (1964) had "fulsomely assured [the] requirement of actual malice in the defamation of public figures"? William Safire comments: "The word 'fulsomely' means 'foully, disgustingly, offensively,' or at the least, 'excessively'; Judge Scalia has too sharp an intellect and too precise a writing style to have lapsed into a misuse of the word to mean 'fully.' " *New York Times,* April 29, 1985.

[3] Judge Bork's rejection of the Supreme Court's privacy decisions as a defense for homosexual conduct is critically analyzed by Ronald Dworkin, "Reagan's Justice," 31 *New York Review of Books* 27 (November 8, 1984).

not to resist it." Frank added: "To use mouth-filling words, cautious extrapolation is in order."[4]

But prediction is a risky enterprise. Guesses, no matter how well-intentioned and well-informed, can be wrong. This risk has led other judges to assert that inferior courts should follow doubtful precedents until the higher court specifically overturns them. As Chief Judge Calvert Magruder of the First Circuit has said: "We should always express a respectful deference to controlling decisions of the Supreme Court, and do our best to follow them. We should leave it to the Supreme Court to overrule its own cases."[5]

If confronted with systematic evasion, the Supreme Court can, as a last resort, invoke its inherent power to punish for contempt in order to coerce either state or federal judges. But this power is almost as unlikely to be used as is the impeachment power of Congress. More probably, the Court would do as John Marshall did in *McCulloch v. Maryland* (1819) when faced with militant state resistance: that is, bring the full weight of its statutory and constitutional authority to bear on the substantive issues in the dispute and make the final determination of the problems itself.

In such a fashion this aspect of judicial decision making comes full circle. The Supreme Court must take into account the reaction of inferior judges, and lower courts must attempt to divine the counter-reaction of the Supreme Court. Meanwhile, both must keep a wary eye on public opinion and maneuverings within the other branches of government to ascertain how these will affect the policy concerned.

POLITICAL CHECKS BY THE PRESIDENT

Federal judges have at their command no physical means of enforcing decisions other than that supplied by the President and Congress. The President even appoints the marshals at the district and circuit court levels, and he can dismiss them at his pleasure. John Marshall and Roger Taney both had experiences with Presidents who refused to execute judicial decrees. Chief Justice Marshall thought that Jefferson was ready to defy the expected decision in *Marbury v. Madison* that Marbury should have his commission. Marshall shrewdly avoided this confrontation. But in 1807 he and Jefferson came close to a second confrontation when, as part of his circuit-riding duties, Marshall presided over the treason trial of Aaron Burr. At the request of Burr's counsel, the Chief Justice ordered Jefferson to produce some correspondence between the President and one of the witnesses for the prosecution. Subsequent events are somewhat unclear, and some his-

---

[4] *Perkins v. Endicott Johnson* (2d. Cir., 1942).
[5] "The Trials and Tribulations of an Intermediate Appellate Court," 44 *Com. L. Q.* 1, 4 (1958).

torians have contended that Jefferson successfully defied the sub-poena. Although Jefferson did not personally appear, as the subpoena commanded, he did submit some of the subpoenaed correspondence —but as a matter of grace, he said.

Chief Justice Taney had a more direct clash with executive power. Following Lincoln's suspension of the writ of habeas corpus and substitution of military for civilian courts in Maryland, a notorious secessionist, John Merryman, was arrested by the military and confined in Fort McHenry. After Taney's effort to serve a writ of habeas corpus on General Cadwalader, the commander of the fort, had been rebuffed, Taney attempted to have the general arrested for contempt; but the marshal was refused admission to the fort. Taney could only lecture the President in a blistering opinion charging Lincoln with violating his oath to support the Constitution.

These were, of course, exceptional cases, but the thread connecting judicial decisions with executive enforcement has often been thin. Andrew Jackson refused to carry out one of the decisions of the Marshall Court protecting the treaty rights of Indians against violation by the state of Georgia. Franklin D. Roosevelt had prepared a radio address to explain why he was not going to comply with an expected Supreme Court decision that the statute taking the United States off the gold standard was unconstitutional. Because, by a vote of five to four, the judges refused to rule against the government's action, FDR did not give the speech. In 1957 when Governor Orval Faubus of Arkansas called out the National Guard to prevent execution of a federal court order to integrate the schools, President Eisenhower was more than willing to compromise and took no action to assist the district court for some days. If the President had not eventually concluded that Faubus was negotiating in bad faith, the *Brown* decision might have become a monument to judicial futility.

Earlier, President Eisenhower had apparently made a clumsy effort to influence the ruling in *Brown.* Earl Warren reports in his memoirs that he was invited to a White House dinner shortly before the decision was due, and that John W. Davis, counsel for the school boards, was also present. During the dinner the President went to great lengths to tell Warren what a "great man" Davis was. He also said that the people in the South were not "bad people. All they are concerned about is to see that their sweet little girls are not required to sit in school alongside some big overgrown Negroes." Not long afterward the Court announced the decision in *Brown,* and, Warren added, "with it went our cordial relations."[6]

Before the Supreme Court's decision in *United States v. Nixon,* (1974), the President's counsel refused to give assurance that Nixon

[6] *The Memoirs of Chief Justice Earl Warren* (New York: Doubleday & Co., 1977), pp. 291–292.

would surrender the Watergate tapes if ordered to do so. Had he in fact refused, the mood of Congress ensured that his impeachment would have quickly ensued.

Aside from the power of nominating new justices, perhaps the most effective impact the executive exerts upon the Court occurs when the President throws the prestige of the White House onto the policy-making scales and openly attacks individual decisions or an entire line of judicial rulings. For various reasons and with varying degrees of success, Jefferson, Jackson, Lincoln, the two Roosevelts, Nixon, and Reagan all undertook to reverse judicial policies by arousing public opposition to them. (Readings 7.5, 7.6, 7.7, and 7.8.)

CONGRESSIONAL RESTRICTIONS

Congressional checks on judicial power are potentially far more effective than those of the President acting alone, although the fact that legislative consensus is required makes their exercise more difficult. The first congressional control is that over the purse strings. While the Constitution provides that a judge's salary shall not be reduced during his term of office, Congress in 1802 simply abolished a whole tier of federal courts and refused to appropriate money to pay the judges' salaries. In 1937 Congress employed a reverse tactic, enacting a statute that offered more favorable retirement benefits and thus encouraging older justices to retire. A threat sometimes made is that Congress will refuse to appropriate funds to carry out particular decisions. A 1975 law sought to undercut enforcement of the *Brown* ruling by forbidding the administration to withhold funds from school districts that refused to participate in "pairing" plans for black and white schools.

As a more important check on the judiciary, Congress can invoke its own lawmaking powers to counter the interpretations of the courts. Any decision construing a federal statute is subject to reversal by legislative adoption of new statutory language. More fundamentally, Congress can propose a constitutional amendment either reversing the Court's constitutional doctrine (as the Fourteenth, Sixteenth, and Twenty-sixth Amendments did) or striking at judicial power itself (as the Eleventh Amendment did).

We have already pointed to other weak spots in the judicial armor. The broad authority that the Constitution gives to Congress over the appellate jurisdiction of the Supreme Court has proved, except for the *McCardle* case, only a scarecrow, like the power of impeachment. (Reading 7.9.) But congressional power over the number of judicial positions and the organization and jurisdiction of the federal courts is a reality.

In 1937 Congress refused to exercise its undoubted power to increase the size of the Supreme Court, as President Roosevelt had proposed. But two decades later Congress embarked on an orgy of "Court-curbing" proposals. The decision in *Brown* had of course aroused the ire of an almost solid front of Southern congressmen. In 1957 the Court raised up additional enemies by decisions limiting congressional investigations of communists and their criminal prosecution under the Smith Act. But with one minor exception all the Court-curbing proposals of this period were defeated, although some by narrow margins.

In the 1960s the Court's adoption of the principle, one person, one vote, and its decisions banning prayers and Bible reading in the public schools generated opposition in the form of proposed constitutional amendments. Resentment against the Warren Court's decisions strengthening the procedural rights of criminal defendants culminated in provisions in the Crime Control and Safe Streets Act of 1968 intended specifically to undo the effects of three of the Court's rulings.

Another serious campaign against the judiciary began in the late 1970s as bills were introduced to strip all federal courts, including the Supreme Court, of jurisdiction in school prayer, abortion, and racial integration cases.[7] While the Reagan administration favored the purpose of such legislation, Attorney General William French Smith warned that "Congress may not . . . consistent with the Constitution, make 'exceptions' to Supreme Court jurisdiction which would intrude upon the core functions of the Supreme Court as an independent and equal branch in our system of separation of powers."

JUDGES AND POLITICIANS

The federal judiciary has its own resources for moderating or thwarting assaults by the political branches. First, elected officials sometimes need a judicial blessing to legitimize political decisions on the margins of constitutionality. Second, although judges inevitably offend some powerful interest groups, in doing so they usually manage to please other groups who can in turn pressure public officials. The relative strength of these sets of groups varies from situation to situation, but the rules of the legislative process give a great advantage to those who only want to preserve the status quo. Here, too, public opinion may become important. The Court's defenders will always charge the Court's attackers with sacrilege. When this charge is joined with hard economic and political interests, it can bestow an aura of righteousness on what would otherwise appear to be self-interest.

---

[7] Lawrence Gene Sager, "Constitutional Limitations on Congress' Authority to Regulate the Jurisdiction of the Federal Courts," 95 *Harvard Law Review* 17 (1981); Laurence H. Tribe, "Jurisdictional Gerrymandering: Zoning Disfavored Rights Out of the Federal Courts," 16 *Harvard Civil Rights-Civil Liberties Law Review* 129 (1981); Gerald Gunther, "Congressional Power to Curtail Federal Court Jurisdiction," 36 *Stanford Law Review* 895 (1984).

Third, federal legislators and administrators compete for political power with each other and with state officials, as well as with federal judges. Congressmen or Presidents who take a long view of their own power position can seldom be certain that in depriving federal judges of power they are not merely transferring that power to another of their rivals.

CHECKS FROM THE STATES

While state executives or legislators have no direct means of limiting federal judicial power, they can utilize their access to Congress or the executive to try to deploy the weapons these institutions have. State judges may, of course, attempt to thwart implementation of federal rulings.

One venerable doctrine of state resistance, nullification, dates back to the Virginia and Kentucky Resolutions of 1798. But the notion that a state has authority to interpose its authority between its citizens and federal officials no longer has any constitutional standing, if indeed it ever did. Despite his authorship of the Virginia Resolutions, James Madison later denounced nullification as a "colossal heresy," a "poison," and a "preposterous and anarchical pretension." In 1955 the attorney general of Mississippi commented that his state's effort to nullify the school segregation decisions was based on "legal poppycock"; earlier the governor of Alabama had characterized his legislators who were proposing nullification as "just a bunch of hound dawgs, bayin' at the moon."

Another tactical advantage of state court judges in relation to the Supreme Court is that the justices of the Supreme Court will review only those cases from state courts in which the decision was based on a substantial federal question. Matters pertaining strictly to state law do not come under federal authority. Thus state judges can sometimes conceal the real basis of a decision from an overworked Supreme Court and so avoid review and reversal.

Considering the differences between state and national interests and outlooks and the perennial friction between trial and appellate judges, a substantial reservoir of potential conflict exists in the judicial system. In 1958, for instance, when attacks on the liberal decisions of the Warren Court had almost produced a constitutional crisis, the Conference of State Chief Justices issued an unprecedented report on federal-state relationships, accusing the Supreme Court of usurping state powers. In the 1970s, by an interesting reversal, the Supreme Court had become rather too conservative for state supreme courts in such states as California, New Jersey, and Hawaii. Courts in those states declined to follow the Burger Court's jurisprudence and relied instead on provisions of their own state constitutions to which they are free to give independent meanings. (Reading 7.10.)

For example, the Burger Court ruled in *San Antonio School District v. Rodriguez* (1973) that the Fourteenth Amendment does not require states to ensure that all public school children receive an equally financed education. But two years earlier the California supreme court had come to the opposite conclusion in *Serrano v. Priest* (1971) on the basis of the state constitution. In spite of *Rodriguez,* the state's policy was subsequently confirmed when the Supreme Court refused review in *Clowes v. Serrano* (1977). Other states followed California's lead in imposing stricter standards than those approved by *Rodriguez.* The New Jersey supreme court imposed an equal-financing requirement in that state by interpreting the state constitutional clause mandating "a thorough and efficient system of free public schools" to mean equally financed public schools.[8]

The concept of an independent judiciary, which can increase the number of jurisdictive collisions between state and national tribunals, is balanced within the national system by an appellate court supervision that helps reduce conflict. A state judge owes his appointment to local political groups and can be removed, if at all, only by state action. Life tenure makes federal judges even more independent, but their inferior position in the hierarchical chain of national authority subjects them to stricter surveillance by the Supreme Court. As the supervisor of the administration of federal justice, the Supreme Court sets more exacting standards for lower courts of the United States than for state tribunals. This supervision lowers the probability of defiance, but federal judges are not mere pawns in a judicial game.

Both state and federal judges are participants in the cult of the robe. They share the mystique of the judicial role. No matter how fierce their rivalries, common possession of this magic distinguishes judges from other persons and gives them interests and outlooks as *judges.* Furthermore, district, circuit, and Supreme Court judges are all *federal* officials and, therefore, in a sense, joint competitors (whether they like it or not) with state judges.

SELECTED REFERENCES

Alsop, Joseph, and Turner Catledge. *The 168 Days.* New York: Doubleday Doran, 1938.

Baker, Leonard. *Back to Back: The Duel Between FDR and the Supreme Court.* New York: Macmillan, 1967.

Berger, Raoul. *Congress v. the Supreme Court.* Cambridge, Massachusetts: Harvard University Press, 1969.

———. "The President, Congress, and the Courts," 83 *Yale Law Journal* 1111 (1974).

Brennan, William J., Jr. "State Constitutions and the Protection of Individual Rights," 90 *Harvard Law Review* 489 (1977).

---

[8] *Robinson v. Cahill* (1976).

Casper, Jonathan D. "The Supreme Court and National Policy Making," 70 *American Political Science Review* 50 (1976).

Dahl, Robert A. "Decision-Making in a Democracy: The Role of the Supreme Court as a National Policy-Maker," 6 *Journal of Public Law* 279 (1958).

Elliott, Sheldon D. "Court Curbing Proposals in Congress," 33 *Notre Dame Lawyer* 597 (1958).

Leuchtenburg, William E. "The Origins of Franklin D. Roosevelt's 'Court-Packing' Plan," in Philip B. Kurland (ed.), *The Supreme Court Review, 1966.* Chicago: University of Chicago Press, 1966. Pp. 347–400.

Mason, Alpheus T. *Harlan Fiske Stone: Pillar of the Law.* New York: Viking, 1956. Chs. 3–6.

Moynihan, Daniel Patrick. "What Do You Do When the Supreme Court Is Wrong?" *The Public Interest,* No. 57 (Fall 1979).

Murphy, Walter F. *Congress and the Court.* Chicago: University of Chicago Press, 1962.

———. "Lower Court Checks on Supreme Court Power," 53 *American Political Science Review* 1017 (1959).

Nagel, Stuart S. "Court-Curbing Periods in American History," 18 *Vanderbilt Law Review* 925 (1965).

Neely, Richard. *Why Courts Don't Work.* New York: McGraw-Hill, 1982.

Note. "Congressional Reversal of Supreme Court Decisions: 1945–1957," 71 *Harvard Law Review* 1324 (1958).

Note. "Evasion of Supreme Court Mandates in Cases Remanded to State Courts Since 1941," 67 *Harvard Law Review* 1251 (1954).

Note. "State Court Evasion of United States Supreme Court Mandates," 56 *Yale Law Journal* 574 (1947).

Pollock, Stewart G. "State Constitutions as Separate Sources of Fundamental Rights," 35 *Rutgers Law Review* 707 (1983).

Pritchett, C. Herman. *Congress Versus the Supreme Court, 1957–1960.* Minneapolis: University of Minnesota Press, 1961.

Schmidhauser, John R., and Larry L. Berg. *The Supreme Court and Congress: Conflict and Interaction, 1945–1968.* New York: Free Press, 1972.

Steamer, Robert J. *The Supreme Court in Crisis: A History of Conflict.* Amherst: University of Massachusetts Press, 1971.

7.1   *"I fear the Court has overstepped."*

[handwritten: an opinion in which the court exercises self control]

FURMAN V. GEORGIA

408 U.S. 238, 92 S. Ct. 2726, 33 L. Ed. 2d 346 (1972)

In this case, five of the justices voted that the death penalty, as then applied in the United States, was unconstitutional. No two of the five, however, could agree on an opinion explaining precisely how capital punishment violated the Constitution, and each member of the majority wrote his own opinion, as did each justice in the minority. (In 1976, after thirty-eight states had enacted new statutes imposing death penalties—most of the acts contained additional procedural safeguards to protect the accused—a different majority of the Court held that capital punishment was not per se unconstitutional. Gregg v. Georgia, 428 U.S. 153.)

from the opinion that the death penalty is unconstitutional

MR. JUSTICE BLACKMUN, dissenting. . . .

he opposes the death penalty but believes that from the constitutional stand, it should continue to be legal

1. Cases such as these provide for me an excruciating agony of the spirit. I yield to no one in the depth of my distaste, antipathy, and, indeed, abhorrence, for the death penalty. . . . That distaste is buttressed by a belief that capital punishment serves no useful purpose that can be demonstrated. For me, it violates childhood's training and life's experiences, and is not compatible with the philosophical convictions I have been able to develop. It is antagonistic to any sense of "reverence for life." Were I a legislator, I would vote against the death penalty. . . .

2. Having lived for many years in a State that does not have the death penalty . . . capital punishment had never been a part of life for me. . . . So far as I can determine, the State, purely from a statistical deterrence point of view, was neither the worse nor the better for its abolition, for, as the majority opinions observe, the statistics prove little, if anything. . . .

4. The several majority opinions acknowledge, as they must, that until today capital punishment was accepted and assumed as not unconstitutional *per se* under the Eighth Amendment or the Fourteenth Amendment. . . .

Suddenly, however, the course of decision is now the opposite way, with the Court evidently persuaded that somehow the passage of time has taken us to a place of greater maturity and outlook. The argument, plausible and high-sounding as it may be, is not persuasive. . . .

The Court has recognized, and I certainly subscribe to the proposition, that the Cruel and Unusual Punishment Clause "may acquire meaning as public opinion becomes enlightened by a humane justice." *Weems v. United States* [1910]. And Mr. Chief Justice Warren, for a plurality of the Court, referred to "the evolving standards of decency that mark the progress of a maturing society." *Trop v. Dulles* [1958].

My problem, however . . . is the suddenness of the Court's perception of progress in the human attitude since decisions of only a short while ago.

5. To reverse the judgments in these cases is, of course, the easy choice. It is easier to strike the balance in favor of life and against death. . . . But it is good argument and it makes sense only in a legislative and executive way and not as a judicial expedient. . . .

I do not sit on these cases, however, as a legislator. . . . Our task here, as must so frequently be . . . re-emphasized, is to pass upon the constitutionality of legislation that has been enacted and that is challenged. This is the sole task for judges. We should not allow our personal preferences as to the wisdom of legislative and congressional action, or our distaste for such action, to guide our judicial decision. . . . The temptations to cross that policy line are very great. In fact, as today's decision reveals, they are almost irresistible. . . .

10. It is not without interest, also, to note, that, although the several opinions for the majority acknowledge the heinous and atrocious character of the offenses committed by the petitioners, none of those opinions makes reference to the misery the petitioners' crimes occasioned to the victims, to the families of the victims, and to the communities where the offenses took place. The arguments for the respective petitioners, particularly the oral arguments, were similarly and curiously devoid of reference to the victims. There is risk, of course, in a comment such as this, for it opens one to the charge of emphasizing the retributive. Nevertheless, these cases are here because offenses to innocent victims were perpetrated. This fact and the terror that occasioned it, and the fear that stalks the streets of many of our cities today, perhaps deserve not to be entirely overlooked. . . .

Although personally I may rejoice at the Court's result, I find it difficult to accept or to justify as a matter of history, of law, or of constitutional pronouncement. I fear the Court has overstepped. It has sought and has achieved an end.

7.2   ". . . the United States Supreme Court has erred in its reading of history."

A FEDERAL DISTRICT JUDGE REVERSES THE SUPREME COURT

Jaffree v. Board of School Commissioners

554 F. Supp. 1104 (1983)

An Alabama law allowed teachers in public schools to begin the school day with a period of silence for meditation or voluntary prayer. A second statute approved a nondenominational prayer to be recited in the classrooms. The U. S. Supreme Court, however, had several times held—see especially *Engel v. Vitale* (1962) and *Abington School District v. Schempp* (1963)—that prayers in public schools violated the First Amendment's prohibition, made applicable to the states through the Fourteenth Amendment, against establishment of religion. In 1982 William B. Hand, chief judge of the United States District Court for the Southern District of Alabama, granted a preliminary injunction against enforcement of the statutes. In January 1983, however, Judge Hand changed his mind, dissolved the injunction, and, in an opinion described by the Solicitor General as one "in which the district judge thumbed his nose at the Supreme Court," explained why the Supreme Court had been wrong. Four months later the Court of Appeals for the Eleventh Circuit reversed and the Supreme Court denied certiorari, but the issue reached the Supreme Court in a companion case, *Wallace v. Jaffree* (1985).

HAND. DISTRICT JUDGE

[There is] previous little historical support for the view that the states were prohibited by the establishment clause of the first amendment from establishing a religion.

More than any other provision of the Constitution, the interpretation by the United States Supreme Court of the establishment clause has been steeped in history. This Court's independent review of the relevant historical documents and its reading of the scholarly analysis convinces it that the United States Supreme Court has erred in its reading of history. Perhaps this opinion will be no more than a voice crying in the wilderness and this attempt to right that which this Court is persuaded is a misreading of history will come to nothing more than blowing in the hurricane, but be that as it may, this Court is persuaded as was Hamilton that "[e]very breach of the fundamental laws, though dictated by necessity impairs the sacred reverence which ought to be maintained in the breast of the rulers towards the constitution." (Federalist No. 25).

Because the establishment clause of the first amendment to the United States Constitution does not prohibit the state from establishing a religion, the prayers offered by the teachers in this case are not unconstitutional. Therefore, the Court holds that the complaint fails to state a claim for which relief could be granted.

CONCLUSION

There are pebbles on the beach of history from which scholars and judges might attempt to support the conclusions that they are wont to reach. That is what Professors Flack, Crosskey and the more modern scholars have done in attempting to establish a beachhead, as did Justice Black, that there is a basis for their conclusions that Congress and the people intended to alter the direction of the country by incorporating the first eight amendments to the Constitution. However, in arriving at this conclusion, they, and each of them, have had to revise established principles of constitutional interpretation by the judiciary. Whether the judiciary, inadvertently or eagerly, walked into this trap is not for discussion. The result is that the judiciary has, in fact, amended the Constitution to the consternation of the republic. As Washington pointed out in his Farewell Address, this clearly is the avenue by which our government can, and ultimately, will be destroyed. We think we move in the right direction today, but in so doing we are denying to the people their right to express themselves. It is not what we, the judiciary want, it is what the people want translated into law pursuant to the plan established in the Constitution as the framers intended. This is the bedrock and genius of our republic. The mantle of office gives us no power to fix the moral direction that this nation will take. When we undertake such course we trample upon the law. In such instances the people have a right to complain. The Court loses its respect and our institution is brought low. This misdirection should be cured now before it is too late. We must give no future generation an excuse to use this same tactic to further their ends which they think proper under the then political climate as for instance did Adolph Hitler when he used the court system to further his goals.

What is past is prologue. The framers of our Constitution, fresh with recent history's teachings, knew full well the propriety of their decision to leave to the peoples of the several states the determination of matters religious. The wisdom of this decision becomes increasingly apparent as the courts wind their way through the maze they have created for themselves by amending the Constitution by judicial fiat to make the first amendment applicable to the states. Consistency no longer exists. Where you cannot recite the Lord's Prayer, you may sing his praises in God Bless America. Where you cannot post the Ten Commandments on the wall for those to read if they do choose, you can require the Pledge of Allegiance. Where you cannot acknowledge the authority of the Almighty in the Regent's prayer, you can acknowledge the existence of the Almighty in singing the verses of America and Battle Hymn of the Republic. It is no wonder that the people perceive that justice is myopic, obtuse, and janus-like.

7.3   *"Should we unhappily be mistaken in our belief that the Supreme Court of Alabama will promptly implement this disposition . . ."*

ALABAMA ATTACKS THE NAACP

". . . Alabama has fallen short of showing a controlling justification. . . ."

National Association for the Advancement of Colored People v. Alabama—1958

357 U.S. 449, 78 S. Ct. 1163, 2 L. Ed. 2d 1488 (1958)

The NAACP's effort to secure implementation of *Brown v. Board of Education* (1954, 1955) led Southern states to search for effective methods of putting the organization out of business. In Alabama the state attorney general sought to enjoin the organization from continuing to operate in the state, charging that it had not met the state's requirements for out-of-state corporations (the NAACP was incorporated in New York) doing business in Alabama. In connection with this suit the state court ordered the NAACP to produce its records, including names and addresses of all its members in Alabama. The NAACP argued that the state law applied only to commercial corporations, but it did nevertheless produce all the records demanded except the membership lists. For failing to comply fully with the state court's order, the trial judge held the organization in contempt, fined it $100,000, and issued an ex parte temporary restraining order forbidding it to operate in the state. Moreover, so long as the NAACP was in contempt, the trial court refused to permit it to litigate any other issues. The state supreme court upheld these rulings, and the NAACP petitioned the United States Supreme Court for a writ of certiorari.

MR. JUSTICE HARLAN delivered the opinion of the Court. . . .

We hold that the immunity from state scrutiny of membership lists which the Association claims on behalf of its members is here so related to the right of the members to pursue their lawful private interests privately and to associate freely with others in so doing as to come within the protection of the Fourteenth Amendment. And we conclude that Alabama has fallen short of showing a controlling justification for the deterrent effect on the free enjoyment of the right to associate which disclosure of membership lists is likely to have. Accordingly, the judgment of civil contempt and the $100,000 fine which resulted from petitioner's refusal to comply with the production order in this respect must fall.

Petitioner joins with its attack upon the production order a challenge to the constitutionality of the State's *ex parte* temporary restraining order preventing it from soliciting support in Alabama, and it asserts that the Fourteenth Amendment precludes such state action. But as noted above, petitioner has never received a hearing on the merits of the ouster suit, and we do not consider these questions properly here. The Supreme Court of Alabama noted in its denial of the petition for certiorari that such petition raised solely a question pertinent to the contempt adjudication. "The ultimate aim and purpose of the litigation is to determine the right of the state to enjoin petitioners from doing business in Alabama. That question, however, is not before us in this proceeding." The proper method for raising questions in the state appellate courts pertinent to the underlying suit for an injunction appears to be by appeal, after a hearing on the merits and final judgment by the lower state court. Only from the disposition of such an appeal can review be sought here.

For the reasons stated, the judgment of the Supreme Court of Alabama must be reversed and the case remanded for proceedings not inconsistent with this opinion.

Reversed.

*"We assume that the State Supreme Court . . . will not fail
to proceed promptly. . . ."*

National Association for the Advancement of Colored People v. Patterson—1959

360 U.S. 240, 79 S. Ct. 1001, 3 L. Ed. 2d 1205 (1959)

PER CURIAM.

The petition for a writ of certiorari is granted.

In our original opinion in this case, we held the Alabama judgment of civil contempt against this petitioner, together with the
$100,000 fine which it carried, constitutionally impermissible in the
circumstances disclosed by the record. We declined, however, to
review the trial court's restraining order prohibiting petitioner from
engaging in further activities in the State, that order then not being
properly before us. Our mandate, issued on August 1, 1958, accordingly remanded the case to the Supreme Court of Alabama "for
proceedings not inconsistent with" our opinion.

In due course the petitioner moved in the Supreme Court of
Alabama that our mandate be forwarded to the Circuit Court of
Montgomery County for the further proceedings which were left
open by our decision. After the motion had been twice renewed the
Supreme Court of Alabama on February 12, 1959, "again affirmed"
the contempt adjudication and $100,000 fine which this Court had
set aside. Finding that the Circuit Court had determined that petitioner had failed to "produce the documents described" in its production order, the State Supreme Court concluded that this Court
was "mistaken" in considering that, except for the refusal to provide
its membership lists, petitioner had complied with such order. This
conclusion was considered as "necessitating another affirmance of
the [contempt] judgment," involving, so the State Court thought,
matters not covered by the opinion and mandate of this Court.

We have reviewed the petition, the response of the State and all
of the briefs and the record filed here in the former proceedings.
Petitioner there claimed that it had satisfactorily complied with the
production order, except as to its membership lists, and this the State
did not deny. In fact, aside from the procedural point, both the State
and petitioner in the certiorari papers posed one identical question,
namely, had the petitioner "the constitutional right to refuse to produce records of its membership in Alabama, relevant to issues in a
judicial proceeding to which it is a party, on the mere speculation
that these members may be exposed to economic and social sanctions
by private citizens of Alabama because of their membership?" The
State made not even an indication that other portions of the produc-

tion order had not been complied with and, therefore, required its affirmance. On the contrary, the State on this phase of the case relied entirely on petitioner's refusal to furnish the "records of its membership." That was also the basis on which the issue was briefed and argued before us by both sides after certiorari had been granted. That was the view of the record which underlay this Court's conclusion that petitioner had "apparently complied satisfactorily with the production order, except for the membership lists." And that was the premise on which the Court disposed of the case. The State plainly accepted this view of the issue presented by the record and by its argument on it, for it did not seek a rehearing or suggest a clarification or correction of our opinion in that regard.

It now for the first time here says that it "has never agreed, and does not now agree, that the petitioner has complied with the trial court's order to produce with the exception of membership. The respondent, in fact, specifically denies that the petitioner has produced or offered to produce in all aspects except for lists of membership." This denial comes too late. The State is bound by its previously taken position, namely, that decision of the sole question regarding the membership lists is dispositive of the whole case.

We take it from the record now before us that the Supreme Court of Alabama evidently was not acquainted with the detailed basis of the proceedings here and the consequent ground for our defined disposition. Petitioner was, as the Supreme Court of Alabama held, obliged to produce the items included in the Circuit Court's order. It having claimed here its satisfactory compliance with the order, except as to its membership lists, and the State having not denied this claim, it was taken as true.

In these circumstances the Alabama Supreme Court is foreclosed from reexamining the grounds of our disposition. "Whatever was before the Court, and is disposed of, is considered as finally settled." *Sibbald v. United States* [1838].

This requires that the judgment of the Supreme Court of Alabama be reversed. Upon further proceedings in the Circuit Court, if it appears that further production is necessary, that court may, of course, require the petitioner to produce such further items, not inconsistent with this and our earlier opinion, that may be appropriate, reasonable and constitutional under the circumstances then appearing.

We assume that the State Supreme Court, thus advised, will not fail to proceed promptly with the disposition of the matters left open under our mandate for further proceedings, and, therefore, deny petitioner's application for a writ of mandamus.

It is so ordered.

Certiorari granted; judgment of Supreme Court of Alabama reversed, and application for writ of mandamus denied.

MR. JUSTICE STEWART took no part in the consideration or decision of this case.

> *". . . we prefer to follow our usual practice and remand the case to the Supreme Court of Alabama. . . ."*

National Association for the Advancement of Colored People v. Alabama—1964

377 U.S. 288, 84 S. Ct. 1302, 12 L. Ed. 2d 325 (1964)

MR. JUSTICE HARLAN delivered the opinion of the Court.

This case, involving the right of the petitioner, the National Association for the Advancement of Colored People, to carry on activities in Alabama, reaches this Court for the fourth time. In 1956 the Attorney General of Alabama brought a suit in equity to oust the association, a New York "membership" corporation, from the State. The basis of the proceeding was the Association's alleged failure to comply with Alabama statutes requiring foreign corporations to register with the Alabama Secretary of State and perform other acts in order to qualify to do business in the State; the complaint alleged also that certain of the petitioner's activities in Alabama, detailed below, were inimical to the well-being of citizens of the State.

On the day the complaint was filed, the Attorney General obtained an *ex parte* restraining order barring the Association, *pendente lite*, from conducting any business within the State and from taking any steps to qualify to do business under state law. Before the case was heard on the merits, the Association was adjudged in contempt for failing to comply with a court order directing it to produce various records, including membership lists. The Supreme Court of Alabama dismissed the petition for certiorari to review the final judgment of contempt on procedural grounds, which this Court, on review, found inadequate to bar consideration of the Association's constitutional claims. Upholding those claims, we reversed the judgment of contempt without reaching the question of the validity of the underlying restraining order.

In the second round of these proceedings the Supreme Court of Alabama, on remand "for proceedings not inconsistent" with this Court's opinion, again affirmed the judgment of contempt which this Court had overturned. This decision was grounded on belief that this Court's judgment had rested on a "mistaken premise." Observing that the premise of our prior decision had been one which the State had "plainly accepted" throughout the prior proceedings here, this Court ruled that the State could not, for the first time on remand, change its stance. We noted that the Supreme Court of Alabama "evidently was not acquainted with the detailed basis of the proceedings here" when it reaffirmed the judgment of contempt . . . and again remanded without considering the validity of the restraining order. In so doing, the Court said: "We assume that the State Supreme Court . . . will not fail to proceed promptly with the disposition of the matters left open under our mandate for further proceedings . . ." rendered in the prior case.

Our second decision was announced on June 8, 1959. Unable to obtain a hearing on the merits in the Alabama courts, the Association, in June 1960, commenced proceedings in the United States District Court to obtain a hearing there. Alleging that the restraining order and the failure of the Alabama courts to afford it a hearing on the validity of the order were depriving it of constitutional rights, the Association sought to enjoin enforcement of the order. Without passing on the merits, the District Court dismissed the action, because it would not assume that the executive and judicial officers of Alabama involved in the litigation would fail to protect "the constitutional rights of all citizens." The Court of Appeals agreed that the matter "should be litigated initially in the courts of the State." It, however, vacated the judgment below and remanded the case to the District Court, with instructions "to permit the issues presented to be determined with expedition in the State courts," but to retain jurisdiction and take steps necessary to protect the Association's right to be heard on its constitutional claims.

The jurisdiction of this Court was invoked a third time. On October 23, 1961, we entered an order as follows:

. . . The judgment below is vacated, and the case is remanded to the Court of Appeals with instructions to direct the District Court to proceed with the trial of the issues in this action unless within a reasonable time, no later than January 2, 1962, the State of Alabama shall have accorded to petitioner an opportunity to be heard on its motion to dissolve the state restraining order of June 1, 1956, and upon the merits of the action in which such order was issued. Pending the final determination of all proceedings in the state action, the District Court is authorized to retain jurisdiction over the federal action and to take such steps as may appear necessary and appropriate to assure a prompt disposition of all issues involved in, or connected with, the state action.

In December 1961, more than five years after it was "temporarily" ousted from Alabama, the Association obtained a hearing on the merits in the Circuit Court of Montgomery County, the court which had issued the restraining order in 1956. On December 29, 1961, the Circuit Court entered a final decree in which the court found that the Association had continued to do business in Alabama "in violation of the Constitution and laws of the state relating to foreign corporations" and that the Association's activities in the State were "in violation of other laws of the State of Alabama and are and have been a usurpation and abuse of its corporate functions and detrimental to the State of Alabama. . . ." The decree permanently enjoined the Association and those affiliated with it from doing "any further business of any description or kind" in Alabama and from attempting to qualify to do business there. The Association appealed to the Supreme Court of Alabama, which, on February 28, 1963, affirmed the judgment below without considering the merits. This Court again granted certiorari. . . .

In the first proceedings in this case, we held that the compelled disclosure of the names of the petitioner's members would entail "the likelihood of a substantial restraint upon the exercise by petitioner's members of their right to freedom of association." It is obvious that the complete suppression of the Association's activities in Alabama which was accomplished by the order below is an even more serious abridgment of that right. The allegations of illegal conduct contained in the . . . charge against the petitioner suggest no legitimate governmental objective which requires such restraint. . . .

There is no occasion in this case for us to consider how much survives of the principle that a State can impose such conditions as it chooses on the right of a foreign corporation to do business within the State, or can exclude it from the State altogether. This case, in truth, involves not the privilege of a corporation to do business in a State, but rather the freedom of individuals to associate for the collective advocacy of ideas. "Freedoms such as . . . [this] are protected not only against heavy-handed frontal attack, but also from being stifled by more subtle governmental interference." Bates v. City of Little Rock [1960]. . . .

The judgment below must be reversed. In view of the history of this case, we are asked to formulate a decree for entry in the state courts which will assure the Association's right to conduct activities in Alabama without further delay. While such a course undoubtedly lies within this Court's power, Martin v. Hunter's Lessee [1816], we prefer to follow our usual practice and remand the case to the Supreme Court of Alabama for further proceedings not inconsistent with this opinion. Such proceedings should include the prompt entry of a decree, in accordance with state procedures, vacating in all respects the permanent injunction order issued by the Circuit Court of Montgomery County, Alabama, and permitting the Association to take all steps necessary to qualify it to do business in Alabama. Should we unhappily be mistaken in our belief that the Supreme Court of Alabama will promptly implement this disposition, leave is given the Association to apply to this Court for further appropriate relief.

Reversed and remanded. *

*Faced with this ultimatum, the Alabama judges dissolved the injunction several months later.—Eds.

7.4

"[We] reject the assumption that the courts of Georgia would allow this man to go to his death. . . ."

GEORGIA V. THE SUPREME COURT

". . . the fact that we have jurisdiction does not compel us to exercise it."

Williams v. Georgia—1955

349 U.S. 375, 75 S. Ct. 814, 99 L. Ed. 1161 (1955)

Aubrey Williams, a black, was convicted of murder in March 1953. In May 1953 the United States Supreme Court reversed the conviction of another black in *Avery v. Georgia,* holding that the method of jury selection had denied the defendant equal protection of the law. The same method of jury selection had been used in *Williams* as in *Avery;* that is, the names of prospective white jurors had been placed on white cards and those of blacks on yellow cards. Six months after the *Avery* decision, Williams's attorney invoked the *Avery* rule to claim that the jury that had convicted his client had been illegally impaneled. The Georgia courts dismissed this appeal on the grounds that under state law a defendant had to challenge a jury when it was "put on" him. The United States Supreme Court granted certiorari.

MR. JUSTICE FRANKFURTER delivered the opinion of the Court. . . .

. . . On oral argument here . . . the State, with commendable regard for its responsibility, agreed that the use of yellow and white tickets in this case was, in light of this Court's decision in *Avery,* a denial of equal protection, so that a new trial would be required but for the failure to challenge the array. We need only add that it was the system of selection and the resulting danger of abuse which was struck down in *Avery* and not an actual showing of discrimination on the basis of comparative numbers of Negroes and whites on the jury lists. The question now before us, in view of the State's concession, is whether the ruling of the Georgia Supreme Court rests upon an adequate nonfederal ground, so that this Court is without jurisdiction to review the Georgia court.

A state procedural rule which forbids the raising of federal questions at late stages in the case, or by any other than a prescribed method, has been recognized as a valid exercise of state power. The principle is clear enough. But the unique aspects of the never-ending new cases that arise require its individual application to particular circumstances. Thus, we would have a different question from that before us if the trial court had no power to consider Williams' constitutional objection at the belated time he raised it. But, where a State allows questions of this sort to be raised at a late stage and be determined by its courts as a matter of discretion, we are not concluded from assuming jurisdiction and deciding whether the state court action in the particular circumstances is, in effect, an avoidance of the federal right. A state court may not, in the exercise of its discretion, decline to entertain a constitutional claim while passing upon kindred issues raised in the same manner.

The Georgia courts have indicated many times that motions for new trial after verdict are not favored, and that extraordinary motions for new trial after final judgment are favored even less. But the Georgia statute provides for such motion, and it has been granted in "exceptional" or "extraordinary" cases. The general rule is that the granting or denying of an extraordinary motion for new trial rests primarily in the discretion of the trial court, and the appellate court will not reverse except for a clear abuse of discretion. In practice, however, the Georgia appellate courts have not hesitated to reverse and grant a new trial in exceptional cases. . . .

We conclude that the trial court and the State Supreme Court declined to grant Williams' motion though possessed of power to do so under state law. Since his motion was based upon a constitutional objection, and one the validity of which has in principle been sustained here, the discretionary decision to deny the motion does not deprive this Court of jurisdiction to find that the substantive issue is properly before us.

But the fact that we have jurisdiction does not compel us to exercise it. . . . In the instant case, there is an important factor which has intervened since the affirmance by the Georgia Supreme Court which impels us to remand for that court's further consideration. This is the acknowledgment by the State before this Court that, as a matter of substantive law, Williams has been deprived of his constitutional rights. . . . We think that orderly procedure requires a remand to the State Supreme Court for reconsideration of the case. Fair regard for the principles which the Georgia courts have enforced in numerous cases and for the constitutional commands binding on all courts compels us to reject the assumption that the courts of Georgia would allow this man to go to his death as the result of a conviction secured from a jury which the State admits was unconstitutionally impaneled. . . .

MR. JUSTICE CLARK, with whom MR. JUSTICE REED and MR. JUSTICE MINTON join, dissenting. . . .

"This court . . . will not supinely surrender sovereign powers of this State."

Williams v. State—1955

88 S. E. 2d 376 (1955)

State Supreme Court

DUCKWORTH, CHIEF JUSTICE.

"The powers not delegated to the United States by the Constitution, or prohibited by it to the States, are reserved to the States respectively, or to the people." Constitution of the United States, 10th Amendment. . . . Even though executives and legislators, not being constitutional lawyers, might often overstep the foregoing unambiguous constitutional prohibition of federal invasion of State jurisdiction, there can never be an acceptable excuse for judicial failure to strictly observe it. This court bows to the Supreme Court on all federal questions of law but we will not supinely surrender sovereign powers of this State. In this case the opinion of the majority of that court recognizes that this court decided the case according to established rules of law, and that no federal jurisdiction existed which would authorize that court to render a judgment either affirming or reversing the judgment of this court, which are the only judgments by that court that this court can constitutionally recognize.

The Supreme Court . . . undertakes to remand the case for further consideration, and in their opinion has pointed to Georgia law vesting in the trial judge discretion in ruling upon an extraordinary motion for new trial and apparently concluded therefrom that this court should reverse the trial court because that discretion was not exercised in the way the Supreme Court would have exercised it. We know and respect the universally recognized rule that the exercise of discretion never authorizes a violation or defiance of law. In this case, as pointed out by us, that law is that the question sought to be raised must be raised before trial and not otherwise.

Not in recognition of any jurisdiction of the Supreme Court to influence or in any manner to interfere with the functioning of this court on strictly State questions, but solely for the purpose of completing the record in this court in a case that was decided by us in 1953, and to avoid further delay, we state that our opinion in *Williams v. State* is supported by sound and unchallenged law, conforms with the State and federal constitutions, and stands as the judgment of all seven of the Justices of this Court.

Judgment of affirmance rendered May 10, 1954, adhered to. All the Justices concur.*

*After this rebuff by the Georgia Supreme Court, Williams's attorneys again petitioned the Supreme Court for review, which was denied on January 16, 1956. Williams died in the electric chair on March 30, 1956.—Eds.

7.5   *"I know of no safe depository of the ultimate powers of the society but the people themselves. . . ."*

THOMAS JEFFERSON TO WILLIAM C. JARVIS

seems to consider the judiciary as too powerful (potentially) and as encroaching on the other branches

I thank you, Sir, for the copy of your *Republican* which you have been so kind as to send me. . . . I have not yet had time to read it seriously, but in looking over it cursorily I see much in it to approve, and shall be glad if it shall lead our youth to the practice of thinking on such subjects and for themselves. That it will have this tendency may be expected, and for that reason I feel an urgency to note what I deem an error in it. . . . You seem . . . to consider the judges as the ultimate arbiters of all constitutional questions; a very dangerous doctrine indeed, and one which would place us under the despotism of an oligarchy. Our judges are as honest as other men, and not more so. They have, with others, the same passions for party, for power, and the privilege of their corps. Their maxim is *"boni judicis est ampliare jurisdictionem"* [the task of a good judge is to expand his jurisdiction], and their power is the more dangerous as they are in office for life, and not responsible, as the other functionaries are, to the elective control. The constitution has erected no such single tribunal, knowing that to whatever hands confided, with the corruptions of time and party, its members would become despots. It has more wisely made all the departments co-equal and co-sovereign within themselves. If the legislature fails to pass laws for a census, for paying the judges and other officers of government, for establishing a militia, for naturalization as prescribed by the constitution, or if they fail to meet in congress, the judges cannot issue their mandamus to them; if the President fails to supply the place of a judge, to appoint other civil or military officers, to issue requisite commissions, the judges cannot force him. They can issue their mandamus or distringas to no executive or legislative officer to enforce the fulfillment of their official duties, any more than the president or legislature may issue orders to the judges or their officers. Betrayed by the English example, and unaware, as it should seem, of the control of our constitution in this particular, they have at times overstepped their limit by undertaking to command executive officers in the discharge of their executive duties; but the constitution, in keeping three departments distinct and independent, restrains the authority of the judges to judiciary organs, as it does the executive and legislative to executive and legislative organs. The judges certainly have more frequent occasion to act on constitutional questions, because the laws of *meum* and *tuum* and of criminal action, forming the great

A. A. Lipscomb (ed.), *The Writings of Thomas Jefferson* (Washington, D.C.: The Thomas Jefferson Memorial Association, 1903), XV, 276–279.

mass of the system of law, constitute their particular department. When the legislative or executive functionaries act unconstitutionally, they are responsible to the people in their elective capacity. The exemption of the judges from that is quite dangerous enough. I know no safe-depository of the ultimate powers of the society but the people themselves; and if we think them not enlightened enough to exercise their control with a wholesome discretion, the remedy is not to take it from them, but to inform their discretion by education. This is the true corrective of abuses of constitutional power. . . . My personal interest in such questions is entirely extinct, but not my wishes for the longest possible continuance of our government on its pure principles; if the three powers maintain their mutual independence on each other it may last long, but not so if either can assume the authorities of the other. . . .

7.6   *"The Congress, the Executive, and the Court must each . . . be guided by its own opinion of the Constitution."*

ANDREW JACKSON'S VETO OF THE BANK BILL

On July 4, 1832, Congress passed an act to continue the Bank of the United States. On July 10, 1832, President Andrew Jackson vetoed the bank bill as unwise, unfair, and unconstitutional. The portion of his veto message dealing with the argument that the constitutionality of the Bank had been definitively settled by the decision of the United States Supreme Court in *McCulloch v. Maryland* (1819) is reprinted here. This part of the message was largely drafted by Roger Brooke Taney, who was soon to succeed John Marshall as Chief Justice of the United States.

It is maintained by the advocates of the bank that its constitutionality in all its features ought to be considered as settled by precedent and by the decision of the Supreme Court. To this conclusion I can not assent. Mere precedent is a dangerous source of authority, and should not be regarded as deciding questions of constitutional power except where the acquiescence of the people and the States can be considered as well settled. So far from this being the case on the subject, an argument against the bank might be based on precedent. One Congress, in 1791, decided in favor of a bank; another, in 1811, decided against. One Congress, in 1815, decided against a bank; another, in 1816, decided in its favor. Prior to the present Congress,

James D. Richardson (ed.), *A Compilation of the Messages and Papers of the Presidents* (Washington, D.C.: Bureau of National Literature and Art, 1908), II, 581–582.

therefore, the precedents drawn from that source were equal. If we resort to the States, the expressions of legislative, judicial, and executive opinions against the bank have been probably to those in its favor as 4 to 1. There is nothing in precedent, therefore, which, if its authority were admitted, ought to weigh in favor of the act before me.

If the opinion of the Supreme Court covered the whole ground of this act, it ought not to control the coordinate authorities of this Government. The Congress, the Executive, and the Court must each for itself be guided by its own opinion of the Constitution. Each public officer who takes an oath to support the Constitution swears that he will support it as he understands it, and not as it is understood by others. It is as much the duty of the House of Representatives, of the Senate, and of the President to decide upon the constitutionality of any bill or resolution which may be presented to them for passage or approval as it is of the supreme judges when it may be brought before them for judicial decision. The opinion of the judges has no more authority over Congress than the opinion of Congress has over the judges, and on that point the President is independent of both. The authority of the Supreme Court must not, therefore, be permitted to control the Congress or the Executive when acting in their legislative capacities, but to have only such influence as the force of their reasoning may deserve.

7.7   *". . . if the policy . . . is to be irrevocably fixed by decisions of the Supreme Court . . . the people will have ceased to be their own rulers. . . ."*

ABRAHAM LINCOLN'S FIRST INAUGURAL ADDRESS, MARCH 4, 1861

. . . A majority, held in restraint by constitutional checks, and limitations, and always changing easily, with deliberate changes of popular opinions and sentiments, is the only true sovereign of a free people. Whoever rejects it, does, of necessity, fly to anarchy or to despotism. Unanimity is impossible; the rule of a minority, as a permanent arrangement, is wholly inadmissible; so that rejecting the majority principle, anarchy, or despotism in some form, is all that is left.

I do not forget the position assumed by some, that constitutional questions are to be decided by the Supreme Court; nor do I deny that such decisions must be binding in any case, upon the parties to a suit, as to the object of that suit, while they are also entitled to a very high

James D. Richardson (ed.), *A Compilation of the Messages and Papers of the Presidents* (Washington, D.C.: Bureau of National Literature and Art, 1908), VI, 9.

respect and consideration, in all parallel cases, by all other departments of government. And while it is obviously possible that such decision may be erroneous in any given case, still the evil effect following it, being limited to that particular case, with the chance that it may be overruled, and never become a precedent for other cases, can better be borne than could the evils of a different practice. At the same time the candid citizen must confess that if the policy of the government, upon vital questions, affecting the whole people, is to be irrevocably fixed by decisions of the Supreme Court, the instant they are made, in ordinary litigation between parties, in personal actions, the people will have ceased to be their own rulers, having to that extent, practically resigned their government, into the hands of that eminent tribunal. Nor is there, in this view, any assault upon the court, or the judges. It is a duty, from which they may not shrink, to decide cases properly brought before them; and it is no fault of theirs, if others seek to turn their decisions to political purposes.

7.8   *"We must find a way to take an appeal from the Supreme Court to the Constitution itself."*

REORGANIZING THE FEDERAL JUDICIARY

Franklin D. Roosevelt

In 1933 you and I knew that we must never let our economic system get completely out of joint again—that we could not afford to take the risk of another great depression.

We also became convinced that the only way to avoid a repetition of those dark days was to have a government with power to prevent and to cure the abuses and the inequalities which had thrown that system out of joint.

We then began a program of remedying those abuses and inequalities—to give balance and stability to our economic system—to make it bombproof against the causes of 1929.

Today we are only part way through that program—and recovery is speeding up to a point where the dangers of 1929 are again becoming possible, not this week or month perhaps, but within a year or two.

National laws are needed to complete that program. Individual or local or State effort alone cannot protect us in 1937 any better than 10 years ago. . . . The American people have learned from the depres-

Speech of March 9, 1937. Senate Report No. 711, 75th Cong., 1st Sess., pp. 41–44.

sion. For in the last three national elections an overwhelming majority of them voted a mandate that the Congress and the President begin the task of providing that protection—not after long years of debate, but now.

The courts, however, have cast doubts on the ability of the elected Congress to protect us against catastrophe by meeting squarely our modern social and economic conditions.

We are at a crisis in our ability to proceed with that protection. It is a quiet crisis. There are no lines of depositors outside closed banks. But to the farsighted it is far-reaching in its possibilities of injury to America.

I want to talk with you very simply about the need for present action in this crisis—the need to meet the unanswered challenge of one-third of a nation ill-nourished, ill-clad, ill-housed.

Last Thursday I described the American form of government as a three-horse team provided by the Constitution to the American people so that their field might be plowed. The three horses are, of course, the three branches of government—the Congress, the executive, and the courts. Two of the horses are pulling in unison today; the third is not. Those who have intimated that the President of the United States is trying to drive that team overlook the simple fact that the President, as Chief Executive, is himself one of the three horses.

It is the American people themselves who are in the driver's seat.

It is the American people themselves who want the furrow plowed.

It is the American people themselves who expect the third horse to pull in unison with the other two.

I hope that you have reread the Constitution of the United States. Like the Bible, it ought to be read again and again.

It is an easy document to understand when you remember that it was called into being because the Articles of Confederation under which the Original Thirteen States tried to operate after the Revolution showed the need of a National Government with power enough to handle national problems. In its preamble the Constitution states that it was intended to form a more perfect Union and promote the general welfare; and the powers given to the Congress to carry out those purposes can be best described by saying that they were all the powers needed to meet each and every problem which then had a national character and which could not be met by merely local action.

But the framers went further. Having in mind that in succeeding generations many other problems then undreamed of would become national problems, they gave to the Congress the ample broad powers "to levy taxes . . . and provide for the common defense and general welfare of the United States."

That, my friends, is what I honestly believe to have been the clear and underlying purpose of the patriots who wrote a Federal Constitution to create a National Government with national power, intended as they said, "to form a more perfect union . . . for ourselves and our posterity." . . .

But since the rise of the modern movement for social and economic progress through legislation, the Court has more and more often and more and more boldly asserted a power to veto laws passed by the Congress and State legislatures in complete disregard of this original limitation.

In the last four years the sound rule of giving statutes the benefit of all reasonable doubt has been cast aside. The Court has been acting not as a judicial body, but as a policy-making body.

When the Congress has sought to stabilize national agriculture, to improve the conditions of labor, to safeguard business against unfair competition, to protect our national resources, and in many other ways to serve our clearly national needs, the majority of the Court has been assuming the power to pass on the wisdom of these acts of the Congress—and to approve or disapprove the public policy written into these laws.

That is not only my accusation. It is the accusation of most distinguished justices of the present Supreme Court. I have not the time to quote to you all the language used by dissenting justices in many of these cases. But in the case holding the Railroad Retirement Act unconstitutional, for instance, Chief Justice Hughes said in a dissenting opinion that the majority opinion was "a departure from sound principles," and placed "an unwarranted limitation upon the commerce clause." And three other justices agreed with him.

In the case holding the A.A.A. unconstitutional, Justice Stone said of the majority opinion that it was a "tortured construction of the Constitution." And two other justices agreed with him.

In the case holding the New York Minimum Wage Law unconstitutional, Justice Stone said that the majority were actually reading into the Constitution their own "personal economic predilections," and that if the legislative power is not left free to choose the methods of solving the problems of poverty, subsistence, and health of large numbers in the community, then "government is to be rendered impotent." And two other justices agreed with him. . . .

In the face of such dissenting opinions, it is perfectly clear that as Chief Justice Hughes has said, "We are under a Constitution, but the Constitution is what the judges say it is."

The Court in addition to the proper use of its judicial functions has improperly set itself up as a third House of the Congress—a super-legislature, as one of the justices has called it—reading into the Constitution words and implications which are not there, and which were never intended to be there.

We have, therefore, reached the point as a Nation where we must take action to save the Constitution from the Court and the Court from itself. We must find a way to take an appeal from the Supreme Court to the Constitution itself. We want a Supreme Court which will do justice under the Constitution—not over it. In our courts we want a government of laws and not of men.

I want—as all Americans want—an independent judiciary as proposed by the framers of the Constitution. That means a Supreme Court that will enforce the Constitution as written—that will refuse to amend the Constitution by the arbitrary exercise of judicial power —amendment by judicial say-so. It does not mean a judiciary so independent that it can deny the existence of facts universally recognized. . . .

What is my proposal? It is simply this: Whenever a judge or justice of any federal court has reached the age of seventy and does not avail himself of the opportunity to retire on a pension, a new member shall be appointed by the President then in office, with the approval, as required by the Constitution, of the Senate of the United States.

That plan has two chief purposes: By bringing into the judicial system a steady and continuing stream of new and younger blood, I hope, first, to make the administration of all federal justice speedier and therefore less costly; secondly, to bring to the decision of social and economic problems younger men who have had personal experience and contact with modern facts and circumstances under which average men have to live and work. This plan will save our National Constitution from hardening of the judicial arteries. . . .

Those opposing this plan have sought to arouse prejudice and fear by crying that I am seeking to "pack" the Supreme Court and that a baneful precedent will be established.

What do they mean by the words "packing the Court"?

Let me answer this question with a bluntness that will end all honest misunderstanding of my purposes.

If by that phrase "packing the Court" it is charged that I wish to place on the bench spineless puppets who would disregard the law and would decide specific cases as I wished them to be decided, I make this answer: That no President fit for his office would appoint, and no Senate of honorable men fit for their office would confirm, that kind of appointees to the Supreme Court.

But if by that phrase the charge is made that I would appoint and the Senate would confirm justices worthy to sit beside present members of the Court who understand those modern conditions; that I will appoint justices who will not undertake to override the judgment of the Congress on legislative policy; that I will appoint justices who will act as justices and not as legislators—if the appointment of such justices can be called "packing the Courts"—then I say that I, and with me the vast majority of the American people, favor doing just that thing—now. . . . Our difficulty with the Court today rises not from the Court as an institution but from human beings within it. But we cannot yield our constitutional destiny to the personal judgment of a few men who, being fearful of the future, would deny us the necessary means of dealing with the present.

This plan of mine is no attack on the Court; it seeks to restore the Court to its rightful and historic place in our system of constitutional government and to have it resume its high task of building anew on the Constitution "a system of living law." . . .

7.9 *"Without jurisdiction the court cannot proceed at all in any cause."*

EX PARTE MCCARDLE

7 Wall. 506, 19 L. Ed. 264 (1869)

In 1866 and 1867 the Supreme Court declared unconstitutional military trials for civilians in areas where regular civil courts were open and also voided a federal statute requiring a "test oath" for admission to certain public professions. These decisions threatened to outlaw the military rule which the Radical Republicans had established in the South. William McCardle, a Mississippi editor, who was being held for trial before a military commission, appealed to the Supreme Court. Ironically, he utilized an 1867 statute intended to protect officials administering the Reconstruction program. To avert a decision that most of the Reconstruction program was unconstitutional, Congress in 1868 repealed—over Johnson's veto—the 1867 act which gave the Supreme Court appellate jurisdiction in the case. The Court heard the *McCardle* case in time to decide it prior to repeal of the statute; but over bitter protests from two justices the majority delayed a decision until after the repeal.

[handwritten margin note: Does this imply that the Reconstruction program was at least held to be unconstitutional?]

ARGUMENT OF COUNSEL . . .

Mr. Sharkey, for the appellant:

The prisoner alleged an illegal imprisonment. The imprisonment was justified under certain acts of Congress. The question then presents a case arising under "the laws of the United States"; and by the very words of the Constitution the judicial power of the United States extends to it. By words of the Constitution, equally plain, that judicial power is vested in one Supreme Court. This court, then, has its jurisdiction directly from the Constitution, not from Congress. The jurisdiction being vested by the Constitution alone, Congress cannot abridge or take it away. The argument which would look to Congressional legislation as a necessity to enable this court to exercise "the judicial power" (any and every judicial power) "of the United States," renders a power, expressly given by the Constitution, liable to be made of no effect by the inaction of Congress. Suppose that Congress never made any exceptions or any regulations in the matter. What, under a supposition that Congress must define when, and where, and how, the Supreme Court shall exercise it, becomes of this "judicial power of the United States," so expressly, by the Constitution, given to this court? It would cease to exist. But this court is coexistent and co-ordinate with Congress, and must be able to exercise the whole judicial power of the United States, though Congress passed no act on the subject. . . .

Now, can Congress thus interfere with cases on which this high tribunal has passed, or is passing, judgment? Is not legislation like this an exercise by the Congress of judicial power? . . .

Messrs. L. Trumbull and M. H. Carpenter, contra:

1. The Constitution gives to this court appellate jurisdiction in any case like the present one was, only with such exceptions and under such regulations as Congress makes.
2. It is clear, then, that this court had no jurisdiction of this proceeding—*an appeal from the Circuit Court*—except under the act of February 5th, 1867. . . .
3. The act conferring the jurisdiction having been repealed, the jurisdiction ceased; and the court had thereafter no authority to pronounce any opinion or render any judgment in this cause. . . .

THE CHIEF JUSTICE [CHASE] delivered the opinion of the court.

The first question necessarily is that of jurisdiction; for, if the act of March, 1868, takes away the jurisdiction defined by the act of February, 1867, it is useless, if not improper, to enter into any discussion of other questions.

It is quite true, as was argued by the counsel for the petitioner, that the appellate jurisdiction of this court is not derived from acts of Congress. It is, strictly speaking, conferred by the Constitution. But it is conferred "with such exceptions and under such regulations as Congress shall make." . . .

The source of that jurisdiction, and the limitations of it by the Constitution and by statute, have been on several occasions subjects of consideration here. In the case of *Durousseau v. The United States* [1810], particularly, the whole matter was carefully examined, and the court held, that while "the appellate powers of this court are not given by the judicial act, but are given by the Constitution," they are, nevertheless, "limited and regulated by that act, and by such other acts as have been passed on the subject." The court said, further, that the judicial act was an exercise of the power given by the Constitution to Congress "of making exceptions to the appellate jurisdiction of the Supreme Court." "They have described affirmatively," said the court, "its jurisdiction, and this affirmative description has been understood to imply a negation of the exercise of such appellate power as is not comprehended with it."

The principle that the affirmation of appellate jurisdiction implies the negation of all such jurisdiction not affirmed having been thus established, it was an almost necessary consequence that acts of Congress, providing for the exercise of jurisdiction, should come to be spoken of as acts granting jurisdiction, and not as acts making exceptions to the constitutional grant of it.

The exception to appellate jurisdiction in the case before us, however, is not an inference from the affirmation of other appellate jurisdiction. . . . The provision of the act of 1867, affirming the appellate jurisdiction of this court in cases of *habeas corpus* is expressly repealed. It is hardly possible to imagine a plainer instance of positive exception.

We are not at liberty to inquire into the motives of the legislature. We can only examine into its power under the Constitution; and the power to make exceptions to the appellate jurisdiction of this court is given by express words.

What, then, is the effect of the repealing act upon the case before us? We cannot doubt as to this. Without jurisdiction the court cannot proceed at all in any cause. Jurisdiction is power to declare the law, and when it ceases to exist, the only function remaining to the court is that of announcing the fact and dismissing the cause. And this is not less clear upon authority than upon principle. . . .

It is quite clear, therefore, that this court cannot proceed to pronounce judgment in this case, for it has no longer jurisdiction of the appeal; and judicial duty is not less fitly performed by declining ungranted jurisdiction than in exercising firmly that which the Constitution and the laws confer.

Counsel seem to have supposed, if effect be given to the repealing act in question, that the whole appellate power of the court, in cases of *habeas corpus,* is denied. But this is an error. The act of 1868 does not except from that jurisdiction any cases but appeals from Circuit Courts under the act of 1867. It does not affect the jurisdiction which was previously exercised.

The appeal of the petitioner in this case must be

Dismissed for want of jurisdiction.

7.10   *"A state's history and traditions should be considered."*

STATE COURTS AND CONSTITUTIONAL RIGHTS IN THE DAY OF THE BURGER COURT

A. E. Dick Howard

. . . Both constitutional history and theory support the case for an independent body of state constitutional law, though they do not help very much in giving direction for specific decisions. History is supportive in that there were state constitutions and state bills of rights long before there was a Federal Constitution. Theory is supportive in that there are inherent differences between state constitutions and the federal document. One important difference is that the Federal Constitution is a grant of power, whereas state charters are a limit on power. State legislatures in nearly every state are held to be able to do whatever is not forbidden them by the state constitution or the Federal Constitution. Consequently, state constitutions are longer and more detailed than their federal counterpart, thus giving more opportunities for the development of an independent body of law.

When specific cases arise, a state judge may wish to consider some of the following factors:

1. The textual language of the state constitution may give cogent ground for a decision different from that which would be arrived at under the Federal Constitution. Frequently a state provision will be more explicit, as with a requirement that mandates a jury of twelve or a religion clause that is detailed on what aid may not flow to church-related schools. Often there will be state provisions that have no explicit federal counterpart at all. Thus, every state constitution dwells at length on education, and most have something to say about conservation and the environment; the Federal Constitution mentions neither. Rights that must, if recognized at all in federal constitutional law, be implied in judicial decisions may be made explicit in a state constitution; such is the case with privacy in Alaska.

A state constitution may openly invite its courts to develop an independent body of law through a provision, such as that added to the California Constitution in 1974, that "[r]ights guaranteed by this Constitution are not dependent on those guaranteed by the United

62 *Virginia Law Review* 873 (1976). Reprinted with permission. A. E. Dick Howard is White Burkett Miller Professor of Law and Public Affairs, University of Virginia School of Law.

States Constitution." Where the rights are procedural in nature, the state's courts may use their rulemaking or supervisory powers to announce rights that the United States Supreme Court does not require.

2. Whether or not the textual language is different from the Federal Constitution, legislative history may reveal an intention that will support reading a state provision independently of federal law. General revisions of a state constitution are accomplished by either a constitutional convention or legislative action, ratified at referendum. In either case there are usually study commission reports and certainly floor debates, which may, in addition to their relevance in interpreting specific provisions, yield statements of philosophy. . . .

3. A state's history and traditions should be considered. Early events often throw considerable light on constitutional interpretation in states tending to strict separation of church and state. In criminal cases, courts in Rhode Island and Maine have dipped thoughtfully into the region's history to decide that a jury must have twelve members and that a jury trial is a right even in trials for minor infractions. A sense of local uniqueness is especially evident in Alaska opinions, several of which have invoked the pioneer philosophy that brought people to Alaska originally.

4. State courts should consider the nature of the subject matter in litigation and the interests affected by the local political process. In *Cooley v. Board of Port Wardens,* the United States Supreme Court did this in concluding that pilotage was not of such a nature as to require a single uniform rule throughout the country. While that approach to commerce cases has been superseded by other analyses, *Cooley* suggests a useful question for state constitutional interpretation: is the subject matter local in character, or does there appear to be a need for national uniformity? . . .

If there is a case to be made for judicial concern about the power of special interest groups to use the legislative process for their own ends, to the detriment of the public interest—a case that, because of its implications for democratic theory, is by no means self-evident— state courts may be better placed to play that role. . . .

5. A state court may be influenced by the extent to which the United States Supreme Court has shown a "hands-off" attitude toward a particular class of problems. The Supreme Court's virtually total abandonment of the use of substantive due process in economic cases invites a closer look by state courts, since if they do not intervene—and they certainly may be persuaded that they should not— there is no federal forum to which to turn. Where state courts are the only effective forum for a particular kind of grievance, they should look more closely before deciding that they, like the Supreme Court, have no role to play.

Conversely, it can be argued that to the extent a subject has been "federalized"—as happened with much of criminal procedure in the 1960's—the state courts should play a deferential and retiring role. This argument should not be overstated, however, for as the trend of Burger Court decisions reminds us, the Federal Constitution places a floor under, rather than a ceiling over, the rights of an accused. The manifestly diverse and specific provisions of state constitutions should not be ignored in the name of uniformity. The values of uniformity should give a state court pause before departing from the federal standard, but they should not be taken to force automatic acquiescence.

6. State constitutions are a peculiarly useful mirror of fundamental values. While the Federal Constitution is amended infrequently and only with great difficulty—witness the travails of the Equal Rights Amendment—state constitutions by contrast are periodically revised to reflect changing values. It is not uncommon for one of the older states, for example, to have had half a dozen constitutions since 1776. Moreover, constitutional revision comes in waves, the era of Jacksonian democracy, the post–Civil War era, and the 1960's being periods of notable activity. Each period of reform and revision has brought with it a new generation's insights, and new values have taken constitutional dimension. . . . With state constitutions thus responding to the felt needs of each generation, there is greater reason for state judges to read those documents as benchmarks for decision.

General revisions aside, state constitutions are far easier to amend than the Federal Constitution. It is hard for the United States Supreme Court to outrage people so much that they amend the Federal Constitution. Critics have tried and failed, as opponents of the Court's school desegregation, one-man one-vote, prayer, and abortion decisions will attest. Supreme Court justices therefore carry an unusually heavy burden when they break new ground. State judges, by contrast, though they should not innovate lightly, should recall that state constitutions are less immutable. At least one state judge has cited the ease of amending state constitutions as a justification for an activist position. Every state legislature can propose amendments to the state constitution, and in a majority of states there is provision for calling a constitutional convention. Additionally, about a quarter of the state constitutions may be amended through popular initiative. After the Supreme Court of California decided that capital punishment violated the California Constitution, the voters promptly amended that document to overturn the court's decision.

7. The tradition of the states as experimenters is an honored one. Justice Brandeis celebrated this tradition when he said that it is "one of the happy incidents of the federal system that a single courageous state may, if its citizens choose, serve as a laboratory; and try novel social and economic experiments without risk to the rest of the coun-

try." . . . [T]he same reasoning supports innovation and diversity among state courts. Legislatures can profit from the experience of sister states, and so can state judges. . . .

The case for an independent role for state courts should not be read as a case for unthinking activism. No judge, state or federal, is a knight errant, whose only concern is to do good. Hence, the state judge, when presented with the invitation to develop a body of state constitutional law, should pause to consider some of the dangers and hazards that may lie along the way.

To be sure, the constraints on state judges are not identical with those upon the federal judiciary. Some considerations that do or should act as a brake upon Supreme Court justices should not really concern a state court judge. For example, however far we may have come since 1789, ours is still a federal union, and the Supreme Court properly takes into account what impact its decisions will have on federalism. It would be false logic, however, for a state court to stay its hand in a given area by pointing to a Supreme Court decision that in fact rested on considerations of federalism. It seems odd, for example, that at least one state court, refusing to intervene in student hair length cases, cited Justice Black's notion that this is a question best left to the states. . . .

There are some genuine concerns, however, that a state judge should mull before mounting an activist horse. Judicial review, even when exercised by elected judges, is never without an antidemocratic flavor. When judges invalidate a legislative act, however correct that judgment, they are thwarting an expression of popular will. What state courts do, then, has clear and significant implications for the political process and for democratic theory. This should weigh on their consciences just as it should upon their distinguished brethren on the federal bench. . . .

Having offered these cautionary notes, one returns to the original theme: that the coming of the Burger Court offers an appropriate time for state courts to reflect on their ancient heritage as interpreters of their state charters of liberty and on the ever growing opportunities to look to those documents to vindicate the rights of the people of the several states. . . .

8
The Impact of
Judicial Decisions

Judicial pronouncements, it has been said, "are not really decisions until they affect the attitudes and behavior of other actors."[1] Traditionally, students of law lost interest in a case after the final decision was handed down. But for those who are concerned with the relation of law to society, the most interesting aspect of the judicial process may be just beginning when a court issues its mandate. For there remains the problem of securing compliance with the ruling; and where a court has taken a position on an important policy issue, the decision is a political event that may set off a chain reaction. If a court miscalculates its ability to alter political behavior, it will stimulate opposition to its policies and perhaps to the judiciary itself. Justice Frankfurter had this possibility in mind when he urged the Supreme Court in *Colegrove v. Green* and *Baker v. Carr* (Readings 5.10 and 8.2) not to enter the "political thicket" of legislative reapportionment. As we have seen in Chapter 7, the opportunities for resistance to Supreme Court decisions, both in the lower courts and in the political arena, are many. One of the most effective of recent approaches to understanding the policy-making roles of the courts has been research into the impact of typical judicial decisions.

Impact, according to Charles A. Johnson and Bradley C. Canon, refers to the general reactions and responses following a judicial decision:

> Judicial decisions are not self-implementing; courts must frequently rely on other courts or on nonjudicial actors in the political system to turn law into action. Moreover, the implementation of judicial decisions is a political process; the actors upon whom courts must

[1] Harold D. Lasswell and Abraham Kaplan, *Power and Society: A Framework for Political Inquiry* (New Haven: Yale University Press, 1950), pp. 74–75.

319

rely to translate law into action are usually *political* actors and are subject to political pressures as they allocate resources to implement a judicial decision.[2] (Reading 8.1.)

COMPLIANCE

In the usual kind of civil litigation, compliance with a decision is routine, at least after all appeals have been exhausted. When a judge determines ownership of property, settles a tax claim, awards compensation, or forbids construction of a dam, the loser typically, if reluctantly, obeys without the court's having to use its coercive power to punish for contempt. If the court's verdict in a criminal case is not guilty, police release the defendant immediately. When the verdict is guilty, and there is no reversal on appeal, judicial personnel, police, and prison officials act together or separately to collect the fine or incarcerate the defendant.

It is when the controversy concerns broad public policy, when interest groups or governmental officials are the litigants, and when a court's final decree and opinion relate directly to future conduct of persons not actually parties to the litigation, that the matter of compliance becomes complex and interesting. In studying such situations, most analysts prefer to use the word "impact" instead of compliance because the importance of what happens after a court's decision may involve a galaxy of private citizens and public officials—including Presidents, governors, state and federal legislators, prosecutors, other judges, and leaders of interest groups.

The immediate effect of a court order, of course, is limited to the proceeding in which it is issued, and it binds only the parties to that proceeding. When the Supreme Court entered its final order in *Brown v. Board of Education* in 1955, the order was directed only to the five defendant school boards or districts; and only these five defendants were under a legal obligation "to admit to public schools on a racially nondiscriminatory basis with all deliberate speed the parties to these cases." But as Chapter 10 will explain in detail, the opinion of any court has status as a precedent under the rule of stare decisis, and because the Supreme Court is the nation's highest tribunal, its decisions on federal matters should be followed by all other courts. But whether, and to what degree, a Supreme Court ruling will be effective outside the confines of the particular case depends upon an extraordinary variety of factors.

Roberts v. United States Jaycees (1984) provides a textbook example of the Supreme Court's effectiveness. In this case the Court upheld the constitutionality of Minnesota's Human Rights Act, which outlawed the practice of the Junior Chamber of Commerce in limiting member-

---

[2] *Judicial Policies: Implementation and Impact* (Washington, D.C.: Congressional Quarterly Press, 1984), p. 25.

ship to males aged from eighteen to thirty-five. The Court rejected the Jaycees' contention that admission of women would violate male members' freedom of intimate and expressive association. Although the Jaycees had long resisted admission of women as a national policy, and the ruling technically applied only to Minnesota, within one month the national society voted to admit women nationwide, and there were only scattered pockets of resistance.

In order to comply with a Supreme Court ruling, officials and interest groups must know that the ruling has been issued and be able to understand it. The Supreme Court has not been particularly helpful in making its opinions intelligible to the public. Until recently the Court handed down opinions only on Mondays, and this bunching made it difficult for the media to report the decisions adequately, particularly toward the end of the term when most of the decisions were announced. Only a few newspapers, notably the *New York Times*, the *Los Angeles Times*, and the *Washington Post*, have reporters competent to handle the legalese in which the opinions are usually written. The press tends to concentrate on controversial items or quotable phrases rather than to give a clear presentation of all the issues. One of the better examples of effective writing, which was widely picked up in media reports of the capital punishment decision, *Furman v. Georgia* (1972), was Justice Stewart's statement, "These death sentences are cruel and unusual in the same way that being struck by lightning is cruel and unusual." The great influence of Justice Holmes was due in part to his masterful style and ability to create quotable phrases such as "clear and present danger."

ANTICIPATED CONSEQUENCES

Concern over the impact of a judicial decision does not begin with the issuance of the final decree. Speculation about possible consequences of a ruling is an inevitable part of the decision-making process. There may be some judges who give no thought to the practical problems a decision would create, who act on the basis of the Latin motto, "Let justice be done, though the heavens fall." But most judges would be reluctant to arrive at a holding that they thought might yield catastrophic results.

Consequently, a normal factor in the decision-making calculus is a weighing of the possible or likely outcomes of alternative rulings. In the Supreme Court one can see concern with consequences at every stage of decision making. Occasionally, as in the School Segregation cases, the justices formally order counsel to focus argument on the most efficacious remedy for a past wrong. A much more typical scene at oral argument shows the justices pressing counsel—often unsuccessfully—to discuss what the practical results would be of the ruling asked for.

At conference the justices also debate likely effects, speculating about probable congressional, presidential, and state responses to possible decisions. When, for instance, the Court was considering *Hirabayashi v. United States* (1943), one justice advised his brethren that if he were the general in charge of the program to place American citizens of Japanese ancestry in concentration camps and a court were to order those people released, he would disobey the decision.[3]

Occasionally, one can see similar though somewhat less brutally candid debates in published opinions. In denying Mississippi's request in 1867 that the Court enjoin President Andrew Johnson from enforcing the Reconstruction Acts, Chief Justice Salmon P. Chase speculated about the likely effects of issuing the injunction:

> If the President refuses obedience, it is needless to observe that the court is without power to enforce its process. If, on the other hand, the President complies with the order of the court and refuses to execute the acts of Congress, is it not clear that a collision may occur between the executive and legislative departments of the government? May not the House of Representatives impeach the President for such refusal? And in that case could this court interfere, in behalf of the President, thus endangered by compliance with its mandate, and restrain by injunction the Senate . . . from sitting as a court of impeachment? Would the strange spectacle be offered to the public wonder of an attempt by this court to arrest proceedings in that court?[4]

Justice Frankfurter's dissent in *Baker v. Carr* (Reading 8.2) voiced a similar warning that courts lacked the means to carry out reapportionment and that even the attempt to do so would lessen judicial prestige by embroiling judges in partisan political debates. Justice Harlan's dissent in *Miranda v. Arizona* (1966) argued that the Court's new rules enlarging the rights of suspected criminals would encourage police to lie about having informed such people of their rights, and, even if successful in ensuring that suspects understood their rights, would exact a fearsome price in unsolved crimes. In *Marsh v. Chambers* (1983) Justice Brennan speculated as to the reactions various persons would have to officially sponsored prayer. (Reading 8.3.)

More positively, one can sometimes see the Court's concern with consequences in decisions that apply new rules only prospectively. The premise on which American courts customarily proceeded was that when a change in constitutional doctrine was announced, it corrected previous errors. All parties who had suffered under the earlier, and now overruled, judicial interpretation were entitled to the benefits of the new ruling.

[3] Alpheus T. Mason, *Harlan Fiske Stone* (New York: Viking, 1956), p. 674.
[4] *Mississippi v. Johnson* (1867).

This prospect weighed heavily on the Warren Court as it revised the constitutional law of criminal trials in the 1960s. Prior to 1961 illegally seized evidence could be used in state prosecutions under the rule of *Wolf v. Colorado* (1949). In *Mapp v. Ohio* (1961) the Court overruled *Wolf* and brought the states under the federal exclusionary rule, which meant that evidence secured in violation of the search and seizure clause would no longer be admissible in state courts. But what about convictions secured prior to 1961 by use of illegal evidence? Under the normal rule of retroactivity these convictions would have been voided, but the Supreme Court drew back from the anticipated consequences of such a holding and ruled in *Linkletter v. Walker* (1965) that *Mapp* would be given only prospective effect. Similarly, in *Johnson v. New Jersey* (1966) the Court declined to apply *Miranda* retroactively. Justice Harlan, who had initially accepted *Linkletter*'s reasoning, later rejected it on the ground that the Court was making a legislative, not a judicial, decision when it decided not to apply constitutional rulings retroactively because of concern about their impact.[5]

ACTUAL CONSEQUENCES

When we speak of the impact of Supreme Court decisions, however, we usually mean actual rather than anticipated consequences. What in fact did happen after the decision was handed down? How and in what way was behavior actually changed by the Court's ruling? Were there problems of enforcement? If so, what form did resistance take— foot dragging, bringing new lawsuits, efforts to reverse the decision by legislation or constitutional amendment, threats against the tenure of the justices, proposals to eliminate some categories of federal court jurisdictions or to limit the appellate jurisdiction of the Supreme Court?

The first thing one notices about the actual consequences of judicial decisions in the United States, even of the Supreme Court, is how varied they have been. The dramatic ruling in the Steel Seizure case during the middle of the Korean War moved President Truman to return quickly though grudgingly the steel mills to their regular managers; and, as everyone had expected, a long and costly strike soon occurred. In 1974 the Court's equally dramatic ruling that Rich-

---

[5] Subsequently, in *United States v. Peltier* (1975) a five-justice majority hostile to the exclusionary rule held a 1973 decision, limiting auto searches by the Border Patrol, inapplicable to a search occurring four months earlier. But in *United States v. Johnson* (1982) a different five-judge majority accepted Harlan's principle "that all 'new' rules of constitutional law must . . . be applied to all those cases which are still subject to direct review by this Court at the time the 'new' decision is handed down." Nevertheless, two years later *Solem v. Stumes* (1984) held that a *Miranda* right recognized in *Edwards v. Arizona* (1981) was not to be applied retroactively. See also *Equal Employment Opportunity Commission v. Allstate Insurance Company* (1984).

ard Nixon should turn over several tapes of conversations in the White House to the special Watergate prosecutor was followed by Nixon's surrender—made far more grudgingly than Truman's. Revelations of what was on the tapes immediately led to nearly unanimous support within the House of Representatives for impeachment, and Nixon resigned in disgrace.

Many rulings have produced mixed results. Some communities blithely ignored the Supreme Court's decisions that religious instruction, prayer, and Bible reading in public schools are all forbidden by the Constitution. Other communities slightly modified their practice; and still others changed their policies to conform to the Court's views. School segregation, of course, presents the richest pattern of diversity. Initially, the Court's edict in *Brown v. Board* did vastly more to get black children into the courts as litigants than into formerly all-white schools as students. But, after a series of bitter political and legal battles that lasted for more than a decade, and especially after passage of the Civil Rights Act of 1964, staunch Southern resistance began to collapse. Ironically, integrated schools became more of a reality in the South than in many eastern, midwestern, and western urban centers, where patterns of housing segregation and later the Burger Court's hostility toward busing helped continue racially segregated education.[6]

The Court's 1973 decisions invalidating state statutes restricting abortion had an impact matched only by the 1954 desegregation ruling. Reacting to *Roe v. Wade* and *Doe v. Bolton,* various state legislatures sought to limit exercise of the abortion right declared in *Roe* by laws requiring parental or husband's consent, a waiting period, abortions only in hospitals, obligations on physicians to explain possible consequences, presence of a second physician, and so on. Such restrictions were generally invalidated by the Supreme Court, most notably in *City of Akron v. Akron Center for Reproductive Health* (1983). But congressional limitations on the use of federal funds to reimburse cost of abortions under state Medicaid programs were upheld in *Harris v. McRae* (1980). Of even greater significance were the concerted efforts to secure a constitutional amendment overturning *Roe* and authorizing states to regulate abortions in their own fashion.

In 1983 the Supreme Court handed down a decision declaring unconstitutional a very common congressional device, the so-called "legislative veto." In scores of statutes, beginning in 1931, Congress had authorized the executive to take certain actions or exercise certain powers, but at the same time it had asserted the authority of one or both houses to veto actions taken under those grants. The purpose of these

[6] *Keyes v. Denver* (1973); *Milliken v. Bradley* (1974); and *ibid* (1977); *Dayton v. Brinkman* (1979); *Armour v. Nix* (1980); *Crawford v. Board of Education* (1982).

vetoes was to avoid resort to ordinary legislation, which under the Constitution requires presidential assent before becoming law.

In *Immigration and Naturalization Service v. Chadha* (1983) the Attorney General had, under statutory authority, suspended the deportation of an alien, but the House had subsequently adopted a resolution vetoing the suspension, also as authorized by statute. The Supreme Court applied in a very literal way the constitutional requirement that all proposed legislation must be presented to the President for his signature or disapproval, and it found this effort to bypass the President unconstitutional.

But Justice White, dissenting and noting that some 200 statutes provided for a legislative veto, contended that this device had

> become a central means by which Congress secures the accountability of executive and independent agencies. Without the legislative veto, Congress is faced with a Hobson's choice; either to refrain from delegating the necessary authority, leaving itself with a hopeless task of writing laws with the requisite specificity to cover endless special circumstances across the entire policy landscape, or in the alternative, to abdicate its lawmaking function to the executive branch and independent agencies. To choose the former leaves major national problems unresolved; to opt for the latter risks unaccountable policymaking by those not elected to fill that role.

In fact, both alternatives were substantially avoided, as congressional committees found various ways to continue their supervision or review of proposed administrative action by other methods. (Reading 8.4.)

Like all decisions, those by judges may have important but unintended effects, as *Dred Scott v. Sandford* (1857) so well illustrates. The doctrines announced by that ruling were, first, that because the framers of the Constitution had not considered black people, whether slave or free, as citizens, a black man could not invoke the jurisdiction of federal courts to hear disputes between citizens of different states. Second, the Court went on to rule that Congress could not prohibit slavery in the territories because such a ban would take away the slave owner's "property" without due process of law. Thus Dred Scott had remained a slave even when his master had taken him into a "free territory."

The justices in the majority had thought that they were solidifying the Union by putting an end to the bitter debate over how Congress should regulate slavery in the territories. However, not only was the actual holding that Scott was still a slave meaningless (his owner immediately freed him), but the Court's opinion on the broader issues only deepened divisions between North and South and helped make bloody civil war more probable. Later, the opening sentence of the Fourteenth Amendment specifically reversed *Dred Scott*'s pronouncement on blacks as noncitizens: "All persons born or naturalized in the United States and subject to the jurisdiction thereof, are citizens of the United States and of the State wherein they reside."

Congress has reversed several other Supreme Court decisions by constitutional amendments. The first was the Eleventh Amendment, adopted in 1795 to override *Chisholm v. Georgia* (1793), which had allowed federal courts to accept jurisdiction of a suit against a state by a citizen of another state. The Sixteenth Amendment, ratified in 1913, reversed *Pollock v. Farmers Loan & Trust Co.* (1895), and authorized the federal government to levy taxes on incomes. The Twenty-sixth Amendment (1971) reversed the holding in *Oregon v. Mitchell* (1970) that Congress could not fix the voting age at 18 for state and local elections. Congress, of course, frequently passes new legislation to expand, limit, reinterpret, or reverse judicial decisions construing federal statutes.

EXPLAINING AND PREDICTING EFFECTS

It is obvious that the Court's decisions have had widely varying results, many of which the justices did not anticipate. The real problem lies in explaining why some decisions have been more effective than others in carrying out the policies immanent in the Court's opinions. So far we have no general theories, at least none that can be rigorously tested. One can say little more than that: (1) if the Court's prestige is high; (2) if the case concerns a matter over which the Court's jurisdiction is clear; (3) if the Court issues a direct order (or commands a lower court to do so) to a named official (4) to perform or not perform a specified act (5) within the official's power to perform or not to perform; and (6) if the Court's decision does not run against the grain of the opinion dominant in the official's constituency, then there is a very high probability that the decision will be carried out. One can place a negative in front of all six circumstances and predict with a high degree of accuracy that the decision will not be carried out. As soon as one of these six circumstances changes, the accuracy of prediction plummets.

Philip B. Kurland has a somewhat simpler set of tests for the effectiveness of a controversial Supreme Court ruling:

I suggest that the ingredients for success of any fundamental decision based on the equal protection clause are three, at least two of which must be present each time for the Court's will to prevail beyond its effect on the immediate parties to the lawsuit. The first requirement is that the constitutional standard be a simple one.

The second is that the judiciary have adequate control over the means of effectuating enforcement. The third is that the public acquiesce—there is no need for agreement, simply the absence of opposition—in the principle and its application.[7]

Part of the problem lies in the constantly reacting nature of the American political system. A judicial decision is usually only one element in a complex battle that may have begun in the private sphere, has been waged in the legislative and executive arenas, and will return to those arenas—if, indeed, it ever completely left them—after judges have had their say. Furthermore, it is likely that most important issues will also reappear in the courts for fresh decisions and do so not once but several times before they are finally settled, forgotten, or superseded by new problems of public policy. "The Supreme Court," James Levine has said, and his observation holds even more strongly for other tribunals, "is better understood as a *catalyst* of change rather than as a singular effector of change."[8]

Unlike physical scientists, those who study political behavior can seldom isolate a single phenomenon and hold all other factors constant. Rather, we typically look at a tangled—and moving—web of events. Pulling the judicial thread out is usually impossible. Earlier we noted that the Civil Rights Act of 1964 was critical in effecting school desegregation in the South; and, we might add, without the civil rights movements of the 1960s, led by people like the Reverend Martin Luther King, Jr., it is highly improbable that there would have been any Civil Rights Act at all in 1964. But without the Court's decision in *Brown* it is equally improbable that there would have been any *effective* civil rights movement in the 1960s.

So far scholars have identified rather than solved such problems, but they continue to chip away. In discussing the effects of decisions, students of the judicial process have made useful distinctions between short- and long-range effects, between effects on the litigants and on public policy, and between effects on immediate policy and on deeply seated ideals and values.

John Marshall's opinion in *McCulloch v. Maryland* (1819) provides an interesting example of the first distinction. The case itself revolved around the Bank of the United States, a corporation chartered by Congress, funded in part by the federal government, and blessed as the depository of the Treasury's assets. Endowed with these advantages as well as ambitious, even ruthless, directors, the Bank's powerful monetary muscle turned the institution into a blazing

---

[7] "Equal Educational Opportunity: The Limits of Constitutional Jurisprudence Undefined," 35 *University of Chicago Law Review* 583 (1968).

[8] James P. Levine, "Methodological Considerations in Studying Supreme Court Efficacy," 4 *Law and Society Review* 583 (1970).

political issue. Its opponents, egged on by smaller bankers, tended to be political liberals, states' righters, westerners, the relatively less well-to-do, and even debtors, who saw the Octopus or the Monster, as they called the Bank, as the cause of many of their woes. Its defenders were likely to be conservatives, easterners, and creditors from the upper-middle and upper classes who viewed the Bank as a bedrock of financial solidity.

Specifically, James McCulloch, the cashier of the Baltimore branch of the Bank, had refused to pay a tax that Maryland had levied to inhibit the Bank's operations. Thus the immediate questions before the Court concerned the authority of Congress to charter the Bank—the Constitution did not list among congressional powers that of incorporating businesses—and the authority of a state to tax a federal instrumentality. For a unanimous Court, Marshall held that the "necessary and proper" clause of Article I of the Constitution conferred ample authority on Congress to charter a bank as a convenient means of collecting taxes, paying national debts, maintaining armed forces, and carrying out all the other tasks prescribed by the Constitution. Furthermore, he ruled that because the federal government was supreme in those areas in which it had authority, the states, as lesser entities, could not tax and possibly hamper or even destroy a federal instrumentality such as the Bank.

McCulloch was a famous victory, but two decades later it was the enemies of the Bank who were gloatingly triumphant. President Andrew Jackson publicly denied that *McCulloch* had been correctly decided, declared that its holding did not bind him (Reading 7.6), ordered federal deposits withdrawn from the Bank, and vetoed a bill to continue the Bank in its existing form. Soon the Bank of the United States was just another of Philadelphia's financial houses. Furthermore, the "new" Supreme Court, led by Roger Brooke Taney, who, as Secretary of the Treasury, had actually withdrawn federal funds from the Bank and, as Attorney General, had drafted Jackson's repudiation of *McCulloch*, was beginning to adopt a theory of federalism very different from Marshall's notions of national supremacy. Taney's concept, which would later be christened "dual federalism," saw the nation and states more as coequal sovereigns than as superior and inferior.

Thus in 1840 *McCulloch* must have seemed to be a monument to judicial impotence. But Marshall's opinion enjoyed a second coming. His dictum, "we must never forget that it is a *constitution* we are expounding," echoes through almost every great case of this century. More important, the Court has accepted his belief in a broad and dominant congressional power inherent in the "necessary and proper" clause as well as in the clause conferring power to regulate "commerce among the several states." In effect, the justices have reaccepted Marshall's theory of federalism.

EFFECTS ON LITIGANTS AND ON PUBLIC POLICY

The distinction between effects on litigants and on public policy can also be sharp. Several studies have shown that less than half of those people who won in the Supreme Court but whose cases required further litigation in state courts actually won when the final decision was reached.[9] *Miranda v. Arizona* provides a case in point. There the Court reversed the conviction of Ernesto Miranda for kidnapping and rape. The prosecution had introduced into evidence at the trial a "confession" that Miranda had made before being informed of his constitutional rights to silence and to an attorney. The Court laid down several principles to govern such situations: Police have an affirmative duty to inform suspects of their rights in clear and unequivocal language, and to warn them that anything they say can be used against them. Further, a suspect who requests an attorney must be allowed to consult with his or her lawyer before being questioned and to have the lawyer present if he or she later decides to answer questions. If a suspect requests a lawyer but cannot afford the fee, the government must supply one.

On retrial, even with the confession excluded, the state was able to produce enough other evidence to convict Miranda again. Thus for him, victory in the Supreme Court meant only a delay in going to prison.[10] On the other hand, despite the Burger Court's modifications of the *Miranda* rules, they have had a real effect on police practices throughout the country. Initially, few police knew what the Court had said and those who knew conformed, if at all, at a minimal level. Gradually, however, police have come to accept—though not necessarily to approve—the *Miranda* rites as another occupational hazard and routinely to inform suspects of their rights.[11] Furthermore, free if badly overworked counsel are usually available at the interrogation. What is less clear is the percentage of suspects availing themselves of their constitutional rights. Complicating all analyses is the harsh fact that a large portion of suspects in criminal cases are simply not very intelligent. Even when the police carefully explain their rights, many of these people, who tend to be the poorest and least educated members of a community, are apt not to comprehend what is being said.

---

[9] Note, "State Court Evasion of United States Supreme Court Mandates," 56 *Yale Law Journal* 574 (1947); Note, "Final Disposition of State Court Decisions Reversed and Remanded by the Supreme Court, October Term, 1931 to October Term, 1940," 55 *Harvard Law Review* 1357 (1942); Note, "Evasion of Supreme Court Mandates in Cases Remanded to State Courts since 1941," 67 *ibid.* 1251 (1954).

[10] Some years later Miranda was killed in a barroom brawl. The first policeman on the scene apprehended the assailant and immediately read him his rights under the *Miranda* rules.

[11] The Burger Court seriously limited *Miranda* in *New York v. Quarles* (1984), holding that the police may omit *Miranda* warnings whenever custodial interrogation concerns "matters of public safety." See also *Minnesota v. Murphy* (1984) and *Berkemer v. McCarty* (1984); *contra, Smith v. Illinois* (1984).

"Plea bargaining" also fogs research here. Few convictions in criminal cases come after full-scale trials; almost all result from a process of bargaining that begins at arrest. In exchange for the police dropping or reducing charges a suspect will often agree to waive his or her rights. Even if the police will not or cannot negotiate, prosecutors may bargain. Their staffs are small and their caseloads sometimes enormous. Furthermore, there is always some risk of losing at a trial, and prosecutors like to be able to display impressive records of convictions. Here one can speculate that the *Miranda* rules give some assistance to the accused in providing them with the opportunity of having an attorney do their negotiating.

Looking at *Miranda* from another angle, one can see the judiciary becoming involved in other coils of the tangled skein of policy making. As had *Gideon v. Wainwright* in 1963, *Miranda* greatly increased the need for public defenders and helped spur enlargement or creation of a series of small bureaucracies of public defenders with their own interests related to but not necessarily identical with those of their clients. Liberal reformers, heartened by the Court's decisions, included in Lyndon Johnson's War against Poverty funds for legal aid for the poor in civil as well as criminal cases, thereby feeding existing offices of public defenders and sometimes spawning new organizations.

Despite a shift in priorities in federal spending since the mid-1960s, these organizations have demonstrated a capacity not just to survive but to grow. To protect legal aid against Richard Nixon's efforts to make peace with poverty, Congress removed the program from the executive branch of government and created a "private," though federally funded, entity, the Legal Services Corporation. The Reagan administration was successful in reducing its budget, but, as of 1985, not in demolishing the corporation.

One cannot reasonably claim that together or singly decisions like *Miranda* or *Gideon* have been directly responsible for such developments; one cannot even substantiate a claim that the justices involved even remotely suspected that their decisions would have such effects. Other factors, such as Ralph Nader's crusade for consumers' rights and "the public be damned" attitudes of many large corporations have probably been more consequential in generating political support for what we just described. But the rulings of the Warren Court forced an opening without which the successes of reformers, consumers' groups, and bureaucrats would have been far more difficult, if possible at all.

EFFECTS ON POLICY AND ON SOCIETY'S IDEALS

The third distinction, that between effects on public policy and effects on a society's ideals and values, may be the fuzziest of the three kinds of impact, since a society's values and ideals are such wonderfully elusive intangibles. But the whole idea of "political culture" from which they spring does not lose importance because it defies precise measurement. In this ghostly realm the Court's writ may also run, for, as Justice Frank Murphy once observed, the Supreme Court is "the great pulpit" in American politics. And no one who heard the constitutional gospel of Earl Warren preached from that pulpit can doubt its *potential* effectiveness.

Earlier we talked about some of the tangible effects that the School Segregation cases helped produce. But one has to have lived in the United States, especially in the Deep South, before and after these decisions fully to appreciate the social revolution that has taken place. Today, even in South Carolina, white taxi drivers will take black passengers, accept tips from them, address them as Mr. and Mrs.—someday, perhaps, Ms—and deliver them to the best hotels and restaurants. Doctors receive black patients in their regular waiting rooms; no longer do they have to wait outside in whatever weather the local gods choose to bestow. None of this behavior sounds even worth noticing thirty years after *Brown*. But a few years before *Brown*—or even a decade after—any one of these actions would have precipitated at least rude conduct and vulgar remarks, probably a boycott, and possibly violence. That few whites notice blacks behaving as free and equal citizens tells far more about the extent of the revolution than does the behavior itself.

No more than any other place on this planet has the Deep South achieved full racial justice; there is still great poverty and much discrimination. But for the first time since the slave ships disgorged their tragic cargo, respect for the dignity of blacks as human beings is now commonplace. That change might have come without Earl Warren and *Brown v. Board,* but there is not a scintilla of evidence that it would have come during the lifetime of any reader of this book.

SELECTED REFERENCES

Baker, Liva. *Miranda: Crime, Law, and Politics.* New York: Atheneum, 1983.

Bass, Jack. *Unlikely Heroes: The Dramatic Story of the Southern Judges of the Fifth Circuit Who Transformed the Supreme Court's* Brown *Decision into a Revolution for Equality.* New York: Simon & Schuster, 1981.

Becker, Theodore L., and Malcolm M. Feeley (eds.). *The Impact of Supreme Court Decisions.* Second ed. New York: Oxford University Press, 1973.

Berkson, Larry Charles. *The Supreme Court and Its Public: The Communication of Policy Decisions.* Lexington, Mass.: Lexington Books, 1978.

Birkby, Robert H. *The Court and Public Policy.* Washington, D.C.: Congressional Quarterly Press, 1983.

Bullock, Charles S., III, and Charles M. Lamb. "Toward a Theory of Civil Rights Implementation," 2 *Policy Perspectives* 376 (1982).

Dolbeare, Kenneth M., and Phillip E. Hammond. *The School Prayer Decisions: From Court Policy to Local Practices.* Chicago: University of Chicago Press, 1971.

Fahlund, G. Gregory. "Retroactivity and the Warren Court," 35 *Journal of Politics* 570 (1973).

Fisher, Louis. "Judicial Misjudgment About the Lawmaking Process: The Legislative Veto," *Public Administration Review* (forthcoming, 1985).

Goldman, Sheldon, and Austin Sarat (eds.). *American Court Systems.* San Francisco: W. H. Freeman, 1978.

Horowitz, Donald L. *The Courts and Social Policy.* Washington, D.C.: The Brookings Institution, 1977. Chs. 3–6.

Johnson, Charles A., and Bradley C. Canon. *Judicial Policies: Implementation and Impact.* Washington, D.C.: Congressional Quarterly, 1984.

Kaplan, Diane S., and Richard Zuckerman. "The *Wyatt* Case: Implementation of a Judicial Decree Ordering Institutional Change," 84 *Yale Law Journal* 1338 (1975).

Krislov, Samuel, *et al.* (eds.). *Compliance and the Law.* Beverly Hills, California: Sage Publications, 1971.

Levine, James P. "Methodological Considerations in Studying Supreme Court Efficacy," 4 *Law & Society Review* 583 (1970).

Medalie, Richard J., Leonard Zeitz, and Paul Alexander. "Custodial Interrogation in Our Nation's Capital: The Attempt to Implement *Miranda,*" 66 *Michigan Law Review* 1347 (1968).

Mishkin, Paul J. "The High Court, the Great Writ, and the Due Process of Time and Law," 79 *Harvard Law Review* 56 (1965).

Muir, William K., Jr. *Law and Attitude Change.* Chicago: University of Chicago Press, 1967.

Murphy, Walter F. *Congress and the Court: A Case Study in the American Political Process.* Chicago: University of Chicago Press, 1962.

Murphy, Walter F., and Joseph Tanenhaus. *The Study of Public Law.* New York: Random House, 1972. Chs. 1–2.

Note. "The Wyatt Case: Implementation of a Judicial Decree Ordering Institutional Change," 84 *Yale Law Journal* 1338 (1975).

Peltason, Jack W. *Fifty-eight Lonely Men: Southern Federal Judges and School Desegregation.* New York: Harcourt, Brace & World, 1961.

Pritchett, C. Herman. *Congress Versus the Supreme Court, 1957–1960.* Minneapolis: University of Minnesota Press, 1961.

Pritchett, C. Herman, and Alan F. Westin (eds.). *The Third Branch of Government: Eight Cases in Constitutional Politics.* New York: Harcourt, Brace & World, 1963.

Romans, Neil T. "The Role of State Supreme Courts in Judicial Policy Making: *Escobedo, Miranda,* and the Use of Judicial Impact Analysis," 27 *Western Political Quarterly* 38 (1974).

Rossum, Ralph A. "New Rights and Old Wrongs: The Supreme Court and the Problem of Retroactivity," 23 *Emory Law Journal* 381 (1974).

Schmidhauser, John R., and Larry L. Berg. *The Supreme Court and Congress: Conflict and Interaction, 1945–1968.* New York: Free Press, 1972.

Sorauf, Frank. *The Wall of Separation: The Constitutional Politics of*

Church and State. Princeton, New Jersey: Princeton University Press, 1976. Chs. 12–15.

Wald, Michael, *et al.* "Interrogations in New Haven: The Impact of Miranda," 76 *Yale Law Journal* 1550 (1967).

Wasby, Stephen L. *The Impact of the United States Supreme Court: Some Perspectives.* Homewood, Illinois: Dorsey Press, 1970.

Wasby, Stephen L., Anthony A. D'Amato, and Rosemary Metrailer. *Desegregation from* Brown *to* Alexander: *An Exploration of Supreme Court Strategies.* Carbondale, Ill.: Southern Illinois University Press, 1977.

Way, H. Frank, Jr. "Survey Research on Judicial Decisions: The Prayer and Bible Reading Cases," 21 *Western Political Quarterly* 189 (1968).

8.1   *". . . we hope to move . . . toward a general theoretical understanding of the events that may follow a judicial decision. . . ."*

RESPONSES TO JUDICIAL POLICIES

Charles A. Johnson and Bradley C. Canon

In this excerpt the authors introduce the notion that judicial decisions are not self-implementing, and that courts must frequently rely on other courts or on nonjudicial actors in the political system to turn law into action. Moreover, the implementation of judicial decisions is a political process; the actors upon whom the courts must rely to translate law into action are usually political actors and are subject to political pressures as they allocate resources to implement a judicial decision.

[O]ur aim is not to study the aftermath of *every* judicial decision; instead, we want to make general statements about what has happened or may happen after *any* judicial decision.* That is, we hope to move away from idiosyncratic, case-by-case or policy-by-policy analyses toward a general theoretical understanding of the events that may follow a judicial decision. . . .

The first step in understanding any political process is to develop a conceptual foundation upon which explanations may be built. We will organize our presentation of what happens after a court decision around two major elements: the *actors* who may respond to the decision and the *responses* that these actors may make. Focusing on

Judicial Policies: Implementation and Impact (Washington, D.C.: Congressional Quarterly Press, 1984), pp. 14–25. Reprinted by permission.

Charles A. Johnson is Associate Professor of Political Science, Texas A&M University. Bradley C. Canon is Professor of Political Science, University of Kentucky.

*The material reprinted here follows the authors' extensive review of reactions to *Roe v. Wade* (1973), holding that a woman has a constitutional right to an abortion at least during the first trimester of her pregnancy. (See Reading 5.8.)—Eds.

these two elements enables us to define more precisely who is reacting and how. In studying the responses to judicial policies we describe and attempt to explain the *behavior* following a court decision —specifically, what the behavior is, its antecedents, and its consequences. Hence, when we discuss "impact," we are describing general reactions following a judicial decision. When we discuss "implementation," we are describing the behavior of lower courts, government agencies, or other affected parties as it relates to enforcing a judicial decision. When we discuss what many would call "compliance/noncompliance" or "evasion," we are describing behavior that is in some way consistent or inconsistent with the behavioral requirements of the judicial decision.

THE INTERPRETING POPULATION

For any appellate court decision, the actor most often charged with responding to a decision is a particular lower court, often a trial court. Moreover, in our common law system many appellate court decisions become policies used in deciding future cases. In a general sense, therefore, a higher court's policy affects all lower courts within its jurisdiction. This set of courts (and in some instances government officials such as attorneys general) is known as the *interpreting population.* The interpreting population, as the name implies, responds to the policy decisions of a higher court by refining the policy announced by the higher court. Such refinements could have the effect of enlarging or of limiting the original policy. This population, in other words, interprets the meaning of the policy and develops the rules for matters not addressed in the original decision. Of course, all populations must "interpret" the decision in order to react to it. Interpretations of lower courts, however, are distinguished from the interpretations of others since theirs are viewed as authoritative in a legal sense by others in the political system. Hence, this population provides "official" interpretations of a court policy applicable to the other populations under their jurisdiction.

The Supreme Court's abortion decision launched the judiciary into a new area of the law, which required considerable refining before complete implementation. Shortly after the decision was announced, lower state and federal courts began hearing cases presenting issues that had not been directly addressed in the *Roe* or *Doe* opinions. In Florida, for example, the issue of a father's rights were raised by a father who brought legal action to restrain the mother of his unborn child from obtaining an abortion. The lower court denied relief and the Florida Supreme Court affirmed that decision, arguing that the Supreme Court's abortion decision was based on the mother's "right of privacy" (*Jones v. Smith,* 1973). The decision to terminate a pregnancy was, therefore, purely the right of the mother and could not be subject to interference by the state or private individuals.

Meanwhile, in Arizona, another matter was before the courts. Arizona law prohibited the advertisement of any medicine or procedures that facilitated abortions. New Times, Inc., a local publisher, was convicted under this statute and appealed to the state supreme court. The conviction was reversed, since the Arizona abortion statutes were found to be similar to the Texas statute struck down in *Roe v. Wade,* even though the issue before the court was different from that decided in the original abortion cases (*State v. New Times, Inc.,* 1973).

In each of these instances the issue before the court had not been addressed directly in the original decision. Consistent with the common law tradition, the lower courts had the responsibility of making authoritative interpretations of policy in light of the original Supreme Court decision. In their interpretations these courts could limit the application of the original policy, as did the Arizona trial court in convicting the publisher, or could facilitate its implementation, as did the Florida courts. . . .

THE IMPLEMENTING POPULATION

The lower courts usually apply a higher court's policy only in cases coming before them. Higher court policies and their interpretation by lower courts quite often affect a wider set of actors. We refer to this set of actors as the *implementing population.* In most instances, this population is made up of authorities whose behavior may be reinforced or sanctioned by the interpreting population. The implementing population usually performs a policing or servicing function in the political system—that is, implementors apply the system's rules to persons subject to their authority. Prominent examples of this population are police officers, prosecutors, university and public school officials, and welfare and social security workers. In many instances, the original policy and subsequent interpretations by lower courts are intended to set parameters on the behavior of the implementing population. A clear example of this activity involves decisions concerning police behavior with regard to the rights of criminal suspects.

Occasionally, the implementing population is composed of private individuals or institutions. This is the case when services provided by private concerns are the subject of a judicial policy. The best example of such a circumstance involves the Supreme Court's abortion decision, for which physicians and hospitals were the actual implementors. When the implementing population falls into this private classification they are usually under a different obligation from most public implementing populations. In the case of public implementing agencies, the court ordinarily *requires* that the agencies change behavior, stop a particular type of service, or provide some new service. Such was the obligation for school systems with regard to *Brown v. Board of Education* and the police with regard to *Miranda v. Arizona* (1966) and *Mapp v. Ohio* (1961). On the other hand, when private concerns are the implementing population, the compulsion to act affirmatively is substantially weaker, if it exists at all. For example, the abortion decision gave women the right to an abortion; hospitals could provide abortions, but hospitals and physicians were not obliged to provide abortion services against their will. Thus, affirmative action implementing a judicial policy by private implementing groups is most often voluntary.

The implementing population may vary from decision to decision. For criminal justice decisions, prosecutors, police officers, and defense attorneys are the primary implementors. For school prayer or busing decisions, the implementors are largely public school officials. Reapportionment decisions usually involve legislators as the implementing population. When judicial decisions require no action by government agencies, nongovernmental service agencies may implement decisions; alternatively, there may be no implementing population at all. . . . [I]n a case such as *New York Times Co. v. Sullivan* (1964), which significantly decreased the applicability of libel law to public officials, there is no implementing population.

The degree to which a court decision actually benefits those it was intended to benefit depends on the actors and institutions who police the activities or provide the services called for in the decision. Women in communities where there were no physicians or hospitals willing to provide abortion services were effectively denied their newly granted right or were forced to go elsewhere to benefit from the judicial policy. As another example, where school officials sanctioned prayers after 1963, they often persisted for years. . . .

THE CONSUMER POPULATION

Those for whom the policies are set forth by the court are identified as the *consumer population*. This population is the set of individuals (usually not affiliated with the government) who would or should receive benefits or suffer disabilities as a result of a judicial decision; that is, they gain or lose desired rights or resources. Criminal suspects, for example, benefit from judicial policies announced by the Supreme Court in *Miranda,* and black students in newly desegregated schools benefit from the *Brown* decision. In other instances, some consumer populations may not benefit from a judicial policy. For example, juvenile court defendants suffer from not being extended the right of trial by jury; stockholders may suffer when their corporation is split up as a result of an antitrust ruling. And there are decisions under which members of the consumer population may either benefit or suffer, depending on their attitudes toward the policy. Under the *Schempp* decision on prayer in public schools, children who want to pray in public school suffer limitations and children who do not want to pray there gain benefits.

The consumer population, depending on the policy involved, may include the entire population of the political system, as with judicial decisions concerning general tax legislation. On the other hand, a very limited population may be directly involved, such as criminal suspects under arrest. When the policy affects a specific sector but supposedly is for the public good (for example, antitrust decisions), a distinction between direct and indirect consumption must sometimes be made.

Specifying the consumer population exactly may be troublesome. . . . [F]ew would dispute that women with unwanted pregnancies are the consumers for the Supreme Court's abortion decision. Those opposed to abortion would likely argue that unborn children are also consumers and receive negative benefits from the abortion decision. Others might argue that fathers of unborn children or parents of underaged, pregnant girls are part of the consumer population. . . .

THE SECONDARY POPULATION

The populations we have discussed so far are those directly affected by a judicial policy or its implementation. The *secondary population* is a residual one. It consists of everyone who is not in the interpreting, implementing, or consumer population. Members of the secondary population are not directly affected by a judicial policy; however, some may react to a policy or its implementation. This reaction usually takes the form of some type of feedback directed toward the original policy maker, another policy maker, the implementing population, or the consumer population.

The secondary population may be divided into four subpopulations: government officials, interest groups, the media, and the public at large. First, there are *government officials*. This subpopulation includes legislators and executive officers who are not immediately affected by the decision. Though usually unaffected directly, these individuals are often in a position to support or hinder the implementation of the original policy. This subpopulation is distinguished from other secondary subpopulations in that its members have direct, legitimate authority in the political system, and they are often the recipients of political pressure from the public. The second subpopulation is *interest groups*, which are often activated by court policies even when they are not directly affected by them. Subsequent actions by these groups may facilitate or block effective implementation of the judicial policy. The third subpopulation is the *media*, which communicate the substance of judicial policies to potentially affected populations. Included here are general and specialized media, which may affect implementation by editorial stance or simply by the way of reporting judicial policies. Media attention to a policy, descriptions of reactions to it, and support or criticism of it can play a large role in determining the amount and direction of feedback behavior. The fourth subpopulation consists of members of the *public at large,* insofar as they do not fall within the consumer population. The most important segment of this subpopulation is attentive citizens—those who are most aware of a judicial policy. This segment includes individuals who may be related to the consumer population (for example, parents of students affected by school prayer decisions), politically active individuals (for example, political party workers), and perhaps knowledgeable or alert individuals.

For the Supreme Court's abortion decision, the secondary population is large and quite varied. . . . [F]ollowing *Roe* . . . most of the reaction came from interest groups and government officials. As to the former, existing institutions or groups such as the Catholic church and many Protestant denominations vigorously denounced the decision, while organizations such as Planned Parenthood, the National Organization for Women, and the American Civil Liberties Union supported it. New groups on both sides devoted solely to the abortion issue also developed quickly. The efforts of these groups produced additional litigation, intensive lobbying, electoral maneuvering, and attempts to mobilize public opinion. Government officials also reacted to the abortion decision by passing restrictive laws, issuing restrictive orders, or, in a few cases, adopting policies that provided opportunities for women to obtain abortions. A fundamental issue for some government officials after *Roe* was whether the government should aid in the implementation of the policy by funding the abortions of poor women. With the eventual approval of the Supreme Court, Congress and several states restricted funding for elective abortions for poor women.

Legislative and executive officials may have considerable influence on the implementation of a judicial policy, even though they are not members of the implementing population (that is, they do not provide policing or implementing services). Legislatures, for instance, may be generous or stinting in appropriating money to carry out a policy, as in funding legal services for the poor. The president and state governors may use their appointing authority to select officials with power over members of the implementing population; or they may use their personal or official influence to encourage either maximum or minimum cooperation in the implementing process, as well as to mobilize public opinion. . . .

FLUIDITY AND LINKAGE AMONG POPULATIONS

The basis for the foregoing classification of populations is primarily functional. We may, therefore, on some occasions find that particular individuals are members of different populations in different circumstances. For example, it is entirely possible for an attorney general to be an interpreter for one judicial policy and an implementor for another. In the former instance, the attorney general would be issuing an authoritative, legally binding statement interpreting a judicial decision; in the latter instance, the attorney general would be charged with the responsibility of applying a judicial policy to some consumer population or of carrying out some order of the court. It is also possible that courts as members of the interpreting population may occasionally be in a position to direct the implementation of judicial policy. Such may be the case when a judge takes direct charge of the implementation of a school desegregation order, as happened in Boston in the 1970s. Teachers are implementors of the prayer decision and consumers of decisions affecting funding levels of public schools. Obviously, private citizens are in both consumer and secondary populations, depending on the nature of the judicial policy.

Attorneys constitute a special set of participants whose function may vary from one setting to another. . . . [They] may insist that other participants follow or implement rules promulgated by a higher court. When they assert the rights of criminal suspects or protect citizens whose constitutional rights have been violated, attorneys are playing a role as quasi-members of the implementing population.

Perhaps even more often, attorneys are called upon to give their interpretations of judicial policies for potential consumers, implementing groups, and, occasionally, secondary groups such as interested citizens or legislative bodies. Such interpretations are not official like those of the interpreting population; however, on many occasions these interpretations are likely to be final, since paying clients assume that the attorneys give a reasoned and fair interpretation of a court decision. . . . Attorneys also serve as interpreters of judicial policies for courts themselves. Because judges cannot read and interpret all higher court policies, they frequently rely on attorneys' briefs to inform them of relevant cases and, sometimes, rival interpretations of those cases.

In a broad sense, attorneys performing these functions serve as linkages between various populations. They provide a link for the communication of decisions downward from higher courts to relevant actors as well as being unofficial interpreters of these decisions. Their linkage activities may also prompt new litigation or feedback to the courts or other agencies, which, in turn, may affect the implementation of a decision.

ACCEPTANCE DECISIONS AND BEHAVIORAL RESPONSES

. . . We may observe a large variety of responses to judicial decisions, so precise distinctions are difficult to make. Nonetheless, we believe two general categories of responses are captured in the concepts of acceptance decisions and behavioral responses.

The *acceptance decision* involves psychological reactions to a judicial policy, which may be generalized in terms of accepting or rejecting the policy. The acceptance decision is shaped by several psychological dimensions: intensity of attitude, regard for the policy-making court, perceptions of the consequences of the decision, and the respondent's own role in society.

The intensity of a person's *attitude toward the policy* prior to the court's decision can be important. Most white southerners, for example, were extremely hostile toward policies of racial integration before *Brown;* thus their unwillingness to accept the decision was not surprising. Many people had similarly intense attitudes about abortion and about prayers in the public schools. Many blacks, feminists, and civil libertarians, respectively, had equally intense attitudes in favor of these policies. For most policies, though, feelings are not so intense. Few people feel strongly about such issues as the size and composition of juries, new doctrines in libel law, or the application of the First Amendment guarantees to commercial advertising. In such instances the acceptance decision is less likely to be governed by prior attitudes.

Another dimension involves *regard for the court* making the decision. People who view the Supreme Court favorably may be more inclined to accept a decision as legitimate and proper. Those who generally view the Court negatively or who believe it has usurped too much authority may transfer these views to particular decisions that the Court makes.

A third dimension relates to a person's *perception of the consequences* of a decision. Those who may not quarrel with a decision in the abstract but believe it will have a serious and detrimental effect on society may be reluctant to accept it. In the 1950s, for example, many citizens feared that the Supreme Court's decisions granting due process to suspected subversives dismissed from government employment would aid the spread of Communism; more recently, many people [have been] disturbed about the exclusion of illegally seized evidence from criminal trials, fearing that criminals might often go without punishment.

Finally, acceptance decisions are shaped by a *person's own role in society.* An ambitious judge or attorney general may be reluctant to accept (publicly, at least) an unpopular judicial policy for fear that it will harm his or her career. Corporate officers or citizens may be unwilling to accept a decision if they think it will reduce their profits or cause them great inconvenience. Conversely, people may accept quite willingly decisions that are popular with the public or that bring them financial or other benefits.

Behavioral responses involve reactions that may be seen or recorded and that may determine the extent to which a court policy is actually realized. These responses are often closely linked to acceptance decisions. Persons who do not accept a judicial policy are likely to engage in behavior designed to defeat the policy or minimize its impact. They will interpret it narrowly, try to avoid implementing it, and refuse or evade its consumption. Those who accept a policy are likely to be more faithful or even enthusiastic in interpreting, implementing, and consuming it. Of course, nonacceptors may not always be in a position to ignore a decision or refuse completely to comply with it. Some behavioral responses may be adjusted to meet the decision's requirements while other, less visible, behavioral responses may more truly reflect their unwillingness to accept the decision. Conversely, acceptors may for reasons of inertia never fully adjust their behavioral responses to a new judicial policy.

Policy changes concern changes in rules, formal norms within an organization, or even informal rules regarding behavior within an organization. Police departments may, for example, adopt formal policies against illegal searches, but may informally wink at violations. Schools may devise strategies to comply with the letter but not the spirit of the Supreme Court's school prayer decision in *Schempp.* Policy changes may also include changes in organizational structure or function. As indicated previously, the delivery of health care services related to abortion changed after *Roe v. Wade* to the extent that currently most abortion services are provided by clinics, not hospitals.

Another dimension of behavioral responses is the activities involved in carrying out the policy. These actions by interpreting and implementing populations may benefit or disadvantage the consumer population; in turn, the consumer population may respond by using, ignoring, or avoiding the policy. . . . We must examine these actions, in addition to such formal responses as written policies, because written policies sometimes bear little relation to a population's behavior.

Feedback . . . is another behavioral response to a judicial policy. It is directed toward the originator of the policy or some other policy-making agency. The purpose of feedback . . . is usually to provide support for or make demands upon other political institutions regarding the judicial policy. Almost immediately after the Supreme Court announced its abortion decision, feedback in the form of letters to the justices began. Also, some members of Congress let the Court know of their displeasure with the abortion decision by introducing amendments to the Constitution to overturn *Roe.* Frequent manifestations of displeasure, as well as some of support, by various interest groups have been directed at the Court and other political institutions, such as Congress and state legislatures. In varying degrees, these attempts at feedback have led to modifications of the policy—as we can see in the Court's approval of the Hyde Amendment passed by Congress, which terminated federal payment for abortions for poor women.

8.2   *"... to promulgate jurisdiction in the abstract is meaningless."*

JUSTICE FRANKFURTER ANTICIPATES THE CONSEQUENCES OF BAKER V. CARR

369 U.S. 186, 82 S. Ct. 691, 7 L. Ed. 2d 663 (1962)

Justice Frankfurter's prevailing opinion in *Colegrove v. Green* (Reading 5.10) warned that courts would enter a "political thicket" if they tried to settle disputes over legislative districting. When *Baker v. Carr* (Reading 5.11) reversed *Colegrove,* Frankfurter predicted dire consequences.

MR. JUSTICE FRANKFURTER, whom MR. JUSTICE HARLAN joins, dissenting.

The Court today reverses a uniform course of decision established by a dozen cases, including one by which the very claim now sustained was unanimously rejected only five years ago. The impressive body of rulings thus cast aside reflected the equally uniform course of our political history regarding the relationship between population and legislative representation—a wholly different matter from denial of the franchise to individuals because of race, color, religion or sex. Such a massive repudiation of the experience of our whole past in asserting destructively novel judicial power demands a detailed analysis of the role of this Court in our constitutional scheme. Disregard of inherent limits in the effective exercise of the Court's "judicial Power" not only presages the futility of judicial intervention in the essentially political conflict of forces by which the relation between population and representation has time out of mind been and now is determined. It may well impair the Court's position as the ultimate organ of "the supreme Law of the Land" in that vast range of legal problems, often strongly entangled in popular feeling, on which this Court must pronounce. The Court's authority—possessed neither of the purse nor the sword—ultimately rests on sustained public confidence in its moral sanction. Such feeling must be nourished by the Court's complete detachment, in fact and in appearance, from political entanglements and by abstention from injecting itself into the clash of political forces in political settlements.

A hypothetical claim resting on abstract assumptions is now for the first time made the basis for affording illusory relief for a particular evil even though it foreshadows deeper and more pervasive difficulties in consequence. The claim is hypothetical and the assumptions are abstract because the Court does not vouchsafe the lower courts—state and federal—guidelines for formulating specific, definite, wholly unprecedented remedies for the inevitable litigations that today's umbrageous disposition is bound to stimulate in connection with politically motivated reapportionments in so many States. In such a setting, to promulgate jurisdiction in the abstract is meaningless. It is devoid of reality as "a brooding omnipresence in the sky" for it conveys no intimation what relief, if any, a District Court is capable of affording that would not invite legislatures to play ducks and drakes with the judiciary. For this Court to direct the District Court to enforce a claim to which the Court has over the years consistently found itself required to deny legal enforcement and at the same time to find it necessary to withhold any guidance to the lower court how to enforce this turnabout, new legal claim, manifests an odd—indeed an esoteric—conception of judicial propriety. One of the Court's supporting opinions, as elucidated by commentary, unwittingly affords a disheartening preview of the mathematical quagmire (apart from divers judicially inappropriate and elusive determinants), into which this Court today catapults the lower courts of the country without so much as adumbrating the basis for a legal calculus as a means of extrication. Even assuming the indispensable intellectual disinterestedness on the part of judges in such matters, they do not have accepted legal standards or criteria or even reliable analogies to draw upon for making judicial judgments. To charge courts with the task of accommodating the incommensurable factors of policy that underlie these mathematical puzzles is to attribute, however flatteringly, omnicompetence to judges. The Framers of the Constitution persistently rejected a proposal that embodied this assumption and Thomas Jefferson never entertained it.

Recent legislation, creating a district appropriately described as "an atrocity of ingenuity," is not unique. Considering the gross inequality among legislative electoral units within almost every State, the Court naturally shrinks from asserting that in districting at least substantial equality is a constitutional requirement enforceable by courts. Room continues to be allowed for weighting. This of course implies that geography, economics, urban-rural conflict, and all the other non-legal factors which have throughout our history entered into political districting are to some extent not to be ruled out in the undefined vista now opened up by review in the federal courts of state reapportionments. To some extent—aye, there's the rub. In effect, today's decision empowers the courts of the country to devise what should constitute the proper composition of the legislatures of the fifty States. If state courts should for one reason or another find themselves unable to discharge this task, the duty of doing so is put on the federal courts or on this Court, if State views do not satisfy this Court's notion of what is proper districting.

We were soothingly told at the bar of this Court that we need not worry about the kind of remedy a court could effectively fashion once the abstract constitutional right to have courts pass on a state-wide system of electoral districting is recognized as a matter of judicial rhetoric, because legislatures would heed the Court's admonition. This is not only an euphoric hope. It implies a sorry confession of judicial impotence in place of a frank acknowledgment that there is not under our Constitution a judicial remedy for every political mischief, for every undesirable exercise of legislative power. The Framers carefully and with deliberate forethought refused so to enthrone the judiciary. In this situation, as in others of like nature, appeal for relief does not belong here. Appeal must be to an informed, civically militant electorate. In a democratic society like ours, relief must come through an aroused popular conscience that sears the conscience of the people's representatives. In any event there is nothing judicially more unseemly nor more self-defeating than for this Court to make *in terrorem* pronouncements, to indulge in merely empty rhetoric, sounding a word of promise to the ear, sure to be disappointing to the hope.

8.3   *"Prayer is serious business. . . ."*

MARSH V. CHAMBERS

463 U.S. 783, 103 S. Ct. 3330, 77 L. Ed. 2d 1019 (1983)

Ernest Chambers, as a member of the state legislature of Nebraska and as a taxpayer, sued in a federal district court for an injunction to stop the legislature's practice of beginning each session with a prayer offered by a chaplain paid out of state funds. The district court refused to ban the prayers but did enjoin the state treasurer from paying the chaplain's salary. The Court of Appeals for the Eighth Circuit held that the entire practice violated the First and Fourteenth Amendments. The Supreme Court granted certiorari and ruled that neither paying the chaplain nor opening legislative sessions with a prayer was unconstitutional. Speaking for six justices, Chief Justice Warren E.

Burger noted that the Continental Congress and the First Congress had followed such a practice:

> In light of the unambiguous and unbroken history of more than two hundred years, there can be no doubt that the practice of opening legislative sessions with prayer has become part of the fabric of our society. To invoke Divine guidance on a public body entrusted with making the laws is not, in these circumstances, an "establishment" of religion or a step toward establishment; it is simply a tolerable acknowledgement of beliefs widely held among the people of this country. As Justice Douglas observed, "[w]e are a religious people whose institutions presuppose a Supreme Being." *Zorach v. Clauson* (1952).

Justice Brennan, joined by Justice Marshall, dissented. (Justice Stevens dissented in a separate opinion.) After arguing that the First Congress' actions did not constitute an authoritative interpretation of the First Amendment, Brennan went on to discuss the practical consequences of legislative prayers.

JUSTICE BRENNAN, with whom JUSTICE MARSHALL joins, dissenting. . . .

Of course, the Court does not rely entirely on the practice of the First Congress in order to validate legislative prayer. There is another theme which, although implicit, also pervades the Court's opinion. It is exemplified by the Court's comparison of legislative prayer with the formulaic recitation of "God save the United States and this Honorable Court." It is also exemplified by the Court's apparent conclusion that legislative prayer is, at worst, a "mere shadow" on the Establishment Clause rather than a "real threat" to it. . . .

Simply put, the Court seems to regard legislative prayer as at most a de minimis violation, somehow unworthy of our attention. I frankly do not know what should be the proper disposition of features of our public life such as "God save the United States and this Honorable Court," "In God We Trust," "One Nation Under God," and the like. I might well adhere to the view expressed in Schempp that such mottos are consistent with the Establishment Clause, not because their import is de minimis, but because they have lost any true religious significance. Legislative invocations, however, are very different.

First of all, as Justice Stevens' dissent so effectively highlights, legislative prayer, unlike mottos with fixed wordings, can easily turn narrowly and obviously sectarian. I agree with the Court that the federal judiciary should not sit as a board of censors on individual prayers, but to my mind the better way of avoiding that task is by striking down all official legislative invocations.

More fundamentally, however, *any* practice of legislative prayer, even if it might look "non-sectarian" to nine Justices of the Supreme Court, will inevitably and continuously involve the state in one or another religious debate. Prayer is serious business—serious theological business—and it is not a mere "acknowledgment of beliefs widely held among the people of this country" for the State to immerse itself in that business. Some religious individuals or groups find it theologically problematic to engage in joint religious exercises predominantly influenced by faiths not their own. Some might object even to the attempt to fashion a "non-sectarian" prayer. Some would find it impossible to participate in any "prayer opportunity" marked by Trinitarian references. Some would find a prayer *not* invoking the name of Christ to represent a flawed view of the relationship between human beings and God. Some might find any petitionary prayer to be improper. Some might find any prayer that lacked a petitionary element to be deficient. Some might be troubled by what they consider shallow public prayer, or non-spontaneous prayer, or prayer without adequate spiritual preparation or concentration. Some might, of course, have *theological* objections to any prayer sponsored by an organ of government. Some might object on theological grounds to the level of political neutrality generally expected of government-sponsored invocational prayer. And some might object on theological grounds to the Court's requirement that prayer, even though religious, not be proselytizing. If these problems arose in the context of a religious objection to some otherwise decidedly secular activity, then whatever remedy there is would have to be found in the Free Exercise Clause. But, in this case, we are faced with potential religious objections to an activity at the very center of religious life, and it is simply beyond the competence of government, and inconsistent with our conceptions of liberty, for the state to take upon itself the role of ecclesiastical arbiter.

The argument is made occasionally that a strict separation of religion and state robs the nation of its spiritual identity. I believe quite the contrary. It may be true that individuals cannot be "neutral" on the question of religion. But the judgment of the Establishment Clause is that neutrality by the organs of *government* on questions of religion is both possible and imperative. Alexis de Tocqueville wrote the following concerning his travels through this land in the early 1830s:

"The religious atmosphere of the country was the first thing that struck me on arrival in the United States. . . .

In France I had seen the spirits of religion and of freedom almost always marching in opposite directions. In America I found them intimately linked together in joint reign over the same land.

My longing to understand the reason for this phenomenon increased daily.

To find this out, I questioned the faithful of all communions; I particularly sought the society of clergymen, who are the depositaries of the various creeds and have a personal interest in their survival. . . . I expressed my astonishment and revealed my doubts to each of them; I found that they all agreed with each other except about details; all thought that the main reason for the quiet sway of religion over the country was the complete separation of church and state. I have no hesitation in stating that throughout my stay in America I met nobody, lay or cleric, who did not agree about that." Democracy in America 295 (G. Lawrence, trans., J. Mayer, ed., 1969).

More recent history has only confirmed de Tocqueville's observations. If the Court had struck down legislative prayer today, it would likely have stimulated a furious reaction. But it would also, I am convinced, have invigorated both the "spirit of religion" and the "spirit of freedom."

I respectfully dissent.

8.4   *"Government requires comity and cooperation among the branches."*

LEGISLATIVE VETOES, PHOENIX STYLE

Louis Fisher

Last June [1983] the U.S. Supreme Court supposedly sounded the death knell for the legislative veto, a key tool used by Congress for decades to control the executive branch. The broadness of *INS v. Chadha* seemed to strip Congress of every variety of legislative veto: two-house, one-house, and committee.

Legislators must now search for substitutes to satisfy the court's belief that the framers intended a "finely wrought and exhaustively considered" process for making law. Instead of using "shortcuts" like the legislative veto, Congress is supposed to act with full deliberation, including action by both houses and presentation of a bill or joint resolution to the president for his signature or veto.

Developments since *Chadha* suggest a different conclusion. Congress will continue to exercise close control over the agencies, but these controls are unlikely to run the gauntlet of the full legislative process. Informal and nonstatutory ways of doing business, perfected over the years by committees and agencies, will persist and probably flourish.

Is this defiance of the Supreme Court? In a way. But a better explanation is that the court reached too far and did not take into account accommodations that have been mutually beneficial to legislators and executive officials. It is unrealistic to think that a single

Reprinted with permission from *Extensions,* a publication of the Carl Albert Congressional Research and Studies Center, Spring 1984. All rights reserved. Louis Fisher is a specialist in American national government in the Congressional Research Service of the Library of Congress.

decision, even by the Supreme Court, will eliminate executive-legislative agreements established over the years.

Part of Congress' response to *Chadha* has been to review statutes that contain legislative vetoes and make them conform to the court's ruling. One-house and two-house legislative vetoes are being deleted and replaced by joint resolutions. This has been the approach with the Foreign Assistance Act, the Export Administration Act, the D.C. Home Rule Bill, Amtrak legislation, the Consumer Product Safety Commission, and the War Powers Resolution.

Joint resolutions are a tempting substitute, a quick way to "doctor" statutes tainted by the legislative veto. However, a joint resolution of disapproval weakens congressional control over the power it delegates. Congress cannot be expected to pass joint resolutions to stop every agency action it dislikes. The workload is too great, and if the president vetoed the joint resolution, members would have to forge a two-thirds majority in each house to override him. Why should Congress produce an extraordinary majority to recapture authority it delegated by majority vote?

On the other hand, a joint resolution of approval shifts the advantage to Congress. The president would have to secure congressional approval within a specific number of days. The results may be ironic. Prior to *Chadha*, it took a two-house legislative veto to disapprove a major arms sale. If Congress now insists on a joint resolution of approval for major sales, they would be "vetoed" if either house refused its support. The administration would face not a two-house but a one-house veto.

Congress has many informal ways of controlling executive agencies. With or without the blessing of the Supreme Court, congressional committees and subcommittees will exercise a veto power over agency actions. And agencies will acquiesce because in return for this level of congressional scrutiny they receive important grants of discretionary power and program flexibility.

It may come as a surprise to some observers in town that Congress has continued to enact legislative vetoes after the *Chadha* decision. Are they constitutional? Not by the court's definition. Will that fact change the behavior between committees and agencies? Probably not. An agency might advise the committee: "As you know, the requirement in this statute for committee prior-approval is unconstitutional under the court's test." Perhaps agency and committee staff will nod their heads in agreement. After which the agency will seek the prior approval of the committee.

Statutes in the future may rely more heavily on "notification" to committees before an agency acts. Notification does not raise a constitutional issue since it falls within the report-and-wait category already sanctioned by prior court rulings. But notification can become a code word for committee prior-approval. Only in highly unusual situations will an agency defy a committee or subcommittee.

Agencies know that harsh penalties await them if they ignore review committees. Certainly we see this pattern over the last three to four decades with regard to reprogramming. As an informal accommodation between the branches, agencies are allowed to shift funds within an appropriation account provided they obtain committee approval for major changes. *Chadha* does not affect these nonstatutory legislative vetoes. They existed in the past and will persist in the future, perhaps in even greater number because of the court's decision. They are not legal in effect. They are, however, in effect legal.

Internal congressional rules are another substitute for the legislative veto. In the 1950s, President Eisenhower objected to statutory provisions that required agencies to "come into agreement" with committees before implementing an administrative action. Congress changed the procedure so that funds could be appropriated for a project only after authorizing committees passed a resolution of approval. The Justice Department accepted the committee resolution as a valid form of action because it was directed at Congress (the Appropriations Committees) rather than the executive branch.

The House of Representatives may also want to rewrite its rule governing limitations (riders) on appropriations bills, making it easier to add them during floor action. Riders allow Congress to veto agency actions simply by denying funds. Since a president would seldom veto an appropriations bill because of an offensive rider, the practical effect is at least a two-house veto. Because of House/Senate accommodations, the result in many cases is a one-house veto.

The court treated a complex issue in simple terms. The unfortunate effect is to convey to the country an impression of government that does not, and cannot, exist in practice. We should not be too surprised or disconcerted if, after the court closed the door to the legislative veto, we heard a number of windows being raised and perhaps new doors constructed, making the executive-legislative structure as accommodating as before for shared power. It may not be a house of aesthetic quality and certainly does not resemble the neat model envisioned by the Supreme Court, but it will go a long way in meeting the basic needs of executive agencies and congressional committees. Government requires comity and cooperation among the branches. Part of this will depend on legislative vetoes in one form or another.*

*By March, 1985, Fisher reported: "In the 16 months between *Chadha* and the end of the 98th Congress, 53 legislative vetoes (generally the committee-veto variety) have been enacted into law in 18 different statutes." Fisher believes that "the Court's prestige has been damaged by a decision that was broader than necessary and unpersuasive in reasoning."—Eds.

PART FOUR
Judicial Decision Making

9
Fact-Finding in the Courts

A judicial decision involves two processes: determining the facts and then choosing (perhaps creating) the appropriate rules of law to apply to these facts. There are, of course, lawsuits in which there is no dispute over the facts. In a criminal case, for example, the defendant may plead guilty and thus relieve the prosecutor of any need to establish a violation of the law. In a civil proceeding both parties may agree about the facts and disagree only about the law applicable to the situation. But trial courts must be prepared to discover the facts in any controversy brought before them, and much of the peculiar character of judicial proceedings is attributable to their fact-finding methods.

Television has probably sensitized much of the American population to the importance of judicial fact-finding, and in this respect, if no other, has performed a public service. Nevertheless, scholars still tend to concentrate on the work of appellate tribunals. The "upper-court myth," as Judge Jerome Frank called it (Reading 9.1), holds that legal rules announced by appellate courts control decisions of trial courts and that trial judges' mistakes can be remedied on appeal. In reality, however, American appellate judges receive a case in the form of a record shaped by the procedural rulings and findings of fact in the trial court. The litigation, like rough dough, has already been partly molded. When the record consists largely of documents, as, for instance, in an antitrust suit, appellate judges may feel at least as competent as the trial judge to weigh the evidence. But when the evidence consists mostly of oral testimony and the witnesses have contradicted each other (as they often do), appellate judges, because they themselves neither saw nor heard those witnesses, are loath to overturn a trial judge's findings. Indeed, the Supreme Court regularly, albeit not universally, adheres to the "two-court rule," that is, the justices will not question facts established by a trial court and accepted by an appellate court in the same case. The "two-court" practice is merely a logical extension of Rule 52a of the Federal Rules of Civil Procedure, which shields from appellate review a district judge's finding of fact unless that finding is "clearly erroneous." By contrast, an appeal in Civil Law systems typically means a complete retrial of alleged facts as well as a review of the applicability of legal rules.

THE ADVERSARY PROCESS

When the common law was in its infancy, the judicial process leaned heavily on the Deity to determine the critical facts in dispute. One method, trial by combat, allowed the litigants to do physical battle with each other.[1] Supposedly, God dropped all other pressing matters in the universe and intervened to bestow victory on the just man. But because at least one of the litigants was unjust and because the Almighty was known to be quite busy and to think in long-range rather than short-range terms, there were risks as well as inconveniences in such trials. To ease these problems, a group of professional champions made themselves available to do combat, albeit for a fee that only the more affluent could afford. Lesser folk in England frequently attracted the Deity's attention by resorting to various trials by ordeal, the hot iron being the most common form. Here during the middle of Mass a litigant grasped a white-hot iron. His smoldering hand was then bandaged and examined three days later. If it was free of infection, God had spared him because he had obviously told the truth; if it was infected, he had lied.

Most Catholic theologians had historically frowned on such practices, and in 1215 the Fourth Lateran Council forbade clergy to participate in them. This ban threw the British law of evidence into chaos, and only after fifty years of experimentation did the jury—in a form familiar to us—come into existence as a substitute for divine fact-finding. An alternative—if to English tastes, peculiar—model existed in the Church and had to an extent been followed in some lay tribunals. In ecclesiastical courts a judge heard witnesses, examined documents, and decided the issues in dispute. He might have prayed for wisdom, but he neither expected, nor apparently habitually received, explicit directions from heaven.

The trial procedures that eventually developed in the common law form an adversary system described in Chapter 2. The trial judge, even when sitting without a jury, properly acts more like a referee than a player in this contest. Opposing counsel carry the burden of uncovering the facts by waging all-out intellectual warfare in order to reveal the truth. Each side calls its own witnesses and questions them about

---

[1] In 1985 two Scottish brothers accused of armed robbery unsuccessfully sought the option of trial by combat with the royal champion. This type of trial was last recorded in 1603, but the honorary office of royal champion still exists, now held by a 54-year-old amateur yachtsman and pianist.

their knowledge of the dispute. Each attorney then has an opportunity to cross-examine, to try to discredit damaging testimony by showing that the witness is mendacious or at least biased, or that the evidence presented is irrelevant to the issues at trial. At the conclusion of these sometimes dramatic confrontations, the judge or the jury is supposed to sort out truth from falsehood and decide what the facts are. (Reading 9.2.)

JURIES

The Sixth and Seventh Amendments to the Constitution confer a right to a trial by jury in all federal cases. The Seventh Amendment, however, excepts civil disputes in which the amount in controversy is $20 or less, and the Supreme Court has exempted criminal prosecutions for "petty offenses," a vague term that usually refers to crimes for which the penalty does not exceed six months' imprisonment. On the other hand, the Court has ruled that trial by jury is so fundamental a constitutional right that the Fourteenth Amendment's due process clause protects it against the states *in criminal cases,* although again not for petty offenses.[2]

The justification for the fundamental nature of the protection of a trial by jury does not lie in a belief that untrained people, selected pretty much at random from the community, are especially adept at findings facts. (Nevertheless, if judges are skilled at discovering the truth, it must follow that most juries are also reasonably capable in that work. The most thorough empirical study—some of whose results are reprinted in Reading 9.3—reported that judges and juries agreed on the verdict in more than three-quarters of the cases studied.[3]) Rather, the real argument for the jury, as eloquently stated by Justice Byron R. White in *Duncan v. Louisiana,* is a political one: "jury trial is granted to criminal defendants in order to prevent oppression by the Government . . . an inestimable safeguard against the corrupt or overzealous prosecutor and against the compliant, biased, or eccentric judge." Another important justification has been that jurors, drawn as they are from the community at large rather than from among lawyers and public officials, may temper enforcement of unpopular, outdated, or harsh laws. (Reading 9.4.)

Although the jury came to America with the English colonists, in Britain today only about one-sixth of indictable offenses are tried by juries. And, despite Justice White's constitutional panegyric to the sacredness of the right, many scholars and jurists have severely criticized the jury for both its expense and its slowness in administering

[2] *Duncan v. Louisiana* (1968); *Baldwin v. New York* (1972).
[3] Harry Kalven and Hans Zeisel, *The American Jury* (Boston: Little, Brown, 1966).

justice. Perhaps partly in response to such criticisms, the Supreme Court has recently permitted experimentation with two historic features of the common law jury—twelve persons and a unanimous verdict. *Williams v. Florida* (1970) found no constitutional objection to the use of a six-person jury in all criminal cases except those in which capital punishment could be imposed. Neither Congress nor the Court has authorized such ultrapetite juries in federal criminal cases, but *Colgrove v. Battin* (1973) approved civil juries of only six people in federal civil trials; and such small panels now sit in most United States district courts. In *Ballew v. Georgia* (1978), however, the Court refused to allow five-person juries in state criminal cases. (Reading 9.5.)

The Court surrendered the principle of unanimity in *Johnson v. Louisiana* (1972), which held that in a state criminal proceeding a verdict of guilty by a nine-to-three vote met the requirements of due process of law. On the other hand, the same opinion insisted—although the issue was not before the Court—that juries in federal criminal cases had to arrive at unanimous verdicts.

Critics have attacked these decisions affecting the size and unanimity of juries as violating historic protections.[4] Smaller juries, it is alleged, are more likely to convict because the number of viewpoints in the jury is reduced and group deliberation is less effective. As for departures from the common law rule of unanimity, Justice Stewart charged that under the *Johnson* decision "nine jurors can simply ignore the view of their fellow panel members of a different race or class." Stewart also contended that unanimity "provides the simple and effective method endorsed by centuries of experience and history to combat the injuries to the fair administration of justice that can be inflicted by community passion and prejudice." The Court in *Burch v. Louisiana* (1979) did agree that the verdict on a six-person jury had to be unanimous.

According to the Sixth Amendment, a jury must be "impartial." Bias, although difficult to guard against, may be thought of as: (1) being simply a matter of individual opinion; or (2) growing out of or being associated with the social or economic status of the jurors. The law protects against bias of the first sort by the *voir dire*, a pretrial proceeding in which opposing counsel, either directly or through the judge, may question prospective jurors about their opinions. If a juror indicates bias in the case, counsel may challenge him or her "for cause"; if the judge believes the lawyer is correct, the challenged person will be dismissed from the panel of potential jurors. The law provides additional protection by allowing each side a certain number

[4] See the materials collected in Wallace D. Loh (ed.), *Social Research and the Judicial Process* (New York: Russell Sage Foundation, 1984), Chs. 7–8.

of "peremptory" challenges, which require no justification.[5] (The number of challenges "for cause" is unlimited.) In extreme cases in which most community members have apparently formed an opinion (perhaps because of extensive pretrial publicity), the defense may ask for a *change of venue,* that is, that the trial be held in another locality.

Courts have guarded against bias in the second sense, attributable to such factors as the juror's race, religion, or ethnicity, through a so-called cross-section principle, which forbids systematic exclusion of identifiable segments of the community from jury panels. A dozen years after adoption of the Fourteenth Amendment, *Strauder v. West Virginia* (1880) held that males could not be excluded from jury service because of race; three-quarters of a century later *Hernandez v. Texas* (1954) extended the ban to cover ethnicity, and, finally, 107 years after the Fourteenth Amendment came into effect, the justices ruled in *Taylor v. Louisiana* (1975) that women as a class could not be excluded or given automatic exemption based solely on sex.

In the Jury Selection and Service Act of 1975, Congress accepted the reasoning behind the Court's rulings and mandated the cross-section principle for federal juries. Jury selection lists are commonly made up from voting registers; this source, however, is likely to underrepresent the young and racial minorities.[6] Some states utilize other sources—motor-vehicle records, telephone and public-utility listings, taxpayer lists, and even public assistance and unemployment rolls. But neither by statute nor judicial decision need a jury be a microcosm of the larger community. Systematic exclusion is taboo, but proportional representation is not required.

The selection of jurors is often a very time-consuming process, sometimes taking longer than the trial itself. The principal reason is that counsel in most states control the voir dire, and they may ask endless questions about each potential juror's occupation, neighbor-

---

[5] In a case where a black was a defendant, the use of peremptory challenges by the prosecution to remove all blacks from the jury venire was held by the Supreme Court not to constitute invidious discrimination; *Swain v. Alabama* (1965). The Court declined to reconsider this issue in *McCray v. New York* (1983). But California, Massachusetts, and Florida courts have ruled that counsel cannot remove members of minority groups from jury pools solely for racial reasons, and the United States Court of Appeals for the Second Circuit agreed when the *McCray* case was retried. The Supreme Court agreed to reconsider the issues in *Batson v. Kentucky* (1985).

Lord Denning, Master of the Rolls (the senior judge of the British appellate system), resigned his post in 1983 after publication of a book in which he argued that all British citizens were no longer qualified to serve on juries because "the English are no longer a homogeneous race. . . . They are white and black, coloured and brown. . . . Some of them come from countries where bribery and graft are accepted and stealing is a virtue so long as you are not found out. They no longer share the same code of morals or religious beliefs." He contended that peremptory challenges were being used to "overload" juries with blacks who were reluctant to convict those of their own race. (*The New York Times,* May 29, 1983.)

[6] In *California v. Harris* (1984) the Supreme Court declined to review a California supreme court decision that barred exclusive reliance on voting lists if it reduced the proportion of racial minorities in the jury pool.

hood, reading habits, hobbies, and acquaintances—all for the purpose of gaining some insight into how they might vote if seated on the jury. In the federal courts such delays are less likely because the judge controls the voir dire, asking questions submitted by counsel.

A recent and subtle challenge to the cross-section principle has come in the form of "jury-stacking." Counsel have always tried to use their challenges to eliminate jurors likely to be unsympathetic to their side, but they have generally proceeded simply on the basis of their experience, judgment, and hunches.[7] More recently—and more expensively—counsel have used public opinion surveys and observation of potential jurors during the voir dire by trained social psychologists to predict jurors' attitudes more accurately. (Reading 9.6.) These experts have a right to be in the courtroom, for in *Press-Enterprise Co. v. Superior Court of California* (1984) the Supreme Court held that trial judges must ordinarily permit the press and public to attend jury selection proceedings.

Defendants in criminal cases may make a "knowing" waiver of the right to jury trial. Moreover, as many as nine out of ten criminal prosecutions are settled by plea bargaining—that is, negotiations between the prosecutor and defense counsel in which the defendant agrees to plead guilty in exchange for the prosecutor's lessening the charge, agreeing to ask the judge for leniency, or both. On the civil side, too, the vast majority of cases filed in court are settled by negotiation; and a judge sitting alone decides a large portion of the remainder.

Operation of the jury system has been a key factor in the Supreme Court's consideration of the constitutionality of capital punishment. The old practice in capital cases was for a judge to hold that a prosecutor could challenge for cause any potential juror who expressed scruples of conscience against the death penalty. *Witherspoon v. Illinois* (1968), however, ruled that this practice violated the cross-section principle.[8] *Crampton v. Ohio* (1971) commended but did not constitutionally require the practice of having guilt and sentence determined in separate jury proceedings.

The next year, *Furman v. Georgia* (1972) unexpectedly held that capital punishment as then applied constituted cruel and unusual punishment. Several of the justices in the majority were deeply concerned about the absence of standards available to guide judges and jurors and the resulting erratic imposition of the penalty. Thirty-eight state legislatures reacted to this decision by establishing new procedures for sentencing prisoners to capital punishment. Some states required

---

[7] See the rules of an experienced trial attorney for selecting jurors, reprinted in Jon Van Dyke, "Voir Dire: How Should It Be Conducted to Ensure That Our Juries Are Representative and Impartial?" 3 *Hastings Constitutional Law Quarterly* 65, 70 (1976).

[8] But in *Wainwright v. Witt* (1985) the Court weakened the *Witherspoon* rule, holding that jurors could be excluded if they expressed views that would "substantially impair" the performance of their duties.

juries to consider certain specified aggravating or mitigating circumstances, while others made death a mandatory penalty for particular offenses. *Gregg v. Georgia* (1976) sustained statutes that set standards and careful procedures in capital cases, but other rulings invalidated statutes that automatically imposed the death penalty.[9]

STANDARDS FOR FACT-FINDING

Courts require varying standards of proof depending on the seriousness of the proceeding. To obtain an indictment (an accusation) from a grand jury, a prosecutor need show only that the facts make a prima facie case, that is, on their face they point toward, without necessarily conclusively proving, the guilt of the accused. That defense counsel may rebut this evidence or produce differing versions or interpretations of the facts does not invalidate an indictment. Similarly, a court applies the standard of a prima facie case when it grants a temporary injunction in an ex parte proceeding, that is, a proceeding in which only the person seeking the injunction comes into court. To secure a conviction on a criminal charge or to obtain a permanent injunction, the standard of proof is much higher, of course.

In civil suits a plaintiff need only show that "the preponderance of the evidence" supports his or her contentions. As its name indicates, this rule requires that on balance the fact finder(s) conclude(s) that more evidence supports than contradicts the plaintiff's allegations of "facts." Much more stringent is the standard required for a conviction in a criminal case: "beyond a reasonable doubt." Here before returning a verdict of guilty, the trial court—either jury or judge—must be convinced that the "facts" presented by the prosecution so overwhelm the "facts" offered by the defense and any alternative explanations of the prosecution's evidence that no reasonable doubt of guilt remains in the fact finders' minds. "Reasonable" is a slippery word that defies precise definition, but trial judges typically instruct juries that it means a doubt of real weight. As one federal judge explained to a jury, a reasonable doubt

> is just such a doubt as the term implies; a doubt for which you can give a reason. It must not arise from a merciful disposition or kindly, sympathetic feeling or desiring to avoid a possibly disagreeable duty. . . . It is a doubt which is created by the want of evidence, or maybe by the evidence itself; not speculative, imaginary, or conjectural.[10]

9 *Woodson v. North Carolina* (1976); *Roberts v. Louisiana* (1976); *Roberts v. Louisiana* (1977); *Lockett v. Ohio* (1978). *Pulley v. Harris* (1984) held that a state appellate court, before affirming a death sentence, is not required to compare the sentence with the penalties imposed in similar cases.

10 *United States v. Olmstead* (U.S. Dist. Ct. for the Western District of Washington, 1926); quoted in Walter F. Murphy, *Wiretapping on Trial* (New York: Random House, 1965), pp. 42–43.

Since the early days of the Republic, courts have routinely insisted that prosecutors meet the standard of "beyond a reasonable doubt"; but neither the Constitution nor any subsequent amendment contains a word about such a requirement. It was not until 1970 that *In re Winship* explicitly ruled that the standard was imbedded in constitutional law. There the Supreme Court said that this strict criterion was inherent in the concept of due process of law expressed in both the Fifth and Fourteenth Amendments and applied to proceedings against juveniles as well as against adults. Nevertheless, the defendant may have to carry the burden of proof under some circumstances. Where, for example, a person offers as a defense that he or she acted under the pressure of an "extreme emotional disturbance" that might explain or excuse the crime, it is constitutional for the trial court to require proof of this defense by a preponderance of the evidence.[11]

ADJUDICATIVE FACTS

Some analysts distinguish between adjudicative and legislative facts.[12] *Adjudicative facts* are of the kind that courts have traditionally had to find to resolve disputes involving a limited number of persons and fairly specific incidents. Controversies over such matters as whether blows were struck, whether a weapon was drawn, or whether a contract was made, are adjudicative facts that can usually be established by ordering persons who were at the scene to testify about what, to their direct knowledge, actually occurred. These are the facts that normally go to a jury. They relate to the parties, their activities, their properties, their businesses. Findings of adjudicative facts must be supported by evidence and, depending on the sort of case, meet either the test of "preponderance of the evidence" or "beyond a reasonable doubt."

Under the strictures of the rule against hearsay, witnesses may testify only about what they themselves have seen or heard. But duly qualified "expert" witnesses, such as people skilled in ballistics, may offer their professional opinions. Efforts to supplement witnesses' testimony by more precise or scientific fact-finding methods have been only minimally successful. On the one hand, courts routinely accept data regarding fingerprints as well as blood and breath tests for drunkenness; on the other hand, judges remain skeptical about lie detectors, voice prints, and narcoanalysis. Interestingly, some judges have per-

---

[11] *Patterson v. New York* (1977).

[12] Donald L. Horowitz prefers the terms "historical facts" and "social facts." He explains: "Historical facts are the events that have transpired between the parties to a lawsuit. *Social facts* are the recurrent patterns of behavior on which policy must be based. Historical facts, as I use the term, have occasionally been called 'adjudicative facts' by lawyers, and social facts have also been called 'legislative facts.' I avoid these terms because of the preconceptions they carry and the division of labor they imply." *The Courts and Social Policy* (Washington, D.C.: The Brookings Institution, 1977), p. 45.

mitted or requested experts on morals or ethics—clergy, philosophers, professors of religion—to testify on such subjects as conscientious objection to military service, the right to die, religious rights of prisoners, and blood transfusions or other medical treatments resisted on moral grounds. (Reading 9.7.)

LEGISLATIVE FACTS AND PUBLIC ISSUES

Contrasting with litigation involving disputes about individual actions are cases where the controversy concerns application or validity of social or economic legislation aimed at establishing governmental control over conduct and the actual, if not formal, litigants are large groups or classes of people. In such cases the "facts" often concern attitudes or opinions or social practices or economic conditions. These are sometimes called *legislative facts*—facts that help the tribunal to exercise its judgment or discretion in determining what course of action to take. Legislative facts are ordinarily general and do not concern merely the immediate parties. When courts must find facts of such breadth, the usual practice of relying on testimony by eyewitnesses or participants becomes both inadequate and inappropriate. As Kenneth C. Davis says, "legislative facts need not be, frequently are not, and sometimes cannot be supported by evidence."[13]

And, as Justice Felix Frankfurter once complained, "the types of cases now calling for decision to a considerable extent require investigation of voluminous literature far beyond the law reports and other legal writings."[14] One needs little imagination to grasp the difficulties of using traditional judicial procedures to obtain information about such broad and complex issues as the potential effect on young children's minds of having a homosexual teacher or a teacher who has had surgery to change his or her sex; the effect on a woman's health of working after the fourth or fifth month of pregnancy; the potential psychic injury to an infant if its mother returns to work within weeks after delivery; whether a war really began at the firing of the first shots, the formal declaration by one of the belligerents, or some time in between; or the potential injury to nearby residents by an accident at a nuclear power plant or a laboratory engaged in recombinant DNA research.

One means judges have used to take broad societal conditions into account is called "judicial notice." The judge merely "notices" certain more or less obvious situations. Such noticing is a long-established judicial tradition, but it has characteristically operated within fairly narrow limits. The Model Code of Evidence of the American Law Institute states that a court may on its own motion take notice, among

---

[13] *Administrative Law and Government* (St. Paul: West Publishing Co., 1960), p. 284.
[14] *Ferguson v. Moore-McCormack Lines,* dis. op. (1957).

other things, of "specific facts so notorious as not to be the subject of reasonable dispute, and . . . specific facts and propositions of generalized knowledge which are capable of immediate and accurate demonstration by resort to easily accessible sources of indisputable accuracy." In *Ohio Bell Telephone Co. v. Public Utilities Commission* (1937), for example, the Supreme Court said it would take notice of the fact that there had been an economic depression and that market values decline during a depression. But litigants would have to prove, by evidence, the precise extent of that decline.

Beyond judicial notice a judge may determine social or economic facts by off-the-bench research, just as in dealing with legal points at issue in a trial. Justice Frankfurter made a significant comment from the bench to counsel during the first reargument of the School Segregation cases:

> Can we not take judicial notice of writing by people who competently deal with these problems? Can I not take judicial notice of [Gunnar] Myrdal's book [*An American Dilemma*] without having him called as a witness? . . . How to inform the judicial mind, as you know, is one of the most complicated problems. It is better to have witnesses, but I did not know that we could not read the works of competent writers.

Such research is not merely a practice of latter-day judges. Justice Louis D. Brandeis generally found the briefs and argument of counsel to be inadequate, and consequently he treated them "as only a starting-point for investigation."[15] James M. Beck, who as Solicitor General handled the important case of *Myers v. United States* (1926) for the government, wrote to Chief Justice Taft after the decision, expressing amazement that Taft had found and used extensive materials not located by counsel for either side.

SOCIAL AND ECONOMIC DATA

Judicial notice is limited in scope, and a busy judge cannot do a great deal of original research. Thus, even together, these two sources of information cannot entirely fulfill a judge's need for information. There are other ways of supplying this need, of course. One way is for counsel to gather relevant data and summarize or analyze them in briefs. Each side can then present and defend its interpretations and attack those of the opposition.

The most celebrated breakthrough involving use of this approach was the brief prepared by Brandeis and presented to the Supreme Court in *Muller v. Oregon* (1908), in which Brandeis was defending

---

15 Alexander M. Bickel, *The Unpublished Opinions of Mr. Justice Brandeis* (Cambridge, Massachusetts: The Belknap Press, 1957), p. xvii.

the constitutionality of a state law setting ten hours as the maximum working day for women. This brief, the usefulness of which the Court specifically acknowledged in its opinion, gathered an enormous amount of information on foreign and American laws limiting hours for women and on governmental reports stressing the dangers to women from long hours of labor. Such laws and opinions "may not be, technically speaking, authorities," the Supreme Court said, but "they are significant of a widespread belief that woman's physical structure, and the functions she performs in consequence thereof, justify special legislation restricting or qualifying the conditions under which she should be permitted to toil." This technique of presenting social data to a court has now become commonplace and, because of its origin, is known as a "Brandeis brief."

A second method, one used in the original School Segregation cases, involves not only inclusion of sociological data in written briefs but use at the trial by one or both sides of social scientists as expert witnesses, much as a prosecutor might call a ballistics technician to testify whether a bullet was fired from a certain gun or as a defense attorney might summon a psychiatrist to testify about a client's mental health. But the social sciences are still "soft" compared to "hard" sciences like chemistry and physics; and in a society in which most educated citizens fancy themselves experts on politics, economics, and sociology, establishing expertise is not always easy.[16] The following colloquy during the trial in the original segregation case from South Carolina illustrates some of the difficulties:

JUDGE [JOHN J.] PARKER: It seems to me that any lawyer or any man who has any experience in government would be just as well qualified as he [Kenneth Clark, a social psychologist] would to express an opinion on that [the effects of segregation on black school children]. He is not a scientist in the field of education. . . . Do you seriously contend he is qualified to testify as an educational expert? What do you say about that, Mr. Marshall?

MR. [THURGOOD] MARSHALL: . . . we have been trying to . . . present as many experts in the field with as many different reasons why we consider that segregation in and of itself is injurious. . . .

JUDGE PARKER: Are you going to offer any more witnesses along this line?

MR. MARSHALL: No sir. The other witnesses are *real* scientists.

JUDGE PARKER: Well, I'll take it for what it's worth. Go ahead.

In the subsequent oral argument before the Supreme Court, Justice Frankfurter expressed what must be a common judicial concern over

16 See Loh, *op. cit.,* Chs. 3–6, 13.

the weight to be given to social science evidence: "I do not mean that I disrespect it. I simply know its character. It can be a very different thing from, as I say, things that are weighed and measured and are fungible. We are dealing here with very subtle things, very subtle testimony."

When the Supreme Court decided the school segregation cases, consolidated under the title of *Brown v. Board of Education,* Chief Justice Warren, in what became a famous footnote, referred to several sociological studies as supporting the Court's conclusion that racial segregation injured the segregated. Opponents of integration utilized these references to charge that the justices were preaching sociology rather than interpreting the Constitution.

SELECTED REFERENCES

Bermant, Gordon. *Jury Selection Procedures in United States District Courts.* Washington, D.C.: Federal Judicial Center, 1982.

Bermant, Gordon, and John Shapard. *The Voir Dire Examination, Juror Challenges, and Adversary Advocacy.* Washington, D.C.: Federal Judicial Center, 1978.

Goodman, Leonard, *et al. Sources and Uses of Social and Economic Data: A Manual for Lawyers.* Washington, D.C.: Bureau of Social Science Research, 1973.

Horowitz, Donald L. *The Courts and Social Policy.* Washington, D.C.: The Brookings Institution, 1977.

Jacob, Herbert. *Justice in America: Courts, Lawyers, and the Judicial Process,* 4th ed. Boston: Little, Brown, 1984.

Kalven, Harry, and Hans Zeisel. *The American Jury.* Boston: Little, Brown, 1966.

Karst, Kenneth L. "Legislative Facts in Constitutional Litigation," 1960 *Supreme Court Review* 75.

Kluger, Richard. *Simple Justice.* New York: Knopf, 1976. Chs. 13–14.

Levin, Betsy, and Willis D. Hawley (eds.). *The Courts, Social Science, and School Desegregation.* New York: Transaction Books, 1977.

Loh, Wallace D. (ed.). *Social Research in the Judicial Process.* New York: Russell Sage Foundation, 1984.

MacRae, Duncan. *The Social Function of Social Science.* New Haven: Yale University Press, 1976.

Nagel, Stuart. "Bringing the Values of Jurors in Line with the Law," 63 *Judicature* 189 (1979).

Note. "The Defendant's Right to Object to Prosecutorial Misuse of the Peremptory Challenge," 92 *Harvard Law Review* 1770 (1979).

Note. "Limiting the Peremptory Challenge: Representation of Groups on Petit Juries," 86 *Yale Law Journal* 1715 (1977).

Note. "Peremptory Challenges and the Meaning of Jury Representation," 89 *Yale Law Journal* 1177 (1980).

Note. "Public Disclosures of Jury Deliberations," 96 *Harvard Law Review* 886 (1983).

O'Brien, David. "The Seduction of the Judiciary: Social Science and the Courts," 64 *Judicature* 8 (1980).

Peltason, Jack W. *Fifty-eight Lonely Men: Southern Federal Judges and School Desegregation.* New York: Harcourt, Brace & World, 1961.

Rosen, Paul L. *The Supreme Court and Social Science.* Urbana: University of Illinois Press, 1972.

Sperlich, Peter W. "Social Science Evidence in the Courts," 63 *Judicature* 280 (1980).

_____. "And Then There Were Six: The Decline of the American Jury," 63 *Judicature* 262 (1980).

9.1

"Our present trial method is . . . the equivalent of throwing pepper in the eyes of a surgeon when he is performing an operation."

THE "FIGHT" THEORY VERSUS THE "TRUTH" THEORY

Jerome Frank

When we say that present-day trial methods are "rational," presumably we mean this: The men who compose our trial courts, judges and juries, in each law-suit conduct an intelligent inquiry into all the practically available evidence, in order to ascertain, as near as may be, the truth about the facts of that suit. That might be called the "investigatory" or "truth" method of trying cases. Such a method can yield no more than a guess, nevertheless an educated guess.

The success of such a method is conditioned by at least these two factors: (1) The judicial inquirers, trial judges or juries, may not obtain all the important evidence. (2) The judicial inquirers may not be competent to conduct such an inquiry. Let us, for the time being, assume that the second condition is met—i.e., that we have competent inquirers—and ask whether we so conduct trials as to satisfy the first condition, i.e., the procuring of all the practically available important evidence.

The answer to that question casts doubt on whether our trial courts do use the "investigatory" or "truth" method. Our mode of trials is commonly known as "contentious" or "adversary." It is based

Excerpts from "The 'Fight' Theory Versus the 'Truth' Theory," in Jerome Frank, *Courts on Trial: Myth and Reality in American Justice* (Copyright 1949 by Jerome Frank, copyright renewed © 1976 by Princeton University Press; Princeton Paperback, 1973), pp. 80–85. Reprinted by permission of Princeton University Press. Jerome Frank was the most famous and controversial of the "legal realists." He served as a judge on the U.S. Court of Appeals for the Second Circuit from 1941 until his death in 1957.

on what I would call the "fight" theory, a theory which derives from the origin of trials as substitutes for private out-of-court brawls.

Many lawyers maintain that the "fight" theory and the "truth" theory coincide. They think that the best way for a court to discover the facts in a suit is to have each side strive as hard as it can, in a keenly partisan spirit, to bring to the court's attention the evidence favorable to that side. Macaulay said that we obtain the fairest decision "when two men argue, as unfairly as possible, on opposite sides," for then "it is certain that no important consideration will altogether escape notice."

Unquestionably that view contains a core of good sense. The zealously partisan lawyers sometimes do bring into court evidence which, in a dispassionate inquiry, might be overlooked. Apart from the fact element of the case, the opposed lawyers also illuminate for the court niceties of the legal rules which the judge might otherwise not perceive. The "fight" theory, therefore, has invaluable qualities with which we cannot afford to dispense.

But frequently the partisanship of the opposing lawyers blocks the uncovering of vital evidence or leads to a presentation of vital testimony in a way that distorts it. I shall attempt to show you that we have allowed the fighting spirit to become dangerously excessive.

This is perhaps most obvious in the handling of witnesses. Suppose a trial were fundamentally a truth-inquiry. Then, recognizing the inherent fallibilities of witnesses, we would do all we could to remove the causes of their errors when testifying. Recognizing also the importance of witnesses' demeanor as clues to their reliability, we would do our best to make sure that they testify in circumstances most conducive to a revealing observation of that demeanor by the trial judge or jury. In our contentious trial practice, we do almost the exact opposite.

No businessman, before deciding to build a new plant, no general before launching an attack, would think of obtaining information on which to base his judgment by putting his informants through the bewildering experience of witnesses at a trial. "The novelty of the situation," wrote a judge, "the agitation and hurry which accompanies it, the cajolery or intimidation to which the witness may be subjected, the want of questions calculated to excite those recollections which might clear up every difficulty, and the confusion of cross-examination . . . may give rise to important errors and omissions." "In the court they stand as strangers," wrote another judge of witnesses, "surrounded with unfamiliar circumstances giving rise to an embarrassment known only to themselves."

In a book by Henry Taft . . . we are told:

Counsel and court find it necessary through examination and instruction to induce a witness to abandon for an hour or two his habitual method of thought and expression, and conform to the rigid ceremonialism of court procedure. It is not strange that frequently truthful witnesses are . . . misunderstood, that they nervously react in such a way as to create the impression that they are either evading or intentionally falsifying. . . . An honest witness testifies on direct examination. He answers questions promptly and candidly and makes a good impression. On cross-examination, his attitude changes. He suspects that traps are being laid for him. He hesitates; he ponders the answer to a simple question; he seems to "spar" for time by asking that questions be repeated; perhaps he protests that counsel is not fair; he may even appeal to the court for protection. Altogether the contrast with his attitude on direct examination is obvious; and he creates the impression that he is evading or withholding.

Yet on testimony thus elicited courts every day reach decisions affecting the lives and fortunes of citizens.

What is the role of the lawyers in bringing the evidence before the trial court? . . . The lawyer considers it his duty to create a false impression, if he can, of any [adverse] witness who gives such testimony. If such a witness happens to be timid, frightened by the unfamiliarity of courtroom ways, the lawyer, in his cross-examination, plays on that weakness, in order to confuse the witness and make it appear that he is concealing significant facts. Longenecker, in his book *Hints on the Trial of a Law Suit* . . . in writing of the "truthful, honest, over-cautious" witness, tells how "a skillful advocate by a rapid cross-examination may ruin the testimony of such a witness." The author does not even hint any disapproval of that accomplishment. Longenecker's and other similar books recommend that a lawyer try to prod an irritable but honest "adverse" witness into displaying his undesirable characteristics in their most unpleasant form, in order to discredit him with the judge or jury. . . .

"An intimidating manner in putting questions," writes Wigmore, "may so coerce or disconcert the witness that his answers do not represent his actual knowledge on the subject. So also, questions which in form or subject cause embarrassment, shame or anger in the witness may unfairly lead him to such demeanor or utterances that the impression produced by his statements does not do justice to its real testimonial value." . . . Sir Frederic Eggleston recently said that . . . "the terrors of cross-examination are such that a party can often force a settlement by letting it be known that a certain . . . counsel has been retained."

The lawyer not only seeks to discredit adverse witnesses but also to hide the defects of witnesses who testify favorably to his client. If, when interviewing such a witness before trial, the lawyer notes that the witness has mannerisms, demeanor-traits, which might discredit him, the lawyer teaches him how to cover up those traits when testifying: He educates the irritable witness to conceal his irritability, the cocksure witness to subdue his cocksureness. In that way, the trial court is denied the benefit of observing the witness's actual normal demeanor, and thus prevented from sizing up the witness accurately.

Lawyers freely boast of their success with these tactics. They boast also of such devices as these: If an "adverse," honest witness, on cross-examination, makes seemingly inconsistent statements, the cross-examiner tries to keep the witness from explaining away the apparent inconsistencies. "When," writes Tracy, counseling trial lawyers, in a much-praised book, "by your cross-examination, you have caught the witness in an inconsistency, the next question that will immediately come to your lips is, 'Now, let's hear you explain.' Don't ask it, for he may explain and, if he does, your point will have been lost. If you have conducted your cross-examination properly (which includes interestingly), the jury will have seen the inconsistency and it will have made the proper impression on their minds. If, on re-direct examination the witness does explain, the explanation will have come later in the case and at the request of the counsel who originally called the witness and the jury will be much more likely to look askance at the explanation than if it were made during your cross-examination." Tracy adds, "Be careful in your questions on cross-examination not to open a door that you have every reason to wish kept closed." That is, don't let in any reliable evidence, hurtful to your side, which would help the trial court to arrive at the truth. . . .

Nor, usually, will a lawyer concede the existence of any facts if they are inimical to his client and he thinks they cannot be proved by his adversary. If, to the lawyer's knowledge, a witness has testified inaccurately but favorably to the lawyer's client, the lawyer will attempt to hinder cross-examination that would expose the inaccuracy. He puts in testimony which surprises his adversary who, caught unawares, has not time to seek out, interview, and summon witnesses who would rebut the surprise testimony. . . .

These, and other like techniques, you will find unashamedly described in the many manuals on trial tactics written by and for eminently reputable trial lawyers. The purpose of these tactics—often effective—is to prevent the trial judge or jury from correctly evaluating the trustworthiness of witnesses and to shut out evidence the trial court ought to receive in order to approximate the truth.

In short, the lawyer aims at victory, at winning in the fight, not at aiding the court to discover the facts. He does not want the trial court to reach a sound educated guess, if it is likely to be contrary to his client's interests. Our present trial method is thus the equivalent of throwing pepper in the eyes of a surgeon when he is performing an operation. . . .

9.2 *". . . they will introduce into their verdict a certain amount . . . of popular prejudice . . ."*

JURIES AS DISCOVERERS OF THE TRUTH

Oliver Wendell Holmes, Jr.

I confess that in my experience I have not found juries specially inspired for the discovery of truth. I have not noticed that they could see further into things or form a saner judgment than a sensible and well trained judge. I have not found them freer from prejudice than an ordinary judge would be. Indeed one reason why I believe in our practice of leaving questions of negligence to them is what is precisely one of their gravest defects from the point of view of their theoretical function: that they will introduce into their verdict a certain amount—a very large amount, so far as I have observed—of popular prejudice, and thus keep the administration of the law in accord with the wishes and feelings of the community.

9.3 *"The jury is . . . an exciting experiment. . . ."*

THE AMERICAN EXPERIMENT

Hans Zeisel and Harry Kalven, Jr.

The Anglo-American jury is a remarkable political institution. It recruits a group of 12 laymen, chosen at random from the widest population; it convenes them for the purpose of the particular trial; it entrusts them with great official powers of decision; it permits them to carry on deliberations in secret and to report out their final judgment without giving reasons for it; and, after their momentary service has been completed, the state orders them to disband and return to private life.

The jury thus represents a deep commitment to the use of laymen in the administration of justice, a commitment that finds its analogue in the widespread use of lay judges in the criminal courts of other countries. It opposes the cadre of professional, experienced judges

Collected Legal Papers (New York: Harcourt, Brace & Howe, 1920), p. 237.

Chicago Today, 3 (Winter 1966), 32–35. Reprinted by permission of the University of Chicago. Hans Zeisel is and Harry Kalven, Jr., was a Professor at the Law School, University of Chicago.

with this transient, ever-changing, ever-inexperienced group of amateurs.

The jury is thus almost by definition an exciting experiment in the conduct of serious human affairs and it is not surprising that, virtually from its inception, it has been the subject of deep controversy, attracting at once the most extravagant praise and the most harsh criticism.

As a matter of both theoretical interest and methodological convenience, we have studied the performance of the jury measured against the performance of the judge as a baseline. Our material is a massive sample of actual criminal jury trials conducted in the United States in recent years. For each of these trials we have the actual decision of the jury and a communication from the trial judge, telling how he would have disposed of that case had it been tried before him without a jury.

For one reason or another the jury feels, at times, that the defendant at the time of the trial has *already* been sufficiently punished so that the addition of any further punishment would be excessive. The readiest occasion is where the defendant himself is hurt as a consequence of the crime. In one case the defendant fires a shot into the family home of his estranged wife. The judge finds him guilty of shooting with intent to kill; the jury convicts only of the lesser charge of pointing and discharging a firearm. The decisive circumstance appears to be that the defendant's shot did not injure anyone, but when the brother-in-law shot back in self-defense, he seriously injured the defendant. The punished-enough theme comes through in the comment of the judge: "Defendant had long experience of marital strife with his wife. Jury felt since the only person hurt was defendant himself they could not punish him further. . . ."

Sometimes, in the jury's eyes, the defendant has been sufficiently punished by the death of a loved one. In a prosecution for negligent auto homicide, the victim is the intended bride of the defendant, a 21-year-old member of the Air Force. It is clear from the judge's description of the case that not only the jury but the parents of the girl feel the defendant has been punished enough by the event: "Her mother and father were character witnesses for the defendant and he makes his home with them when not on duty. Defendant had never been in trouble and it was obvious that the family of the girl did not want him convicted. . . ."

Indeed the jury may respond to this sentiment even where the victim in the case is a stranger to the defendant. Thus, the jury acquits a young boy, a high school senior, who kills a ten-year-old boy while negligently using a rifle. The judge, after describing the boy defendant as of "high moral character, religious, clean-cut appearing," offers as explanation of the disagreement: "The jury felt that having the charge and killing on his conscience was sufficient punishment."

We get just a glimpse here of the profound but disturbing idea that at times the crime may be its own punishment.

The pattern of these cases indicates that the jury is again engaging in a delicate calculus. It is not simplistically treating every injury to every defendant in the course of a crime as punishment. It appears to weigh this factor only where the crime has been a crime of negligence, or where the crime has been limited to an attempt.

The punished-enough theme is found in a second group of cases where there has been long imprisonment while defendant awaited trial. It is customary for the judge in sentencing to give the defendant credit for the time he has already spent in jail; the jury, however, would at times not only give him credit but would set him free. The point is most obvious if the offense itself is considered trivial as in the case where the defendant was charged with stealing two pieces of lumber. He had already spent two months in jail and—"The jury felt sorry for the defendant because he had been in jail for over two months and the lumber allegedly stolen was worth $2.40."

The harm may, however, be quite serious. In a domestic quarrel, the defendant shoots and wounds his common-law wife so seriously that she is in the hospital for almost a year. The trial is not held until she is discharged, with the result that the defendant spends the interval in jail awaiting the trial. This circumstance seems to be a major factor in moving the jury to acquit.

In one set of circumstances the jury carries out the punished-enough theme a wild dimension further. The defendant is charged with rape of his ten-year-old daughter and at the first trial of the case is found guilty and sentenced to life imprisonment. On appeal, a new trial is granted with a change of venue. At the second trial, the jury hangs. The case is tried a third time, and it is for this third trial that we have the actual jury report. At this trial it is disclosed that the defendant has by now been in jail for 13 months. The extraordinary reaction of his third and last jury which acquits is set forth by the judge as follows: "They were out just 30 minutes. The jury took up a collection of $68 and gave it to the defendant after the case was over."

A final variation on the punished-enough theme arises when the defendant has been plagued by such misfortunes, dating from the time of the crime, that the jury feels life or Providence has already punished him sufficiently. This equity is illustrated in a case of income tax evasion, which brings to mind the story of Job. During the period for which the defendant, originally well-to-do, is charged with failing to file tax returns, he is subject to misfortunes which the judge inventories as follows:

Defendant did not testify but the evidence shows that during the years in question his home burned, he was seriously injured, and his son was killed. Later he lost his leg, his wife became seriously ill, and several major operations were necessary. About three years before the trial, his wife gave birth to a premature child which was both blind and spastic. These, however, are only a portion of the calamities the defendant has suffered during the years he failed to file his income tax return. . . .

It is a commonplace that the American society is to an unusual degree not a single homogeneous culture; in a favorite word of social science, the society is pluralistic. Conceivably, the law might recognize cultural differences and apply different norms to subcultures within the society, as indeed British colonialism appears to have done on occasion. But only in rare instances has American law encountered this issue. The examples that come to mind are of religious sects such as the Mormons and the Quakers. In the case of the Mormons the law has forced them to accept the general standard of monogamy, while in the case of the Quakers, when the law recognized their distinctive claim, it did this in the form of a general exemption for conscientious objectors.

In a handful of disagreements the judges' explanations do seem to open suggestively onto this large theme of subculture. But while the judge's comments are insistent, there is a good deal of doubt that this time they succeed in isolating a special jury sentiment.

Not unexpectedly, the cases have a racial cast. In crimes of violence committed by Negroes against Negroes, or Indians against Indians, the jury is, as the judge sees it, moved at times to leniency because it views the defendant as not fully acculturated and, therefore, incapable of white standards of self-control.

It scarcely needs mentioning that this explanation, uncongenial as it is to contemporary mood, tends to speak more in the language of contempt than that of tolerance.

In the end, the theme remains evanescent. The materials are sketchy and crossed with other interpretations. Thus, we do little more here than the reporting out of these cases.

In a case from the south where a Negro woman shoots and kills her husband, the judge would have given the death penalty on a finding of first degree murder, the jury reduces the charge to first degree manslaughter and the judge comments: "Negroes are not held to the same moral responsibility as white people. . . . Negroes kill each other without reason other than the immediate urge at the time. . . . Community regards the law as too severe for some Negro cases because of lack of moral sense."

In another case from the south where a Negro man and woman living in the same house get into a quarrel and the man kills her with a shotgun, the judge explains the disagreement in much the same way: "This verdict in my opinion is due somewhat to the fact that juries give much more latitude to colored folks than to white. They know how liable colored folks are to act on impulse by shooting and cutting. . . ."

The point may not be confined to Negroes. There is more than a suggestion of it in a homicide case where the judge, after giving other reasons for the disagreement, states: "None, except the complaining parties are Indians, and the jury cannot be excited about the fact one Indian kills another."

Despite the emphasis with which the judge's comments have been made there are substantial difficulties with accepting his sub-culture explanation. To begin with, there are not enough cases to persuade. The explanation is couched in simple general terms and requires only Negro parties to a crime of violence; yet we have many *disagreement* cases in intra-racial crimes of violence which the judge explains on other grounds while keeping silent about the sub-culture theme. More troublesome, the few cases we do have here are largely instances of domestic violence between Negroes. We have already seen that the jury is sensitive to domestic tensions and is ready to treat its eruption into violence on generous analogy to self-defense. . . .

As a sort of postscript of dissatisfaction with this line of explanation, we may have one case too many: The defendant, a Negro, shoots the mother of his child. The jury finds murder in the first degree and the judge comments that the verdict "was fully supported by the proof." But he would have found only second degree murder, because the defendant was a Negro and the real reason was "just anger and resentment." He then goes on to say: "The ancestors of this defendant came from the jungle of Africa only a few generations ago. Society expected too much from him. He killed the woman because he had insufficient intelligence to solve his problem any other way." The power with which the judge puts this to explain his own verdict rounds out the doubt that we have located a distinctive jury sentiment.

This is perhaps the appropriate place to note that we originally expected the study to yield considerable evidence on whether or not the jury is color blind. Actually it has been possible to collect only a few scattered findings. The Negro appears as defendant more frequently than the Negro share of the population would predict, although he elects jury trial proportionately. He is at some disadvantage in the quality of counsel, even when we take economic factors into account.

The Negro defendant, furthermore, is less likely to be seen as sympathetic, a factor established as a major influence on jury leniency. The data offer the suggestion that this is aggravated in *inter*racial crimes. Finally, there is the possible offset, examined here, that in *intra*racial crimes the Negro may occasionally be the beneficiary of an unfriendly sentiment.

9.4   *". . . the issue of impartiality is very much alive."*

THE AMERICAN JURY

Jon Van Dyke

The North Carolina jury took only seventy-five minutes to find Joanne Little not guilty of killing her jailer, who (she stated) had tried to assault her sexually. The defense team had spent ten days in July, 1975, to question 150 prospective jurors in an effort to find a panel it considered sympathetic to the young black woman's plea of self-defense. The ten-day examination—similar to others involving significant political and social issues—was the culmination of the nine-month-long Joanne Little Fair Trial Jury Project, an undertaking that cost nearly forty thousand dollars, most of it spent on a seven-member team of professional sociologists, psychologists, and pollsters. The project involved over a thousand telephone interviews, the use of a computer to correlate attitudes and demographic data, and detailed questioning of prospective jurors—with a psychic and body-language expert on hand to be sure that nonverbal clues would not be missed—in order to decide which jurors to remove from the panel through challenges. The forty thousand dollars were only part of the total defense cost of $325,000, most of it raised from citizens around the country in a sophisticated direct-mail campaign.

Is this what it takes to assemble an impartial jury in the United States today? What is the likelihood that a young black woman would find her "peers" on a jury without such an effort? Procedures like those used in the Little trial—and employed in the defense of Angela Davis, John Mitchell and Maurice Stans, the Harrisburg Seven, and others—have been called by some a new form of jury tampering. Not all judges permit attorneys to conduct wide-ranging questioning and challenging, and not all attorneys approve of it. Some critics believe that the challenge efforts employed in some recent well-publicized cases have perverted the process of jury selection, and that the objective of impaneling an impartial jury is more remote than ever when one side can marshal extensive resources to shape the jury to its desires.

But whether or not such procedures go too far is a question that must be seen in light of the reason they take place. Every defendant in a criminal trial in the United States has the right, according to the Constitution, to trial by an "impartial jury." Extensive questioning of

The Center Magazine (Santa Barbara, Calif.: Center for the Study of Democratic Institutions, May/June 1977), p. 36. Reprinted by permission. Jon Van Dyke is Professor of Law, University of Hawaii at Manoa. This excerpt in *The Center Magazine* was taken from *Jury Selection Procedures: Our Uncertain Commitment to Representative Panels* (Cambridge, Mass.: Ballinger Publishing, 1977).

prospective jurors is aimed at eliminating bias in a jury panel, and it would not be necessary if panels could be presumed impartial in the first place. But in many cases they are not. In cases that generate a high level of emotion, as did the Watergate cases, the trials of antiwar activists, and the Joanne Little and Patricia Hearst cases, many prospective jurors have formed opinions about the guilt or innocence of the defendant beforehand, and some effort must be made to ascertain such possible prejudice.

This problem has been compounded in some highly volatile cases by the government's use of the Federal Bureau of Investigation to investigate prospective jurors and provide information to help the prosecution exercise challenges to "shape" the jury the way it desires. An F.B.I. informer was a member of the defense team assisting with jury selection in the "Attica Brothers" trials that followed the 1971 uprising and armed assault in the state prison at Attica, New York, and apparently reported defense strategy regularly to the F.B.I. Even when such methods are not used, the government's clerks supervise jury selection and thus the government has greater control over who is called in the first place. The application of sophisticated social-science methods to jury selection may be an overreaction, casting new doubts about the jury's impartiality, but it was originally, at least, a response to government's actions in the opposite direction.

In the more common, unpublicized cases, jury selection is a less sophisticated contest but still can result in imbalances that, intentional or not, threaten the jury's impartiality. Jurors are supposed to be drawn at random from the community. When they are not, the jury may overrepresent some segments of society and underrepresent others, an imbalance that raises the specter of bias. The concept of the jury requires that neither side exert pressure on the jury, directly or indirectly. Juries today are selected in ways that go much further toward insuring fairness than did those of the past, but the issue of impartiality is very much alive.

9.5   *"... the smaller the group, the less likely it is to overcome the biases of its members. ..."*

BALLEW V. GEORGIA

435 U.S. 223, 98 S. Ct. 1029, 55 L. Ed. 2d 234 (1978)

Claude Davis Ballew, manager of the Paris Adult Theatre in Atlanta, was arrested for distributing obscene materials. As authorized by Georgia law, he was tried and convicted by a five-person jury. State appellate courts affirmed the conviction, and Ballew obtained certiorari from the United States Supreme Court. Despite *Williams v. Florida* (1970), which had upheld use of six-person juries, the Court was unanimous in its judgment to reverse the conviction. The Chief Justice assigned the task of writing the opinion of the Court to Justice Blackmun. He, however, was able to persuade only one other justice to join him; thus there was no opinion for the Court.

MR. JUSTICE BLACKMUN announced the judgment of the Court and delivered an opinion in which **MR. JUSTICE STEVENS** joins. . . .

III

When the Court in *Williams* permitted the reduction in jury size—or, to put it another way, when it held that a jury of six was not unconstitutional—it expressly reserved ruling on the issue whether a number smaller than six passed constitutional scrutiny. See *Johnson v. Louisiana* (1972) (concurring opinion). The Court refused to speculate when this so-called "slippery slope" would become too steep. We face now, however, the two-fold question whether a further reduction in the size of the state criminal trial jury does make the grade too dangerous, that is, whether it inhibits the functioning of the jury as an institution to a significant degree, and, if so, whether any state interest counterbalances and justifies the disruption so as to preserve its constitutionality.

Williams v. Florida and *Colgrove v. Battin* (1973) (where the Court held that a jury of six members did not violate the Seventh Amendment right to a jury trial in a civil case), generated a quantity of scholarly work on jury size.* These writings do not draw or identify a bright line below which the number of jurors would not be able to function as required by the standards enunciated in *Williams.* On the other hand, they raise significant questions about the wisdom and constitutionality of a reduction below six. We examine these concerns:

First, recent empirical data suggest that progressively smaller juries are less likely to foster effective group deliberation. At some point, this decline leads to inaccurate fact-finding and incorrect application of the common sense of the community to the facts. Generally, a positive correlation exists between group size and the quality of both group performance and group productivity. A variety of explanations have been offered for this conclusion. Several are partic-

---

*At this point and elsewhere in his opinion, Justice Blackmun cites and summarizes a large number of studies and research articles concerning the effect of jury size which are too extensive to be reprinted here. The reader is urged to resort to the full opinion for the complete presentation of Blackmun's position.—Eds.

ularly applicable in the jury setting. The smaller the group, the less likely are members to make critical contributions necessary for the solution of a given problem. Because most juries are not permitted to take notes, see Forston, Sense and Non-Sense: Jury Trial Communication, 1975 B.Y.U. L. Rev. 601, 631–633, memory is important for accurate jury deliberations. As juries decrease in size, then, they are less likely to have members who remember each of the important pieces of evidence or argument. Furthermore, the smaller the group, the less likely it is to overcome the biases of its members to obtain an accurate result. When individual and group decisionmaking were compared, it was seen that groups performed better because prejudices of individuals were frequently counterbalanced, and objectivity resulted. Groups also exhibited increased motivation and self-criticism. All these advantages, except, perhaps, self-motivation, tend to diminish as the size of the group diminishes. Because juries frequently face complex problems laden with value choices, the benefits are important and should be retained. In particular, the counterbalancing of various biases is critical to the accurate application of the common sense of the community to the facts of any given case.

Second, the data now raise doubts about the accuracy of the results achieved by smaller and smaller panels. Statistical studies suggest that the risk of convicting an innocent person (Type I error) rises as the size of the jury diminishes. Because the risk of not convicting a guilty person (Type II error) increases with the size of the panel, an optimal jury size can be selected as a function of the interaction between the two risks. Nagel and Neef concluded that the optimal size, for the purpose of minimizing errors, should vary with the importance attached to the two types of mistakes. After weighting Type I error as 10 times more significant than Type II, perhaps not an unreasonable assumption, they concluded that the optimal jury size was between six and eight. As the size diminished to five and below, the weighted sum of errors increased because of the enlarging risk of the conviction of innocent defendants.

Another doubt about progressively smaller juries arises from the increasing inconsistency that results from the decreases. Saks argued that the "more a jury type fosters consistency, the greater will be the proportion of juries which select the correct (i. e., the same) verdict and the fewer 'errors' will be made." Saks 86–87. From his mock trials held before undergraduates and former jurors, he computed the percentage of "correct" decisions rendered by 12-person and 6-person panels. In the student experiment, 12-person groups reached correct verdicts 83% of the time; 6-person panels reached correct verdicts 69% of the time. The results for the former-juror study were 71% for the 12-person groups and 57% for the 6-person groups. *Ibid.* Working with statistics described in H. Kalven & H.

Zeisel, The American Jury 460 (1966), Nagel & Neef tested the average conviction propensity of juries, that is, the likelihood that any given jury of a set would convict the defendant. They found that half of all 12-person juries would have average conviction propensities that varied by no more than 20 points. Half of all 6-person juries, on the other hand, had average conviction propensities varying by 30 points, a difference they found significant in both real and percentage terms. Lempert reached similar results when he considered the likelihood of juries to compromise over the various views of their members, an important phenomenon for the fulfillment of the common-sense function. In civil trials averaging occurs with respect to damages amounts. In criminal trials it relates to numbers of counts and lesser included offenses. And he predicted that compromises would be more consistent when larger juries were employed. For example, 12-person juries could be expected to reach extreme compromises in 4% of the cases, while 6-person panels would reach extreme results in 16%. All three of these post-*Williams* studies, therefore, raise significant doubts about the consistency and reliability of the decisions of smaller juries.

Third, the data suggest that the verdicts of jury deliberation in criminal cases will vary as juries become smaller, and that the variance amounts to an imbalance to the detriment of one side, the defense. Both Lempert and Zeisel found that the number of hung juries would diminish as the panels decreased in size. Zeisel said that the number would be cut in half—from 5% to 2.4% with a decrease from 12 to 6 members. Both studies emphasized that juries in criminal cases generally hang with only one, or more likely two, jurors remaining unconvinced of guilt. Also, group theory suggests that a person in the minority will adhere to his position more frequently when he has at least one other person supporting his argument. In the jury setting the significance of this tendency is demonstrated by the following figures: If a minority viewpoint is shared by 10% of the community, 28.2% of 12-member juries may be expected to have no minority representation, but 53.1% of 6-member juries would have none. Thirty-four percent of 12-member panels could be expected to have two minority members, while only 11% of six-member panels would have two. As the numbers diminish below six, even fewer panels would have one member with the minority viewpoint and still fewer would have two. The chance for hung juries would decline accordingly.

Fourth, what has just been said about the presence of minority viewpoint as juries decrease in size foretells problems not only for jury decisionmaking, but also for the representation of minority groups in the community. The Court repeatedly has held that meaningful community participation cannot be attained with the exclusion of minorities or other identifiable groups from jury service. . . . The exclusion of elements of the community from participation "contravenes the very idea of a jury . . . composed of 'the peers or equals of the person whose rights it is selected or summoned to determine.'" *Carter v. Jury Comm'n* (1970), quoting *Strauder v. West Virginia* (1880). Although the Court in *Williams* concluded that the six-person jury did not fail to represent adequately a cross-section of the community, the opportunity for meaningful and appropriate representation does decrease with the size of the panels. Thus, if a minority group constitutes 10% of the community, 53.1% of randomly selected six-member juries could be expected to have no minority representative among their members, and 89% not to have two. Further reduction in size will erect additional barriers to representation. . . .

IV

While we adhere to, and reaffirm our holding in *Williams v. Florida*, these studies, most of which have been made since *Williams* was decided in 1970, lead us to conclude that the purpose and functioning of the jury in a criminal trial is seriously impaired, and to a constitutional degree, by a reduction in size to below six members. We readily admit that we do not pretend to discern a clear line between six members and five. But the assembled data raise substantial doubt about the reliability and appropriate representation of panels smaller than six. Because of the fundamental importance of the jury trial to the American system of criminal justice, any further reduction that promotes inaccurate and possibly biased decisionmaking, that causes untoward differences in verdicts, and that prevents juries from truly representing their communities, attains constitutional significance.

Georgia here presents no persuasive argument that a reduction to five does not offend important Sixth Amendment interests. . . .

VI

The judgment of the Court of Appeals [of Georgia] is reversed, and the case is remanded for further proceedings not inconsistent with this opinion.

It is so ordered.

MR. JUSTICE STEVENS, concurring. . . .

MR. JUSTICE WHITE, concurring in the judgment.

Agreeing that a jury of fewer than six persons would fail to represent the sense of the community and hence not satisfy the fair cross-section requirement of the Sixth and Fourteenth Amendments, I concur in the judgment of reversal.

MR. JUSTICE POWELL, with whom The CHIEF JUSTICE and MR. JUSTICE REHNQUIST join, concurring in the judgment.

I concur in the judgment, as I agree that use of a jury as small as five members, with authority to convict for serious offenses, involves grave questions of fairness. As the opinion of Mr. Justice Blackmun indicates, the line between five- and six-member juries is difficult to justify, but a line has to be drawn somewhere if the substance of jury trial is to be preserved.

I do not agree, however, that every feature of jury trial practice must be the same in both federal and state courts. *Apodaca v. Oregon* (1972) (Powell, J., concurring). Because the opinion of Mr. Justice Blackmun today assumes full incorporation of the Sixth Amendment by the Fourteenth Amendment contrary to my view in *Apodaca,* I do not join it. Also, I have reservations as to the wisdom —as well as the necessity—of Mr. Justice Blackmun's heavy reliance on numerology derived from statistical studies. Moreover, neither the validity nor the methodology employed by the studies cited was subjected to the traditional testing mechanisms of the adversary process [of Georgia]. The studies relied on merely represent unexamined findings of persons interested in the jury system.

For these reasons I concur only in the judgment.

MR. JUSTICE BRENNAN, with whom MR. JUSTICE STEWART and MR. JUSTICE MARSHALL join.

I join Mr. Justice Blackmun's opinion insofar as it holds that the Sixth and Fourteenth Amendments require juries in criminal trials to contain more than five persons. . . .

JUSTICE BLACKMUN rebuts:
[In a footnote to his opinion Justice Blackmun responded to Justice Powell's "reservations as to the wisdom—as well as the necessity—of Mr. Justice Blackmun's heavy reliance on numerology. . . ."]

We have considered [these statistical studies] carefully because they provide the only basis, besides judicial hunch, for a decision about whether smaller and smaller juries will be able to fulfill the purpose and functions of the Sixth Amendment. Without an examination about how juries and small groups actually work, we would not understand the basis for the conclusion of Mr. Justice Powell that "a line has to be drawn somewhere." We also note that the Chief Justice did not shrink from the use of empirical data in *Williams v. Florida* (1970), when the data were used to support the constitutionality of the six-person criminal jury, or in *Colgrove v. Battin* (1973), a decision also joined by Mr. Justice Rehnquist.

9.6 *". . . the technique raises serious doubts about the very integrity of the jury system. . . ."*

SCIENCE: THREATENING THE JURY TRIAL

Amitai Etzioni

Man has taken a new bite from the apple of knowledge, and it is doubtful whether we will all be better for it. This time it is not religion or the family that are being disturbed by the new knowledge but that venerable institution of being judged by a jury of one's peers. The jury's impartiality is threatened because defense attorneys have discovered that by using social science techniques, they can manipulate the composition of juries to significantly increase the likelihood that their clients will be acquitted.

The problem is not that one may disagree with a particular jury verdict that has resulted in such cases; enough different defendants have been freed with the help of social science jury-stacking to disturb observers on all sides. The trouble is that the technique raises serious doubts about the very integrity of the jury system, that it increases the advantage of rich and prominent defendants over poor and obscure ones and, most ominously, that it may prompt the state to start hiring social scientists of its own. It would seem only a matter of time before prosecutors, with all the resources at their disposal, get fed up with losing cases partly because the defense has scientifically loaded panels with sympathetic jurors.

Prosecutors have already had to swallow a number of such defeats. A team headed by sociologist Jay Schulman and psychologist Richard Christie, for example, took an active role in selecting juries which discharged radical defendants in the Harrisburg Seven case, the Camden 28 trial over a draft-office raid, and the Gainesville Eight case involving Vietnam Veterans Against the War; Schulman is now working in Buffalo, N.Y., for the Attica defendants. A team of black psychologists, moreover, helped choose the jury that acquitted Angela Davis, and nothing of late has done more to publicize scientific intervention in jury selection than the Mitchell-Stans trial in New York.*

In that case, helping to choose the jury was Marty Herbst, a "communication" specialist versed in social science techniques. He

The Washington Post, May 20, 1974. Reprinted with permission. © The Washington Post. Amitai Etzioni is Director of the Center for Policy Research, Washington, D.C.

*The trial of former Attorney General John Mitchell and Maurice Stans, one of Richard Nixon's chief fundraisers, for offenses growing out of the Watergate scandals. The jury acquitted both men, although Mitchell was later convicted after another trial on different charges.—Eds.

advised the defense to seek a jury of working-class persons, of Catholic background, neither poor nor rich ("average income of $8,000 to $10,000"), and readers of New York's *Daily News.* To be avoided were the college-educated, Jews, and readers of the *New York Post* and *The New York Times.* These sociological characteristics are widely associated with conservative politics, respect for authority, and suspicion of the media.

In the original jury, the defense succeeded in getting 11 out of 12 jurors who matched the specifications. By a fluke, the 12th juror became ill and was replaced by another who, though college-educated, was a conservative banker, thus completing the set.

INTERVIEWING ACQUAINTANCES

The more elaborate ways in which social science can help select acquittal-prone juries are illustrated by the Schulman-Christie team's work in the trial of Indian militants at Wounded Knee.

As described in a May, 1973 report, the team first assembled a sociological profile of the community through interviews with 576 persons chosen at random from voter registration lists. The interviews allowed the research team to crosstabulate such characteristics as occupation and education with attitudes favorable toward the defense—especially toward Indians—and to select out the best "predictor variables." Such analysis was needed because people of the same social background hold different attitudes in different parts of the country; hence a generalized sociological model would not suffice. (In Harrisburg, where the Berrigan trial was held, for example, women proved more friendly toward the defense than men, but the reverse was true in Gainesville.)

Next, observers were placed in the courtroom to "psych out" prospective jurors, using anything from the extent to which they talked with other prospective jurors to their mode of dress. (In the Angela Davis case, handwriting experts analyzed the signatures of prospective jurors.)

Information gained in this way was compared to what the computer predicted about the same "type" of person, based on the interview data which had been fed into it. This double reading was further checked, especially when the two sources of information did not concur, by field investigators who interviewed acquaintances of the prospective jurors.

HOW MANY CHALLENGES?

Such information becomes more potent in the hands of defense lawyers the more challenges there are and the more unevenly the challenges are distributed. The number is important because the more persons one can challenge, the more one can select a jury to one's liking. The unevenness is important to prevent the other side from applying the same procedures and nullifying one's work.

The number of challenges varies with the seriousness of the offense and from state to state. A common pattern is that if the prospective penalty is death, each side receives 30 challenges, plus 3 for each of four alternate jurors. If 10 years' imprisonment is at stake, the respective numbers are 20 and 2, and so on down the scale. The original intention was to allow the fairest selections in the weightiest cases. But with the introduction of social science into jury picking, the unwitting result is that the more serious the trial, the more jury-stacking is allowed.

Similarly, uneven challenges are introduced, at the judge's discretion, to make up for other imbalances. While a judge can severely limit the challenges on both sides to avoid a long jury selection process, this significantly increases the chances of having any convictions that might result overturned by a higher court on the ground of a biased jury—and reversals are considered a blot on a judge's record. In the Mitchell-Stans case, the judge allowed the defense 20 peremptory challenges, the prosecution 8, to make up for adverse publicity preceding the trial. This obviously helped the defense lawyers secure the kind of jury they favored.

Social scientists, of course, did not invent the idea of using challenges to help get a favorable jury. But until recently lawyers commonly could not use much more than rules of thumb, hunches, or experience to guide their challenges. As Justice John M. Murtagh put it: "One human being cannot read the mind of another." The lawyers on both sides, moreover, were more or less equal in their ability to exercise this kind of homespun social psychology.

The new methods are quite a bit more accurate, though fortunately they are far from foolproof. People do not always act out their predispositions. Social science data is statistical, not absolute. At best survey techniques, even when supplemented with psychological analysis, can produce only "probabilistic" profiles, not guaranteed results. At the Berrigan trial, two of the defense attorneys' careful selections—one a woman with four conscientious objector sons— held out for a guilty verdict on the conspiracy charge, causing a hung jury.

Nevertheless, the recent spate of acquittals demonstrates that the impact can be considerable and that, on the average, the method will work well. Hence we are surely in for more frequent use of the technique.

IT TAKES MONEY

It might be said that soon both sides to all trials will be equipped with the same capability, and that so long as the granting of an uneven number of challenges is curbed, giving both sides similar selection power, the edge of the social science helpers will be dulled. But the extent to which this takes place will be limited by the costliness of the technique.

Radical defendants have benefited from the free labor of scores of volunteers and the time donations of high-powered consultants, though even they needed expensive computers. As Howard Moore, Jr., Angela Davis's chief counsel, put it: "We can send men to the moon, but not everyone can afford to go. Every unpopular person who becomes a defendant will not have the resources we used in the Davis case." The Mitchell and Stans bills for their social science helpers may run to a five-digit figure.

Clearly, the average defendant cannot avail himself of such aid. Therefore, the net effect of the new technique, as is so often the case with new technology, will be to give a leg up to the wealthy or those who command a dedicated following. This is hardly what the founders of the American judicial system had in mind.

It might also be argued that juries are, on the average, far from representative anyhow; studies do show that too many higher-income, higher-educated people do not serve, that juries end up disproportionately filled with "housewives, clerical workers, craftsmen, and retired persons." Furthermore, the legal defense of those who can pay or otherwise attract top talent has always been much better than that of the average defendant. But a society moving toward greater justice would seek to correct these flaws, not to accentuate them.

Also, it should be noted that up to now the procedure has been used, as far as we know, solely by defense attorneys. The state has not provided any district attorneys with social science teams and computers. However, what would happen if the state did resort to systematic reliance on such techniques? Could any but the wealthiest defendants then compete with the state?

NO GOOD REMEDIES

Unfortunately, one cannot unbite the apple of knowledge. Even sadder is that we see here, as we have seen so often before, that attempting to contain the side-effects of the application of science is costly, at best partially effective, and far from uncontroversial itself. To put it more succinctly, there seem to be no half-good, let alone good, remedies.

Probably the best place to start is with prospective jurors. If fewer persons were excused from jury duty, the universe from which jurors are drawn would be more representative of the community and, to a degree, less easy to manipulate. Next, serious consideration could be given to reducing challenges, especially peremptory ones. This approach, though, constitutes not only a wide departure from tradition, but limits the possibility of uncovering prejudicial attitudes in would-be jurors.

More powerful but even more problematic is to extend the ban on tampering with the jury to all out-of-court investigations of prospective jurors. It could be defined as a serious violation of law to collect data about prospective jurors, to investigate their handwriting, to interview their neighbors and the like, and any discovery of such data-gathering could be grounds for a mistrial. This would not eliminate the lawyers' courtroom use of sociology and psychology or the usefulness of community profiles based on studies of citizens at large. But it could curb the more sophisticated application of those techniques which require homing in on the characteristics of particular jurors.

Another potent but controversial answer is for the judge alone to be allowed to question and remove prospective jurors. In this way the judge could seek both an open-minded jury and one which represents a cross-section of the community, not sociologically loaded dice. To the extent that judges themselves are free of social bias, this would probably work quite well. However, since jury selection has some effect on the outcome of each case, such a relatively active role by the judge flies in the face of the prevalent Anglo-Saxon tradition, according to which the judge is a neutral referee between the sides, not a third party. The challenges, though, could become the task of a specialist attached to the courts.

The most radical remedy would be to follow Britain's lead and restrict the conditions under which citizens are entitled to a jury trial. (In Britain only 2 to 3 per cent of the cases still go to a jury.) Moreover, the jury is considered by many to be a major cause of rising court costs and delays in cases coming to trial. Nor is there any compelling evidence that trial by jury is fairer than trial by judges. These are hardly the days, though, in which reforms entailing less participation by the people and greater concentration of power in the hands of the elected or appointed officials are likely to be either very popular or wise.

But until one remedy or another is applied, the state will almost surely have to do its own research, if only to even the odds. District attorneys or U.S. attorneys cannot be expected to stand by doing nothing while defendants in the most serious cases buy themselves a significant edge in trial after trial. The champions of the technique will have to realize that the days when it could be reserved for their favorite defendants will soon be over.

9.7
"How could ethicists, moralists, or religionists be getting into the courtroom?"

MORAL EXPERTS IN COURT?

Richard Delgado

Arguments concerning right and wrong, good and bad policy, and wise and unwise decisions, have long been regarded as acceptable in courts, at least in certain types of cases. But until recently such arguments were presented by non-experts, that is, by attorneys, rather than by someone purporting to be an expert. They have also been presented by *amici curiae,* friends of the court, who present briefs to call to the court's attention a particular principle or aspect of the case that they feel has not been given adequate attention by the litigants themselves.

There has been in recent years an applied ethics boom in the fields of law and medicine. Professional ethicists and philosophers have been testifying in hearings before national commissions, committees and subcommittees of Congress, and institutional review committees. There has also been a rapid increase in the number of courses in applied ethics in schools of business, journalism, medicine, and law, and in departments of social welfare, religion, and philosophy.

About two years ago, I discovered that in addition to teaching their classes and appearing as official advice-givers, persons with a claim of moral expertise were also appearing in court as expert witnesses. They were offering testimony for the benefit of judge or jury on matters having to do with right and wrong, good and evil, moral judgment, social policy, whether one rule of law was preferable to another rule of law, and the like. This seemed to me extraordinary. After all, courtroom trials—unlike legislative hearings, or meetings of a human subjects review committee, or meetings of the National Commission for the Protection of Human Subjects, which have relatively open formats—are rigidly controlled by detailed rules of evidence and rules of court. How could ethicists, moralists, or religionists be getting into the courtroom? And what were they saying once they were there?

The case that first piqued my interest was *Hart v. Brown,* a kidney transplant case that appears in Michael Shapiro's and Roy Spece, Jr.'s casebook on bioethics and law, a case decided by a Connecticut

The Center Magazine (Santa Barbara, Calif.: Center for the Study of Democratic Institutions, March/April 1984), p. 48. Reprinted with permission. Adapted from Peter G. McAllen and Richard Delgado, "The Moralist as Expert Witness," 62 *Boston University Law Review* 869 (1982). Richard Delgado is Professor of Law, the Law School, University of California, Los Angeles.

superior court in 1972. In *Hart,* the parents of two seven-year-old twins sued for a judicial order authorizing a kidney transplant between the children after local physicians refused to perform the operation without such an order. Apparently no case law within the State of Connecticut approved a nontherapeutic operation, one that would not medically benefit the donor twin. Neither did any case law disapprove such an operation. It was silent. The parents, of course, were willing to give proxy consent for the seven-year-old potential donor; but the court questioned the propriety of letting them make that decision.

In this quandary, the trial judge agreed to hear testimony on whether authorization of the transplant was "morally and ethically sound." One of the experts who testified was a clergyman. He said that the parents' choice was in accord with ethics and morality and that the operation would therefore be justified. The court thus permitted the parents to make the decision, and the operation was performed. The clergyman appears to have testified not as an ordinary witness, but as an expert.

Expert testimony is a form of exception to the usual evidentiary rules in court trials that require that a witness testify from personal knowledge, usually from what he or she heard or saw. An expert may give an opinion—something an ordinary witness may not do—and many also answer hypothetical questions put to him by the judge or attorneys.

Wondering how many other cases there were like *Hart v. Brown,* I went to Lexis—a computer resource that contains most of the recent American court decisions, numbering in the tens of thousands of cases. I came up with about thirty cases, most of them decided in the last five or ten years.

Those who testified fell into certain groups: philosophers, clergy, professors of religion, bioethicists at think tanks and institutes. The range of questions on which they testified was broad. One of the questions was whether a draft registrant's opposition to war was or was not religious and therefore whether conscientious-objector status was warranted. Another was whether a Presbyterian could be a pacifist. Another was whether books or movies that were charged with being obscene did or did not violate community values and morals.

One question was whether transcendental meditation is or is not a religion, the answer determining whether or not it could be taught in public schools without violating the First Amendment doctrine on separation of church and state. Another question concerned whether Hindus or Muslims may eat certain kinds of food, such questions being relevant in prison law cases involving religious dietary restrictions of certain inmates. There was also the case of whether a dying patient's refusal of medical treatment was in accord with Scripture. Another case concerned whether certain religious observances in public schools would be offensive to Jewish students. Still another turned on whether a certain religious group required swimming pools and tennis courts as part of its religious practice.

Some of the cases, like *Hart,* and the Karen Ann Quinlan case (the latter involving maintaining life support for a comatose patient), are agonizing. One sympathizes with the court's dilemma.

Others have a lighter side. *Friedman v. New York* arose when a sixteen-year-old girl and her male companion were stranded in mid-air in a mountain-side chair lift which had closed down for the day without prior warning. Unable to attract attention, they faced the prospect of a chilling night in the mountain air. Rather than stay the night there, the young woman leaped from the lift and fell to the ground, sustaining facial injuries.

She sued the lift operators, who defended themselves by asserting contributory negligence on her part. They claimed that she had not behaved as a reasonable prudent person under the circumstances should have behaved; that is, she had not waited out the night in the lift and got down safely the next morning. To rebut the charge of contributory negligence, the woman introduced a rabbi, who testified that under the circumstances the girl's reaction had been dictated by and conformed to her religious principles, which forbade her from spending the night alone with a man not her husband in an area inaccessible to others. Based in part on this testimony, the court rejected the defense of contributory negligence, and awarded the young woman damages against the ski lift operators.

9.8   *"By George, extraordinary!"*

HOW THE JUSTICES JUDGE DIRTY MOVIES

Nina Totenberg

In cases where publishers, producers, or distributors have been prosecuted for trafficking in obscenity and/or pornography, the Supreme Court has available to it not only the usual briefs and records of the proceedings below, but also the alleged obscene book or movie itself. Thus, if they wish to do so, the justices may on the basis of their own reading or viewing conclude whether the material is in fact obscene, quite independent of findings of fact and law by lower courts.

Whenever the Supreme Court has to decide an obscenity case involving a movie, a showing room is set up in the basement of the

The Washingtonian Magazine, January 1974, p. 42. Reprinted by permission. Nina Totenberg is Legal Affairs Correspondent, National Public Radio.

Court. Considering the limited audience the film caters to, attendance is phenomenal. Justice Douglas never goes because he considers all expression—obscene or not—to be protected by the First Amendment guarantees of free speech. So there is no reason for him to go. Chief Justice Burger is said not to go because he is offended by the stuff. But everyone else shows up.

Justice Blackmun watches in what is described as a "near catatonic state." Justice Marshall usually laughs his way through it all, slapping his knee and wisecracking. Justice White sits rigidly, rocking back and forth in a straight-backed chair; on leaving he has been known to mutter about "filth." Justice Powell, the aristocratic Virginian, was appalled by the first film he saw, *Without A Stitch*, which by today's standards is quite benign. Justice Brennan has gotten used to porn. The late Justice John Harlan used to dutifully attend all the Court's porno flicks—even though he was almost totally blind. Justice Stewart would sit next to Harlan and narrate: "Now she's grabbing . . . now he is taking her . . . now she's . . . now he's. . . ." And about once every five minutes Harlan would exclaim in his proper way: "By George, extraordinary!"

10
Precedents and Legal Reasoning

Not only must a court determine the facts of a case, it must also decide what rules of law control the kind of dispute before it and how to apply those rules. A trial judge may share with a jury responsibility for finding facts, but the judge alone is supposed to determine the law. On occasion, of course, a group of jurors may choose to ignore what the judge tells them is the law, but formal responsibility for selecting appropriate legal rules, interpreting those rules, and even sometimes creating them rests on the judge alone, a burden made abundantly clear by the fact that appellate courts do not use juries at all.

It is customary to say that there are three sources for the law applied by American judges: constitutions (federal and state), statutes (federal and state), and common law. In the sense used here, common law refers to that part of the law of England, the United States, and other English-speaking countries that is found in judicial decisions and in textbooks discussing these decisions, as distinguished from the law enacted by legislatures or constitutional conventions. The common law, as explained in Chapter 1, began in English custom and tradition as interpreted by judges, in contrast to the Civil Law of the Continent, which is based on an all-encompassing code enacted by legislators and expounded by scholars more than by judges.

Here we are not concerned with the substantive rules of the common law, but in the techniques by which judges develop and apply that body of law. The common law's model of decision making is inductive, a process by which judges draw general principles from decisions in particular controversies. Once stated, these principles become controlling *precedents* that judges apply as law in future controversies raising the same sorts of questions. But applying the rule of precedents, or stare decisis, is no automatic process. It involves skill and art—and sometimes an almost occult art. Each new controversy requires a reexamination of precedents in light of the immediate case as well as any

new social conditions. In courts where the common law tradition prevails, judges have a unique responsibility for providing elements of
both stability and change in the law. By force of their commissions
rather than by reason of their competence, as Robert H. Jackson once
noted, they operate as social engineers.

REASONING BY EXAMPLE

The basic technique employed by common law judges to determine
the law is reasoning by example. (Reading 10.1.) Whether the source
of the law applied is statute, constitution, or common law does matter,
and consequently the two following chapters are devoted to the special problems of statutory construction and constitutional interpretation. But the fundamental character of the judicial task is similar in
each instance: a comparison of facts and decisions in related controversies.

Let us take a situation that presents the common law's techniques
of legal reasoning in clearest form. A controversy comes before a
judge in which facts A, B, C, and D are present. The judge searches
earlier cases for similar situations. If he or she finds another case in
which facts A, B, C, and D were present, then that case is a precedent,
and the judge will feel a strong—though not necessarily absolutely
binding—obligation to decide the present case the same way as the
earlier case. When a substantial number of cases involving similar
facts have been decided the same way, judges will say that a rule of
law exists. A general rule has grown from a series of particular instances. Over a period of decades or centuries rules of law covering
a great variety of factual situations develop in this fashion. Periodically, legislatures enact or revise some of these rules of law by adopting them in statutes.

But new controversies constantly question and test these rules. The
facts in a current case never exactly duplicate the facts of an earlier
case. Thus there is constant opportunity to contend that a rule of law
previously applied to an apparently similar case is not really applicable to a current dispute. Counsel may argue, for example, that the facts
in the earlier case were A, B, C, and D, whereas here they are A, B,
C, and E. Judges must then decide whether the similarities are so close
that they should apply the same rule. If so, they must reformulate the
rule to cover situations where the facts are A-B-C-E as well as A-B-C-D.
Alternatively, judges may decide that replacement of D by E so
changes the situation that they must apply a different rule; in that event,
they may merely modify the older rule or create a new one.

Justice Cardozo ridiculed the notion that adherence to precedent
is simply a matter of a judge's "match[ing] the colors of the case at hand
against the colors of many sample cases spread out upon the desk. The
sample nearest in shade supplied the applicable rule." If matching

were all there were to judging, he said, then the judge with the best card index of cases would be the wisest jurist. "It is when the colors do not match, when the references in the index fail, when there is no decisive precedent, that the serious business of the judge begins. He must then fashion law for the litigants before him. In fashioning it for them, he will be fashioning it for others." (Reading 1.5.)

Counsel for the litigants urge on the judges precedents that, they insist, fit the present controversy. Lawyers try to explain away as inapplicable precedents that apparently conflict with the result they are being paid to secure. Counsel as well as judge must thus engage in a complicated process of comparing decisions in a search for similarities that are significant enough to guide judicial wisdom. (Readings 10.2 and 10.3.)

What transpires in a court of common law, then, is not only a controversy about facts. The court is also a forum in which attorneys argue the relevance of previous decisions to current questions and the applicability of rules of law embodied in those earlier decisions. But because rules of law are basically ways of explaining and justifying decisions, the emphasis is typically less on concepts and more on demonstrating how the facts of the present case are similar to or different from those of previous controversies.

THE PRINCIPLE OF THE CASE

To decide whether a previous decision qualifies as a precedent, judges and commentators often say, one must strip away the nonessentials of a case and expose the basic reasons for the court's decision. This process is generally referred to as "establishing the principle of the case," or the *ratio decidendi*. Many jurists have tried to explain how this task can be accurately performed, but no set of rules is very satisfactory. Judges are often imprecise in their language; furthermore, as they learn from experience they or their successors may change their minds about what an earlier case stands for. (Reading 10.4.) With the understanding that judicial principles are elusive targets, we can look at the five rules suggested by Arthur L. Goodhart, which are as useful as any.[1] His first two rules explain how the principle of the case is *not* to be found:

1. The principle of a case is not found in the reasons given in the opinion.
2. The principle is not found in the rule of law set forth in the opinion.

These first two rules suggest that it is not enough to know what the judge said. What is missing in these first two situations is any relation-

[1] "Determining the Ratio Decidendi of a Case," 40 *Yale Law Journal* 161 (1930).

ship between the *facts* of the case and the decision. The principle of a case cannot be established without knowing the facts of that case.

But Goodhart's third rule indicates that there is even more to the problem:

3. The principle is not necessarily found by a consideration of all the ascertainable facts of the case and the judge's decision.

This rule emphasizes that not all of the facts of a case were relevant to establishing the principle of the decision. One must have a standard to determine which facts were relevant. So Goodhart's fourth rule provides:

4. The principle of the case is found by taking account (a) of the facts treated by the judge as material, and (b) his decision as based on them.

Here we finally have a rule on what to look for in the search for the *ratio decidendi.* But Goodhart gives one final guide to relevance.

5. In finding the principle it is also necessary to establish what facts were held to be immaterial by the judge, for the principle may depend as much on exclusion as it does on inclusion.

DICTA

Rule 4, as the basic positive guide, deserves further elaboration. In stressing the relationship between the judge's decision and the facts that he or she treated as material, Goodhart merely reformulated what is generally referred to as the rule of dicta in judicial opinions. A dictum (or obiter dictum; plural: obiter dicta) is any expression in an opinion that is unnecessary to the decision reached in the case or that relates to a factual situation other than the one actually before the court. The task of the judge is to decide the immediate case. Any comments not an integral part of the reasoning necessary to decide that case are, consequently, surplus verbiage and, while sometimes useful, are not authoritative in discovering the principle of that case. A judicial opinion supposedly has value as a precedent only insofar as it is squarely based on the facts of the controversy being adjudicated. As Chief Justice John Marshall explained in *Cohens v. Virginia* (1821):

It is a maxim not to be disregarded, that general expressions in every opinion, are to be taken in connection with the case in which those expressions are used. If they go beyond the case, they may be respected, but ought not to control the judgment in a subsequent suit. . . . The reason of this maxim is obvious. The question actually before the Court is investigated with care, and considered in its full extent. Other principles which may serve to illustrate it, are considered in their relation to the case decided, but their possible bearing on all other cases is seldom completely investigated.

Chief Justice William Howard Taft's opinion in *Myers v. United States* (1926) provides a classic example of dictum. There the Court was dealing with a statute that forbade the President to remove a postmaster from office without the consent of the Senate. For the Court, Taft held that this legislation unconstitutionally restricted the President's authority to direct the executive branch of government. But Taft did not confine his opinion to the office of postmaster. Instead, he declared that the constitutional principles behind the Court's decision applied to all presidential appointees, including heads of federal regulatory commissions.

In 1935 the Supreme Court faced a controversy involving presidential removal of precisely such an official, a member of the Federal Trade Commission. In *Humphrey's Executor v. United States* the Court declared that Taft's broader statement was not controlling in the case of an officer with quasi-legislative and quasi-judicial functions. Justice Sutherland wrote:

The office of a postmaster is so essentially unlike the office now involved that the decision in the *Myers* case cannot be accepted as controlling our decision here. A postmaster is an executive officer restricted to the performance of executive functions. He is charged with no duty at all related to either the legislative or judicial power. The actual decision in the *Myers* case finds support in the theory that such an officer is merely one of the units in the executive department and hence inherently subject to the exclusive and illimitable power of removal by the chief executive, whose subordinate and aide he is. Putting aside dicta, which may be followed if sufficiently persuasive but which are not controlling, the necessary reach of the decision goes far enough to include all purely executive officers. It goes no further. . . .

Alas, the matter of dicta is often not so simply settled. Judges, we have noted, may change their minds or wish to change the rules contained in earlier decisions. When they carry out these wishes, they may find justification for their new directions in the dicta of previous opinions. In time, frequent reliance on logically extraneous words may change the meaning of an earlier case from what its author intended to what its users prefer.

Two shockingly illiberal decisions from World War II provide a pair of illustrations. In *Hirabayashi v. United States* (1943) and *Korematsu v. United States* (1944) the Court sustained, first, the constitutionality of a curfew directed at all persons of Japanese descent living on the West Coast, then upheld a program that forced all such people, including native-born American citizens, to leave their homes and be imprisoned in concentration camps. In justifying the first decision, Chief Justice Harlan Fiske Stone conceded that "distinctions between citizens solely because of their ancestry are by their very nature odious to a free people whose institutions are founded upon the doctrine of equality." But, Stone added: "Because racial discriminations are in most circumstances irrelevant and therefore prohibited, it by no means follows that, in dealing with the perils of war, Congress and the Executive are wholly precluded from taking into account those facts. . . ." Thus the Court found it reasonable for the government in fighting a war against Japan to restrict the movement of people whose ancestors had been born in Japan.

Writing for the Court in *Korematsu,* Justice Hugo Black threw a similar sop to the Bill of Rights, noting that "all legal restrictions which curtail the civil rights of a single racial group are immediately suspect." Then Black, as had Stone, went on to find that the "pressing public necessity" of war could justify imprisonment of citizens of a particular race, even though they had neither been accused nor convicted of any crime.

Because no case has ever again arisen involving such hysteria, the Court has never had a full opportunity to repent its sins. But the justices soon found an indirect way. They have ripped out of context Stone's and Black's dicta about racial equality and cited these sentences as authorities for invalidating a state statute restricting the right of Japanese aliens to own land, for sustaining a state statute forbidding segregated seating in public or private transportation, for forbidding a state court from enforcing an agreement between private citizens not to sell property to blacks, for striking down state efforts to keep ethnic minorities off juries, and for outlawing segregation in public schools.[2] In 1943 or 1944, no one in his right mind, least of all a judge, could have dreamed that *Hirabayashi* and *Korematsu* stood for libertarian principles.

Further complicating analysis, judges may deliberately plant dicta in their opinions, hoping that they themselves or those who come after them will cite these words as authority for changing the law. Although he did not so intend in *Hirabayashi,* Stone was a master of this technique. To gain a majority of votes he would often write an opinion with a very narrow holding, but in the body or footnotes of that opinion he would strew an occasional sentence that he could later pluck out as evidence that the Court had really intended a much broader ruling. As a former law clerk reported, Stone was "like a squirrel storing nuts

---

[2] See Walter F. Murphy, "Civil Liberties and the Japanese American Cases: A Study in the Uses of Stare Decisis," 11 *Western Political Quarterly* 3 (1958).

to be pulled out at some later time. And there was mischief as well as godliness in his delight when his ruse was undetected and the chestnuts safely stored away."[3]

DISTINGUISHING A PRECEDENT

A second method for avoiding application of an earlier ruling that is apparently a precedent for the case at hand is to distinguish it. This process involves demonstrating that the principle of the earlier case is, when properly understood, inapplicable to the present problem. Because the facts of two cases are never identical, it is always possible to find grounds for refusing to follow the earlier decision, although sometimes the reasons offered strain credulity.

Examples are numerous. In *Oyama v. California* (1948) the Supreme Court "assumed" the constitutionality of a California statute forbidding aliens ineligible for American citizenship (that is, Japanese) to acquire agricultural land, though managing to render the act unenforceable on other grounds. Five months later in *Takahashi v. Commission* the Court considered the constitutionality of a similar California law banning alien Japanese from commercial fishing. Justice Stanley Reed thought that "the right to fish is analogous to the right to own land," but Justice Black for the majority managed to distinguish the two statutes. *Oyama* and the cases on which it relied "could not in any event be controlling here. They rested solely upon the power of states to control the devolution and ownership of land within their borders, a power long exercised and supported on reasons peculiar to real property." In other words, land is different from water.

In 1937 Chief Justice Charles Evans Hughes made even less effort to explain how he reconciled *Schechter v. United States* (1935) and *Carter v. Carter Coal Co.* (1936), both denying the federal government's power to regulate labor relations, with *National Labor Relations Board v. Jones & Laughlin Steel Corp.* (1937), upholding the constitutionality of the federal government's authority to regulate labor relations. He merely wrote:

> The question remains as to the effect upon interstate commerce of the labor practice involved. In the *A.L.A. Schechter Poultry Corp.* case, we found that the effect there was so remote as to be beyond the federal power. To find "immediacy or directness" there was to find it "almost everywhere," a result inconsistent with the maintenance of our federal system. In the *Carter* case, the Court was of the opinion that the provisions of the statute relating to production

[3] Memorandum by Herbert Wechsler, Law Clerk File, The Stone Papers, the Library of Congress.

were invalid upon several grounds. . . . These cases are not controlling here.

In trials involving racial minorities, counsel might look for racial prejudice in examining potential jurors. *Ham v. South Carolina* (1973) was such a case, and it appeared to Justice White that the Court's decision laid down a per se rule requiring judges in every such case to ask specific questions on voir dire about racial attitudes. But three years later in *Ristaino v. Ross* the Court held that *Ham* had been decided on the particular facts of that dispute and that it had not announced any general constitutional rule. (Reading 10.5.)

LIMITING A PRECEDENT

Distinguishing a precedent presumably leaves it with full validity for the circumstances to which it originally applied; a judge simply finds it inapplicable to the current controversy. But occasionally reconsideration of a precedent may convince a court that the doctrine of the earlier opinion should be restated in a more limited way to conform to current understandings. *Carter v. Carter Coal Co.* suffered such a fate. As just noted, Chief Justice Hughes merely distinguished it in 1937, and yet it was obvious that much of *Jones & Laughlin* directly contradicted *Carter.* In 1941, in *United States v. Darby Lumber Co.,* the Supreme Court upheld another congressional statute regulating labor relations on grounds that once more contradicted *Carter.* This time the Court thought it well to recognize that something had happened to the vitality of the earlier case and stated that *Carter* was "limited in principle." Although the Court did not explain how the principle was limited, the justices have not since 1936 followed its restrictive interpretation of congressional power.

IGNORING A PRECEDENT

An embarrassing precedent can be handled by simply not mentioning it at all. This technique may seem cowardly and also rather untidy, because it impairs the validity of the ignored precedent and leaves it a derelict on the stream of the law.

In *Lochner v. New York* (1905), for example, the Supreme Court held unconstitutional a state ten-hour law for bakers. Then in *Bunting v. Oregon* (1917) a somewhat differently constituted Court upheld Oregon's ten-hour law for factory workers in a decision that never mentioned *Lochner.* The result of this silence was that when a still different majority of the justices decided in *Adkins v. Children's Hospital* (1923) to invalidate a minimum-wage law for women, they were able to cite *Lochner* as a precedent, contending that "the principles therein stated have never been disapproved." Chief Justice Taft found all this very confusing, for, as he noted in his dissenting opinion in *Adkins,* he had always supposed that *Bunting* had overruled *Lochner* "sub silentio."

Again, in *United States v. Classic* (1941) Justice Stone held that federal primary elections were subject to congressional regulation, without referring at all to *Grovey v. Townsend* (1935), which had asserted that party primaries were outside the protection of the Constitution. Stone had deliberately omitted any reference to *Grovey* because he needed the vote of Justice Owen J. Roberts, who had written the Court's opinion in *Grovey.* Later, in *Smith v. Allwright* (1944), when Roberts's vote was no longer necessary, the Court held that in fact *Grovey* had been dead ever since *Classic.* Realizing that he had been tricked, Roberts protested angrily:

> It is suggested that *Grovey v. Townsend* was overruled *sub silentio* in *United States v. Classic.* If this Court's opinion in the Classic case discloses its method of overruling earlier decisions, I can only protest that, in fairness, it should rather have adopted the open and frank way of saying what it was doing than, after the event, characterize its past action as overruling *Grovey v. Townsend,* though those less sapient never realized the fact.

OVERRULING A PRECEDENT

Lest it be thought that old precedents never die but just fade away, it should be recorded that occasionally a court specifically overrules a case. Overruling is more likely to occur when a precedent has become a notorious political as well as a legal liability. In the decade from 1937 to 1947, as a new Supreme Court liquidated many of the constitutional doctrines of the old Court, the justices overruled at least thirty-two previous decisions, thirty of which turned on issues of constitutional interpretation. One of the most famous victims of this judicial reorientation was *Hammer v. Dagenhart* (1918), in which the Court had by a five-to-four vote declared unconstitutional the federal Child Labor Act of 1916. This ruling was based on such a tortured construction of the Court's previous decisions that its authority had always been slight, and in *United States v. Darby Lumber Co.* (1941) the justices welcomed the opportunity to bury it. For a unanimous Court Justice Stone said:

> The conclusion is inescapable that *Hammer v. Dagenhart* was a departure from the principles which have prevailed in the interpretation of the commerce clause both before and since the decision and that such vitality, as a precedent, as it then had has long since been exhausted. It should be and now is overruled.

Because an overruling of a previous decision often attracts much attention, such events may seem to occur far more frequently than they in fact do. The Supreme Court has many times repeated that it is always ready to reconsider its interpretations of the Constitution, but even there a clean reversal of precedent is unusual. Moreover, where issues essentially involve only private individuals and where many people have in good faith built thick layers of relations around the framework of an earlier rule, judges are reluctant to scrap that rule, even when later research and rethinking show it to have been clearly wrong. Judges have the obvious—and realistic—fear that a sudden switch to the "correct" rule will create chaos. One means of avoiding such horrendous results and still formulating "correct" rules has been "prospective overruling," a declaration by a court that it will decide cases arising in the future by a new principle but will neither upset old decisions nor apply that new principle to disputes that began in the past, when the older rule was in effect.[4]

In addition, Chapter 11 will point out that as a general, but not universal, policy the Supreme Court will not correct its earlier misinterpretations of a congressional statute. Congress, the justices usually say, can undo the Court's error, if error there be, simply by passing a new statute. Other and deeper reasons of policy may lie behind the Court's refusal to overturn a previous decision in any field of the law. For instance, in *Runyon v. McCrary* (1977) Justice John Paul Stevens offered a candid explanation for joining a majority of the Court in a holding that a congressional statute enacted during Reconstruction forbade private citizens to decline to sign a contract with other citizens because of their race. The majority based *Runyon* on *Jones v. Mayer* (1968), but later research convinced Stevens that *Jones* had been wrong. Furthermore, *Jones* had involved a different statute, although Congress had later codified the two as successive sections in the same chapter and title of the United States Code. Despite his view of *Jones* and his misgivings about the differences between the two statutes, Stevens joined the majority, explaining that "even if *Jones* did not accurately reflect the sentiments of the Reconstruction Congress, it surely accords with the prevailing sense of justice today." He continued:

> The policy of the Nation as formulated by the Congress in recent years has moved constantly in the direction of eliminating racial segregation in all sectors of society. This Court has given a liberal and sympathetic construction to such legislation. For the Court now to overrule *Jones* would be a significant step backwards, with effects that would not have arisen from a correct decision in the first

[4] See, for example, *Linkletter v. Walker* (1965) and *Williams v. United States* (1971).

instance. Such a step would be so clearly contrary to my understanding of the mores of today that I think the Court is entirely correct in adhering to *Jones.*

The overruling announced in *Garcia v. San Antonio Metropolitan Transit Authority* (1985) afforded a classic illustration of the deterioration of a precedent. In 1976 the Court had handed down a 5 to 4 decision, *National League of Cities v. Usery,* that federal wage and hour requirements for state and municipal employees were unconstitutional. In so doing, it overruled *Maryland v. Wirtz* (1968) and distinguished *Fry v. United States* (1975), challenged major federal economic legislation for the first time since the 1930s, and appeared to revive the long-abandoned theory of *Hammer v. Dagenhart* (1918) that the federal commerce power is limited by state "sovereignty" and the reserved powers guaranteed by the Tenth Amendment to the "States as States."

Usery generated much litigation and was heavily criticized in the law reviews. The Court failed to follow its logic in two subsequent cases.[5] Then in 1985 Justice Blackmun, the fifth member of the *Usery* majority, concluded that he had been wrong, and with his vote the *Usery* dissenters became the *Garcia* majority. (Reading 10.6.)

EXTENDING A PRECEDENT

So far we have been talking mostly about restricting precedents, but as the meanings of some decisions shrivel or die, the reach of others expands. In fact, Justice Cardozo stressed the "tendency of a principle to expand itself to the limit of its logic," and his opinion in *MacPherson v. Buick Motor Co.* (Reading 10.2) beautifully illustrates the point. *Hirabayashi* and *Korematsu* supply another excellent case study. In the first decision, sustaining the curfew, Justice Stone carefully explained that the Court was restricting itself to deciding that single issue: "It is unnecessary," he wrote, "to consider whether or to what extent such findings [of military danger] would support orders differing from the curfew order." But, the following year, Justice Black in *Korematsu* squarely based his reasoning on "the principles we announced in the *Hirabayashi* Case." In vain Justice Robert H. Jackson dissented: "The Court is now saying that in *Hirabayashi* we did decide the very things we there said that we were not deciding. . . . How far the principle of this case would be extended before plausible reasons would play out, I do not know."

A decade later *Brown v. Board of Education* spoke of the fundamental importance of the public school system to American life and

---

[5] *Hodel v. Virginia Surface Mining and Reclamation Assn.* (1981); *Equal Employment Opportunity Commission v. Wyoming* (1983).

of the deleterious effects of compelling children to attend racially segregated schools. With no further elaboration about the evil effects of segregation in general, the Court used citations from *Brown* to justify invalidating laws requiring racial separation in public parks, golf courses, swimming pools, and transportation.

In sum, when a court makes a decision it brings into being a force that is itself potentially creative. As parents with their children, no judge can foretell how an intellectual offspring will develop. At the hands of other jurists principles may wither, remain healthy, or grow into giants. Indeed, these principles may go through several cycles of expansion and remission as circumstances—and judges—change. Thus, the accordionlike qualities of stare decisis allow judges to adapt the law on an incremental, step-by-step basis, usually preserving some of the old rules while fashioning new ones. (Reading 10.7.) The whole process is much more disorderly and unpredictable than judges sometimes like to admit. "I was much troubled in spirit, in my first years on the bench," Justice Cardozo later wrote, "to find how trackless was the ocean on which I had embarked. I sought for certainty. . . . [But] I have grown to see that the process in its highest reaches is not discovery, but creation. . . ."[6]

SELECTED REFERENCES

Brigham, John. *Constitutional Language: An Interpretation of Judicial Decision.* Westport, Conn.: Greenwood Press, 1978.

Cardozo, Benjamin N. *The Nature of the Judicial Process.* New Haven, Conn.: Yale University Press, 1921.

Carter, Lief H. *Reason in Law.* 2d ed. Boston: Little, Brown, 1984.

Christie, George C. "Objectivity in the Law," 78 *Yale Law Journal* 1311 (1969).

Davis, Kenneth C. "The Future of Judge-Made Law in England," 61 *Columbia Law Review* 201 (1961).

Douglas, William O. "Stare Decisis," 4 *The Record of the Association of the Bar of the City of New York* 152 (1949).

Dworkin, Ronald. *Taking Rights Seriously.* Cambridge, Mass.: Harvard University Press, 1977.

Friedman, Lawrence. "On Legalistic Reasoning," 1968 *Wisconsin Law Review* 148.

Fuller, Lon L. "Reason and Fiat in Case Law," 59 *Harvard Law Review* 376 (1946).

Goodhart, Arthur L. "Determining the Ratio Decidendi of a Case," 40 *Yale Law Journal* 161 (1930).

Leach, W. Barton. "Revisionism in the House of Lords: The Bastion of Rigid Stare Decisis Falls," 80 *Harvard Law Review* 797 (1967).

Levi, Edward H. *An Introduction to Legal Reasoning.* Chicago: University of Chicago Press, 1948.

Llewellyn, Karl N. *The Common Law Tradition: Deciding Appeals.* Boston: Little, Brown, 1960.

---

[6] Benjamin N. Cardozo, *The Nature of the Judicial Process* (New Haven, Conn.: Yale University Press, 1921), p. 166.

Merriman, John Henry. *The Civil Law Tradition: An Introduction to the Legal Systems of Western Europe and Latin America.* Stanford, Calif.: Stanford University Press, 1971.

Monaghan, Henry P. "Foreword: Constitutional Common Law," 89 *Harvard Law Review* 1 (1975).

Pound, Roscoe. "The Theory of Judicial Decision," 36 *Harvard Law Review* 641 (1923).

Shapiro, Martin. "Stability and Change in Judicial Decision-Making: Incrementalism or Stare Decisis?" 2 *Law in Transition Quarterly* 134 (1965).

Wasserstrom, Richard. *The Judicial Decision.* Stanford, Calif.: Stanford University Press, 1961.

10.1 *"The basic pattern of legal reasoning is reasoning by example."*

AN INTRODUCTION TO LEGAL REASONING

Edward H. Levi

. . . [I]t is important that the mechanism of legal reasoning should not be concealed by its pretense. The pretense is that the law is a system of known rules applied by a judge. . . . In an important sense legal rules are never clear, and, if a rule had to be clear before it could be imposed, society would be impossible. The mechanism accepts the differences of view and ambiguities of words. It provides for the participation of the community in resolving the ambiguity by providing a forum for the discussion of policy in the gap of ambiguity. On serious controversial questions, it makes it possible to take the first step in the direction of what otherwise would be forbidden ends. The mechanism is indispensable to peace in a community.

The basic pattern of legal reasoning is reasoning by example. It is reasoning from case to case. It is a three-step process described by the doctrine of precedent in which a proposition descriptive of the first case is made into a rule of law and then applied to a next similar situation. The steps are these: similarity is seen between cases; next the rule of law inherent in the first case is announced; then the rule of law is made applicable to the second case. This is a method of reasoning necessary for the law, but it has characteristics which under other circumstances might be considered imperfections. . . .

The determination of similarity or difference is the function of each judge. Where case law is considered, and there is no statute, he

Reprinted from *An Introduction to Legal Reasoning* by Edward H. Levi, by permission of The University of Chicago Press. Copyright University of Chicago Press, 1948. Pp. 1–7. Edward H. Levi, former President of the University of Chicago and U.S. Attorney General, is now Professor of Law at the University of Chicago.

is not bound by the statement of the rule of law made by the prior judge even in the controlling case. The statement is mere dictum, and this means that the judge in the present case may find irrelevant the existence or absence of facts which prior judges thought important. It is not what the prior judge intended that is of any importance; rather it is what the present judge, attempting to see the law as a fairly consistent whole, thinks should be the determining classification. In arriving at his result he will ignore what the past thought important; he will emphasize facts which prior judges would have thought made no difference. It is not alone that he could not see the law through the eyes of another, for he could at least try to do so. It is rather that the doctrine of dictum forces him to make his own decision.

Thus it cannot be said that the legal process is the application of known rules to diverse facts. Yet it is a system of rules; the rules are discovered in the process of determining similarity or difference. But if attention is directed toward the finding of similarity or difference, other peculiarities appear. The problem for the law is: When will it be just to treat different cases as though they were the same? A working legal system must therefore be willing to pick out key similarities and to reason from them to the justice of applying a common classification. The existence of some facts in common brings into play the general rule. If this is really reasoning, then by common standards, thought of in terms of closed systems, it is imperfect unless some overall rule has announced that this common and ascertainable similarity is to be decisive. But no such fixed prior rule exists. It could be suggested that reasoning is not involved at all; that is, that no new insight is arrived at through a comparison of cases. But reasoning appears to be involved; the conclusion is arrived at through a process and was not immediately apparent. It seems better to say there is reasoning, but it is imperfect.

Therefore it appears that the kind of reasoning involved in the legal process is one in which the classification changes as the classification is made. The rules change as the rules are applied. More important, the rules arise out of a process which, while comparing fact situations, creates the rules and then applies them. . . . In a sense all reasoning is of this type, but there is an additional requirement which compels the legal process to be this way. Not only do new situations arise, but in addition people's wants change. The categories used in the legal process must be left ambiguous in order to permit the infusion of new ideas. And this is true even where legislation or a constitution is involved. The words used by the legislature or the constitutional convention must come to have new meanings. Furthermore, agreement on any other basis would be impossible. In this manner the laws come to express the ideas of the community and even when written in general terms, in statute or constitution, are molded for the specific case.

But attention must be paid to the process. A controversy as to whether the law is certain, unchanging, and expressed in rules, or uncertain, changing, and only a technique for deciding specific cases misses the point. It is both. . . .

Reasoning by example in the law is a key to many things. It indicates in part the hold which the law process has over the litigants. They have participated in the law making. They are bound by something they helped to make. Moreover, the examples or analogies urged by the parties bring into the law the common ideas of the society. The ideas have their day in court, and they will have their day again. This is what makes the hearing fair, rather than any idea that the judge is completely impartial, for of course he cannot be completely so. Moreover, the hearing in a sense compels at least vicarious participation by all the citizens, for the rule which is made, even though ambiguous, will be law as to them.

Reasoning by example shows the decisive role which the common ideas of the society and the distinctions made by experts can have in shaping the law. The movement of common or expert concepts into the law may be followed. . . . The idea achieves standing in the society. It is suggested again to a court. The court this time reinterprets the prior case and in doing so adopts the rejected idea. In subsequent cases, the idea is given further definition and is tied to other ideas which have been accepted by courts. It is now no longer the idea which was commonly held in the society. It becomes modified in subsequent cases. Ideas first rejected but which gradually have won acceptance now push what has become a legal category out of the system or convert it into something which may be its opposite. The process is one in which the ideas of the community and of the social sciences, whether correct or not, as they win acceptance in the community, control legal decisions. Erroneous ideas, of course, have played an enormous part in shaping the law. An idea, adopted by a court, is in a superior position to influence conduct and opinion in the community; judges, after all, are rulers. And the adoption of an idea by a court reflects the power structure in the community. But reasoning by example will operate to change the idea after it has been adopted.

Moreover, reasoning by example brings into focus important similarity and difference in the interpretation of case law, statutes, and the constitution of a nation. There is a striking similarity. It is only folklore which holds that a statute if clearly written can be completely unambiguous and applied as intended to a specific case. . . . Hence reasoning by example operates with all three. But there are important differences. What a court says is dictum, but what a legislature says is a statute. The reference of the reasoning changes. Interpretation of intention when dealing with a statute is the way of describing the attempt to compare cases on the basis of the standard thought to be common at the time the legislation was passed. While this is the attempt, it may not initially accomplish any different result than if the standards of the judge had been explicitly used. Nevertheless, the remarks of the judge are directed toward describing a category set up by the legislature. These remarks are different from ordinary dicta. They set the course of the statute, and later reasoning in subsequent cases is tied to them. As a consequence, courts are less free in applying a statute than in dealing with case law. The current rationale for this is the notion that the legislature has acquiesced by legislative silence in the prior, even though erroneous, interpretation of the court. . . .

Under the United States experience, contrary to what has sometimes been believed when a written constitution of a nation is involved, the court has greater freedom than it has with the application of a statute or case law. . . . The constitution sets up the conflicting ideals of the community in certain ambiguous categories. . . . The constitution, in other words, permits the court to be inconsistent. The freedom is concealed either as a search for the intention of the framers or as a proper understanding of a living instrument, and sometimes as both. But this does not mean that reasoning by example has any less validity in this field.

It may be objected that this analysis of legal reasoning places too much emphasis on the comparison of cases and too little on the legal concepts which are created. It is true that similarity is seen in terms of a word, and inability to find a ready word to express similarity or difference may prevent change in the law. The words which have been found in the past are much spoken of, have acquired a dignity of their own, and to a considerable measure control results. . . . Thus the connotation of the word for a time has a limiting influence—so much so that the reasoning may even appear to be simply deductive.

But it is not simply deductive. In the long run a circular motion can be seen. The first stage is the creation of the legal concept which is built up as cases are compared. The period is one in which the court fumbles for a phrase. Several phrases may be tried out; the misuse or misunderstanding of words itself may have an effect. The concept sounds like another, and the jump to the second is made. The second stage is the period when the concept is more or less fixed, although reasoning by example continues to classify items inside and out of the concept. The third stage is the breakdown of the concept, as reasoning by example has moved so far ahead as to make it clear that the suggestive influence of the word is no longer desired.

The process is likely to make judges and lawyers uncomfortable. It runs contrary to the pretense of the system. It seems inevitable, therefore, that as matters of kind vanish into matters of degree and then entirely new meanings turn up, there will be the attempt to escape to some overall rule which can be said to have always operated and which will make the reasoning look deductive. The rule will be useless. It will have to operate on a level where it has no meaning. . . . It is window dressing. Yet it can be very misleading. Particularly when a concept has broken down and reasoning by example is about to build another, textbook writers, well aware of the unreal aspect of old rules, will announce new ones, equally ambiguous and meaningless, forgetting that the legal process does not work with the rule but on a much lower level. . . .

10.2   *". . . whatever the rule in Thomas v. Winchester may once have been, it has no longer that restricted meaning."*

MACPHERSON V. BUICK MOTOR CO.

217 N.Y. 382, 111 N.E. 1050 (1916) (Court of Appeals of New York)

CARDOZO, J. The defendant is a manufacturer of automobiles. It sold an automobile to a retail dealer. The retailer dealer resold to the plaintiff. While the plaintiff was in the car, it suddenly collapsed. He was thrown out and injured. One of the wheels was made of defective wood, and its spokes crumbled into fragments. The wheel was not made by the defendant; it was bought from another manufacturer. There is evidence, however, that its defects could have been discovered by reasonable inspection, and that inspection was omitted. There is no claim that the defendant knew of the defect and willfully concealed it. . . . The question to be determined is whether the defendant owed a duty of care and vigilance to any one but the immediate purchaser.

The foundations of this branch of the law, at least in this state, were laid in *Thomas v. Winchester.* A poison was falsely labeled. The sale was made to a druggist, who in turn sold to a customer. The customer recovered damages from the seller who affixed the label. "The defendant's negligence," it was said, "put human life in imminent danger." A poison falsely labeled is likely to injure any one who gets it. Because the danger is to be foreseen, there is a duty to avoid injury. Cases were cited by way of illustration in which manufacturers were not subject to any duty irrespective of contract. The distinction was said to be that their conduct, though negligent, was not likely to result in injury to any one except the purchaser. We are not required to say whether the chance of injury was always as remote as the distinction assumes. Some of the illustrations might be rejected to-day. The *principle* of the distinction is for present purposes the important thing.

Thomas v. Winchester became quickly a landmark of the law. In the application of its principle there may at times have been uncertainty or even error. There has never in this state been doubt or disavowal of the principle itself. The chief cases are well known. *Loop v. Litchfield* was the case of a defect in a small balance wheel used on a circular saw. The manufacturer pointed out the defect to the buyer, who wished a cheap article and was ready to assume the risk. The risk can hardly have been an imminent one, for the wheel lasted five years before it broke. In the meanwhile the buyer had made a lease of the machinery. It was held that the manufacturer was not answerable to the lessee. . . . *Losee v. Clute,* the case of the explosion of a steam boiler, must be confined to its special facts. It was put upon the ground that the risk of injury was too remote. The buyer in that case had not only accepted the boiler, but had tested it. The manufacturer knew that his own test was not the final one. The finality of the test has a bearing on the measure of diligence owing to persons other than the purchaser. . . .

These early cases suggest a narrow construction of the rule. Later cases, however, evince a more liberal spirit. First in importance is *Devlin v. Smith.* The defendant, a contractor, built a scaffold for a painter. The painter's servants were injured. The contractor was held liable. He knew that the scaffold, if improperly constructed, was a most dangerous trap. He knew that it was to be used by the workmen. He was building it for that very purpose. Building it for their use, he owed them a duty, irrespective of his contract with their master, to build it with care.

. . . [T]he latest case in this court in which *Thomas v. Winchester* was followed . . . is *Statler v. Ray Mfg. Co.* The defendant manufactured a large coffee urn. It was installed in a restaurant. When heated, the urn exploded and injured the plaintiff. We held that the manufacturer was liable. We said that the urn "was of such a character inherently that, when applied to the purposes for which it was designed, it was liable to become a source of great danger to many people if not carefully and properly constructed."

It may be that *Devlin v. Smith* and *Statler* have extended the rule of *Thomas v. Winchester.* If so, this court is committed to the extension. The defendant argues that things imminently dangerous to life are poisons, explosives, deadly weapons—things whose normal function it is to injure or destroy. But whatever the rule in *Thomas v. Winchester* may once have been, it has no longer that restricted meaning. A scaffold . . . is not inherently a destructive instrument. It becomes destructive only if imperfectly constructed. A large coffee urn . . . may have within itself, if negligently made, the potency of danger, yet no one thinks of it as an implement whose normal function is destruction. . . . We have mentioned only cases in this court. But the rule has received a like extension in our courts of intermediate appeal. . . .

We hold, then, that the principle of *Thomas v. Winchester* is not limited to poisons, explosives, and things of like nature, to things which in their normal operation are implements of destruction. If the nature of a thing is such that it is reasonably certain to place life and limb in peril when negligently made, it is then a thing of danger. Its nature gives warning of the consequences to be expected. If to the element of danger there is added knowledge that the thing will be used by persons other than the purchaser, and used without new tests, then, irrespective of contract, the manufacturer of this thing of danger is under duty to make it carefully. That is as far as we are required to go for the decision of this case. There must be knowledge of a danger, not merely possible, but probable. . . . There must also be knowledge that in the usual course of events the danger will be shared by others than the buyer. Such knowledge may often be inferred from the nature of the transaction. But it is possible that even knowledge of the danger and of the use will not always be enough. The proximity or remoteness of the relation is a factor to be considered. . . . We are not required at this time to say that it is legitimate to go back to the manufacturer of the finished product and hold the manufacturers of the component parts [liable]. . . . We leave that question open. We shall have to deal with it when it arises. . . .

From this survey of the decisions, there thus emerges a definition of the duty of a manufacturer which enables us to measure this defendant's liability. Beyond all question, the nature of an automobile gives warning of probable danger if its construction is defective. This automobile was designed to go fifty miles an hour. Unless its wheels were sound and strong, injury was almost certain. It was as much a thing of danger as a defective engine for a railroad. The defendant knew the danger. It knew also that the car would be used by persons other than the buyer. This was apparent from its size; there were seats for three persons. It was apparent also from the fact that the buyer was a dealer in cars, who bought to resell. The maker of this car supplied it for the use of purchasers from the dealer just as plainly as the contractor in *Devlin v. Smith* supplied the scaffold for use by the servants of the owner. The dealer was indeed the one person of whom it might be said with some approach to certainty that by him the car would not be used. Yet the defendant would have us say that he was the one person whom it was under a legal duty to protect. The law does not lead us to so inconsequent a conclusion. Precedents drawn from the days of travel by stage coach do not fit the conditions of travel to-day. The principle that the danger must be imminent does not change, but the things subject to the principle do change. They are whatever the needs of life in a developing civilization require them to be.

In reaching this conclusion, we do not ignore the decisions to the contrary in other jurisdictions. . . . Some of them, at first sight inconsistent with our conclusion, may be reconciled upon the ground that the negligence was too remote, and that another cause had intervened. But even when they cannot be reconciled, the difference is rather in the application of the principle than in the principle itself. . . .

. . . The English courts . . . agree with ours in holding that one who invites another to make use of an appliance is bound to the exercise of reasonable care. . . . That at bottom is the underlying principle of *Devlin v. Smith.* The contractor who builds the scaffold invites the owner's workmen to use it. The manufacturer who sells the automobile to the retail dealer invites the dealer's customers to use it. . . .

. . . We may find an analogy in the law which measures the liability of landlords. If A leases to B a tumbledown house he [A] is not liable, in the absence of fraud, to B's guests who enter it and are injured. This is because B is then under duty to repair it. . . . But if A leases a building to be used by the lessee at once as a place of public entertainment, the rule is different. There injury to persons other than the lessee is foreseen, and the foresight of the consequences involves the creation of a duty (*Junkermann v. Tilyou R. Co.* and cases there cited).

In this view of the defendant's liability there is nothing inconsistent with the theory of liability on which the case was tried. . . .

The judgment should be affirmed with costs.

WILLARD BARTLETT, CH. J. (dissenting). . . .

HISCOCK, CHASE and **CUDDEBACK, JJ.,** concur with **CARDOZO, J.,** and **HOGAN, J.,** concurs in result; **WILLARD BARTLETT, CH. J.,** reads dissenting opinion; **POUND, J.,** not voting.

Judgment affirmed.

10.3   *". . . government would be impossible if a rule had to be clear before it could be imposed. . . ."*

LAW AS METAPHOR

Timothy J. O'Neill

The practice of law is a linguistic skill: it deals with and works through words. Yet clubs are trumps in law and, therefore, law differs

Excerpted from "The Language of Equality in a Constitutional Order," 75 *American Political Science Review* 626, 631–632 (1981). Reprinted by permission. Timothy J. O'Neill teaches at Wellesley College and is Liberal Arts Fellow in Law and Politics, Harvard Law School.

from most languages in at least one regard—there is a fist behind the legal word. "Fist" implies "action"; law language acts upon the listener both as a sound and as a symbol. Law language is a form of political force, not only in the sense of speech as a physical activity but also in the more important sense of speech as a political act, as an attempt to affect community action. As a subspecies of political language, law language is therefore "conventional" in the most radical sense—it is not only an human artifact but a maker of men and women. The language in which we conceive of legal "things" is decisive in molding our attitudes and behaviors toward those "things." Answers to "what is freedom of speech?" are derived from the legal concepts and usages we have developed to distinguish protected speech from similar but unprotected activities such as obscenity. . . .

While legal words describe nothing perfectly, they are useful in simplifying and clarifying a complex and fluid world. They are necessary abstractions from the bewildering mosaic of reality, attempting to explain complex and seemingly unrelated phenomena by simple and hence, from a realistic standpoint, necessarily incomplete concepts and principles. But the dangers of law language are obvious: the map is offered as a substitute for the territory, the chemical formula for the taste, the diagram for the dance. These dangers are tolerable only so long as the basic nature of law language is remembered by its users.

The abstracting and simplifying character of law language affects its role as a specialized form of political action. Political demands, beliefs, and interests expressed through litigation will be mediated and transformed by the conventions established in law language governing what is sensible. The ways in which particular social problems will be handled in the courtroom will depend not only on the pool of existing ideas and doctrine available to legal actors but also on the ability of the language to apply these existing understandings to new or recurring issues.

Law in the Anglo-American approach has fastened on two devices to provide the flexibility and innovative capacity necessary for change: legal fictions and the process of analogical reasoning. Both are used as means to apply concepts and approaches which have worked satisfactorily in one area to another area. Both are expressions of the curious form of conservatism which permeates the legal system: a prudent recognition of the pitfalls of wholesale innovation harnessed to a cautious realization of the need to adapt to changing circumstances. And both are facets of the metaphorical nature of law language itself.

A legal fiction is a form of "legal pretending." It is a legal contrivance which transforms something known to be false or unreal into an assumed fact. A fiction may be used to broaden or narrow judicial jurisdictions or to modify a substantive rule of law. No matter its goal, however, the fiction is phrased "so as to *look* as if the court merely follows old and legitimate ways. The fiction assimilates the unusual to the usual, the new to the old." Its appeal rests on its ability to disguise change and therefore to allow "for a gentler transition" between the old and the new by treating a new controversy "as if" it fell within a settled aspect of the law. . . .

The second device of metaphorical law language is analogical reasoning—the comparison and contrast of similar and dissimilar things. Analogical reasoning in law presumes that when cases are similar in relevant ways, the judge is warranted in treating them "as if" they were the same. The need for the qualifier "as if" is a recognition of how the interplay between ambiguous words and shifting social circumstances both constrains and liberates legal thinking. Law is not a system of preexisting rules applied by legal experts. Rather, since government would be impossible if a rule had to be clear before it could be imposed, law is a process receptive to differing viewpoints and to ambiguities. Analogical reasoning "provides for the participation of the community in resolving the ambiguity [of rules] by providing a forum" where different policies can be offered by asserting competing analogies. Moreover, since the public participates indirectly in the definition, refinement, and modification of legal rules through analogical reasoning, its loyalty is tied to its legal institutions . . . —one possible explanation for the role and power of courts in American life. But analogical reasoning is not unbounded. It is limited by a taught tradition establishing what procedures and methods are appropriate for drawing analogies—such as the adversarial process of fact-finding in American law—and by specific legal doctrines which constrain the legal actor's freedom to uncover plausible similarities—for example, the axiom that criminal statutes should be construed more strictly than civil statutes. Equally important, but often overlooked, is the influence exerted by the limitations of reasoning based on metaphors.

If analogical reasoning is justified by the ambiguity and shifting contexts of rules and words, it does not follow that a word or rule can mean everything. There is a core of meaning which cannot simply be abandoned without powerful justification. And that "core of meaning" is determined by the inescapable, metaphorical structure of law language.

Both legal fictions and analogical reasoning are metaphorical in form; their power lies in their ability to transfer meanings from a settled portion of the law to an unsettled one. But transference will not work unless there exists a significant likeness between different classes of phenomena . . . which in turn means that the asserted likeness between classes must be accepted as plausible by the existing conventions of what constitutes significant similarities. An example from common law reasoning illustrates this point: a rancher dammed a stream running through his property in order to provide a watering hole for his cattle. An unexpected thunderstorm caused the watering hole to overflow its banks and to flood the croplands of an adjacent farmer. The farmer sued the rancher, holding the rancher responsible for the damage inflicted by the flood waters just as he would be if his cattle had trampled the farmer's crops. The rancher raised in his defense the settled rule that a landowner is not responsible for acts of nature involving his property. The flood was like an act of a wild lion which crossed the rancher's land in order to strike at the farmer's chickens. The court is asked to select from among these competing analogies. Has damming the stream transformed a thing of nature into a thing of man—is a flood more like a wild lion or a domesticated cow? It is of course absurd to speak of a flood as if it were a lion or a cow, but it is the appeal of metaphorical thought that it allows us to transfer through fiction the knowledge and experience accumulated in one area to another area. This willing suspension of disbelief allows us to explain problems in a logical manner by recourse to absurd comparisons. Absurdity serves the vital function of defining the plausibility of an extreme logical argument in law and thereby sets limits to the range of legal logic.

[For example, consider] the limits of the metaphor developed to enrich the meaning of "persons" in the Fourteenth Amendment. At one time, the courts were required to settle the issue whether a corporation was more like an artifact or a human being (the conventional understanding of "person"). By choosing to treat the corporation as if it were a human being, the courts demonstrated their acceptance of the similarities between corporations and human beings as significant and their dismissal of the similarities between corporations and artifacts as irrelevant. The capacity of a corporation to draw upon its human resources in order to plan, to expend its energies prudently, and to adapt to changing circumstances make it plausible to treat it as if it were a living being. Unlike an inanimate object, a corporation is not totally dependent on human action; the body of organizational mores and customs and the structure of decision making mold its human participants into carriers of organizational values. A corporation can be a creator of as well as an instrument for the realization of human values.

But the metaphorical transference of human qualities to the corporation is not without its costs. By investing human abilities and therefore human rights in corporations, law language established limits which make group right claims in a civil rights context appear absurd. The fiction of an autonomous "group" in American law grants the artificial person of the corporation many of the prerogatives of political action and speech but denies it the rights to vote or to campaign for public office. To suggest that General Motors is being deprived of equal protection because it cannot cast a ballot in an election is seen as absurd. Thus, the closer the fiction of the artificial person comes to the core of political practice, the fiercer is the law's attachment to individualism and the less its willingness to entertain the metaphor of the corporate group as "person." . . .

The value of constitutional discourse and decision in political dialogue is often justified by the moral influence exerted by the law on American life. But debates among lawyers are not the same as those among philosophers or economists or members of Congress. Law language narrows the debate and helps to simplify complexities, but it may also impoverish public understanding of serious contro- versies. . . .

This is not an indictment of the law's inadequacies. Legal reason- ing promises plausibility, not certainty, for its conclusions. Nor is this a simple affirmation of the no longer novel insight that judicial deci- sions are poor mechanisms for resolving difficult problems. The in- tent is far more modest: to remind the reader that analyses of [legal] theories . . . are in large part evaluations and explanations of the power of political words. . . .

10.4   ". . . earlier decisions have gravitational force. . . ."

TAKING RIGHTS SERIOUSLY: PRECEDENT

Ronald Dworkin

In the following passage from *Taking Rights Seriously*, Ronald Dworkin invents for purposes of his discussion "a lawyer of superhuman skill, learning, patience and acu- men, whom I shall call Hercules. I suppose that Hercules is a judge in some representa- tive American jurisdiction. I assume that he accepts the main uncontroversial constitutive and regulative rules of the law in his jurisdiction."[1] Earlier Dworkin dis- cussed the English case of *Spartan Steel* as an example of a "hard case, when no settled rule dictates a decision either way. . . . The defendant's employees had broken an electric cable belonging to a power company that supplied power to the plaintiff, and the plaintiff's factory was shut down while the cable was repaired. The court had to decide whether to allow the plaintiff recovery for economic loss following negligent damage to someone else's property."[2]

One day lawyers will present a hard case to Hercules that does not turn upon any statute; they will argue whether earlier common law

Taking Rights Seriously (Cambridge, Mass.: Harvard University Press, 1977), pp. 110–115. Reprinted with permission. Ronald Dworkin, an American lawyer, attended Harvard, Princeton, and Yale, and is University Professor of Jurisprudence at Oxford University and Professor of Law at New York University.

[1]P. 105.
[2]Pp. 83–84.

decisions of Hercules' court, properly understood, provide some party with a right to a decision in his favor. *Spartan Steel* was such a case. The plaintiff did not argue that any statute provided it a right to recover its economic damages; it pointed instead to certain earlier judicial decisions that awarded recovery for other sorts of damage, and argued that the principle behind these cases required a decision for it as well.

Hercules must begin by asking why arguments of that form are ever, even in principle, sound. He will find that he has available no quick or obvious answer. When he asked himself the parallel question about legislation he found, in general democratic theory, a ready reply. But the details of the practices of precedent he must now justify resist any comparably simple theory.

He might, however, be tempted by this answer. Judges, when they decide particular cases at common law, lay down general rules that are intended to benefit the community in some way. Other judges, deciding later cases, must therefore enforce these rules so that the benefit may be achieved. If this account of the matter were a sufficient justification of the practices of precedent, then Hercules could decide these hard common law cases as if earlier decisions were statutes, using the techniques he worked out for statutory interpretation. But he will encounter fatal difficulties if he pursues that theory very far. It will repay us to consider why, in some detail, because the errors in the theory will be guides to a more successful theory.

Statutory interpretation . . . depends upon the availability of a canonical form of words, however vague or unspecific, that set limits to the political decisions that the statute may be taken to have made. Hercules will discover that many of the opinions that litigants cite as precedents do not contain any special propositions taken to be a canonical form of the rule that the case lays down. It is true that it was part of Anglo-American judicial style, during the last part of the nineteenth century and the first part of this century, to attempt to compose such canonical statements, so that one could thereafter refer, for example, to the rule in *Rylands v. Fletcher.* But even in this period, lawyers and textbook writers disagreed about which parts of famous opinions should be taken to have that character. Today, in any case, even important opinions rarely attempt that legislative sort of draftsmanship. They cite reasons, in the form of precedents and principles, to justify a decision, but it is the decision, not some new and stated rule of law, that these precedents and principles are taken to justify. Sometimes a judge will acknowledge openly that it lies to later cases to determine the full effect of the case he has decided.

Of course, Hercules might well decide that when he does find, in an earlier case, a canonical form of words, he will use his techniques of statutory interpretation to decide whether the rule composed of these words embraces a novel case. He might well acknowledge what could be called an enactment force of precedent. He will nevertheless find that when a precedent does have enactment force, its influence on later cases is not taken to be limited to that force. Judges and lawyers do not think that the force of precedents is exhausted, as a statute would be, by the linguistic limits of some particular phrase. If *Spartan Steel* were a New York case, counsel for the plaintiff would suppose that Cardozo's earlier decision in *MacPherson v. Buick,* in which a woman recovered damages for injuries from a negligently manufactured automobile, counted in favor of his client's right to recover, in spite of the fact that the earlier decision contained no language that could plausibly be interpreted to enact that right. He would urge that the earlier decision exerts a gravitational force on later decisions even when these later decisions lie outside its particular orbit.

This gravitational force is part of the practice Hercules' general theory of precedent must capture. In this important respect, judicial practice differs from the practice of officials in other institutions. In chess, officials conform to established rules in a way that assumes full institutional autonomy. They exercise originality only to the extent required by the fact that an occasional rule, like the rule about forfeiture, demands that originality. Each decision of a chess referee, therefore, can be said to be directly required and justified by an established rule of chess, even though some of these decisions must be based on an interpretation, rather than on simply the plain and unavoidable meaning, of that rule.

Some legal philosophers write about common law adjudication as if it were in this way like chess, except that legal rules are much more likely than chess rules to require interpretation. That is the spirit, for example, of Professor Hart's argument that hard cases arise only because legal rules have what he calls 'open texture'.[3] In fact, judges often disagree not simply about how some rule or principle should be interpreted, but whether the rule or principle one judge cites should be acknowledged to be a rule or principle at all. In some cases both the majority and the dissenting opinions recognize the same earlier cases as relevant, but disagree about what rule or principle these precedents should be understood to have established. In adjudication, unlike chess, the argument *for* a particular rule may be more important than the argument *from* that rule to the particular case; and while the chess referee who decides a case by appeal to a rule no one has ever heard of before is likely to be dismissed or certified, the judge who does so is likely to be celebrated in law school lectures.

Nevertheless, judges seem agreed that earlier decisions do con-

[3]H. L. A. Hart, *The Concept of Law,* pp. 121–32.

tribute to the formulation of new and controversial rules in some way other than by interpretation; they are agreed that earlier decisions have gravitational force even when they disagree about what that force is. The legislator may very often concern himself only with issues of background morality or policy in deciding how to cast his vote on some issue. He need not show that his vote is consistent with the votes of his colleagues in the legislature, or with those of past legislatures. But the judge very rarely assumes that character of independence. He will always try to connect the justification he provides for an original decision with decisions that other judges or officials have taken in the past.

In fact, when good judges try to explain in some general way how they work, they search for figures of speech to describe the constraints they feel even when they suppose that they are making new law, constraints that would not be appropriate if they were legislators. They say, for example, that they find new rules immanent in the law as a whole, or that they are enforcing an internal logic of the law through some method that belongs more to philosophy than to politics, or that they are the agents through which the law works itself pure, or that the law has some life of its own even though this belongs to experience rather than logic. Hercules must not rest content with these famous metaphors and personifications, but he must also not be content with any description of the judicial process that ignores their appeal to the best lawyers.

The gravitational force of precedent cannot be captured by any theory that takes the full force of precedent to be its enactment force as a piece of legislation. But the inadequacy of that approach suggests a superior theory. The gravitational force of a precedent may be explained by appeal, not to the wisdom of enforcing enactments, but to the fairness of treating like cases alike. A precedent is the report of an earlier political decision; the very fact of that decision, as a piece of political history, provides some reason for deciding other cases in a similar way in the future. This general explanation of the gravitational force of precedent accounts for the feature that defeated the enactment theory, which is that the force of a precedent escapes the language of its opinion. If the government of a community has forced the manufacturer of defective motor cars to pay damages to a woman who was injured because of the defect, then that historical fact must offer some reason, at least, why the same government should require a contractor who has caused economic damage through the defective work of his employees to make good that loss. We may test the weight of that reason, not by asking whether the language of the earlier decision, suitably interpreted, requires the contractor to pay damages, but by asking the different question whether it is fair for the government, having intervened in the way it did in the first case, to refuse its aid in the second.

Hercules will conclude that this doctrine of fairness offers the only adequate account of the full practice of precedent. He will draw certain further conclusions about his own responsibilities when deciding hard cases. The most important of these is that he must limit the gravitational force of earlier decisions to the extension of the arguments of principle necessary to justify those decisions. If an earlier decision were taken to be entirely justified by some argument of policy, it would have no gravitational force. Its value as a precedent would be limited to its enactment force, that is, to further cases captured by some particular words of the opinion. The distributional force of a collective goal, as we noticed earlier, is a matter of contingent fact and general legislative strategy. If the government intervened on behalf of Mrs. MacPherson, not because she had any right to its intervention, but only because wise strategy suggested that means of pursuing some collective goal like economic efficiency, there can be no effective argument of fairness that it therefore ought to intervene for the plaintiff in *Spartan Steel*.

We must remind ourselves, in order to see why this is so, of the slight demands we make upon legislatures in the name of consistency when their decisions are generated by arguments of policy. Suppose the legislature wishes to stimulate the economy and might do so, with roughly the same efficiency, either by subsidizing housing or by increasing direct government spending for new roads. Road construction companies have no right that the legislature choose road construction; if it does, then home construction firms have no right, on any principle of consistency, that the legislature subsidize housing as well. The legislature may decide that the road construction program has stimulated the economy just enough, and that no further programs are needed. It may decide this even if it now concedes that subsidized housing would have been the more efficient decision in the first place. Or it might concede even that more stimulation of the economy is needed, but decide that it wishes to wait for more evidence—perhaps evidence about the success of the road program—to see whether subsidies provide an effective stimulation. It might even say that it does not now wish to commit more of its time and energy to economic policy. There is, perhaps, some limit to the arbitrariness of the distinctions the legislature may make in its pursuit of collective goals. Even if it is efficient to build all shipyards in southern California, it might be thought unfair, as well as politically unwise, to do so. But these weak requirements, which prohibit grossly unfair distributions, are plainly compatible with providing sizeable incremental benefits to one group that are withheld from others.

There can be, therefore, no general argument of fairness that a government which serves a collective goal in one way on one occasion must serve it that way, or even serve the same goal, whenever a parallel opportunity arises. I do not mean simply that the government may change its mind, and regret either the goal or the means of its earlier decision. I mean that a responsible government may serve different goals in a piecemeal and occasional fashion, so that even though it does not regret, but continues to enforce, one rule designed to serve a particular goal, it may reject other rules that would serve that same goal just as well. It might legislate the rule that manufacturers are responsible for damages flowing from defects in their cars, for example, and yet properly refuse to legislate the same rule for manufacturers of washing machines, let alone contractors who cause economic damage like the damage of *Spartan Steel*. Government must, of course, be rational and fair; it must make decisions that overall serve a justifiable mix of collective goals and nevertheless respect whatever rights citizens have. But that general requirement would not support anything like the gravitational force that the judicial decision in favour of Mrs MacPherson was in fact taken to have.

So Hercules, when he defines the gravitational force of a particular precedent, must take into account only the arguments of principle that justify that precedent. If the decision in favour of Mrs. MacPherson supposes that she has a right to damages, and not simply that a rule in her favor supports some collective goal, then the argument of fairness, on which the practice of precedent relies, takes hold. It does not follow, of course, that anyone injured in any way by the negligence of another must have the same concrete right to recover that she has. It may be that competing rights require a compromise in the later case that they did not require in hers. But it might well follow that the plaintiff in the later case has the same abstract right, and if that is so then some special argument citing the competing rights will be required to show that a contrary decision in the later case would be fair.

10.5   *"Ham's defense was that he had been framed...."*

RACIAL PREJUDICE ON JURIES: TWO CASES

Ham v. South Carolina

409 U.S. 524, 93 S. Ct. 848, 35 L. Ed. 2d 46 (1973)

A bearded young black civil rights activist was charged with possession of marijuana in South Carolina. On voir dire examination of prospective jurors, the judge asked three general questions about bias and prejudice required by statute, but he refused to ask four more specific questions requested by defendant's counsel, including one on possible prejudice against beards.

MR. JUSTICE REHNQUIST delivered the opinion of the Court. . . .
. . . [S]ince a principal purpose of the adoption of the Fourteenth Amendment was to prohibit the States from invidiously discriminating on the basis of race . . . we think that the Fourteenth Amendment required the judge in this case to interrogate the jurors upon the subject of racial prejudice. South Carolina law permits challenges for cause, and authorizes the trial judge to conduct *voir dire* examination of potential jurors. The State having created this statutory framework for the selection of juries, the essential fairness required by the Due Process Clause of the Fourteenth Amendment requires that under the facts shown by this record the petitioner be permitted to have the jurors interrogated on the issue of racial bias. . . .*

Ristaino v. Ross

424 U.S. 589, 96 S. Ct. 1017, 47 L. Ed. 2d 258 (1976)

Two black men were charged in Massachusetts with armed robbery and assault with intent to murder a white security guard. The trial court engaged in a general but thorough inquiry into the impartiality of prospective jurors, but denied defense counsel's motion that a question specifically directed to racial prejudice be asked.

MR. JUSTICE POWELL delivered the opinion of the Court. . . .
. . . The narrow issue [here] is whether, under our recent decision in *Ham v. South Carolina,* respondent was constitutionally entitled to require the asking of a question specifically directed to racial prejudice. The broader issue presented is whether *Ham* announced a requirement applicable whenever there may be a confrontation in a criminal trial between persons of different races or different ethnic origins. We answer both of these questions in the negative. . . .
   The Constitution does not always entitle a defendant to have questions posed during *voir dire* specifically directed to matters that conceivably might prejudice veniremen against him. *Voir dire* "is conducted under the supervision of the court, and a great deal must, of necessity, be left to its sound discretion." This is so because the "determination of impartiality, in which demeanor plays such an important part, is particularly within the province of the trial judge."

*Justice Douglas thought that the judge was also obligated to ask the question concerning "prospective jurors' prejudice to hair growth."—Eds.

Thus, the state's obligation to the defendant to impanel an impartial jury generally can be satisfied by less than an inquiry into a specific prejudice feared by the defendant.

In *Ham,* however, we recognized that some cases may present circumstances in which an impermissible threat to the fair trial guaranteed by due process is posed by a trial court's refusal to question prospective jurors specifically about racial prejudice during *voir dire.* . . . [But] by its terms *Ham* did not announce a requirement of universal applicability. Rather, it reflected an assessment of whether under all the circumstances presented there was a constitutionally significant likelihood that, absent questioning about racial prejudice, the jurors would not be [impartial]. . . .

The circumstances in *Ham* strongly suggested the need for *voir dire* to include specific questioning about racial prejudice. Ham's defense was that he had been framed because of his civil rights activities. His prominence in the community as a civil rights activist, if not already known to the veniremen, inevitably would have been revealed to the members of the jury in the course of his presentation of that defense. Racial issues therefore were inextricably bound up with the conduct of the trial. Furthermore, Ham's reputation as a civil rights activist and the defense he interposed were likely to intensify any prejudice that individual members of the jury might harbor. In such circumstances we deemed a *voir dire* that included questioning specifically directed to racial prejudice, when sought by Ham, necessary to meet the constitutional requirement that an impartial jury be impaneled.

We do not agree with the Court of Appeals that the need to question veniremen specifically about racial prejudice also rose to constitutional dimensions in this case. The mere fact that the victim of the crimes alleged was a white man and the defendants were Negroes was less likely to distort the trial than were the special factors involved in *Ham.* The victim's status as a security officer, also relied upon by the Court of Appeals, was cited by respective defense counsel primarily as a separate source of prejudice, not as an aggravating racial factor . . . and the trial judge dealt with it by his question about law-enforcement affiliations. The circumstances thus did not suggest a significant likelihood that racial prejudice might infect Ross' trial. . . .*

---

*Justice White contended that *Ham* had, contrary to the Court's opinion, "announced a new constitutional rule applicable to federal and state criminal trials," but concurred in the judgment on the ground that "this rule should not be applied retroactively to cases . . . involving trials which occurred prior to the decision in *Ham.*" Justices Marshall and Brennan dissented. Justice Stevens took no part in this decision.

In a footnote Justice Powell said that if this trial had taken place in a federal court, the justices, acting under their "supervisory power" over federal courts, would have required that "questions designed to identify racial prejudice if requested by the

10.6

GARCIA V. SAN ANTONIO METROPOLITAN TRANSIT AUTHORITY

469 U.S. 528, 105 S. Ct. 1005, 83 L. Ed. 2d 1016 (1985)

The Fair Labor Standards Act of 1939 (FLSA) regulated wages and hours of workers in many industries but did not affect state employees. *United States v. Darby Lumber Co.* (1941) sustained the statute as a valid exercise of Congress's authority under Article I, §8, cl. 3, of the Constitution, "to regulate commerce . . . among the several states." Later Congress broadened the Act's coverage and, in 1961, included some state employees. *Wirtz v. Maryland* (1968) upheld this extension. In 1974, Congress further enlarged the Act to include most state employees. Despite *Wirtz,* a group of state and local governments challenged the constitutionality of the 1974 amendment and, in *National League of Cities v. Usery* (1976), persuaded the Court to overrule *Wirtz* and distinguish other rulings. The vote was close, 5–4, with Justice Rehnquist writing for the majority. Over bitter dissents, Rehnquist held that the commerce power was limited by the Tenth Amendment's recognition of state sovereignty.

As the first invalidation of an important piece of economic regulation since the Court's war with the New Deal, *Usery* provoked a great deal of controversy. Many scholars were deeply concerned that the Court was about to read once again an economic theory into the Constitution. These concerns diminished when the justices edged away from *Usery,* distinguishing but not overruling it on several occasions. Justice Blackmun had voted with the majority in *Usery,* but in a separate opinion voiced concern about where its doctrine might lead. It was clear from his vote in *Equal Employment Opportunity Commission v. Wyoming* (1983), in which he joined the four dissenters in *Usery* to erode that ruling, that his concern had not abated.

Thus the stage was set for a new constitutional battle when the U.S. Department of Labor claimed that the San Antonio Metropolitan Transit Authority (SAMTA), a county-owned agency operating a system of mass transit, had to abide by the Fair Labor Standards Act. SAMTA filed suit against the Department of Labor, claiming, on the basis of *Usery,* constitutional immunity from the Act and won in the lower courts. The Department of Labor appealed to the Supreme Court.

JUSTICE BLACKMUN delivered the opinion of the Court.

We revisit in these cases an issue raised in *National League of Cities* v. *Usery* (1976). In that litigation, this Court, by a sharply divided vote, ruled that the Commerce Clause does not empower

---

defendant" be asked. In a subsequent case, *Rosales-Lopez v. United States* (1981), the Court announced that in federal cases where there was a reasonable possibility that racial prejudice would influence the jury, the trial judge must make such an inquiry "when requested by a defendant accused of a violent crime and where the defendant and the victim are members of different racial or ethnic groups." Justice Rehnquist concurred but feared that this "per se rule" would "spawn new litigation over the meaning of these terms and whether the trial court properly assessed the possibility of racial or ethnic prejudice infecting the selection of the jury."—Eds.

Congress to enforce the minimum-wage and overtime provisions of the Fair Labor Standards Act (FLSA) against the States "in areas of traditional governmental functions." Although *National League of Cities* supplied some examples of "traditional governmental functions," it did not offer a general explanation of how a "traditional" function is to be distinguished from a "nontraditional" one. Since then, federal and state courts have struggled with the task, thus imposed, of identifying a traditional function for purposes of state immunity under the Commerce Clause.

In the present cases, a Federal District Court concluded that municipal ownership and operation of a mass-transit system is a traditional governmental function and thus, under *National League of Cities*, is exempt from the obligations imposed by the FLSA. Faced with the identical question, three Federal Courts of Appeals and one state appellate court have reached the opposite conclusion.

Our examination of this "function" standard applied in these and other cases over the last eight years now persuades us that the attempt to draw the boundaries of state regulatory immunity in terms of "traditional governmental function" is not only unworkable but is inconsistent with established principles of federalism and, indeed, with those very federalism principles on which *National League of Cities* purported to rest. That case, accordingly, is overruled. . . .

The prerequisites for governmental immunity under *National League of Cities* were summarized by this Court in *Hodel*. Under that summary, four conditions must be satisfied before a state activity may be deemed immune from a particular federal regulation under the Commerce Clause. First, it is said that the federal statute at issue must regulate "the 'States as States.'" Second, the statute must "address matters that are indisputably 'attribute[s] of state sovereignty.'" Third, state compliance with the federal obligation must "directly impair [the States'] ability 'to structure integral operations in areas of traditional governmental functions.'" Finally, the relation of state and federal interests must not be such that "the nature of the federal interest . . . justifies state submission."

The controversy in the present cases has focused on the third *Hodel* requirement—that the challenged federal statute trench on "traditional governmental functions." The District Court voiced a common concern: "Despite the abundance of adjectives, identifying which particular state functions are immune remains difficult." Just how troublesome the task has been is revealed by the results reached in other federal cases. Thus, courts have held that regulating ambulance services, licensing automobile drivers, operating a municipal airport, performing solid waste disposal, and operating a highway authority are functions *protected* under *National League of Cities*. At the same time, courts have held that issuance of industrial development bonds, regulation of intrastate natural gas sales, regulation of traffic on public roads, regulation of air transportation, operation of a telephone system, leasing and sale of natural gas, operation of a mental health facility, and provision of in-house domestic services for the handicapped are *not* entitled to immunity. We find it difficult, if not impossible, to identify an organizing principle that places each of the cases in the first group on one side of a line and each of the cases in the second group on the other side. The constitutional distinction between licensing drivers and regulating traffic, for example, or between operating a highway authority and operating a mental health facility, is elusive at best.

Thus far, this Court itself has made little headway in defining the scope of the governmental functions deemed protected under *National League of Cities.* In that case the Court set forth examples of protected and unprotected functions, but provided no explanation of how those examples were identified. . . .

We believe, however, that there is a more fundamental problem at work here. . . . The problem is that neither the governmental/proprietary distinction nor any other that purports to separate out important governmental functions can be faithful to the role of federalism in a democratic society. The essence of our federal system is that within the realm of authority left open to them under the Constitution, the States must be equally free to engage in any activity that their citizens choose for the common weal, no matter how unorthodox or unnecessary anyone else—including the judiciary—deems state involvement to be. Any rule of state immunity that looks to the "traditional," "integral," or "necessary" nature of governmental functions inevitably invites an unelected federal judiciary to make decisions about which state policies it favors and which ones it dislikes. . . .

We therefore now reject, as unsound in principle and unworkable in practice, a rule of state immunity from federal regulation that turns on a judicial appraisal of whether a particular governmental function is "integral" or "traditional." Any such rule leads to inconsistent results at the same time that it disserves principles of democratic self-governance, and it breeds inconsistency precisely because it is divorced from those principles. . . .

III

The central theme of *National League of Cities* was that the States occupy a special position in our constitutional system and that the scope of Congress' authority under the Commerce Clause must reflect that position. Of course, the Commerce Clause by its specific language does not provide any special limitation on Congress' actions with respect to the States. See *EEOC* v. *Wyoming* (1983) (concurring opinion). It is equally true, however, that the text of the Constitution provides the beginning rather than the final answer to every inquiry into questions of federalism, for "[b]ehind the words of the constitutional provisions are postulates which limit and control." *Monaco* v. *Mississippi* (1934). *National League of Cities* reflected the general conviction that the Constitution precludes "the National Government [from] devour[ing] the essentials of state sovereignty." *Maryland* v. *Wirtz* (dissenting opinion). In order to be faithful to the underlying federal premises of the Constitution, courts must look for the "postulates which limit and control."

What has proved problematic is not the perception that the Constitution's federal structure imposes limitations on the Commerce Clause, but rather the nature and content of those limitations. . . .

We doubt that courts ultimately can identify principled constitutional limitations on the scope of Congress' Commerce Clause powers over the States merely by relying on *a priori* definitions of state sovereignty. In part, this is because of the elusiveness of objective criteria for "fundamental" elements of state sovereignty, a problem we have witnessed in the search for "traditional governmental functions." There is, however, a more fundamental reason: the sovereignty of the States is limited by the Constitution itself. A variety of sovereign powers, for example, are withdrawn from the States by Article I, § 10. Section 8 of the same Article works an equally sharp contraction of state sovereignty by authorizing Congress to exercise a wide range of legislative powers and (in conjunction with the Supremacy Clause of Article VI) to displace contrary state legislation. By providing for final review of questions of federal law in this Court, Article III curtails the sovereign power of the States' judiciaries to make authoritative determinations of law. Finally, the developed application, through the Fourteenth Amendment, of the greater part of the Bill of Rights to the States limits the sovereign authority that States otherwise would possess to legislate with respect to their citizens and to conduct their own affairs.

The States unquestionably do "retai[n] a significant measure of sovereign authority." *EEOC* v. *Wyoming* (POWELL, J., dissenting). They do so, however, only to the extent that the Constitution has not divested them of their original powers and transferred those powers to the Federal Government. In the words of James Madison to the Members of the First Congress: "Interference with the power of the States was no constitutional criterion of the power of Congress. If the power was not given, Congress could not exercise it; if given, they might exercise it, although it should interfere with the laws, or even the Constitution of the States." . . .

As a result, to say that the Constitution assumes the continued role of the States is to say little about the nature of that role. . . .

When we look for the States' "residuary and inviolable sovereignty," The Federalist No. 39 (J. Madison), in the shape of the constitutional scheme rather than in predetermined notions of sovereign power, a different measure of state sovereignty emerges. Apart from the limitation on federal authority inherent in the delegated nature of Congress' Article I powers, the principal means chosen by the Framers to ensure the role of the States in the federal system lies in the structure of the Federal Government itself. It is no novelty to observe that the composition of the Federal Government was designed in large part to protect the States from overreaching by Congress. The Framers thus gave the States a role in the selection both of the Executive and the Legislative Branches of the Federal Government. The States were vested with indirect influence over the House of Representatives and the Presidency by their control of electoral qualifications and their role in presidential elections. U. S. Const., Art. I, §2, and Art. II, §1. They were given more direct influence in the Senate, where each State received equal representation and each Senator was to be selected by the legislature of his State. Art. I, §3. The significance attached to the States' equal representation in the Senate is underscored by the prohibition of any constitutional amendment divesting a State of equal representation without the State's consent. Art. V. . . .

. . . [W]e are convinced that the fundamental limitation that the constitutional scheme imposes on the Commerce Clause to protect the "States as States" is one of process rather than one of result. Any substantive restraint on the exercise of Commerce Clause powers must find its justification in the procedural nature of this basic limitation, and it must be tailored to compensate for possible failings in the national political process rather than to dictate a "sacred province of state autonomy." *EEOC* v. *Wyoming*.

Insofar as the present cases are concerned, then, we need go no further than to state that we perceive nothing in the overtime and minimum-wage requirements of the FLSA, as applied to SAMTA, that is destructive of state sovereignty or violative of any constitutional provision. . . .

IV

. . . Though the separate concurrence [of Justice Blackmun] providing the fifth vote in *National League of Cities* was "not untroubled by certain possible implications" of the decision, the Court in that case attempted to articulate affirmative limits on the Commerce Clause power in terms of core governmental functions and fundamental attributes of state sovereignty. But the model of democratic decision-making the Court there identified underestimated, in our view, the solicitude of the national political process for the continued vitality of the States. Attempts by other courts since then to draw guidance from this model have proved it both impracticable and doctrinally barren. In sum, in *National League of Cities* the Court tried to repair what did not need repair.

We do not lightly overrule recent precedent. We have not hesitated, however, when it has become apparent that a prior decision has departed from a proper understanding of congressional power under the Commerce Clause. See *United States* v. *Darby* (1941). Due respect for the reach of congressional power within the federal system mandates that we do so now.

National League of Cities v. *Usery* is overruled. The judgment of the District Court is reversed, and these cases are remanded to that court for further proceedings consistent with this opinion.

It is so ordered.

JUSTICE POWELL, with whom THE CHIEF JUSTICE, JUSTICE REHNQUIST, and JUSTICE O'CONNOR join, dissenting. . . .

I

There are, of course, numerous examples over the history of this Court in which prior decisions have been reconsidered and overruled. There have been few cases, however, in which the principle of *stare decisis* and the rationale of recent decisions were ignored as abruptly as we now witness. The reasoning of the Court in *National League of Cities,* and the principle applied there, have been reiterated consistently over the past eight years. Since its decision in 1976, *National League of Cities* has been cited and quoted in opinions joined by every member of the present Court. *Hodel* v. *Virginia Surface Mining & Recl. Assn.* (1981); *United Transportation Union* v. *Long Island R. Co.* (1982); *FERC* v. *Mississippi* (1982). Less than three years ago, in *Long Island R. Co.,* a unanimous Court reaffirmed the principles of *National League of Cities* but found them inapplicable to the regulation of a railroad heavily engaged in interstate commerce. . . .

The Court in that case recognized that the test "may at times be a difficult one," but it was considered in that unanimous decision as settled constitutional doctrine.

As recently as June 1, 1982 the five Justices who constitute the majority in this case also were the majority in *FERC* v. *Mississippi.* In that case, the Court said:

> "In *National League of Cities,* for example, the Court made clear that the State's regulation of its relationship with its employees is an 'undoubted attribute of state sovereignty.' Yet, by holding 'unimpaired' *California* v. *Taylor* (1957), which upheld a federal labor regulation as applied to state railroad employees, *National League of Cities* acknowledged that not all aspects of a State's sovereign authority are immune from federal control."

The Court went on to say that even where the requirements of the *National League of Cities* standard are met, " '[t]here are situations in which the nature of the federal interest advanced may be such that it justifies state submission.' " The joint federal/state system of regulation in *FERC* was such a "situation," but there was no hint in the Court's opinion that *National League of Cities*—or its basic standard—was subject to the infirmities discovered today.

Although the doctrine is not rigidly applied to constitutional questions, "any departure from the doctrine of *stare decisis* demands special justification." *Arizona* v. *Rumsey* (1984). See also *Oregon* v. *Kennedy* (1982) (STEVENS, J., concurring). In the present case, the five Justices who compose the majority today participated in *National League of Cities* and the cases reaffirming it. The stability of judicial decision, and with it respect for the authority of this Court, are not served by the precipitous overruling of multiple precedents that we witness in this case.

Whatever effect the Court's decision may have in weakening the application of *stare decisis,* it is likely to be less important than what the Court has done to the Constitution itself. A unique feature of the United States is the *federal* system of government guaranteed by the Constitution and implicit in the very name of our country. Despite some genuflecting in Court's opinion to the concept of federalism, today's decision effectively reduces the Tenth Amendment to meaningless rhetoric when Congress acts pursuant to the Commerce Clause. . . .

To leave no doubt about its intention, the Court renounces its decision in *National League of Cities* because it "inevitably invites an unelected federal judiciary to make decisions about which state policies its favors and which ones it dislikes." In other words, the extent to which the States may exercise their authority, when Congress purports to act under the Commerce Clause, henceforth is to be determined from time to time by political decisions made by members of the federal government, decisions the Court says will not be subject to judicial review. I note that it does not seem to have occurred to the Court that *it*—an unelected majority of five Justices—today rejects almost 200 years of the understanding of the constitutional status of federalism. In doing so, there is only a single passing reference to the Tenth Amendment. Nor is so much as a dictum of any court cited in support of the view that the role of the States in the federal system may depend upon the grace of elected federal officials, rather than on the Constitution as interpreted by this Court. . . .

JUSTICE O'CONNOR, with whom **JUSTICE POWELL** and **JUSTICE REHNQUIST** join, dissenting.

The Court today surveys the battle scene of federalism and

sounds a retreat. Like JUSTICE POWELL, I would prefer to hold the field and, at the very least, render a little aid to the wounded. I join JUSTICE POWELL's opinion. I also write separately to note my fundamental disagreement with the majority's views of federalism and the duty of this Court. . . .

10.7   *"Legal discourse in the style of* stare decisis . . . *is . . . but an instance of communication with extremely high levels of redundancy."*

TOWARD A THEORY OF STARE DECISIS

Martin Shapiro

I shall propose in this article as a new theory of *stare decisis* (a term I use loosely to mean the practice of courts in deciding new cases in accordance with precedents) that draws upon the insights of communications theory as well as upon some previous work of my own on the decision-making process in tort law. The attempt to apply communications theory to the law is not new, or—given that judicial decision-making is a species of verbal behavior—unexpected. Previous efforts to apply communications theory to problems of judicial decision-making have foundered, however, on a lack of clear conception as to what that theory means and can tell us about the judicial process, and it is with an attempt at clarification of the relevant concepts that I begin.

Communications theory is not a unified body of thought. It has three quite distinct branches. The first, "syntactics," is concerned with the logical arrangement, transmission, and receipt of signals or signs. It is the domain of the electrical engineer; its concern is with the transmission of signals, whatever their meaning. The second is "semantics," which is concerned with the meaning of the signals to people. The third is "pragmatics," which is the study of the impact of signal transmission on human behavior. . . .

The key concepts of syntactics, for our purposes, are "information," "redundancy," and "feedback," of which the first two are best discussed together. For the telegraphic engineer, information is the content of a signal that could not have been predicted by the receiver; it is a probability concept. The more probable the transmission of a given sign, the less information its actual transmission conveys. "Redundancy" is the opposite of information. It is the introduction of repetition or pattern into the message. If the telegrapher

From *The Journal of Legal Studies* 125 (1972). Reprinted by permission. Martin Shapiro is Professor of Law, Boalt Hall, University of California, Berkeley.

sends each message twice, his second sending is redundant and contains less information than his first. If we establish the convention, rule, or pattern that two dashes will always be followed by a dot, then the actual transmission of the dot after the two dashes will be redundant and contain no information because the dot placement in the sequence could always be predicted without actual transmission.

The ideal transmission, then, in terms of pure "information," would contain absolutely no repetition and no pattern. The engineer finds it wise, however, to introduce redundancy at the cost of reducing the information content of a message, because otherwise any loss of information due to malfunctions in the transmission system would be undetectable and irremediable. It is only when we can predict, at least partially, what message we are going to receive that we can spot an erroneous omission or substitution in the message and call for its correction. The ideal message, then, will contain the highest proportion of information and the lowest proportion of redundancy necessary to identify and correct errors in transmission. . . . The concept of redundancy seems to me promising as a further tool in integrating legal discourse into more general discourse.

At the most superficial level, it is obvious that legal discourse organized by the rules of *stare decisis* emphasizes, and itself insists that its success rests upon, high levels of redundancy and, therefore, remembering our original theoretical formulation, low levels of information. The strongest legal argument is that the current case, on its facts, is "on all fours" with a previous case and that the decision in that case is deeply imbedded in a long line of decisions enunciating (repeating) a single legal principle. In other words, the strongest argument is that the current case, treated as an input, is totally redundant, and under the rules of *stare decisis* the duty of the judge is to transmit a message that is equally redundant. Of course the facts of a new case are never exactly on all fours with an old, and no line of precedents is ever totally clear and consistent. The point is that the rules of legal discourse seem to require each attorney to suppress as much information and transmit as much redundancy as possible.

At the semantic level, legal discourse is conducted in terms of highly redundant symbols. The string citation comes to mind in which authorities are piled up endlessly in support of a statement of the law in the opinion, brief, or text. The normal mode of criticizing such citations is to show that they actually contain information: either that (1) the cases in the citation do not say the same thing as the statement in the text or that (2) some of the cases cited do not say the same thing as the other cases cited. If the statement and the cases do not all say exactly the same thing—if the message is not totally redundant after the first bit of information—then a technical error or a violation of the rules of legal craftsmanship has been committed. The rules of the craft are only obeyed to the extent that, having received any portion of the craft message, a second craftsman could have predicted all the remaining portions. . . .

In the "craftsmanlike" appellate opinion or brief, the argument is built sentence by sentence, with each sentence—often many of the phrases within each sentence—supported by a citation. A skilled lawyer, seeing the sequence of citations alone, could predict the argument, or, seeing the argument alone, could predict the citations. Thus, either the argument or the citations are—and are supposed to be—redundant. Furthermore, the optimum situation for authoritative appellate decision-making is one where each citation is to a "leading" case that is "leading" precisely because its reasoning has been repeated (and is itself cited) in many other cases. The citation of a leading case name incorporates, in effect, other synonymous cases so that . . . we may assume that the receiver remembers the synonyms used for a given symbol in the redundant code, and that in future messages these synonyms or alternate codes are understood even though not physically present. Furthermore, recognition of a case as leading assures the lawyer and judge that the issues involved were worked through not once but many times before the system settled on this particular case name as the symbol for its many synonymous treatments of the question. It is significant, too, that a well-constructed legal opinion is likely to make the same point many different ways—in canvassing the issues, in meeting the counterarguments, etc. When a later judicial craftsman cites the previous opinion, he imports the previous internal redundancy of that case into his own well-constructed—that is to say, internally redundant—opinion. Finally, the very practice of citation is the assertion that "I am not saying anything new; I am only repeating what has already been said."

Legal discourse in the style of *stare decisis,* then, is not a unique phenomenon, but an instance of communication with extremely high levels of redundancy. Indeed, what we think of as the "taught tradition" (and thus the peculiar tradition) of the law is largely a set of coding rules for introducing redundancy into legal messages. . . .

In recent years political science has focused not on judicial opinions but on judicial decisions (who won and lost) as keys to understanding judicial attitudes. In legal theory, and legal commentary more generally, there has been much attention to judicial opinions as justifications or explanations, and to what modes of justification and explanation are appropriate to legal discourse. But nearly all the commentators concerned with these problems treat the opinion *in vacuo,* asking whether it meets certain general standards and thus turning the problem into one of logic or philosophy.

Somehow we ignored the fact that appellate courts and the lawyers that serve them spend an overwhelming proportion of their energies in communicating with one another, and that the judicial opinion, itself conforming to the style of *stare decisis,* is the principal mode of communication. This massive pattern of communicative behavior has persisted in the face of our insistence that it is what judges do, not what they say, that counts, in spite of repeated demonstrations that *stare decisis* does not yield single correct solutions, and despite the failure of theorists to provide clear-cut descriptions of what a correct judicial opinion would look like.

It would seem appropriate, therefore, to examine the opinion-writing activity of courts in the context of communication, and once we do, a striking finding emerges. The style of legal discourse that we summarize in the expression *stare decisis* is not a unique phenomenon peculiar to the Anglo-American legal system, not a unique method or form of reasoning or logic, but an instance of redundancy, the standard solution predicted by communications theory for any acute noise problem. And there is a further finding: the characteristic style of Anglo-American legal discourse persists because its rather standard and routine solution to the noise problem of a non-hierarchical organization like the courts yields at the very same time a pattern of redundant communication that is extremely useful, perhaps essential, to the incremental mode of decision-making that organizations of this sort typically adopt. If this suggestion has any merit, it should be possible for social scientists to treat the phenomenon of *stare decisis* as a problem in human communications rather than as exclusively one of logic and/or obfuscation.

11
Statutory Interpretation

The great bulk of law interpreted and applied by American courts today is either statutory law or regulations issued by administrative agencies to implement statutes. Congress, the fifty state legislatures, and thousands of city and county councils annually enact a huge mass of statutes; and administrative agencies daily multiply this brood in reams of supposedly explanatory regulations. This predominance of law based on statutes is characteristic of only the past century. Earlier, judge-made principles of the common law had controlled most social and economic relationships, but democratization, industrialization, and urbanization have motivated legislators to become much more active in formulating social and economic policy.

This shift can be seen in startling clarity in the statistics of the Supreme Court's business. According to the calculations of Felix Frankfurter and James M. Landis,[1] as late as 1875 more than 40 percent of the controversies coming to the Court involved common law litigation; by 1925 only 5 percent of the cases fell into this category. Today the justices would rarely, if ever, accept a case unless it raised an important question of federal constitutional or statutory law, with the latter category including the question whether a given statute authorized a particular administrative regulation.

THE RULE OF STRICT CONSTRUCTION

Judges were initially unhappy about the trend that challenged their legislative primacy. Institutional competition was sharpened because judges tended to represent the status quo and to favor the more conservative forces in society, whereas legislators were more apt to be influenced by reformers. Consequently, for many years a prevalent

---

[1] *The Business of the Supreme Court* (New York: Macmillan, 1928), p. 306.

Oct Terms 35-36

HLR 51:377

judicial tactic in dealing with statutes was to adopt rules that would curtail the effectiveness of new legislation.

Judges' biases were perhaps most obvious in the rule that courts should strictly construe legislation modifying or contradicting the common law. But judges tended to construe strictly any legislation that imposed new burdens or special penalties. Almost every piece of "progressive" legislation in the nineteenth and early twentieth centuries suffered a period of judicial sabotage that took the form not only of outright attacks on the statute's constitutionality but also of interpretations that denied to the law the scope that the legislature had sketched. The Supreme Court, for example, interpreted the Interstate Commerce Act of 1887 so narrowly that within a decade the Interstate Commerce Commission became, Justice John Marshall Harlan, I, protested, "a useless body." The ICC reported to Congress in 1897 that "by virtue of judicial decisions, it [the Commission] has ceased to be a body for the regulation of interstate carriers." It took a series of new statutes and a change in judicial attitudes in the twentieth century to undo this damage.

Although most American judges have outgrown their hostility to legislation, many British judges remain unconvinced of the wisdom if not the legitimacy of statutory law. As a noted authority wrote in 1957, "While it would be going too far to say that our courts read statutes 'in bad faith,' it is difficult to resist the impression that some judges are always ready to think the worst of a statute and of its draftsman."[2]

Even in the United States, judges are still likely to say that they "presume," unless the legislature specifically says otherwise, that a statute accepts judicial definitions of terms (Reading 11.1) and even judicial notions about proper public policy. Moreover, the old rule of strict construction of statutes remains firmly established in criminal law. Penal statutes, judges insist, must be sufficiently specific to define and give adequate notice of the kind of conduct they forbid or penalize. As the Supreme Court said in *Connally v. General Construction Co.* (1926): "A statute which either forbids or requires the doing of an act in terms so vague that men of common intelligence must necessarily guess at its meaning and differ as to its application, violates the first essential of due process of law."

Implementation of these principles of certainty and notice requires courts to resolve any ambiguities of language in criminal statutes in favor of the accused. This rule, as Chief Justice Marshall remarked in *United States v. Wiltberger* (1820), "is founded on the tenderness of the law for the rights of individuals; and on the plain principle that the power of punishment is vested in the legislative, not in the judicial department. It is the legislature, not the Court, which is to define a crime, and ordain its punishment."

---

[2] C. K. Allen, *Law in the Making* (sixth ed.; London: Oxford University Press, 1958), p. 503.

Closely related to this rule of "void for vagueness" is the doctrine of "statutory overbreadth." Both vagueness and overbreadth are grounds for judges' declaring statutes unconstitutional on their face. The charge of overbreadth is typically lodged against statutes touching on the First Amendment, the usual argument being that the law extends beyond the area of legitimate legislative concern and threatens injury to fragile and important freedoms.

THE PROBLEM OF AMBIGUITY

The task of statutory interpretation might seem, on first consideration, to pose fewer problems than the task of reasoning from case law. There is no need to search a sea of precedents for the principle governing the case. There is no need to look for dicta so that they can be excluded from consideration. The court starts with a text, the legislature's effort to state a rule of law in language that will make its meaning clear and plain.

Lawmakers, however, often find it difficult to convey their exact purpose in clear and plain language. It is easy to blame careless draftsmanship, for strange and awkward language abounds in statutes. But some problems are much too technical and complex to be encompassed in words that are intelligible to the nonspecialist. A statute like the Securities and Exchange Act, regulating advertising, buying, and selling of stocks and bonds, must use a great deal of esoteric terminology that has meaning only to experts in the field.

There is the additional problem of language itself. Even rules stated in ordinary words may contain ambiguities. A classic example is the city ordinance that reads: "No vehicle shall enter a public park." Does that ordinance exclude baby buggies? Tricycles? Bicycles? Self-propelled wheelchairs? Mopeds? Skateboards? An ambulance coming to bring an injured person to a hospital? A police car protecting the people enjoying the park? Words, as Judge Jerome Frank explained, "serve as symbols. As such they are necessarily somewhat compressed, condensed. . . . The judges must determine the proper limits of expansion of condensed symbols."[3] Coping with that sort of compressed ambiguity is hardly an easy task.

A third set of complications arises when legislators are deliberately ambiguous. Sometimes lawmakers who cannot agree among themselves on how to attack a problem compromise by choosing obscure language and so toss the basic difficulty to administrators or judges. It may also happen that legislators believe that certain problems are too complex and varied in form to be successfully met by clear, precise language. In such situations, legislators may resort to sweeping phrases, empowering other governmental agencies "to regulate in the public interest," to set "reasonable rates," or to provide "family plan-

[3] *Courts on Trial* (Princeton, N.J.: Princeton University Press, 1950), p. 294.

ning services." During the debate on what became the Sherman Act of 1890, another senator asked John Sherman what he meant by "monopoly." Sherman candidly responded that he had no exact definition:

> it is difficult to define in legal language the precise line between lawful and unlawful combinations. This must be left for the courts to determine in each particular case. All that we, as lawmakers, can do is to declare general principles, and we can be assured that the courts will apply them so as to carry out the meaning of the law. . . .[4]

If Congress had no exact meaning, then judges faced an enormous difficulty in carrying out "the meaning of the law." It is little wonder that the Supreme Court quickly became and remained, as one standard text says, "the ultimate maker of antitrust policy."[5]

At still other times, legislators hastily enact statutes as a means of easing pressure from interest groups and constituents, employing muddy language so as to allow themselves a ready claim of misinterpretation if the legislation proves unwise. As one English judge complained about such a statute, it was "an ill-penned enactment, like too many others, putting Judges in the embarrassing situation of being bound to make sense out of nonsense, and to reconcile what is irreconcilable."[6]

Intentional ambiguity has characterized congressional efforts to enact a standard for exempting conscientious objectors to military service. On the one hand, the older practice of requiring all healthy males to serve required the government to violate the consciences of many of its loyal citizens. On the other hand, excusing members of pacifist religious sects would have violated the establishment clause of the First Amendment. So in 1948 Congress made exemption depend on an individual's relation to a "Supreme Being," leaving it to administrators and judges to interpret this language. *United States v. Seeger* (1965) demonstrates that judges could respond creatively. (Reading 11.2.)

LEGISLATIVE INTENT

Judges normally presume, not always correctly, that a statute has a purpose, that it is a legislative effort to solve a problem in public policy. Thus it is a widely accepted rule that judges should try to discover that purpose so as to interpret specific phrases in light of that overarching objective. As Judge Learned Hand once wrote:

> Of course it is true that the words used, even in their literal sense, are the primary, and ordinarily the most reliable source of interpret-

---

[4] 21 *Congressional Record* 2460.

[5] Merle Fainsod, Lincoln Gordon, and Joseph C. Palamountain, Jr., *Government and the American Economy* (third ed.; New York: Norton, 1959), p. 603.

[6] Quoted in Allen, *Law in the Making*, p. 468.

ing the meaning of any writing: be it a statute, a contract, or anything else. But it is one of the surest indexes of a mature and developed jurisprudence not to make a fortress out of the dictionary; but to remember that statutes always have some purpose or object to accomplish, whose sympathetic and imaginative discovery is the surest guide to their meaning.[7]

This prescription recognizes that judges have a subordinate role to play in applying statutory law; their obligation is to help the legislature achieve its goals.

There have been wide differences of opinion as to the practices a court might employ in attempting to discover legislative purpose. In England the usual rule is that courts must examine nothing but the words of the statute itself. They can take no note of any discussions in Parliament during the passage of the act, nor of any statements of members of the Government in presenting the bill, nor of any committee deliberations on the bill. For generations American practice tended to follow the English example. As late as 1921, a majority of the Supreme Court could claim that it was "well established that the debates in Congress expressive of the views and motives of individual members are not a safe guide . . . in ascertaining the meaning and purpose of the law-making body."[8]

But even then American judges were not universally denying themselves information about a statute's genesis and development, and within little more than a decade courts were routinely looking at legislative reports and debates in an effort to discern what purposes underlay social and economic regulations. Today it is accepted practice for judges to place considerable stress on the legislative history of an act in determining its meaning; and members of Congress, recognizing the important role of legislative history, often take pains to get statements into the *Congressional Record* that will support their interpretation of the legislative language being adopted.[9]

In *Tennessee Valley Authority v. Hill* (1978) the Court concluded that the legislative history and plain language of the Endangered

[7] *Cabell* v. *Markham* (1945).

[8] *Duplex Printing Press Co. v. Deering* (1921).

[9] The Court's decision in *Grove City College v. Bell* (1984) aroused intense opposition in Congress on an issue of statutory interpretation. Title IX of the Education Amendments of 1972 prohibits sex discrimination in "any educational program or activity receiving Federal financial assistance." Its effect in improving financial support for women's athletics was reflected in the performance of U.S. women in the 1984 Olympics. The issue in *Grove City* was whether the act applied to a college that received no direct federal financial aid but where a number of students did receive educational opportunity grants. The Court, complaining about the "sparse legislative history" of Title IX, concluded that the student grants did bring the college within the purview of the statute, but only as to the student aid program. This holding would have removed women's athletics and all other noncomplying programs from the coverage of Title IX, and possibly undermined the enforcement of other major civil rights laws. Legislation to reverse the Court's interpretation in *Grove City* was strongly supported in the 1985 session of Congress.

Species Act of 1973 were so compelling that they mandated what Justice Powell regarded as the "absurd result" of halting a $100 million dam project that was "virtually completed" to protect a small number of three-inch-long fish. (Reading 11.3.) But in *United Steelworkers v. Weber* (1979) a majority of the justices used legislative history and liberal quotations from the Congressional Record to uphold an affirmative-action program that Justice Rehnquist contended violated the plain language of the statute. (Reading 11.4.)

The Supreme Court's interpretation of the Mann Act (1910) may have set new standards for the "sympathetic and imaginative discovery" of legislative purpose for which Judge Learned Hand asked. Although this statute was designated as the "White Slave Traffic Act," and its announced target was commercialized "prostitution or debauchery," it also made illegal crossing state lines "for any other immoral purpose." On the basis of this language the Court in *Caminetti v. United States* (1917) applied the act to two unmarried couples who crossed a state line, and in *Cleveland v. United States* (1946) to six members of a fundamentalist Mormon sect who practiced polygamy. (Reading 11.5.)

LEGISLATIVE RATIFICATION OF JUDICIAL INTERPRETATION

Judges may also seek legislative purpose in legislative inaction. After a statute has been judicially interpreted, courts may study congressional reaction for clues about the correctness of the decision. If disappointed legislators fail to amend the statute, judges often take such inaction as an indication that the original judicial interpretation was correct, at least within limits that Congress considers acceptable.

In *Bob Jones University v. United States* (1983) the Supreme Court upheld denial of a tax exemption by the Internal Revenue Service for a racially discriminatory school, and one of the reasons Chief Justice Burger gave for the ruling was that repeated efforts in Congress to overturn the IRS interpretation of the relevant statute had failed. "Nonaction by Congress is not often a useful guide," he admitted, "but the non-action here is significant." (Reading 11.6.)

Conscientious objection provides an interesting case study. In three separate decisions in 1929 and 1931, the Supreme Court interpreted the statutory oath to "defend" the Constitution, required of aliens wishing to become citizens, as barring conscientious objectors from naturalization. Despite strenuous efforts in Congress to amend the statute to permit conscientious objectors to be naturalized, no change was made in the oath. But in 1946 *Girouard v. United States* reversed earlier holdings and ruled that the oath did *not* exclude conscientious objectors. Chief Justice Stone dissented on the ground that congressional inaction had "adopted and confirmed this Court's earlier construction of the naturalization laws," but, for the Court, Justice Douglas responded: "It is at best treacherous to find in congressional silence alone the adoption of a rule of law."

ADMINISTRATIVE INTERPRETATION

Judges sometimes try to divine a statute's purpose by examining the explanatory rules promulgated by the administrative agency—supposedly staffed by neutral experts—to whom the legislature has assigned the task of enforcing the particular statute. Agencies like the Internal Revenue Service and the National Labor Relations Board issue massive codes of regulations that purport to carry out the will of Congress—a will that, as we have seen, is often expressed in sweeping generalities to meet complex technological, social, and economic problems.

The initial judicial reaction to these agencies was hostile; but, especially since 1937, judges have tended to view administrators more as coworkers than as rivals in the vineyard of statutory construction and to give considerable deference to their interpretations of congressional intent. Indeed, on occasion, dissenting judges have accused their brethren of abdicating their functions to administrators. But, courts retain full authority to modify or reject administrative interpretations of statutes and sometimes exercise that authority.

LEGISLATIVE MOTIVATION

Words like purpose, intent, goal, and objective all refer to *what* the legislature tried to accomplish. Motivation refers to *why* the legislature wanted to enact a statute. Confusing the *what* and the *why* can cause serious problems. Unhappily for those who like logic, judges often use terms like "purpose" and "motivation" interchangeably.

To avoid the sticky practical difficulties of separating purpose from motivation, judges have frequently asserted that they will not look at the reasons why legislators voted as they did, only at legislative authority. *McCray v. United States* (1904) is the classic case. There Congress had levied a tax of ten cents a pound on oleomargarine colored yellow to look like butter, but only one-quarter of a cent a pound on uncolored margarine. Ignoring the obvious fingerprints of the dairy lobby that were smeared on the margins of the statute, the Court held that it could not consider "the motives" of Congress, only its constitutional power to tax.

Several generations later, *Palmer v. Thompson* (1971)[10] arrived at a similar conclusion. That case concerned the closing by the city

[10] See the two articles by Paul Brest: "Palmer v. Thompson: An Approach to the Problem of Unconstitutional Legislative Motive," 1971 *Supreme Court Review* 95; and "The Conscientious Legislator's Guide to Constitutional Interpretation," 27 *Stanford Law Review* 585 (1975).

council of Jackson, Mississippi, of all five of its municipal swimming pools. The Supreme Court refused to declare this action unconstitutional on the ground that the council had really been trying to avoid racial integration. As Justice Black said for the Court:

> there is an element of futility in a judicial attempt to invalidate a law because of the bad motives of its supporters. If the law is struck down for this reason . . . it would presumably be valid as soon as the legislature or relevant governing body repassed it for different reasons.

The judicial record, however, is not so consistent as these dogmatic pronouncements indicate. *Bailey v. Drexel Furniture Co.* (1922) invalidated a congressional tax on businesses employing children because, Chief Justice Taft claimed, the motivation behind the statute was not to collect taxes but to regulate child labor. During the 1960s, in striking down state statutes that discriminated on the basis of race, the Warren Court sometimes looked at legislative motive. More recently, the Burger Court has continued that practice in race cases, but with results opposite from those of the Warren Court. The official doctrine now holds that a statute that on its face does not discriminate, but does affect races differently, will be judged unconstitutional only if the legislative *motive* was to discriminate. Two cases illustrate the new trend. *Washington v. Davis* (1976) upheld a test for applicants for the police force in Washington, D.C., that had been challenged because many more blacks than whites failed it. *Arlington Heights v. Metropolitan Housing Corp.* (1977) sustained restrictive zoning ordinances that in effect excluded low- and middle-income families from the community. In both cases, the Court found that "proof of racially discriminatory intent" was absent.

How to establish "intent" in the sense of motivation poses grave problems, but in *Arlington Heights* Justice Lewis F. Powell faced up to the issue:

> The historical background of the decision is one evidentiary course, particularly if it reveals a series of official actions taken for invidious purposes. . . . Departures from the normal procedural sequence also might afford evidence that improper purposes are playing a role. . . . The legislative or administrative history may be highly relevant, especially where there are contemporary statements by members of the decisionmaking body, minutes of its meetings, or reports. In some extraordinary instances the members might be called to the stand at trial to testify concerning the purpose of the official action, although even then such testimony frequently will be barred by privilege.

AVOIDING CONSTITUTIONAL QUESTIONS

A rule of interpretation frequently utilized by judges and highly recommended by the Supreme Court requires that whenever possible legislation be interpreted in such a way as to avoid constitutional questions. Involved here is a recognition of the need to use very cautiously judicial power to declare legislative acts unconstitutional, particularly acts of Congress, a policy to be discussed in more detail in the next chapter. In *Ashwander v. Tennessee Valley Authority* (1936), Justice Louis Brandeis listed for the Court's benefit a "series of rules under which it has avoided passing upon a large part of all the constitutional questions pressed upon it for decision." The seventh rule read:

> When the validity of an act of the Congress is drawn in question and even if a serious doubt of constitutionality is raised, it is a cardinal principle that this Court will first ascertain whether a construction of the statute is fairly possible by which the question may be avoided.

Often, of course, judges will disagree on how far they may legitimately go in interpreting a statute so as to make it constitutional. The principle of judicial self-restraint may give conflicting advice. The rule that a judge should not declare a statute invalid if he can avoid doing so may be challenged by the rule that a judge should not redraft what Congress has enacted. For a court to rewrite a statute in order to make it constitutional may be a more unwarranted exercise of judicial power than to take the legislation at its face value and declare it invalid.

One of the many notable instances of judicial difference on this issue occurred in *Scales v. United States* (1961). The Supreme Court was reviewing the conviction of a communist under the provision of the Smith Act making it a crime for anyone, "knowing the purposes thereof," to become a member of or affiliate with "any society, group, or assembly of persons" advocating, abetting, advising, or teaching "the duty, necessity, desirability or propriety" of violent overthrow of the government of the United States or of any state or territory in the United States. Speaking for the majority, Justice John M. Harlan, II, tried to skirt the First Amendment's protection of freedom of association by interpreting the statute as affecting only "active" members who had the "specific intent" of carrying out the proscribed activities, not just nominal members who knew of a group's illegal aims. In dissent Justice Black protested that:

> the Court has practically rewritten the statute . . . by treating the requirements of "activity" and "specific intent" as implicit in words that plainly do not include them. . . . It seems clear to me that neither

petitioner nor anyone else could ever have guessed that this law would be held to mean what this Court now holds it does mean. For that reason, it appears that petitioner has been convicted under a law that is, at best, unconstitutionally vague and, at worst, ex post facto.

STATUTORY LAW AND JUDICIAL LAW MAKING

This discussion should have made it obvious that judges may have at least as much leeway in interpreting statutes as in working within the interstices of their own previous decisions. Seeking legislative purpose is frequently a bootless hunt. As Monroe Smith observed several generations ago:

> the possibilities of lawfinding under cover of interpretation are very great. A distinguished German jurist, Windscheid, has remarked that in interpreting legislation modern courts may and habitually do "think over again the thought which the legislator was trying to express," but that the Roman jurist went further and "thought out the thought which the legislator was trying to think."[11]

The difficulties of discerning legislative purpose have moved American jurists to refer to the process of statutory interpretation as an "art." Judge Jerome Frank took this analogy and Windscheid's observation to heart. Only half-smiling, Frank suggested that judges should read a statute like a musician reads a score, as something to be interpreted rather than mechanically applied. "The conscientious, intelligent judge," he continued,

> will consider government a sort of orchestra, in which, in symphonies authorized by the people, the courts and the legislature each play their parts. The playing may sometimes be bad. There may, occasionally, be some disharmonies. But, after all, modern music has taught us that a moderate amount of cacaphony need not be altogether unpleasant.[12]

Whether or not Frank's analogy pleases judges, it is apparent that their roles will, of necessity, be creative when reading many statutes —and the "many" will probably include those most important to a particular generation. A court can make as much law by reading a statute too strictly as it can by reading it too loosely, and "too" in each instance defies objective definition. As a result, the "disharmonies"

---

[11] Quoted by Thomas Reed Powell, "The Logic and Rhetoric of Constitutional Law," 15 *Journal of Philosophy, Psychology, and Scientific Method* 654 (1918).
[12] *Courts on Trial*, pp. 207–208.

that result as judges rule for or against particular interests may be far more frequent—and painful—than Frank cared to admit.

SELECTED REFERENCES

Beaney, William M. "Civil Liberties and Statutory Construction," 8 *Journal of Public Law* 66 (1959).

Bickel, Alexander M., and Harry H. Wellington. "Legislative Purpose and the Judicial Process: The Lincoln Mills Case," 71 *Harvard Law Review* 1 (1957).

Binion, Gayle. " 'Intent' and Equal Protection: A Reconsideration," in Philip B. Kurland et al. (eds.), *1983 Supreme Court Review* 397. Chicago: University of Chicago Press, 1984.

Brest, Paul. "Palmer v. Thompson: An Approach to the Problem of Unconstitutional Legislative Motive," in Philip B. Kurland (ed.), *1971 Supreme Court Review* 95. Chicago: University of Chicago Press, 1981.

———. "The Conscientious Legislator's Guide to Constitutional Interpretation," 27 *Stanford Law Review* 585 (1975).

——— and Sanford V. Levinson (eds.). *Processes of Constitutional Decisionmaking: Cases and Materials.* 2d ed. Boston: Little, Brown, 1983.

Calabresi, Guido. *A Common Law for the Age of Statutes.* Cambridge, Mass.: Harvard University Press, 1982.

Ely, John Hart. "Legislative and Administrative Motivation in Constitutional Law," 79 *Yale Law Journal* 1207 (1970).

Frank, Jerome. *Law and the Modern Mind.* New York: Brentano's, 1930. Chs. 3, 4.

———. "Words and Music: Some Remarks on Statutory Interpretation," 47 *Columbia Law Review* 1259 (1947).

Interpretation Symposium. 28 *Southern California Law Review* 1 (1985).

Kaufman, Irving R. "Divining the Legislative Will," 53 *Fordham Law Review* 1 (1985).

Mantel, Howard N. "The Congressional Record: Fact or Fiction of the Legislative Process," 12 *Western Political Quarterly* 981 (1959).

Mendelson, Wallace. "Mr. Justice Frankfurter on the Construction of Statutes," 43 *California Law Review* 652 (1955).

Miller, Arthur S. "Statutory Language and the Purposive Use of Ambiguity," 42 *Virginia Law Review* 23 (1956).

Pound, Roscoe. "Common Law and Legislation," 21 *Harvard Law Review* 383 (1908).

Symposium on Statutory Construction, 3 *Vanderbilt Law Review* 365 (1950).

Symposium: Law and Literature. 60 *Texas Law Review* 373 (1982).

11.1   *". . . judges are not unfettered glossators."*

SOME REFLECTIONS ON THE READING OF STATUTES

Felix Frankfurter

. . . Anything that is written may present a problem of meaning, and that is the essence of the business of judges in construing legislation. The problem derives from the very nature of words. They are symbols of meaning. But unlike mathematical symbols, the phrasing of a document, especially a complicated enactment, seldom attains more than approximate precision. If individual words are inexact symbols, with shifting variables, their configuration can hardly achieve invariant meaning or assured definiteness. Apart from the ambiguity inherent in its symbols, a statute suffers from dubieties. It is not an equation or a formula representing a clearly marked process, nor is it an expression of individual thought to which is imparted the definiteness a single authorship can give. A statute is an instrument of government partaking of its practical purposes but also of its infirmities and limitations, of its awkward and groping efforts. . . . The imagination which can draw an income tax statute to cover the myriad transactions of a society like ours, capable of producing the necessary revenue without producing a flood of litigation, has not yet revealed itself. Moreover, government sometimes solves problems by shelving them temporarily. The legislative process reflects that attitude. Statutes as well as constitutional provisions at times embody purposeful ambiguity or are expressed with a generality for future unfolding. . . .

The intrinsic difficulties of language and the emergence after enactment of situations not anticipated by the most gifted legislative imagination, reveal doubts and ambiguities in statutes that compel judicial construction. The process of construction, therefore, is not an exercise in logic or dialectic: The aids of formal reasoning are not irrelevant; they may simply be inadequate. The purpose of construction being the ascertainment of meaning, every consideration brought to bear for the solution of that problem must be devoted to that end alone. To speak of it as a practical problem is not to indulge a fashion in words. It must be that, not something else. Not, for instance, an opportunity for a judge to use words as "empty vessels into which he can pour anything he will"—his caprices, fixed notions,

2 *Record of the Association of the Bar of the City of New York* 213 (1947).

even statesmanlike beliefs in a particular policy. Nor, on the other hand, is the process a ritual to be observed by unimaginative adherence to well-worn professional phrases. . . .

. . . The area of free judicial movement is considerable. . . . The difficulty is that the legislative ideas which laws embody are both explicit and immanent. And so the bottom problem is: What is below the surface of the words and yet fairly a part of them? Words in statutes are not unlike words in a foreign language in that they too have "associations, echoes, and overtones." Judges must retain the associations, hear the echoes, and capture the overtones. . . .

Even within their area of choice the courts are not at large. They are confined by the nature and scope of the judicial function in its particular exercise in the field of interpretation. They are under the constraints imposed by the judicial function in our democratic society. As a matter of verbal recognition certainly, no one will gainsay that the function in construing a statute is to ascertain the meaning of words used by the legislature. To go beyond it is to usurp a power which our democracy has lodged in its elected legislature. . . . A judge must not rewrite a statute, neither to enlarge nor to contract it. . . .

This duty of restraint, this humility of function as merely the translator of another's command, is a constant theme of our Justices. . . . In short, judges are not unfettered glossators. They are under a special duty not to over-emphasize the episodic aspects of life and not to undervalue its organic processes—its continuities and relationships. For judges at least it is important to remember that continuity with the past is not only a necessity but even a duty. . . .

Let me descend to some particulars.

The text.   Though we may not end with the words in construing a disputed statute, one certainly begins there. . . . The Court no doubt must listen to the voice of Congress. But often Congress cannot be heard clearly because its speech is muffled. Even when it has spoken, it is as true of Congress as of others that what is said is what the listener hears. Like others, judges too listen with what psychologists used to call the apperception mass, which I take it means in plain English that one listens with what is already in one's head. One more caution is relevant when one is admonished to listen attentively to what a statute says. One must also listen attentively to what it does not say.

We must, no doubt, accord the words the sense in which Congress used them . . . we assume that Congress uses common words in their popular meaning, as used in the common speech of men. The cases speak of the "meaning of common understanding," "the normal and spontaneous meaning of language," "the common and appropriate use," "the natural straightforward and literal sense," and similar variants. . . .

Sometimes Congress supplies its own dictionary. It did so in 1871 in a statute defining a limited number of words for use as to all future enactments. . . . Or there may be indications from the statute that words in it are the considered language of legislation. "If Congress has been accustomed to use a certain phrase with a more limited meaning than might be attributed to it by common practice, it would be arbitrary to refuse to consider that fact when we come to interpret a statute." . . . Or words may acquire scope and function from the history of events which they summarize or from the purpose which they serve. . . . Words of art bring their art with them. They bear the meaning of their habitat whether it be a phrase of technical significance in the scientific or business world, or whether it be loaded with the recondite connotations of feudalism. . . . The peculiar idiom of business or of administrative practice often modifies the meaning that ordinary speech assigns to language. And if a word is obviously transplanted from another legal source, whether the common law or other legislation, it brings the old soil with it.

The context. Legislation is a form of literary composition. But construction is not an abstract process equally valid for every composition, not even for every composition whose meaning must be judicially ascertained. The nature of the composition demands awareness of certain presuppositions. . . . And so, the significance of an enactment, its antecedents as well as its later history, its relation to other enactments, all may be relevant to the construction of words for one purpose and in one setting but not for another. Some words are confined to their history; some are starting points for history. Words are intellectual and moral currency. They come from the legislative mint with some intrinsic meaning. Sometimes it remains unchanged. Like currency, words sometimes appreciate or depreciate in value.

Frequently the sense of a word cannot be got except by fashioning a mosaic of significance out of the innuendoes of disjointed bits of statute. Cardozo phrased this familiar phenomenon by stating that "the meaning of a statute is to be looked for, not in any single section, but in all the parts together and in their relation to the end in view." . . .

You may have observed that I have not yet used the word "intention." All these years I have avoided speaking of the "legislative intent" and I shall continue to be on my guard against using it. The objection to "intention" was indicated in a letter by Mr. Justice Holmes which the recipient kindly put at my disposal:

Only a day or two ago—when counsel talked of the intention of a legislature, I was indiscreet enough to say I don't care what their intention was. I only want to know what the words mean. . . .

Legislation has an aim; it seeks to obviate some mischief, to supply an inadequacy, to effect a change of policy, to formulate a plan of government. That aim, that policy is not drawn, like nitrogen, out of the air; it is evinced in the language of the statute, as read in the light of other external manifestations of purpose. That is what the judge must seek and effectuate. . . .

The difficulty in many instances where a problem of meaning arises is that the enactment was not directed towards the troubling question. The problem might then be stated, as once it was by Mr. Justice Cardozo, "which choice is it the more likely that Congress would have made?" . . . But the purpose which a court must effectuate is not that which Congress should have enacted, or would have. It is that which it did enact, however inaptly, because it may fairly be said to be imbedded in the statute, even if a specific manifestation was not thought of, as is often the very reason for casting a statute in very general terms.

Often the purpose or policy that controls is not directly displayed in the particular enactment. Statutes cannot be read intelligently if the eye is closed to considerations evidenced in affiliated statutes, or in the known temper of legislative opinion. Thus, for example, it is not lightly to be presumed that Congress sought to infringe on "very sacred rights." This improbability will be a factor in determining whether language, though it should be so read if standing alone, was used to effect such a drastic change. . . .

Nor can canons of construction save us from the anguish of judgment. Such canons give an air of abstract intellectual compulsion to what is in fact a delicate judgment, concluding a complicated process of balancing subtle and elusive elements. . . . Insofar as canons of construction are generalizations of experience, they all have worth. In the abstract, they rarely arouse controversy. Difficulties emerge when canons compete in soliciting judgment, because they conflict rather than converge. For the demands of judgment underlying the art of interpretation, there is no vade-mecum. . . .

The quality of legislative organization and procedure is inevitably reflected in the quality of legislative draftsmanship. Representative Monroney told the House last July [1947] that "ninety-five percent of all the legislation that becomes law passes the Congress in the shape that it came from our committees. Therefore if our committee work is sloppy, if it is bad, if it is inadequate, our legislation in ninety-five percent of the cases will be bad and inadequate as well." . . . But what courts do with legislation may in turn deeply affect what Congress will do in the future. Emerson says somewhere that mankind is as lazy as it dares to be. Loose judicial reading makes for loose legislative writing. It encourages the practise illustrated in a recent cartoon in which a senator tells his colleagues "I admit this new bill is too complicated to understand. We'll just have to pass it to find out what it means." . . .

But there are more fundamental objections to loose judicial reading. In a democracy the legislative impulse and its expression should come from those popularly chosen to legislate, and equipped to devise policy, as courts are not. The pressure on legislatures to discharge their responsibility with care, understanding and imagination should be stiffened, not relaxed. Above all, they must not be encouraged in irresponsible or undisciplined use of language. In the keeping of legislatures perhaps more than any other group is the well-being of their fellow-men. Their responsibility is discharged ultimately by words. . . .

11.2   *"No party claims to be an atheist. . . ."*

UNITED STATES V. SEEGER
380 U.S. 163, 85 S. Ct. 850, 13 L. Ed. 2d 733 (1965)

The Draft Act of 1917 exempted objectors affiliated with a "well-recognized religious sect or organization . . . whose existing creed or principles [forbids] its members to participate in war in any form." This definition raised obvious constitutional questions regarding establishment of a religion, and the 1940 Selective Training and Service Act made it unnecessary to belong to a pacifist religious sect if the claimant's own opposition to war was based on "religious training and belief." This phrase was defined in Section 6(j) of the 1948 act as follows: "an individual's belief in a relation to a Supreme Being involving duties superior to those arising from any human relation, but [not including] essentially political, sociological, or philosophical views or a merely personal moral code."

This case involved three young men, none of whom was a member of an orthodox religious group or willing to declare a belief in a Supreme Being. None, however, was avowedly an atheist.

MR. JUSTICE CLARK delivered the opinion of the Court. . . .

1. The crux of the problem lies in the phrase "religious training and belief." . . . In assigning meaning to this statutory language we may narrow the inquiry by noting briefly those scruples expressly excepted from the definition. The section excludes those persons who, disavowing religious belief, decide on the basis of essentially political, sociological or economic considerations that war is wrong

and that they will have no part of it. These judgments have historically been reserved for the Government, and in matters which can
be said to fall within these areas the conviction of the individual has
never been permitted to override that of the State. *United States v.
Macintosh* (dissenting opinion) [1931]. The statute further excludes
those whose opposition to war stems from a "merely personal moral
code," a phrase to which we shall have occasion to turn later in
discussing the application of § 6 (j) to these cases. We also pause to
take note of what is not involved in this litigation. No party claims
to be an atheist or attacks the statute on this ground. The question
is not, therefore, one between theistic and atheistic beliefs. We do
not deal with or intimate any decision on that situation in this case.
Nor do the parties claim the monotheistic belief that there is but one
God; what they claim . . . is that they adhere to theism, as opposed
to atheism, which is "the belief in the existence of a god or gods;
belief in superhuman powers or spiritual agencies in one or many
gods," as opposed to atheism. Our question, therefore, is the narrow
one: Does the term "Supreme Being" as used in § 6(j) mean the
orthodox God or the broader concept of a power or being, or a faith,
"to which all else is subordinate or upon which all else is ultimately
dependent"? In considering this question we resolve it solely in relation to the language of § 6(j) and not otherwise.

2. Few would quarrel, we think, with the proposition that in no
field of human endeavor has the tool of language proved so inadequate in the communication of ideas as it has in dealing with the
fundamental questions of man's predicament in life, in death or in
final judgment and retribution. This fact makes the task of discerning
the intent of Congress in using the phrase "Supreme Being" a complex one. Nor is it made the easier by the richness and variety of
spiritual life in our country. Over 250 sects inhabit our land. Some
believe in a purely personal God, some in a supernatural deity; others
think of religion as a way of life envisioning as its ultimate goal the
day when all men can live together in perfect understanding and
peace. There are those who think of God as the depth of our being;
others, such as the Buddhists, strive for a state of lasting rest through
self-denial and inner purification; in Hindu philosophy, the Supreme
Being is the transcendental reality which is truth, knowledge and
bliss. Even those religious groups who have traditionally opposed
war in every form have splintered into various denominations. . . .
This vast panoply of beliefs reveals the magnitude of the problem
which faced the Congress when its set about providing an exemption
from armed service. It also emphasizes the care that Congress realized was necessary in the fashioning of an exemption which would
be in keeping with its long-established policy of not picking and
choosing among religious beliefs.

In spite of the elusive nature of the inquiry, we are not without certain guidelines. In amending the 1940 Act, Congress adopted almost intact the language of Chief Justice Hughes in *United States v. Macintosh:*

> "The essence of religion is belief in a relation to *God* involving duties superior to those arising from any human relation." (Emphasis supplied.)

By comparing the statutory definition with those words, however, it becomes readily apparent that the Congress deliberately broadened them by substituting the phrase "Supreme Being" for the appellation "God." And in so doing it is also significant that Congress did not elaborate on the form or nature of this higher authority which it chose to designate as "Supreme Being." By so refraining it must have had in mind the admonitions of the Chief Justice when he said in the same opinion that even the word "God" had myriad meanings for men of faith. . . .

Moreover, the Senate Report on the bill specifically states that § 6(j) was intended to re-enact "substantially the same provisions as were found" in the 1940 Act. That statute, of course, refers to "religious training and belief" without more. Admittedly, all of the parties here purport to base their objection on religious belief. It appears, therefore, that we need only look to this clear statement of congressional intent as set out in the report. Under the 1940 Act it was necessary only to have a conviction based upon religious training and belief; we believe that is all that is required here. Within that phrase would come all sincere religious beliefs which are based upon a power or being, or upon a faith, to which all else is subordinate or upon which all else is ultimately dependent. The test might be stated in these words: A sincere and meaningful belief which occupies in the life of its possessor a place parallel to that filled by the God of those admittedly qualifying for the exemption comes within the statutory definition. This construction avoids imputing to Congress an intent to classify different religious beliefs, exempting some and excluding others, and is in accord with the well-established congressional policy of equal treatment for those whose opposition to service is grounded in their religious tenets. . . .

5. We recognize the difficulties that have always faced the trier of fact in these cases. We hope that the test that we lay down proves less onerous. The examiner is furnished a standard that permits consideration of criteria with which he has had considerable experience. While the applicant's words may differ, the test is simple of application. It is essentially an objective one, namely, does the claimed belief occupy the same place in the life of the objector as an orthodox belief in God holds in the life of one clearly qualified for exemption?

Moreover, it must be remembered that in resolving these exemption problems one deals with the beliefs of different individuals who will articulate them in a multitude of ways. In such an intensely personal area, of course, the claim of the registrant that his belief is an essential part of a religious faith must be given great weight. . . . The validity of what he believes cannot be questioned. Some theologians, and indeed some examiners, might be tempted to question the existence of the registrant's "Supreme Being" or the truth of his concepts. But these are inquiries foreclosed to Government. As Mr. Justice Douglas stated in *United States v. Ballard* (1944): "Men may believe what they cannot prove. They may not be put to the proof of their religious doctrines or beliefs. Religious experiences which are real as life to some may be incomprehensible to others." Local boards and courts in this sense are not free to reject beliefs because they consider them "incomprehensible." Their task is to decide whether the beliefs professed by a registrant are sincerely held and whether they are, in his own scheme of things, religious. . . .

MR. JUSTICE DOUGLAS, concurring.

If I read the statute differently from the Court, I would have difficulties. For then those who embraced one religious faith rather than another would be subject to penalties; and that kind of discrimination, as we held in *Sherbert v. Verner* [1963] would violate the Free Exercise Clause of the First Amendment. It would also result in a denial of equal protection by preferring some religions over others—an invidious discrimination that would run afoul of the Due Process Clause of the Fifth Amendment. See *Bolling v. Sharpe* [1954].

The legislative history of this Act leaves much in the dark. But it is, in my opinion, not a *tour de force* if we construe the words "Supreme Being" to include the cosmos, as well as an anthropomorphic entity. If it is a *tour de force* so to hold, it is no more so than other instances where we have gone to extremes to construe an Act of Congress to save it from demise on constitutional grounds. In a more extreme case than the present one we said that the words of a statute may be strained "in the candid service of avoiding a serious constitutional doubt." *United States v. Rumely* [1953].

When the Congress spoke in the vague general terms of a Supreme Being I cannot, therefore, assume that it was so parochial as to use the words in the narrow sense urged on us. I would attribute tolerance and sophistication to the Congress, commensurate with the religious complexion of our communities. In sum, I agree with the Court that any person opposed to war on the basis of a sincere belief, which in his life fills the same place as a belief in God fills in the life of an orthodox religionist, is entitled to exemption under the statute. . . .*

11.3
"To sustain that position . . . we would be forced to ignore the ordinary meaning of plain language."

TENNESSEE VALLEY AUTHORITY V. HILL
437 U.S. 153, 98 S. Ct. 2279, 57 L. Ed. 2d 117 (1978)

In 1967 Congress authorized the Tennessee Valley Authority to construct the Tellico Dam on the Little Tennessee River. The project encountered serious opposition from the locality and from conservationists, but Congress continued appropriations and by 1973 the dam was practically completed but not closed. In that year Congress passed the Endangered Species Act, the legislative history of which clearly indicated that Congress intended to halt and reverse the trend toward extinction of certain species, whatever the cost. Protection of endangered species was given priority over the "primary mission" of federal agencies, even if this required the agencies to alter ongoing projects.

Soon after the passage of the act a species of perch called the snail darter was discovered in a stretch of the Little Tennessee that would be flooded by the dam. On the petition of environmental groups and others, the Secretary of the Interior listed the snail darter as an endangered species in 1976, as authorized by statute, and declared this area of the river to be its "critical habitat." Failing in efforts to transplant the snail darter, the TVA argued that the statute did not apply to a project that was more than 50 percent completed. The federal district court accepted this view, and in 1976 Congress again appropriated funds for the project. But in January 1977 the court of appeals issued a permanent injunction halting all activities that would destroy or modify the critical habitat of the snail darter. TVA sought and obtained certiorari from the Supreme Court.

MR. CHIEF JUSTICE BURGER delivered the opinion of the Court. . . .

We begin with the premise that operation of the Tellico Dam will either eradicate the known population of snail darters or destroy their critical habitat. Petitioner does not now seriously dispute this fact. In any event, under § 4(a)(1) of the Act, the Secretary of the Interior is vested with exclusive authority to determine whether a species such as the snail darter is "endangered" or "threatened" and to ascertain the factors which have led to such a precarious existence. By § 4(d) Congress has authorized—indeed commanded—the Secretary to "issue such regulations as he deems necessary and advisable

---

*Reacting to *Seeger,* Congress amended the act to delete "Supreme Being," while retaining the ambiguous test of "religious training and belief." In *Welsh v. United States* (1970), the Court applied the amended statute so broadly as to lead Justice Harlan, who had voted with the majority in *Seeger,* to complain that his brethren had performed "a lobotomy" on the statute.—Eds.

to provide for the conservation of such species." As we have seen, the Secretary promulgated regulations which declared the snail darter an endangered species whose critical habitat would be destroyed by creation of the Tellico Reservoir. Doubtless petitioner would prefer not to have these regulations on the books, but there is no suggestion that the Secretary exceeded his authority or abused his discretion in issuing the regulations. . . .

Starting from the above premise, two questions are presented: (a) would TVA be in violation of the Act if it completed and operated the Tellico Dam as planned?; (b) if TVA's actions would offend the Act, is an injunction the appropriate remedy for the violation? For the reasons stated hereinafter, we hold that both questions must be answered in the affirmative.

It may seem curious to some that the survival of a relatively small number of three-inch fish among all the countless millions of species extant would require the permanent halting of a virtually completed dam for which Congress has expended more than $100 million. The paradox is not minimized by the fact that Congress continued to appropriate large sums of public money for the project, even after congressional appropriations committees were apprised of its apparent impact upon the survival of the snail darter. We conclude, however, that the explicit provisions of the Endangered Species Act require precisely that result.

One would be hard pressed to find a statutory provision whose terms were any plainer than those in § 7 of the Endangered Species Act. Its very words affirmatively command all federal agencies "to *insure* that actions *authorized, funded,* or *carried out* by them do not *jeopardize* the continued existence" of an endangered species or *"result* in the destruction or modification of habitat of such species. . . ." (Emphasis added.) This language admits of no exception. Nonetheless, petitioner urges, as do the dissenters, that the Act cannot reasonably be interpreted as applying to a federal project which was well under way when Congress passed the Endangered Species Act of 1973. To sustain that position, however, we would be forced to ignore the ordinary meaning of plain language. It has not been shown, for example, how TVA can close the gates of the Tellico Dam without "carrying out" an action that has been "authorized" and "funded" by a federal agency. Nor can we understand how such action will *"insure"* that the snail darter's habitat is not disrupted. Accepting the Secretary's determinations, as we must, it is clear that TVA's proposed operation of the dam will have precisely the opposite effect, namely the *eradication* of an endangered species.

Concededly, this view of the Act will produce results requiring the sacrifice of the anticipated benefits of the project and of many millions of dollars in public funds. But examination of the language, history and structure of the legislation under review here indicates beyond doubt that Congress intended endangered species to be afforded the highest of priorities.

When Congress passed the Act in 1973, it was not legislating on a clean slate. The first major congressional concern for the preservation of the endangered species had come with passage of the Endangered Species Act of 1966 . . . [which] directed all federal agencies both to protect these species and *"insofar as is practicable and consistent with the[ir] primary purposes . . .* preserve the habitats of such threatened species on lands under their jurisdiction." (Emphasis added.) The 1966 statute was not a sweeping prohibition on the taking of endangered species, however, except on federal lands, and even in those federal areas the Secretary was authorized to allow the hunting and fishing of endangered species.

In 1969 Congress enacted the Endangered Species Conservation Act, which continued the provisions of the 1966 Act while at the same time broadening federal involvement in the preservation of endangered species. Under the 1969 legislation, the Secretary was empowered to list species "threatened with worldwide extinction"; in addition, the importation of any species so recognized into the United States was prohibited. . . .

Despite the fact that the 1966 and 1969 legislation represented "the most comprehensive of its type to be enacted by any nation" up to that time, Congress was soon persuaded that a more expansive approach was needed if the newly declared national policy of preserving endangered species was to be realized. By 1973, when Congress held hearings on what would later become the Endangered Species Act of 1973, it was informed that species were still being lost at the rate of about one per year, and "the pace of disappearance of species" appeared to be "accelerating." Moreover, Congress was also told that the primary cause of this trend was something other than the normal process of natural selection. . . . Congress did not view these developments lightly. . . . The legislative proceedings in 1973 are, in fact, replete with expressions of concern over the risk that might lie in the loss of *any* endangered species. Typifying these sentiments is the report of the House Committee on Merchant Marine and Fisheries on H.R. 37, a bill which contained the essential features of the subsequently enacted Act of 1973; in explaining the need for the legislation, the report stated:

> "As we homogenize the habitats in which these plants and animals evolved, and as we increase the pressure for products that they are in a position to supply (usually unwillingly) we threaten their—and our own —genetic heritage.
>
> *"The value of this genetic heritage is, quite literally, incalculable.*
>
> "From the most narrow possible point of view, *it is in the best interests of mankind to minimize the losses of genetic variations.* The reason is simple: they are potential resources. They are keys to puzzles which we

cannot solve, and may provide answers to questions which we have not yet learned to ask. . . ."

As it was finally passed, the Endangered Species Act of 1973 represented the most comprehensive legislation for the preservation of endangered species ever enacted by any nation. Its stated purposes were "to provide a means whereby the ecosystems upon which endangered species and threatened species depend may be conserved," and "to provide a program for the conservation of such . . . species. . . ." In furtherance of these goals, Congress expressly stated in § 2(c) that "all Federal departments and agencies *shall* seek *to conserve endangered species* and threatened species. . . ." (Emphasis added.) Lest there be any ambiguity as to the meaning of this statutory directive, the Act specifically defined "conserve" as meaning "to use and the use of *all methods and procedures which are necessary* to bring *any endangered species or threatened species* to the point at which the measures provided pursuant to this Act are no longer necessary." . . .

Section 7 of the Act, which of course is relied upon by respondents in this case, provides a particularly good gauge of congressional intent. As we have seen, this provision had its genesis in the Endangered Species Act of 1966, but that legislation qualified the obligation of federal agencies by stating that they should seek to preserve endangered species only *"insofar as is practicable and consistent with the[ir] primary purposes. . . ."* Likewise, every bill introduced in 1973 contained a qualification similar to that found in the earlier statutes. Exemplary of these was the Administration Bill, H.R. 4758, which in § 2(b) would direct federal agencies to use their authorities to further the ends of the Act *"insofar as is practicable and consistent with the[ir] primary purposes. . . ."* (Emphasis added.) Explaining the idea behind this language, an Administration spokesman told Congress that it "would signal to . . . all agencies of the Government that this is the *first priority, consistent with their primary objectives."* (Emphasis added.) This type of language did not go unnoticed by those advocating strong endangered species legislation. A representative of the Sierra Club, for example, attacked the use of the phrase "consistent with the primary purpose" in proposed H.R. 4758, cautioning that the qualification "could be construed to be a declaration of congressional policy that other agency purposes are necessarily more important than protection of endangered species and would always prevail if conflict were to occur."

What is very significant in this sequence is that the final version of the 1973 Act carefully omitted all of the reservations described above. . . .

It is against this legislative background that we must measure

TVA's claim that the Act was not intended to stop operation of a project which, like Tellico Dam, was near completion when an endangered species was discovered in its path. While there is no discussion in the legislative history of precisely this problem, the totality of congressional action makes it abundantly clear that the result we reach today is wholly in accord with both the words of the statute and the intent of Congress. The plain intent of Congress in enacting this statute was to halt and reverse the trend toward species extinction, whatever the cost. This is reflected not only in the stated policies of the Act, but in literally every section of the statute. . . . In addition, the legislative history undergirding § 7 reveals an explicit congressional decision to require agencies to afford first priority to the declared national policy of saving endangered species. . . .

It is not for us to speculate, much less act, on whether Congress would have altered its stance had the specific events of this case been anticipated. [But] it is clear Congress foresaw that § 7 would, on occasion, require agencies to alter ongoing projects in order to fulfill the goals of the Act. . . .

One might dispute the applicability of these examples to the Tellico Dam by saying that in this case the burden on the public through the loss of millions of unrecoverable dollars would greatly outweigh the loss of the snail darter. But neither the Endangered Species Act nor Art. III of the Constitution provides federal courts with authority to make such fine utilitarian calculations. On the contrary, the plain language of the Act, buttressed by its legislative history, shows clearly that Congress viewed the value of endangered species as "incalculable." Quite obviously, it would be difficult for a court to balance the loss of a sum certain—even $100 million—against a congressionally declared "incalculable" value, even assuming we had the power to engage in such a weighing process, which we emphatically do not.

In passing the Endangered Species Act of 1973, Congress was also aware of certain instances in which exceptions to the statute's broad sweep would be necessary. Thus, § 10 . . . creates a number of limited "hardship exemptions," none of which would even remotely apply to the Tellico Project. . . .

Notwithstanding Congress' expression of intent in 1973, we are urged to find that the continuing appropriations for Tellico Dam constitute an implied repeal of the 1973 Act, at least insofar as it applies to the Tellico Project. In support of this view, TVA points to the statements found in various House and Senate appropriations committees' reports; those reports generally reflected the attitude of the *committees* either that the Act did not apply to Tellico or that the dam should be completed regardless of the provisions of the Act. Since we are unwilling to assume that these latter committee statements constituted advice to ignore the provisions of a duly enacted law, we assume that these committees believed that the Act simply was not applicable in this situation. But even under this interpretation of the committees' actions, we are unable to conclude that the Act has been in any respect amended or repealed.

There is nothing in the appropriations measures, as passed, which state that the Tellico Project was to be completed irrespective of the requirements of the Endangered Species Act. These appropriations, in fact, represented relatively minor components of the lump sum amounts for the *entire* TVA budget. To find a repeal of the Endangered Species Act under these circumstances would surely do violence to the "cardinal rule . . . that repeals by implication are not favored." *Morton v. Mancari* (1974). . . .

Having determined that there is an irreconcilable conflict between operation of the Tellico Dam and the explicit provisions of § 7 of the Endangered Species Act, we must now consider what remedy, if any, is appropriate. . . . [We] are urged to view the Endangered Species Act "reasonably," and hence shape a remedy "that accords with some modicum of commonsense and the public weal." But is that our function? We have no expert knowledge on the subject of endangered species, much less do we have a mandate from the people to strike a balance of equities on the side of the Tellico Dam. Congress has spoken in the plainest of words, making it abundantly clear that the balance has been struck in favor of affording endangered species the highest of priorities, thereby adopting a policy which it described as "institutionalized caution."

Our individual appraisal of the wisdom or unwisdom of a particular course consciously selected by the Congress is to be put aside in the process of interpreting a statute. Once the meaning of an enactment is discerned and its constitutionality determined, the judicial process comes to an end. We do not sit as a committee of review, nor are we vested with the power of veto. The lines ascribed to Sir Thomas More by Robert Bolt are not without relevance here:

> "The law, Roper, the law. I know what's legal, not what's right. And I'll stick to what's legal. . . . I'm *not* God. The currents and eddies of right and wrong, which you find such plain-sailing, I can't navigate, I'm no voyager. But in the thickets of the law, oh there I'm a forester. . . . What would you do? Cut a great road through the law to get after the Devil? . . . And when the last law was down, and the Devil turned round on you—where would you hide, Roper, the laws all being flat? This country's planted thick with laws from coast to coast—Man's laws, not God's—and if you cut them down . . . d'you really think you could stand upright in the winds that would blow then? Yes, I'd give the Devil benefit of law, for my own safety's sake." Bolt, A Man for All Seasons, Act I, at 147 (Heinemann ed. 1967).

We agree with the Court of Appeals that in our constitutional system the commitment to the separation of powers is too fundamental for us to pre-empt congressional action by judicially decreeing what accords with "commonsense and the public weal." Our Constitution vests such responsibilities in the political Branches.

Affirmed.

MR. JUSTICE POWELL, with whom MR. JUSTICE BLACKMUN joins, dissenting.

The Court today holds that § 7 of the Endangered Species Act requires a federal court, for the purpose of protecting an endangered species or its habitat, to enjoin permanently the operation of any federal project, whether completed or substantially completed. This decision casts a long shadow over the operation of even the most important projects, serving vital needs of society and national defense, whenever it is determined that continued operation would threaten extinction of an endangered species or its habitat. This result is said to be required by the "plain intent of Congress" as well as by the language of the statute.

In my view § 7 cannot reasonably be interpreted as applying to a project that is completed or substantially completed when its threat to an endangered species is discovered. Nor can I believe that Congress could have intended this Act to produce the "absurd result"—in the words of the District Court—of this case. If it were clear from the language of the Act and its legislative history that Congress intended to authorize this result, this Court would be compelled to enforce it. It is not our province to rectify policy or political judgments by the Legislative Branch, however egregiously they may disserve the public interest. But where the statutory language and legislative history, as in this case, need not be construed to reach such a result, I view it as the duty of this Court to adopt a permissible construction that accords with some modicum of commonsense and the public weal. . . .

11.4

"Thus, by a tour de force reminiscent . . . of escape artists such as Houdini, the Court eludes clear statutory language. . . ."

UNITED STEELWORKERS V. WEBER

443 U.S. 193, 99 S. Ct. 2721, 61 L. Ed. 2d 480 (1979)

The Kaiser Aluminum company had reserved for minorities half of all positions in its nationwide training program for skilled craft jobs. Brian F. Weber, a white employee, who had more seniority than several black employees chosen, was not selected. As a private employer Kaiser was not bound by the equal protection clause of the Fourteenth Amendment, but Title VII of the 1964 Civil Rights Act bars racial discrimination in private employment.

MR. JUSTICE BRENNAN delivered the opinion of the Court. . . .

We emphasize at the outset the narrowness of our inquiry. Since the Kaiser-USWA plan does not involve state action, this case does not present an alleged violation of the Equal Protection Clause of the Constitution. Further, since the Kaiser-USWA plan was adopted voluntarily, we are not concerned with what Title VII requires or with what a court might order to remedy a past proven violation of the Act. The only question before us is the narrow statutory issue of whether Title VII *forbids* private employers and unions from voluntarily agreeing upon bona fide affirmative action plans that accord racial preferences in the manner and for the purpose provided in the Kaiser-USWA plan. That question was expressly left open in *McDonald v. Santa Fe Trail Trans. Co.* (1976) which held, in a case not involving affirmative action, that Title VII protects whites as well as blacks from certain forms of racial discrimination.

Respondent argues that Congress intended in Title VII to prohibit all race-conscious affirmative action plans. Respondent's argument rests upon a literal interpretation of §§ 703(a) and (d) of the Act. Those sections make it unlawful to "discriminate . . . because of . . . race" in hiring and in the selection of apprentices for training programs. Since, the argument runs, *McDonald v. Santa Fe Trail Trans. Co.* settled that Title VII forbids discrimination against whites as well as blacks, and since the Kaiser-USWA affirmative action plan operates to discriminate against white employees solely because they are white, it follows that the Kaiser-USWA plan violates Title VII.

Respondent's argument is not without force. But it overlooks the significance of the fact that the Kaiser-USWA plan is an affirmative action plan voluntarily adopted by private parties to eliminate traditional patterns of racial segregation. In this context respondent's reliance upon a literal construction of § 703(a) and (d) and upon *McDonald* is misplaced.

. . . It is a "familiar rule that a thing may be within the letter of the statute and yet not within the statute, because not within its spirit nor within the intention of its makers." *Holy Trinity Church v. United States* (1892). The prohibition against racial discrimination in §§ 703(a) and (d) of Title VII must therefore be read against the background of the legislative history of Title VII and the historical context from which the Act arose. Examination of those sources makes clear that an interpretation of the sections that forbade all race-conscious affirmative action would "bring about an end completely at variance with the purpose of the statute" and must be rejected.

Congress' primary concern in enacting the prohibition against racial discrimination in Title VII of the Civil Rights Act of 1964 was with "the plight of the Negro in our economy." (Remarks of Sen.

Humphrey.) Before 1964, blacks were largely relegated to "unskilled and semi-skilled jobs." (Remarks of Sens. Humphrey, Clark, [and] Kennedy.) Because of automation the number of such jobs was rapidly decreasing. (See Remarks of Sens. Humphrey [and] Clark.) As a consequence "the relative position of the Negro worker [was] steadily worsening. In 1947 the non-white unemployment rate was only 64 percent higher than the white rate; in 1962 it was 124 percent higher." *Id.* (Remarks of Sen. Humphrey.) See also remarks of Sen. Clark. Congress considered this a serious social problem. As Senator Clark told the Senate:

> "The rate of Negro unemployment has gone up consistently as compared with white unemployment for the past 15 years. This is a social malaise and a social situation which we should not tolerate. That is one of the principal reasons why this bill should pass."

Congress feared that the goals of the Civil Rights Act—the integration of blacks into the mainstream of American society—could not be achieved unless this trend were reversed. And Congress recognized that that would not be possible unless blacks were able to secure jobs "which have a future." (Remarks of Sen. Clark.) See also remarks of Sen. Kennedy. As Senator Humphrey explained to the Senate:

> "What good does it do a Negro to be able to eat in a fine restaurant if he cannot afford to pay the bill? What good does it do him to be accepted in a hotel that is too expensive for his modest income? How can a Negro child be motivated to take full advantage of integrated educational facilities if he has no hope of getting a job where he can use that education?" . . .
>
> "Without a job, one cannot afford public convenience and accommodations. Income from employment may be necessary to further a man's education, or that of his children. If his children have no hope of getting a good job, what will motivate them to take advantage of educational opportunities?"

These remarks echoed President Kennedy's original message to Congress upon the introduction of the Civil Rights Act in 1963.

> "There is little value in a Negro's obtaining the right to be admitted to hotels and restaurants if he has no cash in his pocket and no job."

Accordingly, it was clear to Congress that "the crux of the problem [was] to open employment opportunities for Negroes in occupations which have been traditionally closed to them," . . . (remarks of Sen. Humphrey), and it was to this problem that Title VII's prohibition against racial discrimination in employment was primarily addressed.

It plainly appears from the House Report accompanying the Civil Rights Act that Congress did not intend wholly to prohibit private and voluntary affirmative action efforts as one method of solving this problem. The Report provides:

"No bill can or should lay claim to eliminating all of the causes and consequences of racial and other types of discrimination against minorities. There is reason to believe, however, that national leadership provided by the enactment of Federal legislation dealing with the most troublesome problems *will create an atmosphere conducive to voluntary or local resolution of other forms of discrimination.*"

Given this legislative history, we cannot agree with respondent that Congress intended to prohibit the private sector from taking effective steps to accomplish the goal that Congress designed Title VII to achieve. The very statutory words intended as a spur or catalyst to cause "employers and unions to self-examine and to self-evaluate their employment practices and to endeavor to eliminate, so far as possible, the last vestiges of an unfortunate and ignominious page in this country's history," *Albemarle v. Moody* (1975), cannot be interpreted as an absolute prohibition against all private, voluntary, race-conscious affirmative action efforts to hasten the elimination of such vestiges. It would be ironic indeed if a law triggered by a Nation's concern over centuries of racial injustice and intended to improve the lot of those who had "been excluded from the American dream for so long" (remarks of Sen. Humphrey), constituted the first legislative prohibition of all voluntary, private, race-conscious efforts to abolish traditional patterns of racial segregation and hierarchy.

Our conclusion is further reinforced by examination of the language and legislative history of § 703(j) of Title VII. Opponents of Title VII raised two related arguments against the bill. First, they argued that the Act would be interpreted to *require* employers with racially imbalanced work forces to grant preferential treatment to racial minorities in order to integrate. Second, they argued that employers with racially imbalanced work forces would grant preferential treatment to racial minorities, even if not required to do so by the Act. See remarks of Sen. Sparkman. Had Congress meant to prohibit all race-conscious affirmative action, as respondent urges, it easily could have answered both objections by providing that Title VII would not require or *permit* racially preferential integration efforts. But Congress did not choose such a course. Rather Congress added § 703(j) which addresses only the first objection. The section provides that nothing contained in Title VII "shall be interpreted to *require* any employer . . . to grant preferential treatment . . . to any group because of the race . . . of such . . . group on account of" a de facto racial imbalance in the employer's work force. The section does *not* state that "nothing in Title VII shall be interpreted to *permit*" voluntary affirmative efforts to correct racial imbalances. The natural inference is that Congress chose not to forbid all voluntary race-conscious affirmative action.

The reasons for this choice are evident from the legislative record. Title VII could not have been enacted into law without substantial support from legislators in both Houses who traditionally resisted federal regulation of private business. Those legislators demanded as a price for their support that "management prerogatives and union freedoms . . . be left undisturbed to the greatest extent possible." Section 703(j) was proposed by Senator Dirksen to allay any fears that the Act might be interpreted in such a way as to upset this compromise. The section was designed to prevent § 703 of Title VII from being interpreted in such a way as to lead to undue "Federal Government interference with private businesses because of some Federal employee's ideas about racial balance or imbalance." Clearly, a prohibition against all voluntary, race-conscious, affirmative action efforts would disserve these ends. Such a prohibition would augment the powers of the Federal Government and diminish traditional management prerogatives while at the same time impeding attainment of the ultimate statutory goals. In view of this legislative history and in view of Congress' desire to avoid undue federal regulation of private businesses, use of the word "require" rather than the phrase "require or permit" in § 703(j) fortifies the conclusion that Congress did not intend to limit traditional business freedom to such a degree as to prohibit all voluntary, race-conscious affirmative action.

We therefore hold that Title VII's prohibition in §§ 703(a) and (d) against racial discrimination does not condemn all private, voluntary, race-conscious affirmative action plans.

III

We need not today define in detail the line of demarcation between permissible and impermissible affirmative action plans. It suffices to hold that the challenged Kaiser-USWA affirmative action plan falls on the permissible side of the line. The purposes of the plan mirror those of the statute. Both were designed to break down old patterns of racial segregation and hierarchy. Both were structured to "open employment opportunities for Negroes in occupations which have been traditionally closed to them."

At the same time the plan does not unnecessarily trammel the interests of the white employees. The plan does not require the discharge of white workers and their replacement with new black hires. Cf. *McDonald v. Santa Fe Trail Trans. Co.* Nor does the plan create an absolute bar to the advancement of white employees; half of those trained in the program will be white. Moreover, the plan is a temporary measure; it is not intended to maintain racial balance, but simply to eliminate a manifest racial imbalance. Preferential selection of craft trainees at the Gramercy plant will end as soon as the percentage of black skilled craft workers in the Gramercy plant approximates the percentage of blacks in the local labor force.

We conclude, therefore, that the adoption of the Kaiser-USWA plan for the Gramercy plant falls within the area of discretion left by Title VII to the private sector voluntarily to adopt affirmative action plans designed to eliminate conspicuous racial imbalance in traditionally segregated job categories. Accordingly, the judgment of the Court of Appeals for the Fifth Circuit is

Reversed.

MR. JUSTICE POWELL and MR. JUSTICE STEVENS took no part in the consideration or decision of this case.

MR. JUSTICE BLACKMUN, concurring. . . .

MR. JUSTICE REHNQUIST, with whom CHIEF JUSTICE [BURGER] joins, dissenting.

In a very real sense, the Court's opinion is ahead of its time: it could more appropriately have been handed down five years from now, in 1984, a year coinciding with the title of a book from which the Court's opinion borrows, perhaps subconsciously, at least one idea. Orwell describes in his book a governmental official of Oceania, one of the three great world powers, denouncing the current enemy, Eurasia, to an assembled crowd:

> "It was almost impossible to listen to him without being first convinced and then maddened. . . . The speech had been proceeding for perhaps twenty minutes when a messenger hurried onto the platform and a scrap of paper was slipped into the speaker's hand. He unrolled and read it without pausing in his speech. Nothing altered in his voice or manner, or in the content of what he was saying, but suddenly the names were different. Without words said, a wave of understanding rippled through the crowd. Oceania was at war with Eastasia! . . . The banners and posters with which the square was decorated were all wrong! . . .
>
> "[T]he speaker had switched from one line to the other actually in mid-sentence, not only without a pause, but without even breaking the syntax." G. Orwell, Nineteen Eighty-Four, 182–183 (1949).

Today's decision represents an equally dramatic and equally unremarked switch in this Court's interpretation of Title VII.

The operative sections of Title VII prohibit racial discrimination in employment *simpliciter.* Taken in its normal meaning and as understood by all Members of Congress who spoke to the issue during the legislative debates, . . . this language prohibits a covered employer from considering race when making an employment decision, whether the race be black or white. Several years ago, however, a United States District Court held that "the dismissal of white employees charged with misappropriating company property while not dismissing a similarly charged Negro employee does not raise a claim upon which Title VII relief may be granted." *McDonald v. Santa Fe Trail Transp. Co.* (1976). This Court unanimously reversed, concluding from the "uncontradicted legislative history" that "[T]itle VII prohibits racial discrimination against the white petitioners in this case upon the same standards as would be applicable were they Negroes. . . ."

We have never wavered in our understanding that Title VII "prohibits *all* racial discrimination in employment, without exception for any particular employees." In *Griggs v. Duke Power Co.* (1971), our first occasion to interpret Title VII, a unanimous court observed that "[d]iscriminatory preference, for any group, minority or majority, is precisely and only what Congress has proscribed." And in our most recent discussion of the issue, we uttered words seemingly dispositive of this case: "It is clear beyond cavil that the obligation imposed by Title VII is to provide an equal opportunity for *each* applicant regardless of race, without regard to whether members of the applicant's race are already proportionately represented in the work force." *Furnco Construction Corp. v. Waters* (1978) (emphasis in original).

Today, however, the Court behaves much like the Orwellian speaker earlier described, as if it had been handed a note indicating that Title VII would lead to a result unacceptable to the Court if interpreted here as it was in our prior decisions. Accordingly, without even a break in syntax, the Court rejects "a literal construction of § 703(a)" in favor of newly discovered "legislative history," which leads it to a conclusion directly contrary to that compelled by the "uncontradicted legislative history" unearthed in *McDonald* and our other prior decisions. Now we are told that the legislative history of Title VII shows that employers are free to discriminate on the basis of race: an employer may, in the Court's words, "trammel the interests of white employees" in favor of black employees in order to eliminate "racial imbalance." Our earlier interpretations of Title VII, like the banners and posters decorating the square in Oceania, were all wrong.

As if this were not enough to make a reasonable observer question this Court's adherence to the oft-stated principle that our duty is to construe rather than rewrite legislation, *United States v. Rutherford* (1979), the Court also seizes upon § 703(j) of Title VII as an independent, or at least partially independent, basis for its holding. Totally ignoring the wording of that section, which is obviously addressed to those charged with the responsibility of interpreting the law rather than those who are subject to its proscriptions, and totally ignoring the months of legislative debates preceding the section's introduction and passage, which demonstrate clearly that it was enacted to prevent precisely what occurred in this case, the Court infers from § 703(j) that "Congress chose not to forbid all voluntary race-conscious affirmative action."

Thus, by a *tour de force* reminiscent not of jurists such as Hale, Holmes, and Hughes, but of escape artists such as Houdini, the Court eludes clear statutory language, "uncontradicted" legislative history and uniform precedent in concluding that employers are, after all, permitted to consider race in making employment decisions. It may be that one or more of the principal sponsors of Title VII would have preferred to see a provision allowing preferential treatment of minorities written into the bill. Such a provision, however, would have to have been expressly or impliedly excepted from Title VII's explicit prohibition on all racial discrimination in employment. There is no such exception in the Act. And a reading of the legislative debates concerning Title VII, in which proponents and opponents alike uniformly denounced discrimination in favor of, as well as discrimination against, Negroes, demonstrates clearly that any legislator harboring an unspoken desire for such a provision could not possibly have succeeded in enacting it into law. . . .

11.5

"Where the language is plain and admits of no more than one meaning the duty of interpretation does not arise . . ."

INTERPRETATION OF THE MANN ACT

In 1910 Congress passed the Mann Act, which according to its own terms "shall be known and referred to as the 'White Slave Traffic Act.'" It provides in its essential portion:

> **Any person who shall knowingly transport or cause to be transported, or aid or assist in obtaining transportation for, or in transporting, in interstate or foreign commerce or in any territory or in the District of Columbia, any woman or girl for the purpose of prostitution or debauchery, or for any other immoral purpose, or with the intent and purpose to induce, entice or compel such woman or girl to become a prostitute, or to give herself up to debauchery, or to engage in any other immoral practice . . . shall be deemed guilty of a felony.**

The Supreme Court upheld the constitutionality of the act in *Hoke v. United States* (1913), as a regulation of interstate commerce. The argument against the act was that it was "a subterfuge and an attempt to interfere with the police power of the States to regulate the morals of their citizens," but the Court replied that the act was concerned with "a domain which the States cannot reach and over which Congress alone has power."

Caminetti v. United States

242 U.S. 470, 37 S. Ct. 192, 61 L. Ed. 442 (1917)

Four men were convicted under the Mann Act, two for taking their mistresses across a state line and two for inducing and coercing a young girl under eighteen to go from Oklahoma to Kansas with the intent of getting her to engage in immoral practices.

MR. JUSTICE DAY delivered the opinion of the Court. . . .

It is contended that the Act of Congress is intended to reach only "commercialized vice" or the traffic in women for gain, and that the conduct for which the several petitioners were indicted and convicted, however reprehensible in morals, is not within the purview of the statute when properly construed in the light of its history and the purposes intended to be accomplished by its enactment. In none of the cases was it charged or proved that the transportation was for gain or for the purpose of furnishing women for prostitution for hire, and it is insisted that, such being the case, the acts charged and proved, upon which conviction was had, do not come within the statute.

It is elementary that the meaning of a statute must, in the first instance, be sought in the language in which the act is framed, and if that is plain, and if the law is within the constitutional authority of the law-making body which passed it, the sole function of the courts is to enforce it according to its terms.

Where the language is plain and admits of no more than one meaning the duty of interpretation does not arise and the rules which are to aid doubtful meanings need no discussion. There is no ambiguity in the terms of this act. It is specifically made an offense to knowingly transport or cause to be transported, etc., in interstate commerce, any woman or girl for the purpose of prostitution or debauchery, or for "any other immoral purpose," or with the intent or purpose, to induce any such woman or girl to become a prostitute or to give herself up to debauchery, or to engage in any other immoral practice.

Statutory words are uniformly presumed, unless the contrary appears, to be used in their ordinary and usual sense. . . . To cause a woman or girl to be transported for the purposes of debauchery, and for an immoral purpose, to-wit, becoming a concubine or mistress . . . or to transport an unmarried woman, under eighteen years of age, with the intent to induce her to engage in prostitution, debauchery and other immoral practices . . . would seem by the very statement of the facts to embrace transportation for purposes denounced by the act, and therefore fairly within its meaning.

While such immoral purpose would be more culpable in morals and attributed to baser motives if accompanied with the expectation of pecuniary gain, such considerations do not prevent the lesser offense against morals of furnishing transportation in order that a woman may be debauched, or become a mistress or a concubine from being the execution of purposes within the meaning of this law. To say the contrary would shock the common understanding of what constitutes an immoral purpose. . . .

But it is contended that though the words are so plain that they cannot be misapprehended when given their usual and ordinary interpretation, and although the sections in which they appear do not in terms limit the offense defined and punished to acts of "commercialized vice," or the furnishing or procuring of transportation of women for debauchery, prostitution or immoral practices for hire, such limited purpose is to be attributed to Congress and engrafted upon the act in view of the language of § 8 and the report which accompanied the law upon its introduction into and subsequent passage by the House of Representatives.

In this connection, it may be observed that while the title of an act cannot overcome the meaning of plain and unambiguous words used in its body, the title of this act embraces the regulation of interstate commerce "by prohibiting the transportation therein for immoral purposes of women and girls, and for other purposes." It is true that § 8 of the act provides that it shall be known and referred to as the "White-slave traffic Act," and the report accompanying the introduction of the same into the House of Representatives set forth the fact that a material portion of the legislation suggested was to meet conditions which had arisen in the past few years, and that the legislation was needed to put a stop to a villainous interstate and international traffic in women and girls. Still, the name given to an act by way of designation or description, or the report which accompanies it, cannot change the plain import of its words. . . . *Despite the obvious reasoning behind the statute, the words and history must be observed*

Reports to Congress accompanying the introduction of proposed laws may aid the courts in reaching the true meaning of the legislature in cases of doubtful interpretation. But, as we have already said, and it has been so often affirmed as to become a recognized rule, when words are free from doubt they must be taken as the final expression of the legislative intent, and are not to be added to or subtracted from by considerations drawn from titles or designating names or reports accompanying their introduction, or from any extraneous source. In other words, the language being plain, and not leading to absurd or wholly impracticable consequences, it is the sole evidence of the ultimate legislative intent. . . .

The judgment in each of the cases is

Affirmed.

MR. JUSTICE MCREYNOLDS took no part in the consideration or decision of these cases.

MR. JUSTICE MCKENNA, with whom concurred the CHIEF JUSTICE [WHITE] and MR. JUSTICE CLARKE, dissenting.

Undoubtedly in the investigation of the meaning of a statute we resort first to its words, and when clear they are decisive. The principle has attractive and seemingly disposing simplicity, but that it is not easy of application or, at least, encounters other principles, many cases demonstrate. The words of a statute may be uncertain in their signification or in their application. If the words be ambiguous, the problem they present is to be resolved by their definition; the subject-matter and the lexicons become our guides. But here, even, we are not exempt from putting ourselves in the place of the legislators. If the words be clear in meaning but the objects to which they are addressed be uncertain, the problem then is to determine the uncertainty. And for this a realization of conditions that provoked the statute must inform our judgment. . . .

The transportation which is made unlawful is of a woman or girl "to become a prostitute or to give herself up to debauchery, or to engage in any other immoral practice." Our present concern is with the words "any other immoral practice," which, it is asserted, have a special office. The words are clear enough as general descriptions; they fail in particular designation. . . . "Immoral" is a very comprehensive word. It means a dereliction of morals. In such sense it covers every form of vice, every form of conduct that is contrary to good order. It will hardly be contended that in this sweeping sense it is used in the statute. But if not used in such sense, to what is it limited and by what limited? If it be admitted that it is limited at all, that ends the imperative effect assigned to it in the opinion of the court. But not insisting quite on that, we ask again, By what is it limited? By its context, necessarily, and the purpose of the statute.

For the context I must refer to the statute; of the purpose of the statute Congress itself has given us illumination. It devotes a section to the declaration that the "Act shall be known and referred to as the 'White-slave traffic Act.' " And its prominence gives it prevalence in the construction of the statute. It cannot be pushed aside or subordinated by indefinite words in other sentences, limited even there by the context. . . . The designation "White-slave traffic" has the sufficiency of an axiom. If apprehended, there is no uncertainty as to the conduct it describes. It is commercialized vice, immoralities having a mercenary purpose, and this is confirmed by other circumstances.

The author of the bill was Mr. Mann, and in reporting it from the House Committee on Interstate and Foreign Commerce he declared for the Committee that it was not the purpose of the bill to interfere with or usurp in any way the police power of the States, and further that it was not the intention of the bill to regulate prostitution or the places where prostitution or immorality was practiced, which were said to be matters wholly within the power of the States and over which the federal government had no jurisdiction. And further explaining the bill, it was said that the sections of the act had been "so drawn that they are limited to cases in which there is the act of transportation in interstate commerce of women for purposes of prostitution." And again:

. . . The legislation is needed to put a stop to a villainous interstate and international traffic in women and girls. . . . It does not attempt to regulate the practice of voluntary prostitution, but aims solely to prevent panderers and procurers from compelling thousands of women and girls against their will and desire to enter and continue in a life of prostitution. . . .

⌊In other words, it is vice as a business at which the law is directed,⌋ using interstate commerce as a facility to procure or distribute its victims. . . .

This being the purpose, the words of the statute should be construed to execute it, and they may be so construed even if their literal meaning be otherwise. . . .

"To accomplish its purpose the statute enumerates the prohibited acts in broad language capable of application beyond that intended by the legislative framers."

Mortensen v. United States

322 U.S. 369, 64 S. Ct. 1037, 88 L. Ed. 1331 (1944)

Mr. and Mrs. Hans Mortensen, operators of a house of ill fame in Grand Island, Nebraska, took two of their prostitutes along on their vacation to Yellowstone National Park and Salt Lake City. On their return to Grand Island, the girls renewed their activities in the Mortensens' employ. Shortly thereafter, the Mortensens were indicted and convicted under the Mann Act for bringing the girls back to Nebraska. There was no charge that any immoral acts had occurred during the vacation or that the Mortensens had used any pressure to persuade the girls to return.

MR. JUSTICE MURPHY delivered the opinion of the Court. . . .

⌊The primary issue before us is whether there was any evidence from which the jury could rightly find that petitioners transported the girls from Salt Lake City to Grand Island for an immoral purpose in violation of the Mann Act.⌋

The penalties of § 2 of the Act are directed at those who knowingly transport in interstate commerce "any woman or girl for the purpose of prostitution or debauchery, or for any other immoral purpose, or with the intent and purpose to induce, entice, or compel such woman or girl to become a prostitute or to give herself up to debauchery, or to engage in any other immoral practice." The statute thus aims to penalize only those who use interstate commerce with a view toward accomplishing the unlawful purposes. To constitute a violation of the Act, it is essential that the interstate transportation have for its object or be the means of effecting or facilitating the proscribed activities. An intention that the women or girls shall engage in the conduct outlawed by § 2 must be found to exist before the conclusion of the interstate journey and must be the dominant motive of such interstate movement. And the transportation must be designed to bring about such result. Without that necessary intention and motivation, immoral conduct during or following the journey is insufficient to subject the transporter to the penalties of the act. . . .

It may be assumed that petitioners anticipated that the two girls would resume their activities as prostitutes upon their return to Grand Island. But we do not think it is fair or permissible under the evidence adduced to infer that this interstate vacation trip, or any part of it, was undertaken by petitioners for the purpose of, or as a means of effecting or facilitating, such activities. The sole purpose of the journey from beginning to end was to provide innocent recreation and a holiday for petitioners and the two girls. . . . What Congress has outlawed by the Mann Act, however, is the use of interstate commerce as a calculated means for effectuating sexual immorality. In ordinary speech an interstate trip undertaken for an innocent vacation purpose constitutes the use of interstate commerce for that innocent purpose. Such a trip does not lose that meaning when viewed in light of a criminal statute outlawing interstate trips for immoral purposes.

The fact that the two girls actually resumed their immoral practices after their return to Grand Island does not, standing alone, operate to inject a retroactive illegal purpose into the return trip to Grand Island. Nor does it justify an arbitrary splitting of the round trip into two parts so as to permit an inference that the purpose of the drive to Salt Lake City was innocent while the purpose of the homeward journey to Grand Island was criminal. The return journey under the circumstances of this case cannot be considered apart from its integral relation with the innocent round trip as a whole. There is no evidence of any change in the purpose of the trip during its course. If innocent when it began it remained so until it ended. . . .

To punish those who transport inmates of a house of prostitution on an innocent vacation trip in no way related to the practice of their commercial vice is consistent neither with the purpose nor with the language of the Act. Congress was attempting primarily to eliminate the "white-slave" business. . . . To accomplish its purpose the statute enumerates the prohibited acts in broad language capable of application beyond that intended by the legislative framers. But even such broad language is conditioned upon the use of interstate transportation for the purpose of, or as a means of effecting or facilitating, the commission of the illegal acts. Here the interstate round trip had no such purpose and was in no way related to the subsequent immoralities in Grand Island. In short, we perceive no statutory purpose or language which prohibits petitioners under these circumstances from using interstate transportation for a vacation or for any other innocent purpose.

The judgment of the court below is

Reversed.

MR. CHIEF JUSTICE STONE:
MR. JUSTICE BLACK, MR. JUSTICE REED, MR. JUSTICE DOUGLAS and I think the judgment should be affirmed.

Courts have no more concern with the policy and wisdom of the Mann Act than of the Labor Relations Act or any other which Congress may constitutionally adopt. Those are matters for Congress to determine, not the courts. . . .

The fact that petitioners, who were engaged in an established business of operating a house of prostitution in Nebraska, took some of its women inmates on a transient and innocent vacation trip to other states, is in no way incompatible with the conclusion that petitioners, in bringing them back to Nebraska, purposed and intended that they should resume there the practice of commercial vice, which in fact they did promptly resume in petitioners' establishment. The record is without evidence that they engaged or intended to engage in any other activities in Nebraska, or that anything other than the practice of their profession was the object of their return. . . .

> *"Whether an act is immoral within the meaning of the statute is not to be determined by the accused's concepts of morality."*

Cleveland v. United States

329 U.S. 14, 67 S. Ct. 13, 91 L. Ed. 12 (1946)

Six members of a fundamentalist Mormon sect that practiced polygamy were convicted under the Mann Act for transporting their several wives across state lines.

MR. JUSTICE DOUGLAS delivered the opinion of the Court. . . .

The Act makes an offense the transportation in interstate commerce of "any woman or girl for the purpose of prostitution or debauchery, or for any other immoral purpose." The decision turns on the meaning of the latter phrase, "for any other immoral purpose." . . .

It is argued that the *Caminetti* decision gave too wide a sweep to the Act; that the Act was designed to cover only the white slave business and related vices; that it was not designed to cover voluntary actions bereft of sex commercialism; and that in any event it should not be construed to embrace polygamy which is a form of marriage and, unlike prostitution or debauchery or the concubinage involved in the *Caminetti* case, has as its object parenthood and the creation and maintenance of family life. . . .

While *Mortensen v. United States* [1944] rightly indicated that the Act was aimed "primarily" at the use of interstate commerce for the conduct of the white slave business, we find no indication that a profit motive is a *sine qua non* to its application. Prostitution, to be sure, normally suggests sexual relations for hire. But debauchery has no such implied limitation. In common understanding the indulgence which that term suggests may be motivated solely by lust. And so we start with words which by their natural import embrace more than commercialized sex. What follows is "any other immoral purpose." Under the *ejusdem generis* rule of construction the general words are confined to the class and may not be used to enlarge it. But we could not give the words a faithful interpretation if we confined them more narrowly than the class of which they are a part.

That was the view taken by the Court in [earlier] cases. We do not stop to reexamine the *Caminetti* case to determine whether the Act was properly applied to the facts there presented. But we adhere to its holding . . . that the Act, while primarily aimed at the use of interstate commerce for the purposes of commercialized sex, is not restricted to that end.

We conclude, moreover, that polygamous practices are not excluded from the Act. They have long been outlawed in our society. As stated in *Reynolds v. United States* [1879]:

> Polygamy has always been odious among the northern and western nations of Europe, and, until the establishment of the Mormon Church, was almost exclusively a feature of the life of Asiatic and of African people. At common law, the second marriage was always void (2 Kent, Com. 79), and from the earliest history of England polygamy has been treated as an offence against society. . . .

. . . Polygamy is a practice with far more pervasive influences in society than the casual, isolated transgressions involved in the *Caminetti* case. The establishment or maintenance of polygamous households is a notorious example of promiscuity. . . . We could conclude that Congress excluded these practices from the Act only if it were clear that the Act is confined to commercialized sexual vice. Since we cannot say it is, we see no way by which the present transgressions can be excluded. These polygamous practices have long been branded as immoral in the law. Though they have different ramifications, they are in the same genus as the other immoral practices covered by the Act. . . .

It is also urged that the requisite criminal intent was lacking since petitioners were motivated by a religious belief. That defense claims too much. If upheld, it would place beyond the law any act done under claim of religious sanction. But it has long been held that the fact that polygamy is supported by a religious creed affords no defense in a prosecution for bigamy. *Reynolds v. United States.* Whether an act is immoral within the meaning of the statute is not to be determined by the accused's concepts of morality. Congress has provided the standard. The offense is complete if the accused intended to perform, and did in fact perform, the act which the statute condemns. . . .

Affirmed.

[handwritten marginalia: Silence of Congress doesn't mean assent - possibly exhausted work load.]

MR. JUSTICE BLACK and MR. JUSTICE JACKSON think that the cases should be reversed. They are of opinion that affirmance requires extension of the rule announced in the *Caminetti* case and that the correctness of that rule is so dubious that it should at least be restricted to its particular facts.

[handwritten marginalia: but thought Caminetti should be overruled]

MR. JUSTICE RUTLEDGE, concurring. . . .

MR. JUSTICE MURPHY, dissenting.

Today another unfortunate chapter is added to the troubled history of the White Slave Traffic Act. It is a chapter written in terms that misapply the statutory language and that disregard the intention of the legislative framer. It results in the imprisonment of individuals whose actions have none of the earmarks of white slavery, whatever else may be said of their conduct. . . .

It is not my purpose to defend the practice of polygamy or to claim that it is morally the equivalent of monogamy. But it is essential to understand what it is, as well as what it is not. Only in that way can we intelligently decide whether it falls within the same genus as prostitution or debauchery.

There are four fundamental forms of marriage: (1) monogamy; (2) polygyny, or one man with several wives; (3) polyandry, or one woman with several husbands; and (4) group marriage. The term "polygamy" covers both polygyny and polyandry. Thus we are dealing here with polygyny, one of the basic forms of marriage. Historically, its use has far exceeded that of any other form. It was quite common among ancient civilizations and was referred to many times by the writers of the Old Testament; even today it is to be found frequently among certain pagan and non-Christian peoples of the world. We must recognize, then, that polygyny, like other forms of marriage, is basically a cultural institution rooted deeply in the religious beliefs and social mores of those societies in which it appears. It is equally true that the beliefs and mores of the dominant culture of the contemporary world condemn the practice as immoral and substitute monogamy in its place. To those beliefs and mores I subscribe, but that does not alter the fact that polygyny is a form of marriage built upon a set of social and moral principles. . . .

The Court states that polygamy is "a notorious example of promiscuity." The important fact, however, is that despite the differences that may exist between polygamy and monogamy, such differences do not place polygamy in the same category as prostitution or debauchery. When we use those terms we are speaking of acts of an entirely different nature, having no relation whatever to the various forms of marriage. It takes no elaboration here to point out that marriage, even when it occurs in a form of which we disapprove, is not to be compared with prostitution or debauchery or other immoralities of that character.

The Court's failure to recognize this vital distinction and its insistence that polygyny is "in the same genus" as prostitution and debauchery do violence to the anthropological factors involved. Even etymologically, the words "polygyny" and "polygamy" are quite distinct from "prostitution," "debauchery" and words of that ilk. There is thus no basis in fact for including polygyny within the phrase "any other immoral purpose" as used in this statute. . . .

11.6   *"The purpose of a charitable trust may not be illegal or violate established public policy."*

BOB JONES UNIVERSITY V. UNITED STATES

461 U.S. 574, 103 S. Ct. 2017, 76 L. Ed. 2d 157 (1983)

By §501(c)(3) of the Internal Revenue Code, Congress has exempted from federal taxation:

> [c]orporations, and any community chest fund, or foundation, organized and operated exclusively for religious, charitable, scientific, testing for public safety, literary, or educational purposes, or to foster national or international amateur sports . . . or for the prevention of cruelty to children or animals.

Congress has added the proviso that organizations entitled to exemptions may not be operated for profit and may not engage in lobbying or other political activities, but Congress made no mention of institutions' racial policies. Section 170(c) parallels the language of §501(c)(3) by providing that taxpayers may deduct from their taxable income contributions to such organizations. This section is also silent about racial policies.

Until 1970 the Internal Revenue Service granted tax-exempt status under these provisions to private schools without regard to their racial policies. In January of that year, however, the United States District Court for the District of Columbia issued a preliminary injunction against the IRS, forbidding it to accord tax exemptions to private schools in Mississippi that accepted only white students. Within a few months the IRS changed its policy and announced new regulations denying tax-exempt status to all private schools that discriminated by race.

Bob Jones University, a fundamentalist Christian institution whose sponsors believe the Bible forbids interracial dating and marriage, had completely excluded blacks until 1971. Faced with IRS's new regulations, the university then began to admit blacks married to other blacks. Following another judicial ruling—*McCrary v. Runyon* (1975) —Bob Jones permitted unmarried blacks to enroll, but it still forbade interracial dating and marriage. In 1976 the IRS formally revoked the school's tax-exempt status, made the revocation retroactive to 1970, and assessed federal unemployment taxes of approximately $500,000. The local federal district court held that the IRS had exceeded its powers, but the court of appeals reversed, ruling that Bob Jones was not a charitable institution in the common law's sense of that term because it violated the strong national public policy against racial discrimination. The university petitioned the Supreme Court for certiorari, and the justices granted the writ.

The Reagan administration agreed with the district court, and the solicitor general, whose office usually handles all litigation for the government before the Supreme Court, refused to argue for the IRS. The Court then appointed William T. Coleman, Jr., a prominent black Republican attorney, to present the case for the IRS.

CHIEF JUSTICE BURGER delivered the opinion of the Court. . . .

It is a well-established canon of statutory construction that a court should go beyond the literal language of a statute if reliance on that language would defeat the plain purpose of the statute. . . .

Section 501(c)(3) therefore must be analyzed and construed within the framework of the Internal Revenue Code and against the background of the Congressional purposes. Such an examination reveals unmistakable evidence that, underlying all relevant parts of the Code, is the intent that entitlement to tax exemption depends on meeting certain common law standards of charity—namely, that an institution seeking tax-exempt status must serve a public purpose and not be contrary to established public policy. . . .

Tax exemptions for certain institutions thought beneficial to the social order of the country as a whole, or to a particular community, are deeply rooted in our history, as in that of England. The origins of such exemptions lie in the special privileges that have long been extended to charitable trusts.

More than a century ago, this Court announced the caveat that is critical in this case:

"[I]t has now become an established principle of American law, that courts of chancery will sustain and protect . . . a gift . . . to public charitable uses, *provided the same is consistent with local laws and public policy. . . .*" *Perin v. Carey* (1861) (emphasis added).

Soon after that, in 1878, the Court commented:

"A charitable use, *where neither law nor public policy forbids,* may be applied to almost any thing *that tends to promote the well-doing and well-being of social man." Ould v. Washington Hospital for Found-lings* (emphasis added).

In 1891, in a restatement of the English law of charity which has long been recognized as a leading authority in this country, Lord Mac-Naghten stated:

> " 'Charity' in its legal sense comprises four principal divisions: trusts for the relief of poverty; *trusts for the advancement of education;* trusts for the advancement of religion; and trusts for *other purposes beneficial to the community,* not falling under any of the preceding heads." *Commissioners v. Pemsel* (emphasis added).

These statements clearly reveal the legal background against which Congress enacted the first charitable exemption statute in 1894: charities were to be given preferential treatment because they provide a benefit to society.

What little floor debate occurred on the charitable exemption provision of the 1894 Act and similar sections of later statutes leaves no doubt that Congress deemed the specified organizations entitled to tax benefits because they served desirable public purposes.

In enacting the Revenue Act of 1938 Congress expressly reconfirmed this view with respect to the charitable deduction provision:

> "The exemption from taxation of money and property devoted to charitable and other purposes is based on the theory that the Government is compensated for the loss of revenue by its relief from financial burdens which would otherwise have to be met by appropriations from other public funds, and by the benefits resulting from the promotion of the general welfare."

A corollary to the public benefit principle is the requirement, long recognized in the law of trusts, that the purpose of a charitable trust may not be illegal or violate established public policy. In 1861, this Court stated that a public charitable use must be "consistent with local laws and public policy," *Perin v. Carey.* Modern commentators and courts have echoed that view.

When the Government grants exemptions or allows deductions all taxpayers are affected; the very fact of the exemption or deduction for the donor means that other taxpayers can be said to be indirect and vicarious "donors." Charitable exemptions are justified on the basis that the exempt entity confers a public benefit—a benefit which the society or the community may not itself choose or be able to provide, or which supplements and advances the work of public institutions already supported by tax revenues. History buttresses logic to make clear that, to warrant exemption under § 501(c)(3), an institution must fall within a category specified in that section and must demonstrably serve and be in harmony with the public interest.

The institution's purpose must not be so at odds with the common community conscience as to undermine any public benefit that might otherwise be conferred.

We are bound to approach these questions with full awareness that determinations of public benefit and public policy are sensitive matters with serious implications for the institutions affected; a declaration that a given institution is not "charitable" should be made only where there can be no doubt that the activity involved is contrary to a fundamental public policy. But there can no longer be any doubt that racial discrimination in education violates deeply and widely accepted views of elementary justice. Prior to 1954, public education in many places still was conducted under the pall of *Plessy v. Ferguson* (1896); racial segregation in primary and secondary education prevailed in many parts of the country. This Court's decision in *Brown v. Board of Education* (1954) signalled an end to that era. Over the past quarter of a century, every pronouncement of this Court and myriad Acts of Congress and Executive Orders attest a firm national policy to prohibit racial segregation and discrimination in public education.

An unbroken line of cases following *Brown v. Board of Education* establishes beyond doubt this Court's view that racial discrimination in education violates a most fundamental national public policy, as well as rights of individuals.

> "The right of a student not to be segregated on racial grounds in schools . . . is indeed so fundamental and pervasive that it is embraced in the concept of due process of law." *Cooper v. Aaron* (1958).

In *Norwood v. Harrison* (1973), we dealt with a non-public institution:

> "[A] private school—even one that discriminates—fulfills an important educational function; *however, . . . [that] legitimate educational function cannot be isolated from discriminatory practices . . . [D]iscriminatory treatment exerts a pervasive influence on the entire educational process.*" (Emphasis added.) . . .

Congress, in Titles IV and VI of the Civil Rights Act of 1964, . . . clearly expressed its agreement that racial discrimination in education violates a fundamental public policy. Other sections of that Act, and numerous enactments since then, testify to the public policy against racial discrimination. . . .

The Executive Branch has consistently placed its support behind eradication of racial discrimination. Several years before this Court's decision in *Brown v. Board of Education*, President Truman issued Executive Orders prohibiting racial discrimination in federal employment decisions, and in classifications for the Selective Service. In 1957, President Eisenhower employed military forces to ensure compliance with federal standards in school desegregation programs. . . . And in 1962, President Kennedy announced:

> "[T]he granting of federal assistance for . . . housing and related facilities from which Americans are excluded because of their race, color, creed, or national origin is unfair, unjust, and inconsistent with the public policy of the United States as manifested in its Constitution and laws."

These are but a few of numerous Executive Orders over the past three decades demonstrating the commitment of the Executive Branch to the fundamental policy of eliminating racial discrimination.

Few social or political issues in our history have been more vigorously debated and more extensively ventilated than the issue of racial discrimination, particularly in education. Given the stress and anguish of the history of efforts to escape from the shackles of the "separate but equal" doctrine of *Plessy v. Ferguson*, it cannot be said that educational institutions that, for whatever reasons, practice racial discrimination, are institutions exercising "beneficial and stabilizing influences in community life," *Walz v. Tax Comm'n* (1970), or should be encouraged by having all taxpayers share in their support by way of special tax status.

There can thus be no question that the interpretation of § 170 and § 501(c)(3) announced by the IRS in 1970 was correct. That it may be seen as belated does not undermine its soundness. It would be wholly incompatible with the concepts underlying tax exemption to grant the benefit of tax-exempt status to racially discriminatory educational entities, which "exer[t] a pervasive influence on the entire educational process." *Norwood v. Harrison*. Whatever may be the rationale for such private schools' policies, and however sincere the rationale may be, racial discrimination in education is contrary to public policy. Racially discriminatory educational institutions cannot be viewed as conferring a public benefit within the "charitable" concept discussed earlier, or within the Congressional intent underlying § 170 and § 501(c)(3). . . .

The actions of Congress since 1970 leave no doubt that the IRS reached the correct conclusion in exercising its authority. It is, of course, not unknown for independent agencies or the Executive Branch to misconstrue the intent of a statute; Congress can and often does correct such misconceptions, if the courts have not done so. Yet for a dozen years Congress has been made aware—acutely aware—of the IRS rulings of 1970 and 1971. As we noted earlier, few issues have been the subject of more vigorous and widespread debate and discussion in and out of Congress than those related to racial segregation in education. Sincere adherents advocating contrary views have ventilated the subject for well over three decades. Failure of Congress to modify the IRS rulings of 1970 and 1971, of which Congress was, by its own studies and by public discourse, constantly reminded; and Congress' awareness of the denial of tax-exempt status for racially discriminatory schools when enacting other and related legislation make out an unusually strong case of legislative acquiescence in and ratification by implication of the 1970 and 1971 rulings. . . .

Non-action by Congress is not often a useful guide, but the non-action here is significant. During the past 12 years there have been no fewer than 13 bills introduced to overturn the IRS interpretation of § 501(c)(3). Not one of these bills has emerged from any committee, although Congress has enacted numerous other amendments to § 501 during this same period, including an amendment to § 501(c)(3) itself. It is hardly conceivable that Congress—and in this setting, any Member of Congress—was not abundantly aware of what was going on. In view of its prolonged and acute awareness of so important an issue, Congress' failure to act on the bills proposed on this subject provides added support for concluding that Congress acquiesced in the IRS rulings of 1970 and 1971. . . .

The judgments of the Court of Appeals are, accordingly, affirmed.

MR. JUSTICE POWELL, concurring in the judgment. . . .

I . . . concur in the Court's judgment that tax-exempt status under §§170(c) and 501(c)(3) is not available to private schools that concededly are racially discriminatory. I do not agree, however, with the Court's more general explanation of the justifications for the tax exemptions provided to charitable organizations. . . .

MR. JUSTICE REHNQUIST, dissenting. . . .

In approaching this statutory construction question the Court quite adeptly avoids the statute it is construing. This I am sure is no accident, for there is nothing in the language of §501(c)(3) that supports the result obtained by the Court. . . .

One way to read the opinion handed down by the Court today leads to the conclusion that [Congress's] long and arduous refining process of §501(c)(3) was certainly a waste of time, for when enacting the original 1894 statute Congress intended to adopt a common law term of art and intended that this term of art carry with it all of the common law baggage which defines it. Such a view, however, leads also to the unsupportable idea that Congress has spent almost a century adding illustrations simply to clarify an already defined common law term.

Another way to read the Court's opinion leads to the conclusion that even though Congress has set forth *some* of the requirements of a §501(c)(3) organization, it intended that the IRS additionally require that organizations meet a higher standard of public interest, not stated by Congress, but to be determined and defined by the IRS and the courts. This view I find equally unsupportable. Almost a century of statutory history proves that Congress itself intended to decide what §501(c)(3) requires. Congress has expressed its decision in the plainest of terms in §501(c)(3) by providing that tax-exempt status is to be given to any corporation, or community chest fund, or foundation that is organized for one of the eight enumerated purposes, operated on a nonprofit basis, and uninvolved in lobbying activities or political campaigns. . . . Congress has left it to neither the IRS nor the courts to select or add to the requirements of §501(c)(3). . . .

Perhaps recognizing the lack of support in the statute itself, or in its history, for the 1970 IRS change, the Court finds that "[t]he actions of Congress since 1970 leave no doubt that the IRS reached the correct conclusion in exercising its authority," concluding that there is "an unusually strong case of legislative acquiescence in and ratification by implication of the 1970 and 1971 rulings." . . . These bills and related hearings indicate little more than that a vigorous debate has existed in Congress concerning the new IRS position. . . .

This Court continuously has been hesitant to find ratification through inaction. See *United States v. Wise* [1962]. . . . Few cases would call for more caution than the present one. The new IRS interpretation is not only far less than a long standing administrative policy, it is at odds with a position maintained by IRS, and unquestioned by Congress, for several decades prior to 1970. The interpretation is unsupported by the statutory language, it is unsupported by legislative history, the interpretation has led to considerable controversy in and out of Congress, and the interpretation gives to the IRS a broad power which until now Congress has kept for itself. Where in addition to these circumstances Congress has shown time and again that it is ready to enact positive legislation to change the tax code when it desires, this Court has no business finding that Congress has adopted the new IRS position by failing to enact legislation to reverse it.

I have no disagreement with the Court's finding that there is a strong national policy in this country opposed to racial segregation. I agree with the Court that Congress has the power to further this policy by denying §501(c)(3) status to organizations that practice racial discrimination. But as yet Congress has failed to do so. Whatever the reasons for this failure, this Court should not legislate for Congress. . . .

12
Constitutional Interpretation

Interpreting a constitution is the highest function that judges perform. Because a constitution embodies some of a nation's fundamental choices among values, spells out the processes by which other values are to be chosen and describes the qualifications (typically popular election of some sort) of the immediate choosers, and divides authority among those choosers, any convincing explanation of what that set of arrangements means can shape the general political beliefs of society as well as affect many specific public policies.

The difficulties of constitutional interpretation are commensurate with its importance. Constitutions and amendments thereto are drafted by human beings who, living at given moments in history, are usually trying to solve concrete problems. Transferring meaning to later—and unforeseen—problems is no easy task. Moreover, as we have already seen with judicial opinions and statutory provisions, there are limits to the clarity of language, limits that become appallingly obvious when we look at constitutional clauses that forbid "unreasonable searches and seizures" or government's depriving people of their rights to life, liberty, and property "without due process of law." Because, as John Marshall wrote in *McCulloch v. Maryland* (1819), a constitution is "intended to endure for ages to come," its terms tend to sketch broadly rather than etch sharply rights, duties, and powers. They speak, as Ronald Dworkin says, (Reading 12.7), in general concepts rather than in particularistic conceptions. A constitution, Marshall explained in *McCulloch:*

> to contain an accurate detail of all the subdivisions of which its great powers will admit, and of all the means by which they may be carried into execution, would partake of the prolixity of a legal code, and could scarcely be embraced by the human mind. . . . Its nature, therefore, requires, that only its great outlines should be

479

marked, its important objects designated, and the minor ingredients which compose those objects, be deduced from the nature of the objects themselves.

Such breadth of draftsmanship may well make it possible for a constitution "to be adapted to the various *crises* of human affairs"; but that breadth also throws heavy responsibility on fallible human beings.

Given the nature of a constitution, the question is not whether it should be interpreted, for that is a necessity. Rather, the question is: by whom shall it be interpreted? To some extent, all public officials and all politically active citizens share an obligation to interpret their own constitution. If legislators are intelligent, rational, and dedicated, they must decide whether any bill before the house meets minimal constitutional standards. A conscientious administrator has to make a similar judgment when carrying out a statutory command or formulating a more specific directive. Indeed, one can cogently argue that not only *should* all public officials interpret the constitution, but also that they *must* do so, for even a decision that squaring a bill or an order with the constitution is someone else's responsibility is itself an interpretation of the fundamental law.

The extent to which the framers and ratifiers of the American Constitution meant to confer on the judiciary authority to assess the validity of congressional and presidential interpretations of the Constitution is something about which we can never be fully certain. It is clear, however, from the amending clause and the various institutional limitations of judicial power (see Chapter 7) that the founding fathers had no intention whatever of making judges omnipotent or imbuing them with infallibility in this or any other area of law and policy.

But whatever scope and authority the framers meant to give judges, the plain fact is that since John Marshall's opinion in *Marbury v. Madison* (1803) (Reading 1.3), the United States has managed to live with a broad measure of judicial authority to invalidate acts of coordinate branches of government. Marshall's logic may have been tenuous. The Constitution itself may be silent about the validity of certain kinds of governmental action. And silence, Marshall's shaky logic, and political restraints may move American judges to use their power cautiously. But when all these things are said and resaid, emphasized and reemphasized, American judges still exercise the authority to strike down statutes and executive orders, federal as well as state. And the authority of the Supreme Court as constitutional interpreter is so firmly established that it can precipitate the resignation of a President or declare over 200 congressional statutory provisions unconstitutional in one fell swoop. (Readings 12.1 and 12.2.)

JUDICIAL REVIEW ABROAD

This sort of authority is not unique to the United States, although it is fair to say that the prestige of the American Supreme Court has provided a model and incentive for other countries. By the middle of the nineteenth century the Judicial Committee of the British Privy Council was functioning as a kind of constitutional arbiter for colonial governments within the British Empire—but not, of course, for the United Kingdom itself. Then Canada in the late nineteenth century and Australia in the first years of the twentieth century created their systems of constitutional review, although the Canadians allowed the Judicial Committee to sit as a "supreme" supreme court until 1949.

In the nineteenth century Argentina also modeled its Corte Suprema on that of the United States and even instructed its judges to pay special attention to precedents of the American tribunal. In this century Austria, Ireland, India, and the Philippines adopted judicial review, and variations of this power can be found in Switzerland, much of Latin America, some of Africa, and in a formal if not real sense even in countries such as Pakistan and Yugoslavia.

After World War II the three defeated Axis powers—Italy, Japan, and West Germany—all institutionalized judicial review in their new constitutions. This development was due in part to a revulsion against recent experiences with unchecked executive power and in part to the influence of American occupying authorities. Japan, whose constitution was to some extent drafted by Americans, follows the "decentralized" model[1] of the United States: the power of judicial review is diffused throughout the entire system of courts. All courts of general jurisdiction can declare a legislative or executive act invalid.

Germany and Italy, however, followed a "centralized" model first adopted in the Austrian constitution of 1920. Each country has a single constitutional court (although the German tribunal sits in two divisions, or "senates") that has a judicial monopoly on interpreting the fundamental law. When in litigation before the ordinary courts judges must apply a law whose constitutionality they doubt, they are obliged to send the case directly to the constitutional court. This tribunal receives evidence on the constitutional issue, hears argument, and hands down a decision—but only on the constitutional question—and publishes an opinion justifying the ruling and explaining the controlling principles. German and Italian public officials may also bring suits in their constitutional court to challenge the legitimacy of legislative, executive, or judicial acts. Under some circumstances private citizens in West Germany (but not in Italy) may start similar litigation. Where judicial action is challenged, the constitutional court in effect reviews a decision of another court, but the form of the action is very different from an appeal in the United States.

The case for a decentralized system is basically that stated by Marshall in *Marbury.* Judges often face the problem of conflicting laws

[1] Mauro Cappelletti, *Judicial Review in the Contemporary World* (Indianapolis: Bobbs-Merrill, 1971), pp. 46ff.; see also Walter F. Murphy and Joseph Tanenhaus (eds.), *Comparative Constitutional Law* (New York: St. Martin's Press, 1977), Chs. 1–6.

and must decide which will prevail. If the laws have equal normative force (for example, statutes adopted by Congress), there are general rules to apply—such as, the later law must prevail or a particularized law supersedes a general law. But if the laws are not of equal normative force, the superior law must outrank the lesser. If a judge cannot give preference to a constitutional provision over ordinary legislation, the judicial role is seriously circumscribed.

The countries that have rejected Marshall's rationale tend to use the Civil Law, which takes more seriously the myth of separation of powers and endorses a notion of the supremacy of statutory law over judicial rulings. These countries have accepted the charge that invalidation of a statute on constitutional grounds is an act of high policy, inappropriate for a general court. So even Civil Law nations like Italy and West Germany that have accepted a centralized form of judicial review require all courts except one to apply the law as they find it. The most ordinary judges can do when a constitutional issue is raised is to refer the problem to the specialized constitutional court.

THE BRITISH ALTERNATIVE

The British alternative to judicial review is parliamentary supremacy. It may be true that the British Parliament tends to be more responsive to citizens' demands than the American Congress, and the integral relationship between the British executive and the legislature through the device of ministerial responsibility prevents the deadlock and irresponsibility that often characterize American institutional arrangements. But because Parliament can pass any legislation it wishes—and on occasion it has wished to abridge civil liberties—the citizen has few, if any, constitutional rights enforceable in court against the government.[2] Still, as we noted earlier, the British may be closer to a form of judicial review than they realize. In joining the European Economic Community (EEC, or Common Market), Britain agreed to accept the jurisdiction of the EEC Court of Justice. This tribunal has authority to determine the validity—under the treaties establishing the Common Market—of a wide range of domestic policies of each member nation.[3]

THE NATURE OF THE CONSTITUTION

As Chapters 5 and 11 explained, one approach to constitutional interpretation used by American judges has been avoidance. The justices

[2] For this reason, it was astonishing that in 1984 a judge of the High Court struck down the government's ban on trade unions in sensitive defense installations on the grounds that such action, taken without consulting the unions, was contrary to "natural justice." (*New York Times,* July 17, 1984.) The ruling was promptly reversed on appeal. (*New York Times,* August 7, 1984.)

[3] See Werner J. Feld and Elliot E. Slotnick, " 'Marshalling' the European Community Court," 25 *Emory Law Journal* 317 (1976).

have sometimes asserted a formal doctrine—usually one not in the constitutional document itself—such as "political questions," "standing to sue," or "equitable abstention," to place responsibility for interpreting particular parts of the Constitution on other governmental officials. The Supreme Court's control over its own docket allows the justices, without any explanation whatever, to refuse to decide constitutional (or other) issues that they think are not yet ripe for adjudication, too politically explosive, too difficult, or too trivial.

When a court does decide to face a constitutional problem, there are several preliminary questions that judges must answer before addressing the specific issue that the case presents. First of all, they must decide just what a constitution is. For instance, is it a contract among sovereign states or an agreement among the individual citizens of the entire country? Since 1865, American judges would almost unanimously agree with John Marshall's ruling in *McCulloch v. Maryland* and opt for the second meaning. But it took a bloody civil war to eliminate the first definition, and it is not completely clear that the first was historically wrong.

Another set of preliminary questions concerns the scope of the term "constitution." Does it include only the original document plus its various amendments or are there some concepts within those words that were so obvious to the framers as not to need mentioning? Further, have some usages become such integral parts of the political tradition as to take on constitutional status? Do some documents have such a hallowed nature that they too are part of a country's basic heritage? Before American judges choose the easy answer, "only the constitutional document and its amendments," they must carefully consider that one looks in vain in the Constitution for any mention of some principles such as the rule of law, presumption of innocence, and the importance of human dignity that we take for granted. Among the more constitutionally consequential usages not mentioned in the Constitution is judicial review itself; neither is there a word about "executive privilege," "senatorial courtesy," or political parties. Moreover, the ideas of the Declaration of Independence, certainly its second paragraph's paean to freedom and equality, and Lincoln's Gettysburg Address are more than mere artifacts of intellectual history. Indeed, the constitutional philosophy behind the Warren Court's reapportionment decisions formulating and applying the principle of "one person, one vote" depended far more on Jefferson and Lincoln than on any particular clause in the constitutional document.

A third set of preliminary questions concerns the stability of constitutional commands. Is the Constitution the supreme law "equally in war and peace," or, if a constitution is "to be adapted to the various *crises* in human affairs," do emergencies relax its strictures on governmental authority? Survival, after all, is from one point of view the highest national value. It was Jefferson, not Hamilton, who argued that "to lose our country by scrupulous adherence to written law, would be to lose the law itself, with life, liberty, property and all those who are enjoying them with us; thus absurdly sacrificing the end to the means."[4] Lest a judge think that that sentiment is constitutionally conclusive, he or she need only remember that this was Richard Nixon's ultimate rationale for his crimes. One might ask, what doth it profit a nation to survive if the cost of survival is the loss of the reason for its existence?

MODES OF INTERPRETATION

Once judges have answered to their satisfaction these and similar questions, they can intelligently address the problem of milking meaning from the "constitution." The most obvious approach is to look at the words of the document itself. Clear wording may end many problems, though this possibility is less likely to help judges than other officials. For if the words of the document are unambiguous and if there are no contrary understandings and usages, officials are apt to face no dilemma, and private citizens are not likely to challenge the official's action in the courts—at the ballot box, perhaps, but not in the courts.

Unhappily for the peace of mind of all concerned, the meaning of words, especially in a constitution, is not likely to be so obvious that "he who runs can read." We need not rehearse all that Chapter 11 said about ambiguity of statutory language. The plain words of the Fourteenth Amendment, "nor [shall any state] deny to any person within its jurisdiction the equal protection of the laws," was of scant help to the Court in determining in the *Bakke* case the constitutionality of a plan for "affirmative action."[5] But one must also keep in mind that the American Constitution was drafted in the eighteenth century. English grammar and syntax as well as the meanings of many words have changed in the intervening two centuries. For example, according to one authority[6] the word "among" was then more often a synonym for "within" than "between more than two." If true, Article I, Section 8's grant of power to Congress to regulate "commerce *among* the several states" was vastly more sweeping than judicial decisions indicated until recent decades. Similarly, the term "due process of law" initially referred only to procedure—*how* government did something. Today,

---

[4] Letter to J. B. Colvin, September 20, 1810; Andrew A. Lipscomb (ed.), *The Writings of Thomas Jefferson* (Washington, D.C.: The Thomas Jefferson Memorial Association, 1903), XII, 418.

[5] In *Regents of the University of California v. Bakke* (1978) the Court, by a vote of five to four, held that a numerical quota for admission of minorities to a medical school was unconstitutional as an explicit racial classification, but that it would be proper to take race into account as one factor in achieving a diverse student body.

[6] W. W. Crosskey, *Politics and the Constitution* (Chicago: University of Chicago Press, 1953), I, Ch. 3.

however, "due process" includes substance—*what* government does —as well as procedure.

Among the more serious difficulties is that even where individual words are clear in their meaning, they may become opaque when combined with other words to form clauses and sentences. What does Congress' power "to declare war" and to "raise and support armies" include? Does it allow locking up innocent civilians in concentration camps because their ancestors were born in what is for the time being an enemy country? Does it allow Congress to draft young people into the military, despite the Thirteenth Amendment's prohibition of "involuntary servitude"? Does it allow drafting Quakers and other religious conscientious objectors even though the First Amendment forbids Congress to abridge the "free exercise" of religion?

INTENT

When interpreters find little nourishment in "plain words," they might seek clarification in the "intent" of the framers. But that can contains even more wiggly worms than the search for legislative intent behind a statute. Such a search makes two assumptions. The first is that the framers' specific intentions—rather than only the concepts and principles they actually proposed—should bind future generations.

The second assumption is that the framers had a single intention— as opposed to many different and perhaps irreconcilable intentions— and that it is possible to discover that intent. Both parts of this assumption are tenuous. "Every man," William Anderson has noted, "being a different individual, unavoidably has intentions that are somewhat different from those of someone else. Such a thing as a solid, unified intention of all the members in any group would be hard if not impossible to find."[7]

Such a set of intentions is particularly hard to find for the fifty-five men who met at Philadelphia to frame the original Constitution. The convention itself kept neither official nor unofficial verbatim records. Historians usually depend largely on James Madison's notes, but by Madison's own admission his notes were incomplete. He wrote some at night after debate and others after the convention had adjourned. Several other members of the convention also kept notes. These are more fragmentary than Madison's, but on some points they disagree with his.

Even when judges have full and accurate accounts of the debates, as they do with many constitutional amendments, problems hardly vanish. Relatively few senators and congressmen speak during the legislative proceedings, and those who do seldom agree fully with

[7] "The Intention of the Framers: A Note on Constitutional Interpretation," 49 *American Political Science Review* 340, 343 (1955).

each other. One can often only hazard a guess about what was transpiring in the minds of those who were silent. And there remains the fundamental point that we alluded to in discussing statutory interpretation: in the end, as Felix Frankfurter once noted, legislators voted on the proposed amendment, not on the speeches. As William Anderson concluded: "The transition that needs to be made from the enduring and objective facts of the written words used to the fleeting, largely unexpressed, and subjective facts of the intentions of the framers who passed away many years ago is beyond human capacity to make. . . ."

There are other objections to using intent, based on democratic theory and on pragmatism. Whatever the framers had in their minds, the democratic argument runs, the people of the times accepted—and we, by opting to remain in the country and to support the Constitution, have accepted—only what the framers *said,* not what they *meant* to say.

The pragmatic argument was best stated by Justice Benjamin N. Cardozo in an opinion he decided not to publish. At issue had been the validity of a Minnesota statute, enacted to combat the Great Depression, providing for a moratorium on foreclosures on farms whose owners were unable to pay their mortgages. Whatever its wisdom, the statute ran afoul not only of the plain words of Article I, §10 of the Constitution, "No State shall . . . pass any law impairing the obligations of contracts," but also of the "intent" of the framers as evidenced from contemporary writings. Nevertheless, the Supreme Court by a five-to-four vote, sustained the statute. Chief Justice Hughes's opinion for the Court was a mishmash of reasoning, partly based on a distinction between the obligation of a contract and the remedy for enforcing a contract and also partly on the notion that the Constitution's meaning changes over time. Cardozo had wanted to put the issue more bluntly:

> To hold this [statute constitutional] may be inconsistent with things that men said in 1787 when expounding to compatriots the newly written constitution. They did not see the changes in the relation between states and nation or in the play of social forces that lay hidden in the womb of time. It may be inconsistent with things that they believed or took for granted. Their beliefs to be significant must be adjusted to the world they knew.

Nevertheless, judges and scholars still often look to the "intent of the framers" as a mystic touchstone for constitutional interpretation. In *Minneapolis Star & Tribune v. Minnesota Commissioner of Revenue* (1983), where the state had levied a special sales tax on paper and ink used by newspapers, Justice O'Connor said in her opinion for the Court striking down the tax: "There is substantial evidence that differential taxation of the press would have troubled the Framers of the First

Amendment." To that statement she appended a footnote about constitutional interpretation generally:

> It is true that our opinions rarely speculate on precisely how the Framers would have analyzed a given regulation of expression. In general . . . we have only limited evidence of exactly how the Framers intended the First Amendment to apply. There are no recorded debates in the Senate or in the States, and the discussion in the House of Representatives was couched in general terms, perhaps in response to Madison's suggestion that the representatives not stray from simple acknowledged principles. Consequently, we ordinarily simply apply those general principles. . . . But when we do have evidence that a particular law would have offended the Framers, we have not hesitated to invalidate it on that ground alone.

Moreover, the concept of the "Framers" can be extended both backward and forward in time from 1787. In *Marsh v. Chambers* (1983) where, as already noted, the Court upheld the practice of legislative prayers, Chief Justice Burger's justification for the ceremony was that the Continental Congress in 1774 and both houses of the First Congress in 1789 had opened their sessions with prayers offered by a paid chaplain. (Reading 12.3.)

POLLS OF OTHER JURISDICTIONS

As a variant on the historical approach, a judge might probe English traditions or early colonial or state practices to determine how public officials of the times—or later—interpreted similar words or phrases. The Supreme Court has frequently used such evidence. For instance, when *Wolf v. Colorado* (1949) presented the Court with the question whether the Fourth Amendment, as applied to the states by the due process clause of the Fourteenth Amendment, barred use in state courts of evidence obtained through an unconstitutional search, Justice Felix Frankfurter surveyed the law in all the states and in ten jurisdictions within the British Commonwealth. He used this poll to bolster a conclusion that, while the Constitution forbade unreasonable searches and seizures, it did not prohibit state officials from using such ill-gotten evidence against a defendant.

In 1952, however, when *Rochin v. California* confronted the justices with the question whether a state could use evidence it had obtained from a defendant by pumping out his stomach—evidence admissible in the overwhelming majority of states—Frankfurter declined to call the roll. Instead he declared that gathering evidence by a stomach pump was "conduct that shocks the conscience" and so its fruits could not be used in courts, state or federal.

When in 1961 *Mapp v. Ohio* overruled *Wolf* and held all unconstitutionally obtained evidence inadmissible in state courts, the justices again surveyed the field. For the Court Justice Clark said: "While in 1949 ... almost two-thirds of the States were opposed to the exclusionary rule, now, despite the *Wolf* Case, more than half of those since passing upon it, by their own legislative or judicial decision, have wholly or partly adopted or adhered to the Weeks [exclusionary] rule."

The point of this set of examples is not that Frankfurter or the Court was inconsistent, but that the method itself, while it offers insights, is far from foolproof. First of all, the Constitution rejected many English and some colonial and state practices. Second, even a steady stream of precedents from the states may mean no more than that busy judges imitated each other under the rubric of stare decisis. Third, if one is seeking for original intent, it is difficult to imagine the relevance of state practices in the twentieth century to what was in the minds of people in the eighteenth century. If one wants to know what other judges, now and in the recent past, have thought about the Constitution, polls are useful. Nevertheless, they say nothing about the correctness of those thoughts—and the correctness of a lower court's interpretation may be precisely the issue before the Supreme Court.

BALANCING OF INTERESTS

In places the Constitution makes apparently conflicting authorizations and prohibitions. The First Amendment, for example, forbids Congress to abridge freedom of the press, while the Sixth Amendment guarantees a defendant in a criminal case a trial by "an impartial jury." Writers and commentators in the various mass media may so blanket the news with unfavorable publicity that a defendant could not obtain an impartial jury, at least near his home. Similarly, Article I, Section 8 authorizes Congress to "provide for the common defence," while the First Amendment bans laws abridging freedom of speech. Does that prohibition mean that those who urge the violent overthrow of the government cannot be jailed?

Justice Hugo L. Black asserted that the plain words of the First Amendment controlled both sorts of situations. That amendment was phrased in absolute terms: "Congress shall make no Law," and, to Black, "no law" meant no law at all. Other judges, like John Marshall Harlan II, have claimed that in cases involving a clash of constitutional values courts must "balance" the interests involved.

There are serious difficulties with both approaches. Literalism, we have already seen, quickly runs into a stone wall. Potentially conflicting constitutional clauses may be equally absolute; the First and Sixth Amendments provide a case in point. More important for Black's own broader constitutional philosophy, a literal interpretation of the First Amendment, since it restricts only Congress, would leave open the possibility of judges or administrators being legitimately able to abridge free speech.

For their part, the "balancers" have yet to explain the nature of the scale on which they weigh competing interests or, more important, the weights attached to various values. If no one knows how the scale is calibrated or has any precise notion of even the relative weights of the values involved until after a decision is announced, it is difficult to escape the conclusion that the judge has by fiat decided that one value is more important than another. The particular decision may be wise and even in keeping with some general philosophy that infuses the Constitution, but it would seem preferable both to prove intellectual honesty and to establish guidelines for future conduct that the judge say so and say so candidly.

HIERARCHY OF VALUES

Perhaps what the balancers are groping toward is the notion that certain values are more important than others and that extracting them from the tangled web of litigation makes their relative importance clearer. Some justices have openly said that they find in the Constitution such a hierarchy and have tried to identify at least some of the "more basic" values. Harlan Stone, for instance, looked on the freedoms enshrined in the First Amendment as having a "preferred position" in the Constitution's galaxy. He—and later liberal justices like Hugo L. Black, William O. Douglas, and William J. Brennan—justified extending judicial protection of these rights as a means of preserving the democratic aspects of the American political system, a means of keeping open the lines of communication among citizens so that today's minority might have a chance of becoming tomorrow's majority. As Black once put it:

> I view the guaranties of the First Amendment as the foundation upon which our governmental system rests and without which it could not continue to endure as conceived and planned. Freedom to speak and write about public questions is as important to the life of our government as the heart is to the human body. In fact, this privilege is the heart of our government. If that heart be weakened, the result is debilitation; if it be stilled, the result is death.[8]

There is some intellectual unity in the clauses protecting the rights to speak and write and to vote. To this list, however, the Court has added freedom to: marry, worship or not worship, have or not have children, travel, retain one's citizenship, enjoy privacy, and perhaps receive a minimal education. Few people would deny that some values

[8] *Milk Wagon Drivers Union v. Meadowmoor Dairies* (1941).

protected by the Constitution are more worthwhile than others. It would be passing strange to equate the right to a trial by jury in a civil suit involving more than $20 with the right to worship or not worship as one sees fit. The question remains, however: why the particular values listed above? These may, indeed, all be fundamental but neither judge nor commentator has yet convincingly explained how they fit together, why they are, as a group, more precious than other rights, or how one justifies their primacy in terms of constitutional doctrine.

COST-BENEFIT ANALYSIS

In Chapter 8 we discussed the anticipated impact of judicial decisions on events in the real world, and we noted how judges inevitably appraise alternative rulings by anticipating their consequences. The same concern for consequences can of course be a factor in deciding between alternative constitutional interpretations.

One of the serious issues on the Burger Court concerned application of the exclusionary rule, which forbids the use in criminal proceedings of evidence secured in violation of the Fourth Amendment. Public perception that the rule is a major factor in hampering the conviction of criminals has inevitably affected judicial attitudes, as Justice White frankly admitted in *United States v. Leon* (1984): "The substantial social costs exacted by the exclusionary rule for the vindication of Fourth Amendment rights have long been a source of concern." In the *Leon* case the Court majority applied a "cost-benefit" calculus to justify a "good faith" seizure by police on an invalid search warrant. (Readings 12.4 and 12.5.)

CONSTITUTIONAL ENGINEERING

One could make a much longer list of methods—and criticisms of those methods—of constitutional interpretation. But no method or rule of interpretation, either singly or in combination with others, offers much hope of attaining final "truth." Acceptance of this fact has caused judges and scholars to react in ways that can be arranged along a broad spectrum. At one end is endorsement of a judicial role of breathing life into the vague terms of the Constitution so that it is "relevant to solutions of current problems"—in sum a judicial license to make the Constitution a "living" reality. The other extreme posits for elected officials and the amending process the task of modernizing the Constitution and leaves to judges the ostensibly simple function of "saying what the law is." (Readings 12.6, 12.7.)

One encounters occasional judicial statements like Earl Warren's refusal in the School Segregation cases to "turn the clock back to 1868 when the [Fourteenth] Amendment was adopted," or Oliver Wendell Holmes's assertion that a case "must be considered in the light of our whole experience and not merely in that of what was said a hundred years ago."[9] Nevertheless, the two extreme positions on this spectrum are more likely to be populated by scholars than by judges, who tend to scatter somewhat nearer the center.

Any position along this spectrum poses severe problems for its occupant. There is some evidence, albeit inconclusive, that the framers of the Bill of Rights meant federal judges to be the peculiar protectors of the values embodied there. (See Frank Johnson's quotation from Madison in Reading 2.4.) On the other hand, the line between active judicial protection and government by judiciary can be exceedingly fine, as some of the discussion in earlier chapters explained in detail. Even when judges pass on to other officials the duty of making choices, those judges are choosing not only to interpret the Constitution as giving authority to others, but they are also, in effect, accepting or rejecting certain particular public policies. When judges offer their own solution to a problem, judicial involvement in policy making becomes more obvious, but it does not necessarily become more important. "The most important thing we do," Justice Brandeis once commented, "is not doing."

More bothersome to judges and commentators alike is that there is no honest way of avoiding the fact that whatever choice is made, judges' own values inevitably have colored perceptions of the issues and estimates of the chances of success as well as of the intrinsic worth of particular solutions. Just as in finding facts and interpreting previous decisions and statutory provisions, judges' values color what they see and how they choose in discovering the Constitution's commands. "We may try to see things as objectively as we please," Cardozo said. "None the less, we can never see them with any eyes except our own." (Reading 1.5.)

Coupled with judges' knowledge that their own values are limiting their options and shaping their choices is the realization that the task of constitutional interpretation, to an even greater degree than the rest of judging, involves much more than legal craftsmanship. In the final analysis, the Civil Law scholars have been right: to the extent that a constitution is a charter for government, its interpretation is a high act of policy making. Involved are the skills of the politician—who, when successful is dubbed a statesman, and when unsuccessful is called a hack. Requiring as it does large measures of political wisdom as well as legal learning, constitutional interpretation remains an art, not a science.

SELECTED REFERENCES

Ackerman, Bruce A. "Beyond *Carolene Products,*" 98 *Harvard Law Review* 713 (1985).

[9] *Missouri v. Holland* (1920).

Agresto, John. *The Supreme Court and Constitutional Democracy.* Ithaca, N.Y.: Cornell University Press, 1984.

Anastaplo, George. *The Constitutionalist: Notes on the First Amendment.* Dallas: Southern Methodist University Press, 1971.

Barber, Sotirios A. *On What the Constitution Means.* Baltimore: Johns Hopkins University Press, 1984.

Berger, Raoul. *Government by Judiciary: The Transformation of the Fourteenth Amendment.* Cambridge, Massachusetts: Harvard University Press, 1977.

Beth, Loren P. *The Development of the American Constitution, 1877–1917.* New York: Harper & Row, 1971.

Bickel, Alexander M. *The Least Dangerous Branch.* Indianapolis: Bobbs-Merrill, 1962.

———. *The Supreme Court and the Idea of Progress.* New York: Harper & Row, 1970.

Blasi, Vincent (ed.). *The Burger Court: The Counter-Revolution That Wasn't.* New Haven: Yale University Press, 1983.

Bobbitt, Philip. *Constitutional Fate: Theory of the Constitution.* New York: Oxford University Press, 1982.

Brest, Paul, and Sanford V. Levinson (eds.). *Processes of Constitutional Decisionmaking: Cases and Materials.* 2d ed. Boston: Little, Brown, 1983.

Brigham, John. *Civil Liberties and American Democracy.* Washington, D.C.: Congressional Quarterly, 1984.

Cannon, Mark W. and David M. O'Brien. *Views from the Bench: The Judiciary and Constitutional Politics.* Chatham, N.J.: Chatham House, 1985.

Choper, Jesse H. *Judicial Review and the National Political Process.* Chicago: University of Chicago Press, 1980.

Cortner, Richard C. *The Supreme Court and the Second Bill of Rights.* Madison: University of Wisconsin Press, 1981.

Crosskey, William W. *Politics and the Constitution in the History of the United States.* 2 vols. Chicago: University of Chicago Press, 1953. Ch. 1.

Dahl, Robert A. "Decision-Making in a Democracy: The Supreme Court as a National Policy-Maker," 6 *Journal of Public Law* 279 (1957).

Elliott, E. Donald. "*INS v. Chadha:* The Administrative Constitution, the Constitution, and the Legislative Veto," in Philip B. Kurland et al. (eds.), *1983 Supreme Court Review* 125. Chicago: University of Chicago Press, 1984.

Ely, John Hart. *Democracy and Distrust: A Theory of Judicial Review.* Cambridge, Mass.: Harvard University Press, 1980.

Emerson, Thomas I. *Toward a General Theory of the First Amendment.* New York: Random House, 1966.

Harris, William F., II. "Bonding Word and Polity: The Logic of American Constitutionalism," 76 *American Political Science Review* 34 (1982).

Lusky, Louis. *By What Right? A Commentary on the Supreme Court's Power to Revise the Constitution.* Charlottesville, Virginia: The Michie Co., 1975.

Mason, Alpheus T. *The Supreme Court from Taft to Burger.* Baton Rouge: Louisiana State University Press, 1979.

McCloskey, Robert G. *The American Supreme Court.* Chicago: University of Chicago Press, 1960.

McWhinney, Edward. *Judicial Review.* 4th ed. Toronto: University of Toronto Press, 1969.

Miller, Charles A. *The Supreme Court and the Uses of History.* Cambridge, Mass.: Harvard University Press, 1969.

Monaghan, Henry P. "Foreword: Constitutional Common Law," 89 *Harvard Law Review* 1 (1975).

Murphy, Paul L. *The Constitution in Crisis Times, 1918–1969.* New York: Harper & Row, 1972.

Murphy, Walter F. "The Art of Constitutional Interpretation," in M. Judd Harmon (ed.), *Essays on the Constitution.* Port Washington, N. Y.: Kennikat Press, 1978.

———. "An Ordering of Constitutional Values," 53 *Southern California Law Review* 703 (1980).

———. "Constitutional Interpretation: Text, Values, and Processes," 9 *Reviews in American History* 7 (1981).

Murphy, Walter F., James E. Fleming, and William F. Harris II (eds.). *American Constitutional Interpretation.* Mineola, N.Y.: Foundation Press, 1986.

Murphy, Walter F., and Joseph Tanenhaus. *The Study of Public Law.* New York: Random House, 1972, Chs. 2–6.

Murphy, Walter F., and Joseph Tanenhaus (eds.). *Comparative Constitutional Law: Cases and Commentaries.* New York: St. Martin's Press, 1977.

Perry, Michael J. *The Constitution, the Courts, and Human Rights.* New Haven, Conn.: Yale University Press, 1982.

Powell, H. Jefferson. "The Original Understanding of Original Intent." 98 *Harvard Law Review* 885 (1985).

Pritchett, C. Herman *Constitutional Civil Liberties.* Englewood Cliffs, N.J.: Prentice-Hall, Inc., 1984.

———. *Constitutional Law of the Federal System.* Englewood Cliffs, N.J.: Prentice-Hall, Inc., 1984.

Schrock, Thomas S., and Robert C. Welsh. "Reconsidering the Constitutional Common Law," 91 *Harvard Law Review* 1117 (1978).

Interpretation Symposium. 58 *Southern California Law Review* 1 (1985).

Thayer, James Bradley. "The Origin and Scope of the American Doctrine of Constitutional Law," 7 *Harvard Law Review* 129 (1893).

Tribe, Laurence H. *American Constitutional Law.* Mineola, N.Y.: Foundation Press, 1978.

———. *Constitutional Choices.* Cambridge, Mass.: Harvard University Press, 1985.

Wechsler, Herbert. "Toward Neutral Principles of Constitutional Law," 73 *Harvard Law Review* 1 (1959).

12.1   *". . . this presumptive privilege must be considered in light of our historic commitment to the rule of law."*

UNITED STATES V. NIXON

418 U.S. 683, 94 S. Ct. 3090, 41 L. Ed. 2d 1039 (1974)

On several occasions during the so-called Watergate affair, President Nixon had claimed "executive privilege" to justify refusal to submit White House tape recordings and other records demanded by congressional committees, the Watergate special prosecutor, and judges in several proceedings. This case arose in connection with the criminal prosecution of former Attorney General John N. Mitchell and six other Watergate figures. In preparation for the case, Special Prosecutor Archibald Cox had caused a subpoena to be issued requiring Nixon to produce tapes and other documents relating to his conversations with the defendants. Nixon resisted the subpoena, but his claim of executive privilege was rejected in the district court, and his appeal to the court of appeals was aborted when the Supreme Court took the unusual action of granting the prosecutor's petition for a writ of certiorari before judgment.

CHIEF JUSTICE BURGER delivered the opinion of the Court. . . .

IV

A

. . . [W]e turn to the claim that the subpoena should be quashed because it demands "confidential conversations between a President and his close advisors that it would be inconsistent with the public interest to produce." The first contention is a broad claim that the separation of powers doctrine precludes judicial review of a President's claim of privilege. The second contention is that if he does not prevail on the claim of absolute privilege, the court should hold as a matter of constitutional law that the privilege prevails over the subpoena *duces tecum.*

In the performance of assigned constitutional duties each branch of the Government must initially interpret the Constitution, and the interpretation of its powers by any branch is due great respect from the others. The President's counsel, as we have noted, reads the Constitution as providing an absolute privilege of confidentiality for all presidential communications. Many decisions of this Court, however, have unequivocally reaffirmed the holding of *Marbury v. Madison* (1803) that "it is emphatically the province and duty of the judicial department to say what the law is."

No holding of the Court has defined the scope of judicial power specifically relating to the enforcement of a subpoena for confidential presidential communications for use in a criminal prosecution, but other exercises of powers by the Executive Branch and the Legislative Branch have been found invalid as in conflict with the Constitution. *Powell v. McCormack* (1969); *Youngstown Sheet & Tube Co. v. Sawyer* (1952). In a series of cases, the Court interpreted the explicit immunity conferred by express provisions of the Constitution on Members of the House and Senate by the Speech or Debate Clause, U.S. Const. Art. I, § 6. . . . Since this Court has consistently exercised the power to construe and delineate claims arising under express powers, it must follow that the Court has authority to interpret claims with respect to powers alleged to derive from enumerated powers.

Our system of government "requires that federal courts on occasion interpret the Constitution in a manner at variance with the construction given the document by another branch." *Powell v. McCormack.* And in *Baker v. Carr* the Court stated: "[D]eciding whether a matter has in any measure been committed by the Constitution to another branch of government, or whether the action of that branch exceeds whatever authority has been committed, is itself a delicate exercise in constitutional interpretation, and is a responsibility of this Court as ultimate interpreter of the Constitution.

Notwithstanding the deference each branch must accord the others, the "judicial power of the United States" vested in the federal courts by Art. III, § 1 of the Constitution can no more be shared with the Executive Branch than the Chief Executive, for example, can share with the Judiciary the veto power, or the Congress share with the Judiciary the power to override a presidential veto. Any other conclusion would be contrary to the basic concept of separation of powers and the checks and balances that flow from the scheme of a tripartite government. The Federalist, No. 47. We therefore reaffirm that it is "emphatically the province and the duty" of this Court "to say what the law is" with respect to the claim of privilege presented in this case. *Marbury v. Madison.*

B

In support of his claim of absolute privilege, the President's counsel urges two grounds one of which is common to all governments and one of which is peculiar to our system of separation of powers. The first ground is the valid need for protection of communications between high government officials and those who advise and assist them in the performance of their manifold duties; the importance of this confidentiality is too plain to require further discussion. Human experience teaches that those who expect public dissemination of their remarks may well temper candor with a concern for appearances and for their own interests to the detriment of the decision-making process. Whatever the nature of the privilege of confidentiality of presidential communications in the exercise of Art. II powers the privilege can be said to derive from the supremacy of each branch within its own assigned area of constitutional duties. Certain powers and privileges flow from the nature of enumerated powers; the protection of the confidentiality of presidential communications has similar constitutional underpinnings.

The second ground asserted by the President's counsel in support of the claim of absolute privilege rests on the doctrine of separation of powers. Here it is argued that the independence of the Executive Branch within its own sphere . . . insulates a president from a judicial subpoena in an ongoing criminal prosecution, and thereby protects confidential presidential communications.

However, neither the doctrine of separation of powers, nor the need for confidentiality of high level communications, without more, can sustain an absolute, unqualified presidential privilege of immunity from judicial process under all circumstances. The President's need for complete candor and objectivity from advisers calls for great deference from the courts. However, when the privilege depends solely on the broad, undifferentiated claim of public interest in the confidentiality of such conversations, a confrontation with other values arises. Absent a claim of need to protect military, diplomatic or sensitive national security secrets, we find it difficult to accept the argument that even the very important interest in confidentiality of presidential communications is significantly diminished by production of such material for *in camera* inspection with all the protection that a district court will be obliged to provide.

The impediment that an absolute, unqualified privilege would place in the way of the primary constitutional duty of the Judicial Branch to do justice in criminal prosecutions would plainly conflict with the function of the courts under Art. III. In designing the structure of our Government and dividing and allocating the sovereign power among three coequal branches, the Framers of the Constitution sought to provide a comprehensive system, but the separate powers were not intended to operate with absolute independence. . . . To read the Art. II powers of the President as providing an absolute privilege as against a subpoena essential to enforcement of criminal statutes on no more than a generalized claim of the public interest in confidentiality of nonmilitary and nondiplomatic discussions would upset the constitutional balance of "a workable government" and gravely impair the role of the courts under Art. III.

C

Since we conclude that the legitimate needs of the judicial process may outweigh presidential privilege, it is necessary to resolve those competing interests in a manner that preserves the essential functions of each branch. The right and indeed the duty to resolve that question does not free the judiciary from according high respect to the representations made on behalf of the President. *United States v. Burr* (1807).

The expectation of a President to the confidentiality of his conversations and correspondence, like the claim of confidentiality of judicial deliberations, for example, has all the values to which we accord deference for the privacy of all citizens and added to those values the necessity for protection of the public interest in candid, objective, and even blunt or harsh opinions in presidential decisionmaking. A President and those who assist him must be free to explore alternatives in the process of shaping policies and making decisions and to do so in a way many would be unwilling to express except privately. These are the considerations justifying a presumptive privilege for presidential communications. The privilege is fundamental to the operation of government and inextricably rooted in the separation of powers under the Constitution. In *Nixon v. Sirica* (1973), the Court of Appeals held that such presidential communications are "presumptively privileged," and this position is accepted by both parties in the present litigation. We agree with Mr. Chief Justice Marshall's observation, therefore, that "in no case of this kind would a court be required to proceed against the President as against an ordinary individual." *United States v. Burr.*

But this presumptive privilege must be considered in light of our historic commitment to the rule of law. This is nowhere more profoundly manifest than in our view that "the twofold aim [of criminal justice] is that guilt shall not escape or innocence suffer." *Berger v. United States* (1935). We have elected to employ an adversary system of criminal justice in which the parties contest all issues before a court of law. The need to develop all relevant facts in the adversary system is both fundamental and comprehensive. The ends of criminal justice would be defeated if judgments were to be founded on a partial or speculative presentation of the facts. The very integrity of the judicial system and public confidence in the system depend on full disclosure of all the facts, within the framework of the rules of evidence. To insure that justice is done, it is imperative to the function of courts that compulsory process be available for the production of evidence needed either by the prosecution or by the defense.

Only recently the Court restated the ancient proposition of law, albeit in the context of a grand jury inquiry rather than a trial,

> " 'that the public . . . has a right to every man's evidence' except for those persons protected by a constitutional, common law, or statutory privilege. *United States v. Bryan* (1950)."

The privileges referred to by the Court are designed to protect weighty and legitimate competing interests. Thus, the Fifth Amendment to the Constitution provides that no man "shall be compelled in any criminal case to be a witness against himself." And, generally, an attorney or a priest may not be required to disclose what has been revealed in professional confidence. These and other interests are recognized in law by privileges against forced disclosure, established in the Constitution, by statute, or at common law. Whatever their origins, these exceptions to the demand for every man's evidence are

not lightly created nor expansively construed, for they are in deroga-
tion of the search for truth.

In this case the President challenges a subpoena served on him
as a third party requiring the production of materials for use in a
criminal prosecution on the claim that he has a privilege against
disclosure of confidential communications. He does not place his
claim of privilege on the ground they are military or diplomatic
secrets. As to these areas of Art. II duties the courts have traditionally
shown the utmost deference to presidential responsibilities. . . . No
case of the Court, however, has extended this high degree of deference to a President's generalized interest in confidentiality. Nowhere in the Constitution, as we have noted earlier, is there any
explicit reference to a privilege of confidentiality, yet to the extent
this interest relates to the effective discharge of a President's powers,
it is constitutionally based.

The right to the production of all evidence at a criminal trial
similarly has constitutional dimensions. The Sixth Amendment explicitly confers upon every defendant in a criminal trial the right "to
be confronted with the witnesses against him" and "to have compulsory process for obtaining witnesses in his favor." Moreover, the Fifth
Amendment also guarantees that no person shall be deprived of
liberty without due process of law. It is the manifest duty of the
courts to vindicate those guarantees and to accomplish that it is
essential that all relevant and admissible evidence be produced.

In this case we must weigh the importance of the general privilege of confidentiality of presidential communications in performance of his responsibilities against the inroads of such a privilege on
the fair administration of criminal justice. The interest in preserving
confidentiality is weighty indeed and entitled to great respect. However we cannot conclude that advisers will be moved to temper the
candor of their remarks by the infrequent occasions of disclosure
because of the possibility that such conversations will be called for in
the context of a criminal prosecution.

On the other hand, the allowance of the privilege to withhold
evidence that is demonstrably relevant in a criminal trial would cut
deeply into the guarantee of due process of law and gravely impair
the basic function of the courts. A President's acknowledged need for
confidentiality in the communications of his office is general in nature, whereas the constitutional need for production of relevant evidence in a criminal proceeding is specific and central to the fair
adjudication of a particular criminal case in the administration of
justice. Without access to specific facts a criminal prosecution may be
totally frustrated. The President's broad interest in confidentiality of
communications will not be vitiated by disclosure of a limited number of conversations preliminarily shown to have some bearing on
the pending criminal cases.

We conclude that when the ground for asserting privilege as to subpoenaed materials sought for use in a criminal trial is based only on the generalized interest in confidentiality, it cannot prevail over the fundamental demands of due process of law in the fair administration of criminal justice. The generalized assertion of privilege must yield to the demonstrated, specific need for evidence in a pending criminal trial. . . .

E

. . . Since this matter came before the Court during the pendency of a criminal prosecution, and on representations that time is of the essence, the mandate shall issue forthwith.

Affirmed.

MR. JUSTICE REHNQUIST took no part in the consideration or decision of these cases.

12.2   *"Convenience and efficiency are not the primary objectives—or the hallmarks—of democratic government . . ."*

IMMIGRATION AND NATURALIZATION SERVICE V. CHADHA

462 U.S. 919, 103 S. Ct. 2764, 77 L. Ed. 2d 317 (1983)

Section 244(c)(2) of the Immigration and Nationality Act allowed a single house of Congress to overturn certain decisions made by the Immigration and Naturalization Service. In this instance, the House of Representatives annulled an administrative decision to suspend deportation of an alien, which had been approved by the Attorney General. This action was an instance of the so-called "legislative veto," which had been provided for in one form or another in over 200 statutes since first employed in 1932 as a device for legislative review and control over actions of the administrative branch.

CHIEF JUSTICE BURGER delivered the opinion of the Court. . . .

III

A

We turn now to the question whether action of one House of Congress under § 244(c)(2) violates strictures of the Constitution. We begin, of course, with the presumption that the challenged statute is valid. Its wisdom is not the concern of the courts; if a challenged action does not violate the Constitution, it must be sustained:

> "Once the meaning of an enactment is discerned and its constitutionality determined, the judicial process comes to an end. We do not sit as a committee of review, nor are we vested with the power of veto." *Tennessee Valley Authority v. Hill* (1978).

By the same token, the fact that a given law or procedure is efficient, convenient, and useful in facilitating functions of government, standing alone, will not save it if it is contrary to the Constitution. Convenience and efficiency are not the primary objectives—or the hallmarks—of democratic government and our inquiry is sharpened rather than blunted by the fact that Congressional veto provisions are appearing with increasing frequency in statutes which delegate authority to executive and independent agencies. . . .

Justice WHITE undertakes to make a case for the proposition that the one-House veto is a useful "political invention," and we need not challenge that assertion. We can even concede this utilitarian argument although the long range political wisdom of this "invention" is arguable. It has been vigorously debated and it is instructive to compare the views of the protagonists. See, e.g., Javits & Klein, Congressional Oversight and the Legislative Veto: A Constitutional Analysis, 52 N.Y.U. L.Rev. 455 (1977), and Martin, The Legislative Veto and the Responsible Exercise of Congressional Power, 68 Va.L.Rev. 253 (1982). But policy arguments supporting even useful "political inventions" are subject to the demands of the Constitution which defines powers and, with respect to this subject, sets out just how those powers are to be exercised.

Explicit and unambiguous provisions of the Constitution prescribe and define the respective functions of the Congress and of the Executive in the legislative process. Since the precise terms of those familiar provisions are critical to the resolution of this case, we set them out verbatim. Art. I provides:

> "All legislative Powers herein granted shall be vested in a Congress of the United States, which shall consist of a Senate and a House of Representatives." Art. I, § 1. (Emphasis added.)
>
> "Every Bill which shall have passed the House of Representatives *and* the Senate, *shall,* before it becomes a Law, be presented to the President of the United States; . . ." Art. I, § 7, cl. 2. (Emphasis added.)
>
> "*Every* Order, Resolution, or Vote to which the Concurrence of the Senate and House of Representatives may be necessary (except on a question of Adjournment) *shall be* presented to the President of the United States; and before the Same shall take Effect, *shall be* approved by him, or being disapproved by him, *shall be* repassed by two thirds of the Senate and House of Representatives, according to the Rules and

Limitations prescribed in the Case of a Bill." Art. I, § 7, cl. 3. (Emphasis added.)

These provisions of Art. I are integral parts of the constitutional design for the separation of powers. We have recently noted that "[t]he principle of separation of powers was not simply an abstract generalization in the minds of the Framers: it was woven into the documents that they drafted in Philadelphia in the summer of 1787." *Buckley v. Valeo* [1976]. Just as we relied on the textual provision of Art. II, § 2, cl. 2, to vindicate the principle of separation of powers in *Buckley,* we find that the purposes underlying the Presentment Clauses, Art. I, § 7, cls. 2, 3, and the bicameral requirement of Art. I, § 1 and § 7, cl. 2, guide our resolution of the important question presented in this case. The very structure of the articles delegating and separating powers under Arts. I, II, and III exemplify the concept of separation of powers and we now turn to Art. I.

B

The Presentment Clauses   The records of the Constitutional Convention reveal that the requirement that all legislation be presented to the President before becoming law was uniformly accepted by the Framers. Presentment to the President and the Presidential veto were considered so imperative that the draftsmen took special pains to assure that these requirements could not be circumvented. During the final debate on Art. I, § 7, cl. 2, James Madison expressed concern that it might easily be evaded by the simple expedient of calling a proposed law a "resolution" or "vote" rather than a "bill." As a consequence, Art. I, § 7, cl. 3 was added.

The decision to provide the President with a limited and qualified power to nullify proposed legislation by veto was based on the profound conviction of the Framers that the powers conferred on Congress were the powers to be most carefully circumscribed. It is beyond doubt that lawmaking was a power to be shared by both Houses and the President. In The Federalist No. 73 Hamilton focused on the President's role in making laws:

"If even no propensity had ever discovered itself in the legislative body to invade the rights of the Executive, the rules of just reasoning and theoretic propriety would of themselves teach us that the one ought not to be left to the mercy of the other, but ought to possess a constitutional and effectual power of self-defense." . . .

The President's role in the lawmaking process also reflects the Framers' careful efforts to check whatever propensity a particular Congress might have to enact oppressive, improvident, or ill-considered measures. The President's veto role in the legislative process was described later during public debate on ratification:

> "It establishes a salutary check upon the legislative body, calculated to guard the community against the effects of faction, precipitancy, or of any impulse unfriendly to the public good which may happen to influence a majority of that body. . . . The primary inducement to conferring the power in question upon the Executive is to enable him to defend himself; the secondary one is to increase the chances in favor of the community against the passing of bad laws through haste, inadvertence, or design." The Federalist No. 73 (A. Hamilton).

The Court also has observed that the Presentment Clauses serve the important purpose of assuring that a "national" perspective is grafted on the legislative process:

> "The President is a representative of the people just as the members of the Senate and of the House are, and it may be, at some times, on some subjects, that the President elected by all the people is rather more representative of them all than are the members of either body of the Legislature whose constituencies are local and not countrywide." . . . *Myers v. United States* (1926).

C

Bicameralism The bicameral requirement of Art. I, §§ 1, 7 was of scarcely less concern to the Framers than was the Presidential veto and indeed the two concepts are interdependent. By providing that no law could take effect without the concurrence of the prescribed majority of the Members of both Houses, the Framers reemphasized their belief, already remarked upon in connection with the Presentment Clauses, that legislation should not be enacted unless it has been carefully and fully considered by the Nation's elected officials. In the Constitutional Convention debates on the need for a bicameral legislature, James Wilson, later to become a Justice of this Court, commented:

> "Despotism comes on mankind in different shapes. Sometimes in an Executive, sometimes in a military, one. Is there danger of a Legislative despotism? Theory & practice both proclaim it. If the Legislative authority be not restrained, there can be neither liberty nor stability; and it can only be restrained by dividing it within itself, into distinct and independent branches. In a single house there is no check, but the inadequate one, of the virtue & good sense of those who compose it."

Hamilton argued that a Congress comprised of a single House was antithetical to the very purposes of the Constitution. Were the Nation to adopt a Constitution providing for only one legislative organ, he warned:

"we shall finally accumulate, in a single body, all the most important prerogatives of sovereignty, and thus entail upon our posterity one of the most execrable forms of government that human infatuation ever contrived. Thus we should create in reality that very tyranny which the adversaries of the new Constitution either are, or affect to be, solicitous to avert." The Federalist No. 22.

This view was rooted in a general skepticism regarding the fallibility of human nature later commented on by Joseph Story:

"Public bodies, like private persons, are occasionally under the dominion of strong passions and excitements; impatient, irritable, and impetuous. . . . If [a legislature] feels no check but its own will, it rarely has the firmness to insist upon holding a question long enough under its own view, to see and mark it in all its bearings and relations to society."

These observations are consistent with what many of the Framers expressed, none more cogently than Hamilton in pointing up the need to divide and disperse power in order to protect liberty:

"In republican government, the legislative authority necessarily predominates. The remedy for this inconveniency is to divide the legislature into different branches; and to render them, by different modes of election and different principles of action, as little connected with each other as the nature of their common functions and their common dependence on the society will admit." The Federalist No. 51.

We see therefore that the Framers were acutely conscious that the bicameral requirement and the Presentment Clauses would serve essential constitutional functions. The President's participation in the legislative process was to protect the Executive Branch from Congress and to protect the whole people from improvident laws. The division of the Congress into two distinctive bodies assures that the legislative power would be exercised only after opportunity for full study and debate in separate settings. The President's unilateral veto power, in turn, was limited by the power of two thirds of both Houses of Congress to overrule a veto thereby precluding final arbitrary action of one person. It emerges clearly that the prescription for legislative action in Art. I, §§ 1, 7 represents the Framers' decision that the legislative power of the Federal government be exercised in accord with a single, finely wrought and exhaustively considered, procedure.

IV

The Constitution sought to divide the delegated powers of the new federal government into three defined categories, legislative, executive and judicial, to assure, as nearly as possible, that each Branch of government would confine itself to its assigned responsibility. The hydraulic pressure inherent within each of the separate Branches to exceed the outer limits of its power, even to accomplish desirable objectives, must be resisted.

Although not "hermetically" sealed from one another, *Buckley v. Valeo,* the powers delegated to the three Branches are functionally identifiable. When any Branch acts, it is presumptively exercising the power the Constitution has delegated to it. When the Executive acts, it presumptively acts in an executive or administrative capacity as defined in Art. II. And when, as here, one House of Congress purports to act, it is presumptively acting within its assigned sphere.

Beginning with this presumption, we must nevertheless establish that the challenged action under § 244(c)(2) is of the kind to which the procedural requirements of Art. I, § 7 apply. Not every action taken by either House is subject to the bicameralism and presentment requirements of Art. I. Whether actions taken by either House are, in law and fact, an exercise of legislative power depends not on their form but upon "whether they contain matter which is properly to be regarded as legislative in its character and effect."

Examination of the action taken here by one House pursuant to § 244(c)(2) reveals that it was essentially legislative in purpose and effect. In purporting to exercise power defined in Art. I, § 8, cl. 4 to "establish an uniform Rule of Naturalization," the House took action that had the purpose and effect of altering the legal rights, duties and relations of persons, including the Attorney General, Executive Branch officials and Chadha, all outside the legislative branch. Section 244(c)(2) purports to authorize one House of Congress to require the Attorney General to deport an individual alien whose deportation otherwise would be cancelled under § 244. The one-House veto operated in this case to overrule the Attorney General and mandate Chadha's deportation; absent the House action, Chadha would remain in the United States. Congress has *acted* and its action has altered Chadha's status.

The legislative character of the one-House veto in this case is confirmed by the character of the Congressional action it supplants. Neither the House of Representatives nor the Senate contends that, absent the veto provision in § 244(c)(2), either of them, or both of them acting together, could effectively require the Attorney General to deport an alien once the Attorney General, in the exercise of legislatively delegated authority, had determined the alien should remain in the United States. Without the challenged provision in § 244(c)(2), this could have been achieved, if at all, only by legislation requiring deportation. Similarly, a veto by one House of Congress under § 244(c)(2) cannot be justified as an attempt at amending the standards set out in § 244(a)(1), or as a repeal of § 244 as applied to Chadha. Amendment and repeal of statutes, no less than enactment, must conform with Art. I.

The nature of the decision implemented by the one-House veto in this case further manifests its legislative character. After long experience with the clumsy, time consuming private bill procedure, Congress made a deliberate choice to delegate to the Executive Branch, and specifically to the Attorney General, the authority to allow deportable aliens to remain in this country in certain specified circumstances. It is not disputed that this choice to delegate authority is precisely the kind of decision that can be implemented only in accordance with the procedures set out in Art. I. Disagreement with the Attorney General's decision on Chadha's deportation—that is, Congress' decision to deport Chadha—no less than Congress' original choice to delegate to the Attorney General the authority to make that decision, involves determinations of policy that Congress can implement in only one way: bicameral passage followed by presentment to the President. Congress must abide by its delegation of authority until that delegation is legislatively altered or revoked.

Finally, we see that when the Framers intended to authorize either House of Congress to act alone and outside of its prescribed bicameral legislative role, they narrowly and precisely defined the procedure for such action. There are but four provisions in the Constitution, explicit and unambiguous, by which one House may act alone with the unreviewable force of law, not subject to the President's veto:

(a) The House of Representatives alone was given the power to initiate impeachments. Art. I, § 2, cl. 6;

(b) The Senate alone was given the power to conduct trials following impeachment on charges initiated by the House and to convict following trial. Art. I, § 3, cl. 5;

(c) The Senate alone was given final unreviewable power to approve or to disapprove presidential appointments. Art. II, § 2, cl. 2;

(d) The Senate alone was given unreviewable power to ratify treaties negotiated by the President. Art. II, § 2, cl. 2.

Clearly, when the Draftsmen sought to confer special powers on one House, independent of the other House, or of the President, they did so in explicit, unambiguous terms. These carefully defined exceptions from presentment and bicameralism underscore the difference between the legislative functions of Congress and other unilateral but important and binding one-House acts provided for in the Constitution. These exceptions are narrow, explicit, and separately justified; none of them authorize the action challenged here. On the contrary, they provide further support for the conclusion that Congressional authority is not to be implied and for the conclusion that the veto provided for in § 244(c)(2) is not authorized by the constitutional design of the powers of the Legislative Branch.

Since it is clear that the action by the House under § 244(c)(2) was not within any of the express constitutional exceptions authorizing one House to act alone, and equally clear that it was an exercise of legislative power, that action was subject to the standards prescribed in Article I. The bicameral requirement, the Presentment Clauses, the President's veto, and Congress' power to override a veto were intended to erect enduring checks on each Branch and to protect the people from the improvident exercise of power by mandating certain prescribed steps. To preserve those checks, and maintain the separation of powers, the carefully defined limits on the power of each Branch must not be eroded. To accomplish what has been attempted by one House of Congress in this case requires action in conformity with the express procedures of the Constitution's prescription for legislative action: passage by a majority of both Houses and presentment to the President.

The veto authorized by § 244(c)(2) doubtless has been in many respects a convenient shortcut; the "sharing" with the Executive by Congress of its authority over aliens in this manner is, on its face, an appealing compromise. In purely practical terms, it is obviously easier for action to be taken by one House without submission to the President; but it is crystal clear from the records of the Convention, contemporaneous writings and debates, that the Framers ranked other values higher than efficiency. The records of the Convention and debates in the States preceding ratification underscore the common desire to define and limit the exercise of the newly created federal powers affecting the states and the people. There is unmistakable expression of a determination that legislation by the national Congress be a step-by-step, deliberate and deliberative process.

The choices we discern as having been made in the Constitutional Convention impose burdens on governmental processes that often seem clumsy, inefficient, even unworkable, but those hard choices were consciously made by men who had lived under a form of government that permitted arbitrary governmental acts to go unchecked. There is no support in the Constitution or decisions of this Court for the proposition that the cumbersomeness and delays often encountered in complying with explicit Constitutional standards may be avoided, either by the Congress or by the President. See *Youngstown Sheet & Tube Co. v. Sawyer* (1952). With all the obvious flaws of delay, untidiness, and potential for abuse, we have not yet found a better way to preserve freedom than by making the exercise of power subject to the carefully crafted restraints spelled out in the Constitution. . . .

JUSTICE POWELL concurring in the judgment. . . .
JUSTICE WHITE dissenting.

Today the Court not only invalidates § 244(c)(2) of the Immigration and Nationality Act, but also sounds the death knell for nearly 200 other statutory provisions in which Congress has reserved a "legislative veto." For this reason, the Court's decision is of surpassing importance. And it is for this reason that the Court would have been well-advised to decide the case, if possible, on the narrower grounds of separation of powers, leaving for full consideration the constitutionality of other congressional review statutes operating on such varied matters as war powers and agency rulemaking, some of which concern the independent regulatory agencies.

The prominence of the legislative veto mechanism in our contemporary political system and its importance to Congress can hardly be overstated. It has become a central means by which Congress secures the accountability of executive and independent agencies. Without the legislative veto, Congress is faced with a Hobson's choice: either to refrain from delegating the necessary authority, leaving itself with a hopeless task of writing laws with the requisite specificity to cover endless special circumstances across the entire policy landscape, or in the alternative, to abdicate its lawmaking function to the executive branch and independent agencies. To choose the former leaves major national problems unresolved; to opt for the latter risks unaccountable policymaking by those not elected to fill that role. Accordingly, over the past five decades, the legislative veto has been placed in nearly 200 statutes. The device is known in every field of governmental concern: reorganization, budgets, foreign affairs, war powers, and regulation of trade, safety, energy, the environment and the economy. . . .

12.3   *"Standing alone, historical patterns cannot justify contemporary violations of constitutional guarantees. . . ."*

MARSH V. CHAMBERS

463 U.S. 783, 103 S. Ct. 3330, 77 L. Ed. 2d 1019 (1983)

It was the long-established practice of the one-house Nebraska legislature to begin each session with a prayer offered by a chaplain paid from public funds. The same Presbyterian minister had served in this capacity since 1965. As a member of the legislature and a taxpayer, Ernest Chambers sued to enjoin the legislative prayers as violating the Establishment Clause of the First Amendment. The district court held that the clause was not violated by the prayers, but that it was violated by payment to the chaplain out of public funds. The court of appeals, applying the Supreme Court's reasoning in *Lemon v. Kurtzman* (1971), held that the entire practice was unconstitutional.

CHIEF JUSTICE BURGER delivered the opinion of the Court. . . .

We granted certiorari limited to the challenge to the practice of opening sessions with prayers by a State-employed clergyman, . . . and we reverse.

The opening of sessions of legislative and other deliberative public bodies with prayer is deeply embedded in the history and tradition of this country. From colonial times through the founding of the Republic and ever since, the practice of legislative prayer has coexisted with the principles of disestablishment and religious freedom. In the very courtrooms in which the United States District Judge and later three Circuit Judges heard and decided this case, the proceedings opened with an announcement that concluded, "God save the United States and this Honorable Court." The same invocation occurs at all sessions of this Court.

The tradition in many of the colonies was, of course, linked to an established church, but the Continental Congress, beginning in 1774, adopted the traditional procedure of opening its sessions with a prayer offered by a paid chaplain. . . . Although prayers were not offered during the Constitutional Convention, the First Congress, as one of its early items of business, adopted the policy of selecting a chaplain to open each session with prayer. Thus, on April 7, 1789, the Senate appointed a committee "to take under consideration the manner of electing Chaplains." On April 9, 1789, a similar committee was appointed by the House of Representatives. On April 25, 1789, the Senate elected its first chaplain, the House followed suit on May 1, 1789. A statute providing for the payment of these chaplains was enacted into law on Sept. 22, 1789.

On Sept. 25, 1789, three days after Congress authorized the appointment of paid chaplains, final agreement was reached on the language of the Bill of Rights. Clearly the men who wrote the First Amendment Religion Clause did not view paid legislative chaplains and opening prayers as a violation of that Amendment, for the practice of opening sessions with prayer has continued without interruption ever since that early session of Congress. It has also been followed consistently in most of the states, including Nebraska, where the institution of opening legislative sessions with prayer was adopted even before the State attained statehood. . . .

Standing alone, historical patterns cannot justify contemporary violations of constitutional guarantees, but there is far more here than simply historical patterns. In this context, historical evidence sheds light not only on what the draftsmen intended the Establishment Clause to mean, but also on how they thought that Clause applied to the practice authorized by the First Congress—their actions reveal their intent. An act

"passed by the first Congress assembled under the Constitution, many of whose members had taken part in framing that instrument, . . . is contemporaneous and weighty evidence of its true meaning." *Wisconsin v. Pelican Ins. Co.* (1888).

In *Walz v. Tax Comm'n* (1970), we considered the weight to be accorded to history:

> "It is obviously correct that no one acquires a vested or protected right in violation of the Constitution by long use, even when that span of time covers our entire national existence and indeed predates it. Yet an unbroken practice . . . is not something to be lightly cast aside."

No more is Nebraska's practice of over a century, consistent with two centuries of national practice, to be cast aside. It can hardly be thought that in the same week Members of the First Congress voted to appoint and to pay a Chaplain for each House and also voted to approve the draft of the First Amendment for submission to the States, they intended the Establishment Clause of the Amendment to forbid what they had just declared acceptable. In applying the First Amendment to the states through the Fourteenth Amendment, *Cantwell v. Connecticut* (1940), it would be incongruous to interpret that clause as imposing more stringent First Amendment limits on the States than the draftsmen imposed on the Federal Government.

This unique history leads us to accept the interpretation of the First Amendment draftsmen who saw no real threat to the Establishment Clause arising from a practice of prayer similar to that now challenged. We conclude that legislative prayer presents no more potential for establishment than the provision of school transportation, *Everson v. Board of Education* (1946), beneficial grants for higher education, *Tilton v. Richardson* (1971), or tax exemptions for religious organizations.

Respondent cites Justice Brennan's concurring opinion in *Abington School Dist. v. Schempp* (1963), and argues that we should not rely too heavily on "the advice of the Founding Fathers" because the messages of history often tend to be ambiguous and not relevant to a society far more heterogeneous than that of the Framers. Respondent also points out that John Jay and John Rutledge opposed the motion to begin the first session of the Continental Congress with prayer. Brief for Respondent 60.

We do not agree that evidence of opposition to a measure weakens the force of the historical argument; indeed it infuses it with power by demonstrating that the subject was considered carefully and the action not taken thoughtlessly, by force of long tradition and without regard to the problems posed by a pluralistic society. Jay and Rutledge specifically grounded their objection on the fact that the delegates to the Congress "were so divided in religious sentiments . . . that [they] could not join in the same act of worship." Their objection was met by Samuel Adams, who stated that "he was no bigot, and could hear a prayer from a gentleman of piety and virtue, who was at the same time a friend to his country." . . .

This interchange emphasizes that the delegates did not consider opening prayers as a proselytizing activity or as symbolically placing the government's "official seal of approval on one religious view." Rather, the Founding Fathers looked at invocations as "conduct whose . . . effect . . . harmonize[d] with the tenets of some or all religions." *McGowan v. Maryland* (1961). The Establishment Clause does not always bar a state from regulating conduct simply because it "harmonizes with religious canons." . . . Here, the individual claiming injury by the practice is an adult, presumably not readily susceptible to "religious indoctrination." . . .

In light of the unambiguous and unbroken history of more than 200 years, there can be no doubt that the practice of opening legislative sessions with prayer has become part of the fabric of our society. To invoke Divine guidance on a public body entrusted with making the laws is not, in these circumstances, an "establishment" of religion or a step toward establishment; it is simply a tolerable acknowledgment of beliefs widely held among the people of this country. As Justice Douglas observed, "[w]e are a religious people whose institutions presuppose a Supreme Being." *Zorach v. Clauson (1952).* . . .

The judgment of the Court of Appeals is reversed.

JUSTICE BRENNAN, with whom **JUSTICE MARSHALL** joins, dissenting. . . .

The Court's main argument for carving out an exception sustaining legislative prayer is historical. The Court cannot—and does not —purport to find a pattern of "undeviating acceptance," *Walz* (Brennan, J., concurring), of legislative prayer. It also disclaims exclusive reliance on the mere longevity of legislative prayer. . . . The Court does, however, point out that, only three days before the First Congress reached agreement on the final wording of the Bill of Rights, it authorized the appointment of paid chaplains for its own proceedings, and the Court argues that in light of this "unique history," the actions of Congress reveal its intent as to the meaning of the Establishment Clause. I agree that historical practice is "of considerable import in the interpretation of abstract constitutional language." This is a case, however, in which—absent the Court's invocation of history—there would be no question that the practice at issue was unconstitutional. And despite the surface appeal of the Court's argument, there are at least three reasons why specific historical practice should not in this case override that clear constitutional imperative.

First, it is significant that the Court's historical argument does not rely on the legislative history of the Establishment Clause itself. Indeed, that formal history is profoundly unilluminating on this and most other subjects. Rather, the Court assumes that the Framers of the Establishment Clause would not have themselves authorized a practice that they thought violated the guarantees contained in the clause. This assumption, however, is questionable. Legislators, influenced by the passions and exigencies of the moment, the pressure of constituents and colleagues, and the press of business, do not always pass sober constitutional judgment on every piece of legislation they enact, and this must be assumed to be as true of the members of the First Congress as any other. Indeed, the fact that James Madison, who voted for the bill authorizing the payment of the first congressional chaplains, later expressed the view that the practice was unconstitutional, is instructive on precisely this point. Madison's later views may not have represented so much a change of *mind* as a change of *role,* from a member of Congress engaged in the hurley-burley of legislative activity to a detached observer engaged in unpressured reflection. Since the latter role is precisely the one with which this Court is charged, I am not at all sure that Madison's later writings should be any less influential in our deliberations than his earlier vote.

Second, the Court's analysis treats the First Amendment simply as an Act of Congress, as to whose meaning the intent of Congress is the single touchstone. Both the Constitution and its amendments, however, became supreme law only by virtue of their ratification by the States, and the understanding of the States should be as relevant to our analysis as the understanding of Congress. . . .

This observation is especially compelling in considering the meaning of the Bill of Rights. The first 10 Amendments were not enacted because the members of the First Congress came up with a bright idea one morning; rather, their enactment was forced upon Congress by a number of the States as a condition for their ratification of the original Constitution. To treat any practice authorized by the First Congress as presumptively consistent with the Bill of Rights is therefore somewhat akin to treating any action of a party to a contract as presumptively consistent with the terms of the contract. The latter proposition, if it were accepted, would of course resolve many of the heretofore perplexing issues in contract law.

Finally, and most importantly, the argument tendered by the Court is misguided because the Constitution is not a static document whose meaning on every detail is fixed for all time by the life experience of the Framers. We have recognized in a wide variety of constitutional contexts that the practices that were in place at the time any particular guarantee was enacted into the Constitution do not necessarily fix forever the meaning of that guarantee. To be truly faithful to the Framers, "our use of the history of their time must limit itself to broad purposes, not specific practices." *Abington School Dist. v. Schempp* (Brennan, J., concurring). Our primary task must be to translate "the majestic generalities of the Bill of Rights, conceived as part of the pattern of liberal government in the eighteenth century, into concrete restraints on officials dealing with the problems of the twentieth century. . . ." *West Virginia State Bd. of Education v. Barnette* (1943).

The inherent adaptability of the Constitution and its amendments is particularly important with respect to the Establishment Clause. "[O]ur religious composition makes us a vastly more diverse people than were our forefathers. . . . In the face of such profound changes, practices which may have been objectionable to no one in the time of Jefferson and Madison may today be highly offensive to many persons, the deeply devout and the nonbelievers alike." *Schempp* (Brennan, J., concurring). President John Adams issued during his Presidency a number of official proclamations calling on all Americans to engage in Christian prayer. Justice Story, in his treatise on the Constitution, contended that the "real object" of the First Amendment "was, not to countenance, much less to advance Mahometanism, Judaism, or infidelity, by prostrating Christianity; but to exclude all rivalry among Christian sects. . . ." Whatever deference Adams' actions and Story's views might once have deserved in this Court, the Establishment Clause must now be read in a very different light. Similarly, the members of the First Congress should be treated, not as sacred figures whose every action must be emulated, but as the authors of a document meant to last for the ages. Indeed, a proper respect for the Framers themselves forbids us to give so static and lifeless a meaning to their work. To my mind, the Court's focus here on a narrow piece of history is, in a fundamental sense, a betrayal of the lessons of history.

JUSTICE STEVENS, dissenting.

12.4
"The substantial social costs exacted by the exclusionary rule for the vindication of Fourth Amendment rights have long been a source of concern."

UNITED STATES V. LEON
468 U.S. 897, 104 S. Ct. 3405, 82 L. Ed. 2d 677 (1984)

Weeks v. United States (1914) excluded from use in federal trials evidence obtained by unlawful searches and seizures. *Mapp v. Ohio* (1961) extended this exclusionary rule to state trials and provoked bitter and long-lasting opposition by police, prosecutors, and many other public officials, including state and federal judges. In this case, police had obtained a facially valid search warrant to seize evidence linking Alberto Leon to large-scale drug dealing. Partially on the basis of this evidence, a federal grand jury indicted him for conspiracy to possess and distribute cocaine. At a pretrial hearing, however, the district judge found that, although the police had acted in good faith, the affidavit on which the warrant was based had been insufficient to establish "probable cause," as required by the Fourth Amendment. Thus the district judge ruled that the seized evidence must be excluded from the trial. The Department of Justice appealed to the Court of Appeals for the Ninth Circuit and, after that tribunal affirmed, sought and obtained certiorari from the United States Supreme Court.

JUSTICE WHITE delivered the opinion of the Court. . . .

Language in opinions of this Court and of individual Justices has sometimes implied that the exclusionary rule is a necessary corollary of the Fourth Amendment, *Mapp v. Ohio* (1961); *Olmstead v. United States* (1928), or that the rule is required by the conjunction of the Fourth and Fifth Amendments. These implications need not detain us long. The Fifth Amendment theory has not withstood critical analysis or the test of time, see *Andersen v. Maryland* (1976), and the Fourth Amendment "has never been interpreted to proscribe the introduction of illegally seized evidence in all proceedings or against all persons." *Stone v. Powell* (1976).

The Fourth Amendment contains no provision expressly precluding the use of evidence obtained in violation of its commands, and an examination of its origin and purposes makes clear that the use of fruits of a past unlawful search or seizure "work[s] no new Fourth Amendment wrong." *United States v. Calandra* (1974). The wrong condemned by the Amendment is "fully accomplished" by the unlawful search or seizure itself, *ibid.*, and the exclusionary rule is neither intended nor able to "cure the invasion of the defendant's rights which he has already suffered." *Stone v. Powell* (WHITE, J., dissenting). The rule thus operates as "a judicially created remedy designed to safeguard Fourth Amendment rights generally through its deterrent effect, rather than a personal constitutional right of the person aggrieved." *United States v. Calandra.*

Whether the exclusionary sanction is appropriately imposed in a particular case, our decisions make clear, is "an issue separate from the question whether the Fourth Amendment rights of the party seeking to invoke the rule were violated by police conduct." *Illinois v. Gates* [1983]. Only the former question is currently before us, and it must be resolved by weighing the costs and benefits of preventing the use in the prosecution's case-in-chief of inherently trustworthy tangible evidence obtained in reliance on a search warrant issued by a detached and neutral magistrate that ultimately is found to be defective.

The substantial social costs exacted by the exclusionary rule for the vindication of Fourth Amendment rights have long been a source of concern. "Our cases have consistently recognized that unbending application of the exclusionary sanction to enforce ideals of governmental rectitude would impede unacceptably the truth-finding functions of judge and jury." *United States v. Payner* (1980). An objectionable collateral consequence of this interference with the criminal justice system's truth-finding function is that some guilty defendants may go free or receive reduced sentences as a result of favorable plea bargains. Particularly when law enforcement officers have acted in objective good faith or their transgressions have been minor, the magnitude of the benefit conferred on such guilty defendants offends basic concepts of the criminal justice system. *Stone v. Powell.* Indiscriminate application of the exclusionary rule, therefore, may well "generat[e] disrespect for the law and the administration of justice." Accordingly, "[a]s with any remedial device, the application of the rule has been restricted to those areas where its remedial objectives are thought most efficaciously served." *United States v. Calandra.* . . .

Close attention to those remedial objectives has characterized our recent decisions concerning the scope of the Fourth Amendment exclusionary rule. The Court has, to be sure, not seriously questioned, "in the absence of a more efficacious sanction, the continued application of the rule to suppress evidence from the [prosecution's] case where a Fourth Amendment violation has been substantial and deliberate. . . ." *Franks v. Delaware* (1978), *Stone v. Powell.* Nevertheless, the balancing approach that has evolved in various contexts— including criminal trials—"forcefully suggest[s] that the exclusionary rule be more generally modified to permit the introduction of evidence obtained in the reasonable good-faith belief that a search or seizure was in accord with the Fourth Amendment." *Illinois v. Gates.* (WHITE, J., concurring in the judgment).

JUSTICE BRENNAN, with whom **JUSTICE MARSHALL** joins, dissenting.

Ten years ago in *United States v. Calandra* (1974), I expressed the fear that the Court's decision "may signal that a majority of my colleagues have positioned themselves to reopen the door [to evidence secured by official lawlessness] still further and abandon altogether the exclusionary rule in search-and-seizure cases." Since then, in case after case, I have witnessed the Court's gradual but determined strangulation of the rule. It now appears that the Court's victory over the Fourth Amendment is complete. That today's decision represents the *piece de resistance* of the Court's past efforts cannot be doubted, for today the Court sanctions the use in the prosecution's case-in-chief of illegally obtained evidence against the individual whose rights have been violated—a result that had previously been thought to be foreclosed.

The Court seeks to justify this result on the ground that the "costs" of adhering to the exclusionary rule in cases like those before us exceed the "benefits." But the language of deterrence and of cost/benefit analysis, if used indiscriminately, can have a narcotic effect. It creates an illusion of technical precision and ineluctability. It suggests that not only constitutional principle but also empirical data supports the majority's result. When the Court's analysis is examined carefully, however, it is clear that we have not been treated to an honest assessment of the merits of the exclusionary rule, but have instead been drawn into a curious world where the "costs" of excluding illegally obtained evidence loom to exaggerated heights and where the "benefits" of such exclusion are made to disappear with a mere wave of the hand.

The majority ignores the fundamental constitutional importance of what is at stake here. While the machinery of law enforcement and indeed the nature of crime itself have changed dramatically since the Fourth Amendment became part of the Nation's fundamental law in 1791, what the Framers understood then remains true today—that the task of combatting crime and convicting the guilty will in every era seem of such critical and pressing concern that we may be lured by the temptations of expediency into forsaking our commitment to protecting individual liberty and privacy. It was for that very reason that the Framers of the Bill of Rights insisted that law enforcement efforts be permanently and unambiguously restricted in order to preserve personal freedoms. In the constitutional scheme they ordained, the sometimes unpopular task of ensuring that the government's enforcement efforts remain within the strict boundaries fixed by the Fourth Amendment was entrusted to the courts. . . .

JUSTICE STEVENS [concurring in *Leon* and dissenting in a similar case decided the same day]. . . .

It is appropriate to begin with the plain language of the Fourth Amendment:

> "The right of the people to be secure in their persons, houses, papers, and effects, against unreasonable searches and seizures, shall not be violated; and no Warrants shall issue but upon probable cause, supported by Oath or affirmation, and particularly describing the place to be searched, and the persons or things to be seized."

The Court assumes that the searches in these cases violated the Fourth Amendment, yet refuses to apply the exclusionary rule because the Court concludes that it was "reasonable" for the police to conduct them. In my opinion an official search and seizure cannot be both "unreasonable" and "reasonable" at the same time. The doctrinal vice in the Court's holding is its failure to consider the separate purposes of the two prohibitory clauses in the Fourth Amendment.

The first clause prohibits unreasonable searches and seizures and the second prohibits the issuance of warrants that are not supported by probable cause or that do not particularly describe the place to be searched and the persons or things to be seized. We have, of course, repeatedly held that warrantless searches are presumptively unreasonable, and that there are only a few carefully delineated exceptions to that basic presumption. But when such an exception has been recognized, analytically we have necessarily concluded that the warrantless activity was not "unreasonable" within the meaning of the first clause. Thus, any Fourth Amendment case may present two separate questions: whether the search was conducted pursuant to a warrant issued in accordance with the second clause, and, if not, whether it was nevertheless "reasonable" within the meaning of the first. On these questions, the constitutional text requires that we speak with one voice. We cannot intelligibly assume arguendo that a search was constitutionally unreasonable but that the seized evidence is admissible because the same search was reasonable.

I . . .

In *Leon,* there is also a substantial question whether the warrant complied with the Fourth Amendment. There was a strong dissent on the probable cause issue when *Leon* was before the Court of Appeals, and that dissent has been given added force by this Court's intervening decision in *Illinois v. Gates* (1983), which constituted a significant development in the law. It is probable, though admittedly not certain, that the Court of Appeals would now conclude that the warrant in *Leon* satisfied the Fourth Amendment if it were given the opportunity to reconsider the issue in the light of *Gates.* Adherence to our normal practice following the announcement of a new rule would therefore postpone, and probably obviate, the need for the promulgation of the broad new rule the Court announces today. . . .

Judges, more than most, should understand the value of adherence to settled procedures. By adopting a set of fair procedures, and then adhering to them, courts of law ensure that justice is administered with an even hand. "These are subtle matters, for they concern the ingredients of what constitutes justice. Therefore, justice must satisfy the appearance of justice." *Offutt v. United States* (1954). Of course, this Court has a duty to face questions of constitutional law when necessary to the disposition of an actual case or controversy. *Marbury v. Madison* (1803). But when the Court goes beyond what is necessary to decide the case before it, it can only encourage the perception that it is pursuing its own notions of wise social policy, rather than adhering to its judicial role. I do not believe the Court should reach out to decide what is undoubtedly a profound question concerning the administration of criminal justice before assuring itself that this question is actually and of necessity presented by the concrete facts before the Court. Although it may appear that the Court's broad holding will serve the public interest in enforcing obedience to the rule of law, for my part, I remain firmly convinced that "the preservation of order in our communities will be best insured by adherence to established and respected procedures." *Groppi v. Leslie* (CA7 1971) (en banc) (Stevens, J., dissenting), rev'd (1972). . . .

IV . . .

The exclusionary rule is designed to prevent violations of the Fourth Amendment. "Its purpose is to deter—to compel respect for the constitutional guaranty in the only effectively available way, by removing the incentive to disregard it." *Elkins v. United States* (1960). If the police cannot use evidence obtained through warrants issued on less than probable cause, they have less incentive to seek those warrants, and magistrates have less incentive to issue them.

Today's decisions do grave damage to that deterrent function. Under the majority's new rule, even when the police know their warrant application is probably insufficient, they retain an incentive to submit it to a magistrate, on the chance that he may take the bait. No longer must they hesitate and seek additional evidence in doubtful cases. . . .

The Court is of course correct that the exclusionary rule cannot deter when the authorities have no reason to know that their conduct is unconstitutional. But when probable cause is lacking, then by definition a reasonable person under the circumstances would not believe there is a fair likelihood that a search will produce evidence of a crime. Under such circumstances well-trained professionals must know that they are violating the Constitution. The Court's approach —which, in effect, encourages the police to seek a warrant even if they know the existence of probable cause is doubtful—can only lead to an increased number of constitutional violations.

Thus, the Court's creation of a double standard of reasonableness inevitably must erode the deterrence rationale that still supports the exclusionary rule. But we should not ignore the way it tarnishes the role of the judiciary in enforcing the Constitution. For the original rationale for the exclusionary rule retains its force as well as its relevance:

> "The tendency of those who execute the criminal laws of the country to obtain conviction by means of unlawful seizures . . . should find no sanction in the judgments of the courts which are charged at all times with

the support of the Constitution and to which people of all conditions have a right to appeal for the maintenance of such fundamental rights." *Weeks v. United States* (1914).

Thus, "Courts which sit under our Constitution cannot and will not be made party to lawless invasions of the constitutional rights of citizens by permitting unhindered governmental use of the fruits of such invasions. . . ." *Terry v. Ohio* (1968). . . . Today, for the first time, this Court holds that although the Constitution has been violated, no court should do anything about it at any time and in any proceeding. In my judgment, the Constitution requires more. Courts simply cannot escape their responsibility for redressing constitutional violations if they admit evidence obtained through unreasonable searches and seizures, since the entire point of police conduct that violates the Fourth Amendment is to obtain evidence for use at trial. If such evidence is admitted, then the courts become not merely the final and necessary link in an unconstitutional chain of events, but its actual motivating force. "If the existing code does not permit district attorneys to have a hand in such dirty business it does not permit the judge to allow such iniquities to succeed." *Olmstead v. United States* (1928) (Holmes, J., dissenting). Nor should we so easily concede the existence of a constitutional violation for which there is no remedy. To do so is to convert a Bill of Rights into an unenforced honor code that the police may follow in their discretion. The Constitution requires more; it requires a *remedy*. If the Court's new rule is to be followed, the Bill of Rights should be renamed.

It is of course true that the exclusionary rule exerts a high price —the loss of probative evidence of guilt. But that price is one courts have often been required to pay to serve important social goals. That price is also one the Fourth Amendment requires us to pay, assuming as we must that the Framers intended that its strictures "shall not be violated." For in all such cases, as Justice Stewart has observed, "the same extremely relevant evidence would not have been obtained had the police officer complied with the commands of the fourth amendment in the first place."

> "[T]he forefathers thought this was not too great a price to pay for that decent privacy of home, papers and effects which is indispensable to individual dignity and self-respect. They may have overvalued privacy, but I am not disposed to set their command at naught." *Harris v. United States* (1947) (Jackson, J., dissenting).

We could, of course, facilitate the process of administering justice to those who violate the criminal laws by ignoring the commands of the Fourth Amendment—indeed, by ignoring the entire Bill of Rights—but it is the very purpose of a Bill of Rights to identify values that may not be sacrificed to expediency. In a just society those who govern, as well as those who are governed, must obey the law. . . .

". . . the technocratic approach of the policy analyst is ill-suited to the judicial task of construing law—especially the law of the Constitution."—Laurence H. Tribe

12.5 *"All goods are scarce. . . . Judges must respond to scarcity."—Frank H. Easterbrook*

ECONOMIC REASONING AND CONSTITUTIONAL INTERPRETATION

In the November 1984 issue of the *Harvard Law Review,* Frank H. Easterbrook published an article entitled "Foreword: The Court and the Economic System." In it he argued that economic principles of reasoning permeated the Supreme Court's work and defended this approach to legal problems. Soon thereafter, Laurence H. Tribe wrote a rebuttal and Easterbrook a reply.

Constitutional Calculus: Equal Justice or Economic Efficiency?

Laurence H. Tribe

The Constitution cannot be cabined in any calculus of costs and benefits. Yet in his Foreword to the Supreme Court issue of this journal, Professor Frank Easterbrook, an exponent of an increasingly influential school of thought regarding the relationship of law to economics, comes to the defense of a recent Supreme Court trend toward discharging the federal judicial mission in the manner of an economic manager armed with the hard-edged tools of cost-benefit analysis. Whether the Court actually uses those tools as aids to decisionmaking, or merely employs them to legitimate decisions arrived at in other ways, the thrust of my critique is that the substantive values implicit in the Court's emerging approach are deeply at odds with the constitutional enterprise. Professor Easterbrook's spirited defense of the Supreme Court's increasingly apparent affinity for a technocratic perspective is welcome because it renders transparent what might otherwise have been obscure. And because it comes from an unabashed advocate rather than a critic of the new approach, the Easterbrook analysis helps to rebut any suggestion that the managerial mode neither motivates the Court's actions nor provides a mask for the Court's decisions, but is only a mirage conjured by observers unsympathetic with the substantive results of a series of recent decisions.

98 *Harvard Law Review* 592 (1985). Copyright © 1985 by the Harvard Law Review Association. Laurence H. Tribe is Tyler Professor of Constitutional Law, Harvard Law School.

Like Professor Easterbrook, I will be concerned here less with the outcomes of selected Supreme Court cases than with the Court's methods and the premises on which those methods necessarily rest. Specifically, I will focus on what sorts of questions the Court asks or fails to ask both itself and us about power and powerlessness, about public purposes and private interests, about the nature of laws and constitutions, and about the mission of courts in our political system.

In Professor Easterbrook's world, the Supreme Court is little more than a "regulator": a "governor of the government." Its Justices, like all judges, are pulled in opposite directions by their work. From one side, the nature of litigation invites judges to apply an ex post approach to dispute resolution, an approach that requires a court to take the positions of the parties as given and to apportion losses and profits fairly among them. From the other side, sophisticated judges who "appreciate" the economic system are pulled toward an ex ante approach, in which a court is interested less in doing justice in the case at hand than in creating sound rules to govern the behavior of the world at large. In the Easterbrook vision, rule creation is thus forward-looking and, in his felicitous phrase, the rule "knows not its subjects."

One salient feature of Professor Easterbrook's distinction is that concern for fairness surfaces principally in the ex post, not the ex ante, approach. That is, if courts seek to do justice among the parties actually before them by merely slicing up the pie fairly, they must forfeit the opportunity to expand the pie as a whole by formulating an appropriate forward-looking and general legal rule. For, in Professor Easterbrook's opinion, a focus on the equities in the individual case "almost invariably" leads to the promulgation of rules that tend to impoverish people generally, by snatching from them the opportunity to order their activities more efficiently in the future. According to Professor Easterbrook, the lawyer's concept of fairness is a "'suitcase full of bottled ethics from which one freely chooses to blend his own type of justice'"; only those unable to appreciate the importance of increasing overall productivity will engage in such childish pursuits. It is instrumental rather than moral values that truly matter.

Given this perspective on the role of the judiciary in general, it is unsurprising that Professor Easterbrook concentrates primarily on nonconstitutional adjudication. The Supreme Court's constitutional rules, as he sees them, are addressed solely to the lower courts and only remotely and indirectly influence anyone's behavior or shape any aspect of the public's general attitudes. But regardless of whom constitutional decisions are thought to address, and regardless of whether Professor Easterbrook believes that his instrumental lens is primarily suited to the analysis of statutory decisions, he apparently considers utilitarian policy analysis to be appropriate in constitutional cases as well. According to Professor Easterbrook, it is not for the judiciary to concern itself with criticizing or changing the distribution of wealth and power, or to decide what is to count as a cost or a benefit; those matters are solely the province of the political branches, whose legislative deals the judiciary must faithfully enforce. Whatever the subject matter of a rule, be it securities regulation or freedom of expression, Professor Easterbrook endorses a nearly exclusive focus on each rule's marginal impact—its probable incremental effect on a suitably weighted sum of the variables made relevant by the political compromises the judiciary is charged to effectuate.

But to treat the underlying choice of variables, and the social reality they represent, as beyond the judiciary's proper concern is to render the answer derived by a court both trivial and at best half-right. Professor Easterbrook tells us that what we need to ask is what effect the alternative rules will have on the future behavior of individuals; but he does not bother to inquire how those same alternatives will affect the future distribution of power and wealth among those individuals, nor does he care to know how the parties actually before the court initially arrived at their unequal positions. This disregard of the *distributional* dimension of any given problem is characteristic of the entire law-and-economics school of thought, which assumes a world in which no one is economically coerced and in which individuals who do not "buy" things are said to be "unwilling," rather than unable, to do so.

Treating a constitutional court's task as merely one of toting up marginal costs and benefits also ignores the crucial questions of what *counts* as a cost or a benefit—and who gets to decide that issue. The approach applauded by Professor Easterbrook thus fails to recognize the *constitutive* dimension of constitutional decisions: the fact that constitutional choices affect, and hence require consideration of, the way in which a polity wishes to *constitute* itself. In making such choices, we reaffirm and create, select and shape, the values and truths we hold sacred. Such decisions determine much about how we define our society and specify much about what we stand for and what sort of country we wish to become. Contrary to Professor Easterbrook's assumption, the constitutional decisions of courts—and, to a lesser but still significant degree, all legal decisions—serve not merely to implement "given" systems of acknowledged values, but also to define and reshape the values—indeed, the very identity—of the nation. A court not only chooses *how* to achieve preexisting ends, but also affects *what* those ends are to be and *who* we are to become.

It is for this reason above all others that the technocratic approach of the policy analyst is ill-suited to the judicial task of construing law

—especially the law of the Constitution. The instrumental methods of which Professor Easterbrook is so fond are incapable of grasping and addressing that dimension of human choice that permits the simultaneous transformation of the system of ends and values that characterizes the chooser; such methods cannot address the question of what the chooser's system of ends *should be*. Yet the core of the Supreme Court's function, in any but the most shallow conception, must rotate precisely about these questions of value, not merely about questions of relative efficiency.

The appeal of utilitarian policy analysis, as well as its power, lies in its ability to reduce the various dimensions of a problem to a common denominator. The inevitable result is not only that "soft" variables—such as the value of vindicating a fundamental right or preserving human dignity—tend to be ignored or understated, but also that entire problems are reduced to terms that misstate their structure and that ignore the nuances that give these problems their full character. Thus, for example, the law-and-economics school of thought typically argues that rights should be awarded on grounds of efficiency to reflect the discontinuous preferences of those who would refuse any inducement to cede those "rights." Even if this analytic approach occasionally generates a result with which most of us would agree, by assigning a right in accord with the individual feelings and collective traditions that underlie those discontinuous preferences, the *method* nonetheless remains defective and distorting. Being "assigned" a right on efficiency grounds, after an appraisal of the relevant cost curves, hardly satisfies the particular human need that can be met only by a shared social and legal understanding that the right belongs to the individual because the capacity and opportunity it embodies are organically and historically a part of the person that she is, and *not* for any purely contingent and essentially managerial reason. As Justice Stewart concisely put the matter for the Court in *Faretta v. California,* "Personal liberties are not rooted in the law of averages."

One final flaw in the utilitarian approach championed by Professor Easterbrook is its embrace of one of the most persistent myths of policy analysis: that the analytical techniques *in themselves* lack significant substantive bias or controversial content—that the techniques are neutral in regard to matters of value precisely because such matters may simply be inserted in the analysis. But the disregard of those techniques for distributive and other constitutive concerns cannot be corrected merely by punching in one or more dummy variables labeled "values." The cost-benefit comparisons and marginal analyses are already engineered, whether intentionally or not, to serve a specific agenda. The intellectual and social heritage of these ideas, as well as their natural tendency, lies in the classical

eighteenth and nineteenth century economics of unfettered contract, consumer sovereignty, social Darwinism, and perfect markets
—the classical economics that the Supreme Court in fact exalted as
federal constitutional law from the 1890s to 1937. This brings those
ideas within a paradigm of actions guided by a preexisting set of
personal preferences—a paradigm inclined toward the exaltation of
possessive individualism, "efficient" resource allocation, and maximum productivity, as against respect for distributive justice,
procedural fairness, and the irreducible and sometime inalienable
values associated with personal rights and public goods. It is thus
little wonder that Professor Easterbrook's courts, cut adrift from the
Constitution's emphasis on fundamental rights as well as its structural concern for a democratic separation of powers, are but passive
and empty vessels.

In this respect, the myth that judges are but "honest agents,"
"faithfully executing decisions made by others," is a cornerstone both
of Professor Easterbrook's argument and of the judicial approach
that arguments like his are calculated to encourage and to legitimate.
But surely courts cannot enhance the quality of constitutional adjudication by abdicating responsibility for the difficult choices such adjudication inevitably entails. We must thus examine with the deepest
skepticism any claim that there exists some neutral technique that,
if followed with care and competence, can serve to make our judges
mere agents of political bargains struck on our behalf by others.

The not-so-hidden premise of the methods that Professor Easterbrook endorses must therefore be that process, structure, distribution, and constitutive notions of what count as costs or benefits are
somehow "given" in advance and therefore need not actively concern those who are charged with construing and enforcing laws and
constitutions. But, as will by now be apparent, I believe that precisely
those dimensions of constitutional—and general judicial—decisionmaking should be of paramount concern. Relegating them to an
unexamined background entails self-deception, ensures the triumph
of extant distributions of wealth and power, and abdicates responsibility for the choices that courts and others necessarily make in accepting or rejecting competing claims to legal protection. Indeed, in
a political era increasingly dominated by narcissistic inattention to
the public realm, and marked particularly by a lack of concern for
the least powerful within society, the Supreme Court's failure to
address the plight of those most in need reinforces what I see as a
dismal moral vacuum.

A final point deserves reiteration. Nothing in my critique makes
it necessary to prove that the Supreme Court's increasingly frequent
invocation of cost-benefit modes of analysis and argument actually
mirrors the thought processes that motivate the Court's decisions.

The vital fact is that the Court's actions, like the steely cost-benefit analyses with which they comport so well, are sadly insensitive to constitutional concerns bearing on the distribution of wealth and power and to the broader constitutive dimensions of all legal decisions. Because it is those concerns and dimensions that should be most prominent on the agenda of a court dealing with constitutional issues, the Supreme Court's failure to take such concerns seriously is no less troubling if the cost-benefit patina is but a mask for substantive judgments arrived at through other means, than it is if the cost-benefit imagery genuinely mirrors what the Court understands itself to be doing. . . .

Method, Result, and Authority: A Reply

Frank H. Easterbrook

I.

All good things are scarce. Self-interested conduct is the handmaiden of scarcity. These are facts of life. Given scarcity, judicial decisions inevitably create, transfer, or destroy valuable things and affect people's decisions. Even justice is scarce. Disputes about attorneys' fees stem from the high costs of litigation, and rules about harmless error grow out of the costs of retrials (including the delay other litigants encounter when one case receives extra process).

Judges must respond to scarcity. The effects of a court's decision on who gets how much of what good things may or may not be what the judges anticipated. Private and public responses to the decision may or may not undercut what the judges sought to achieve.

The foundation of my Foreword is the belief that knowledge of potential effects and responses is preferable to ignorance. The Foreword contains three principal normative propositions:

(1) judges should be aware that their decisions create incentives influencing conduct ex ante, and that attempts to divide the stakes fairly ex post will alter or reverse the signals that are desirable from an ex ante perspective;

(2) judges should be aware that marginal effects, and not average effects, influence the responses to their decisions, and that responses are pervasive; and

(3) judges should be aware of the interest-group nature of much legislation, for this influences its meaning.

98 *Harvard Law Review* 622 (1985). Copyright © 1985 by the Harvard Law Review Association. Frank H. Easterbrook is Lee and Brena Freeman Professor of Law, University of Chicago.

Appreciation of each of these propositions is an essential ingredient in any intelligent response to the problem of scarcity.

The Foreword also offers two descriptive propositions:

(1) the Justices are better aware of these three principles and act on them more intelligently than they used to do; and
(2) their recognition and action cuts across many parts of the law.

Both of these propositions seem to me reasons to applaud the Justices.

A number of propositions do not appear in the Foreword. The following are among the missing:

(a) all human concerns can be monetized in practice and deployed by courts in a grand cost-benefit analysis;
(b) an application of the three normative principles leads to a determinate outcome in all (or even most) cases; and
(c) utilitarian principles should govern all kinds of disputes.

Professor Tribe's Article largely agrees with the Foreword's descriptive propositions. He does not question my analysis of how the Court's thinking has changed, though he obviously would prefer that the Court follow a noninstrumental path. He also does not question much of the normative analysis, though his preference for noninstrumental values leads him to think that the analysis turns judges' heads in the wrong direction.

Most of the bite in Professor Tribe's Comment comes from his vigorous denial of propositions (a), (b), and (c). He believes, for example, that many human concerns cannot be (or ought not to be) monetized, that cost-benefit calculations may be indeterminate, and that the Constitution often instructs judges to disregard utilitarian calculations in favor of recognizing personal rights and reshaping preferences.

I am delighted to agree. My Foreword does not mention "cost-benefit analysis," for example; judges have neither the information nor the incentive to do such analysis well, and even a dispassionate analysis done by a team of superb economists is apt to be incomplete and misleading. . . .

. . . I think Professor Tribe's Comment is based on the belief that those interested in the economics of legal institutions *must* believe propositions (a), (b), and (c), even if they deny them. Why be interested in economic analysis if it does not give universal answers? Professor Tribe's reaction is common among those who see red whenever someone mentions economics. I therefore think it helpful briefly to explore why people ask economic questions even if they do not think the inquiry will yield dispositive answers to all legal disputes.

II.

Law is not a closed logical system. Every legal dispute worth having involves some propositions about the state of the world. These disputes have answers, though they may be very hard to find. Professor Tribe tells us, for example, that if people can sleep in the parks near the White House, the homeless will become better off because they likely will get some income transfers in their favor. This may or may not be true—whether it is true depends on the reactions of other, competing lobbyists, on the substitution among programs of income redistribution, and so forth. The effects of an increase in one group's public exposure are hard to calculate. We need some way to evaluate Professor Tribe's assertion, as we need a way to evaluate the other predictions that are the stuff of litigation.

No litigant argues before the Supreme Court without making predictions about how the decision will affect society. Few opinions omit predictions about effects. Litigants and judges alike believe that these effects are important in determining the outcome of the case. These predictions usually rest on a tacit economic analysis. Better to make the analysis express, to give more knowledge of these consequences.

It really does not matter that the ex ante perspective, attention to marginal effects, and recognition of the interest-group character of legislation are not *dispositive* in this search. No one insists that any single method or piece of evidence be dispositive. In litigation we call evidence "relevant" if it makes the truth of a pertinent fact more or less likely; we do not demand that each piece of evidence be dispositive. In the design of aircraft, the principles of aerodynamics and fluid motion are important but not dispositive, because no computer is powerful enough to model all aspects of the flow of air over an airfoil. Some designs therefore lead to crashes. Yet only a fool would argue that because aerodynamics is not dispositive, it should be discounted as a useful source of knowledge in the design of aircraft.

It is the same with economic analysis. The consideration of marginal effects in deciding cases is not apt to be dispositive, but it is informative and in many instances will tip the balance. Because more knowledge is better than less, economic analysis is valuable. The alternative ways of predicting effects of decisions—often unfounded guesses, counterfactual beliefs, and superstition—do not become more attractive just because economic analysis is incomplete.

Professor Tribe appears to believe, however, that economic inquiry contains *mis*information that imposes unwarranted costs on the legal process. . . . He thinks that economic analysis directs attention toward what is monetizable and away from personal rights and the goal of changing values. Perhaps it does for some; any tool can be misused. Knives can kill people as well as cut the food at dinner. But economics need not mislead. Economics is about maximization subject to constraints. Economics is applied rationality. Someone can name the maximand (say, freedom of speech and the value of proposing new political arrangements) or the constraint (usually scarcity of some valuable thing) without affecting the nature of the analysis. True, there are formal models that have no room for personal relationships, but there is also an economics of the family in which altruism, concern for future generations, and the development of more fulfilling lives play the central role. Economists have no difficulty understanding education, although the role of education in changing the values of those being educated is an essential part of the venture. People often want to change their own preferences, and anything they want to do—even if they do not know where they will end up —can be evaluated. Nothing in the approach requires the exclusion of other values. . . .

III.

Finally, we are entitled to ask why courts are authorized to pursue the path marked for them by Professor Tribe—marching off toward reconstituting society. Why is this a part of the judicial mission? Legislatures "reconstitute society" daily; they are the mechanism for aggregating preferences, setting change in motion, and expressing aspirations. The Civil Rights Act of 1964 is a profound and increasingly successful effort to overcome and reshape preferences. Judges have a different role. The argument for judicial review in *The Federalist* and in *Marbury v. Madison* is that judges serve as a brake on the other branches by insisting that they pursue their goals in ways that respect both the structure of government and the rights won in the Revolution and Civil War. The idea that judges should spur the other branches on to ever greater reconstitutions of society is alien to the original design.

It is here that Professor Tribe and I conclusively part company. The difference between us is not so much about the role of economics in judging as it is about the role of judges in society. Our differences could not be deeper if neither of us had heard of Adam Smith. . . .

Judges have no authority to reconstitute the values of the people or to exalt redistribution at the expense of competing objectives selected by the political branches. Our Constitution is based on the ideas of Locke and Montesquieu, not the view of Rousseau that the state should imbue its citizens with the "true" values they "ought" to hold. The framers were skeptical about both the existence of such values and the wisdom of trusting the government to choose among them. They rejected the arguments of the anti-Federalists, which were very similar to those of Rousseau and Professor Tribe. The choice made in 1789 was to separate powers, not to give judges the functions of both making and executing decisions about the fundamental values of society. As Hamilton quoted Montesquieu in *The Federalist* No. 78, "[T]here is no liberty, if the power of judging be not separated from the legislative and executive powers." The choice was to recognize and rely on the self-interest of factions—public and private—rather than to scorn faction and seek the instruction of Platonic guardians.

The Constitution demands that all power be authorized. It is not enough to say that judicial decisions are about "how we define our society and specify much about what we stand for and what sort of country we wish to become." "We the People" speak through the Constitution itself, through representatives in the legislature, through the amending process. Judges are granted tenure to *insulate* them from the wishes of today's majorities, not to enable them to claim inspiration about the "true will" of the people. The passage of time cannot make Rousseau the courts' guiding star—not, at least, without another revolution. The Court's drift from economic substantive due process to other forms of substantive intervention did not occur because of a new grant of legitimate authority. Judges applying the Constitution we have, rather than the one Professor Tribe wishes we had, must take their guidance and authority from decisions made elsewhere. Otherwise they speak with the same authority they and Professor Tribe and I possess when we fill the law reviews with our speculations and desires: none. And the other branches owe no obedience to those who speak without authority.

This is not to say that the judicial process is mechanical. Far from it. The process involves the most delicate assessment of meaning. Knowledge is ephemeral, and doubts about both the meaning of words and the effects of rules tax the greatest interpreters. But none of this changes the source of the power to decide. Judges can legitimately demand to be obeyed only when their decisions stem from fair interpretations of commands laid down in the texts. This principle—the real source of the disagreement between Professor Tribe and myself, and between Tribe and the Court—has nothing to do with economics. Professor Tribe would be dismayed no matter why judges took a restricted view of the considerations they deemed to be appropriate in deciding cases. Professor Tribe would not be happy with a Court staffed by Justices with Felix Frankfurter's view of the role of judges, even though Justice Frankfurter thought ill of economics. An understanding of economics does not cause people to invent limits on the role of judges. Causation runs the other way. Those who believe that judges have but a limited role to play in government are also more likely to be comfortable using the liberal, individualist premises that Professor Tribe rightly sees as important parts of economic thought.

IV.

Determining how "we reaffirm and create, select and shape, the values and truths we hold sacred" is the most pressing task for the political society. But the execution of this task falls on the people and their representatives. The delicacy and indeterminacy of the task is no reason for judges to pretend that there is no scarcity.

Once they must deal with scarcity, they must deal with economics. They may discharge this obligation expressly or by implication, well or poorly, but deal with it they will. Utopian visions yield political aspiration, but aspiration and adjudication must be separated. Hopes for a better society do not justify unreflective treatment of the tradeoffs we must make in a world of scarcity.

12.6 *"Surely there is no justification for a third legislative branch in the federal government. . . ."*

THE NOTION OF A LIVING CONSTITUTION

William H. Rehnquist

At least one of the more than half-dozen persons nominated during the past decade to be an Associate Justice of the Supreme Court of the United States has been asked by the Senate Judiciary Committee at his confirmation hearings whether he believed in a living Constitution. It is not an easy question to answer; the phrase "living Constitution" has about it a teasing imprecision that makes it a coat of many colors. . . .

. . . The phrase is really a shorthand expression that is susceptible of at least two quite different meanings.

The first meaning was expressed . . . by Mr. Justice Holmes in *Missouri v. Holland* [1920] . . .:

. . . When we are dealing with words that also are a constituent act, like the Constitution of the United States, we must realize that they have called into life a being the development of which could not have been foreseen completely by the most gifted of its begetters. It was enough for

54 *Texas Law Review* 693 (1976). Quoted with the permission of the copyright owner, *Texas Law Review*, The University of Texas School of Law, 2500 Red River, Austin, Texas 78705. William H. Rehnquist has been an Associate Justice of the U.S. Supreme Court since 1971.

them to realize or to hope that they had created an organism; it has taken a century and has cost their successors much sweat and blood to prove that they created a nation.

. . . The framers of the Constitution wisely spoke in general language and left to succeeding generations the task of applying that language to the unceasingly changing environment in which they would live. . . . Merely because a particular activity may not have existed when the Constitution was adopted, or because the framers could not have conceived of a particular method of transacting affairs, cannot mean that general language in the Constitution may not be applied to such a course of conduct. Where the framers of the Constitution have used general language, they have given latitude . . . to make that language applicable to cases that the framers might not have foreseen.

. . . I have sensed a second connotation of the phrase "living Constitution." . . . Embodied in its most naked form, it recently came to my attention in some language from a brief that had been filed in a United States District Court on behalf of state prisoners asserting that the conditions of their confinement offended the United States Constitution . . . :

> We are asking a great deal of the Court because other branches of government have abdicated their responsibility. . . . Prisoners are like other "discrete and insular" minorities for whom the Court must spread its protective umbrella because no other branch of government will do so. . . . This Court, as the voice and conscience of contemporary society, as the measure of the modern conception of human dignity, must declare that the [named prison] and all it represents offends the Constitution of the United States and will not be tolerated.

Here we have a living Constitution with a vengeance. Although the substitution of some other set of values for those which may be derived from the language and intent of the framers is not urged in so many words, that is surely the thrust of the message. Under this brief writer's version of the living Constitution, nonelected members of the federal judiciary may address themselves to a social problem simply because other branches of government have failed or refused to do so. These same judges, responsible to no constituency whatever, are nonetheless acclaimed as "the voice and conscience of contemporary society."

. . . [T]hose who have pondered the matter have always recognized that the ideal of judicial review has basically antidemocratic and antimajoritarian facets that require some justification in this Nation, which prides itself on being a self-governing representative democracy. . . .

All who have studied law, and many who have not, are familiar with John Marshall's classic defense of judicial review in his opinion for the Court in *Marbury v. Madison.* . . . [W]hile it supports the Holmes version of the phrase "living Constitution," it also suggests some outer limits for the brief writer's version.

The ultimate source of authority in this Nation, Marshall said, is not Congress, not the states, not for that matter the Supreme Court. . . . The people are the ultimate source of authority; they have parceled out the authority that originally resided entirely with them by adopting the original Constitution and by later amending it. . . .

In addition, Marshall said that if the popular branches of government . . . are operating within the authority granted to them by the Constitution, their judgment and not that of the Court must obviously prevail. When these branches overstep the authority given them by the Constitution . . . or invade protected individual rights, and a constitutional challenge to their action is raised in a lawsuit brought in federal court, the Court must prefer the Constitution to the government acts.

John Marshall's justification for judicial review makes the provision for an independent federal judiciary not only understandable but also thoroughly desirable. Since the judges will be merely interpreting an instrument framed by the people, they should be detached and objective. A mere change in public opinion since the adoption of the Constitution, unaccompanied by a constitutional amendment, should not change the meaning of the Constitution. . . .

Clearly Marshall's explanation contains certain elements of either ingenuousness or ingeniousness. . . . The Constitution is in many of its parts obviously not a specifically worded document but one couched in general phraseology. There is obviously wide room for honest difference of opinion over the meaning of general phrases in the Constitution; any particular Justice's decision when a question arises under one of these general phrases will depend to some extent on his own philosophy of constitutional law. One may nevertheless concede all of these problems . . . yet feel that [Marshall's] justification for nonelected judges exercising the power of judicial review is the only one consistent with democratic philosophy of representative government. . . .

One senses no . . . connection with a popularly adopted constituent act in . . . the brief writer's version of the living Constitution. The brief writer's version seems instead to be based upon the proposition that federal judges, perhaps judges as a whole, have a role . . . , quite independent of popular will, to play in solving society's problems. Once we have abandoned the idea that the authority of the courts to declare laws unconstitutional is somehow tied to the language of the Constitution that the people adopted, a judiciary exercising the power of judicial review appears in a quite different light. Judges then are no longer the keepers of the covenant; instead they are a small group of fortunately situated people with a roving commission to second-guess Congress, state legislatures, and state and federal administrative officers concerning what is best for the country. Surely there is no justification for a third legislative branch in the federal government, and there is even less justification for a federal legislative branch's reviewing on a policy basis the laws enacted by the legislatures of the fifty states. . . . If there is going to be a council of revision, it ought to have at least some connection with popular feeling. Its members either ought to stand for reelection on occasion, or their terms should expire and they should be allowed to continue serving only if reappointed by a popularly elected Chief Executive and confirmed by a popularly elected Senate.

The brief writer's version of the living Constitution is seldom presented in its most naked form, but is instead usually dressed in more attractive garb. The argument in favor of this approach generally begins with a sophisticated wink—why pretend that there is any ascertainable content to the general phrases of the Constitution as they are written since, after all, judges constantly disagree about their meaning? . . . We all know the basis of Marshall's justification for judicial review, the argument runs, but it is necessary only to keep the window dressing in place. Any sophisticated student of the subject knows that judges need not limit themselves to the intent of the framers, which is very difficult to determine in any event. Because of the general language used in the Constitution, judges should not hesitate to use their authority to make the Constitution relevant and useful in solving the problems of modern society. . . .

At least three serious difficulties flaw the brief writer's version of the living Constitution. First, it misconceives the nature of the Constitution, which was designed to enable the popularly elected branches of government, not the judicial branch, to keep the country abreast of the times. Second, the brief writer's version ignores the Supreme Court's disastrous experiences when in the past it embraced contemporary, fashionable notions of what a living Constitution should contain. Third, however socially desirable the goals sought to be advanced by the brief writer's version, advancing them through a freewheeling, nonelected judiciary is quite unacceptable in a democratic society.

It seems to me that it is almost impossible, after reading the record of the Founding Fathers' debates in Philadelphia, to conclude that they intended the Constitution itself to suggest answers to the manifold problems that they knew would confront succeeding generations. The Constitution that they drafted was indeed intended to endure indefinitely, but the reason for this very well-founded hope was the general language by which national authority was granted to Congress and the Presidency. These two branches were to furnish the motive power within the federal system, which was in turn to coexist with the state governments. . . . Limitations were indeed placed upon both federal and state governments. . . . These limitations, however, were not themselves designed to solve the problems of the future, but were instead designed to make certain that the constituent branches, when *they* attempted to solve those problems, should not transgress these fundamental limitations.

Although the Civil War Amendments [XIII–XV] were designed more as broad limitations on the authority of state governments, they too were enacted in response to practices that the lately seceded states engaged in to discriminate against and mistreat the newly emancipated freed men. To the extent that the language of these amendments is general, the courts are of course warranted in giving them an application coextensive with their language. Nevertheless, I greatly doubt that even men like Thad Stevens and John Bingham, leaders of the radical Republicans in Congress, would have thought any portion of the Civil War Amendments, except section five of the fourteenth amendment,[1] was designed to solve problems that society might confront a century later. I think they would have said that those amendments were designed to prevent from ever recurring abuses in which the states had engaged prior to that time.

The brief writer's version of the living Constitution, however, suggests that if the states' legislatures and governors, or Congress and the President, have not solved a particular social problem, then the federal court may act. I do not believe that this argument will withstand rational analysis. Even in the face of a conceded social evil, a reasonably competent and reasonably representative legislature may decide to do nothing. It may decide that the evil is not of sufficient magnitude to warrant any governmental intervention. It may decide that the financial cost of eliminating the evil is not worth the benefit which would result from its elimination. It may decide that the evils which might ensue from the proposed solution are worse than the evils which the solution would eliminate.

Surely the Constitution does not put either the legislative branch or the executive branch in the position of a television quiz show contestant so that when a given period of time has elapsed and a problem remains unsolved by them, the federal judiciary may press a buzzer and take its turn at fashioning a solution.

The second difficulty with the brief writer's version of the living Constitution lies in its inattention to or rejection of the Supreme Court's historical experience gleaned from similar forays into problem solving. . . .

The third difficulty with the brief writer's notion of the living Constitution is that it seems to ignore totally the nature of political

[1]"The Congress shall have power to enforce, by appropriate legislation, the provisions of this article." U.S. Const. amend. XIV, § 5.

value judgments in a democratic society. If such a society adopts a constitution and incorporates in that constitution safeguards for individual liberty, these safeguards indeed do take on a generalized moral rightness or goodness. They assume a general social acceptance neither because of any intrinsic worth nor because of any unique origins in someone's idea of natural justice but instead simply because they have been incorporated in a constitution by the people. Within the limits of our Constitution, the representatives of the people in the executive branches of the state and national governments enact laws. The laws that emerge after a typical political struggle in which various individual value judgments are debated likewise take on a form of moral goodness. . . . It is the fact of their enactment that gives them whatever moral claim they have upon us as a society, however, and not any independent virtue they may have in any particular citizen's own scale of values.

Beyond the Constitution and the laws in our society, there simply is no basis other than the individual conscience of the citizen that may serve as a platform for the launching of moral judgments. There is no conceivable way in which I can logically demonstrate to you that the judgments of my conscience are superior to the judgments of your conscience, and vice versa. Many of us necessarily feel strongly and deeply about our own moral judgments, but they remain only personal moral judgments until in some way given the sanction of law. . . .

. . . Representative government is predicated upon the idea that one who feels deeply upon a question as a matter of conscience will seek out others of like view or will attempt to persuade others who do not initially share that view. When adherents to the belief become sufficiently numerous, he will have the necessary armaments required in a democratic society to press his views upon the elected representatives of the people, and to have them embodied into positive law.

Should a person fail to persuade the legislature, or should he feel that a legislative victory would be insufficient because of its potential for future reversal, he may seek to run the more difficult gauntlet of amending the Constitution. . . .

I know of no other method compatible with political theory basic to democratic society by which one's own conscientious belief may be translated into positive law and thereby obtain the only general moral imprimatur permissible in a pluralistic, democratic society. It is always time consuming, frequently difficult, and not infrequently impossible to run successfully the legislative gauntlet. . . . It is even more difficult for either a single individual or indeed for a large group of individuals to succeed in having such a value judgment embodied in the Constitution. All of these burdens and difficulties are entirely consistent with the notion of a democratic society. It should not be easy for any one individual or group of individuals to impose by law their value judgments upon fellow citizens who may disagree with those judgments. Indeed, it should not be easier just because the individual in question is a judge. . . .

The brief writer's version of the living Constitution, in the last analysis, is a formula for an end run around popular government. To the extent that it makes possible an individual's persuading one or more appointed federal judges to impose on other individuals a rule of conduct that the popularly elected branches of government would not have enacted and the voters have not and would not have embodied in the Constitution, the brief writer's version of the living Constitution is genuinely corrosive of the fundamental values of our democratic society.

12.7   *"Those who ignore the distinction between concepts and conceptions ... are forced to argue in a vulnerable way."*

TAKING RIGHTS SERIOUSLY: CONSTITUTIONAL CASES

Ronald Dworkin

. . .[I]n what follows I shall use the name 'Nixon' to refer, not to Nixon, but to any politician holding the set of attitudes about the Supreme Court that he made explicit in his political campaigns. There was, fortunately, only one real Nixon, but there are, in the special sense in which I use the name, many Nixons.

What can be the basis of this composite Nixon's opposition to the controversial decisions of the Warren Court? He cannot object to these decisions simply because they went beyond prior law, or say that the Supreme Court must never change its mind. Indeed the Burger Court itself seems intent on limiting the liberal decisions of the Warren Court. . . . The Constitution's guarantee of 'equal protection of the laws', it is true, does not in plain words determine that 'separate but equal' school facilities are unconstitutional, or that segregation was so unjust that heroic measures are required to undo its effects. But neither does it provide that as a matter of constitutional law the Court would be wrong to reach these conclusions. It leaves

Abridged by permission of the author and publishers from *Taking Rights Seriously* by Ronald Dworkin, Cambridge, Mass.: Harvard University Press, Copyright © 1972, 1977 by Ronald Dworkin. Ronald Dworkin, an American lawyer, attended Harvard, Princeton, and Yale, and is at present University Professor of Jurisprudence at Oxford and Professor of Law, New York University.

these issues to the Court's judgment, and the Court would have made law just as much if it had, for example, refused to hold [segregation] unconstitutional. . . .

So we must search further to find a theoretical basis for Nixon's position. . . .

2

The constitutional theory on which our government rests is not a simple majoritarian theory. The Constitution, and particularly the Bill of Rights, is designed to protect individual citizens and groups against certain decisions that a majority of citizens might want to make, even when that majority acts in what it takes to be the general or common interest. Some of these constitutional restraints take the form of fairly precise rules. . . . But other constraints take the form of what are often called 'vague' standards, for example, the provision that the government shall not deny men due process of law, or equal protection of the laws.

This interference with democratic practice requires a justification. The draftsmen of the Constitution assumed that these restraints could be justified by appeal to moral rights which individuals possess against the majority, and which the constitutional provisions, both 'vague' and precise, might be said to recognize and protect.

The 'vague' standards were chosen deliberately . . . in place of the more specific and limited rules that they might have enacted. But their decision . . . has caused a great deal of legal and political controversy, because even reasonable men of good will differ when they try to elaborate, for example, the moral rights that the due process clause or the equal protection clause brings into the law. They also differ when they try to apply these rights, however defined, to complex matters of political administration. . . .

The practice has developed of referring to a 'strict' and a 'liberal' side to these controversies, so that the Supreme Court might be said to have taken the 'liberal' side in the segregation cases and its critics the 'strict' side. Nixon has this distinction in mind when he calls himself a 'strict constructionist'. But the distinction is in fact confusing because it runs together two different issues that must be separated. Any case that arises under the 'vague' constitutional guarantees can be seen as posing two questions: (1) Which decision is required by strict, that is to say faithful, adherence to the text of the Constitution or to the intention of those who adopted that text? (2) Which decision is required by a political philosophy that takes a strict, that is to say narrow, view of the moral rights that individuals have against society? Once these questions are distinguished, it is plain that they may have different answers. The text of the First Amendment, for example, says that Congress shall make *no* law abridging the freedom of speech, but a narrow view of individual rights would permit many such laws. . . .

In the case of the 'vague' provisions, however, like the due process and equal protection clauses, lawyers have run the two questions together because they have relied, largely without recognizing it, on a theory of meaning that might be put this way: If the framers of the Constitution use vague language . . . then what they 'said' or 'meant' is limited to the instances of official action that they had in mind as violations, or, at least, to those instances that they would have thought were violations if they had had them in mind. . . .

This theory makes a strict interpretation of the text yield a narrow view of constitutional rights, because it limits such rights to those recognized by a limited group of people at a fixed date of history. . . .

But the theory of meaning on which this argument depends is far too crude; it ignores a distinction that philosophers have made but lawyers have not yet appreciated. Suppose I tell my children simply that I expect them not to treat others unfairly. I no doubt have in mind examples of the conduct I mean to discourage, but I would not accept that my 'meaning' was limited to these examples, for two reasons. First I would expect my children to apply my instructions to situations I had not and could not have thought about. Second, I stand ready to admit that some particular act I had thought was fair when I spoke was in fact unfair, or vice versa, if one of my children is able to convince me of that later; in that case I should want to say that my instructions covered the case he cited, not that I had changed my instructions. I might say that I meant the family to be guided by the *concept* of fairness, not by any specific *conception* of fairness I might have had in mind.

This is a crucial distinction. . . . Suppose a group believes in common that acts may suffer from a special moral defect which they call unfairness, and which consists in a wrongful division of benefits and burdens, or a wrongful attribution of praise or blame. Suppose also that they agree on a great number of standard cases of unfairness and use these as benchmarks against which to test other, more controversial cases. In that case, the group has a concept of unfairness, and its members may appeal to that concept in moral instruction or argument. But members of that group may nevertheless differ over a large number of these controversial cases, in a way that suggests that each either has or acts on a different theory of *why* the standard cases are acts of unfairness. They may differ, that is, on which more fundamental principles must be relied upon to show that a particular division or attribution is unfair. In that case, the members have different conceptions of fairness.

If so, then members of this community who give instructions or set standards in the name of fairness may be doing two different things. First they may be appealing to the concept of fairness, simply by instructing others to act fairly; in this case they charge those whom they instruct with the responsibility of developing and applying their own conception of fairness as controversial cases arise. That is not the same thing, of course, as granting them a discretion to act as they like; it sets a standard which they must try—and may fail—to meet. . . . The man who appeals to the concept in this way may have his own conception . . . but he holds this conception only as his own theory of how the standard he set must be met, so that when he changes his theory he has not changed that standard.

On the other hand, the members may be laying down a particular conception of fairness; I would have done this, for example, if I had listed my wishes with respect to controversial examples or if, even less likely, I had specified some controversial and explicit theory of fairness. . . . The difference is a difference not just in the *detail* of the instructions given but in the *kind* of instructions given. When I appeal to the concept of fairness I appeal to what fairness means, and I give my views on that issue no special standing. When I lay down a conception of fairness, I lay down what I mean by fairness, and my view is therefore the heart of the matter. . . .

Once this distinction is made it seems obvious that we must take what I have been calling 'vague' constitutional clauses as representing appeals to the concepts they employ, like legality, equality, and cruelty. . . .

Those who ignore the distinction between concepts and conceptions . . . are forced to argue in a vulnerable way. If those who enacted the broad clauses had meant to lay down particular conceptions, they would have found the sort of language conventionally used to do this, that is, they would have offered particular theories of the concepts in question.

Indeed the very practice of calling these clauses 'vague' . . . can now be seen to involve a mistake. The clauses are vague only if we take them to be botched or incomplete or schematic attempts to lay down particular conceptions. If we take them as appeals to moral concepts they could not be made more precise by being more detailed.

The confusion I mentioned between the two senses of 'strict' construction is therefore very misleading indeed. If courts try to be faithful to the text of the Constitution, they will for that very reason be forced to decide between competing conceptions of political morality. So it is wrong to attack the Warren Court, for example, on the ground that it failed to treat the Constitution as a binding text. On the contrary, if we wish to treat fidelity to that text as an overriding requirement of constitutional interpretation, then it is the conservative critics of the Warren Court who are at fault, because their philosophy ignores the direction to face issues of moral principle that the logic of the text demands.

I put the matter in a guarded way because we may *not* want to accept fidelity to the spirit of the text as an overriding principle of constitutional adjudication. It may be more important for courts to decide constitutional cases in a manner that respects the judgments of other institutions of government, for example. Or it may be more important for courts to protect established legal doctrines, so that citizens and the government can have confidence that the courts will hold to what they have said before. But it is crucial to recognize that these other policies compete with the principle that the Constitution is the fundamental and imperative source of constitutional law. They are not, as the 'strict constructionists' suppose, simply consequences of that principle.

3

Once the matter is put in this light . . . we are able to assess these competing claims of policy, free from the confusion imposed by the popular notion of 'strict construction'. For this purpose I want now to compare and contrast two very general philosophies of how the courts should decide difficult or controversial constitutional issues. I shall call these two philosophies by the names they are given in the legal literature—the programs of 'judicial activism' and 'judicial restraint'—though it will be plain that these names are in certain ways misleading.

The program of judicial activism holds that courts should accept the directions of the so-called vague constitutional provisions in the spirit I described. . . . They should work out principles of legality, equality, and the rest, revise these principles from time to time in the light of what seems to the Court fresh moral insight, and judge the acts of Congress, the states, and the President accordingly. . . .

The program of judicial restraint, on the contrary, argues that courts should allow the decisions of other branches of government to stand, even when they offend the judges' own sense of the principles required by the broad constitutional doctrines, except when these decisions are so offensive to political morality that they would violate the provisions on any plausible interpretation, or, perhaps, when a contrary decision is required by clear precedent. . . .

The Supreme Court followed the policy of activism rather than restraint in cases like the segregation cases because the words of the equal protection clause left it open whether the various educational practices of the states concerned should be taken to violate the Constitution, no clear precedent held that they did, and reasonable men might differ on the moral issues involved. . . . But the program of restraint would not always act to provide decisions that would please political conservatives. In the early days of the New Deal . . . it was the liberals who objected to Court decisions that struck down acts of Congress in the name of the due process clause.

It may seem, therefore, that if Nixon has a legal theory it depends crucially on some theory of judicial restraint. We must now, however, notice a distinction between two forms of judicial restraint, for there are two different, and indeed incompatible, grounds on which that policy might be based.

The first is a theory of political *skepticism* that might be described in this way. The policy of judicial activism presupposes a certain objectivity of moral principle; in particular it presupposes that citizens do have certain moral rights against the state, like a moral right to equality of public education or to fair treatment by the police. Only if such moral rights exist in some sense can activism be justified as a program based on something beyond the judge's personal preferences. The skeptical theory attacks activism at its roots; it argues that in fact individuals have no such moral rights against the state. They have only such *legal* rights as the Constitution grants them, and these are limited to the plain and uncontroversial violations of public morality that the framers must have had actually in mind, or that have since been established in a line of precedent.

The alternative ground of a program of restraint is a theory of judicial *deference.* Contrary to the skeptical theory, this assumes that citizens do have moral rights against the state beyond what the law expressly grants them, but it points out that the character and strength of these rights are debatable and argues that political institutions other than courts are responsible for deciding which rights are to be recognized.

This is an important distinction, even though the literature of constitutional law does not draw it with any clarity. The skeptical theory and the theory of deference differ dramatically in the kind of justification they assume, and in their implications for the more general moral theories of the men who profess to hold them. These theories are so different that most American politicians can consistently accept the second, but not the first.

A skeptic takes the view . . . that men have no moral rights against the state and only such legal rights as the law expressly provides. But what does this mean, and what sort of argument might the skeptic make for his view? . . . I shall rely, in trying to answer these questions, on a low-keyed theory of moral rights against the state. . . . Under that theory, a man has a moral right against the state if for some reason the state would do wrong to treat him in a certain way, even though it would be in the general interest to do so. . . .

I want to say a word about the virtues of this way of looking at moral rights against the state. . . . [I]t simply shows a claim of right to be a special, in the sense of a restricted, sort of judgment about what is right or wrong for governments to do.

Moreover, this way of looking at rights avoids some of the notorious puzzles associated with the concept. It allows us to say, with no sense of strangeness, that rights may vary in strength and character from case to case, and from point to point in history. If we think of rights as things, these metamorphoses seem strange, but we are used to the idea that moral judgments about what it is right or wrong to do are complex and are affected by considerations that are relative and that change.

The skeptic who wants to argue against the very possibility of rights against the state of this sort has a difficult brief. He must rely, I think, on one of three general positions: (a) He might display a more pervasive moral skepticism, which holds that even to speak of an act being morally right or wrong makes no sense. . . . (b) He might hold a stark form of utilitarianism, which assumes that the only reason we ever have for regarding an act as right or wrong is its impact on the general interest. Under that theory, to say that busing may be morally required even though it does not benefit the community generally would be inconsistent. (c) He might accept some form of totalitarian theory, which merges the interest of the individual in the good of the general community, and so denies that the two can conflict.

Very few American politicians would be able to accept any of these three grounds. . . .

I do not want to suggest, however, that no one would in fact argue for judicial restraint on grounds of skepticism; on the contrary, some of the best known advocates of restraint have pitched their arguments entirely on skeptical grounds. In 1957, for example, the great judge Learned Hand . . . argued for judicial restraint, and said that the Supreme Court had done wrong to declare school segregation illegal. . . . It is wrong to suppose, he said, that claims about moral rights express anything more than the speakers' preferences. If the Supreme Court justifies its decisions by making such claims, rather than by relying on positive law, it is usurping the place of the legislature, for the job of the legislature, representing the majority, is to decide whose preferences shall govern.

This simple appeal to democracy is successful if one accepts the skeptical premise. . . . But a very different, and much more vulnerable, argument from democracy is needed to support judicial restraint if it is based not on skepticism but on deference, as I shall try to show.

4

. . . [A] theory of restraint based . . . on deference [holds] that courts ought not to decide controversial issues of political morality because they ought to leave such decisions to other departments of government. . . .

There is one very popular argument in favor of the policy of deference, which might be called the argument from democracy. It is at least debatable, according to this argument, whether a sound conception of equality forbids segregated education or requires measures like busing to break it down. Who ought to decide these debatable issues of moral and political theory? Should it be a majority of a court in Washington, whose members are appointed for life and are not politically responsible to the public whose lives will be affected by the decision? Or should it be the elected and responsible state or national legislators? A democrat, so this argument supposes, can accept only the second answer.

But the argument from democracy is weaker than it might first appear. The argument assumes, for one thing, that state legislatures are in fact responsible to the people in the way that democratic theory assumes. But in all the states, though in different degrees and for different reasons, that is not the case. . . . I want to pass that point, however, because it does not so much undermine the argument from democracy as call for more democracy. . . . I want to fix attention on the issue of whether the appeal to democracy in this respect is even right in principle.

The argument assumes that in a democracy all unsettled issues, including issues of moral and political principle, must be resolved only by institutions that are politically responsible in the way that courts are not. Why should we accept that view of democracy? To say that that is what democracy means does no good, because it is wrong to suppose that the word, as a word, has anything like so precise a meaning. Even if it did, we should then have to rephrase our question to ask why we should have democracy, if we assume that is what it means. Nor is it better to say that that view of democracy is established in the American Constitution, or so entrenched in our political tradition that we are committed to it. We cannot argue that the Constitution, which provides no rule limiting judicial review to clear cases, establishes a theory of democracy that excludes wider review, nor can we say that our courts have in fact consistently accepted such a restriction. . . .

So the argument from democracy is not an argument to which we are committed either by our words or our past. We must accept it, if at all, on the strength of its own logic. In order to examine the arguments more closely, however, we must make a further distinction. The argument . . . might be continued in two different ways: one might argue that judicial deference is required because democratic institutions, like legislatures, are in fact likely to make *sounder* decisions than courts . . . about the nature of an individual's moral right against the state.

Or one might argue that it is for some reason *fairer* that a democratic institution rather than a court should decide such issues. . . . The distinction between these two arguments would make no sense to a skeptic, who would not admit that someone could do a better or worse job at identifying moral rights against the state, any more than someone could do a better or worse job of identifying ghosts. But a lawyer who believes in judicial deference rather than skepticism must acknowledge the distinction. . . .

I shall start with the second argument, that legislatures and other democratic institutions have some special title to make constitutional decisions. . . . One might say that the nature of this title is obvious, because it is always fairer to allow a majority to decide any issue than a minority. But that . . . ignores the fact that decisions about rights against the majority are not issues that in fairness ought to be left to the majority. Constitutionalism—the theory that the majority must be restrained to protect individual rights—may be a good or bad political theory, but the United States has adopted that theory, and to make the majority judge in its own cause seems inconsistent and unjust. So principles of fairness seem to speak against, not for, the argument from democracy.

Chief Justice Marshall recognized this . . . in *Marbury v. Madison*. . . . He argued that since the Constitution provides that the Constitution shall be the supreme law of the land, the courts . . . must have power to declare statutes void that offend that Constitution. Many legal scholars regard his argument as a *non sequitur,* because, they say, although constitutional constraints are part of the law, the courts, rather than the legislature itself, have not necessarily been given authority to decide whether in particular cases that law has been violated. But the argument is not a *non sequitur* if we take the principle that no man should be judge in his own cause to be so fundamental a part of the idea of legality that Marshall would have been entitled to disregard it only if the Constitution had expressly denied judicial review.

Some might object that it is simple-minded to say that a policy of deference leaves the majority to judge its own cause. Political decisions are made, in the United States, not by one stable majority but by many different political institutions each representing a different constituency which itself changes its composition over time. The decision of one branch of government may well be reviewed by another branch that is also politically responsible, but to a larger or different constituency. . . .

But this objection is itself too glib, because it ignores the special character of disputes about individual moral rights as distinct from other kinds of political disputes. Different institutions do have different constituencies when, for example, labor or trade or welfare issues are involved. . . . But this is not generally the case when individual constitutional rights, like the rights of accused criminals, are at issue. It has been typical of these disputes that the interests of those in political control of the various institutions of the government have been both homogeneous and hostile. Indeed that is why political theorists have conceived of constitutional rights as rights against the 'state' or the 'majority' as such, rather than against any particular body or branch of government. . . .

It does seem fair to say, therefore, that the argument from democracy asks that those in political power be invited to be the sole judge of their own decisions. . . . That is not a final proof that a policy of judicial activism is superior to a program of deference. . . . But the point does undermine the argument that the majority, in fairness, must be allowed to decide the limits of its own power.

We must therefore turn to the other continuation of the argument from democracy, which holds that democratic institutions, like legislatures, are likely to reach *sounder* results about the moral rights of individuals than would courts. In 1969 the late Professor Alexander Bickel . . . argued for the program of judicial restraint in a novel and ingenious way. He allowed himself to suppose, for purposes of argument, that the Warren Court's program of activism could be justified if in fact it produced desirable results. He appeared, therefore, to be testing the policy of activism on its own grounds, because he took activism to be precisely the claim that the courts have the moral right to improve the future, whatever legal theory may say. . . . Bickel accepted it, at least provisionally, but he argued that activism fails its own test.

The future that the Warren Court sought has already begun not to work, Bickel said. The philosophy of racial integration it adopted was too crude, for example, and has already been rejected by the more imaginative leaders of the black community. Its thesis of simple and radical equality has proved unworkable in many other ways as well; its simple formula for one-man-one-vote for passing on the fairness of election districting, for instance, has produced neither sense nor fairness.

Why should a radical Court that aims at improving society fail even on its own terms? Bickel has this answer: Courts, including the Supreme Court, must decide blocks of cases on principle, rather than responding in a piecemeal way to a shifting set of political pressures. They must do so not simply because their institutional morality requires it, but because their institutional structure provides no means by which they might gauge political forces even if they wanted to. But government by principle is an inefficient and in the long run fatal form of government, no matter how able and honest the statesmen who try to administer it. For there is a limit to the complexity that any principle can contain and remain a recognizable principle, and this limit falls short of the complexity of social organization.

The Supreme Court's reapportionment decisions, in Bickel's view, were not mistaken just because the Court chose the wrong principle. One-man-one-vote is too simple, but the Court could not have found a better, more sophisticated principle that would have served as a successful test for election districting across the country, or across the years, because successful districting depends upon accommodation with thousands of facts of political life, and can be reached, if at all, only by the chaotic and unprincipled development of history. Judicial activism cannot work as well as government by the more-or-less democratic institutions, not because democracy is required by principle, but, on the contrary, because democracy works without principle, forming institutions and compromises as a river forms a bed on its way to the sea.

What are we to make of Bickel's argument? His account of recent history can be, and has been, challenged. It is by no means plain, certainly not yet, that racial integration will fail as a long-term strategy; and he is wrong if he thinks that black Americans, of whom more still belong to the NAACP than to more militant organizations, have rejected it. No doubt the nation's sense of how to deal with the curse of racism swings back and forth as the complexity and size of the problem become more apparent, but Bickel may have written at a high point of one arc of the pendulum.

He is also wrong to judge the Supreme Court's effect on history as if the Court were the only institution at work, or to suppose that if the Court's goal has not been achieved the country is worse off than if it had not tried. . . . Nor do we have much basis for supposing that the racial situation in America would now be more satisfactory, on balance, if the Court had not intervened, in 1954, and later, in the way that it did.

But there is a very different, and for my purpose much more important, objection to take to Bickel's theory. His theory is novel because it appears to concede an issue of principle to judicial activism, namely that the Court is entitled to intervene if its intervention produces socially desirable results. But the concession is an illusion, because his sense of what is socially desirable is inconsistent with the presupposition of activism that individuals have moral rights against the state. In fact, Bickel's argument cannot succeed, even if we grant his facts and his view of history, except on a basis of a skepticism about rights as profound as Learned Hand's.

I presented Bickel's theory as an example of one form of the argument from democracy, the argument that since men disagree about rights, it is safer to leave the final decision about rights to the political process, safer in the sense that the results are likely to be sounder. Bickel suggests a reason why the political process is safer. He argues that the endurance of a political settlement about rights is some evidence of the political morality of that settlement. He argues that this evidence is better than the sorts of argument from principle that judges might deploy if the decision were left to them. . . .

. . . [Bickel] argues that the organic political process will secure the genuine rights of men more certainly if it is not hindered by the artificial and rationalistic intrusion of the courts. In this view, the rights of blacks, suspects, and atheists will emerge through the process of political institutions responding to political pressures in the normal way. If a claim of right cannot succeed in this way, then for that reason it is, or in any event it is likely to be, an improper claim or right. But this bizarre proposition is only a disguised form of the skeptical point that there are in fact no rights against the state.

Perhaps, as Burke and his modern followers argue, a society will produce the institutions that best suit it only by evolution and never by radical reform. But rights against the state are claims that, if accepted, require society to settle for institutions that may not suit it so comfortably. The nerve of a claim of right . . . is that an individual is entitled to protection against the majority even at the cost of the general interest. Of course the comfort of the majority will require some accommodation for minorities but only to the extent necessary to preserve order; and that is usually an accommodation that falls short of recognizing their rights.

Indeed the suggestion that rights can be demonstrated by a process of history rather than by an appeal to principle shows either a confusion or no real concern about what rights are. A claim of right presupposes a moral argument and can be established in no other way. Bickel paints the judicial activists . . . as eighteenth-century philosophers who appeal to principle because they hold the optimistic view that a blueprint may be cut for progress. But this picture confuses two grounds for the appeal to principle and reform, and two senses of progress.

It is one thing to appeal to moral principle in the silly faith that ethics as well as economics moves by an invisible hand, so that individual rights and the general good will coalesce, and law based on principle will move the nation to a frictionless utopia. . . . But it is quite another matter to appeal to principle *as* principle, to show, for example, that it is unjust to force black children to take their public education in black schools, even if a great many people *will* be worse off if the state adopt the measures needed to prevent this.

This is a different version of progress. It is moral progress, and though history may show how difficult it is to decide where moral progress lies, and how difficult to persuade others once one has decided, it cannot follow from this that those who govern us have no responsibility to face that decision or to attempt that persuasion.

5

This has been a complex argument, and I want to summarize it. Our constitutional system rests on a particular moral theory, namely, that men have moral rights against the state. The difficult clauses of the Bill of Rights, like the due process and equal protection clauses, must be understood as appealing to moral concepts rather than laying down particular conceptions; therefore a court that undertakes the burden of applying these clauses fully as law must be an activist court, in the sense that it must be prepared to frame and answer questions of political morality.

It may be necessary to compromise that activist posture to some extent, either for practical reasons or for competing reasons of principle. But Nixon's public statements about the Supreme Court suggest that the activist policy must be abandoned altogether, and not merely compromised, for powerful reasons of principle. If we try to state these reasons of principle, we find that they are inconsistent with the assumption of a constitutional system, either because they leave the majority to judge its own cause, or because they rest on a skepticism about moral rights that neither Nixon nor most American politicians can consistently embrace.

So Nixon's jurisprudence is a pretense and no genuine theory at all. . . . Constitutional law can make no genuine advance until it isolates the problem of rights against the state and makes that problem part of its own agenda. That argues for a fusion of constitutional law and moral theory, a connection that, incredibly, has yet to take place. . . .

13
The Processes of Judicial Decision Making

As previous chapters have shown, judicial decision making is far from being a mechanical act. Fact-finding in the courts differs from the search for truth in a laboratory or a library; judicial reasoning is not like the formal logic of the philosopher; and trial and appellate procedures differ in structure from those of legislatures and administrative agencies. Together these processes and structures narrow the alternatives that judges are likely to perceive and from among which they will choose; but singly or together these peculiar processes channel, rather than determine, judicial behavior. They leave room for the play of personal values, including conceptions of proper judicial functions, weighings of probable effects of a decision, and perceptions of the political environment and likely reactions of other actors.

DECISIONS OF TRIAL COURTS

A trial judge must often give a decision almost as a reflex action. During the course of a trial, a lawyer may object to an opponent's questioning and ask the judge for a ruling. Especially when a jury is present, judges do not like to suspend proceedings while they research and meditate, although they sometimes must because of the complexity of the issue. In contrast to the necessity for quick decisions while a trial is in progress, the judge has some opportunity to reflect on the instructions to be given to the jurors at the close of the trial. The judge may also ask the lawyers on each side to assist him by drafting proposed instructions. Because the final decision in the case is the jury's, these instructions are usually not published, although they are kept with the records of the trial so that they may be reviewed in the event of an appeal. The sole record of the jury's deliberative process is the verdict itself.

Because proceedings before a judge sitting without a jury are much less formal than those with a jury present, the trial judge has to make relatively fewer rulings on procedural technicalities. After hearing the evidence and argument and reading any briefs submitted, the judge will decide the case either immediately or after deliberation that often lasts as long as several weeks and occasionally several months. That decision will be accompanied by a written opinion that will consist of at least two parts, findings of fact and conclusions of law; it may also include a statement explaining the reasoning by which the court arrived at these results.[1]

THE SUPREME COURT

On appellate courts the decision-making process takes place under the much more complex conditions of group life. Of necessity our analysis will concentrate on the decisional experience of the United States Supreme Court.

The Court's term begins on the first Monday in October and runs until sometime in June or July, and the justices carry undecided cases over to the next term. Normally, the Court sits for two-week periods to hear arguments and announce decisions and then adjourns for two weeks to allow the justices to research, think, and write their opinions. During the weeks the Court is sitting, the justices meet a few minutes before ten in the robing room behind the courtroom. Precisely at ten the maroon velvet curtains part, and the justices take their places behind the bench as the crier gavels the courtroom to attention and chants:

> The Honorable, the Chief Justice and Associate Justices of the Supreme Court of the United States! Oyez, Oyez, Oyez! All persons having business before the Honorable, the Supreme Court of the United States are admonished to draw near and give their attention, for the Court is now sitting. God save the United States and this Honorable Court.

The Court receives over 5,000 appeals and petitions for certiorari each term.[2] For example, in the 1983 term it disposed of 4,162 cases and carried over 993 to the next term. During the term the Court decided 266 appeals and petitions on the merits, and denied or dis-

---

[1] The West Publishing Company, the commercial firm that prints the *Federal Supplement* (abbreviated F. Supp.) and the *Federal Rules Decisions* (abbreviated F.R.D.), the only generally available volumes of rulings by U.S. district courts, publishes only opinions that its editors believe will be of wide interest to the legal profession. Thus most district court opinions can be found only in the files of individual courthouses. In the *Federal Reporter* (now in its Second Series and abbreviated F. 2d), West publishes most, but still not all, rulings of the various U.S. courts of appeals.

[2] From the 5,311 cases docketed in the 1981 term, there was a slight decrease to 5,079 in the 1982 term, and 5,100 in the 1983 term.

missed 1,902.[3] The remaining cases were *in forma pauperis* (filed without payment), originated mostly by convicts in state and federal prisons, and often hand-written. Most of these cases present no substantial grounds for review, but occasionally one will raise a significant issue, as in *Gideon v. Wainwright* (1963) wherein the Court held that defendants in all serious criminal prosecutions had a right to counsel, appointed and paid for by the government if defendants were too poor to afford their own attorneys. In the 1983 term, 1,968 IFP petitions were denied or withdrawn, and only 19 were decided on the merits.

CASE SELECTION: THE ROLE OF LAW CLERKS

Most of the justices have found it possible to handle this huge workload only by giving major case selection responsibilities to their law clerks. The first clerk was hired by Justice Horace Gray in 1882 at his own expense. But before long it became an established practice for each justice to have one clerk, with two for the chief justice. The number has now been increased to four (five for the chief justice). The method of selection is entirely a personal matter for the justices, who often have had a preference for graduates of particular law schools (usually Ivy League) or residents of certain states or areas. Recently there has been a tendency to prefer law graduates with experience as clerk to a judge of a federal court of appeals or state supreme court. Law clerks generally serve for one term, but there have been notable exceptions. (Reading 13.1.)

Most justices delegate responsibility for initial review of all appeals and petitions to their clerks, who prepare for each case a summary of the facts, questions presented, and a recommended course of action.[4] In 1972, as the workload mounted, a majority of the justices had their clerks join a "cert pool." Filings were divided among the clerks in the pool, and a single clerk's memo would then be circulated to all the participating justices. By 1984 six justices—Burger, White, Blackmun, Powell, Rehnquist, and O'Connor—were participating in the pool. Justice Stevens relied on his own clerks; he expected them to select about 20 percent of the petitions for him to see. Only Justice Brennan continued to do the entire task himself, except during the summer recess.[5]

[3] 98 *Harvard Law Review* 311 (1984).

[4] An interesting example: "Petitioner is a big Cadillac dealer who got caught buying the local Alderman; he has been fighting conviction for four years; his case has no merit and his brief is replete with overstatements, innuendo, speculation, and almost untruth. It would be a crime to touch this case." Doris Marie Provine, *Case Selection in the United States Supreme Court* (Chicago: University of Chicago Press, 1980), p. 22.

[5] As noted in Chapter 3, Chief Justice Burger has maintained that the Supreme Court is overburdened and has proposed the creation of a new judicial panel composed of nine appellate judges to review conflicting rulings of the federal courts of appeals. But

CONFERENCE ACTION: THE RULE OF FOUR

Case selection is made by the justices in conference. The chief justice circulates a list of petitions that he proposes should be discussed. If all justices agree the other petitions pending are denied without discussion.

As noted in Chapter 3, the Court is required by statute to accept appeals, but in fact many are dismissed as failing to present a substantial federal question. Petitions for certiorari are granted on the affirmative vote of four justices. The Court's Rule 17 states: "A review on writ of certiorari is not a matter of right, but of sound judicial discretion, and will be granted only where there are special and important reasons therefor." The "rule of four" has no statutory standing. It rests simply on practice and assurances given by Chief Justice Taft and other members of the Court to Congress in 1925, when access to the Court was made largely discretionary, that the Court would not abuse its new freedom.

But allowing a minority of the Court to determine what cases it will consider does create some problems. As Justice Stevens has said: "The Rule of Four must inevitably enlarge the size of the Court's argument docket and cause it to hear a substantial number of cases that a majority of the Court deems unworthy of review." It occasionally happens that a case placed on the docket by a vote of four justices will be dismissed by vote of the other five justices as "improvidently granted."[6] (Reading 13.2.) It appears, however, that some 80 percent of all the Court's decisions on certiorari are unanimous, and that only 2 percent are accepted by less than a majority.

Refusal to grant certiorari does not necessarily mean that the justices have approved the decision below. As Justice Frankfurter said in *State v. Baltimore Radio Show* (1950), it means only that four justices did not deem the case important enough, for whatever reason, to justify the Court's attention. Nevertheless, it cannot be denied that refusal to grant certiorari does lend some credence to the lower court ruling.

Analysis of the votes on granting certiorari reveals wide variations in judicial attitudes. Provine's intensive study of certiorari voting during the 1947–1957 terms showed a range from Frank Murphy (1940–

---

two New York University law professors concluded on the basis of an extensive study that the Court's problems were self-inflicted. They found that only 48 percent of the 1982 term's decisions met standards set by the researchers for cases that truly required Supreme Court action. Another 28 percent fell into a middle category of cases that were not top priority but that the Court could legitimately choose to hear if it had time. The remaining 24 percent they regarded as cases that were not worth the Court's time. Among the cases denied review, they found only thirteen that should have been added as top priority. John Sexton and Samuel Estreicher, NYU Supreme Court Project, "A Managerial Theory of the Supreme Court's Responsibilities" (mimeo.). See *Wall Street Journal,* March 7, 1985.

6 In *United States v. Shannon* (1952) Justice Douglas protested that such action would impair the "integrity of the four-vote rule."

49), who voted to grant 59.1 percent of the petitions, to Sherman Minton (1949–56) at 13.2 percent.[7] She also found a substantial correlation between judicial votes and the issues involved in the petitions.

In deciding which cases to decide, the Court is expressing its view about which issues are of national importance. Proposals to allow some new intermediate court to make these decisions and thus determine the Court's agenda, noted in Chapter 3, would seriously limit the Court in discharging its responsibility for national policymaking.

ORAL ARGUMENT

If the Court grants certiorari, the clerk puts the case on the docket and schedules oral argument. Well before that date, each side submits written briefs detailing its contentions and reprinting relevant portions of the record from lower courts. Once again, it is not always possible for the justices to read all the material. They examine the briefs with care; but since it is not unusual for a trial record in a complicated case to run to several thousand pages, the justices have to learn which parts can be skipped or perused and which need close study. The Supreme Court's Rules require that briefs contain specific page citations to those parts of the record being discussed, but there are limits to specificity. *Sacher v. United States* (1952), for example, involved review of convictions for contempt of court by several lawyers for their general conduct during a trial whose record took up 13,000 pages.

The justices hear oral argument from 10:00 A.M. until noon on Mondays, Tuesdays, and Wednesdays, then recess for an hour for lunch, and return for two more hours of argument at 1:00 P.M. Although the Court will grant exceptions in unusually important cases, counsel for each side usually have only thirty minutes. Thus the Court can hear an average of twelve cases each week it sits.

The attorney stands at a lectern facing the justices in their high-backed leather chairs. A white light flashes when counsel has five minutes left, and when time is up, a red light goes on. Although lavishly generous with its time during its initial decades, in this century the Court has been miserly. The story is told that Chief Justice Charles Evans Hughes once cut a prominent lawyer off in the middle of the word "if."

Oral argument can be an arduous experience for counsel. Especially if an attorney merely repeats what is already written in the brief,

---

[7] *Op. cit.*, p. 115. Some dissents to denial of certiorari are full-fledged opinions on the case. When the Court majority denies certiorari in death sentence cases, Justices Brennan and Marshall invariably dissent with this formula: "Adhering to our views that the death penalty is in all circumstances cruel and unusual punishment prohibited by the Eighth and Fourteenth Amendments . . . we would grant certiorari and vacate the death sentence in this case." In *Glass v. Louisiana* (1985) their dissent included graphic descriptions of death by electrocution, which they charged was "nothing less than the contemporary technological equivalent of burning people at the stake."

the justices may stare impassively at the draperies, chat among themselves, write notes, read, send pages for law reports, or even occasionally nap, apparently bored by what is being said to them. On the other hand, they may suddenly turn a turgid presentation into an exciting debate by posing a rapid series of piercing questions and counterquestions. Trying to race along with nine different minds going off in several directions provides strenuous mental exercise. When he was Solicitor General, before his own appointment to the Court, Stanley Reed once fainted dead away while arguing a case, and many other lawyers have suffered obvious intellectual blackouts.

It should be understood that all cases accepted by the Court do not go to oral argument. Many are summarily disposed of on the basis of the original petitions for certiorari or the jurisdictional statement in appeals. (Reading 13.3.) Even though no opinion is written, summary disposition is a decision on the merits and binding on the lower courts. In *Goldwater v. Carter* (1979) the Court, without hearing argument, rejected Senator Goldwater's attack on the President's termination of a defense treaty with Taiwan, but nevertheless eight justices filed statements of their views on the issues and two protested deciding the case without oral argument.

By custom, any justice who is not present for oral argument does not participate in decision of the case, making a tie vote possible. A tie vote automatically affirms the judgment of the lower court, creates no precedent, and is binding only on the parties to the actual dispute. How the justices voted is not revealed. The Court, however, can reschedule the case for new argument, if it regards decision of the controversy essential.[8]

Justices may recuse (disqualify) themselves if they have had some previous relation with the controversy or with parties or counsel in the case. But the decision to recuse is an individual one each justice makes for him- or herself. In *Laird v. Tatum* (1972) Justice Rehnquist filed a memorandum declining to disqualify himself in a case involving the Army's surveillance over private citizens and public officials, even though, prior to his Court appointment, as an official in the Department of Justice he had general knowledge of these practices and had defended them before a congressional committee.

THE JUDICIAL CONFERENCE

For a short time on Wednesday afternoons after oral argument and all day on Fridays when the Court is sitting, the justices meet in conference to decide the cases just argued. The conference room is austerely

[8] During Justice Powell's prolonged recovery from surgery in 1985, the Court decided seven cases by tie votes and rescheduled four for reargument. *New York Times,* April 3, 1985.

furnished with a long table and nine chairs, law books, a portrait of John Marshall, a marble fireplace, a desk for the chief justice in one corner, and an undiverting view of Second Street, N.E. When the justices meet there, they lock themselves in. The junior justice answers all knocks at the door, and no one is allowed in except a waiter who brings in desperately needed coffee. Even he is quickly relieved of his burden by one of the justices.

Before discussion begins, each justice shakes hands with every other, a reminder that they remain colleagues even though they may soon be bitterly arguing. The chief justice presides and has the difficult and delicate duty of allowing adequate discussion of each case while moving the Court efficiently through its docket. To accomplish this task, he must have the skill to encourage meaningful intellectual debate and still prevent discussion from degenerating into invective or filibustering. The chief justice gives his views first, and then the other justices speak in order of seniority of service on the Court. Traditionally, when the chief called discussion to a close, the justices voted in reverse order of seniority, with the newest justice going first and the chief last. This procedure conferred on the chief the advantage of being able to vote with the majority. During his last years on the bench, however, Chief Justice Earl Warren persuaded his brethren to vote in the same order as they had spoken. This procedure has continued under Warren Burger.

If he votes with the majority, the chief assigns the task of writing the opinion of the Court. If the chief justice is in the minority, the senior associate justice makes the assignment. Before John Marshall the Court had generally followed the British practice, whereby each judge who had the time or inclination wrote his own opinion. There was seldom an institutional opinion of the Court. Marshall, believing that the appearance of monolithic unity of reasoning as well as of result would give greater impact to judicial decisions, made it standard practice to designate one judge, usually himself, to act as spokesman for the whole Court.

WRITING OPINIONS

The power to choose the opinion writer provides a source of real power for the chief justice, because he can designate that member of the majority, including himself, who, he believes, will write the opinion that best fits the situation. Chief justices have adopted various strategies in opinion assignment. The chief will usually feel it incumbent on himself to write the opinion in the major cases, as Warren did in the *Brown* case and Burger did in *United States v. Nixon.* (Reading 12.1.) Where the Court is badly divided and it is uncertain whether a narrow majority can be held together, chief justices have usually thought it desirable to have one of the Court's more diplomatic justices write the opinion.

The justices and their law clerks have been described by Justice Powell as "nine small, independent law firms." [9] Each justice and his or her own staff tend to run separate operations, with little direct interaction. All the justices rely heavily on their clerks to do the research and to edit if not prepare drafts of the opinions they have been assigned to write, though actual practices vary widely.

When the opinion writer has a draft ready, it is circulated to all the justices, no matter how they voted. Each can make comments and suggestions for change. Any justice who believes that the opinion writer is taking an undesirable path is free to write a separate opinion, concurring or dissenting, or join with another justice in so doing. If enough justices behave in that fashion, the original opinion writer may wind up alone, perhaps even in dissent, with someone else writing for the Court.

The very existence of the possibility of a concurring or dissenting opinion—not considered proper in Civil Law countries like France or Italy and only recently allowed on a single tribunal in West Germany, the Constitutional Court—is an important facet of legal systems based on the common law. When judges publicly disagree about the meaning of law and perhaps also of the Constitution, "the Law" loses the appearance of majestic certainty. Jurists may disagree among themselves whether such a loss is desirable, but there can be no doubt that dissenting opinions sometimes provide powerful forces for legal, social, and political change. Actually a dissenter has an easier task than the justice who speaks for the Court or even one who writes a concurring opinion, for a dissenter speaks without the authority and therefore without the responsibility of representing a coordinate branch of the federal government. As Justice Cardozo once said:

> The spokesman of the Court is cautious, timid, fearful of the vivid word, the heightened phrase. He dreams of an unworthy brood of scions, the spawn of careless *dicta,* disowned by the *ratio decidendi.* . . . The result is to cramp and paralyze. One fears to say anything when the peril of misunderstanding puts a warning finger to the lips. Not so, however, the dissenter. . . . Deep conviction and warm feeling are saying their last say with knowledge that the cause is lost. . . . The dissenter speaks to the future, and his voice is pitched to a key that will carry through the years.[10]

Whether because of the eloquence of dissenters, the complexity of the issues, or the stubbornness of individual justices, it sometimes hap-

9 "What the Justices Are Saying," 62 *American Bar Association Journal* 1454 (1976).
10 "Law and Literature," 14 *Yale Review* 699, 715–716 (1925).

pens that they cannot agree on an opinion that at least five of them can sign. In that situation, the Court announces its decision, either through a brief *per curiam* (unsigned) order that merely states the result or through the justice in the majority whose opinion attracted the most votes (called the "plurality opinion"). Under such circumstances, each justice may write an opinion or clusters of several justices may join together.[11] But, whatever these divisions, any opinion that does not command the assent of a majority of the justices who participate in a decision—and at least six justices are necessary for a quorum—does not speak for the Supreme Court of the United States. Such an opinion is an expression of the views of one or more members of the Court and is entitled to respect. But its reasoning need not be accepted as controlling by other judges, public officials, or private citizens. Thus as we shall see in a few pages, the stage is set for negotiations within the Court. (See Readings 13.4 and 13.5.)

Dissenting and concurring opinions, if there are any, are also circulated among all the justices, and authors may make changes to meet points raised by other opinions. When he feels that the justices are satisfied that they can fruitfully say no more to each other, the chief justice brings the case up again at conference. If he hears no request for additional time, the chief puts the case on the list of those whose decision will be announced during the next week the Court is in session.

NEGOTIATING AND BARGAINING

The preceding discussion fails to convey a realistic sense of the interplay among the justices as they work their way toward a consensus, if that is possible, or toward an effective statement of and support for conflicting views. The judicial conferences are secret, of course, but the notes and papers of the Court's members have provided insight into the group life of the Court. Few justices have been so insensitive to their responsibilities as simply to plow their own furrows, write their own opinions, and ignore the accommodation of views essential on a collegial tribunal. Rather, justices generally seek to persuade their colleagues of the rightness—even righteousness—of their views.

[11] The result can be a confusing hodge-podge, as the beginning of *United Jewish Organizations v. Carey* (1977) indicates:

Mr. Justice WHITE announced the judgment of the Court and filed an opinion, all of which is joined by Mr. Justice STEVENS, Parts I, II, and III of which are joined by Mr. Justice BRENNAN, and Parts I and IV of which are joined by Mr. Justice REHNQUIST.

To complicate matters further, Justice Brennan wrote a special concurring opinion, as did Justice Stewart (joined by Justice Powell). Chief Justice Burger wrote a dissenting opinion. Justice Marshall did not participate in the decision.

Where possible, they use reason, where necessary they use emotional appeal and/or bargaining.[12]

Negotiation and compromise are facts of life on appellate courts. To bargain effectively one must have something to trade as well as a sanction to apply if the offer is rejected. The most significant items with which judges can negotiate are their votes and concurrences in opinions. Conversely, threats to change votes or write separate opinions, dissenting or concurring, are the sanctions most generally available to judges. The effectiveness of each depends in part on the division within the Court and the skills of the particular jurist. When, for instance, the Supreme Court is divided five to four, any justice in the majority can exercise great influence by dropping hints of a switch in vote. When the vote is nine to zero or eight to one, any justice has much less clout. Similarly, a threat from a judge whose writing style is dull and whose reasoning is not noted for awesome power is not likely to carry much weight unless the vote is very close. On the other hand, a dissent—even the possibility of a lone dissent—from a judge with the skill of a Holmes, a Brandeis, a Black, a Jackson, a Frankfurter, or a Harlan is likely to give the majority pause.

Negotiation may be explicit or tacit. One of the most common opportunities for compromise occurs when judges circulate drafts of opinions ("slip opinions," as they are called in the Supreme Court) to colleagues for comments. The other judges may then suggest changes, with everyone understanding that the opinion writer ignores these suggestions at the risk of losing support for the opinion. The threat to pull out normally need not be expressed, though some judges prefer to be very explicit. Stone, for example, once wrote Frankfurter: "If you wish to write, placing the case on the ground which I think tenable and desirable, I shall cheerfully join you. If not, I will add a few observations for myself." Only slightly less direct was the note attached to a draft of a concurring opinion that Stone sent Roberts:

> I doubt if we are very far apart in the Cantwell case, but in order that you might get exactly my views, I have written them out and enclosed them herewith.
>
> If you feel that you could agree with me, I think you would find no difficulty in making some changes in your opinion which would make it unnecessary for me to say anything.

While it is probably true that accommodation more often prevents a majority from splintering into concurring factions, compromise can also serve to mute dissent. In either circumstance, the threat of a separate opinion may create a bargaining situation in which both may gain something. Fearing that publication of a dissent or concurrence might cause the author of the prevailing opinion to make his or her pronouncements more rigid or perhaps draw attention to and emphasize an "erroneous" ruling, a judge in the minority might reason that it would be more prudent to suppress disagreement if concessions can be won from the majority. As Justice William Johnson, a contemporary of John Marshall, explained his vote in *Sturges v. Crowninshield* (1819): "The Court was, in that case, greatly divided in their views of the doctrine, and the judgment partakes as much of a compromise as of a legal adjudication. The minority thought it better to yield something than risk the whole."[13]

As an integral part of this process, publication of a dissent and circulation within a court of a separate opinion serve two different functions. The latter is essentially an effort to resolve conflict within the family by, in one fashion or another, persuading other judges. The former is basically an attempt to shift the arena of combat. Having lost within the Court, a published dissenting opinion is, as Justice Cardozo said, an appeal to history, particularly to future judges. But a dissent can be more. Whether or not the author intends it, a dissent can become an appeal to contemporaries—to members of Congress, to the President and executive officials, to lower-court judges, to the bar or other interest groups, or to the public at large—to change the decision of the majority. As Frankfurter explained to Murphy in discussing a dissent in *Harris v. United States:*

> This is a protest opinion—a protest at the Bar of the future—but also an effort to make the brethren realize what is at stake. Moreover, a powerful dissent in a case like that is bound to have an effect on the lower courts as well as on the officers of the law, just as a failure to speak out vigorously against what the Court is doing will only lead to further abuse. And so in order to impress our own brethren, the lower courts and enforcement officers, it seems to me vital to make the dissent an impressive document.

Although dissent is a cherished part of the common law tradition, a judge who persistently refuses collegial accommodation may soon be regarded as an obstructionist. Similarly, colleagues may regard as disloyal to the bench a judge whose dissents frequently become levers for legislative or administrative action reversing judicial policies. It is likely that either appraisal would curtail the influence of a justice. Even in his despair over the course of constitutional adjudication after John Marshall's death, Justice Joseph Story thought this consideration limited the frequency with which he could dissent. He told James Kent that he would stay on the bench and continue to express his—and

---

[13] It was in *Ogden v. Saunders* (1827) that Johnson explained his earlier vote in *Sturges.*

Marshall's—opinions, "But I shall naturally be silent on many occasions from an anxious desire not to appear contentious, or dissatisfied, or desirous of weakening the [word unclear] influence of the court." (Reading 13.6.)

Another factor that might prod a minority judge into accepting compromise is psychological. Most people suffer anxiety when they find themselves in severe disagreement with a group with whom they are intimately associated. Appellate judges tend to be highly independent and individualistic people, but they may not be completely immune to dislike of isolation. Their professional socialization—especially their legal training and the accepted norms of judicial behavior—to some extent encourages judges to express their own views, but only to some extent. This socialization also encourages judges to strive for harmony and teamwork with colleagues.

On the other hand, there are factors that push the majority, especially the opinion writer, to accept compromise. As already noted, an eloquent, tightly reasoned dissent can be an upsetting force. Writing without institutional authority—and responsibility—a clever dissenter can sometimes wreak intellectual mayhem on the essay that an opinion writer for the Court has had to patch together out of the not always compatible views of the other justices. The majority may therefore find it profitable to mute criticism from within the Court by giving in to the minority on some issues.

The judge who has the task of writing the opinion of the Court may assume the role of a broker adjusting the interests of the group. The problems, of course, are dynamic rather than static. By making a change in an opinion to pick up one vote, another may be lost. Moreover, compromising and incorporating several different lines of reasoning in the opinion may encourage an even more damaging dissent.

Most important, a judge will want to avoid watering down an opinion to the point where it ceases to be an operational doctrine—though dilution may be the only alternative to outright rejection. The opinion writer can supply a sort of marginal analysis to the alternatives confronted. The minimum need—the essential need—is for enough votes to win a majority so that the result and opinion will carry the institutional authority of the Court. Thus, given the high value of these votes, the opinion writer should be willing to pay a relatively high price in accommodation to secure them. Once, however, a majority acquiesces, the marginal value of any additional vote declines, as does the price that an opinion writer should be willing to pay. The marginal value of another vote, however, is never zero, though the price may exceed its real value.

The idea of a justice looking over his shoulder at Congress, the President, or judges of lower courts while negotiating with other justices conflicts with the image of a Supreme Court composed of austere and aloof demigods standing above the dark earth of politics. Although most informed students of the judicial process concede (sometimes grudgingly) the accuracy of such a description of what actually goes on in many collegial tribunals, many of those scholars—and judges themselves—perceive serious moral and ethical problems. Inevitably the question arises: How far can a judge compromise without betraying the oath to support the Constitution?

In 1979 *The Brethren* purported to reveal the inside story of the Burger Court's decisional history over seven terms.[14] One of the authors, Bob Woodward, had earned his reputation as an ace investigative reporter in the Watergate affair. The book, according to the hyperbole on the dust jacket, was "the first detailed behind-the-scenes account of the Supreme Court in action." The authors, their advertising claimed, had "pierced the secrecy to give us an unprecedented view of the Chief and Associate Justices—maneuvering, arguing, politicking, compromising, and making the decisions that affect every major area of American life."

No reader, having come this far in *Courts, Judges, and Politics,* would be shocked by the notion that judges argue and compromise, and that constitutional principles are subject to continual reexamination as they challenge and are challenged by a disordered world. Indeed, such a description is likely to seem as exceptional as the notion that professional football is a physical sport. Two rather contrasting views of *The Brethren* are reprinted at the close of this chapter. (Readings 13.7 and 13.8.)

SELECTED REFERENCES

Alito, Samuel A. "The 'Released Time' Cases Revisited: A Study of Group Decisionmaking by the Supreme Court," 83 *Yale Law Journal* 1202 (1974).

Atkinson, David N. "Justice Sherman Minton and Behavior Patterns Inside the Supreme Court," 69 *Northwestern University Law Review* 716 (1975).

Bartee, Alice F. *Cases Lost, Causes Won.* New York: St. Martin's Press, 1984.

Baum, Lawrence. "Policy Goals in Gatekeeping: A Proximity Model of Discretionary Jurisdiction," 21 *American Journal of Political Science* 13 (1977).

Bickel, Alexander. *The Unpublished Opinions of Mr. Justice Brandeis.* Cambridge, Massachusetts: The Belknap Press, 1957.

Danelski, David J. "Values as Variables in Judicial Decision-Making: Notes Toward a Theory," 19 *Vanderbilt Law Review* 721 (1966).

Frank, Jerome. *Law and the Modern Mind.* New York: Brentano's, 1930.

Frankfurter, Felix. "Chief Justices I Have Known," 39 *Virginia Law Review* 883 (1953).

[14] Bob Woodward and Scott Armstrong, *The Brethren: Inside the Supreme Court* (New York: Simon and Schuster, 1979).

Howard, J. Woodford, Jr. *Mr. Justice Murphy: A Political Biography.* Princeton, New Jersey: Princeton University Press, 1968. Part II.

————, "On the Fluidity of Judicial Choice," 62 *American Political Science Review* 43 (1968).

Kluger, Richard. *Simple Justice.* New York: Knopf, 1976. Ch. 25.

Mason, Alpheus T. *Harlan Fiske Stone: Pillar of the Law.* New York: Viking, 1956. Parts III–VIII.

————. "The Chief Justice of the United States: Primus Inter Pares," 17 *Journal of Public Law* 20 (1968).

————. *William Howard Taft: Chief Justice.* New York: Simon and Schuster, 1965.

McElwain, Edwin. "The Business of the Supreme Court as Conducted by Chief Justice Hughes," 63 *Harvard Law Review* 5 (1949).

Menez, Joseph F. *Decision Making in the Supreme Court of the United States.* Lanham, Md.: University Press of America, 1984.

Murphy, Walter F. *Elements of Judicial Strategy.* Chicago: University of Chicago Press, 1964. Especially Chs. 3 and 7.

Murphy, Walter F., and Joseph Tanenhaus. *The Study of Public Law.* New York: Random House, 1972. Chs. 3, 5, and 6.

Oakley, John B., and Robert S. Thompson. *Law Clerks and the Judicial Process.* Berkeley, Calif.: University of California Press, 1981.

Powell, Lewis F., Jr. "What Really Goes on at the Supreme Court," 66 *American Bar Association Journal* 721 (1980).

Pritchett, C. Herman. *Civil Liberties and the Vinson Court.* Chicago: University of Chicago Press, 1954.

————. *The Roosevelt Court: A Study in Judicial Politics and Values, 1937–1947.* New York: Macmillan, 1948.

Provine, D. Marie. *Case Selection in the United States Supreme Court.* Chicago: University of Chicago Press, 1980.

————. "Deciding What to Decide: How the Supreme Court Sets Its Agenda," 64 *Judicature* 320 (1981).

Rohde, David W., and Harold J. Spaeth. *Supreme Court Decision Making.* San Francisco: Freeman, 1976.

Schubert, Glendon. *The Judicial Mind: Attitudes and Ideologies of Supreme Court Justices, 1946–1963.* Evanston, Ill.: Northwestern University Press, 1965.

————. *The Judicial Mind Revisited: Psychometric Analysis of Supreme Court Ideology.* New York: Oxford University Press, 1974.

Slotnick, Elliot E. "Who Speaks for the Court? Majority Opinion Assignment from Taft to Burger," 23 *American Journal of Political Science* 60 (1979).

Spaeth, Harold J. "Distributive Justice: Majority Opinion Assignment in the Burger Court," 67 *Judicature* 299 (1984).

Tanenhaus, Joseph, *et al.* "The Supreme Court's Certiorari Jurisdiction: Cue Theory," in Glendon Schubert (ed.), *Judicial Decision-Making.* New York: Free Press, 1963.

Ulmer, S. Sidney. "Earl Warren and the Brown Decision," 33 *Journal of Politics* 689 (1971).

Ulmer, S. Sidney, William Hintze, and Louise Kirklowsky. "The Decision to Grant or Deny Certiorari: Further Considerations of Cue Theory," 6 *Law & Society Review* 637 (1972).

Wilkinson, J. Harvie, III. *Serving Justice: A Supreme Court Clerk's View.* New York: Charterhouse, 1974.

13.1   *"Felix Frankfurter was fond of joking that Harlan ran a sweatshop."*

MR. JUSTICE HARLAN

Charles Nesson

I hesitate to write about the Justice. It seems impossible to capture the respect and affection which all his clerks have for him. He, of course, would frown at any such silly notion. Always a man who believed in pushing against the adversities of life, great and small, he would have me put hesitation aside and set about it.

In a sense that was the spirit of my year as the Justice's law clerk; a wonderful year, full of hard work done with a steadiness and firmness of purpose characteristic of the Justice. Felix Frankfurter was fond of joking that Harlan ran a sweatshop. In a sense, he did: the work poured out, yet we felt anything but driven. The Justice was not a taskmaster. He taught by example; a calm, gentlemanly man, hardworking, exceedingly warm and honest, with a capacity for absorbing and complementing the energies of others. He wanted his clerks to share fully in the job he was doing and in the pleasures he took from it. His great love was the craft of lawyering—breaking down a problem by research and analysis to uncover the essential questions which called for his judgment. I can remember spending hours in his office, arguing back and forth to get to the nub. The Justice prepared for these discussions, as he prepared for everything else. Quiet and measured in his approach to the cases, he would state his tentative conclusions and offer the framework of his analysis, then open each problem for response and discussion. When a case was particularly tough to crack, the Justice would take the briefs and memos home with him for the evening, assuring us that it would "succumb to a little bourbon." And inevitably it did.

Circumstance and philosophy made Harlan a dissenter. I was never sure whether he enjoyed the role. By nature he was a winner, bred in the traditions of Wall Street, entirely at ease with power, people and lawyerly competition, accustomed to having results respond to his ministrations. On Friday afternoons when he returned to chambers from the Court conference and reported the votes, I thought I sometimes caught a hint of resignation to the loneliness of his position—but just as many times I saw a gleam of mischief and fun as he mapped out a dissent. Never one to hold his fire or to play for alliances on the Court, he believed in stating his differences frankly,

84 *Harvard Law Review* 390 (1971). Copyright © 1971 by the Harvard Law Review Association. Charles Nesson is Professor of Law at the Harvard Law School.

and was respected for it, even and perhaps especially by those with whom he differed most fundamentally.

The Justice played an important, unseen role on the Court, often improving the quality of its opinions. He believed firmly that a Court opinion should honestly explain the judgment; that if a result was inexplicable, the judgment was probably wrong; and his sense of quality and his pride in the Court's work took precedence over personal recognition. In one of the first dissents I worked on, he circulated a draft packed with research, opening gaping holes in the majority draft opinion. When, shortly afterwards, a new majority draft was circulated incorporating much of our work but turning it at crucial points to patch some of the majority's chinks, I felt frustrated and outmaneuvered. But not the Justice. Even though his truncated dissent would now carry less sting, he was pleased that our opinion had had effect, that the issue had been joined more closely, and that the dialogue of the Court had worked to produce a more substantial job. His frustration came in just the opposite and, unfortunately, not unusual situation when his dissent would cry out for response and receive none. Typically this signified only that by the time he circulated his draft at least four Justices had already sent their "join" notes to the majority writer, who, with a solid Court, saw no need to respond. The practice offended the Justice's sense of craft —and, after some teaching from him, mine too.

It was this sense of straightforwardness which bound his law clerks to him. In my case I came slowly to realize that here was a truly kind and honest man, confident of his own abilities, yet modest and willing to give of himself at every point of contact.

13.2 *". . . The Rule of Four is a valuable, though not immutable device. . . ."*

THE RULE OF FOUR: NEW YORK V. UPLINGER

467 U.S. 246, 104 S. Ct. 2332, 81 L. Ed. 2d 201 (1984)

PER CURIAM. We granted certiorari to review a decision of the New York Court of Appeals concerning New York State Penal Law § 240.35-3, which prohibits loitering "in a public place for the purpose of engaging, or soliciting another person to engage, in deviate sexual intercourse or other sexual behavior of a deviate nature." Respondents, charged with violating the statute, challenged its constitutionality and the Court of Appeals sustained their claim. The court concluded that § 240.35-3 is "a companion statute to the consensual sodomy statute . . . which criminalized acts of deviate sexual inter-course between consenting adults" and noted that it had previously held the latter statute unconstitutional in *People v. Onofre* (1980), which we declined to review. Construing the loitering statute as intended "to punish conduct anticipatory to the act of consensual sodomy," the Court of Appeals reasoned that "[i]nasmuch as the conduct ultimately contemplated by the loitering statute may not be deemed criminal, we perceived no basis upon which the State may continue to punish loitering for that purpose."

As the diverse arguments presented in the briefs have demon-strated, the opinion of the Court of Appeals is fairly subject to varying interpretations, leaving us uncertain as to the precise federal consti-tutional issue the court decided. . . .

Under these circumstances, we are persuaded that this case pro-vides an inappropriate vehicle for resolving the important constitu-tional issues raised by the parties. We therefore dismiss the writ of certiorari as improvidently granted.

It is so ordered.

JUSTICE STEVENS, concurring.

Although the origins of the Rule of Four are somewhat obscure, its administration during the past 60 years has undergone a number of changes. Even though our decision today makes no change in the Rule, I regard it as sufficiently significant to warrant these additional comments.

I first note that I agree with the reasons set forth in the Per Curiam opinion for not deciding this case. . . .

Four Members of the Court believe, however, that the merits "should be addressed." They do not, however, address the merits themselves. Nor do they attempt to refute the sound reasons offered by the majority for dismissing the writ as improvidently granted. As long as we adhere to the Rule of Four, four Justices have the power to require that a case be briefed, argued, and considered at a post-argument conference. Why, then, should they not also have the power to command that its merits be decided by the Court?

The difference in the character of the decision to hear a case and the decision to decide it justifies a difference in the way the decision should be made. As long as we act prudently in selecting cases for review, there is relatively little to be lost, and a great deal to be gained, by permitting four Justices who are convinced that a case should be heard to have it placed on the calendar for argu-ment. It might be suggested that the case must be decided unless there has been an intervening development that justifies a dismis-sal. I am now persuaded, however, that there is *always* an important intervening development that may be decisive. The Members of the Court have always considered a case more carefully after full briefing and argument on the merits than they could at the time of the certiorari conference, when almost 100 petitions must be considered each week. Nevertheless, once a case has been briefed, argued, and studied in chambers, sound principles of judicial economy normally outweigh most reasons advanced for dismissing a case. Indeed, in many cases, the majority may remain convinced that the case does not present a question of general significance warranting this Court's review, but nevertheless proceed to decide the case on the merits because there is no strong countervailing reason to dismiss after the large investment of resources by the parties and the Court.

A decision on the merits does, of course, have serious consequences, particularly when a constitutional issue is raised, and most especially when the constitutional issue presents questions of first impression. The decision to decide a constitutional question may be the most momentous decision that can be made in a case. Fundamental principles of constitutional adjudication counsel against premature consideration of constitutional questions and demand that such questions be presented in a context conducive to the most searching analysis possible. See generally *Ashwander v. Tennessee Valley Authority* (1936) (Brandeis, J., concurring). The policy of judicial restraint is most salient in this Court given its role as the ultimate expositor of the meaning of the Constitution, and "perhaps the most effective implement for making the policy effective has been the certiorari jurisdiction conferred upon this Court by the Congress." If a majority is convinced after studying the case that its posture, record or presentation of issues makes it an unwise vehicle for exercising the "gravest and most delicate" function that this Court is called upon to perform, the Rule of Four should not reach so far as to compel the majority to decide the case.

In conclusion, the Rule of Four is a valuable, though not immutable, device for deciding when a case must be argued, but its force is largely spent once the case has been heard. At that point, a more fully informed majority of the Court must decide whether some countervailing principle outweighs the interest in judicial economy in deciding the case.

JUSTICE WHITE, with whom The Chief Justice, **JUSTICE REHNQUIST,** and **JUSTICE O'CONNOR** join, dissenting.

As I see it, the New York statute was invalidated on federal constitutional grounds, and the merits of that decision are properly before us and should be addressed. Dismissing this case as improvidently granted is not the proper course. . . .

13.3   *"We are far too busy to review every claim of error. . . ."*

SUMMARY DISPOSITIONS: TWO CASES

The Supreme Court typically accepts more cases than it can schedule for oral argument. Some of these it will put off until the next term; others the justices decide by summary disposition, that is, solely on the basis of the briefs and papers submitted by the parties in their request for and opposition to review by the Court. Thus the parties not only have no chance to present oral argument, they also have no opportunity to prepare written briefs that fully argue the issues on their merits.

Illinois v. Batchelder

463 U.S. 1112, 103 S. Ct. 3513, 77 L. Ed. 2d 1267 (1983)

An Illinois trial court denied the state's request to suspend Milton Batchelder's driving license for driving while intoxicated because the arresting officer's affidavit did not comply with state law. The state intermediate appellate court held the affidavit was valid under state law but did not "comport with the [U. S.] Constitution, specifically the Fourth and Fourteenth Amendments thereof." The state supreme court refused review, and the prosecutor petitioned the United States Supreme Court for certiorari.

PER CURIAM. . . .
. . . The petition for certiorari is granted, the judgment of the Appellate Court of Illinois, Third Judicial District, is reversed. . . . JUSTICE STEVENS, with whom JUSTICE BRENNAN and JUSTICE MARSHALL join, dissenting.

This case comes to us from an intermediate Illinois appellate court. It is a case that the Illinois Supreme Court declined to review. Its practical consequences concern the amount of detail that Illinois police officers in the Third Appellate District must include in an affidavit supporting a petition to suspend a driver's license. In final analysis the only question presented relates to how an Illinois statute is to be implemented in one part of the state. I suspect that the Illinois Supreme Court may have decided not to take this case because it preferred to address the question presented in a case in which both parties would be adequately represented.

The only paper filed in behalf of the losing party in this Court reads, in full, as follows:

"Court Clerk;
      Re: Illinois vs: Milton D. Batchelder
      No: 82–947
      "In regard to your letter of 3–31–83 pertaining to the above captioned matter.
      "I have a heart problem and am unemployed.
      "I do not have the funds to hire an attorney.

"Is it possible for the court to appoint me counsel or for the court to rule on the record that is on appeal?

"I am unlearned at law and have had little formal education.

"Unless the court can give me some help I will not be able to pursue this matter.

"This letter written by;
Donald E. Worlow
302 Pontiac Rd.
Marquette Hgts., Ill.
"For Milton D. Batchelder
/s/ Milton Batchelder"

If a case is important enough to merit a decision on the merits by this Court, I believe it also should be important enough to justify the appointment of counsel to represent the party defending the judgment of the court below. I respectfully dissent from the Court's summary disposition.

California v. Beheler
463 U. S. 1121, 103 S. Ct. 3517, 77 L. Ed. 2d 1275 (1983)

A California court convicted Jerry Beheler of aiding and abetting a murder, partially on the basis of statements he had made to the police after he voluntarily came to the station house. An intermediate state court of appeals reversed the conviction because the police had not read Beheler his "*Miranda* rights" before he gave his statement. The state supreme court refused review, and the prosecutor petitioned the United States Supreme Court for certiorari.

PER CURIAM.

The question presented in this petition . . . is whether *Miranda* warnings are required if the suspect is not placed under arrest, voluntarily comes to the police station, and is allowed to leave unhindered by the police after a brief interview. Because this question has already been settled clearly by past decisions of this Court, we reverse a decision of the California Court of Appeal holding that *Miranda* warnings are required in these circumstances. . . .

JUSTICE STEVENS, with whom JUSTICE BRENNAN and JUSTICE MARSHALL join, dissenting.

This case comes to us from an intermediate appellate court in California. It is a case that the Supreme Court of California deemed unworthy of review. It is a case in which the California Appellate Court wrote a 38-page opinion, most of which was devoted to an analysis of the question whether, under all of the relevant facts, the respondent was "in custody" under the test set forth in *People v. Blouin* (1978). . . .

Today, without receiving briefs or arguments on the merits, this Court summarily reverses the decision of the intermediate appellate court of California. In doing so the Court notes that "the circumstances of each case must certainly influence a determination of whether a suspect is 'in custody' " and that the ultimate inquiry is whether the restraint on freedom of movement is "of the degree associated with a formal arrest." . . . I believe that other courts are far better equipped than this Court to make the kind of factual study that must precede such a determination. We are far too busy to review every claim of error by a prosecutor who has been unsuccessful in presenting his case to a state appellate court. Moreover, those courts are far better equipped than we are to assess the police practices that are highly relevant to the determination whether particular circumstances amount to custodial interrogation. I therefore respectfully dissent from the Court's summary decision of the merits of this case.

13.4   ". . . 'lead us not into temptation.' "

THE INFLUENCE OF THE CHIEF JUSTICE IN THE DECISIONAL PROCESS

David J. Danelski

The Chief Justice of the United States has a unique opportunity for leadership in the Supreme Court. He presides in open court and over the secret conferences where he usually presents each case to his associates, giving his opinion first and voting last. He assigns the Court's opinion in virtually all cases when he votes with the majority; and when the Court is divided, he is in a favorable position to seek unity. But his office does not guarantee leadership. His actual influence depends upon his esteem, ability, and personality and how he performs his various roles.

IN CONFERENCE

The conference is the matrix of leadership in the Court.[1] The Court member who is able to present his views with force and clarity and defend them successfully is highly esteemed by his associates. When

This is an abridged version of a paper delivered in New York City at the 1960 annual meeting of the American Political Science Association. David J. Danelski is Dean of the Faculty and Vice President for Academic Affairs at Occidental College.

[1] This study is based largely on private papers of members of the Supreme Court from 1921 to 1946. The theory of conference leadership is derived primarily from the work of Robert F. Bales. See his "Task Roles and Social Roles in Problem-Solving Groups" in Maccoby *et al.*, *Readings in Social Psychology* (New York: Holt, Rinehart and Winston, 1958), pp. 437–447.

perplexing questions arise, they turn to him for guidance. He usually makes more suggestions than his colleagues, gives more opinions, and orients the discussion more frequently, emerging as the Court's task leader. In terms of personality, he is apt to be somewhat reserved; and, in concentrating on the decision of the Court, his response to the emotional needs of his associates is apt to be secondary.

Court members frequently disagree in conference and argue their positions with enthusiasm, seeking to persuade their opponents and the undecided brethren. And always, when the discussion ends, the vote declares the victor. All of this gives rise to antagonism and tension, which, if allowed to get out of hand, would make intelligent, orderly decision of cases virtually impossible. However, the negative aspects of conference interaction are more or less counterbalanced by activity which relieves tension, shows solidarity, and makes for agreement. One Court member usually performs more such activity than the others. He invites opinions and suggestions. He attends to the emotional needs of his associates by affirming their value as individuals and as Court members, especially when their views are rejected by the majority. Ordinarily he is the best-liked member of the Court and emerges as its social leader. While the task leader concentrates on the Court's decision, the social leader concentrates on keeping the Court socially cohesive. In terms of personality, he is apt to be warm, receptive, and responsive. Being liked by his associates is ordinarily quite important to him; he is also apt to dislike conflict.

As presiding officer of the conference, the Chief Justice is in a favorable position to assert task and social leadership. His presentation of cases is an important task function. His control of the conference's process makes it easy for him to invite suggestions and opinions, seek compromises, and cut off debate which appears to be getting out of hand, all important social functions.

It is thus possible for the Chief Justice to emerge as both task and social leader of the conference. This, however, requires the possession of a rare combination of qualities plus adroit use of them. Normally, one would expect the functions of task and social leadership to be performed by at least two Court members, one of whom might or might not be the Chief Justice. As far as the Chief Justice is concerned, the following leadership situations are possible:

	TASK LEADERSHIP	SOCIAL LEADERSHIP
I	+	+
II	−	+
III	+	−
IV	−	−

In situation I, the Chief Justice is a "great man" leader, performing both leadership functions. The consequences of such leadership, stated as hypotheses, are: (1) conflict tends to be minimal; (2) social cohesion tends to increase; (3) satisfaction with the conference tends to increase; (4) production, in terms of number of decisions for the time spent, tends to increase. The consequences in situations II and III are the same as in I, particularly if the Chief Justice works in coalition with the associate justice performing complementary leadership functions. However, in situation IV, unless the task and social functions are adequately performed by associate justices, consequences opposite to those in situations I, II, and III tend to occur. . . .

Situation II prevailed in the Taft Court (1921–1930): Chief Justice Taft was social leader, and his good friend and appointee, Justice Van Devanter, was task leader. Evidence of Van Devanter's esteem and task leadership is abundant. Taft, for example, frequently asserted that Van Devanter was the ablest member of the Court. If the Court were to vote, he said, that would be its judgment too. The Chief Justice admitted that he did not know how he could get along without Van Devanter in conference, for Van Devanter kept the Court consistent with itself, and "his power of statement and his immense memory make him an antagonist in conference who generally wins against all opposition." At times, Van Devanter's ability actually embarrassed the Chief Justice, and he wondered if it might not be better to have Van Devanter run the conference himself. "Still," said Taft, "I must worry along until the end of my ten years, content to aid in the deliberation when there is a difference of opinion." In other words, Taft was content to perform the social functions of leadership. And he did this well. His humor soothed over the rough spots in conference. "We are very happy with the present Chief," said Holmes in 1922. "He is good-humored, laughs readily, not quite rapid enough, but keeps things moving pleasantly."

Situation I prevailed in the Hughes Court (1930–1941): task and social leadership were combined in Chief Justice Hughes. He was the most esteemed member of his Court. This was due primarily to his performance in conference. Blessed with a photographic memory, he would summarize comprehensively and accurately the facts and issues in each case he presented. When he finished, he would look up and say with a smile: "Now I will state where I come out." Then he would outline his views as to how the case should be decided. Sometimes that is all the discussion a case received, and the justices proceeded to vote for the disposition suggested by the Chief. Where there was discussion, the other Court members gave their views in order of seniority without interruption, stating why they concurred or dissented from the views of the Chief Justice. After they had their say, Hughes would review the discussion, pointing out his agreement and disagreement with the views expressed. Then he would call for a vote.

As to the social side of Hughes' leadership, there is the testimony of Justice Roberts: never in the eleven years Roberts sat with Hughes in conference did he see him lose his temper. Never did he hear him pass a personal remark or even raise his voice. Never did he witness him interrupting or engaging in controversy with an associate. Despite Hughes' popular image of austerity, several of his associates have said that he had a keen sense of humor which aided in keeping differences in conference from becoming discord. Moreover, when discussion showed signs of deteriorating into wrangling, Hughes would cut it off. On the whole, he was well liked. Justice Roberts said: "Men whose views were as sharply opposed as those of Van Devanter and Brandeis, or those of Sutherland and Cardozo, were at one in their admiration and affectionate regard for their presiding officer." Roberts could have well added Justices Holmes, Black, Reed, Frankfurter, Douglas, McReynolds, and perhaps others.

Situation IV prevailed during most of Stone's Chief Justiceship (1941–1946). When Stone was promoted to the center chair, Augustus Hand indicated in a letter to Hughes that Stone did not seem a sure bet as task leader because of "a certain inability to express himself orally and maintain a position in a discussion." Hand proved to be correct. Stone departed from the conference role cut out by Hughes. When he presented cases, he lacked the apparent certitude of his predecessor; and, at times, his statement indicated that he was still groping for a solution. In that posture, cases were passed on to his associates for discussion. Court members spoke out of turn, and Stone did little to control their debate. Instead, according to Justice Reed, he would join in the debate with alacrity, "delighted to take on all comers around the conference table." "Jackson," he would say, "that's damned nonsense." "Douglas, *you* know better than that."

In other words, Stone was still acting like an associate justice. Since he did not assume the Chief Justice's conference role as performed by Hughes, task leadership began to slip from his grasp. Eventually, Justice Black emerged as the leading contender for task leadership. Stone esteemed Black, but distrusted his unorthodox approach; thus no coalition occurred as in the Taft Court. Justices Douglas, Murphy, Rutledge, and, to a lesser degree, Reed acknowledged Black's leadership which he was able to reinforce by generally speaking before them in conference. Justices Roberts, Frankfurter, and Jackson, however, either looked to Stone for leadership or competed for it themselves.

The constant vying for task leadership in the Stone conference led to serious conflict, ruffled tempers, severe tension, and antagonism. A social leader was badly needed. Stone was well-liked by his associates and could have performed this function well, but he did not. He did not use his control over the conference process to cut off debates leading to irreconcilable conflict. He did not remain neutral when controversies arose so that he could later mediate them. As his biographer, Alpheus T. Mason, wrote: "He was totally unprepared to cope with the petty bickering and personal conflict in which his Court became engulfed." At times, when conference discussion became extremely heated, Justice Murphy suggested that further consideration of certain cases be postponed, but in this regard, Stone was a failure.

A consideration of the personalities of the task and social leaders on the Court from 1921 to 1946 is revealing. Of his friend, task leader Van Devanter, William D. Mitchell said: "Many thought him unusually austere, but he was not so with his friends. He was dignified and reserved." Of task leader Black, his former law clerk, John P. Frank, wrote: "Black has firm personal dignity and reserve.... [He] is a very, very tough man. When he is convinced, he is cool hard steel.... His temper is usually in close control, but he fights, and his words may occasionally have a terrible edge. He can be a rough man in an argument." On the other hand, social leader Taft was a warm, genial, responsive person who disliked conflict of any kind. Stone had a similar personality. He, too, according to Justice Jackson, "dreaded conflict." Hughes' personality contained elements conducive to both task and social leadership. He was "an intense man," said Justice Roberts; when he was engrossed in the work of the Court, "he had not time for lightness and pleasantry." Nonetheless, added Roberts, Hughes' relations with "his brethren were genial and cordial. He was considerate, sympathetic, and responsive."

The consequences of the various Court leadership configurations from 1921 to 1946 may be summarized as follows:

	TAFT (II)	HUGHES (I)	STONE (IV)
CONFLICT	Present but friendly.	Present but bridled by C.J.	Considerable; unbridled and at times unfriendly.
COHESION	Good; teamwork and compromise.	Fair; surface personal cordiality; less teamwork than in Taft Court.	Poor; least cohesion in 25-year period; personal feuds in the Court.
SATISFACTION	Considerable.	Mixed; Stone dissatisfied prior to 1938; Frankfurter, Roberts, and others highly satisfied.	Least in 25-year period; unrelieved tension and antagonism.

	TAFT (II)	HUGHES (I)	STONE (IV)
PRODUCTION	Fair; usually one four- to five-hour conference a week with some items carried over.	Good; usually one conference a week.	Poor; frequently more than one conference a week; sometimes three and even four.

Except in production, the Taft Court fared better than the Courts under his two successors. The consequences of leadership in the Stone Court were predictable from the hypotheses, but Hughes' "great man" leadership should have produced consequences more closely approximating those in the Taft Court. The difference in conflict, cohesion, and satisfaction in the two courts can be perhaps attributed to the fact that Taft was a better social leader than Hughes.

OPINION ASSIGNMENT

The Chief Justice's power to assign opinions is significant because his designation of the Court's spokesman may be instrumental in:

1. Determining the value of a decision as a precedent, for the grounds of a decision frequently depend upon the justice assigned the opinion.
2. Making a decision as acceptable as possible to the public.
3. Holding the Chief Justice's majority together when the conference vote is close.
4. Persuading dissenting associates to join in the Court's opinion.

The Chief Justice has maximal control over an opinion when he assigns it to himself; undoubtedly Chief Justices have retained many important cases for that reason. The Chief Justice's retention of "big cases" is generally accepted by his associates. In fact, they expect him to speak for the Court in those cases so that he may lend the prestige of his office to the Court's pronouncement.

When the Chief Justice does not speak for the Court, his influence lies primarily in his assignment of important cases to associates who generally agree with him. From 1925 to 1930, Taft designated his fellow conservatives, Sutherland and Butler, to speak for the Court in about half of the important constitutional cases[2] assigned to asso-

---

[2]"Important constitutional cases" were determined by examination of four recent leading works on the Constitution. If a case was discussed in any two of the works, it was considered an "important constitutional case."

ciate justices. From 1932 to 1937, Hughes, who agreed more with Roberts, Van Devanter, and Sutherland than the rest of his associates during this period, assigned 44 per cent of the important constitutional cases to Roberts and Sutherland. From 1943 to 1945, Stone assigned 55.5 per cent of those cases to Douglas and Frankfurter. During that period, only Reed agreed more with Stone than Frankfurter, but Douglas agreed with Stone less than any other justice except Black. Stone had high regard for Douglas' ability, and this may have been the Chief Justice's overriding consideration in making these assignments.

It is possible that the Chief Justice might seek to influence dissenting justices to join in the Court's opinion by adhering to one or both of the following assignment rules:

Rule 1: Assign the case to the justice whose views are the closest to the dissenters on the ground that his opinion would take a middle approach upon which both majority and minority could agree.

Rule 2: Where there are blocs on the Court and a bloc splits, assign the opinion to a majority member of the dissenters' block on the grounds that (a) he would take a middle approach upon which both majority and minority could agree and (b) the minority justices would be more likely to agree with him because of general mutuality of agreement.

There is some evidence that early in Taft's Chief Justiceship he followed Rule 1 occasionally and assigned himself cases in an effort to win over dissenters. An analysis of his assignments from 1925 to 1930, however, indicates that he apparently did not adhere to either of the rules with any consistency. The same is true for Stone's assignments from 1943 to 1945. In other words, Taft and Stone did not generally use their assignment power to influence their associates to unanimity. However, an analysis of Hughes' assignments from 1932 to 1937 indicates that he probably did. He appears to have followed Rule 1 when either the liberal or conservative blocs dissented intact. When the liberal bloc dissented, Roberts, who was then a center judge, was assigned 46 per cent of the opinions. The remaining 54 per cent were divided among the conservatives, apparently according to their degree of conservatism: Sutherland, 25 per cent; Butler, 18 per cent; McReynolds, 11 per cent. When the conservative bloc dissented, Hughes divided 63 per cent of those cases between himself and Roberts.

Hughes probably also followed Rule 2. When the left bloc split, Brandeis was assigned 22 per cent of the cases he could have received compared with his 10 per cent average for unanimous cases. When the right bloc split, Sutherland was assigned 16 per cent of the decisions he could have received compared with his 11 per cent average for unanimous cases. He received five of the six cases assigned the conservatives when their bloc split.

Of course, there are other considerations underlying opinion assignment by the Chief Justice, such as equality of distribution, ability, and expertise. It should be noted that opinion assignment may also be a function of social leadership.

UNITING THE COURT

One of the Chief Justice's most important roles is that of Court unifier. Seldom has a Chief Justice had a more definite conception of that role than Taft. His aim was unanimity, but he was willing to admit that at times dissents were justifiable and perhaps even a duty. Dissents were proper, he thought, in cases where a Court member strongly believed the majority erred in a matter involving important principle or where a dissent might serve some useful purpose, such as convincing Congress to pass certain legislation. But, in other cases, he believed a justice should be a good member of the team, silently acquiesce in the views of the majority, and not try to make a record for himself by dissenting.

Since Taft's conception of the function of the dissent was shared by most of his associates, his efforts toward unity were well received. Justices joining the Taft Court were indoctrinated in the "no dissent unless absolutely necessary" tradition, most of them learning it well. Justice Butler gave it classic expression on the back of one colleague's opinions in 1928:

> I voted to reverse. While this sustains your conclusion to affirm, I still think reversal would be better. But I shall in silence acquiesce. Dissents seldom aid in the right development or statement of the law. They often do harm. For myself I say: "lead us not into temptation."

Hughes easily assumed the role of Court unifier which Taft cut out for him, for his views as to unanimity and dissent were essentially the same as Taft's. Believing that some cases were not worthy of dissent, he would join in the majority's disposition of them, though he initially voted the other way. For example, in a 1939 case involving statutory construction, he wrote to an associate: "I choke a little at swallowing your analysis, still I do not think it would serve any useful purpose to expose my views."

Like Taft, Hughes mediated differences of opinion between contending factions, and in order to get a unanimous decision, he would try to find common ground upon which all could stand. He was willing to modify his own opinions to hold or increase his majority; and if this meant he had to put in some disconnected thoughts or sentences, in they went. In cases assigned to others, he would readily suggest the addition or subtraction of a paragraph in order to save a dissent or a concurring opinion.

When Stone was an associate justice, he prized the right to dissent and occasionally rankled under the "no dissent unless absolutely necessary" tradition of the Taft and Hughes Courts. As Chief Justice, he did not believe it appropriate for him to dissuade Court members from dissenting in individual cases by persuasion or otherwise. A Chief Justice, he thought, might admonish his associates generally to exercise restraint in the matter of dissents and seek to find common ground for decision, but beyond that he should not go. And Stone usually went no further. His activity or lack of it in this regard gave rise to new expectations on the part of his associates as to their role and the role of the Chief Justice regarding unanimity and dissent. In the early 1940's, a new tradition of freedom of individual expression displaced the tradition of the Taft and Hughes Courts. This explains in part the unprecedented number of dissents and separate opinions during Stone's Chief Justiceship.

Nonetheless, Stone recognized that unanimity was desirable in certain cases. He patiently negotiated a unanimous decision in the Nazi Saboteurs case.[3] It should be pointed out, however, that this case was decided early in his Chief Justiceship before the new tradition was firmly established. By 1946, when he sought unanimity in the case of General Yamashita,[4] the new tradition of freedom was so well established that Stone not only failed to unite his Court, but his dissenters, Murphy and Rutledge, apparently resented his attempt to do so.

The unprecedented number of dissents and concurrences during Stone's Chief Justiceship can be only partly attributed to the displacing of the old tradition of loyalty to the Court's opinion. A major source of difficulty appears to have been the free-and-easy expression of views in conference. Whether the justices were sure of their grounds or not, they spoke up and many times took positions from which they could not easily retreat; given the heated debate which sometimes occurred in the Stone conference, the commitment was not simply intellectual. What began in conference frequently ended with elaborate justification as concurring or dissenting opinions in the United States Reports. This, plus Stone's passiveness in seeking to attain unanimity, is probably the best explanation for what Pritchett characterized as "the multiplication of division" in the Stone Court.

CONCLUSION

Interpersonal influence in the Supreme Court is an important aspect of the judicial process which has been given little attention. Of course, the "why" of the Court's decisions cannot be explained solely or even predominantly in those terms. Yet interpersonal influence is

[3] *Ex parte Quirin* (1942).
[4] *In re Yamashita* (1946).

a variable worthy of consideration. Take, for example, the Court's about-face in the flag salute cases. With task leader Hughes presiding in 1940, not a single justice indicated in conference that he would dissent in the Gobitis[5] case. Subsequently, Stone registered a solo dissent, but such militant civil libertarians as Black, Douglas, and Murphy remained with Hughes. Only three years later, the Court reversed itself in the Barnette[6] case with Black, Douglas, and Murphy voting with Stone. One might seriously ask whether the presence of Hughes in the first case and not in the second had something to do with the switch. Much more work has to be done in this area, but it appears that in future analyses of the Court's work, task and social leadership will be useful concepts.

The importance of the Chief Justice's power to assign opinions is obvious. Equally if not more important is his role in unifying the Court. Taft's success in this regard greatly contributed to the Court's prestige, for unanimity reinforces the myth that the law is certain. In speaking of the Court in 1927, Hughes said that "no institution of our government stands higher in public confidence." As Court unifier, he sought to maintain that confidence after his appointment in 1930. That the Court's prestige is correlated with unanimity was demonstrated in Stone's Chief Justiceship: as dissent rose, the Court's prestige declined.

Thus the activity of the Chief Justice can be very significant in the judicial process. If he is the Court's task leader, he has great influence in the allocation of political values which are inevitably involved in many of the Court's decisions. More than any of his associates, his activity is apt to affect the Court's prestige; this is important, for ultimately the basis of the Court's power is its prestige.

13.5   *"What is significant about opinions for the Court . . . is that they are . . . a compromised, bargained rationalization for an institutional decision and policy."*

OPINIONS FOR THE COURT: THE NIXON CASE

David M. O'Brien

Opinions announcing the judgment of the Court are negotiated documents, built on compromises forged from the collective deliber-

---

[5]*Minersville School District v. Gobitis* (1940).

[6]*West Virginia v. Barnette* (1943).

Based on materials in the author's forthcoming book on the Supreme Court (New York: W. W. Norton & Company, 1986). Reprinted by permission. David M. O'Brien is Associate Professor of Political Science, University of Virginia.

ations and ideological divisions within the Court. This has always been true, though the extent of collective deliberations, negotiations and compromises varies throughout the Court's history and from case to case. For, "the opinion which is to be delivered as the opinion of the Court is," Chief Justice Marshall explained, "previously submitted to the consideration of all the judges; and, if any part of the reasoning be disapproved, it must be so modified as to receive the approbation of all, before it can be delivered as the opinion of all." Drafting the Court's opinion, as crisply put by Justice Holmes, requires that a "judge can dance the sword dance; that is he can justify an obvious result without stepping on either blade of opposing fallacies."

Opinions for the Court may either be unsigned *(per curiam)* or, in most and most important cases, signed by the justice who undertook principal responsibility for and delivered the opinion. In extraordinary cases, like *Cooper v. Aaron,* all of the justices may sign an opinion to emphasize their agreement on the decision and its rationalization. What is significant about opinions for the Court, then, is that they are not a statement of an individual justice's personal jurisprudence; instead a compromised, bargained rationalization for an institutional decision and policy. The Court's opinion is the principal vehicle for communicating its institutional decisions, but also for conveying the politically symbolic values of certainty, stability and impartiality in the law. If a would-be author reaches the limits of compromise, the opinion is usually given up for reassignment. In unusual circumstances, a justice delivering the Court's opinion may add a few words of his own in a separate opinion, as Justice Brennan once did. Traditionally, though, justices have sought compromise, if not pride of authorship, precisely because the Court's opinion must serve as an institutional justification for a collective decision.

The unanimous opinion on executive privilege in *United States v. Nixon* provides a good, if somewhat extreme, example of the justices working toward an institutional decision *and* opinion. Justice Rehnquist, a former assistant attorney general during the Nixon administration, disqualified himself from participating not because of the case at hand; rather due to "close professional association with three of the named defendants" in a related criminal prosecution against the U.S. Attorney General, John Mitchell. In conference on May 31, 1974, Justices Blackmun and White wanted to deny certiorari, yet all came to agree that the Court had jurisdiction, that the case did not raise a non-justiciable "political question," and that they should decide the case as promptly as possible. All eight justices furthermore agreed that President Nixon's claim of executive privilege could not withstand judicial scrutiny, but their differences in approach and deference to the President had to be reconciled during the opinion-writing process. With unanimity on the outcome, the shared understanding of the import of a ruling at a time when Congress was investigating the "cover-up" of the Watergate break-in, as well as the symbolism and tactical advantages of drafting the Court's opinion, the Chief Justice took the case for himself.

What followed in the weeks after conference, however, was truly a process of collective deliberation and drafting. It soon became clear that the Chief was too deferential to the President, who had appointed him for his "strict constructionism" and position on judicial self-restraint. An exchange of memoranda suggesting possible treatment of various sections of the opinion circulated from chamber to chamber. "My effort to accommodate everyone by sending out 'first drafts' is not working out." Chief Justice Burger at one point was driven to respond, "I do not contemplate sending out any more material until it is *ready.*" But individual justices had been working on drafts for the opinion. Even before the Court heard oral arguments Justice Powell had circulated a proposed outline and draft of some sections for the opinion, and the importance of the case compelled them to continue to arrive, if possible, at an acceptable opinion for all. Justice Blackmun worked on the statement of facts, for example, and Justice Douglas offered suggestions of issues of standing. Justices Powell and Stewart focused on sharpening the treatment of the merits of the claim of executive privilege and refining language to establish firmly, unequivocably that any such privilege is qualified and neither absolute nor unreviewable.

In the evenings and during the weekends, the justices met "in the interest of a cooperative effort" to find common ground. "After individually going over the circulation," Justice Stewart explained, "we collected our joint and several specific suggestions and met with the Chief Justice in order to convey these suggestions to him." When submitting another revision of a section to the Chief, Justice Powell wrote Justice Brennan, "I have tried to move fairly close to your original memo on this point, as I understand it and what you said at conference." In such circumstances, when there is an implicit agreement on the import of achieving a unanimous opinion for the Court, the spirit of cooperation prevails. At the same time, threats of a concurring or dissenting opinion carry more weight.

The Chief's draft was not merely deferential but weak in treating the authority and power of judicial review. According to Chief Justice Burger, judicial review and executive privilege are on the same constitutional footing—neither is specifically mentioned in the Constitution but both derive their legitimacy from historical practice and the operation of government. Justice Stewart offered some revisions, which Justice White then supported in a memorandum to the Chief stating that

> Because I am one of those who thinks that the Constitution on its face provides for judicial review; especially if construed in the light of what those who drafted it said at the time or later, I always wince when it is

inferred that the Court created the power or even when it is said that the "power of judicial review [was] first announced in *Marbury v. Madison.*" See page 4 of your draft. But perhaps this is only personal idiosyncrasy.

"Perhaps none of these matters is of earthshaking importance," he concluded, "but it is likely that I shall write separately if your draft becomes the opinion of the Court." What emerged as a unanimous opinion delivered by Chief Justice Burger was in fact the result of complex negotiations and compromises in which each justice played some role, made some substantial contribution, to the final published opinion.

13.6   *"Dissenting opinions function analogously to acts of civil disobedience. . . ."*

THE SPIRIT OF DISSENT

J. Louis Campbell III

Since the advent of collegial courts minority-view judges have used published dissents to register their objections and reservations to majority judgments. This has been particularly true of the U.S. Supreme Court, where in fact, the first reported opinion of a justice was a dissent, coming as the justices delivered their opinions *seriatim.* Chief Justice Marshall, though highly regarded for his dissent in *Ogden v. Saunders,* fostered a preference against dissents and secured the Court tradition of one majority opinion standing as the last word on the law.

Marshall's leadership and a rather homogeneous tribunal militated against dissents for some time. Then with Marshall's death and the ascendency of Chief Justice Taney (1836), the era of dissent began. The great dissenters in the Court's history have since included some of our most illustrious justices, such as Holmes, Brandeis, and Douglas.

Notwithstanding, there remains a bias in the legal community against dissent. There seems in particular to be some question about its efficacy. Prominent legal philosopher H. L. A. Hart has written that "A supreme tribunal has the last word in saying what the law is, and when it has said it, the statement that the Court was 'wrong' has no consequence within the system: no one's rights are thereby altered."

66 *Judicature* 306 (1983). Reprinted from *Judicature,* the journal of the American Judicature Society. J. Louis Campbell III is Assistant Professor of Speech Communication, Pennsylvania State University.

Nevertheless, statements that the Court was wrong, I propose, do have important consequences apart from direct and immediate alteration of rights and duties, and these consequences may be found within the system. Dissenting opinions function analogously to acts of civil disobedience in offering protest and securing systemic change. "Institutional disobedience" is a good term to characterize dissents and their authors. That is, in writing and publishing dissents, judges are protesting as authorities within institutional roles, analogous to civilians in non-institutional roles who physically enact their protest. Dissent can influence change in both the judicial system and the larger political milieu, and many legal professionals have provided corroborative evidence for this theory of dissent.

The roots of Civil Disobedience

First, what is "civil disobedience"? Civil disobedience is an appeal to controlling authorities and to the general public "to alter certain laws or policies that the minority takes to be incompatible with the fundamental principles of morality, principles to which it believes the majority is committed," according to Marshall Cohen. In self-governing communities its essence is:

> . . . propositional, stipulative, suggestive. Discovery, harangue, advocacy are its instruments of corrective persuasion of the beliefs and desires of others . . . Its central function is not directly to change the law . . . by forcing new policy . . . its function is to *locate* wrong, *inform* the public of such wrong, and *persuade* the electorate to reconsider.

Perception, identification, criticism, persuasion—these are the mechanisms of civil disobedience as a means of social change, influence, and coordination toward a point of view. It is not purposeless, reckless, or anarchistic. On the contrary, the civil disobedient has chosen to participate in democratically sanctioned processes for democratically praiseworthy ends.

A civilly disobedient person serves two such democratic ends: First, the reinforcement of the ideal of self-choice, the freedom to arrive at one's own perspective, "a fundamental condition of free government and of all moral judgment"; and second, persuasion of others to join the cause celebre. The cause of the disobedient is:

> concerned with improving the existing legal system. He envisions his role as therapeutic rather than destructive. He believes that the ideal of justice is being violated in some way in the existing laws . . . He therefore makes of himself a martyr, bearing witness to the truth, and hoping thereby to educate and enlighten and to move men of good will.

The civilly disobedient person appeals to the Democratic Ethos:

> [He is] a man who defies that law out of conscience or moral belief . . . If he acts out of conscience it is important to remember that he appeals to it as

well. . . . It is to protest the fact that the majority has violated these principles that the disobedient undertakes his disobedience.

The form of civil disobedience need not, and indeed some would argue that it must not, be violent. It is a "quiet, symbolic act . . . aimed at peaceful revision of attitude." Acts that run counter to the majority can be justified as civil disobedience only when they are acts of political speech, appeals, a form of persuasion as opposed to coercion.

Institutional Disobedience

It is this non-violent quality of civil disobedience that has allowed modern democracies to provide *institutional* means of protest to minorities in recognition of their prerogative to oppose majority viewpoints. This type of dissension can "observe, or follow, lines of political 'due process.'" In fact, contemporary scholars suggest that instead of perceiving civil disobedience as essentially contrary to the ideas of authority and obligation, "we might consider building into the very idea of authority and obligation in a democracy a conception of allowable civil disobedience." Dissenting opinions, indeed, may be seen in just this kind of light, as inherent, disparate, due process "acts" allowed to system authorities on behalf of minority viewpoints, or in other words, as institutional disobedience.

Dissents are protestual, propositional, stipulative, and suggestive in appealing to the authority of conscience, with the hope of a future remedy for a present wrong. They thus militate against monolithic solidarity in the judiciary, reflecting the innate nature and exigence of law in contemporary society as a mosaic. Dissents offer an avenue of representation for perceptions at variance with the dominant vision. They locate wrong in the majority, inform the audience of such wrong, and persuade the audience to reconsider. Thus in this respect dissents function analogously to civil disobedience in our society.

Further as the world changes so must the law. And the dissenting opinion is "one of the processes that aids that development as the law meets and solves new situations." The dissent initiates and presses change in the system, again analogous to civil disobedience. Without the judicial dissent, "boulders which are fused together with time-defying cement form a wall which could some day obstruct the passage of a needed road to the City of the Realized Hope of Man."

Though there may be various bases for dissent, many dissents are grounded in moral or ethical terms, just as is civil disobedience. These subsets of judicial opinion move beyond the purely legal world "by placing the imprimatur of respectable moral leadership upon controversial social or economic reforms." The appeal is to conscience. Justice Douglas wrote that dissents "may salvage for tomorrow the principle that was sacrificed or forgotten today. Their discussion and propagation of the great principles of our Charter may keep the democratic ideal alive in the days of regression, uncertainty, despair."

Contesting the imprimatur of infallibility for majority opinions, dissents are foresighted. Chief Justice Hughes pointed to the conscience inherent in minority opinions, regardless of specific rationale, when he wrote, "The dissent is an appeal to the brooding spirit of the law, to the intelligence of a future day. . . ." Advocacy is the instrument of this corrective persuasion. Dissents are evidence that the minority view has been heard—the wrong located, the public informed and persuaded. Though the minority view has not triumphed, it has been endowed with a quality of permanence for constant review by sympathetic advocates and system authorities.

The symbolic means of protest is an area of difference between civil and institutional disobedients. Civil disobedients use acts to oppose, such as sit-ins. Judges, on the other hand, use rhetoric. This difference does not make either civil or institutional disobedience inherently more effective. Rather, it reflects a strategic awareness of which symbols, acts or words, can best facilitate protest given the different contexts. . . .

13.7 *"In both conception and execution,* The Brethren *seems misguided and naive."*

EAVESDROPPING ON JUSTICE

Alpheus Thomas Mason

Runaway best-seller *The Brethren* paints an irreverent portrait of America's most hallowed institution, the United States Supreme Court. The image, bizarre in its highlights, is that of nine quarrelsome, backbiting, foulmouthed intellectual lightweights with little or no appreciation of the crucial role they play in our constitutional system. The major target, Chief Justice Warren Burger, is pictured as a devious, pompous, humorless "dummy" who used the Court's center chair to promote himself, usurp his colleagues' prerogatives, and befuddle constitutional issues.

By and large, reviewers—lawyers, political scientists, historians,

95 *Political Science Quarterly* 295 (1980). Reprinted by permission. Alpheus Thomas Mason is McCormick Professor of Jurisprudence Emeritus at Princeton University. He is the author of many books on the Supreme Court, including biographies of Justices Louis Dembitz Brandeis, Harlan Fiske Stone, and William Howard Taft.

and journalists—have been critical. Ironically, the book's shortcomings underscore its significance. Few dismiss it as unimportant.

"Its excellence is in its reporting," Jethro K. Lieberman concludes. "It is the most comprehensive inside story ever written of the most important court in the world. For this reason alone it is required reading."

In both conception and execution, *The Brethren* seems misguided and naive. Apparently, the authors had not realized that Supreme Court justices are sometimes limited in competence and character. They seem surprised to discover that the Court is politically oriented and, on occasion, considers whether a particular decision will be "good for the country." Why assume that justices are beyond reproach, never surrendering to the frailties that afflict other mortals? From John Jay to Warren Burger the Court has consisted largely of politicians, appointed by politicians, confirmed by politicians, and empowered to decide controversial public issues.

The authors, one of whom had struck gold in the Watergate exposé, *All the President's Men,* evidently believed that spilling the judiciary's carefully guarded secrets would be equally fruitful. In terms of dollars and cents, the book is a huge success. In what may be presumed to be a more elevated goal, it is a complete failure. A mountain of muckraking journalism labored and yielded nary a mouse of corruption or scandal, previously unknown. The smoking gun, if any, is yet to be discovered.

The Brethren is based largely on backstairs gossip and hearsay, sometimes once or twice removed. Interviews with scores of law clerks, evidently a major source, precluded citations. The most sensational disclosures, divining the justices' innermost feelings—"suspicious," "furious," "dumbfounded," "distressed," "paranoid," rarely in good humor—would be difficult to verify and document. Somehow the authors discovered that Justice Powell, finding no guidance in the Constitution for deciding the Abortion case, "felt he would just have to vote his 'gut.'"

A notable exception to freewheeling journalism is the informed and illuminating discussion of *United States v. Nixon,* the 1974 tapes case. Significantly, it draws heavily on a document—Justice Brennan's seventy-seven-page record, apparently obtained surreptitiously or stolen. Positive and negative inferences may be drawn. Heretofore, authors of books in this genre have been circumscribed by the legitimate use of authoritative records, by sensitivity to the proprieties and canons of good taste.

Ironically, a book designed to display the Court at its worst, sometimes reveals it at its best. In the Nixon tapes case, where judicial temperament was strained to the limit, the Burger Court reached a principled decision. Even the much-maligned chief justice proved capable of meeting certain requirements of statesmanship.

The Brethren is not the first book to explore the Court's inside history, even the carefully guarded conference room. Walter Murphy's *Elements of Judicial Strategy,* a major contribution, was doomed to attract a relatively small audience by the author's low-key objective: "this book is neither an effort to debunk or belittle, nor an effort to praise or defend. It is an attempt to understand." Murphy demonstrates how the black-robed jurists resort to all sorts of devices —bargaining, flattery, emotional appeal—in support of preferred goals. Far from faulting such procedures, he takes them for granted.

The authors seem to feel that negotiation and compromise, common in other political forums, are reprehensible in the councils of the judiciary. By featuring short tempers, emotional flare-ups, and crude language, Woodward and Armstrong overlook the benefits Edmund Burke attributed to give-and-take, rough-and-tumble debate, whatever the forum: "He that wrestles with us strengthens our nerves, and sharpens our skill. Our antagonist is our helper."

Differences, opposition, and dissent are essential to the discovery of that most elusive measure of value—the common interest. Tucked away in a footnote of Rousseau's *Social Contract* is this gem of wisdom: "If there were no different interests, the common interest would be barely felt, as it would encounter no obstacle: all would go of its own accord and politics would cease to be an art." The Constitution itself is "a bundle of compromises."

Crucial Supreme Court cases rarely pose the simple issue of right and wrong. Usually involved is a tragic conflict that troubled the ancient Greeks, a clash of rights. For its resolution we have no calculus, no slide rule.

The Constitution's Framers were not strangers to the hazards of constitutional interpretation. In *Federalist* No. 37, Madison recalls that "among the difficulties encountered by the convention" was "combining the requisite stability and energy in government, with the inviolable attention due to liberty and to the republican form." In attempting to achieve this delicate balance, two other difficulties were encountered: "imperfection in the organ of conception [and] inadequateness of the vehicle of ideas." Dramatizing the snares that plagued the Framers in 1787 and Supreme Court justices throughout our history, Madison observed: "When the Almighty himself condescends to address mankind in their own language, his meaning, luminous as it must be, is rendered dim and doubtful by the cloudy medium through which it is communicated."

Small wonder that judicial decisions are informed by briefs of counsel on both sides and in crucial cases, such as *Brown* and *Bakke,* by amicus curiae briefs. Supreme Court opinions—majority, concurring, and dissenting—often the product of exhaustive research and profound learning, are published, open to professional analysis and public scrutiny. It is difficult to be arbitrary when rulings are destined to be subjected to such a wide range of critical examination. Unlike members of Congress, Supreme Court justices are not surrounded by well-financed lobbyists, hired to advance special interests. *The Brethren* turned up only one case in which pressure was exerted on individual Supreme Court justices. The culprit was FDR's "Tommy the Cork," a veteran legislative lobbyist. Not surprisingly, Corcoran was unceremoniously ejected from the judicial chambers.

The Founding Fathers, realizing the delicacy of the Court's role, provided judges with life tenure, thus freeing them from the political pressures that naturally influence the conduct of elected officials. The Framers were not unaware, however, that even judges might on occasion be culpable. Consequently, they made them subject to impeachment.

In *Federalist* No. 78, Hamilton anticipated possible abuse of judicial power: "The Courts must declare the sense of the law; and if they should be disposed to exercise *will* instead of *judgement,* the consequence would equally be the substitution of their pleasure to that of the legislative body." *Federalist* No. 81 assures us that impeachment "alone is a complete security" for "deliberate usurpation on the authority of the legislative." In light of largely unchecked judicial aggrandizement, Hamilton's expectations border on the naive.

Speculating on how judges might be kept within the narrow bounds of objectivity, Hamilton wrote: "To avoid an arbitrary discretion in the courts, it is indispensable that they should be bound down by strict rule and precedents, which serve to define and point out their duty in every particular case which comes before them; . . . the records of those precedents must unavoidably swell to a very considerable bulk, and must demand long and laborious study to acquire a competent knowledge of them. Hence it is that there can be but few men in the society who will have sufficient skill in the laws to qualify them for the stations of judges."

On the whole, Hamilton's prediction has been borne out. Few would deny that, in terms of character and competence, Supreme Court justices are of higher caliber than run-of-the-mill legislators and presidents. The accumulated historical record—nearly 500 volumes of Supreme Court Reports—stands as a living testimonial to depth of reasoning, dedication, and learning. Certain justices—Brandeis is but one notable example—have taken special pains to make their opinions instructive. No other branch of our government has made a comparable contribution to college, university, and law school education.

Certain judicial procedures are properly screened from the public eye. The reason is the same one that prompted members of the Constitutional Convention to keep their deliberations secret. Privacy of the conference room, at least while the case is pending, is a must. Later on, however, the work of Supreme Court justices, no less than the deliberations of any other branch of government, aided by the research of responsible scholars, should be subjected to public scrutiny. There is a very special reason for such studies. Supreme Court justices alone are politically nonresponsible. Because they are not directly restrained by the voters, the justices should be restrained by the informed verdict of history.

Nor has the Court suffered from such investigations. Documented research to date demonstrates the accuracy of Charles Evans Hughes's observation: "In the conferences of the Justices of the Supreme Court of the United States, there is exhibited a candor, a comprehensiveness, a sincerity, and a complete devotion to their task that I am sure would be most gratifying to the entire people of the Union, could they know more intimately what actually takes place."

"I have no patience," Justice Stone commented, "with the complaint that criticism of judicial action involves any lack of respect for the courts. Where the courts deal, as ours do, with great public questions, the only protection against unwise decisions, and even judicial usurpation, is careful scrutiny of their action and fearless comment on it." Authoritative research seems to confirm Justice Brandeis's claim that "the reason the public thinks so much of the Justices of the Supreme Court is that they are almost the only people in Washington who do their own work."

Karl Llewellyn's caustic wit demolishes the purblind notion that judicial proceedings should be shrouded with an impenetrable veil of secrecy:

> It is well to remember that neither secrecy of the Court's deliberation nor later secrecy about what went on during that deliberation rests in the nature of things on any ordinance of God. The roots of each are either practical or accidental, and it is only either ignorance or tradition which makes us feel that we have here something untouchable, a semiholy arcanum. . . . Thus the storied sanctity of the conference room represents to me as pragmatic and nonmystic a phase of appellate judicial work as the handling of the docket.

It is ironical, indeed, that Chief Justice Burger, outspoken critic of *authorized* studies of the Court's internal workings, should have himself become the victim of hit-and-run vilification by the use of *unauthorized* sources. By keeping a tight lid on their papers or destroying them, the justices themselves invite books like *The Brethren.* Its authors may have been egged on by the fact that the Supreme Court has been less disposed than elected officials to "allow its decision-making to become public" and "has by and large escaped public scrutiny."

Although the time is past when any body of men, including Supreme Court justices, can be set on a pedestal and decorated with a halo, there is certain advantage in maintaining the public image of the Court as somehow above the fray. Human nature seems to crave an object of veneration; mystery and mysticism are its handmaidens. America, unlike England, has no king or queen on the throne. Yet, like any free society, we can profit from a symbolic element. English publicist Walter Bagehot reminds us that those elements in the governing process that "excite the most easy reverence are theatrical elements—that which is mystic in its claims; that which is occult in its mode of action; that which is brilliant to the eye." The Supreme Court occupies vis-à-vis the people a position not unlike that of the British crown. The difference—a big one—is that the Court wields power. With neither purse nor sword it can bring presidents, Congress, state legislatures, and governors to heel. . . .

Constitutional interpretation is an art. Judicial review enables the Constitution to respond to the changing needs and aspirations of a free society. It involves the discovery of meanings revealed only to judges. For them the Constitution is a sort of brooding omnipresence. To others, whether legislators or executives, its meaning is hidden, obscure—speculative. Thus a paradox lies at the core of the judicial process: while wearing the magical habiliments of *the* law, Supreme Court justices take sides on vital social and political issues. Justice Robert H. Jackson shattered esoteric constitutional orthodoxy —the Supreme Court considered as the mouthpiece of self-interpreting, self-enforcing law—when in a moment of rare judicial candor he confessed: "We are not final because we are infallible, but we are infallible only because we are final."

Needed is not confirmation of what we already know, that Supreme Court justices are fallible, motivated by passion and drives common to other mortals. Essential in a free society are responsible and documented studies of the give-and-take of the judicial process. We know far less of the forces and factors that shape judicial action than we do of the workings of Congress and the presidency. The intimacies of the conference room—for Felix Frankfurter "the workshop of the living Constitution"—have been largely denied to the historian and biographer. "Until we have penetrating studies of the influence of these men [Supreme Court justices]," Frankfurter challenged, "we shall not have an adequate history of the Supreme Court, and, therefore, of the United States. . . . Divisions on the Court and clarity of view and candor of expression to which they give rise, are especially productive of insight. . . . Much life may be found to stir beneath even the decorous surface of unanimous opinions."

After a certain lapse of time—opinions vary as to how long that should be—the Court and country would gain from informed and responsible disclosures of its internal proceedings. Not least among the advantages would be correction of the distorted picture of the

Court and its members in books such as Pearson and Allen's *Nine Old Men* and *The Brethren.*

The Supreme Court is our final arbiter, always open to change, the forum and focus of never-ending dialogue, not entirely oblivious to the election returns. *The Brethren,* a monstrous blemish on a highly revered institution, is not likely to inflict permanent injury. Even the most striking example of judicial capriciousness did no lasting harm. In 1937, within a period of only a few weeks without change of a single justice, the Court, under FDR's misguided Court-packing threat, sustained New Deal legislation heretofore ruled invalid. From the Court itself the public learned that judicial decisions are not babies delivered by constitutional storks.

The Brethren, a disservice to the Court in both its practical and ceremonial aspects, suffers most conspicuously from lack of grounding in history and sophisticated understanding of the judicial process. Warren Burger is not the first chief justice to take advantage of the Court's center chair. Marshall, Taft, and Hughes used the chief justiceship with an eye to their place in history and to promote cherished values. Contemporary attacks, though sometimes harsh, did not descend, however, to *The Brethren*'s level of character assassination.

When FDR's all-out attack on the "Nine Old Men" ran into a ground swell of public opposition, Professor Frankfurter tried to stiffen the president's resolve: "People have been taught to believe that when the Supreme Court speaks, it is not they who speak but the Constitution, whereas, of course, in so many vital cases, it is *they* (the justices) who speak, and *not* the Constitution. And I verily believe that that is what the country needs most to understand." Purblind realism thus encouraged the president to persist in a battle in which "black-robed reactionary justices won over the master liberal politician of our day." Determined to penetrate, by whatever means, the judiciary's inner sanctum, the authors of *The Brethren* were lured into the same trap.

Like FDR in 1937, Woodward and Armstrong seem not to realize that the Supreme Court is not only an instrument of government but also the symbol of an ideal—in the public eye, with certain justification, on the heights of Olympus. . . .

13.8

". . . the mistakes of fact and even of judgment are far outweighed by the book's potential for creating a more realistic appraisal of the Court's role. . . ."

A POLITICAL SCIENTIST WRITES IN DEFENSE OF *THE BRETHREN*

Albert P. Melone

The Brethren has been both widely read and generally criticized. The former is commendable; the latter should not go unchallenged. As is usually the case with ambitious and worthwhile projects, the authors, Bob Woodward and Scott Armstrong, have made some errors. Yet the mistakes of fact and even of judgment are far outweighed by the book's potential for creating a more realistic appraisal of the Court's role in the American political system.

The Brethren is indeed gossipy and reveals little-known and sometimes embarrassing information about the personal habits and tastes of the Supreme Court justices. Woodward and Armstrong have extended the current journalistic analysis of executive and legislative officials to the judiciary. But however distasteful the analysis might be, one must certainly admit that judges, like other political leaders, are mere mortals. Their quest for power, their egocentricity, and their petty behavior can hardly be considered unusual in contemporary society.

The authors have made technical errors in the book, even to the point of misstating the facts and the Court's holdings in a few opinions. These errors are undoubtedly disconcerting to serious students of constitutional law. However, the book is clearly intended as a journalistic account of judicial politics and not a legal treatise. The authors highlight not the law as such but rather the judicial decision-making process, and they thus focus on how justices negotiate for a given result and how and why they may trade a vote today for one tomorrow.

If the naive view prevailed that a justice always votes his conscience, then institutional paralysis would surely result. Indeed, no political system could long endure without compromise, logrolling, and the formation of alliances. What Woodward and Armstrong do is to show that the Supreme Court must also use these methods.

The use of information supplied by the law clerks is a common criticism of this book, and perhaps the authors do place too much

64 *Judicature* 140 (1980). Reprinted from *Judicature,* the journal of the American Judicature Society. Albert P. Melone is Professor of Political Science, Southern Illinois University, Carbondale.

reliance on the clerks' self-inflating words. In one instance, some 30 clerks have specifically repudiated a report attributed to them by the authors. The accuracy of the information thus is attacked not only because the critics allege that the sources are unreliable but also because the sources themselves—the clerks—claim that the authors have misrepresented the facts. Woodward and Armstrong have anticipated this criticism by stressing that they always verified the story with other sources, such as different clerks, unpublished written materials, other Court employees, and some of the justices themselves.

The Rules of the Game

While the issue of the validity of authors' information is often raised, what especially irritates critics is that the clerks violated the rules of the game. Clerks are not only well-situated institutionally to learn how the decision-making process works but also to participate in it to a limited extent. The clerks are bearers of gossip and informal messages between and among the chambers of the justices. Given the volume of their work, the justices cannot perform their duties without the aid of competent assistants.

In light of their privileged position, critics think the clerks who washed the Court's dirty linen in public violated the norms of polite society concerning discretion and silence. Apparently many clerks, and probably some of the justices, broke this gentlemen's code.

But the consequences of unbecoming conduct are not as ruinous as one might suppose. Although justices may suppress any open display of hostility, they can hardly suppress hostility, especially in a group as small as the Supreme Court. But so what? In the unlikely event that some justices are shocked and embarrassed by the revelations of the book, one need not conclude that the justices will now become even less cooperative than they were before. Surely mature and experienced public figures understand that sometimes lofty argument degenerates into personal animosity and ill-will. Moreover, they recognize the importance of putting such unprofessional feelings aside and getting on with the public's business. It is doubtful that the Court will now experience less internal cohesion.

The possible diminution of public respect for the Marble Palace is a greater source of concern. In light of the book's revelations about the Court's internal workings and personalities, might we surmise that public support for the judicial system will wane and that the rule of law will be questioned? It is true that myths are often functional for the maintenance of social and political systems. But democratic theory assumes that the political system functions best with a well-informed citizenry.

The Myth behind the Judiciary

The Brethren attacks the myth that judges only discover the law, they do not make it. Like most other myths, the judicial myth is useful for gaining the kind of unreasoning, blind obedience and respect that parents might expect from children. The book's popular appeal is its irreverent and clear message that the Supreme Court is a political institution. Defenders of mystery and magic may flinch at the suggestion, but the American public is fully capable of acquiring a realistic knowledge of the judicial system without growing alienated or, worse, rebellious in the process.

As lawyers know very well, the rules contained in constitutions, statutes, or case law are often vague, ambiguous, or otherwise not self-evident. Justices are compelled to give meaning to so-called principles such as "due process of law," "unreasonable restraint of trade," or "obscenity." Only by drawing upon those values and attitudes grounded in their life experiences and world views can they arrive at a decision in a given case or controversy.

This is not to say that the justices are without restraint, and that they can come to any decision they wish. They must provide justification in the form of written opinions. But the mere existence of written opinions does not make the reasoning any less teleological. *The Brethren* is replete with examples of how the justices first decided on the most desirable outcome for a case and then spent arduous hours justifying it and building the coalition necessary to win a majority vote.

The Court's 1972 abortion decision provides a graphic example of how justices sometimes agonize over the paucity of legal principles or rules to guide their decision-making behavior. Justice Harry Blackmun, working for many months on the abortion question during the Court's 1971 term, could not produce an acceptable draft opinion. When the Court's summer interlude began, Justice Blackmun began studying the question intensely at the world-famous Mayo Clinic in Rochester, Minnesota. Because he had served the clinic as counsel for many years, he was remarkably familiar with the field of medicine. Hence, it should come as no surprise that the medical distinction of the trimester pregnancy is now as much a part of Blackmun's opinion as the tenuous legal concept of the right to privacy.

Thus, the state's constitutional ability to interfere with a woman's right to an abortion today turns on a medically-based formula to protect the woman's health in the second trimester of pregnancy and to protect the potential life of the fetus after the beginning of the last trimester. Because the phrase "right to privacy" does not appear in the Constitution and because it is such a new judicial concept, one might say that in this case—as in many others before it—the Court could no longer sustain the idea of mechanical jurisprudence as a description of the judicial process: it simply lacks intellectual viability.

The Appearance of Impartiality

Though they must choose among competing sets of ideas, it does not necessarily follow that justices are guilty of personal favoritism, prejudice, or bias toward the particular litigants coming before the Court. The authors make this point by noting the many instances in which justices disqualified themselves from participation in cases where even the slightest hint of personal bias might be suspected.

For example, because his old law firm had once been the bond counsel for the Denver School Board, and even though he had been away from there for 13 years, Justice White felt compelled to disqualify himself from the Denver school desegregation case *(Keyes v. School District No. 1)*.

Likewise, because he had been chairman of the Richmond, Virginia School Board from 1952 to 1961, Justice Powell felt it necessary to disqualify himself in a 1972 case involving a federal district court-ordered city-suburb merger of the Richmond School district.

As an official of the Justice Department, William Rehnquist had drafted President Nixon's original position on executive privilege; he had also worked closely with both Haldeman and Ehrlichman and was a close personal friend of Kleindienst. Without offering any reason (and none was necessary under the circumstances), Justice Rehnquist disqualified himself from the Watergate tapes case involving the President. However, as Justice Rehnquist has suggested, in the attempt to appear more virtuous than Caesar's wife, a preoccupation with the appearance of impartiality may result in the justices failing to perform their fundamental responsibility to decide cases.

The authors provide a concrete example of how impartial members of the Court can be. Justices Black and Brennan responded quickly to overt lobbying on behalf of a client by Thomas B. Corcoran, a former official of the Roosevelt Administration and a well-known Washington lawyer. When Corcoran strolled into the justices' offices to argue for a rehearing petition that was pending before the Court, both Black and Brennan asked Corcoran to leave, and Brennan later disqualified himself from the case. Thus, Woodward and Armstrong demonstrate that the justices are impartial toward the litigants, though they are hardly neutral toward the great issues of the day. Impartiality to litigants reinforces the Court's reputation for fairness, but neutrality on issues denies the necessity of choice in the cases the Court encounters each term.

Interpersonal Relationships

The Brethren directs public attention to the interpersonal influences and small group dynamics of the Supreme Court. It alerts the general public to what students of the Court have long understood, namely, judicial policy-making is significantly affected by the quality of the personal and professional interactions among Court members. Identifying the quality of interactions is important for understanding the Court as a social and political organization.

Most commentators point to the unusual social and task leadership traits of John Marshall as a significant basis for the development of the Supreme Court as a powerful political institution. As a talented social leader, Marshall minimized interpersonal conflicts; as a task leader he improved the Court's internal procedures and offered forceful intellectual guidance.

Chief Justice Taft is best understood as a mediator of social conflict within the Court but not as a particularly gifted intellectual or task leader; he depended upon Associate Justice Van Devanter to guide the Court as a group through the intellectual nooks and crannies of the day's great constitutional labyrinth. Compared to Hughes, Chief Justice Stone is remembered as both an ineffective social and task leader.

In this book, critics interpret the authors' focus upon Warren Burger's leadership traits as an attempt to victimize him, suggesting that these liberal journalists are guilty of malicious intent or that they are using *ad hominen* arguments. But the authors present an engrossing and vivid account of Burger's personal, social, political and organizational style, and, though it seems unflattering, it furnishes the discerning reader with a sufficient number of cues to create sympathy for Burger because of the difficulty of the tasks confronting him.

As Woodward and Armstrong point out, Burger succeeded a very popular leader of the Court, Earl Warren, who was certainly the first among equals, personally charming to all and intellectually compatible with the liberal bloc. In contrast, Burger was appointed by a President who was almost universally despised by liberals on and off the Court. Since Burger interpreted his appointment as a conservative mandate to change the Court's liberal course, he could expect little else but trouble from the confirmed liberals such as Black, Douglas, Brennan, and Marshall.

Through his prerogatives as Chief Justice, Burger has manipulated his institutional power—especially assigning opinions—to achieve conservative goals. But ever since John Marshall did away with seriatim opinions and assigned most cases to himself, chief justices have recognized and employed, with varying degrees of acu-

men and success, their institutional authority to achieve desired political ends. Burger is no exception.

In addition to dealing with the disputatious liberals, Burger has
had to cope with independent-oriented moderates, such as Stewart
and White, and with his intellectually arrogant fellow conservative,
Rehnquist. It is little wonder that Burger welcomed as a relief the
nomination to the Court of Harry Blackmun, his childhood friend. All
in all, Woodward and Armstrong present sufficient information for
the objective reader to come to the fair conclusion that given the
times and cast of characters, it would be most difficult for any human
being to perform both task and social duties with great distinction.

Is *The Brethren* Useful?

Some critics condemn *The Brethren* as unscholarly because it lacks
the kind of documentation that directs scholars to law libraries or
computer centers. But the authors do not pretend to be constitutional lawyers, historians, or even political scientists. Their *modus
operandi* is that of investigative journalists, and their writing style is
designed to gain the attention of the reading public, not to cultivate
specialist audiences. In light of its obvious scholarly limitations, is *The
Brethren* useful to serious students of the judiciary? The answer is a
qualified yes.

Scholars should regard *The Brethren* as a searching mission (not
search and destroy) to uncover and construct testable propositions.
From a theoretical perspective, it is not particularly significant that
Justice X holds Justice Y in high or low esteem. What is significant is
that personal interactions have public consequences; in this respect,
The Brethren offers nothing new.

In at least one research area, however, the authors compel us to
consider seriously the organizational roles of the law clerks. Heretofore, scholars have tended to minimize the roles of the clerks; textbook writers might mention how clerks are chosen and the roles they
play in certiorari decisions, and an occasional author would recite the
long-standing debate whether clerks are influential in policy-making.
But generally, conventional wisdom maintains that the evidence is
inconclusive.

Woodward and Armstrong remind us, however, that the clerks
are at the center of a communication network. They facilitate the
work of the individual justices by carrying informal messages from
chamber to chamber, saving justices from intellectual embarrass-
ments and helping to create necessary coalitions for deciding cases.
The clerks may both facilitate and impair the decision-making process, however; they lubricate the system and yet contribute to its
friction. Because Woodward and Armstrong rely so heavily on information provided by the clerks, the clerks' influence may be over-

stated. Exaggeration or not, *The Brethren* should encourage renewed scholarly interest in the roles the clerks play.

Overall, *The Brethren* is a worthwhile venture. A mature and realistic understanding of our political institutions is what we need today. Over time, reason and not myth is the best support for the rule of law. Genuine respect and support for our most honorable political institution should be based upon knowledge, not mystery. With this relatively short book, two journalists have made a valuable contribution to public awareness.

PART FIVE

Courts and Constitutional Democracy

14
The Search for Standards

A republic, John Adams said, has "a government of laws, and not of men"; and the notion of "a rule of law," another phrase for the same phenomenon, has long been a cherished American ideal. Yet earlier chapters in this book have argued that judicial precedents, statutory language, and constitutional clauses are typically blurred at the edges. Where problems are most likely to arise—where public policies clash with putative rights—legal rules are usually at their most imprecise, leaving room for discretion, judicial as well as legislative and executive. Indeed, in many of the more important controversies that come before them, judges must either choose among a wide variety of potentially pertinent rules, modify one or more of those rules, or create new ones. Their only real alternatives to discretion are resignation or retirement.

This hard fact of judicial discretion raises all sorts of problems: what happens to the "rule of law" if judges not only can but must pick, choose, and occasionally create new principles? If federal judges—appointed for what amounts to life tenure and responsible to no electorate—help shape, make, and unmake public policy, what happens to democratic government? There are no easy answers to either of these questions; moreover, these are not mere academic inquiries designed for the seminar room rather than the real world of politics. On the contrary, they raise issues that touch the lives of judges, other public officials, and all citizens affected by particular public policies.

JUDICIAL POWER AND CONSTITUTIONAL DEMOCRACY

We attack the second question first. Earlier chapters have shown that, while judges have real power in American politics, they are hardly omnipotent. Judges of trial courts often share authority to decide cases with jurors; and those judges, along with jurists on intermediate appellate courts, are subject to review within the judicial system. The decisions of all appellate courts, including the United States Supreme Court, must be applied to future disputes by a judicial bureaucracy whose juristic views may or may not coincide with those of the highest oracles of the law. Chapter 7 detailed the web of potential political restraints spun around federal judges, such as impeachment, congressional control over jurisdiction, absence of judicial power to enforce decisions, increase in numbers of judges, and appointment of ideologically different men and women to the bench. State judges, most of whom are subject to some kind of public election for limited terms, face similar sets of limitations.

These checks and counterchecks allow popularly elected officials to curb judges whose decisions persistently and dramatically differ from politically prevalent standards about legal rules. More important, however, in analyzing the undemocratic nature of judicial power is, as Chapter 1 pointed out, the fact that American government is not a pure democracy nor is it merely a representative democracy. Rather, it is a constitutional democracy, blending sometimes smoothly, sometimes lumpily, the ideals of popular participation and equality with the concept of limited government and individual liberty. Formal institutions such as the electoral college, the Senate, and federalism, all—if one believes James Madison's boasts in *The Federalist* Nos. 10, 39, 51, and 63—have as one of their chief purposes making it difficult for a majority to exercise full governmental control. Judicial power, even judicial review, fits neatly into this pattern of institutions checking each other as they restrain the will of the majority of the people.

Thus tension between democracy and judicial power is not only inevitable; if one views the political system as a structure uniting democracy and constitutionalism, that tension is also functional in helping to fulfill one of the system's basic purposes: limiting power. The continued existence of vast judicial power and its occasional operation as a restraining force on popularly elected officials are a credit to the ingenuity of the framers and a monument to the continued distrust that succeeding generations have felt toward unrestricted majority rule. "One person, one vote" may be an ideal of American politics, but only when those equally weighted votes can have but a limited impact on public policy. This formal institutional context may do nothing to lessen tensions between judicial power and democratic government, but it does make clear that that tension is an integral part of the political system and not an aberration for which judges need apologize.

It is important to keep in mind that to accept judicial power as a legitimate counterweight to popular political sentiment does not imply that judges are free to ignore the limits on and traditions of the judicial process. Those traditions impose loose reins rather than iron fetters, but they do indicate restrictions on discretion. Without a doubt judges sometimes make law and policy, but they do so in ways different from and more limited than those of other public officials.

And yet however functional in systemic terms are the tensions between judicial power and democratic ideals, those tensions tug at judges' sleeves and whisper in their ears that they are strange creatures in a land of popular government. Judges are widely divergent in their political outlooks as Owen Roberts, Hugo Black, Felix Frankfurter, William O. Douglas, Harlan Fiske Stone, John Marshall Harlan II, and William H. Rehnquist have remarked about the restraining force of that tension. Here again, one might argue, it operates in a functional fashion, limiting judicial power even as it pits judicial power against legislative or executive power, reminding judges that they, too, are fallible and warning them of the perils of substituting their wisdom for that of elected officials. Indeed, one might contend that the judges' self-restraint restricts judicial power more effectively than any other check.

In sum, one can live more comfortably—which is not to say easily—with the tensions between judicial power and democracy if one understands the nature of the political system within which that tension exists. That understanding, however, need not, perhaps should not, move one to assume that judges—or legislators, or executive officials—will always operate only within their proper domains. Nor should one assume that judges, any more than legislators or administrators, will habitually be guided by wisdom informed by self-restraint, channeled by constitutional principles, and nurtured by cultural ideals. The possibility of error, deliberate as well as inadvertent, is as real in the judicial process as in any other phase of human coexistence.

THE RULE OF LAW

The "rule of law" presents even thornier problems. The "pure" form of a clear and precise set of rules, established and known beforehand, that officials will apply to each other and to private citizens, cannot exist in a society that is experiencing social and technological change. As long as such conditions shift, law must also change if it is to be an effective means of social control. Legislation can mandate changes for the future, and judicial *opinions* may also address problems yet to arise. But judicial *decisions* normally evaluate—approve, disapprove, or punish—actions begun and usually completed in the past. Thus, to some extent—and to losing litigants to a great extent—a judicial change in legal rules, especially a change based on judges' choices among competing values, smacks of a government of men and not of laws.

No one with even the remotest familiarity with American political history can deny that the personal values of judges have made immense differences in the triumph of particular principles of law. What made judges like John Marshall, Joseph Story, Joseph Bradley, Stephen Field, Samuel Miller, James Kent, Lemuel Shaw, Benjamin Cardozo, Roger Traynor, and Earl Warren important figures in legal development was not merely, as Holmes once implied, that they were "there." After all other people were "there," too; and still others, with very different ideas, were anxiously waiting to take their places. As this book has so often indicated, in the common law tradition judges frequently act as social engineers; they are not animate memory banks who regurgitate previous decisions, statutory provisions, and constitutional clauses at appropriate times. Judging is, at least at times, a creative process. Insofar as it is creative it involves subjective choices and generates uncertainty. Creativity, subjectivity, and uncertainty are incongruent with a "pure" notion of the rule of law. No legal system in a modern changing world could produce—for long—such a "pure" or rigid rule of law. Not even the elaborate codes in Civil Law countries have yet succeeded in stifling the operation of or the need for judicial discretion.

Indeed, one might well pause to wonder whether such a "pure" rule of law would be desirable. If all members of a society shared very much the same fundamental and secondary values, if all were content with the status quo, if technological advances threatened no established procedures and vested interests, then a pure rule of law might seem attractive. But to the extent that any one of those elements disappears or perceptibly changes, a pure rule of law loses some of its appeal.

THE QUEST FOR BASIC PRINCIPLES

To say that a pure rule of law is a chimerical and perhaps not even a desirable goal no more means that judges should willy-nilly indulge their personal values to fashion and refashion rules than does an understanding of constitutional democracy imply that judges should treat legislative or executive decisions contemptuously. There is a middle ground, a wide middle ground, between a judicial robot and an eccentric, freewheeling policy maker who happens to wear black robes. Judges' options may be restrained without thereby being preordained.

In a broad sense, a written constitution is an effort to establish a rule of law by marking some of the outer limits of public authority and by making some choices among fundamental values. No constitution—not those of Australia, Canada, India, Ireland, Italy, Japan, Switzerland, West Germany, or the United States—has made an exhaustive or even permanent listing of such limits and choices. But if a written constitution does not predetermine all judicial decisions, at least it channels most of them by narrowing the options from which judges may legitimately select. Moreover, as with the notion of democracy, many judges experience a serious, if not frightening, tension between their freedom to choose and create on the one hand, and their emotional commitment to the rule of law on the other. For one may reasonably suppose that, because they have been trained in a tradition that exalts the rule of law, judges' frequent paeans to this ideal represent far more than an empty ritual.

Another set of emotional phenomena reinforce this sort of pull: perhaps just simple pride, or a less conscious desire to be accepted and admired by those one considers as peers. There is no reason to suppose that judges want—and need—the approval of those whom they respect any less than does the rest of mankind. As educated and intelligent men and women, they realize that in the Western world judges who can ground their decisions in general jurisprudential principles—or create a general framework for jurisprudence—receive much more esteem than jurists who appear to decide cases on an ad hoc basis.

Similarly, on a strictly prudential level, most judges have also understood that to a great extent their power rests on their ability to persuade others—other judges, other public officials, leaders of interest groups, news analysts, writers of law review articles, and the legal profession generally as well as ordinary citizens—that their decisions are not mere exercises in willfulness but are rooted in tradition, supported by statutory and constitutional provisions, structured by informed intelligence, and guided by general principles of law. Thus professional socialization, psychic needs, and a desire to realize their full potential push judges to try to lock their decisions and opinions onto the tracks of durable, if not immutable, general principles—if possible, "objective standards." And by accepting such standards—even if they had a part in creating them—judges restrain their own power by narrowing their options.

OBJECTIVITY, RESTRAINT, AND STANDARDS

Although their intertwining courses are most visible in constitutional adjudication, quests for objectivity, restraint, and congruence with the notion of a rule of law are by no means confined to that field. In fact, one might cogently argue that these efforts so permeate all adjudication that analyzing them separately distorts their centrality to the judicial process. But we, like most readers, can analyze only one set of strands at a time, even while trying to keep in mind the essential unity of decision making.

American debates on objectivity, restraint, and the rule of law reach back at least to Jefferson's attack on John Marshall for allegedly turning the Constitution into "a thing of putty, to be moulded into any shape that he will." Marshall's response was a less than candid denial of judicial discretion, a tactic that judges have often repeated:

Judicial power, as contradistinguished from the power of the law, has no existence. Courts are the mere instruments of the law, and can will nothing. . . . Judicial power is never exercised for the purpose of giving effect to the will of the Judge; always for the purpose of giving effect to the will of the Legislature; or, in other words, to the will of the law.[1]

Within the Supreme Court the debate over objectivity and restraint crescendoed during the 1930s, when a conservative majority attempted to stop the New Deal. Since the early 1890s the Court had been writing the economic doctrines of laissez faire into the margins of the Constitution. The justices typically found state regulations of business to run afoul of the due process clause of the Fourteenth Amendment; and, less often, but still not infrequently, they invalidated congressional regulations as usurping state power guaranteed by the Tenth Amendment. The right to property, the Court held, included "freedom of contract," and governmental efforts to regulate wages and hours were "mere meddlesome interferences" with that right. As long as the economic system worked reasonably well, it was difficult to muster sufficient political power to overturn these decisions. Oliver Wendell Holmes was simply wrong, at least for his time, when he said that "the Fourteenth Amendment does not enact Mr. Herbert Spencer's Social Statics," for by judicial fiat the Fourteenth Amendment did precisely that. For many years Holmes's complaint to his brethren that there was "no limit but the sky" to what economic doctrines they could discover in the Constitution went unheeded. But the Great Depression smashed the prevailing economic system, bolstered the courage of dissenting judges, and enormously increased the political power of opponents outside the judiciary.

In the Court's deliberations over the constitutionality of the New Deal, Harlan Fiske Stone carried on Holmes's reasoning. Since the Fifth and Fourteenth Amendments did not absolutely forbid deprivations of life, liberty, or property but only prohibited such denials "without due process of law," the proper function of judges in economic matters was limited to ensuring that a reasonable man could conclude that a given regulation was, indeed, reasonable. Reasonableness of legislative action marked the full extent of the Constitution's economic doctrine. With the awesome might of Franklin D. Roosevelt and the twentieth century supporting Stone's dissents, the conservatives lost the battle.

The passing of the old guard signaled a shift in tone rather than an end to the search for general principles. In the *Carolene Products* case of 1938 (Reading 14.1) Stone laid the basis for a new jurisprudence.

[1] *Osborn v. Bank of the United States* (1824).

He distinguished between economic rights on the one hand and, on the other, rights pertaining to freedom of speech, press, and assembly, to equal protection of the laws, and those others encompassed in the Bill of Rights. The last three sets of rights, he thought, were entitled to greater judicial protection than were economic rights. More particularly, he would later claim, the rights touching on political communication deserved a "preferred position" that would overcome the usual presumption by judges that a challenged statute was constitutional.

Along similar lines, Justice Benjamin Cardozo had spoken in *Palko v. Connecticut* (1937) of a hierarchy of values in the Constitution. The Fourteenth Amendment, he said, had made binding on the states those provisions of the Bill of Rights (but only those provisions) that were "of the very essence of a scheme of ordered liberty." Most especially, Cardozo spoke of the guarantees of the First Amendment as "the matrix, the indispensable condition, of nearly every other form of freedom."

Soon the justices were in full argument over acceptance of Stone's and Cardozo's concepts. The opposing leaders through the 1940s and 1950s were Felix Frankfurter and Hugo L. Black. Frankfurter rejected Stone's ordering of values within the Constitution insofar as that ordering gave primacy to political communication and imposed a judicial obligation to exercise closer scrutiny over legislation that touched rights listed under the First Amendment.[2] A constitutional clause was a clause was a clause. On the other hand, Frankfurter accepted Cardozo's concept that, where the obligations of the states under the Fourteenth Amendment were concerned, some values in the Constitution were more essential to free government than others and were, therefore, protected against state as well as federal action. But even so, Frankfurter denied that within that special class of rights freedom of speech rated extraordinary judicial protection.

In contrast, Hugo Black endorsed and extended Stone's ideas. Black saw freedom of speech as "the heart of democratic government" and therefore entitled to special judicial protection as a preferred constitutional value. At the same time, Black categorically rejected Cardozo's formula for picking and choosing among provisions of the Bill of Rights that were binding on the states. He claimed that the Fourteenth Amendment had "incorporated" verbatim the first eight amendments but, curiously, not the Ninth—not, at least, if it had any substantive meaning. Black opposed any notion that judges should have discretion to impose on the country their own concepts of what rights were more or less constitutionally valued.

In short, Black would have required a literal reading of the Consti-

---

[2] For a time Frankfurter did accept Stone's ideas. Later, however, Frankfurter repented this acceptance, and he spent much of the next twenty years explaining how and why he disagreed. See Reading 14.2.

tution, with the concept of constitution confined to the document of 1787 and its amendments. The judicial task, Black said, quoting from a nineteenth-century decision, was "to place ourselves as nearly as possible in the condition of the men who framed that instrument," and that instrument was immutable, except by formal amendment.

In his search for objectivity and restraint, Frankfurter sought guidance from the development of the common law in England, America, and the Commonwealth nations. In addition, he prescribed deference mixed with rigorous psychological self-analysis. Humility, he wrote in *Haley v. Ohio* (1948) was a necessary judicial attribute:

> Humility in this context means an alert self-scrutiny so as to avoid infusing into the vagueness of a Constitutional command one's own merely private notions. Like other mortals, judges, though unaware, may be in the grip of prepossessions. The only way to relax such a grip, the only way to avoid finding in the Constitution the personal bias one has placed in it, is to explore the influences that have shaped one's unanalyzed views. . . .

Black's approach was simpler: to read the Constitution literally and to apply its provisions exactly as (Hugo Black saw them) written. When the Warren Court, in one of its most far-reaching decisions, discovered a "right to privacy" that judges were authorized to protect by "penumbras" of no less than five amendments to the Constitution, Black protested the expansion of judicial power by this "shocking doctrine." (Reading 14.3.)

In this jurisprudential debate scholars have been as active and as acerbic as judges. The most provocative scholarly contribution of recent decades was made by Herbert Wechsler in 1959 when he called for "neutral principles" to control constitutional decisions.[3] Wechsler fully accepted judicial review as part of the American system; but, he argued, judges

> are bound to function otherwise than as a naked power organ; they participate as courts of law. This calls for facing how determinations of this kind can be asserted to have any legal quality. The answer, I suggest, inheres primarily in that they are—or are obliged to be —entirely principled. A principled decision, in the sense I have in mind, is one that rests on reasons with respect to all the issues in the case, reasons that in their generality and their neutrality transcend any immediate result that is involved. When no sufficient reasons of this kind can be assigned for overturning value choices of the other branches of the Government or of a state, those choices must, of course, survive.

[3] "Toward Neutral Principles of Constitutional Law," 73 *Harvard Law Review* 1 (1959).

Perhaps because he questioned the principled nature, although not the actual holding, of the School Segregation decisions, or perhaps because the notion of neutral principles (a notion that Wechsler carefully avoided defining precisely) has such a romantic appeal to many scholars and such an aura of naïveté to others, Wechsler triggered a torrent of replies, rebuttals, and reiterations. The vagueness of the concept of neutral principles did nothing to slacken the pace of argument. In one of the first and most direct challenges both to neutral principles and a "pure" notion of the rule of law, Arthur S. Miller and Ronald F. Howell stated that "adherence to neutral principles, in the sense of principles that do not refer to value choices, is impossible in the constitutional adjudicatory process." Moreover, Miller and Howell attacked the basic idea of "neutral principles" as "the worst sort of anthropomorphism." Neutrality,

> if it means anything, can only refer to the thought processes of identifiable human beings. Principles cannot be neutral or biased or prejudiced or impersonal—obviously. The choices that are made by judges in constitutional cases always involve value consequences, thus making value choice unavoidable. The principles which judges employ in projecting their choices to the future, or in explaining them, must also refer to such value alternatives, if given empirical reference.[4]

Not content with attempting to rebut Wechsler, Miller and Howell urged that judges adopt a "purposive" or "teleological jurisprudence," one that would basically evaluate alternative decisions by their likely results, rather than primarily by their "coincidence with a set of allegedly consistent doctrinal principles or by an impossible reference to neutrality of principle." The Supreme Court, they asserted, "*is* a power organ which aids in the shaping of community values. . . . The only question is not whether it should be so but whether it should be *outwardly* so, and whether it should try to be so systematically, rather than in a helter skelter manner." The main function of the Court as they saw it "must be that of an active participant in government, assisting in furthering the democratic ideal. Acting at least in part as a national conscience, the Court should help articulate in broad principle the goals of American society."

In response to his numerous critics, Wechsler said that he had no intention of denying that constitutional provisions protected certain values. His point was that those values should

> be determined by a general analysis that gives no weight to accidents of application, finding a scope that is acceptable whatever

---

[4] "The Myth of Neutrality in Constitutional Adjudication," 27 *University of Chicago Law Review* 661 (1960).

interest, group, or person may assert the claim. So too, when there is conflict among values having constitutional protection . . . I argue that the principle of resolution must be neutral in a comparable sense. . . . Issues of federalism, for example, such as those involved in the interpretation of the commerce clause, may not be made to turn on the material interest that is affected, be it that of labor or of management, producers or consumers, or whatever other faction is at bar.[5]

Wechsler's formula finds heady support in the rhetoric of judicial opinions. All judges like to think themselves neutral between the parties to a case, though few would be so naïve as to claim neutrality between those values that they see the law as protecting and those they think it condemns. Yet, as we have previously noted, there is no doubt that judges, while speaking Wechsler's script, have often acted according to Miller and Howell's scenario. To seek is not always to find.

By the early 1970s Felix Frankfurter and John Marshall Harlan II, who had elegantly carried on and improved Frankfurter's reasoning, were dead, as was Hugo Black. The storm over Wechsler's neutral principles had also subsided. But on the new Court the lines of battle were reforming, with Justices William J. Brennan and William Rehnquist emerging as opposing intellectual leaders.

With four Nixon appointees, a conservative majority was presumptively in control of the Court. But during the decade no wholesale reversal of Warren Court holdings occurred. In fact, the declaration of a constitutional right to abortion, and the ban on capital punishment as then practiced, more than matched the activism of the Warren Court. The Burger Court of the 1970s also took advanced positions on sex discrimination and the rights of prisoners and inmates of mental institutions. It continued to uphold desegregation of public schools, and in *Bakke* approved the use of race, though not racial quotas, as a factor in academic admissions. Indeed, *United Steelworkers v. Weber* (1979) permitted a racial quota in private employment, and in *Fullilove v. Klutznick* (1981) Chief Justice Burger reasoned that a statute requiring 10 percent of federal funds granted for local public works projects to be used for services or supplies from minority group businesses did not, "on its face," violate the Constitution.

But the changed mood of the 1980s that elected and reelected Ronald Reagan was felt almost immediately on the Court, as Sandra Day O'Connor replaced moderate Potter Stewart. The landmarks of the Warren Court began to be undermined, distinguished, or reversed. The basic abortion decision, *Roe v. Wade,* survived, perhaps temporarily, by reason of Justice Powell's respect for stare decisis.[6] But the

[5] *Principles, Politics, and Fundamental Law* (Cambridge, Massachusetts: Harvard University Press, 1961), pp. xiii–xiv.

[6] *City of Akron v. Akron Center for Reproductive Health, Inc.* (1984).

wall of separation between church and state, which had been historically justified as protecting religion from state control, began instead
to be viewed as a symbol of hostility to religion and a limitation on
religious freedom.[7]

The Court also began to reconsider decisions that had confirmed
the constitutional rights of criminal defendants. Six justices held that
the exclusionary rule did not apply where search with an invalid warrant was undertaken by the police in "good faith."[8] The same six
justices also decided that if "public safety" would be promoted, state
officials could violate the *Miranda* rules.[9] Seven justices ruled that
evidence secured by illegal questioning could nevertheless be used
in court if its eventual discovery would have been "inevitable."[10]
Prisoners were stripped of Fourth Amendment rights.[11] (Reading
14.4.) The Court ceased to find technical objections to carrying out the
death penalty.[12] The early Burger Court denied executive privilege to
Richard Nixon, but the later Court permitted Ronald Reagan to deny
Americans the right to visit Cuba.[13]

As the conservative political and economic philosophy of President
Reagan makes itself felt in the selection of federal judges, the issues
may change from judicial activism in defense of constitutional rights to
judicial acquiescence in the dismantling of four decades of libertarian
doctrine. Those who had charged the Court with making law will hail its
return to a strict interpretation of the Constitution. The particular issues
generating conflict will change, but the American system will continue
to reverberate a basic tension between the demands of representative
democracy that the people shall govern and the demands of constitutionalism that all government, even by the people, shall be limited by
the fundamental rights of individual citizens. That tension is inherent in
the nature of a polity that takes itself seriously as a constitutional
democracy. (Readings 14.5, 14.6.)

SELECTED REFERENCES

Bickel, Alexander M. *The Least Dangerous Branch.* Indianapolis:
Bobbs-Merrill, 1962.

[7] *Lynch v. Donnelly* (1984). But see *Grand Rapids v. Ball* (1985), *Aguilar v. Felton*
(1985), *Wallace v. Jaffree* (1985), and *Thornton v. Caldor, Inc.* (1985).

[8] *United States v. Leon* (1984).

[9] *New York v. Quarles* (1984).

[10] *Nix v. Williams* (1984).

[11] *Hudson v. Palmer* (1984). Only in two criminal justice cases during the 1983–84 term
did the Court rule in favor of the defendant.

[12] *Pulley v. Harris* (1984); *Spaziano v. Florida* (1984); *Barefoot v. Estelle* (1983); *Zant
v. Stephens* (1983); *Barclay v. Florida* (1983).

[13] *Regan v. Wald* (1984).

————. *The Morality of Consent.* New Haven, Connecticut: Yale University Press, 1975.

————. *The Supreme Court and the Idea of Progress.* New York: Harper & Row, 1970.

Blasi, Vincent (ed.). *The Burger Court: The Counter-Revolution That Wasn't.* New Haven: Yale University Press, 1983.

Choper, Jesse H. *Judicial Review and the National Political Process.* Chicago: University of Chicago Press, 1980.

Dahl, Robert A. "Decision-Making in a Democracy: The Role of the Supreme Court as a National Policy-Maker," 6 *Journal of Public Law* 279 (1957).

Dorsen, Norman, and Joel Gara. "Free Speech, Property, and the Burger Court: Old Values, New Balances," in Philip B. Kurland et al. (eds.), *1982 Supreme Court Review* 195. Chicago: University of Chicago Press, 1983.

Dworkin, Ronald M. *Taking Rights Seriously.* Cambridge, Mass.: Harvard University Press, 1977.

Easterbrook, Frank H. "Ways of Criticizing the Court," 95 *Harvard Law Review* 802 (1982).

Ely, John Hart. *Democracy and Distrust: A Theory of Judicial Review.* Cambridge, Mass.: Harvard University Press, 1980.

Gunther, Gerald. "The Subtle Vices of the Passive Virtues—A Comment on Principle and Expediency in Judicial Review," 64 *Columbia Law Review* 1 (1964).

Hand, Learned. *The Bill of Rights.* Cambridge, Massachusetts: Harvard University Press, 1958.

Mason, Alpheus T. *The Supreme Court from Taft to Warren.* 3d ed. Baton Rouge: Louisiana State University Press, 1979.

Meiklejohn, Alexander. *Free Speech and Its Relation to Self-Government.* New York: Harper, 1948.

Miller, Arthur S., and Ronald F. Howell. "The Myth of Neutrality in Constitutional Adjudication," 27 *University of Chicago Law Review* 661 (1960).

Murphy, Walter F. *Elements of Judicial Strategy.* Chicago: University of Chicago Press, 1964. Chs. 3, 7.

Perry, Michael J. *The Constitution, the Courts, and Human Rights.* New Haven: Yale University Press, 1982.

Posner, Richard A. *Economic Analysis of Law.* Boston: Little, Brown, 1972.

————. *The Economics of Justice.* Cambridge, Mass.: Harvard University Press, 1981.

Pritchett, C. Herman. "Libertarian Motivations on the Vinson Court," 47 *American Political Science Review* 321 (1953).

Rehnquist, William H. "Observation: The Notion of a Living Constitution," 54 *Texas Law Review* 693 (1976).

Reich, Charles. "Mr. Justice Black and the Living Constitution," 76 *Harvard Law Review* 673 (1963).

Schwartz, Bernard. "The Constitution and Cost-Benefit Analysis," in Philip B. Kurland et al. (eds.), *1981 Supreme Court Review* 291. Chicago: University of Chicago Press, 1982.

————. *Super Chief: Earl Warren and His Supreme Court.* New York: New York University Press, 1982.

Thayer, James Bradley. "The Origin and Scope of the American Doctrine of Constitutional Law," 7 *Harvard Law Review* 129 (1893).

Wechsler, Herbert. *Principles, Politics, and Fundamental Law.* Cambridge, Massachusetts: Harvard University Press, 1961.

———. "Toward Neutral Principles of Constitutional Law," 73 *Harvard Law Review* 1 (1959).

Wright, J. Skelly. "Professor Bickel, the Scholarly Tradition, and the Supreme Court," 84 *Harvard Law Review* 769 (1971).

14.1   "*. . . more exacting judicial scrutiny . . .*"

UNITED STATES V. CAROLENE PRODUCTS COMPANY

304 U.S. 144, 58 S. Ct. 778, 82 L. Ed. 1234 (1938)

In this apparently unimportant case the Supreme Court by a six-to-one vote sustained the constitutionality of a federal statute prohibiting interstate commerce in "filled milk." In his opinion for the majority, however, Justice Stone laid the groundwork for his preferred freedoms doctrine. To the statement that even in the absence of specific legislative findings of fact "the existence of facts supporting the legislative judgment is to be presumed," Stone appended the following footnote. (Actually the second and third paragraphs of the footnote were drafted by Stone's clerk, Louis Lusky, and the first paragraph was added by Charles Evans Hughes.)

There may be narrower scope for operation of the presumption of constitutionality when legislation appears on its face to be within a specific prohibition of the Constitution, such as those of the first ten amendments, which are deemed equally specific when held to be embraced within the Fourteenth.

It is unnecessary to consider now whether legislation which restricts those political processes which can ordinarily be expected to bring about a repeal of undesirable legislation, is to be subjected to more exacting judicial scrutiny under the general prohibitions of the Fourteenth Amendment than are most other types of legislation. . . .

Nor need we inquire whether similar considerations enter into the review of statutes directed at particular religious, or national, or racial minorities; whether prejudice against discrete and insular minorities may be a special condition, which tends seriously to curtail the operation of those political processes ordinarily to be relied upon to protect minorities, and which may call for a correspondingly more searching judicial inquiry.*

*See Bruce A. Ackerman, "Beyond *Carolene Products,*" 98 *Harvard Law Review* 713 (1985).

14.2   *". . . we act in these matters not by authority of our competence but by force of our commissions."*

THE CONTROVERSY OVER THE COMPULSORY FLAG SALUTE

". . . I cannot resist the conviction that we ought to let the legislative judgment stand . . ."

Justice Frankfurter to Justice Stone

In 1940 the Supreme Court decided *Minersville School District v. Gobitis* (310 U.S. 586, 60 S. Ct. 1010, 84 L. Ed. 1375). A local Pennsylvania school board had required all children attending public schools to participate in a flag-salute ceremony. Such a salute ran counter to the religious beliefs of Jehovah's Witnesses, but by an eight-to-one vote the Supreme Court sustained the constitutionality of the flag-salute requirement. Before the decision was announced, Justice Frankfurter, author of the majority opinion, wrote a memorandum to Justice Stone, the sole dissenter.

May 27, 1940

Dear Stone:

Were No. 690 [*Minersville School District v. Gobitis*] an ordinary case I should let the opinion speak for itself. But that you should entertain doubts has naturally stirred me to an anxious re-examination of my own views, even though I can assure you that nothing has weighed as much on my conscience, since I have come on this Court, as has this case. . . . After all, the vulgar intrusion of law in the domain of conscience is for me a very sensitive area. For various reasons . . . a good part of my mature life has thrown whatever weight it has had against foolish and harsh manifestations of coercion and for the amplest expression of dissident views, however absurd or offensive these may have been to my own notions of rationality and decency. . . .

But no one has more clearly in his mind than you, that even when it comes to these ultimate civil liberties . . . we are not in the domain of absolutes. Here, also, we have an illustration of what the Greeks thousands of years ago recognized as a tragic issue, namely, the clash

This letter is reprinted in Alpheus T. Mason, *Security Through Freedom* (Ithaca, N.Y.: Cornell University Press, 1955), pp. 217–220. It is reprinted with the permission of the author, the publisher, and Mr. Justice Frankfurter.

of rights, not the clash of wrongs. For resolving such clash we have no calculus. But there is for me, and I know also for you, a great makeweight for dealing with this problem, namely, that we are not the primary resolvers of the clash. We are not exercising an independent judgment; we are sitting in judgment upon the judgment of the legislature. I am aware of the important distinction which you so skillfully adumbrated in your footnote 4 (particularly the second paragraph of it) in the *Carolene Products Co.* case. I agree with that distinction; I regard it as basic. . . .

What weighs with me strongly in this case is my anxiety that, while we lean in the direction of the libertarian aspect, we do not exercise our judicial power unduly, and as though we ourselves were legislators by holding too tight a rein on the organs of popular government. In other words, I want to avoid the mistake comparable to that made by those whom we criticized when dealing with the control of property. I hope I am aware of the different interests that are compendiously summarized by opposing "liberty" to "property." But . . . I cannot rid myself of the notion that it is not fantastic, although I think foolish and perhaps worse, for school authorities to believe . . . that to allow exemption to some of the children goes far towards disrupting the whole patriotic exercise. . . .

For time and circumstances are surely not irrelevant considerations in resolving the conflicts that we do have to resolve in this particular case. . . .

For my intention . . . was to use this opinion as a vehicle for preaching the true democratic faith of not relying on the Court for the impossible task of assuring a vigorous, mature, self-protecting and tolerant democracy by bringing the responsibility for a combination of firmness and toleration directly home where it belongs—to the people and their representatives themselves.

I have tried in this opinion really to act on what will, as a matter of history, be a lodestar for due regard between legislative and judicial powers, to wit, your dissent in the *Butler* case. . . . The duty of compulsion [in the flag-salute requirement] being as minimal as it is for an act, the normal legislative authorization of which certainly cannot be denied, and all channels of affirmative free expression being open to both children and parents, I cannot resist the conviction that we ought to let the legislative judgment stand and put the responsibility for its exercise where it belongs. . . .

Faithfully yours,
Felix Frankfurter

"The very purpose of a Bill of Rights was to withdraw certain subjects from the vicissitudes of political controversy. . . ."

West Virginia State Board of Education v. Barnette

319 U.S. 624, 63 S. Ct. 1178, 87 L. Ed. 1628 (1943)

This case involved the constitutionality of a West Virginia statute similar to that in *Minersville*. Two important changes had taken place in the Court in the meantime, however. Justices Black, Douglas, and Murphy, in a separate opinion in another case concerning Jehovah's Witnesses, had confessed that they had erred in the first flag-salute case. Moreover, two members of the *Gobitis* majority, McReynolds and Hughes, had retired, and the two new members of the Court, Jackson and Rutledge, were thought to be hostile to the compulsory flag salute. Jehovah's Witnesses brought a suit to enjoin enforcement of the flag-salute regulation. Noting the changes on the Supreme Court, a special three-judge federal district court granted the injunction. State officials appealed.

MR. JUSTICE JACKSON delivered the opinion of the Court. . . .

The freedom asserted by these appellees does not bring them into collision with rights asserted by any other individual. It is such conflicts which most frequently require intervention of the State to determine where the rights of one end and those of another begin. But the refusal of these persons to participate in the ceremony does not interfere with or deny rights of others to do so. Nor is there any question in this case that their behavior is peaceable and orderly. The sole conflict is between authority and rights of the individual. The State asserts power to condition access to public education on making a prescribed sign and profession and at the same time to coerce attendance by punishing both parent and child. The latter stand on a right of self-determination in matters that touch individual opinion and personal attitude. . . .

There is no doubt that, in connection with the pledges, the flag salute is a form of utterance. Symbolism is a primitive but effective way of communicating ideas. The use of an emblem flag to symbolize some system, idea, institution, or personality, is a short cut from mind to mind. Causes and nations, political parties, lodges and ecclesiastical groups seek to knit the loyalty of their followings to a flag or banner, a color or design. The State announces rank, function, and authority through crowns and maces, uniforms and black robes; the church speaks through the Cross, the Crucifix, the altar and shrine, and clerical raiment. Symbols of State often convey political ideas just as religious symbols come to convey theological ones. Associated with many of these symbols are appropriate gestures of acceptance or respect: a salute, a bowed or bared head, a bended knee. A person gets from a symbol the meaning he puts into it, and what is one man's comfort and inspiration is another's jest and scorn. . . .

It is also to be noted that the compulsory flag salute and pledge requires affirmation of a belief and an attitude of mind. . . . It is now a commonplace that censorship or suppression of expression of opinion is tolerated by our Constitution only when the expression presents a clear and present danger of action of a kind the State is empowered to prevent and punish. It would seem that involuntary affirmation could be commanded only on even more immediate and urgent grounds than silence. But here the power of compulsion is invoked without any allegation that remaining passive during a flag salute ritual creates a clear and present danger that would justify an effort even to muffle expression. To sustain the compulsory flag salute we are required to say that a Bill of Rights which guards the individual's right to speak his own mind, left it open to public authorities to compel him to utter what is not in his mind. . . .

The *Gobitis* opinion reasoned that this is a field "where courts possess no marked and certainly no controlling competence," that it is committed to the legislatures as well as the courts to guard cherished liberties and that it is constitutionally appropriate to "fight out the wise use of legislative authority in the forum of public opinion and before legislative assemblies rather than to transfer such a contest to the judicial arena," since all the "effective means of inducing political changes are left free." . . .

The very purpose of a Bill of Rights was to withdraw certain subjects from the vicissitudes of political controversy, to place them beyond the reach of majorities and officials and to establish them as legal principles to be applied by the courts. One's right to life, liberty, and property, to free speech, a free press, freedom of worship and assembly, and other fundamental rights may not be submitted to vote; they depend on the outcome of no elections. . . .

Nor does our duty to apply the Bill of Rights to assertions of official authority depend upon our possession of marked competence in the field where the invasion of rights occurs. True, the task of translating the majestic generalities of the Bill of Rights, conceived as part of the pattern of liberal government in the eighteenth century, into concrete restraints on officials dealing with the problems of the twentieth century, is one to disturb self-confidence. . . . But we act in these matters not by authority of our competence but by force of our commissions. We cannot, because of modest estimates of our competence in such specialties as public education, withhold the judgment that history authenticates as the function of this Court when liberty is infringed. . . .

If there is any fixed star in our constitutional constellation, it is that no official, high or petty, can prescribe what shall be orthodox in politics, nationalism, religion, or other matters of opinion or force citizens to confess by word or act their faith therein. . . .

The decision of this Court in *Minersville School District v. Gobitis* and the holdings of those few *per curiam* decisions which preceded and foreshadowed it are overruled, and the judgment enjoining enforcement of the West Virginia Regulation is

Affirmed.

MR. JUSTICE ROBERTS and **MR. JUSTICE REED** adhere to the views expressed by the Court in *Minersville School District v. Gobitis* . . . and are of the opinion that the judgment below should be reversed.

MR. JUSTICE BLACK and **MR. JUSTICE DOUGLAS**, concurring. . . .

MR. JUSTICE FRANKFURTER, dissenting.

One who belongs to the most vilified and persecuted minority in history is not likely to be insensible to the freedoms guaranteed by our Constitution. Were my purely personal attitude relevant I should wholeheartedly associate myself with the general libertarian views in the Court's opinion, representing as they do the thought and action of a lifetime. But as judges we are neither Jew nor Gentile, neither Catholic nor agnostic. We owe equal attachment to the Constitution and are equally bound by our judicial obligations whether we derive our citizenship from the earliest or the latest immigrants to these shores. As a member of this Court I am not justified in writing my private notions of policy into the Constitution, no matter how deeply I may cherish them or how mischievous I may deem their disregard. The duty of a judge who must decide which of two claims before the Court shall prevail, that of a State to enact and enforce laws within its general competence or that of an individual to refuse obedience because of the demands of his conscience, is not that of the ordinary person. It can never be emphasized too much that one's own opinion about the wisdom or evil of a law should be excluded altogether when one is doing one's duty on the bench. The only opinion of our own even looking in that direction that is material is our opinion whether legislators could in reason have enacted such a law. In the light of all the circumstances, including the history of this question in this Court, it would require more daring than I possess to deny that reasonable legislators could have taken the action which is before us for review. . . .

The admonition that judicial self-restraint alone limits arbitrary exercise of our authority is relevant every time we are asked to nullify legislation. The Constitution does not give us greater veto power when dealing with one phase of "liberty" than with another, or when dealing with grade school regulations than with college regulations that offend conscience. . . . In neither situation is our function comparable to that of a legislature or are we free to act as though we were a super-legislature. Judicial self-restraint is equally necessary whenever an exercise of political or legislative power is challenged. There is no warrant in the constitutional basis of this Court's authority for attributing different roles to it depending upon the nature of the challenge to the legislation. Our power does not vary according to the particular provision of the Bill of Rights which is invoked. The right not to have property taken without just compensation has, so far as the scope of judicial power is concerned, the same constitutional dignity as the right to be protected against unreasonable searches and seizures, and the latter has no less claim than freedom of the press or freedom of speech or religious freedom. In no instance is this Court the primary protector of the particular liberty that is invoked. . . .

When Mr. Justice Holmes, speaking for this Court, wrote that "it must be remembered that legislatures are ultimate guardians of the liberties and welfare of the people in quite as great a degree as the courts" . . . he went to the very essence of our constitutional system and the democratic conception of our society. He did not mean that for only some phases of civil government this Court was not to supplant legislatures and sit in judgment upon the right or wrong of a challenged measure. He was stating the comprehensive judicial duty and role of this Court in our constitutional scheme whenever legislation is sought to be nullified on any ground, namely, that responsibility for legislation lies with legislatures, answerable as they are directly to the people, and this Court's only and very narrow function is to determine whether within the broad grant of authority vested in legislatures they have exercised a judgment for which reasonable justification can be offered. . . .

The reason why from the beginning even the narrow judicial authority to nullify legislation has been viewed with a jealous eye is that it serves to prevent the full play of the democratic process. The fact that it may be an undemocratic aspect of our scheme of government does not call for its rejection or its disuse. But it is the best of reasons, as this Court has frequently recognized, for the greatest caution in its use. . . .

Under our constitutional system the legislature is charged solely with civil concerns of society. If the avowed or intrinsic legislative purpose is either to promote or to discourage some religious community or creed, it is clearly within the constitutional restrictions imposed on legislatures and cannot stand. But it by no means follows that legislative power is wanting whenever a general non-discriminatory civil regulation in fact touches conscientious scruples or religious beliefs of an individual or a group. Regard for such scruples or beliefs undoubtedly presents one of the most reasonable claims for the exertion of legislative accommodation. . . . But the real question is, who is to make such accommodations, the courts or the legislature? . . .

The subjection of dissidents to the general requirement of saluting the flag, as a measure conducive to the training of children in good citizenship, is very far from being the first instance of exacting obedience to general laws that have offended deep religious scruples. Compulsory vaccination, food inspection regulations, the obligation to bear arms, testimonial duties, compulsory medical treatment— these are but illustrations of conduct that has often been compelled in the enforcement of legislation of general applicability even though the religious consciences of particular individuals rebelled at the exaction.

Law is concerned with external behavior and not with the inner life of man. It rests in large measure upon compulsion. Socrates lives in history partly because he gave his life for the conviction that duty of obedience to secular law does not presuppose consent to its enactment or belief in its virtue. The consent upon which free government rests is the consent that comes from sharing in the process of making and unmaking laws. The state is not shut out from a domain because the individual conscience may deny the state's claim. The individual conscience may profess what faith it chooses. It may affirm and promote that faith—in the language of the Constitution, it may "exercise" it freely—but it cannot thereby restrict community action through political organs in matters of community concern, so long as the action is not asserted in a discriminatory way either openly or by stealth. One may have the right to practice one's religion and at the same time owe the duty of formal obedience to laws that run counter to one's beliefs. . . .

One's conception of the Constitution cannot be severed from one's conception of a judge's function in applying it. The Court has no reason for existence if it merely reflects the pressures of the day. Our system is built on the faith that men set apart for this special function, freed from the influences of immediacy and from the deflections of worldly ambition, will become able to take a view of longer range than the period of responsibility entrusted to Congress and legislatures. We are dealing with matters as to which legislators and voters have conflicting views. Are we as judges to impose our strong convictions on where wisdom lies? . . .

Of course patriotism can not be enforced by the flag salute. But neither can the liberal spirit be enforced by judicial invalidation of illiberal legislation. Our constant preoccupation with the constitutionality of legislation rather than with its wisdom tends to preoccupation of the American mind with a false value. The tendency of focussing attention on constitutionality is to make constitutionality synonymous with wisdom, to regard a law as all right if it is constitutional. Such an attitude is a great enemy of liberalism. Particularly in legislation affecting freedom of thought and freedom of speech much which should offend a free-spirited society is constitutional. Reliance for the most precious interests of civilization, therefore, must be found outside of their vindication in courts of law. Only a persistent positive translation of the faith of a free society into the convictions and habits and actions of a community is the ultimate reliance against unabated temptations to fetter the human spirit.

> "... specific guarantees in the Bill of Rights have penumbras, formed by emanations from those guarantees that help give them life and substance."—Justice Douglas

> "... I get nowhere in this case by talk about a constitutional 'right of privacy' as an emanation from one or more constitutional provisions."—Justice Black

14.3

GRISWOLD V. CONNECTICUT

381 U.S. 479, 85 S. Ct. 1678, 14 L. Ed. 2d 510 (1965)

The Executive Director of the Planned Parenthood League of Connecticut and a physician teaching at the Yale Medical School were convicted in a state court for giving birth control information to a married couple. Connecticut law made the use of contraceptive devices as well as counseling, aiding, or abetting such use a criminal offense. State courts sustained the conviction, and the defendants appealed to the United States Supreme Court. (For earlier efforts to test this statute, see *Tileston v. Ullman* and *Poe v. Ullman*, Reading 5.7.)

MR. JUSTICE DOUGLAS delivered the opinion of the Court. . . .

Coming to the merits, we are met with a wide range of questions that implicate the Due Process Clause of the Fourteenth Amendment. . . . We do not sit as a super-legislature to determine the wisdom, need, and propriety of laws that touch economic problems, business affairs, or social conditions. This law, however, operates directly on an intimate relation of husband and wife and their physician's role in one aspect of that relation.

The association of people is not mentioned in the Constitution nor in the Bill of Rights. The right to educate a child in a school of the parents' choice—whether public or private or parochial—is also not mentioned. Nor is the right to study any particular subject or any foreign language. Yet the First Amendment has been construed to include certain of those rights.

By *Pierce v. Society of Sisters* [1925], the right to educate one's children as one chooses is made applicable to the States by the force of the First and Fourteenth Amendments. By *Meyer v. Nebraska* [1923], the same dignity is given the right to study the German language in a private school. In other words, the State may not, consistently with the spirit of the First Amendment, contract the spectrum of available knowledge. The right of freedom of speech and press includes not only the right to utter or to print, but the right to distribute, the right to receive, the right to read (*Martin v. Struthers* [1943]) and freedom of inquiry, freedom of thought, and freedom to teach (see *Wieman v. Updegraff* [1952])—indeed the freedom of the entire university community. *Sweezy v. New Hampshire* [1957]. Without those peripheral rights the specific rights would be less secure. And so we reaffirm the principle of the *Pierce* and the *Meyer* cases.

In *NAACP v. Alabama* [1958], we protected the "freedom to associate and privacy in one's associations," noting that freedom of association was a peripheral First Amendment right. Disclosure of membership lists of a constitutionally valid association, we held, was invalid "as entailing the likelihood of a substantial restraint upon the exercise by petitioner's members of their right to freedom of association." . . . In like context, we have protected forms of "association" that are not political in the customary sense but pertain to the social, legal, and economic benefit of the members. *NAACP v. Button* [1963]. In *Schware v. Board of Bar Examiners* [1957], we held it not permissible to bar a lawyer from practice, because he had once been a member of the Communist Party. The man's "association with that Party" was not shown to be "anything more than a political faith in a political party" . . . and was not action of a kind proving bad moral character. . . .

The foregoing cases suggest that specific guarantees in the Bill of Rights have penumbras, formed by emanations from those guarantees that help give them life and substance. . . . Various guarantees create zones of privacy. The right of association contained in the penumbra of the First Amendment is one. . . . The Third Amendment in its prohibition against the quartering of soldiers "in any house" in time of peace without the consent of the owner is another facet of that privacy. The Fourth Amendment explicitly affirms the "right of the people to be secure in their persons, houses, papers, and effects, against unreasonable searches and seizures." The Fifth Amendment in its Self-Incrimination Clause enables the citizen to create a zone of privacy which government may not force him to surrender to his detriment. The Ninth Amendment provides: "The enumeration in the Constitution, of certain rights, shall not be construed to deny or disparage others retained by the people."

The Fourth and Fifth Amendments were described in *Boyd v. United States* [1886] as protection against all governmental invasions "of the sanctity of a man's home and the privacies of life." We recently referred in *Mapp v. Ohio* [1961] to the Fourth Amendment as creating a "right to privacy, no less important than any other right carefully and particularly reserved to the people." See Beaney, The Constitutional Right to Privacy, 1962 Sup. Ct. Rev. 212; Griswold, The Right to be Let Alone, 55 Nw. UL Rev. 216 (1960). . . .

The present case, then, concerns a relationship lying within the zone of privacy created by several fundamental constitutional guarantees. And it concerns a law which, in forbidding the *use* of contraceptives rather than regulating their manufacture or sale, seeks to achieve its goals by means having a maximum destructive impact upon that relationship. Such a law cannot stand in light of the familiar principle, so often applied by this Court, that a "governmental purpose to control or prevent activities constitutionally subject to state regulation may not be achieved by means which sweep unnecessarily broadly and thereby invade the area of protected freedoms." *NAACP v. Alabama.* Would we allow the police to search the sacred precincts of marital bedrooms for telltale signs of the use of contraceptives? The very idea is repulsive to the notions of privacy surrounding the marriage relationship.

We deal with a right of privacy older than the Bill of Rights—older than our political parties, older than our school system. Marriage is a coming together for better or for worse, hopefully enduring, and intimate to the degree of being sacred. It is an association that promotes a way of life, not causes; a harmony in living, not political faiths; a bilateral loyalty, not commercial or social projects. Yet it is an association for as noble a purpose as any involved in our prior decisions.

Reversed.

MR. JUSTICE GOLDBERG, whom the CHIEF JUSTICE [WARREN] and MR. JUSTICE BRENNAN join, concurring.

. . . Although I have not accepted the view that "due process" as used in the Fourteenth Amendment incorporates all of the first eight Amendments . . . I do agree that the concept of liberty protects those personal rights that are fundamental, and is not confined to the specific terms of the Bill of Rights. My conclusion that the concept of liberty . . . embraces the right of marital privacy though that right is not mentioned explicitly in the Constitution[1] is supported both by numerous decisions of this Court, referred to in the Court's opinion, and by the language and history of the Ninth Amendment. In reach-

[1]My Brother Stewart dissents on the ground that he "can find no . . . general right of privacy in the Bill of Rights, in any other part of the Constitution, or in any case ever before decided by this Court." He would require a more explicit guarantee than the one which the court derives from several constitutional amendments. This Court, however, has never held that the Bill of Rights or the Fourteenth Amendment protects only those rights that the Constitution specifically mentions by name. To the contrary, this Court, for example, in *Bolling v. Sharpe* [1954], while recognizing that the Fifth Amendment does not contain the "explicit safeguard" of an equal protection clause, nevertheless derived an equal protection principle from that Amendment's Due Process Clause. And in *Schware v. Board of Bar Examiners*, the Court held that the Fourteenth Amendment protects from arbitrary state action the right to pursue an occupation, such as the practice of law.

ing the conclusion that the right of marital privacy is protected, as being within the protected penumbra of specific guarantees of the Bill of Rights, the Court refers to the Ninth Amendment. . . . I add these words to emphasize the relevance of that Amendment to the Court's holding. . . .

The Ninth Amendment reads, "The enumeration in the Constitution, of certain rights, shall not be construed to deny or disparage others retained by the people." . . .

In presenting the proposed Amendment, Madison said:

> It has been objected also against a bill of rights, that, by enumerating particular exceptions to the grant of power, it would disparage those rights which were not placed in that enumeration; and it might follow by implication, that those rights which were not singled out, were intended to be assigned into the hands of the General Government, and were consequently insecure. This is one of the most plausible arguments I have ever heard urged against the admission of a bill of rights into this system; but, I conceive, that it may be guarded against. I have attempted it, as gentlemen may see by turning to the last clause of the fourth resolution [the Ninth Amendment]. . . .

While this Court has had little occasion to interpret the Ninth Amendment, "[i]t cannot be presumed that any clause in the constitution is intended to be without effect." *Marbury v. Madison*. . . . The Ninth Amendment to the Constitution may be regarded by some as a recent discovery and may be forgotten by others, but since 1791 it has been a basic part of the Constitution which we are sworn to uphold. To hold that a right so basic and fundamental and so deep-rooted in our society as the right of privacy in marriage may be infringed because that right is not guaranteed in so many words by the first eight amendments to the Constitution is to ignore the Ninth Amendment and to give it no effect whatsoever. . . .

A dissenting opinion suggests that my interpretation of the Ninth Amendment somehow "broaden[s] the powers of this Court." With all due respect, I believe that it misses the import of what I am saying. . . . The Ninth Amendment simply shows the intent of the Constitution's authors that other fundamental personal rights should not be denied such protection or disparaged in any other way simply because they are not specifically listed in the first eight constitutional amendments. I do not see how this broadens the authority of the Court: rather it serves to support what this Court has been doing in protecting fundamental rights.

Nor am I turning somersaults with history in arguing that the Ninth Amendment is relevant in a case dealing with a *State*'s infringement of a fundamental right. While the Ninth Amendment—and indeed the entire Bill of Rights—originally concerned restrictions upon *federal* power, the subsequently enacted Fourteenth

Amendment prohibits the States as well from abridging fundamental personal liberties. And, the Ninth Amendment, in indicating that not all such liberties are specifically mentioned in the first eight amendments, is surely relevant in showing the existence of other fundamental personal rights, now protected from state, as well as federal, infringement. . . .

In determining which rights are fundamental, judges are not left at large to decide cases in light of their personal and private notions. Rather, they must look to the "traditions and [collective] conscience of our people" to determine whether a principle is "so rooted [there] . . . as to be ranked as fundamental." . . .

I agree fully with the Court that, applying these tests, the right of privacy is a fundamental personal right, emanating "from the totality of the constitutional scheme under which we live." . . .

MR. JUSTICE HARLAN, concurring in the judgment.

I fully agree with the judgment of reversal, but find myself unable to join the Court's opinion. The reason is that it seems to me to evince an approach to this case very much like that taken by my Brothers Black and Stewart in dissent, namely: the Due Process Clause of the Fourteenth Amendment does not touch this Connecticut statute unless the enactment is found to violate some right assured by the letter or penumbra of the Bill of Rights.

In other words, what I find implicit in the Court's opinion is that the "incorporation" doctrine may be used to *restrict* the reach of Fourteenth Amendment Due Process. . . .

In my view, the proper constitutional inquiry in this case is whether this Connecticut statute infringes the Due Process Clause of the Fourteenth Amendment because the enactment violates basic values "implicit in the concept of ordered liberty," *Palko v. Connecticut* [1937]. For reasons stated at length in my dissenting opinion in *Poe v. Ullman* [1961], I believe that it does. While the relevant inquiry may be aided by resort to one or more of the provisions of the Bill of Rights, it is not dependent on them or any of their radiations. The Due Process Clause of the Fourteenth Amendment stands, in my opinion, on its own bottom. . . .

Judicial self-restraint will not, I suggest, be brought about in the "due process" area by the historically unfounded incorporation formula long advanced by my Brother Black, and now in part espoused by my Brother Stewart. It will be achieved in this area, as in other constitutional areas, only by continual insistence upon respect for the teachings of history, solid recognition of the basic values that underlie our society, and wise appreciation of the great roles that the doctrines of federalism and separation of powers have played in establishing and preserving American freedoms. . . . Adherence to these principles will not, of course, obviate all constitutional differences of opinion among judges, nor should it. Their continued recognition will, however, go farther toward keeping most judges from roaming at large in the constitutional field than will the interpolation into the Constitution of an artificial and largely illusory restriction on the content of the Due Process Clause.

MR. JUSTICE WHITE, concurring in the judgment. . . .

MR. JUSTICE BLACK, with whom MR. JUSTICE STEWART joins, dissenting.

. . . I do not to any extent whatever base my view that this Connecticut law is constitutional on a belief that the law is wise or that its policy is a good one. . . . There is no single one of the graphic and eloquent strictures and criticisms fired at the policy of this Connecticut law either by the Court's opinion or by those of my concurring Brethren to which I cannot subscribe—except their conclusion that the evil qualities they see in the law make it unconstitutional. . . .

The Court talks about a constitutional "right of privacy" as though there is some constitutional provision or provisions forbidding any law ever to be passed which might abridge the "privacy" of individuals. But there is not. There are, of course, guarantees in certain specific constitutional provisions which are designed in part to protect privacy at certain times and places with respect to certain activities. Such, for example, is the Fourth Amendment's guarantee against "unreasonable searches and seizures." But I think it belittles that Amendment to talk about it as though it protects nothing but "privacy." To treat it that way is to give it a niggardly interpretation, not the kind of liberal reading I think any Bill of Rights provision should be given. The average man would very likely not have his feelings soothed any more by having his property seized openly than by having it seized privately and by stealth. He simply wants his property left alone. And a person can be just as much, if not more, irritated, annoyed and injured by an unceremonious public arrest by a policeman as he is by a seizure in the privacy of his office or home.

One of the most effective ways of diluting or expanding a constitutionally guaranteed right is to substitute for the crucial word or words of a constitutional guarantee another word or words more or less flexible and more or less restricted in meaning. . . . "Privacy" is a broad, abstract and ambiguous concept which can easily be shrunken in meaning but which can also, on the other hand, easily be interpreted as a constitutional ban against many things other than searches and seizures. . . . For these reasons I get nowhere in this case by talk about a constitutional "right of privacy" as an emanation from one or more constitutional provisions. I like my privacy as well as the next one, but I am nevertheless compelled to admit that government has a right to invade it unless prohibited by some specific constitutional provision. . . .

The due process argument which my Brothers Harlan and White adopt here is based . . . on the premise that this Court is vested with power to invalidate all state laws that it considers to be arbitrary, capricious, unreasonable, or oppressive, or this Court's belief that a particular state law under scrutiny has no "rational or justifying" purpose, or is offensive to a "sense of fairness and justice." If these formulas based on "natural justice," or others which mean the same thing, are to prevail, they require judges to determine what is or is not constitutional on the basis of their own appraisal of what laws are unwise or unnecessary. The power to make such decisions is of course that of a legislative body. . . . I do not believe that we are granted power by the Due Process Clause or any other constitutional provision or provisions to measure constitutionality by our belief that legislation is arbitrary, capricious or unreasonable, or accomplishes no justifiable purpose, or is offensive to our own notions of "civilized standards of conduct." Such an appraisal of the wisdom of legislation is an attitude of the power to make laws, not of the power to interpret them. The use by federal courts of such a formula or doctrine or what not to veto federal or state laws simply takes away from Congress and States the power to make laws based on their own judgment of fairness and wisdom and transfers that power to this Court for ultimate determination—a power which was specifically denied to federal courts by the convention that framed the Constitution. . . .

My Brother Goldberg has adopted the recent discovery that the Ninth Amendment as well as the Due Process Clause can be used by this Court as authority to strike down all state legislation which this Court thinks violates "fundamental principles of liberty and justice," or is contrary to the "traditions and [collective] conscience of our people." He also states, without proof satisfactory to me, that in making decisions on this basis judges will not consider "their personal and private notions." One may ask how they can avoid considering them. Our Court certainly has no machinery with which to take a Gallup Poll. And the scientific miracles of this age have not yet produced a gadget which the Court can use to determine what traditions are rooted in the "[collective] conscience of our people." Moreover, one would certainly have to look far beyond the language of the Ninth Amendment to find that the Framers vested in this Court any such awesome veto powers over lawmaking, either by the States or by the Congress. Nor does anything in the history of the Amendment offer any support for such a shocking doctrine. The whole history of the adoption of the Constitution and Bill of Rights points the other way, and the very material quoted by my Brother Goldberg shows that the Ninth Amendment was intended to protect against the idea that "by enumerating particular exceptions to the grant of power" to the Federal Government, "those rights which were not singled out, were intended to be assigned into the hands of the General Government [the United States], and were consequently insecure." That Amendment was passed, not to broaden the powers of this Court or any other department of "the General Government," but, as every student of history knows, to assure the people that the Constitution in all its provisions was intended to limit the Federal Government to the powers granted expressly or by necessary implication. If any broad, unlimited power to hold laws unconstitutional because they offend what this Court conceives to be the "[collective] conscience of our people" is vested in this Court by the Ninth Amendment, the Fourteenth Amendment, or any other provision of the Constitution, it was not given by the Framers, but rather has been bestowed on the Court by the Court. . . .

I realize that many good and able men have eloquently spoken and written, sometimes in rhapsodical strains, about the duty of this Court to keep the Constitution in tune with the times. The idea is that the Constitution must be changed from time to time and that this Court is charged with a duty to make those changes. For myself, I must with all deference reject that philosophy. The Constitution makers knew the need for changes and provided for it. Amendments suggested by the people's elected representatives can be submitted to the people or their selected agents for ratification. That method of change was good for our Fathers, and being somewhat old-fashioned I must add it is good enough for me. And so, I cannot rely on the Due Process Clause or the Ninth Amendment or any mysterious and uncertain natural law concept as a reason for striking down this state law. . . .

MR. JUSTICE STEWART, whom MR. JUSTICE BLACK joins, dissenting.

. . . I think this is an uncommonly silly law. As a practical matter, the law is obviously unenforceable, except in the oblique context of the present case. As a philosophical matter, I believe the use of contraceptives in the relationship of marriage should be left to personal and private choice, based upon each individual's moral, ethical, and religious beliefs. As a matter of social policy, I think professional counsel about methods of birth control should be available to all, so that each individual's choice can be meaningfully made. But we are not asked in this case to say whether we think this law is unwise, or even asinine. We are asked to hold that it violates the United States Constitution. And that I cannot do.

In the course of its opinion the Court refers to no less than six Amendments to the Constitution: the First, the Third, the Fourth, the Fifth, the Ninth, and the Fourteenth. But the Court does not say which of these Amendments, if any, it thinks is infringed by this Connecticut law.

We *are* told that the Due Process Clause of the Fourteenth Amendment is not, as such, the "guide" in this case. With that much I agree. . . .

As to the First, Third, Fourth, and Fifth Amendments, I can find nothing in any of them to invalidate this Connecticut law, even assuming that all those Amendments are fully applicable against the States. It has not even been argued that this is a law "respecting an establishment of religion, or prohibiting the free exercise thereof." And surely, unless the solemn process of constitutional adjudication is to descend to the level of a play on words, there is not involved here any abridgement of "that freedom of speech, or of the press; or the right of the people peaceably to assemble, and to petition the Government for a redress of grievances." No soldier has been quartered in any house. There has been no search, and no seizure. Nobody has been compelled to be a witness against himself.

The Court also quotes the Ninth Amendment, and my Brother Goldberg's concurring opinion relies heavily upon it. But to say that the Ninth Amendment has anything to do with this case is to turn somersaults with history. The Ninth Amendment, like its companion the Tenth, which this Court held "states but a truism that all is retained which has not been surrendered," *United States v. Darby* [1941], was framed by James Madison and adopted by the States simply to make clear that the adoption of the Bill of Rights did not alter the plan that the *Federal* Government was to be a government of express and limited powers, and that all rights and powers not delegated to it were retained by the people and the individual States. Until today no member of this Court has ever suggested that the Ninth Amendment meant anything else, and the idea that a federal court could ever use the Ninth Amendment to annul a law passed by the elected representatives of the people of the State of Connecticut would have caused James Madison no little wonder. . . .

At the oral argument in this case we were told that the Connecticut law does not "conform to current community standards." But it is not the function of this Court to decide cases on the basis of community standards. We are here to decide cases "agreeably to the Constitution and laws of the United States." It is the essence of judicial duty to subordinate our own personal views, our own ideas of what legislation is wise and what is not. If, as I should surely hope, the law before us does not reflect the standards of the people of Connecticut, the people of Connecticut can freely exercise their true Ninth and Tenth Amendment rights to persuade their elected representatives to repeal it. That is the constitutional way to take this law off the books.

14.4   *"... that trivial residue may mark the difference between slavery and humanity."*

HUDSON V. PALMER

468 U.S. 517, 104 S. Ct. 3194, 82 L. Ed. 2d 393 (1984)

A Virginia prison inmate filed an action in federal court against an official of the prison alleging that the official had conducted an unreasonable search of the prisoner's cell and destroyed some noncontraband personal property during the search.

CHIEF JUSTICE BURGER delivered the opinion of the Court. . . .

II

A

The first question we address is whether respondent has a right of privacy in his prison cell entitling him to the protection of the Fourth Amendment against unreasonable searches. As we have noted, the Court of Appeals held that the District Court's summary judgment in petitioner's favor was premature because respondent had a "limited privacy right" in his cell that might have been breached. The court concluded that, to protect this privacy right, shakedown searches of an individual's cell should be performed only "pursuant to an established program of conducting random searches . . . reasonably designed to deter or discover the possession of contraband" or upon reasonable belief that the prisoner possesses contraband. Petitioner contends that the Court of Appeals erred in holding that respondent had even a limited privacy right in his cell, and urges that we adopt the "bright line" rule that prisoners have no legitimate expectation of privacy in their individual cells that would entitle them to Fourth Amendment protection.

We have repeatedly held that prisons are not beyond the reach of the Constitution. No "iron curtain" separates one from the other. *Wolff v. McDonnell* (1974). Indeed, we have insisted that prisoners be accorded those rights not fundamentally inconsistent with imprisonment itself or incompatible with the objectives of incarceration. For example, we have held that invidious racial discrimination is as intolerable within a prison as outside, except as may be essential to "prison security and discipline." *Lee v. Washington* (1968) *(per curiam).* Like others, prisoners have the constitutional right to petition the Government for redress of their grievances, which includes a reasonable right of access to the courts. *Johnson v. Avery* (1969). Prisoners must be provided "reasonable opportunities" to exercise their religious freedom guaranteed under the First Amendment. *Cruz v. Beto* (1972) *(per curiam).* Similarly, they retain those First Amendment rights of speech "not inconsistent with [their] status as . . . prisoner[s] or with the legitimate penological objectives of the corrections system." *Pell v. Procunier* (1974). They enjoy the protection of due process. *Wolff v. McDonnell; Haines v. Kerner* (1972). And the Eighth Amendment ensures that they will not be subject to "cruel and unusual punishments." *Estelle v. Gamble* (1976). The continuing guarantee of these substantial rights to prison inmates is testimony to a belief that the way a society treats those who have transgressed against it is evidence of the essential character of that society.

However, while persons imprisoned for crime enjoy many protections of the Constitution, it is also clear that imprisonment carries with it the circumscription or loss of many significant rights. These constraints on inmates, and in some cases the complete withdrawal of certain rights, are "justified by the considerations underlying our penal system." *Price v. Johnston* (1948); see also *Bell v. Wolfish* [1979], *Wolff v. McDonnell.* The curtailment of certain rights is necessary, as a practical matter, to accommodate a myriad of "institutional needs and objectives" of prison facilities, chief among which is internal security, see *Pell v. Procunier* (1974). Of course, these restrictions or retractions also serve, incidentally, as reminders that, under our system of justice, deterrence and retribution are factors in addition to correction.

We have not before been called upon to decide the specific question whether the Fourth Amendment applies within a prison cell, but the nature of our inquiry is well defined. We must determine here, as in other Fourth Amendment contexts, if a 'justifiable' expectation of privacy is at stake. *Katz v. United States* (1967). The applicability of the Fourth Amendment turns on whether "the person invoking its protection can claim a 'justifiable,' a 'reasonable,' or a 'legitimate expectation of privacy' that has been invaded by government action." *Smith v. Maryland* (1979), and cases cited. We must decide, in Justice Harlan's words, whether a prisoner's expectation of privacy in his prison cell is the kind of expectation that "society is prepared to recognize as 'reasonable.' " *Katz* (concurring opinion).

Notwithstanding our caution in approaching claims that the Fourth Amendment is inapplicable in a given context, we hold that society is not prepared to recognize as legitimate any subjective expectation of privacy that a prisoner might have in his prison cell and that, accordingly, the Fourth Amendment proscription against unreasonable searches does not apply within the confines of the prison cell. The recognition of privacy rights for prisoners in their individual cells simply cannot be reconciled with the concept of incarceration and the needs and objectives of penal institutions.

Prisons, by definition, are places of involuntary confinement of persons who have a demonstrated proclivity for antisocial criminal, and often violent, conduct. Inmates have necessarily shown a lapse in ability to control and conform their behavior to the legitimate standards of society by the normal impulses of self-restraint; they have shown an inability to regulate their conduct in a way that reflects either a respect for law or an appreciation of the rights of others. Even a partial survey of the statistics on violent crime in our Nation's prisons illustrates the magnitude of the problem. During 1981 and the first half of 1982, there were over 120 prisoners murdered by fellow inmates in state and federal prisons. A number of prison personnel were murdered by prisoners during this period. Over 29 riots or similar disturbances were reported in these facilities for the same time frame. And there were over 125 suicides in these institutions. . . .

Within this volatile "community," prison administrators are to take all necessary steps to ensure the safety of not only the prison staffs and administrative personnel, but visitors. They are under an obligation to take reasonable measures to guarantee the safety of the inmates themselves. They must be ever alert to attempts to introduce drugs and other contraband into the premises which, we can judicially notice, is one of the most perplexing problems of prisons today; they must prevent, so far as possible, the flow of illicit weapons into the prison; they must be vigilant to detect escape plots, in which drugs or weapons may be involved, before the schemes materialize. In addition to these monumental tasks, it is incumbent upon these officials at the same time to maintain as sanitary an environment for the inmates as feasible, given the difficulties of the circumstances.

The administration of a prison, we have said, is "at best an extraordinarily difficult undertaking." *Wolff v. McDonnell; Hewitt v. Helms* (1983). But it would be literally impossible to accomplish the prison objectives identified above if inmates retained a right of privacy in their cells. Virtually the only place inmates can conceal weapons, drugs, and other contraband is in their cells. Unfettered access to these cells by prison officials, thus, is imperative if drugs and contraband are to be ferreted out and sanitary surroundings are to be maintained.

Determining whether an expectation of privacy is "legitimate" or "reasonable" necessarily entails a balancing of interests. The two interests here are the interest of society in the security of its penal institutions and the interest of the prisoner in privacy within his cell. The latter interest, of course, is already limited by the exigencies of the circumstances: A prison "shares none of the attributes of privacy of a home, an automobile, an office, or a hotel room." *Lanza v. New*

York (1962). We strike the balance in favor of institutional security, which we have noted is "central to all other corrections goals," *Pell v. Procunier.* A right of privacy in traditional Fourth Amendment terms is fundamentally incompatible with the close and continual surveillance of inmates and their cells required to ensure institutional security and internal order. We are satisfied that society would insist that the prisoner's expectation of privacy always yield to what must be considered the paramount interest in institutional security. We believe that it is accepted by our society that "[l]oss of freedom of choice and privacy are inherent incidents of confinement." *Bell v. Wolfish.*

The Court of Appeals was troubled by the possibility of searches conducted solely to harass inmates; it reasoned that a requirement that searches be conducted only pursuant to an established policy or upon reasonable suspicion would prevent such searches to the maximum extent possible. Of course, there is a risk of maliciously motivated searches, and of course, intentional harassment of even the most hardened criminals cannot be tolerated by a civilized society. However, we disagree with the court's proposed solution. The uncertainty that attends random searches of cells renders these searches perhaps the most effective weapon of the prison administrator in the constant fight against the proliferation of knives and guns, illicit drugs, and other contraband. The Court of Appeals candidly acknowledged that "the device [of random cell searches] is of . . . obvious utility in achieving the goal of prison security."

A requirement that even random searches be conducted pursuant to an established plan would seriously undermine the effectiveness of this weapon. It is simply naive to believe that prisoners would not eventually decipher any plan officials might devise for "planned random searches," and thus be able routinely to anticipate searches. The Supreme Court of Virginia identified the shortcomings of an approach such as that adopted by the Court of Appeals and the necessity of allowing prison administrators flexibility:

> "For one to advocate that prison searches must be conducted only pursuant to an enunciated general policy or when suspicion is directed at a particular inmate is to ignore the realities of prison operation. Random searches of inmates, individually or collectively, and their cells and lockers are valid and necessary to ensure the security of the institution and the safety of inmates and all others within its boundaries. This type of search allows prison officers flexibility and prevents inmates from anticipating, and thereby thwarting, a search for contraband." *Marrero v. Commonwealth* (1981).

We share the concerns so well expressed by the Supreme Court and its view that wholly random searches are essential to the effective security of penal institutions. We, therefore, cannot accept even the concededly limited holding of the Court of Appeals.

Respondent acknowledges that routine shakedowns of prison cells are essential to the effective administration of prisons. He contends, however, that he is constitutionally entitled not to be subjected to searches conducted only to harass. The crux of his claim is that "because searches and seizures to harass are unreasonable, a prisoner has a reasonable expectation of privacy not to have his cell, locker, personal effects, person invaded for such a purpose." This argument, which assumes the answer to the predicate question whether a prisoner has a legitimate expectation of privacy in his prison cell at all, is merely a challenge to the reasonableness of the particular search of respondent's cell. Because we conclude that prisoners have no legitimate expectation of privacy and that the Fourth Amendment's prohibition on unreasonable searches does not apply in prison cells, we need not address this issue.

Our holding that respondent does not have a reasonable expectation of privacy enabling him to invoke the protections of the Fourth Amendment does not mean that he is without a remedy for calculated harassment unrelated to prison needs. Nor does it mean that prison attendants can ride roughshod over inmates' property rights with impunity. The Eighth Amendment always stands as a protection against "cruel and unusual punishments." By the same token, there are adequate state tort and common-law remedies available to respondent to redress the alleged destruction of his personal property. . . .

Palmer does not seriously dispute the adequacy of the existing state-law remedies themselves. He asserts in this respect only that, because certain of his legal papers allegedly taken "may have contained things irreplacable [sic], and incompensable" or "may also have involved sentimental items which are of equally intangible value," a suit in tort, for example, would not "necessarily" compensate him fully. If the loss is "incompensable," this is as much so under § 1983 as it would be under any other remedy. In any event, that Palmer might not be able to recover under these remedies the full amount which he might receive in a § 1983 action is not, as we have said, determinative of the adequacy of the state remedies. . . .

III

We hold that the Fourth Amendment has no applicability to a prison cell. We hold also that, even if petitioner intentionally destroyed respondent's personal property during the challenged shakedown search, the destruction did not violate the Fourteenth Amendment since the Commonwealth of Virginia has provided respondent an adequate postdeprivation remedy.

Accordingly, the judgment of the Court of Appeals reversing and remanding the District Court's judgment on respondent's Fourth and Fourteenth Amendments claim is reversed. The judgment affirming the District Court's decision that respondent has not been denied due process under the Fourteenth Amendment is affirmed.

It is so ordered.

JUSTICE O'CONNOR, concurring. . . .

JUSTICE STEVENS, * with whom JUSTICE BRENNAN, JUSTICE MARSHALL, and JUSTICE BLACKMUN join, concurring in part and dissenting in part. . . .

Measured by the conditions that prevail in a free society, neither the possessions nor the slight residuum of privacy that a prison inmate can retain in his cell, can have more than the most minimal value. From the standpoint of the prisoner, however, that trivial residuum may mark the difference between slavery and humanity. On another occasion, THE CHIEF JUSTICE wrote:

> "It is true that inmates lose many rights when they are lawfully confined, but they do not lose all civil rights. Inmates in jails, prisons, or mental institutions retain certain fundamental rights of privacy; they are not like animals in a zoo to be filmed and photographed at will by the public or by media reporters, however 'educational' the process may be for others." *Houchins v. KQED, Inc.* (1978) (plurality opinion).

Personal letters, snapshots of family members, a souvenir, a deck of cards, a hobby kit, perhaps a diary or a training manual for an apprentice in a new trade, or even a Bible—a variety of inexpensive items may enable a prisoner to maintain contact with some part of his past and an eye to the possibility of a better future. Are all of these items subject to unrestrained perusal, confiscation or mutilation at the hands of a possibly hostile guard? Is the Court correct in its perception that "society" is not prepared to recognize *any* privacy or possessory interest of the prison inmate—no matter how remote the threat to prison security may be? . . . .

It is well-settled that the discretion accorded prison officials is not absolute. A prisoner retains those constitutional rights not inconsistent with legitimate penological objectives. There can be no penological justification for the seizure alleged here. There is no contention that Palmer's property posed any threat to institutional security. Hudson had already examined the material before he took and destroyed it. The allegation is that Hudson did this for no reason save spite; there is no contention that under prison regulations the material was contraband, and in any event as I have indicated above the Constitution prohibits a State from treating letters and legal materials as contraband. The Court agrees that intentional harassment of prisoners by guards is intolerable. That being the case, there is no

---

*Justice Stevens took the unusual step of reading this dissent from the bench on July 3, 1984.—Eds.

room for any conclusion but that the alleged seizure was unreasonable. The need for "close and continual surveillance of inmates and their cells" in no way justifies taking and destroying noncontraband property; if material is examined and found not to be contraband, there can be no justification for its seizure. When, as here, the material at issue is not contraband it simply makes no sense to say that its seizure and destruction serves "legitimate institutional interests." Such seizures are unreasonable.

The Court's holding is based on its belief that society would not recognize as reasonable the possessory interests of prisoners. Its perception of what society is prepared to recognize as reasonable is not based on any empirical data; rather it merely reflects the perception of the four Justices who have joined the opinion that the Chief Justice has authored. On the question of what seizures society is prepared to consider reasonable, surely the consensus on that issue in the lower courts is of some significance. Virtually every federal judge to address the question over the past decade has concluded that the Fourth Amendment does apply to a prison cell. There is similar unanimity among the commentators. The Court itself acknowledges that "intentional harassment of even the most hardened criminals cannot be tolerated by a civilized society." That being the case, I fail to see how a seizure that serves no purpose except harassment does not invade an interest that society considers reasonable, and that is protected by the Fourth Amendment.

The Court rests its view of "reasonableness" almost entirely upon its assessment of the security needs of prisons. Because deference to institutional needs is so critical to the Court's approach, it is worth inquiring as to the view prison administrators take toward conduct of the type at issue here. On that score the Court demonstrates a remarkable lack of awareness as to what penologists and correctional officials consider "legitimate institutional interests." I am unaware that any responsible prison administrator has ever contended that there is a need to take or destroy noncontraband property of prisoners; the Court certainly provides no evidence to support its conclusion that institutions require this sort of power. To the contrary, it appears to be the near-universal view of correctional officials that guards should neither seize nor destroy noncontraband property. For example, the Federal Bureau of Prisons' regulations state that only items which may not be possessed by a prisoner can be seized by prison officials. They also provide that prisoners can retain property consistent with prison management, specifically including clothing, legal materials, hobbycraft materials, commissary items, radios and watches, correspondence, reading materials, and personal photos. Virginia law and its Department of Corrections' regulations similarly authorize seizure of contraband items alone. I am aware of no prison system with a different practice; the standards for prison administration which have been promulgated for correctional institutions invariably require prison officials to respect prisoners' possessory rights in noncontraband personal property.

Depriving inmates of any residuum of privacy or possessory rights is in fact plainly *contrary* to institutional goals. Sociologists recognize that prisoners deprived of any sense of individuality devalue themselves and others and therefore are more prone to violence toward themselves or others. At the same time, such an approach undermines the rehabilitative function of the institution: "Without the privacy and dignity provided by Fourth Amendment coverage, an inmate's opportunity to reform, small as it may be, will further be diminished. It is anomalous to provide a prisoner with rehabilitative programs and services in an effort to build self-respect while simultaneously subjecting him to unjustified and degrading searches and seizures." . . .

To justify its conclusion, the Court recites statistics concerning the number of crimes that occur within prisons. For example, it notes that over an 18-month period approximately 120 prisoners were murdered in state and federal facilities. At the end of 1983 there were 438,830 inmates in state and federal prisons. The Court's homicide rate of 80 per year yields an annual prison homicide rate of 18.26 persons per 100,000 inmates. In 1982, the homicide rate in Miami was 51.98 per 100,000; in New York it was 23.50 per 100,000; in Dallas 31.53 per 100,000; and in the District of Columbia 30.70 per 100,000. Thus, the prison homicide rate, it turns out, is significantly lower than that in many of our major cities. I do not suggest this type of analysis provides a standard for measuring the reasonableness of a search or seizure within prisons, but I do suggest that the Court's use of statistics is less than persuasive.

The size of the inmate population also belies the Court's hypothesis that all prisoners fit into a violent, incorrigible stereotype. Many, of course, become recidivists. But literally thousands upon thousands of former prisoners are now leading constructive law-abiding lives. The nihilistic tone of the Court's opinion—seemingly assuming that all prisoners have demonstrated an inability "to control and conform their behavior to the legitimate standards of society by the normal impulses of self-restraint" is consistent with its conception of prisons as sterile warehouses, but not with an enlightened view of the function of a modern prison system. . . .

. . . Once it is agreed that random searches of a prisoner's cell are reasonable to ensure that the cell contains no contraband, there can be no need for seizure and destruction of noncontraband items found during such searches. To accord prisoners any less protection is to declare that the prisoners are entitled to no measure of human dignity or individuality—not a photo, a letter, nor anything except standard-issue prison clothing would be free from arbitrary seizure and destruction. Yet that is the view the Court takes today. It declares prisoners to be little more than chattels, a view I thought society had outgrown long ago. . . .

Today's holding cannot be squared with the text of the Constitution, nor with common sense. The Fourth Amendment is of "general application," and its text requires that every search and seizure of "papers and effects" be evaluated for its reasonableness. . . . More fundamentally, in its eagerness to adopt a rule consistent with what it believes to be wise penal administration, the Court overlooks the purpose of a written Constitution and its Bill of Rights. That purpose, of course, is to ensure that certain principles will not be sacrificed to expediency; these are enshrined as principles of fundamental law beyond the reach of governmental officials or legislative majorities. The Fourth Amendment is part of that fundamental law; it represents a value judgment that unjustified search and seizure so greatly threatens individual liberty that it must be forever condemned as a matter of constitutional principle. The courts, of course, have a special obligation to protect the rights of prisoners. Prisoners are truly the outcasts of society. Disenfranchised, scorned and feared, often deservedly so, shut away from public view, prisoners are surely a "discrete and insular minority." In this case, the destruction of Palmer's property was a seizure; the Judiciary has a constitutional duty to determine whether it was justified. The Court's conclusive presumption that all conduct by prison guards is reasonable is supported by nothing more than its idiosyncratic view of the imperatives of prison administration—a view not shared by prison administrators themselves. Such a justification is nothing less than a decision to sacrifice constitutional principle to the Court's own assessment of administrative expediency. . . .

14.5   *"That abstinence from giving his own desires free play, that continuing and self-conscious renunciation of power, that is the morality of the jurist."*

TRADITION AND MORALITY IN CONSTITUTIONAL LAW

Robert H. Bork

We are entering, I believe, a period in which our legal culture and constitutional law may be transformed, with even more power accru-

The Francis Boyer Lectures on Public Policy, American Enterprise Institute for Public Policy Research (1984). Copyright © 1985, American Enterprise Institute. Reprinted with permission. All rights reserved. Robert H. Bork, a former professor of law at Yale, is Judge, United States Court of Appeals for the District of Columbia Circuit.

ing to judges than is presently the case. There are two reasons for that. One is that constitutional law has very little theory of its own and hence is almost pathologically lacking in immune defenses against the intellectual fevers of the larger society as well as against the disorders generated by its own internal organs.

The second is that the institutions of the law, in particular the schools, are becoming increasingly converted to an ideology of the Constitution that demands just such an infusion of extraconstitutional moral and political notions. A not untypical example of the first is the entry into the law of the first amendment of the old, and incorrect, view that the only kinds of harm that a community is entitled to suppress are physical and economic injuries. Moral harms are not to be counted because to do so would interfere with the autonomy of the individual. That is an indefensible definition of what people are entitled to regard as harms.

The result of discounting moral harm is the privatization of morality, which requires the law of the community to practice moral relativism. It is thought that individuals are entitled to their moral beliefs but may not gather as a community to express those moral beliefs in law. Once an idea of that sort takes hold in the intellectual world, it is very likely to find lodgment in constitutional theory and then in constitutional law. The walls of the law have proved excessively permeable to intellectual osmosis. Out of prudence, I will give but one example of the many that might be cited.

A state attempted to apply its obscenity statute to a public display of an obscene word. The Supreme Court majority struck down the conviction on the grounds that regulation is a slippery slope and that moral relativism is a constitutional command. The opinion said, "The principle contended for by the State seems inherently boundless. How is one to distinguish this from any other offensive word?" One might as well say that the negligence standard of tort law is inherently boundless, for how is one to distinguish the reckless driver from the safe one? The answer in both cases is, by the common sense of the community. Almost all judgments in the law are ones of degree, and the law does not flinch from such judgments except when, as in the case of morals, it seriously doubts the community's right to define harms. Moral relativism was even more explicit in the majority opinion, however, for the Court observed, apparently thinking the observation decisive: "One man's vulgarity is another's lyric."* On that ground, it is difficult to see how law on any subject can be permitted to exist.

But the Court immediately went further, reducing the whole question to one of private preference, saying: "We think it is largely

---

*The reference is to Justice John Marshall Harlan's opinion for the Court in *Cohen v. California* (1971).—Eds.

because governmental officials cannot make principled distinctions in this area that the Constitution leaves matters of taste and style so largely to the individual." Thus, the community's moral and aesthetic judgments are reduced to questions of style and those are then said to be privatized by the Constitution. It testifies all the more clearly to the power of ideas floating in the general culture to alter the Constitution that this opinion was written by a justice generally regarded as moderate to conservative in his constitutional views.

George Orwell reminded us long ago about the power of language to corrupt thought and the consequent baleful effects upon politics. The same deterioration is certainly possible in morality. But I am not concerned about the constitutional protection cast about an obscene word. Of more concern is the constitutionalizing of the notion that moral harm is not harm legislators are entitled to consider. As Lord Devlin said, "What makes a society is a community of ideas, not political ideas alone but also ideas about the way its members should behave and govern their lives." A society that ceases to be a community increases the danger that weariness with turmoil and relativism may bring about an order in which many more, and more valuable, freedoms are lost than those we thought we were protecting.

I do not know the origin of the notion that moral harms are not properly legally cognizable harms, but it has certainly been given powerful impetus in our culture by John Stuart Mill's book *On Liberty*. Mill, however, was a man of two minds and, as Gertrude Himmelfarb has demonstrated, Mill himself usually knew better than this. Miss Himmelfarb traces the intellectual themes of *On Liberty* to Mill's wife. It would be ironic, to put it no higher, if we owed major features of modern American constitutional doctrine to Harriet Taylor Mill, who was not, as best I can remember, one of the framers at Philadelphia.

It is unlikely, of course, that a general constitutional doctrine of the impermissibility of legislating moral standards will ever be framed. So the development I have cited, though troubling, is really only an instance of a yet more worrisome phenomenon, and that is the capacity of ideas that originate outside the Constitution to influence judges, usually without their being aware of it, so that those ideas are elevated to constitutional doctrine. We have seen that repeatedly in our history. If one may complain today that the Constitution did not adopt John Stuart Mill's *On Liberty*, it was only a few judicial generations ago, when economic laissez faire somehow got into the Constitution, that Justice Holmes wrote in dissent that the Constitution "does not enact Mr. Herbert Spencer's Social Statics."

Why should this be so? Why should constitutional law constantly be catching colds from the intellectual fevers of the general society? The fact is that the law has little intellectual or structural resistance to outside influences, influences that should properly remain outside. The striking, and peculiar, fact about a field of study so old and so intensively cultivated by men and women of first-rate intelligence is that the law possesses very little theory about itself. . . . This theoretical emptiness at its center makes law, particularly constitutional law, unstable, a ship with a great deal of sail but a very shallow keel, vulnerable to the winds of intellectual or moral fashion, which it then validates as the commands of our most basic compact.

This weakness in the law's intellectual structure may be exploited by new theories of moral relativism and egalitarianism now the dominant mode of constitutional thinking in a number of leading law schools. The attack of these theories upon older assumptions has been described by one Harvard law professor as a "battle of cultures," and so it is. It is fair to think, then, that the outcome of this confused battle may strongly affect the constitutional law of the future and hence the way in which we are governed.

The constitutional ideologies growing in the law schools display three worrisome characteristics. They are increasingly abstract and philosophical; they are sometimes nihilistic; they always lack what law requires, democratic legitimacy. These tendencies are new, much stronger now than they were even ten years ago, and certainly nothing like them appeared in our past.

Up to a few years ago most professors of constitutional law would probably have agreed with Joseph Story's dictum in 1833: "Upon subjects of government, it has always appeared to me, that metaphysical refinements are out of place. A constitution of government is addressed to the common-sense of the people, and never was designed for trials of logical skill or visionary speculation." . . .

. . . Academic lawyers are not going to solve the age-old problems of political and moral philosophy any time soon, but the articulated premise of their abstract enterprise is that judges may properly reason to constitutional decisions in that way. But judges have no mandate to govern in the name of contractarian or utilitarian or what-have-you philosophy rather than according to the historical Constitution. Judges of this generation, and much more, of the next generation, are being educated to engage in really heroic adventures in policy making.

This abstract, universalistic style of legal thought has a number of dangers. For one thing, it teaches disrespect for the actual institutions of the American polity. These institutions are designed to achieve compromise, to slow change, to dilute absolutisms. They embody wholesome inconsistencies. They are designed, in short, to do things that abstract generalizations about the just society tend to bring into contempt.

More than this, the attempt to define individual liberties by abstract reasoning, though intended to broaden liberties, is actually